The Criminal Justice System and Women

Women Offenders ● Victims ● Workers

The Criminal Justice System and Women

Women Offenders • Victims • Workers

Edited and Compiled by

Barbara Raffel Price
Natalie J. Sokoloff

Clark Boardman Company, Ltd.
New York, New York
1982

Library of Congress Cataloging in Publication Data
Main entry under title:

The Criminal justice system and women.

(Law & society)
1. Sex discrimination in criminal justice administration—United
States—Addresses, essays, lectures. 2. Female offenders—United
States—Addresses, essays, lectures. 3. Women—United States—Crimes
against—Addresses, essays, lectures. I. Price, Barbara R. II. Sokoloff,
Natalie J. III. Series.

HV6791.C754	364'.088042	81-18040
ISBN 0-87632-368-9		AACR2

List of Contributors

Geoffrey Alpert
Gail Armstrong
Phyllis Jo Baunach
Dorothy H. Bracey
Sandra Butler
Irene Diamond
Claudia Dreifus
Laurie Engelberg
Clarice Feinman
Susan P. Gavin
Ruth Glick
Susan Griffin
Jennifer James
Andrew Karmen

Dorie Klein
Meda Chesney-Lind
Catharine A. MacKinnon
Del Martin
Elena Natalizia
Susan Ness
Virginia V. Neto
Michelle Patterson
Cheryl Bowser Petersen
Nicole Hahn Rafter
Gerald D. Robin
Carol Smart
Darrell Steffensmeier
Roi D. Townsey

v

About the Editors

BARBARA RAFFEL PRICE is a graduate of Smith College and has a doctorate from The Pennsylvania State University. She is Professor of Criminal Justice at John Jay College of Criminal Justice in the Department of Law, Police Science and Criminal Justice Administration. She has been associated with police executive and supervisory training programs in Pennsylvania and was co-director of a nationwide study of local jails. Active in the American Society of Criminology, Dr. Price has been a member of its executive board since 1972 and is now Vice-President of the Society. She has been on the editorial board of *Criminology* and is also on the editorial board of *The Journal of Criminal Justice Ethics*. She is the author of *Police Professionalism: Rhetoric and Action*, co-author of *Jails and Drug Treatment*, and co-editor of *Criminal Justice Research*. In her published articles she has discussed police corruption, police training, women police executives, jail services and police community relations. Her current research is on police administrative practices.

NATALIE J. SOKOLOFF is Associate Professor of Sociology at the John Jay College of Criminal Justice, where she teaches in the Sociology Department and the Thematic Studies Program, an interdisciplinary team-taught program focusing on civil rights, civil liberties, and the criminal justice system. Formerly associated with the New York State Division for Youth in its research evaluation program (New York City) and the Mount Sinai School of Medicine in its Department of Community Medicine (New York City), she holds a bachelor's degree from the University of Michigan, a master's degree from Brown University, and her doctorate from the City University of New York, Graduate Center.

Professor Sokoloff is the author of *Between Money and Love: The Dialectics of Women's Home and Market Work* (Praeger, 1980) and was the recipient of a grant from the American Sociological Association's Problems in the Discipline Program to develop an on-going interdisciplinary workshop among experts in the field of women and work. She has published in numerous journals, including: *Women: A Journal of Liberation, Resources for Feminist Research; Quest: A Feminist Quarterly; Current Perspectives in Social Theory;* and the *International Journal of Health Services*, as well as in several anthologies on the relationship between family and labor force participation for women. Professor Sokoloff is a feminist activist and scholar whose work is oriented toward examining, analyzing, and fighting against discrimination against women in the U.S. labor force.

About the Contributors

GEOFFREY ALPERT received his Ph.D. in sociology from Washington State University. He is Director of the Center for the Study of Law and Society and teaches in the department of sociology at the University of Miami. Alpert is the author of *The Legal Rights of Prisoners*.

GAIL ARMSTRONG received her bachelor's degree from Indiana University and attended its graduate school. She is assistant editor with the University of Delaware Publications Office.

PHYLLIS JO BAUNACH is a correctional research specialist at the National Institute of Justice in Washington, D.C. and teaches at the University of Maryland. She received her Ph.D. from the University of Minnesota. Currently co-chairperson of the Division on Women and Crime and a board member of the American Society of Criminology, Baunach is the 1982-83 recipient of the American Association of University Women's Young Scholar Award. Her publications include "Sex Role Operations: Strategies for Women Working in the Criminal Justice System" (with Nicole Rafter) in *Judge, Lawyer, Victim, and Thief*, by Rafter and Stanko.

DOROTHY H. BRACEY is professor of anthropology at the John Jay College of Criminal Justice. In addition to a Ph.D. in anthropology from Harvard University, she received a master's degree in law from Yale Law School. She is President of the Academy of Criminal Justice Sciences and an editor of *Police Studies*. Bracey's publications include *Baby-Pros: Preliminary Profiles of Juvenile Prostitutes*.

SANDRA BUTLER is author of *Conspiracy of Silence: The Trauma of Incest*.

IRENE DIAMOND is assistant professor of political science at Purdue University. She received her Ph.D. from Princeton University. She is the author of two books: *Sex Roles in the State House* and *Families, Politics, and Public Policy: A Feminist Dialogue on Women and the State*.

CLAUDIA DREIFUS is a professional writer and journalist. She has written three books, the last of which is an edited book of readings entitled, *Seizing Our Bodies: The Politics of Women's Health*. Her articles appear regularly in *Redbook, Playboy, Ms., Newsday,* and *Mademoiselle*.

LAURIE ENGELBERG has been an advanced graduate student and teaching associate at the University of California, Los Angeles. She is the author of a number of papers addressing the role of women in contemporary society. Her primary interest is in women's health care, and she has served as a consultant to the Department of Health, Education and Welfare in an evaluation of the use of female paramedics in obstetrical and gynecological settings.

CLARICE FEINMAN has a doctorate in social and urban history from New York University and has published on the incarceration of women in New York City jails. She is an assistant professor for the Department of Criminal Justice at Trenton State College. She has written a book, *Women in Criminal Justice,* on women offenders and professionals in criminal justice.

SUSAN P. GAVIN has a master's degree from The Pennsylvania State University and is an affiliate instructor in the Administration of Justice Program at that university. Gavin is concerned with promoting the integration of women within the various criminal justice professions.

RUTH GLICK received her Ph.D. from the University of California, Los Angeles and has worked in both the corrections and health fields. She is the administrator of a family planning and abortion services clinic in Reno, Nevada.

SUSAN GRIFFIN is a writer who studies at San Francisco University, where she received her master's degree. She has published two books: *Rape: The Power of Consciousness* and *Pornography and Silence: Culture's Revenge Against Nature.*

JENNIFER JAMES, associate professor of psychiatry and behavioral sciences at the University of Washington Medical School, received her Ph.D. in urban cultural anthropology from the University of Washington. She has published numerous articles on prostitutes and prostitution.

ANDREW KARMEN, assistant professor of sociology at John Jay College of Criminal Justice, received his Ph.D. in sociology from Columbia University. He has written several articles in the area of victimology and is working on a text entitled *Crime Victims: An Introduction to Victimology.*

DORIE KLEIN received her Ph.D. from the University of California, Berkeley. She has been a post-doctoral fellow with the Alcohol Research Group at the University of California and has taught in women's studies at California State University, Sacramento. Klein is the author of many well-known articles on women and criminal justice.

MEDA CHESNEY-LIND is a researcher and assistant professor of sociology at the Youth Development Research Center for the School of Social Work at the University of Hawaii and at Honolulu Community College. She received her Ph.D. from the University of Hawaii. She has published widely in the field of criminology on the sexist treatment of women and girls by the criminal justice system.

CATHARINE A. MacKINNON, visiting assistant professor of law at Stanford Law School, is a lawyer, teacher, and writer. She received her J.D. from Yale University, where she is a doctoral candidate in political science. In 1976 she helped establish the New Haven Law Collective, where she has practiced since being admitted to the Connecticut Bar in 1978. MacKinnon is the author of *Sexual Harrassment of Working Women: A Case of Sex Discrimination.*

DEL MARTIN is an author, lecturer, and consultant who writes about violence against women, its origins, and prevention strategies, as well as the relationship between the criminal justice system and domestic violence. She has been active in the feminist movement since 1967 as a member of the National Organization for Women (NOW), the National Women's Political Caucus, and as an International Women's Year delegate to the Women's National Conference in Houston. She serves on the California Commission on Crime Control and Violence Prevention.

ELENA NATALIZIA is a field organizer with Network, a Catholic social justice lobby in Washington, D.C. She has a master's degree in criminal justice from Northeastern University and is a member of the Sisters of Mercy, a Roman Catholic religious community.

SUSAN NESS, an attorney and legal consultant, is Director of the Judicial Appointments Project for the National Women's Political Caucus. She received her J.D. from Boston College Law School. The Judicial Appointments Project, which she founded in 1977, seeks to increase the representation of women on the state and federal judiciaries.

VIRGINIA V. NETO, a criminal justice consultant and researcher for the past fifteen years, has specialized in women's issues since 1974 when she became Research Director of the first national study of female offenders and correctional programs affecting women. In 1980-81 she conducted a second survey of programs for women in prison. Neto has a bachelor's degree from Creighton University and did graduate work at Washington University.

MICHELLE PATTERSON has been an assistant professor of sociology at the University of California, Santa Barbara. She has written and lectured on women in higher education and the professions.

CHERYL BOWSER PETERSEN is assistant deputy superintendent of the Middlesex County Sheriff's Department, Jail and House of Corrections, in Billerica, Massachusetts. With a master's degree from the University of Wisconsin, she is now completing her doctorate in sociology at Boston College.

NICOLE HAHN RAFTER is assistant professor at the College of Criminal Justice, Northeastern University. She received her Ph.D. from the State University of New York at Albany. She is currently completing a history of the women's prison system and has authored numerous articles on criminology and women.

GERALD D. ROBIN is professor of criminal justice at the University of New Haven, Connecticut. He also served as Director of Research and Evaluation for the Philadelphia regional office of the Law Enforcement Assistance Administration. Robin is the author of numerous articles on criminal justice and *Introduction to the Criminal Justice System.*

CAROL SMART is a research fellow for the Centre for Criminological and Socio-Legal Studies at the University of Sheffield in England, and has a master's degree in criminology from that university. Smart has written several books and articles on women, deviance, and social control. She is the author of *Women, Crime and Criminology: A Feminist Critique.*

DARRELL STEFFENSMEIER, an associate professor of sociology at The Pennsylvania State University, received his Ph.D. from the University of Iowa. He has published widely in major sociological and criminological journals.

ROI D. TOWNSEY is a former Director of the National Information Research Center on Women in Policing of the Police Foundation. She received her Ph.D. from the State University of New York, Stony Brook. Now an assistant professor at John Jay College of Criminal Justice, she is concentrating on sociolegal issues pertaining to the incarceration of minorities and the use of deadly force by police. Townsey is the author of *Women Police Officers: A Personnel Study.*

Preface

This book provides the reader with a perspective on the treatment of women in the criminal justice system—as offenders, as victims of crime, and as working members of the system. Typically only one or two of these areas are covered in a single volume, rarely all three. In organizing and teaching college courses related to these subjects, we have found that much of the available literature fails to provide a comprehensive overview of the issues and full development of the problems. This volume was developed to offer a complete treatment of women as they affect and are affected by crime and the criminal justice system.

Rather than focusing only on the discipline of criminology as a major source of materials, various sources have been drawn on from a number of different disciplines and perspectives to reflect both historical and recent developments in understanding the criminal justice system and its impact on women. Articles have been included by sociologists, anthropologists, and other social scientists as well as criminologists; practitioners, administrators, and activists as well as academics; journalists as well as scholars; and most importantly, feminists from a wide range of social and political perspectives.

Criminologists find themselves in considerable disagreement as to the proper scope of their discipline. Historically, in the United States criminology has been confined to a study of the causes of crime and the offender, with a focus on developing theory to explain why crime occurs. In Europe the emphasis in the eighteenth and nineteenth centuries was also on crime causation, although there was a heavy orientation toward examining criminal law (this study was known as the study of social control). At the same time, most of the work through the mid-twentieth century dealt with male offenders and was done by male researchers. In recent decades, especially after the establishment of the federal Law Enforcement Assistance Administration (LEAA), which was created to control crime by providing money to the criminal justice system to upgrade its performance, criminologists mapped out a wider terrain for criminology. Some chose to study the criminal justice system; the subjects of analysis included law enforcement agencies, criminal courts, juvenile justice systems, probation agencies, parole systems, jails and prisons. Others began to examine the victim, again spurred by LEAA, which began collecting victimization data in 1972. By this time, feminists and the women's movement in general were demonstrating a particular interest in women victims of rape and other crimes, an area long neglected by the system. Today victimization studies are done at all levels by women and men researchers.

The influence of feminism is extremely important in understanding how these latter two areas of study—the criminal justice system and the victim —have emerged in recent years to equal the past interest of criminologists in crime causation and the offender. By sparking an interest in the condition of women as offenders, victims, and system workers, feminism has contributed to the broader scope of criminology today. And this book, by providing studies of each of these three areas, will contribute toward moving the study of women and crime out of the "special issues" category and into mainstream criminology.

THEMES OF THE BOOK

The readings are structured to illustrate several important themes common to all the various criminal justice system roles of women. Most important in the planning of this book was a concern that students be able to explore not only the roles of women as offenders, victims, and workers, but also to understand and question socially structured systems in which these roles operate. In addition, it is important that readers ask questions about how women participate not only in perpetuating but also in changing the system.

This book addresses broad issues surrounding the criminal justice system as it pertains to women. It specifically identifies issues that have yet to be recognized as critical in an understanding of how and why the system operates to the disadvantage of women. For example, the section on women offenders does not stop at the simple fact that women are not immune to criminal activities. Instead, questions are raised that focus on *why* women become criminals. Of course, they break laws as do male criminals. But why do they break laws? Who created those laws and in whose interest? What pressures women to commit certain types of crimes and not others? In addition, we must question whether women are more or less protected by the laws than men. If we find that women are less protected by these laws, then the reasons for unequal protection must be studied.

In a search for answers to these and many other questions, the criminal justice system must be viewed as a set of institutions that are very much a part of the larger society. As such, the system both reflects and perpetuates society's values. Where society is sexist, it should not be a surprise to find sexism in the criminal justice system. One of the prevailing themes, then, in this book is sexism and its effect on women offenders, victims, and criminal justice workers. For example, women are clearly oppressed by rape. However, instead of accepting the sexist interpretation that a rape is in some respects the victim's fault—she was out too late, her skirt was too short, her reputation was far from pure—many women have banded to-

gether in anti-rape groups to demand that rape be recognized, uncondi-
tionally, as a horrendous crime against women. In regard to occupational
discrimination, some women have fought their way into traditional male
positions, such as policing and corrections. Their full acceptance, however,
has yet to be established and related issues of values and practices within
the organization need to be exposed. For example, the issue of police and
correctional officers' roles as social control agents of the poor and of
minority groups must be resolved at the same time as efforts toward
achieving better representation of women in the more prestigious male
jobs continue.

The purpose of the criminal justice system is to control people's behavior by judging the accused and punishing the guilty. An elaborate structure
of rules and enforcers of these rules (police, courts, and corrections) have
been developed to make people comply to society's standards. We will
focus on the woman and show that she is treated differently than the man
within the context of the criminal justice system. First, as an offender she
is judged by different standards than men, convicted for different behavior, and has different needs when she returns to society; second, she is
victimized by crime in different ways than men and has special needs as
a victim; and third, her treatment and opportunities as a worker in the
criminal justice system are different.

The readings in this book will also describe how sexism, racism, and the
class structure associated with capitalism have negative effects on women
in relation to the criminal justice system. *Sexism* is defined in this book as
the socially organized cultural beliefs, practices, and institutions that result
in systematic male superiority and male domination over women as a
group. In this context women are treated on the basis of their socially
defined "female nature." *Racism* is similar; this term refers to the socially
organized attitudes, policies, and institutions that result in systematic
domination of one race over another. Finally, *capitalism* refers to the economic and political ways in which private ownership of productive property and production of goods and services are organized in the interest of
profit making for the relative few. In each case a group—women, racial
minorities, or poor and working class people—are severely disadvantaged
in the daily operations of our society.

The reader must understand that there are no easy answers and no
consensus as to what causes the greatest difficulties for women in regard
to the criminal justice system's treatment and response. Indeed, the two
editors of this book emphasize different factors that contribute to women's
unfavorable situation as compared to men. One of us has the perspective
that cross-cultural oppression of women is the first and most basic cause
of domination by one group over another: all present political and economic systems in our society are sexist and therefore what is most important

is to bring about changes in the sexist ideology and socially structured relations between men and women. The other of us sees capitalism as one of the basic causes for women's oppression in our society and that basic changes in the profit-making system, as well as a total reordering of the sexist social relations between men and women on an egalitarian basis, are necessary. Whatever our differences in these perspectives, there is the common understanding that a need exists for a thorough analysis of the social organization of sex, class, and race in the United States if we are to better understand and change the conditions of women in relation to the criminal justice system.

ORGANIZATION OF THE BOOK

This book is divided into four sections: Part 1, Theories and Facts about Women Offenders; Part 2, Women Victims of Crime; Part 3, Women Workers in the Criminal Justice System; and Part 4, The Future.

In Part 1 the topic of women offenders is presented first by examining existing theories about female criminality. In asking why women commit crimes, it is necessary to first consider some basic notions about criminal law. Law is defined in this book as governmental social control. In light of that definition, the first chapter explores how law is created and changed as well as how law has affected and been affected by women. Following that chapter several authors are presented who discuss issues of crime causation, especially in reference to women and girls (Chapters 2-4). Chapters 5-7 discuss the relationship, if any, between the women's liberation movement and criminality of women, and Chapters 8-10 describe the woman offender once she is convicted. These last three chapters in Part 1 give the reader a factual picture of the convicted woman, her treatment, and her situation as a prisoner.

Part 2 examines women crime victims. The Introduction to this section was written by Andrew Karmen, who specializes in victimology. He focuses on those crimes which have long victimized women but have been made public only recently as a result of the women's movement—rape, wife battering, and sexual harassment. In Chapters 11-14, the victimization of women in general is covered; specific crimes such as rape and wife battering are also presented in this section. Chapters 15-16 take a unique approach to the area of female prostitution. Rather than regarding prostitutes as criminals, both James and Bracey contend that these offenders are victims of a sexist society in general, and a discriminatory system of law enforcement specifically. Finally, the three concluding chapters in this section focus on practices that seriously victimize women physically and psychologically—incest (Chapter 17), pornography (Chapter 18), and sexual harassment (Chapter 19).*

Part 3 considers women as working members of the criminal justice system. The Introduction provides an overview of how women are influencing the entire criminal justice system by their interest in the woman offender and victim, by their determination to work in traditionally male jobs, and by their challenges to the sexism they encounter as workers within the system. This section discusses the many barriers set up by our social structure and institutionalized over time that limit women's entrance into many work positions and jeopardize their success once they are employed. Chapter 20 begins this part with a chapter that examines the selection process which keeps women out of judgeships—positions of the highest status in the criminal justice system. The topic of Chapter 21 is the female lawyer and how the profession itself participates in sexual discrimination. Chapters 22-24 are on the subject of women in policing. Here special attention is given not only to the discrimination experienced by women officers but the added discrimination experienced by black policewomen. These chapters are followed by a previously unpublished and powerful chapter on women correctional officers in all-male facilities.

Part 4, "The Future," should be seen as a modest beginning, not an ending. This section provides a summary for the volume and a look into possible future steps toward transforming the system and fostering broader social changes to deal with sexism and the criminal justice system. The remaining chapters for this section need to be written. We leave that challenge to our readers.

We feel that special acknowledgments are in order for those women who have been important to us personally and important to the movement toward transforming the sexist nature of our criminal justice system. This book is for Inez Garcia, Joan Little, Yvonne Wainrow, and Desi Woods, all imprisoned for protecting themselves against male attackers; for Kitty Genovese, Greta Rideout, Diane Williams, and Carmita Wood, all victims of male assaults and intimidations; for Rhonda Copelon, Eleanor Holmes Norton, Constance Baker Motley, Kathyrn Rorabach, Margaret Burnham, Felicia Spritzer, Gertrude Schimmel, and Julia Tucker, all women working for change in the criminal justice system. We also dedicate this book to Charlotte Carlin Sokoloff in the hope that, unlike many women in the past, all women will be able to use their skills, knowledge, and training in the future, and to Sarah F. Price for being her mother's inspiration as she helps to shape that future.

---

* Although there is a great need for more serious investigation of homicide (e.g., an emerging pattern of marginally employed men killing young, successful businesswomen), robbery, and assault perpetrated against women, little work has been done to date. Articles on these crimes, then, were not available.

We want to thank John Jay College of Criminal Justice in general, and specifically the departments of Thematic Studies, Law and Police Science and Sociology for providing the kind of environment that promotes interdisciplinary analysis. It was in such a context that the two editors of this book came together over their concern for women in the criminal justice system.

Working with Candice Piaget of the Clark Boardman Company, Ltd., has been satisfying not only because of her professional skills as an editor, but also because she shares much of our philosophy and concern about what happens to women in this society.

For their continuing sustenance and encouragement, for serving as intellectual advisors, and for their willingness to assume many of the time consuming tasks essential to the creation of this volume, we are indebted to Bob Price and Fred Pincus.

Table of Contents

PART 1

Theories and Facts
About Women Offenders

Introduction[1]

The contributions to criminology by women have had a growing impact in recent years. While their full extent can not yet be evaluated, two aspects are of particular significance. First, the influence of women is being felt in the development of criminological theory about crime causation. Second, women are beginning to make an impact on social policy and practical reforms as a result of their research findings and social activism. Both of these areas are well illustrated in Chapters 1-10.

As the women's liberation movement gained momentum in the mid-1960s, feminists turned scholarly attention to a critical analysis of women and crime. Feminism is a social movement which seeks the attainment of social, political, and economic equality for women. The movement has focused particularly on the institutional nature of discrimination and has generated in-depth analysis of the condition of women in western society. In criminology the movement precipitated a reevaluation of old theories about crime causation as they pertain to women. In so doing, the sexist foundations of these theories were clearly exposed. At one point the women's movement was accused of creating women criminals. In part as a response to such charges, researchers have been taking a fresh look at the crimes women commit, the social structural conditions surrounding those crimes, the nature of the charges brought against women, and the conditions and types of punishment women receive. Thus, the women's movement, and the researchers influenced by it, are making contributions to criminology as they study the social structural conditions which lead to crimes by women.

In Part 1 the chapters examine three aspects of women and crime: first, theories about crime causation as they pertain to women; second, the relationship between the women's liberation movement and crime; and third, women in prison.

1. *Theories About Crime Causation: The Development of Criminological Theory.* It is frequently noted that there is an on-going tension between theory and data: fresh information exposes the inadequacies of existing theory while new theories call into question past observations and methods of collecting information. The resulting tension between theory and data is a useful phenomenon because it helps assure that scholarly disciplines, such as sociology and criminology, are self-critical and productive.

One of the observations made by feminists about women's crime was that almost all past theories of crime causation were developed following

3

analysis of patterns of male criminality. As a result, the theories were not very useful in explaining female crime and the particular forms that it takes. The recent attention to women's role in crime, an area almost totally neglected in the past by criminologists, has stimulated the expansion of information about societal conditions that lead to crimes by women, the condition and experience of the women themselves, and society's responses to those crimes. Feminists in their writings continue to extend our formulations for greater understanding of the socially structured circumstances related to women's participation or non-participation in crime. In the process knowledge is also being gained about males and factors that prevent or incline them to crime and so criminologists will need to continue to evaluate and scrutinize old, generally accepted theories of crime. The effort should ultimately lead to a broader and more useful understanding of crime generally, whether committed by women or men.

With growing numbers of scholarly investigations being conducted on the causes of female criminality, new empirical data will emerge requiring the present theory be reassessed, in some instances to be rejected, in others to be revised. It is generally the case that theory shapes what scholars study and, to an extent, what they find. In part, crimes by women and against women are being "discovered" because the women's movement has criticized traditional criminologists for either ignoring women or for imposing preconceived notions on criminological studies about women, their behavior in the home, within the family, and in the larger outside world. In short, the women's movement has prompted social scientists to explore more carefully both the sexism inherent in their theories and the particular relationship of women to the criminal justice system. In so doing, women criminologists, who are either feminists or influenced by them, are playing a significant part in furthering the body of knowledge.[2]

2. *The Impact of the Women's Movement on Crime.* The earliest effect of the current women's movement on criminology was a backlash or response to feminists by those who articulated an "emancipation argument," also called a "liberation theory." This theory states that as women assume the same roles in society as men, their criminal behavior will become like that of men. It is not an original theory: William Adrian Bonger, a Dutch sociologist at the turn of the century, first proposed the idea. Even pioneer criminologists such as Lombroso and Ferri, who unquestionably were sexist in their own understanding of women and criminality, had identified the impact of society on criminal behavior by the early 1900s. But in the early 1970s it was an idea that had come to fruition. Certainly the crime statistics showed that crimes by women were rising. The women's movement was gaining momentum, encouraging women to assume new roles outside the home, which alarmed many politically conservative people and groups. Thus, conditions led them to make an overly simplistic cause and

effect theory associating rising female crime with the growth of the women's movement. This position particularly appealed to those against changes in society to provide equality for women. This emancipation argument has been described in a cynical vein as the "as women follow men into the factories and offices, so too will they follow them into the prisons syndrome."[3]

It was a seductive theory but not supported by facts. In fact, despite all the charges of increased female crime, women in local jails remained constant at six percent from 1972 to 1978.[4] However, to those intent on discrediting the movement and its purposes the theory provided good ammunition and so they argued that the crime rate was high enough without women adding to the rate as they became "liberated."

More thoughtful analysts responded to this emancipation or liberation argument by cautioning against drawing hasty conclusions from gross crime statistics.[5] They cited, first, the problems (both reporting and recording) of relying on the accuracy of official crime statistics when building theory. They pointed out, also, that careful analysis of official data showed increases only in certain crime categories: low-level forgery, fraud, and petty larcenies (see Chapter 6). On second examination, the growth in women's crime seemed to be a case of recording more credit card and check writing crimes along with a rise in shoplifting. It should be pointed out that these crimes coincided with social conditions associated with a rise in both inflation and unemployment. The so-called traditional male crimes of violence, robbery, assault, murder, had not risen among women. Where was the evidence that the liberated new woman criminal had arrived on the scene? Finally, other analysts argued that what was important was not to look at the individual women who were caught engaging in criminal behavior per se, but the overall conditions in society.[6]

3. *Women in Prison.* Simultaneous with the dissemination of these findings on the limited rise in female crime, women researchers studied the actual composition of jail and prison inmates who were women. They reported that incarcerated women were untouched by the women's movement, at least in any direct and visible way. Women inmates still came from the poor, the uneducated, and racial minority groups as they had for decades (see Chapter 8). Quite clearly, women from these sectors were not the women who had been changed or become liberated by the movement. They were not arrested in the course of seeking self-fulfillment and new roles; nor were they possessed of recently acquired self-confidence and determination to make their own way independently in the world.

Not only were women inmates not directly affected by the women's movement, but their treatment within the criminal justice system by its members reinforced their previous acculturation of playing traditional roles of dependency and working in traditional female occupations. Researchers uncovered many interesting facts on the handling of women prisoners. They found, for example, that extremes of treatment were common, ranging from apparent protective chivalrous treatment to excessively harsh sentences compared to those given men. Unjust and disparate (in relation to males) treatment of female status offenders was also documented by researchers. In addition, many studies uncovered shockingly bad living conditions in women's facilities with no services or very minimal levels and inadequate medical care—worse than that available to men inmates, which itself is often substandard.

There are several implications of the criminal justice system's response to women prisoners: first, it indicates that women are regarded by officials as more despicable than men who are sent to jail or prison; second, the system and those appointed to run it, have capitalized on the fact that women are less prone than men to riot and to use violent forms to protest harsh conditions; third, women emerge from their incarceration no better prepared to cope with the world than when they entered prison, and with less of a chance than the male inmate who has been released. Not only has the woman in prison had less opportunity to receive job training, educational programs or counseling, but the socializing that she does receive is inappropriate. It is designed to convince her that her proper role is only that of "good" housewife, mother, and homemaker—roles that she can only fill if she succeeds in learning how to support herself (and any children she may have since 80 percent of all incarcerated women are unmarried).

The material in this section on women offenders covers theories about women offenders in Chapters 1-4, challenges to the contention of a relationship between the women's movement and crime by women in Chapters 5-6, and the conditions of women prisoners in Chapters 7-10. Taken together, these three parts provide an overview with considerable illustrative detail on the current status of women offenders in the United States.

Notes

1 The material in this introduction is based, in part, on Barbara Raffel Price, "The Impact of Feminism on Criminology" (paper delivered at the 1980 meeting of the American Society of Criminology, San Francisco).

2 For example, Freda Adler's *Sisters in Crime*, which argued the thesis that women were becoming more like men not only in their legitimate pursuits but in their illegitimate activities, stimulated criticism and research by many others.

3 Barbara Raffel Price, "Women and Crime," *Bulletin of the American Academy of Psychiatry and the Law* 2, no. 2 (1979).

4 *Profile of Jail Inmates: Sociodemographic Findings from the 1978 Survey of Inmates of Local Jails* (Washington, D.C.: U.S. Government Printing Office, 1980), p. 3. There was, however, a sharp

increase in the number of females in state and federal prisons. Up 2 percent from 4 to 6 percent in federal prisons and up 1 percent from 3 to 4 percent in state prisons. These figures are up 113 percent and 71 percent respectively.

5 Among those social scientists are such women as Sue Titus Reid, *Crime and Criminology* (New York: Holt, Rinehart & Winston, 1982); Carol Smart, *Women, Crime, and Criminology: A Feminist Critique* (London: Routledge, Kegan Paul, 1976); Laura Crites, ed., *Women Offenders* (Lexington: Lexington Books, 1976); Laurel Rans, "Women's Crime—Much Ado about Nothing," *Federal Probation,* March 1978; Ruth Glick (see Chapter 8 herein); Nanci Koser Wilson, "The Masculinity of Violent Crime—Some Second Thoughts," *Criminal Justice,* vol. 9 no. 2, 1981.

6 Dorie Klein and June Kress, "Any Woman's Blues: A Critical Overview of Women, Crime and Criminal Justice," *Crime and Social Justice,* Spring 1976.

1

The Criminal Law and Women[1]

Natalie J. Sokoloff and Barbara Raffel Price

We chose to begin this section on women offenders with a piece written specifically for this volume. All too often, books and articles dealing with offenders—including the few focusing particularly on women—fail to ask what historical, political, and social processes influence the development of laws which determine who will be defined as criminal and for what types of offenses.

Offenders become offenders because they break laws (and are caught). But who makes these laws? In whose interest? At what expense to certain groups, such as women, workers, poor people, and people of color? Which kinds of laws affect women most? How well are they enforced? What kinds of laws are women most likely to break? And how does a sexist legal system treat such law breakers?

Criticisms of criminal justice injustices are becoming more and more commonplace; only the naive would assert that the criminal justice system provides equal justice. It would also be simplistic to argue that a major overhaul of the system is possible in the foreseeable future, given immediate attention to its innumerable problems—that once the system is forced to recognize its ills, justice will reassert itself.

Our society is complex, and the causes of crime are deep-seated. There are no simple explanations, and there are no simple solutions to preventing or controlling crime. Nevertheless, reforms are in order. But to effect realistic reforms that address the system's most serious weaknesses, society must understand: *why* injustices occur through an institution premised on "equal justice for all"; *how* the system itself perpetuates these injustices; and *what* needs to be done to maximize the system's strengths without sacrificing its ideals. Finally, and perhaps most importantly, we must begin to understand that the future integrity of the system depends as much on broad social change as on conscientious reform efforts within the criminal justice system.

This book, and Part 1 specifically, addresses one of the more serious and blatant failings of the criminal justice system: its treatment of women in relation to our society's legal framework. Of interest here are women

9

offenders, women who break the law; women victims, women who are harmed by others who break the law; and women professionals and para-professionals who enforce the law. Before discussing women who break laws and become criminals in the process, the law itself needs careful scrutiny.

First, let us begin by asking who is responsible for making the laws under which women are convicted. Why have these laws been made? In whose interest were these laws created? Which groups of women are more likely to be punished for violating these laws? Second, rather than looking solely at the motivation, behavior, or immediate social environment of the individuals who break laws, let us examine some of the ways in which society is organized to promote the conditions that cause behavior defined as criminal in this society. Third, a context is provided for understanding criminal law in relation to women, with an emphasis on the relationship between criminal, civil, and administrative law and the differential impact of these laws on women. And finally, this chapter supports the belief that the legal system, like the criminal justice system, operates under the class, race, and sex biases inherent in the larger society. How this operates specifically in regard to women offenders is a question of special concern in this chapter, and is a question that prepares the reader for the chapters that follow in this section.

The problems that women face within the legal system are neither specific nor intrinsic features of the system. Rather, they are related to broader issues in American life of sexism, racism, and capitalism—which are reflected in the organization and administration of the legal system itself.

In order to better understand these concerns about the law and its relationship to women, this chapter considers the following basic notions about the law: (1) The Law: What Is It? Who Makes It? Who Is Affected By It?; (2) Types of Law; (3) Theories of Crime Causation Affecting the Development of the Law; (4) Women Under the Law; and (5) Social Movements Affecting Women and the Law.

THE LAW

What Is It?

Law, in the broadest sense, is a set of formalized and codified rules that govern people's behavior and carry negative sanctions for violation. Laws are enacted norms; they are explicitly brought into being by legislation generated by elected public officials. In part laws are considered formal norms because they are written down. They are also considered formal norms because public agencies (police, courts, and corrections) have been created to enforce the laws (Almquist et al., 1978). As one observer argues, the technique of criminal law consists primarily in announcing certain standards of conduct and attaching unpleasant consequences to acts (or omissions) violating those standards, thereby hoping to motivate people to conform (Hart, 1968).

Informal norms which are not part of the law also guide behavior and also may be negatively sanctioned. For example, someone may avoid talking with you or refuse you a job if you are too loud or dress in a way that is regarded as objectionable. Penalties for violating the law, however, are much more severe than are those for violating most norms. In criminal law, penalities range all the way from a money fine to probation, to a jail or prison sentence, and in some states, to death.

The law is organized in such a way that it is primarily individuals rather than corporations whose behavior is controlled by negative sanctions. This is due in part to the fact that the legal system and its criminal law are grounded in the protection of private property and the accumulation of private and corporate profits, as much as in the physical security of individual citizens. In fact the criminal law was developed to apply to individual human behavior and motivation. It has since been applied to the actions of corporations; but it is still the case today that the criminal law is most often used against individuals. Some harms done by corporations, many of which have caused illness or death, have been subjected to civil actions, criminal prosecutions, or the new hybrid "civil penalties," but punishment has usually been in a monetary form (Stone, 1975). Several examples of how the law impacts upon individuals in contrast to corporations are instructive.

On the one hand, if an individual is found to have murdered another person, it is likely that s/he will be imprisoned, and the possibility exists that the offender's life could be taken by the state. On the other hand, although it has been proven that cigarette smoking definitely leads to cancer, which in turn, often leads to death, the tobacco industry remains a thriving trade. Birth control pills are another example. Even though research is finding that birth control pills cause physical harm to women and can cause deformities in children, they continue to be made readily available to the public. Of course, tobacco companies and birth control manufacturers are now required to supply warnings with their products. If consumers continue to smoke or to take the pill, it is at their own risk. But does this truly absolve these industries of guilt when cigarette smokers succumb to lung disease or when women are paralyzed by strokes? When a person is murdered, is the murderer's guilt somewhat mitigated because of society's constant warnings that citizens must protect themselves against crime? Even though intent is a key element in the case of one individual killing another, the examples given here are nonetheless disconcerting.

Although the deterrent effect of criminal sanctions is often debated, there is no doubt that possibility of punishment does not overly intimidate corporations. This is due in part because corporations are never certain if they will be accused of any wrongdoing, in part because the fines are too low to be a meaningful deterrent, and in part because the stigmatization of being taken to court is absent or minimal as compared to the loss of face that a person might experience if accused of a crime. Further, the requirement of *mens rea*, i.e., that for some crimes the state must demonstrate that an actor intended to behave in a manner defined as illegal (Gibbons, 1968), makes prosecuting a large corporation a difficult, if not impossible matter. U.S. corporations are interested in profits. The law works well to protect their property rights; it works far less well to protect people from the harmful impact of their often admittedly unintended acts. Typically, intent must be found in an identifiable high officer of the corporation— hardly an easy charge to prove.

In these and other ways, the law defines which behavior will be punished, how it will be punished, and who will be punished. In so doing, the law protects what those in power value most.

Who Makes the Law?

Women, racial/ethnic minorities, the poor, and working class people rarely benefit from the law. A brief look at which groups of people make laws will demonstrate the truth of this unfortunate reality. On the surface, the facts are clear: rich white men are most influential in creating laws. Criminal law in our society consists of the regulations of behavior by those invested with the authority to act in the name of society. Much of the criminal law is written by state legislatures and the United States Congress, whose members are overwhelmingly male. In 1981 the Congress had only 21 women members (4 percent) out of a total of 535 seats (National Directory of Women Elected Officials, 1981). The state legislatures have slightly more women, averaging 12 percent nationally, but there is great variation from state to state (NDWEO, 1981).

It has long been argued by both mainstream and radical political theorists that the state and thus the legal system and its criminal laws operate in the interests of the dominant class in a capitalist society. In the United States the dominant class may be considered the wealthy business class. Those who write the laws either belong to or represent this dominant class. In a democratically controlled Senate under former President Carter, the majority of senators owned at least a quarter million dollars in stocks and assets, while at least 22 out of 100 senators reported themselves to be millionaires ("The Millionaire Contingent in Congress," 1980). Under a more open "big business-favored" administration with President Ronald Reagan, four out of five of his very influential cabinet level officials were at least half-millionaires, and more than half (10 out of 17) are worth more than one million dollars ("Financial Reports Show that 10 Members . . . ," 1981). Not only do the wealthy exercise disproportionate power in government directly; they also do so indirectly. The concentration of corporate and banking power, with a concomitant political power in relatively few hands, is a critical consideration in a realistic analysis of the criminal law.

It still comes as a surprise to many people that in the United States less than one percent of the entire population owns half of all corporate stock. In terms of families, the top 5 percent of all families own over half of the country's wealth, while the bottom 60 percent, the mass of all families, own only 8 percent. In terms of corporations, the 200 largest corporations (far less than one percent) hold 59 percent of all corporate manufacturing assets and receive more than three-fourths of all profits made by U.S. corporations. Finally, less than one percent of the 15,000 banks in this country control over half of all assets (Statistical Abstract of the United States, 1980; Rose, 1979; Babson and Brigham, 1977).

In short, it has been argued by some that:

> . . . the law became the ultimate means by which the state secures the interests of the governing class. Laws institutionalize and legitimize property relations. It is through the legal system, then, that the state explicitly and forcefully protects the interests of the capitalist class. Crime control becomes the coercive means of checking threats to its economic arrangements . . . . The state did not appear as a third party in the conflict between classes [as pluralists have argued], but arose to protect and promote the interests of the dominant economic class, which owns and controls the means of production (Quinney, 1975 p. 290).

While it is certainly the case that some individuals who participate in making the laws have come from the poor and working classes, as well as from racial/ethnic minorities, the system of law making itself is controlled by those with vested interests in private property and directed toward the protection of individual and corporate wealth or those who represent those interests.

Moreover, it is important to remember that despite the alliance between the wealthy business class and the legal system (see Domhoff, 1967; Miller, 1978, for a discussion of corporate and government interlocks), the law is not static. Challenges are constantly being made by those who believe the ruling elite to be indifferent to or in conflict with their interests. For example, the working class has won many rights and labor reforms previously denied them under the law, such as the right to strike and the right to unionize. In addition, even elite factions are sometimes in conflict on certain issues. One clear example has been the long-standing conflict between land conservationists who come from the wealthy upper class and lumbering and mining interests.

Who Becomes a 'Criminal'?

The law, created in large part by and for the dominant class in society, defines which behavior is punishable and thereby determines which groups of people are most likely to be punished.

In our society people are most commonly arrested for crimes against property (burglary, larceny), crimes against the public order (prostitution, gambling, narcotics possession, disorderly conduct, vagrancy), and crimes against persons (assault, murder). Those most likely to be arrested and convicted of these crimes are poor and working class people who are also disproportionately members of racial/ethnic minority groups.

Class, then, is an obvious consideration here. People from lower socioeconomic backgrounds are much more likely to be found guilty and receive harsher sentences for similar acts than those from higher socioeconomic backgrounds. In fact, the favorable treatment of middle and upper class people is found to exist at all stages of the criminal justice process, including arrest, preliminary hearing, pretrial release, pretrial detainment, trial, sentence, and parole. The poor will be less likely to have a private attorney, to have reasonable bail set, to have a jury trial, to have the case dismissed or to be acquitted, to receive probation or a suspended sentence, and if convicted, to receive a relatively short sentence if jailed (Nagel and Weitzman, 1972).

For example, according to one estimate of jail populations (see Wright, 1973) only 14 percent of the prison population are white collar employees, while 43 percent of the prisoners are low-level manual workers or service workers. Among the general labor force the figures are reversed: 41 percent are white collar and 17 percent labor force. People from poorer socioeconomic classes tend to be involved in behavioral patterns that automatically have a greater probability of being handled officially as criminal in our system than do people from higher socioeconomic classes. Thus people from lower socioeconomic origins are more likely to engage in activities that result in charges of drunkenness, assault, disorderly conduct, burglary, and robbery. In contrast, middle and upper class people tend to be involved in activities not traditionally dealt with by the criminal justice system, even though they may be defined as criminal acts. For example, although criminal laws extend to such white collar activities as fraud, falsification of records, evasion of taxes, misuse of funds, malpractice, and the acts of corporations, these acts are not typically handled by criminal justice procedures. Nor are corporate offenders likely to be apprehended.

Sufficient resources are rarely alloted to federal and state agencies to enforce regulations affecting corporations. The U.S. Environmental Protection Agency offers an example of the problem. This agency is responsible for enforcing regulations on toxic waste dumping which often causes serious harm to people and the environment. However, the E.P.A., with over 12,000 employees, currently has only three criminal investigators (Krajick, 1981). This is but another example of the way in which the law is organized and carried out to protect the dominant business class.

In asking who becomes a criminal, bias against racial/ethnic minorities cannot be ignored. The condition, for instance, of blacks in relation to the law and at each stage of the criminal justice process is significantly worse than it is for whites (see Nagel and Weitzman, 1972). The racial distribution of inmates in local jails is one indicator of the significance of racism to this discussion. The figures have remained relatively constant over the past decade: 40 percent of all males in jail are black in this country; this rises to 50 percent of all women in jail. Yet consider the fact that blacks comprise only 12 percent of the general population (Bureau of Justice Statistics, 1980).

Singer (1973) wrote about women in prison saying "mounting evidence supports the conclusion that the criminal justice system as a whole screens out the middle class offender, while leaving the poor and often the racial minorities to be dealt with by imprisonment . . . anyone who has spent time in women's prisons would agree that they are not institutions for the rich" (p. 295). After a survey of prisons for women, The Director of Women's Bureau of the Department of Labor in 1971 stated that: "most women offenders come from the city ghettos. A disproportionate number are from minority populations . . . they are poor . . . very poor" (statement of Elizabeth Koontz before the D.C. Commission on the Status of Women). And for black women the situation is even worse. A study of the District of Columbia Women's Detention Center concluded that "the criminal justice system of the District appears to penalize black female offenders with disproportionate severity. At every stage in the criminal justice process, black women are retained in the system at higher rates than white women" (Barros, 1971 p. ii). Prostitution acts as a vivid example. Only 5 percent of all inmates are female. Yet 30 percent of women in jail are convicted prostitutes. And black women are seven times more likely to be arrested for the crime of prostitution than women of other races (Haft, 1975).

Who Becomes a Victim?

It is interesting to note that despite the most recent attempts at crime control, and despite the common belief that it is the white middle class and upper class that are most likely to be victims of street crime, the data show that the poor and minority groups are the most common victims of violent crime. Murder, aggravated assault, armed robbery, and forcible rape happen most often to people from lower socioeconomic backgrounds (Criminal Victimization in the United States, 1977). While a citizen has a probability of being a victim of a violent crime only once in 400 years, that probability changes to once in 2,000 years if the citizen is white and middle class. If, however, the person is black or hispanic the chances of being violently victimized rise to once in 80 years—or once in a lifetime (Haskell and Yablonsky, 1974). Further in a study of 17 cities, 55 percent of all murder victims and 72 percent of all victims of criminal homicide were black (Mulvihill & Tumin, 1969). For black women racism is compounded by sexism. Black women are two to three times more likely to be raped than women in general (Bowker, 1981); yet black rape victims are believed less often by the police than white rape victims (see Chapter 13, herein). And while black women are clearly more likely to suffer crimes of violence than white or hispanic women, women of all races, ethnic and class groups who are "unattached" (never married, divorced, widowed, separated) are much more likely to be victims of violent crime than married women. For example, separated, divorced, or never married women are six to seven times more likely to be raped than married women (Bowker, 1981).

The victimization data also tells us that men and women are most likely to be victimized by people of the same sex or from the same social class and racial background. However, for women, they are victimized more by men than by other women. Victimization also appears related to being away from the home and family, but in the same neighborhood (Hindelang et al., 1978; see also Chapter 11, herein). However, many crimes against women occur in the home and with known assailants (e.g., rape and wife battering) than occur for men but are not reported.

This chapter began by asking what is law and who makes it. The discussion proceeded from a general definition of law to a discussion about who becomes a criminal and who is victimized. It was demonstrated that women did not do very well—they are under-represented in the making of the law, yet badly over-represented in harms done to them. Women, along with poor people and minorities, have been historically under-protected by the law and seem relatively powerless to obtain equitable treatment before the criminal law. A brief discussion of the different types of law that exist follows.

TYPES OF LAW[2]

Laws can be distinguished by their sources. These may be legislatures, courts, or administrative agencies; we speak correspondingly of statute, case, and regulatory law. The last category, sometimes referred to as administrative law, includes the regulations governing the activities of parole boards as well as the Internal Revenue Service; some of these regulations define crimes. Laws can also be distinguished by relations between the wrongs they address and the remedies they provide. In *criminal law* the state brings an action against a person (whether individual or corporation); the remedy sought is punishment for the harm done. In *civil law* a complainant brings an action against a defendant; the remedy sought is compensation to the complainant (or "to be made whole") for the harm done; punitive damages may be awarded as well. In *administrative law* agencies may bring actions against persons; the remedy sought is compliance with agency regulations. These actions are to be distinguished from those brought by the state or with the state's concurrence to punish persons who have committed crimes defined by regulatory agencies (sometimes called "administrative crimes"). In addition, the courts may impose penalties in order to obtain compliance with their rulings and their codes of conduct, e.g., perjury.

Many acts may make their authors liable to criminal, civil, and administrative actions. Thus a canner whose negligence causes botulism poisoning in an individual may have to: (1) defend against a civil action brought by the poisoned person's family asking monetary support as a remedy; (2) defend a criminal action brought by the state for manslaughter and imposing a fine or prison sentence as a remedy; and (3) defend against actions brought by federal agencies seeking compliance with their packing regulations. Theoretically, then, the same behavior can be covered by different laws.

Statutory Law, Case Law, and Regulatory Law

When legislative action is taken, typically at the state or federal level, the result is *statutory law;* when court decisions and opinions are handed down, a body of precedents which influences subsequent interpretations of the law and is known as *case law* results; when government agencies are empowered by legislatures to write rules and regulations binding on specific persons and organizations, the result is *regulatory* and *administrative law.*

The criminal codes are statutory law. There are 51 separate limited jurisdiction criminal codes in this country, one for each state and the District of Columbia, as well as a federal criminal code, which has national applicability and is the responsibility of the Congress. In addition local jurisdictions have authority, delegated or assumed, to define crimes; regulatory agencies may also define crimes. Together these criminal codes make up the criminal statutes of the land and are a part of statutory law. Besides statutory law there is a body of case law both at the state and federal level which has been created over time.[3] An important third kind of law is regulatory law, which includes regulations that criminal justice agencies issue, and those of other government agencies, such as the Environmental Protection Agency. Once an agency is formed, it is possible that it be empowered to write its own rules, regulations, or guidelines based on law and to hold quasi-judicial hearings.[4]

Criminal and Non-Criminal Law

Civil law refers in large part to the body of law concerned with resolving private conflicts, particularly those concerning private property such as contracts, as well as divorce, child support, and so on. Criminal law, on the other hand, is assumed to be a crime against the state, rather than against an individual person or corporation—even though the act may have been committed against an individual. This is because criminal law applies to acts which are considered so serious and important to the general welfare that the state initiates the prosecution. These crimes may be defined in criminal or regulatory codes or laws. At issue in criminal law is the restoration of public order (Richardson, 1980). In some cases the victim may bring a civil action against the defendant as well. For example, the crime of rape is a felony under criminal law in every jurisdiction, and the state prosecutes the accused. However, the victim, who may have served as a witness at the criminal trial, can only initiate an action in civil court demanding compensation for injury suffered. Thus criminal and civil law overlap, although there are important distinctions between the two types of law.

What this means in practical terms is that if an individual threatens another person on the street for his or her money, holds up a bank, or shoplifts, s/he will be punished as a criminal if caught and convicted. If, on the other hand, an automobile company makes a car with faulty parts and many people are injured or killed as a result, the typical procedure will be that the company is sued for civil and not criminal damages; that is, the company is usually fined or reprimanded (civil), but no one in the corporation is seen as responsible (as a "criminal") and ends up going to jail.

Further, in criminal law if an individual or corporation has been wronged, the wrong is interpreted as a "social wrong," as a crime against society. As such, the state musters all its force and brings suit against the violator; that is, the force and machinery is deployed in the interest of the "victim." In civil law, however, the state interprets a violation as a private wrong against an individual, and therefore it is the individual's duty to redress. Since the violation is not regarded by the state as a social wrong, it is up to the individual to take his or her case to the courts. Typically, the most that happens here is some kind of "reprimand" or fine.

In this discussion of the distinction between criminal law and civil law, it becomes obvious that the criminal law works against specific groups (typically the less powerful) while the civil law operates to the advantage of powerful interest groups or corporations. Again, how these two bodies of law affect women demonstrates our point. For example, there is a tendency to restrict attention to acts done *by* individual women and presently defined in criminal codes, such as prostitution, shoplifting, and writing checks with insufficient funds. There is little discussion, on the other hand, about harms done by corporations and professionals *to* large groups of women, but which are not defined as criminal. Examples of some of these harms to women include the following: brown lung disease among female cotton mill workers; the production of medical devices (especially such contraceptives as birth control pills and intrauterine devices, which endanger health and often life); and questionable medical procedures (e.g., half of all hysterectomies have been found to be medically unnecessary). These are serious, life-threatening abuses against women which are not considered crimes against women by the law. The government does not assign significant personnel either to enforce existing law where criminal law could apply or to review ways to enact laws and protect the public where the law does not yet apply. In discussing violence against both women and men in our society, then, the existing use of formalized criminal law and its administration represents only the "tip of the iceberg."

In short, criminal law tends to focus on individual street crime or organized crime; it does not focus on the widespread abuses of powerful interest groups and wealthy corporations that are harmful to vast numbers of people. Such actions are more likely to be covered under the less punitive common civil law in this country. Most of the laws enacted as a result of the recent political efforts of the women's movement, such as affirmative action hiring and equitable education admissions, fail to extend significantly the criminal law. Cases of employment discrimination and education admission discrimination normally come under civil and administrative law. The instititution or corporation responsible for a violation is generally liable only for compensation, the loss of federal monies or court orders directed toward compliance. Even where there are punitive penalties the offender frequently risks incurring the penalty rather than change and conform to the law, given the limited burdens imposed by the law and its limited enforcement. Stone (1975) points out that even in cease-and-desist orders only monetary threats exist since the corporation is not imprisonable.

The limitations of criminal law are therefore far-reaching, particularly for women, who are systematically discriminated against. Consider as a last example that impressive legislation was passed in the 1970s banning discrimination against women faculty, administrators, service workers, and students in educational institutions receiving federal funds. Thousands of cases of discrimination were brought by individual women (or groups of women) at colleges and universities throughout the country (e.g., see Lichtenstein, 1977, on backlog of over 3,000 complaints for 1977 alone). Despite hundreds of complaints that went beyond individual educational institutions and ultimately were filed with the Department of Health, Education and Welfare (now the Department of Education) against institutions of education for discrimination against women through Title IX of the Education Amendments Act of 1972, there has not been a single instance in which funds have been withheld by the federal government from a university or college found to be engaging in sex discriminatory practices.[5] Thus, the violator is never punished with the threat of jail or a criminal action of any severity. Yet, even here, the less severe penalties permitted under the law (until 1981) for actions harmful to women are seldom, and in this case never, applied.

THEORIES OF CRIME CAUSATION

The law and the penalties prescribed for violations of the criminal law reflect particular theories of crime causation (Gibbons, 1968, Chapter 6; Cohn, 1976, Chapter 22). The four most common theories, the first three of which justify and interpret the law, are: (1) the classical school; (2) the neoclassical school; (3) the positivist school; and (4) the radical or marxist criminology school.

The classical approach holds that people have "free will," are responsible for their acts, and for the most part will be rational in their behavior, thus avoiding punishment where foreseeable by abiding by the law. Accordingly, law clearly states both penalties and crimes (making punishment severe enough to encourage right behavior), anticipating the general compliance of the public. The classical school, therefore, "fit" penalties to crimes and understood punishment as a way to deter or prevent certain behavior. Law and punishment, according to the classical school, must be swift and certain so that people will be clear about the relationship between their acts and punishment.

The neoclassical school holds that the classical school is too rigid. While they agree that having specified penalties for specified crimes is important, they maintain that the law must also allow for exceptions whenever "free will" is not fully present. How can a four-year-old or a retarded person exercise "free will"? Therefore, the neoclassical position argues that the criminal law must apply to such persons only in limited degree; penalties could not be "fitted" to the act without taking the actor into account. Thus, with regard to married women, the law at one time did not hold them fully responsible for their actions; it therefore exempted them from certain penalties because of the marriage bond. Neoclassical theory was the foundation for such special treatment of married women.

A third philosophy of crime causation also shapes our criminal law. It is known as the positivist school; positivists state that criminal behavior is caused by measurable factors, such as brain characteristics, body structure, specific physical features, sex, physical processes, and even the social environment. While the members of the positivist school denied "free will," emphasizing "scientific" causes, especially hereditary factors, they considered criminals legally and socially responsible for their acts (Cohn, 1976). They established the idea of examining the criminal in order to locate the cause of the crime. Their early work emphasized biology and biological causes, but they did not exclude among their causal factors society and its institutions—the family, religion, and the school. Women were readily "explained" when they came into conflict with the law as victims of their own unique biology which made them either irrational or irresponsible or both (see Chapter 2, herein).

The positivists held that the purpose of punishment is rehabilitation; in their "medical models" punishment and treatment are indistinguishable. The law must focus on the offender's resocialization—psychological help or training in a vocation—whatever is needed to turn the offender into a law-abiding citizen. In explaining crime causation, the positivist school also points to inequality in socialization, citing lack of opportunities in life. Again, the implication for women is that they should be rehabilitated or resocialized so that they can "fit in" to society according to the prevailing norms. The traditional role of women in society was not questioned and women's prisons typically trained prisoners, if they were trained at all, in basic homemaking skills and some rudimentary sex-stereotyped occupational skills: cooking, cleaning, sewing, laundry, beauty care and, more recently, typing and key punch operating.

These three theories, classical, positivist, and neoclassical, have been the ones most commonly used to explain crime by men (and women when they were included at all). Criminologists within these traditions accept the legal or state definitions of crime. For them, crime causation was located in the individual offender who is understood as pathological, abnormal, or deviant. As positivism predominated, the conclusion was drawn "that ill-adjusted individuals in conflict with society, in other words, 'deviants,' must be psychologically 'rehabilitated' by the criminal justice system" (Klein and Kress, 1976).

When demands arose in recent years from women influenced by the women's movement that they be included in research and analysis, new theories were not developed; rather, women were simply "added on" to existing theories (see Sokoloff, 1980, Chapter 1, for an example of how this applies to research on women and work). Thus, female criminality has generally been analyzed as a result of innate biological or psychological characteristics of women. Social and economic characteristics were only superficially acknowledged; but even when they were recognized, the ultimate explanation reverted back to the individual woman: akin to the "victim-blaming" approach discussed by Karmen in the Introduction to Part 2 of this book. In short, a woman's biological or reproductive capacities were identified as the defining characteristics on which her criminality (as well as her normality) depended.

In contrast to the above theories which not only shape the criminal law under which we live but also accept the confines of the existing social system is the more recent school of radical or marxist criminology. This fourth theory of crime causation attributes much crime to injustices in the organization and production of criminal law. It cites ruling class control of all major institutions (e.g., business, legislatures, courts) and the social relations between the rich and powerful and the working class and poor as the focal point. It is radical criminology which maintains that those in power create the legal code—in their own interest—defining some acts as serious crimes while ignoring or reducing others to violations of administrative regulations.

Although radical criminology recognizes that street crime is a serious matter to be attended by the law, it does not focus its analysis on developing strategies to deter individual criminals, as the three earlier theories did. Rather, this school is concerned with how the political economic system itself promotes the conditions that cause typical criminal behavior (i.e., poverty) (Platt, 1974). At the same time, radical criminology emphasizes how the system ignores, in large part, the economic and social exploitation of workers, minorities, and poor people by factory owners, big business, government officials, and others in power.

Radical criminology calls for a transformation of the entire political economic system. This approach argues for changing the criminal justice and legal systems by changing the underlying social relations between dominant and subordinate groups in society, particularly between the business class and the working class, but also between whites and racial/ethnic minorities as well as between men and women.

With regard to women, a radical or marxist analysis tries to understand the impact of women's economic dependence in the family on her formally labeled criminal behavior. It maintains that women's inferior economic and political status causes some women to resort to check cashing fraud, shoplifting, prostitution and other crimes in order to support themselves and their children. Finally, rather than trying to change the women and their criminal behavior, marxist criminologists draw attention to changing social, economic, and political conditions which lead to such acts rather than simply altering the law and the way it is administered.

WOMEN UNDER THE LAW

How does the system of criminal and civil law relate to women in the United States? Women have historically been treated in the law as property, first of their fathers and then of their husbands. It is only recently, during the 20th century, that women have acquired independent legal rights in western societies. In the United States it was not until 1971 that the Supreme Court ruled that women were to be interpreted as persons under the Constitution, Reed v. Reed, 404 U.S. 71, 92 S.Ct. 251, 30 L.Ed.2d 225 (1971). Thus, along with the mentally incompetent and the very young, women too have been considered in the past not fully responsible for their acts. The concept of *mens rea* mentioned earlier is applicable here since the law often required the state to prove a person intended to do an act before it can prosecute. Women were once not viewed as mentally capable of intending to do anything; they were seen as too childlike. On this basis historically they have been exempted from the penalties which many laws imposed. However, this "chivalrous" attitude toward women should be understood as just that: a "special protection" of women by men which provides women with dubious privileges "in return for curtailment of their rights and restriction of their activities" (Klein and Kress, 1976).[6]

For example, when the first woman in Wisconsin thought that she might have the right to practice law in 1875, the court turned her down in the following way:

> The law of nature destines and qualifies the female sex for the bearing and nurture of the children of our race and for the custody of the homes of the world . . . [A]ll life-long callings of women, inconsistent with these radical and sacred duties of their sex, as is the profession of the law, are departures from the order of nature; and when voluntary, treason against it . . . The peculiar qualities of womanhood, its genteel graces, its quick sensibility, its subordination of hard reason to sympathetic feeling, are surely not qualifications for forensic strife. Nature has tempered women as little for the juridicial conflicts of the courtroom, as for the physical conflict of the battle field . . . [In re Goddell, 39 Wisc. 232, 245 (1875)]

It should be noted that only white, native-born women associated with middle income and well-to-do men were thought of as "delicate flowers" in need of "chivalrous protection." Women from poor, working class and slave origins have always had to work hard in order to survive and were never considered delicate.

While today women increasingly are seen as equal before the law, the fact that women in the United States have always been defined in the law primarily by their patriarchal relation to the home as wife and mother has had important consequences for how they are treated in the larger society. For example, a man cannot be convicted for raping his wife in forty-one states if they are living together. In nine states, even if they are legally separated, the man cannot by law be charged with rape (Barden, 1981). This is the case in spite of estimates which suggest that at least 600,000 wives are sexually assaulted each year by their husbands. Currently five states (California, Massachusetts, Michigan, Connecticut, and New Jersey) have laws under which forcible sexual relations between married couples is a crime (Barden, 1981); to date, no husband has been convicted and punished for raping his wife.

Ideas about the proper role of women in society are not static: women have fought hard throughout the course of our history to better their conditions. In the legal system in particular, women have long sought changes that would improve their lives. However, the members of the legal system are for the most part men. Thus, even if many laws were not sexist, the fact that those who make the laws (federal and state legislators, government administrators, and judges) and those who enforce the laws (police and courts) are overwhelmingly male, affects in major ways how women are thought of and treated by the legal system. Even when the criminal law does not formally discriminate against women, in practice—as the law operates in the processing of women from police to courts to jails—the law very often does discriminate.

An excellent example of such discriminatory treatment is the processing of female juveniles apprehended for status offenses. A status offense is one that allows the state to intervene in a juvenile's life for behavior which if done by an adult would not be prosecutable. Running away from home, incorrigibility, being in danger of falling into vice, are examples of status offenses. Girls are much more likely than boys to be brought into juvenile court for status offenses and they are punished more severely than youngsters who commit more serious property crimes or even some violent offenses (see Chapter 4, herein). The girls are punished for failing to be submissive, docile and, most importantly, for lacking "sexual purity." The wording of the statutory law may not discriminate against girls, but the way the law is carried out often does.

Since the law was especially lenient toward some women and certain kinds of misbehavior which did not violate standards of "femininity," those women who were not dealt with informally but instead came before the court were considered to have been especially bad and hardened criminals. The court's view, therefore, was that such women needed severe handling. It was as if the very presence of women offenders might explode the myths surrounding attitudes about women concerning their "delicate nature" and "innate goodness." Apparently, the preservation of these attitudes required that women offenders be kept out of public sight and sent to prison for long terms, not to be released until they were deemed fully rehabilitated, i.e., "knew their place" as women in society (see Chapters 2 and 7, herein). Since low income, minority women, and juvenile girls were more often convicted of crimes, we can assume that one important element operating is that these women and girls do not meet the white and middle class standards of femininity of the society (Klein and Kress, 1976).

The creation and differential application of the law to the detriment of women has been discussed in this section. Attention has been given to the way in which the law is particularly disadvantageous to poor, working class and ethnic minority women. In the past women have been viewed by the law as incompetent, childlike, and in need of protection; males were seen as the protectors and financial caretakers of women. Husbands and wives were even treated as "one" under the law—and that "one" was the male. Finally, the double standard of morality based on biological determinism was built into the legal process itself. The myth of purity prevailed: women criminals were said to offend because they were women; for them chivalry gave way to vengeance.

SOCIAL MOVEMENTS

Criminal laws which are sexually discriminatory have gradually been modified or eliminated at the state and federal levels. At least three different but somewhat related social movements or developments are responsible. The one which is most directly responsible is, of course, the women's movement and is made up of women from several different political, economic, and social change perspectives (Freeman, 1975). Much of this change has occurred through individual and group efforts, including such activities as establishing consciousness raising groups, public education programs, working with local groups, public demonstrations and litigation specifically challenging laws that discriminate against women. The second movement, the prisoners' rights movement, has taken a similar course and it, too, is a grass roots effort led by those most directly affected by obtaining its goals—prisoners. The third development, sentencing reform, is essentially different in that it is not a grass roots social movement but rather a concerned interest group of professionals working in the criminal justice system, including elected officials in the legislatures, who create official task forces to study the issues and propose changes.

The Women's Movement

The most important social movement specifically directed to improving women's status in society in general and in the law specifically has been the women's movement. It has focused its efforts in several directions: obtaining new legislation, abolishing discriminatory law and discriminatory practices in the public and private sectors, and educating the public about the harmful effects of sex discrimination.

A primary effort has been to secure passage of an Equal Rights Amendment to the federal constitution. Thirty-six states have already passed their own equal rights amendments to state constitutions. When such an amendment is passed, the legislature is supposed to examine all of its laws so that they conform to the new standard of nondiscrimination. For the criminal code it should remove all sexist language in the law, thereby ensuring that men and women are punished for the same crimes and with the same amount of punishment. Thus far, however, only 11 of the 36 states have taken this step. Within criminal law, then, the majority of women are still not well-protected from legal discrimination. It should be apparent that as important as the national Equal Rights Amendment is, if it were to be passed it would not solve all of women's problems in our society.[7] The existence of formal legal rights is only the beginning; until they are exercised in daily life little meaningful change exists.

Another important way that the women's movement has brought about change in the law is through its pressure on Congress. As a result, federal legislation prohibiting sex discrimination in employment, education, credit, insurance, taxes, pensions, and the military has been passed. However, the enforcement of these laws is seriously jeopardized in cities and regions across the country because of fiscal problems and conservative decision makers. Moreover in the 1980s our society is experiencing a strong conservative trend politically which has supported reduced federal protection in civil rights laws generally and a movement toward severely weakening affirmative action requirements. The law itself is moving back to the position where it fails to protect women and minorities under these conditions. In addition to the threats against a national Equal Rights Amendment, the rights of women to control over their bodies is under attack as conservatives attempt to criminalize abortion once again, as well as to take away the ability of women (either alone or with partners) to provide the most basic necessities of life with severe cutbacks in essential social services. It may well be that a perception of many in this country that the women's movement has been too successful is now producing a powerful backlash —to the detriment of all women. One possible consequence, according to some observers, is a strengthening of the women's movement by renewing its determination to achieve its objectives and by attracting more support for its goals.

The Prisoners' Rights Movement

A second but smaller movement intent on changing laws and the criminal justice system is one of prison reform. The prisoners' rights movement began in the mid-1960s, a period of intense social activism. It hoped to direct public attention to the fact that prisoners in the United States are entitled to, but very often fail to receive, the benefits of the rights and privileges that the constitution extends to all citizens (Alpert, 1976). The purposes of the movement are many: to improve the often horrendous conditions in prisons; to gain the right to medical care, nutritious food, work for pay, work furlough programs; to obtain protection against the use of force; to provide prisoners with support both inside and outside the prison; to educate the public in order to gain support for changing the conditions of prison life; and to develop an analysis of the underlying political, economic, and social conditions of prisoners and prison life. The prisoners' rights movement has worked through the courts, through the educational and lobbying efforts of ex-offender groups, as well as through inmate strikes, demonstrations, and riots (see No More Cages).

The focus of this movement has been primarily on class and race oppression of prisoners, not on sexism in prisons. Women prisoners have not generally been as active in the movement as men (see Chapter 10 herein, for discussion of some of the reasons for this lower profile of women inmates; see also Burkhart, 1973, and Resnik and Shaw, 1980). For women, the situation is particularly difficult, since their small numbers in prison, only 5 percent of the entire prison population, has left those women incarcerated invisible to the public. Some litigation by women prisoners has occurred most notably over the validity of longer sentences imposed on women and more recently for improved medical services (see Resnik and Shaw, 1980).[8] Women inmates have also expressed their resistance by rioting on occasion (Female Offenders, 1979). Several examples follow:

One serious disturbance occurred at the federal prison for women in Alderson, West Virginia in 1971, the same year that the Attica riot took place. The women at Alderson staged a memorial demonstration and work stoppage "in memory of the brothers murdered at . . . Attica." A building occupation followed, the women issued 42 demands, and about 500 of the 529 prisoners stopped work and school at the prison for five days (Eisen, 1977). In response to that riot women identified as the ring leaders by the authorities were punished and were transferred to an all-male federal prison in Fort Worth, Texas. As a consequence of this action, however, the women became integrated into the general inmate population for their work assignments and for meals and recreation. Ironically, this was the beginning of "co-corrections" in the United States, an experiment which not only has had some successes, but has spread to some state prisons and local jails.

Another rebellion took place in the early 1970s in a jail outside Detroit, Michigan where many women inmates were assigned to laundry work, washing not only all clothing from the women's jail but also all from the men's jail nearby, the Detroit House of Corrections. The women resisted by destroying most of the equipment and the laundry itself, in protest over the work. The authorities closed the operation, sent the laundry to a commercial service, and reassigned the women to work in the neighboring state mental hospital doing various menial tasks.

In another case of women prisoners' resistance, the response of the institution was more mixed. The conditions leading to the rebellion at Raleigh, North Carolina is specified by Eisen (1977):

> The rebellion at Raleigh began in March 1975, with a 1-day work stoppage protesting the intolerable heat, slippery floors, 200-pound loads and unsanitary work conditions at the prison laundry. Many of the 400 women at Raleigh are forced to work at this laundry, which serves the various state hospitals. Other demands included humane medical treatment, improved work conditions, increase in pay, end to harassment by guards known to be Ku Klux Klan members, and improved visiting conditions (p. 10).

In this case, authorities responded predictably by transferring the 34 "ringleaders" to a men's prison and putting 95 more in a lock-up. However, some of the worst conditions improved as a consequence of the uprising; for example, the women now get some pay for their work.

While the prisoners' rights movement and the women's movement have many goals in common, most notably protection under the law from arbitrary and unfair treatment, the activities of the two groups do not usually overlap. Yet there are several examples where the two movements have coalesced to work for change. Some small indications may be found in the recent announcement by the Federal Bureau of Prisons that women will have an opportunity to be trained in nontraditional work (Female Offenders, 1979), and some interest has been expressed in state prisons in programs for inmate-mothers (see Chapter 9, herein). In addition, "prison support groups, defense committees and women's groups across the country have formed in solidarity with women struggling inside prison" (Eisen, 1977). An example are the women's groups working at the California Institute for Women (CIW). Not only have they done general support work, but they have alerted the public to the dehumanizing and punitive behavior modification program that CIW wanted to institute several years ago. In 1976, these women's groups helped to organize mass support against this behavior modification program, which was never opened. A year later these groups rallied against the threatened construction of a new women's prison in the state. Better programs and opportunities, not more prisons, was the goal of these groups.

The Sentencing Reform Movement

A third and much smaller development within criminal law is the recent attention to reforming the criminal codes as they specify punishments in sentencing. The current reform interest is in reducing the disparity of sentences (see Newman, 1978; Allen, 1978).

"Disparity in sentencing" refers to the practice of allowing judges to give very different sentences to offenders convicted of exactly the same crime under similar conditions. The issue of disparity has been seen as a problem by those in the criminal justice system as well as by offenders; it offends a sense of basic fairness. As interest in this issue has grown, some states have completely revised their criminal codes so that judges have much less discretion at time of sentencing. We have here a return to the classical position on punishment.

As the sentencing laws are changed, the sexually discriminatory parts of the law may also be changed or removed, particularly when groups within the women's movement monitor the revisions. Thus, at the time of sentencing, women, at least, should not be treated more harshly than men under reformed criminal codes. However the issue of sentencing reform is complex.[9] While it is essential that men and women be treated similarly in sentencing and that judges not treat women more severely, it is also the case that until overall treatment of women in the criminal justice system is altered they may continue to be discriminated against once arrested (see Chapter 15, herein).

This section has described three separate social movements or developments in the United States, each working for specific objectives—women's equality, prisoner's rights, and reformed sentencing laws—but these objectives overlap and each has the potential to improve the conditions of women offenders, victims, and workers in the criminal justice system.

In this chapter the reader has been introduced to the criminal law as it relates to women, racial/ethnic groups, and the poor and working classes. The chapter began by explaining the law in terms of the purposes it serves. This led to an explanation of what acts are defined as criminal, with a focus on what groups are most affected by the law and what groups are most likely to be either victims of crime or victims of the law itself. Theories developed to explain crime were identified as traditional rationales which have served to justify legal definitions of crime; the school of radical or marxist criminology was singled out as the only theory of crime causation which generally locates the causes of criminal behavior not in the individual offender, but at the political and economic arrangements of a capitalist society. The impact of the law in relation to minority groups generally and women specifically was then explained, concluding with a brief look at social movements which have arisen in response to this society's inequitable system of law and justice.

The basic point of this chapter is that the law is not simple, value-free, or static. As you read through the chapters in this book, it is important that you ask how the conditions of sex, race, and class in the larger society affect the relationship between women and the criminal justice system.

Notes

1 The authors gratefully acknowledge the critical comments and helpful suggestions made by Sid Harring, William Heffernan, Fred L. Pincus, Robert G. Price, and Norma K. Raffel in the writing of this chapter.

2 Two discussions which were helpful to the authors and will be helpful to the reader are Reid (1979) and Sigler (1981), chapters 3 and 6.

3 Case law consists of court decisions and court interpretations of statutory law which heavily influence future decisions. Even where statutes have codified areas previously left to case law, the terms of the codes themselves are often defined through previous and subsequent cases.

4 Such is the case, for example, with parole boards. Some of their operational authority is specified in statutory law but much is left for the board to develop such as rules on eligibility for parole, required conditions to stay on parole and hearing procedures to revoke parole. In this way the agency or board writes the guidelines for its own operation. These affect the behavior of its clients as well as its own organization's members. Because these "laws" take the form of written "statutes" or regulations and "case" determinations by administrators or administrative law courts, administrative law has much in common with case and statutory law. Keep in mind that some of these regulations, typically through authority delegated by statute but sometimes under what is know as "home rule" (in the case of, e.g., municipal ordinances), define crimes.

5 In 1981, the Reagan administration excluded employment discrimination altogether from Title IX, providing women with that much less protection.

6 This "protectionist" attitude prevails in many spheres of the law today. Thus, much like "protective labor" legislation for women at the turn of the century, legislation is being proposed today which will "protect women" from traditionally well-paying male jobs. Jobs in the lead industry, for example, which are high paying can be extremely harmful to a fetus if a pregnant woman is employed there. However, it is only women of childbearing ages (15-44) who are denied employment. Yet male workers and nonpregnant women are exposed to harmful substances and conditions in the workplace, many of which can be transmitted to an unborn fetus by men as well as women (Chavkin, 1979).

7 It is important for the reader to understand that formal legal rights for women is only the first step in the long struggle for women's rights, equality and liberation. With an Equal Rights Amendment, a much needed instrument, women would then be "free," like men, to be unequal by race, class and sexual orientation. For example, so long as there is class inequality, working class and poor women will be able to achieve equality—but typically with their low status, poorly paid male partners who lack decision making control in their jobs and much of their lives. So long as racism is a basic structure of relations in our society, women of color will be able to achieve economic, educational, political, social and sexual equality primarily with their racially discriminated against men of color. And so forth.

8 See, e.g., Commonwealth v. Daniels(1) 210 Pa. Super. 156, 232 A.2d 247 (1967) and Commonwealth v. Daniels (111) 430 Pa. 642, 243 A.2d 400 (1968) and Todaro v. Ward, 431F. Supp. 1129 (S.D.N.Y.), aff'd, 565 F.2d 48 (2d. Cir. 1977).

9 It is of course important to remember that limiting judges' discretion also can have potentially harmful effects. For example, the laws themselves might become quite harsh and the judge would have no power to modify punishment. Typically the criminal justice system "corrects" somewhat for these situations by the discretion exercised by the prosecutor in the charge made; in òther cases, with jury trials, juries may be reluctant to convict if the punishment is deemed too severe. However, several states that have revised their criminal codes reducing judicial discretion have, in effect, increased the length of incarceration time and those sentences are being imposed by the courts. The state of New Jersey is an example of this result. This problem is further complicated by the fact that limiting judges' discretion so that sentences may be increased has been a tactic of conservatives whose aim has been to push for harsher sentences of offenders instead of trying to change the underlying conditions in society that might lead to the crime in the first place.

References

Allen, Harry E. and Clifford E. Simonson. Corrections in America: An Introduction. Enceno, CA: Glencoe Press, 1978.

Almquist, Elizabeth, Janet S. Chafetz, Barbara J. Chance, and Judy Corder-Bolz. Sociology: Women, Men and Society. St. Paul, MI: West Publishing Co., 1978.

Alpert, Geoffrey P. "Prisoners right of access to courts; planning for legal aid," Washington Law Rev. 51:653-675, 1976.

Babson, Steve and Nancy Brigham. Why Do We Spend So Much Money? Somerville, MA: Popular Economics Press, 1977.

Barden, J.C. "Confronting the moral and legal issues of marital rape," The New York Times (June 1): B5, 1981.

Barros, Slaven, McArthur, and Adams. "Movement and characteristics of women's detention center admissions," Research Re. 39:ii, 1971.

Bowker, Lee. Women, Crime and the Criminal Justice System. Lexington, MA: Lexington Books, 1978.

————, ed. Women and Crime in America. New York: Macmillan, 1981.

Bureau of Justice Statistics. "Profile of jail inmates: sociodemographic findings from the 1978 survey of inmates of local jails," National Prisoner Statistics Report. Washington, D.C.: U.S. Government Printing Office, 1980.

Burkhart, Kathyrn Watterson. Women in Prison. New York: Popular Library and Doubleday & Co., 1973.

Cargan, Leonard and Mary A. Coates. "The indeterminate sentence and judicial bias," Crime and Delinquency 20 (April) 2: 144-156, 1974.

Chavkin, Wendy. "Occupational hazards to reproduction: a review essay and annotated bibliography," Feminist Studies (Summer) 310-325, 1974.

Cohn, Alvin. Crime and Justice Administration. Philadelphia: J.B. Lippincott, 1976.

Criminal Victimization in the United States: A National Crime Survey Report. Washington, D.C.: National Criminal Justice Information and Statistics Service, 1977.

Domhoff, William. Who Rules America? Englewood Cliffs, N.J.: Prentice-Hall, 1967.

Eisen, Arlene. "Rebellions rock women's prisons," Guardian (May 25), p. 10, 1977.

Female Offenders: Who are They and What Are Their Problems Confronting Them? Washington, D.C.: General Accounting Office, 1979.

"Financial reports show that 10 members of cabinet are worth $1 million or more," New York Times, (January 26), p.24, 1981.

Freeman, Jo. The Politics of Women's Liberation: A Case Study of an Emerging Social Movement and Its Relation to the Policy Process. New York: David McKay Co, 1975.

Gibbons, Don C. Society, Crime, and Criminal Careers. Englewood Cliffs, NJ: Prentice-Hall, 1967.

Haft, Marylin. "Legal arguments: prostitution laws and the constitution," in The Politics of Prostitution, by Jennifer James, Jean Withers, Marilyn Haft and Sara Theiss. Seattle: Social Research Associates, 1975.

Hart, H.L.A. Prolegomenon to the principles of punishment, in Punishment and Responsibility. New York: Oxford City University Press, 1968.

Haskell, M. and L. Yablonsky. Criminology: Crime and Criminality. Chicago: Rand McNally, 1974.

Lichtenstein, Grace. "Men hold most top college jobs 5 years after U.S. order on bias," New York Times (December 6), p. 18, 1977.

Martindale, Don A. The Nature and Types of Sociological Theory. Boston: Houghton Mifflin, 1960.

Marx, Karl. Capital: A Critique of Political Economy, vol. 1 (1886), reprint. New York: International Publishing Co, 1967.

Miller, Judith. "Interlocking directorates flourish," New York Times, (April 23), p. D23, 1978.

Mulvihill, Donald J. and Melvin M. Tumin. Crimes of Violence, vol. II. A Staff Report submitted to the National Commission on the Causes and Prevention of Violence. Washington, D.C.: U.S. Government Printing Office, 1969.

Nagel, S. and Lenore Weitzman. "Double standard of american justice," in Transaction: Social Science and Modern Society (18): 18-25, 62, 1972.

National Directory of Women Elected Officials 1981. Washington, D.C.: Women's Political Caucus, 1981.

The New York Times, January 26, 1981.

Newman, Donald J. Introduction to Criminal Justice. Philadelphia: J.B. Lippincott, 1978.

No More Cages: A Bi-monthly Women's Prison Newsletter. Women Free Women in Prison, P.O. Box 90, Brooklyn, NY 11215.

Platt, Tony. "Prospects for a radical criminology in the United States," Crime and Social Justice (1) (Spring-Summer), 1974.

Quinney, Richard. Criminology: Analysis and Critique of Crime in America. Boston: Little, Brown and Co., 1970, 1975.

_____. Class, State and Crime: On the Theory and Practice of Criminal Justice. New York: Longman, 1977.

Reid, Sue Titus. Crime and Criminology. New York: Holt, Reinhart, and Winston, 1979.

Resnik, Judy and Nancy Shaw. "Prisoners of their sex: health problems of incarcerated women." New York: Clark Boardman Co., 1980.

Richardson, Laurel Walum. The Dynamics of Sex and Gender: A Sociological Perspective. Boston: Houghton Mifflin Co., 1977, 1981.

Rose, Stephen J. "Social stratification in the United States: an analytic guidebook." Social Graphics Co., 1120 Riverside Ave., Baltimore, Md. 21230, 1979.

Sigler, Jay A. Understanding Criminal Law. Boston: Little, Brown and Co., 1981.

Singer, Linda. "Women and the correctional process," American Criminal Law Rev. (11):295,-297, 1973.

Sokoloff, Natalie J. Between Money and Love: The Dialectics of Women's Home and Market Work. New York: Praeger, 1980.

Stone, Christopher D. Where the Law Ends. New York: Harper & Row, 1975.

"The millionaire contingent in congress," U.S. News & World Report (March 17), p.4, 1980.

U.S. Bureau of the Census, Statistical Abstract of the United States: 1980 (101st ed.), Washington, D.C., 1980.

Weber, Max. Economy and Society. Edited by Gunther Roth and Claus Wittich, translated by Ephraim Fischoff et al. New York: Bedminster Press, 1968.

Wright, Erik Olin. The Politics of Punishment: A Critical Analysis of Prisons in America. New York: Harper & Row, 1973.

2

The Etiology of Female Crime: A Review of the Literature

Dorie Klein

This article on women offenders, a classic in the field, provides an historical overview of the major theories of women and their criminality. This chapter ties in with many points made in the first chapter in Klein's description of how writers have always brought sexist, racist, and classist assumptions to their studies of women criminals. In reading this chapter, pay attention to the rationales and explanations given by different writers over the years to explain why women commit crimes. Consider the arguments which correspond to each of these writers' views.

For the student of women and crime the importance of this chapter is in its discussion on explanations of crime by women and the author's demonstration that these have been neither well-researched nor well-documented. According to Klein, past theories depend on the ultimate idea that criminality is a result of individual characteristics (such as one's biology—read sexuality for women—or psychology). At bottom, this is equally as true for both early as well as many contemporary sociologists. Thus strategies for rehabilitating the offender tend to focus on individual adjustment to the socially acceptable "legal world," not on social change of the broader society itself. Klein, instead, extends her historical analysis to question the impact of the political economy, racism, and sexism on the causes and definitions of female crime.

The criminality of women has long been a neglected subject area of criminology. Many explanations have been advanced for this, such as women's low official rate of crime and delinquency and the preponderance of male theorists in the field. Female criminality has often ended up as a footnote to works on men that purport to be works on criminality in general.

There has been, however, a small group of writings specifically concerned with women and crime. This paper will explore those works con-

From *Crime and Social Justice: Issues in Criminology,* Fall 1973, pp. 3–30. Copyright © Crime and Social Justice, P.O. Box 4373, Berkeley, California, 94704. Reprinted by permission.

cerned with the etiology of female crime and delinquency, beginning with the turn-of-the-century writing of Lombroso and extending to the present. Writers selected to be included have been chosen either for their influence on the field, such as Lombroso, Thomas, Freud, Davis and Pollak, or because they are representative of the kinds of work being published, such as Konopka, Vedder and Somerville, and Cowie, Cowie and Slater. The emphasis is on the continuity between these works, because it is clear that, despite recognizable differences in analytical approaches and specific theories, the authors represent a tradition to a great extent. It is important to understand, therefore, the shared assumptions made by the writers that are used to laying the groundwork for their theories.

The writers see criminality as the result of *individual* characteristics that are only peripherally affected by economic, social and political forces. These characteristics are of a *physiological* or *psychological* nature and are uniformly based on implicit or explicit assumptions about the *inherent nature of women*. This nature is *universal*, rather than existing within a specific historical framework.

Since criminality is seen as an individual activity, rather than as a condition built into existing structures, the focus is on biological, psychological and social factors that would turn a woman toward criminal activity. To do this, the writers create two distinct classes of women: good women who are "normal" noncriminals, and bad women who are criminals, thus taking a moral position that often masquerades as a scientific distinction. The writers, although they may be biological or social determinists to varying degrees, assume that individuals have *choices* between criminal and noncriminal activity. They see persons as atomistically moving about in a social and political vacuum; many writers use marketplace models for human interaction.

Although the theorists may differ on specific remedies for individual criminality, ranging from sterilization to psychoanalysis (but always stopping far short of social change), the basic thrust is toward *individual adjustment*, whether it be physical or mental, and the frequent model is rehabilitative therapy. Widespread environmental alterations are usually included as casual footnotes to specific plans for individual therapy. Most of the writers are concerned with *social harmony* and the welfare of the existing social structure rather than with the women involved or with women's position in general. None of the writers come from anything near a "feminist" or "radical" perspective.

In *The Female Offender*, originally published in 1903, Lombroso described female criminality as an inherent tendency produced in individuals that could be regarded as biological atavisms, similar to cranial and facial features, and one could expect a withering away of crime if the atavistic people were prohibited from breeding. At this time criminality was widely regarded as a physical ailment, like epilepsy. Today, Cowie, Cowie and Slater (1968) have identified physical traits in girls who have been classified as delinquent, and have concluded that certain traits, such as bigness, may lead to aggressiveness. This theme of physiological characteristics has been developed by a good number of writers in the last seventy years, such as the Gluecks (1934). One sees at the present time a new surge of "biological" theories of criminality; for example, a study involving "violence-prone" women and menstrual cycles has recently been proposed at UCLA.[1]

Thomas, to a certain degree, and Freud extend the physiological explanation of criminality to propose a psychological theory. However, it is critical to understand that these psychological notions are based on assumptions of universal *physiological* traits of women, such as their reproductive instinct and passivity, that are seen as invariably producing certain psychological reactions. Women may be viewed as turning to crime as a *perversion of* or *rebellion against* their *natural feminine roles*. Whether their problems are biological, psychological or social-environmental, the point is always to return them to their roles. Thomas (1907; 1923), for example, points out that poverty might prevent a woman from marrying, whereby she would turn to prostitution as an alternative to carry on her feminine service role. In fact, Davis (1961) discusses prostitution as a parallel illegal institution to marriage. Pollak (1950) discusses how women extend their service roles into criminal activity due to inherent tendencies such as deceitfulness. Freud (1933; Jones, 1961) sees any kind of rebellion as the result of a failure to develop healthy feminine attitudes, such as narcissism, and Konopka (1966) and Vedder and Somerville (1907) apply Freudian thought to the problem of female delinquency.

The specific characteristics ascribed to women's nature and those critical to theories of female criminality are uniformly *sexual* in their nature. Sexuality is seen as the root of female behavior and the problem of crime. Women are defined as sexual beings, as sexual capital in many cases, physiologically, psychologically and socially. This definition *reflects* and *reinforces* the economic position of women as reproductive and domestic workers. It is mirrored in the laws themselves and in their enforcement, which penalize sexual deviations for women and may be more lenient with economic offenses committed by them, in contrast to the treatment given men. The theorists accept the sexual double standard inherent in the law, often noting that "chivalry" protects women, and many of them build notions of the universality of *sex repression* into their explanations of women's position. Women are thus the sexual backbone of civilization.

In setting hegemonic standards of conduct for all women, the theorists define *femininity*, which they equate with healthy femaleness, in classist, racist and sexist terms, using their assumptions of women's nature, specifically their sexuality, to justify what is often in reality merely a defense of the existing order. Lombroso, Thomas and Freud consider the upper-class white woman to be the highest expression of femininity, although she is inferior to the upper-class white man. These standards are adopted by later writers in discussing femininity. To most theorists, women are inherently inferior to men at masculine tasks such as thought and production, and therefore it is logical that their sphere should be reproductive.

Specific characteristics are proposed to bolster this sexual ideology, expressed for example by Freud, such as passivity, emotionalism, narcissism and deceitfulness. In the discussions of criminality, certain theorists, such as Pollak, link female criminality to these traits. Others see criminality as an attempt away from femininity into masculinity, such as Lombroso, although the specifics are often confused. Contradictions can be clearly seen, which are explained by the dual nature of "good" and "bad" women and by the fact that this is a mythology attempting to explain real behavior. Many explanations of what are obviously economically motivated offenses, such as prostitution and shoplifting, are explained in sexual terms, such as prostitution being promiscuity, and shoplifting being "kleptomania" caused by women's inexplicable mental cycles tied to menstruation. Different explanations have to be made for "masculine" crimes, e.g., burglary, and for "feminine" crimes, e.g., shoplifting. Although this distinction crops up consistently, the specifics differ widely.

The problem is complicated by the lack of knowledge of the epidemiology of female crime, which allows such ideas as "hidden crime," first expressed by Pollak (1950), to take root. The problem must be considered on two levels: women, having been confined to certain tasks and socialized in certain ways, are *in fact* more likely to commit crime related to their lives which are sexually oriented; yet even nonsexual offenses are *explained* in sexual terms by the theorists. The writers ignore the problems of poor and Third World women, concentrating on affluent white standards of femininity. The experiences of these overlooked women, who *in fact* constitute a good percentage of women caught up in the criminal justice system, negate the notions of sexually motivated crime. These women have real economic needs which are not being met, and in many cases engage in illegal activities as a viable economic alternative. Furthermore, chivalry has never been extended to them.

The writers largely ignore the problems of sexism, racism and class, thus their work is sexist, racist and classist in its implications. Their concern is adjustment of the woman to society, not social change. Hence, they represent a tradition in criminology and carry along a host of assumptions about women and humanity in general. It is important to explore these assumptions and traditions in depth in order to understand what kinds of myths have been propagated around women and crime. The discussions of each writer or writers will focus on these assumptions and their relevance to criminological theories. These assumptions of universal, biological/psychological characteristics, of individual responsibility for crime, of the necessity for maintaining social harmony, and of the benevolence of the state link different theories along a continuum, transcending political labels and minor divergencies. The road from Lombroso to the present is surprisingly straight.

LOMBROSO: "THERE MUST BE
SOME ANOMALY . . . . "

Lombroso's work on female criminality (1920) is important to consider today despite the fact that his methodology and conclusions have long been successfully discredited. Later writings on female crime by Thomas, Davis, Pollak and others use more sophisticated methodologies and may proffer more palatable liberal theories. However, to varying degrees they rely on those sexual ideologies based on *implicit* assumptions about the physiological and psychological nature of women that are *explicit* in Lombroso's work. Reading the work helps to achieve a better understanding of what kinds of myths have been developed for women in general and for female crime and deviance in particular.

One specific notion of women offered by Lombroso is women's physiological immobility and psychological passivity, later elaborated by Thomas, Freud and other writers. Another ascribed characteristic is the Lombrosian notion of women's adaptability to surroundings and their capacity for survival as being superior to that of men. A third idea discussed by Lombroso is women's amorality: they are cold and calculating. This is developed by Thomas (1923), who describes women's manipulation of the male sex urge for ulterior purposes; by Freud (1933), who sees women as avenging their lack of a penis on men; and by Pollak (1950), who depicts women as inherently deceitful.

When one looks at these specific traits, one sees contradictions. The myth of compassionate women clashes with their reputed coldness; their frailness belies their capacity to survive. One possible explanation for these contraditions is the duality of sexual ideology with regard to "good" and "bad" women.[2] Bad women are whores, driven by lust for money or for men, often essentially "*masculine*" in their orientation, and perhaps afflicted with a touch of penis envy. Good women are chaste, "feminine," and usually not prone to criminal activity. But when they are, they commit crime in a most *ladylike* way such as poisoning. In more sophisticated theory, all women are seen as having a bit of both tendencies in them. Therefore, women can be compassionate *and* cold, frail *and* sturdy, pious *and* amoral, depending on which path they choose to follow. They are seen

as rational (although they are irrational, too!), atomistic individuals making choices in a vacuum, prompted only by personal, physiological/psy-
chological factors. These choices relate only to the *sexual* sphere. Women
have no place in any other sphere. Men, on the other hand, are not held
sexually accountable, although, as Thomas notes (1907), they are held
responsible in *economic* matters. Men's sexual freedom is justified by the
myth of masculine, irresistible sex urges. This myth, still worshipped
today, is frequently offered as a rationalization for the existence of prostitution and the double standard. As Davis maintains, this necessitates the
parallel existence of classes of "good" and "bad" women.

These dual moralities for the sexes are outgrowths of the economic,
political and social *realities* for men and women. Women are primarily
workers within the family, a critical institution of reproduction and socialization that services such basic needs as food and shelter. Laws and codes
of behavior for women thus attempt to maintain the smooth functioning
of women in that role, which requires that women act as a conservative
force in the continuation of the nuclear family. Women's main tasks are
sexual, and the law embodies sexual limitations for women, which do not
exist for men, such as the prohibition of promiscuity for girls. This explains
why theorists of female criminality are not only concerned with sexual
violations by female offenders, but attempt to account for even *nonsexual*
offenses, such as prostitution, in sexual terms, e.g., women enter prosit" +
"tion for sex rather than for money. Such women are not only economic
offenders but are sexual deviants, falling neatly into the category of "bad"
women.

The works of Lombroso, particularly *The Female Offender* (1920), are a
foremost example of the biological explanation of crime. Lombroso deals
with crime as an atavism, or survival of "primitive" traits in individuals,
particularly those of the female and nonwhite races. He theorizes that
individuals develop differentially within sexual and racial limitations
which differ hierarchically from the most highly developed, the white
men, to the most primitive, the nonwhite women. Beginning with the
assumption that criminals must be atavistic, he spends a good deal of time
comparing the crania, moles, heights, etc. of convicted criminals and prostitutes with those of normal women. Any trait that he finds to be more
common in the "criminal" group is pronounced an atavistic trait, such as
moles, dark hair, etc., and women with a number of these telltale traits
could be regarded as potentially criminal, since they are of the atavistic
type. He specifically rejects the idea that some of these traits, for example
obesity in prostitutes, could be the *result* of their activities rather than an
indicator of their propensity to them. Many of the traits are depicted as
"anomalies," such as darkness and shortness, and characteristic of certain
racial groups, such as the Sicilians, who undoubtedly comprise an op-

pressed group within Italy and form a large part of the imprisoned population.

Lombroso traces an overall pattern of evolution in the human species that accounts for the uneven development of groups: the white and non-white races, males and females, adults and children. Women, children and nonwhites share many traits in common. There are fewer variations in their mental capacities: "even the female criminal is monotonous and uniform compared with her male companion, just as in general woman is inferior to man" (Ibid.:122), due to her being "atavistically nearer to her origin than the male" (Ibid.:107). The notion of women's mediocrity, or limited range of mental possibilities, is a recurrent one in the writings of the twentieth century. Thomas and others note that women comprise "fewer genuises, fewer lunatics and fewer morons" (Thomas 1907:45); lacking the imagination to be at either end of the spectrum, they are conformist and dull . . . not due to social, political or economic constraints on their activities, but because of their innate physiological limitations as a sex. Lombroso attributes the lower female rate of criminality to their having fewer anomalies, which is one aspect of their closeness to the lower forms of less differentiated life.

Related characteristics of women are their passivity and conservatism. Lombroso admits that women's traditional sex roles in the family bind them to a more sedentary life. However, he insists that women's passivity can be directly traced to the "immobility of the ovule compared with the zoosperm" (1920:109), falling back on the sexual act in an interesting anticipation of Freud.

Women, like the lower races, have greater powers of endurance and resistance to mental and physical pain than men. Lombroso states: "denizens of female prisoners . . . have reached the age of 90, having lived within those walls since they were 29 without any grave injury to health" (Ibid.:125). Denying the humanity of women by denying their capability for suffering justifies exploitation of women's energies by arguing for their suitability to hardship. Lombroso remarks that "a duchess can adapt herself to new surroundings and become a washerwoman much more easily than a man can transform himself under analogous conditions" (Ibid.:272). The theme of women's adaptability to physical and social surroundings, which are male initiated, male controlled, and often expressed by saying that women are actually the "stronger" sex, is a persistent thread in writings on women.

Lombroso explains that because women are unable to feel pain, they are insensitive to the pain of others and lack moral refinement. His blunt denial of the age-old myth of women's compassion and sensitivity is modified, however, to take into account women's low crime rate:

Women have many traits in common with children; that their moral sense is deficient; that they are revengeful, jealous . . . In ordinary cases these defects are neutralized by piety, maternity, want of passion, sexual coldness, weakness and an undeveloped intelligence (Ibid.:151).

Although women lack the higher sensibilities of men, they are thus restrained from criminal activity in most cases by lack of intelligence and passion, qualities which *criminal* women possess as well as all *men*. Within this framework of biological limits of women's nature, the female offender is characterized as *masculine* whereas the normal woman is *feminine*. The anomalies of skull, physiognomy and brain capacity of female criminals, according to Lombroso, more closely approximate that of the man, normal or criminal, than they do those of the normal woman; the female offender often has a "virile cranium" and considerable body hair. Masculinity in women is an anomaly itself, rather than a sign of development, however. A related notion is developed by Thomas, who notes that in "civilized" nations the sexes are more physically different.

What we look for most in the female is femininity, and when we find the opposite in her, we must conclude as a rule that there must be some anomaly . . . Virility was one of the special features of the savage woman . . . In the portraits of Red Indian and Negro beauties, whom it is difficult to recognize for women, so huge are their jaws and cheekbones, so hard and coarse their features, and the same is often the case in their crania and brains (Ibid.:112).

The more highly developed races would therefore have the most feminized women with the requisite passivity, lack of passion, etc. This is a *racist* and *classist* definition of femininity—just as are almost all theories of *femininity* and as, indeed, is the thing itself. The ideal of the lady can only exist in a society built on the exploitation of labor to maintain the woman of leisure who can *be* that ideal lady.

Finally, Lombroso notes women's lack of *property sense*, which contributes to their criminality.

In their eyes theft is . . . an audacity for which compensation is due to the owner . . . as an individual rather than a social crime, just as it was regarded in the primitive periods of human evolution and is still regarded by many uncivilized nations (Ibid.:217).

One may question this statement on several levels. Can it be assumed to have any validity at all, or is it false that women have a different sense of property than men? If it is valid to a degree, is it related to women's lack of property ownership and nonparticipation in the accumulation of capitalist wealth? Indeed, as Thomas (1907) points out, women are considered property themselves. At any rate, it is an interesting point in Lombroso's book that has only been touched on by later writers, and always in a manner supportive of the institution of private property.

THOMAS: "THE STIMULATION SHE CRAVES"

The works of W. I. Thomas are critical in that they mark a transition from purely physiological explanations such as Lombroso's to more sophisticated theories that embrace physiological, psychological and social-structural factors. However, even the most sophisticated explanations of female crime rely on implicit assumptions about the *biological* nature of women. In Thomas' *Sex and Society* (1907) and *The Unadjusted Girl* (1923), there are important contradictions in the two approaches that are representative of the movements during that period between publication dates: a departure from biological Social-Darwinian theories to complex analyses of the interaction between society and the individual, i.e., societal repression and manipulation of the "natural" wishes of persons.

In *Sex and Society* (1907), Thomas poses basic biological differences between the sexes as his starting point. Maleness is "katabolic," the animal force which is destructive of energy and allows men the possibility of creative work through this outward flow. Femaleness is "anabolic," analogous to a plant which stores energy, and is motionless and conservative. Here Thomas is offering his own version of the age-old male/female dichotomy expressed by Lombroso and elaborated on in Freud's paradigm, in the structural-functionalist "instrumental-expressive" duality, and in other analyses of the status quo. According to Thomas, the dichotomy is most highly developed in the most civilized races, due to the greater differentiation of sex roles. This statement ignores the hard physical work done by poor *white* women at home and in the factories and offices in "civilized" countries, and accepts a *ruling-class* definition of femininity.

The cause of women's relative decline in stature in more "civilized" countries is a subject on which Thomas is ambivalent. At one point he attributes it to the lack of "a superior fitness on the motor side" in women (Ibid.:94); at another point, he regards her loss of *sexual freedom* as critical, with the coming of monogamy and her confinement to sexual tasks such as wifehood and motherhood. He perceptively notes:

> Women were still further degraded by the development of property and its control by man, together with the habit of treating her as a piece of property, whose value was enhanced if its purity was assured (Ibid.:297).

However, Thomas' underlying assumptions in his explanations of the inferior status of women are *physiological ones.* He attributes to men high amounts of sexual energy, which lead them to pursue women for their sex, and he attributes to women maternal feelings devoid of sexuality, which lead *them* to exchange sex for domesticity. Thus monogamy, with chastity for women, is the *accommodation* of these basic urges, and women are domesticated while men assume leadership, in a true market exchange.

Why, then, does Thomas see problems in the position of women? It is because modern women are plagued by "irregularity, pettiness, ill health and inserviceableness" (Ibid.:245). Change is required to maintain *social harmony*, apart from considerations of women's needs, and women must be educated to make them better wives, a theme reiterated throughout this century by "liberals" on the subject. Correctly anticipating a threat, Thomas urges that change be made to stabilize the family, and warns that "no civilization can remain the highest if another civilization adds to the intelligence of its men the intelligence of its women" (Ibid.:314). Thomas is motivated by considerations of social integration. Of course, one might question how women are to be able to contribute much if they are indeed anabolic. However, due to the transitional nature of Thomas' work, there are immense contradictions in his writing.

Many of Thomas' specific assertions about the nature of women are indistinguishable from Lombroso's; they both delineate a biological hierarchy along race and sex lines.

> Man has, in short, become more somatically specialized an animal than women, and feels more keenly any disturbance of normal conditions with which he has not the same physiological surplus as woman with which to meet the disturbance . . . It is a logical fact, however, that the lower human races, the lower classes of society, women and children show something of the same quality in their superior tolerance of surgical disease (Ibid.:36).

Like Lombroso, Thomas is crediting women with superior capabilities of survival because they are further down the scale in terms of evolution. It is significant that Thomas includes the lower classes in his observation; is he implying that the lower classes are in their position *because* of their natural unfitness, or perhaps that their *situation* renders them less sensitive to pain? At different times, Thomas implies both. Furthermore, he agrees with Lombroso that women are more nearly uniform than men, and says that they have a smaller percentage of "genius, insanity and idiocy" (Ibid.:45) than men, as well as fewer creative outbursts of energy.

Dealing with female criminality in *Sex and Society* (1907), Thomas begins to address the issue of morality, which he closely links to legality from a standpoint of maintaining social order. He discriminates between male and female morality:

> Morality as applied to men has a larger element of the contractual, representing the adjustment of his activities to those of society at large, or more particularly to the

activities of the male members of society; while the morality which we think of in connection with women shows less of the contractual and more of the personal, representing her adjustment to men, more particularly the adjustment of her person to men (Ibid.:172).

Whereas Lombroso barely observes women's lack of participation in the institution of private property, Thomas' perception is more profound. He points out that women *are* property of men and that their conduct is subject to different codes.

> Morality, in the most general sense, represents the code under which activities are best carried on and is worked out in the school of experience. It is preeminently an adult and male system, and men are intelligent enough to realize that neither women nor children have passed through this school. It is on this account that man is merciless to woman from the standpoint of personal behavior, yet he exempts her from anything in the way of contractual morality, or views her defections in this regard with allowance and even with amusement (Ibid.:234).

Disregarding his remarks about intelligence, one confronts the critical point about women with respect to the law: because they occupy a *marginal* position in the productive sphere of exchange commodities outside the home, they in turn occupy a marginal position in regard to "contractual" law which regulates relations of property and production. The argument of differential treatment of men and women by the law is developed in later works by Pollak and others, who attribute it to the "chivalry" of the system which is lenient to women committing offenses. As Thomas notes, however, women are simply not a serious *threat* to property, and are treated more "leniently" because of this. Certain women do become threats by transcending (or by being denied) their traditional role, particularly many Third World women and political rebels, and they are *not* afforded chivalrous treatment! In fact, chivalry is reserved for the women who are least likely to ever come in contact with the criminal justice system: the ladies, or white middle-class women. In matters of *sexual* conduct, however, which embody the double standard, women are rigorously prosecuted by the law. As Thomas understands, this is the sphere in which women's functions *are* critical. Thus it is not a matter of "chivalry" how one is handled, but of different forms and thrusts of social control applied to men and women. Men are engaged in productive tasks and their activities in this area *are* strictly curtailed.

In *The Unadjusted Girl* (1923), Thomas deals with female delinquency as a "normal" response under certain social conditions, using assumptions about the nature of women which he leaves unarticulated in this work. Driven by basic "wishes," an individual is controlled by society in her activities through institutional transmission of codes and mores. Depending on how they are manipulated, wishes can be made to serve social or antisocial ends. Thomas stresses the institutions that socialize, such as the family, giving people certain "definitions of the situation." He confidently —and defiantly—asserts:

> There is no individual energy, no unrest, no type of wish, which cannot be sublimated and made socially useful. From this standpoint, the problem is not the right of society to protect itself from the disorderly and antisocial person, but the right of the disorderly and antisocial person to be made orderly and socially valuable . . . The problem of society is to produce the right attitudes in its members (Ibid.:232-233).

This is an important shift in perspective, from the traditional libertarian view of protecting society by punishing transgressors, to the *rehabilitative* and *preventive* perspective of crime control that seeks to control *minds* through socialization rather than to merely control behavior through punishment. The autonomy of the individual to choose is seen as the product of his environment which the state can alter. This is an important refutation of the Lombrosian biological perspective, which maintains that there are crime-prone individuals who must be locked up, sterilized or otherwise incapacitated. Today, one can see an amalgamation of the two perspectives in new theories of "behavior control" that use tactics such as conditioning and brain surgery, combining biological and environmental viewpoints.[3]

Thomas proposes the manipulation of individuals through institutions to prevent antisocial attitudes, and maintains that there is no such person as the "crime prone" individual. A hegemonic system of belief can be imposed by sublimating natural urges and by correcting the poor socialization of slum families. In this perspective, the *definition* of the situation rather than the situation *itself* is what should be changed; a situation is what someone *thinks* it is. The response to a criminal woman who is dissatisfied with her conventional sexual roles is to change not the roles, which would mean widespread social transformations, but to change her attitudes. This concept of civilization as repressive and the need to adjust is later refined by Freud.

Middle class women, according to Thomas, commit little crime because they are socialized to sublimate their natural desires and to behave well, treasuring their chastity as an investment. The poor woman, however, "is not immoral, because this implies a loss of morality, but amoral" (Ibid.:98). Poor women are not objectively driven to crime; they long for it. Delinquent girls are motivated by the desire for excitement or "new experience," and forget the repressive urge of "security." However, these desires are well within Thomas' conception of *femininity:* delinquents are not rebelling against womanhood, as Lombroso suggests, but merely acting it out illegally. Davis and Pollak agree with this notion that delinquent women are not "different" from nondelinquent women.

Thomas maintains that it is not sexual desire that motivates delinquent girls, for they are no more passionate than other women, but they are *manipulating* male desires for sex to achieve their own ulterior ends.

> The beginning of delinquency in girls is usually an impulse to get amusement, adventure, pretty clothes, favorable notice, distinction, freedom in the larger world . . . The girls have usually beco ne 'wild' before the development of sexual desire, and their casual sex relations do not usually awaken sex feeling. Their sex is used as a condition of the realization of other wishes. It is their capital (Ibid.:109).

Here Thomas is expanding on the myth of the manipulative woman, who is cold and scheming and vain. To him, good female sexual behavior is a protective measure—"instinctive, of course" (1907:241), whereas male behavior is uncontrollable as men are caught by helpless desires. This is the common Victorian notion of the woman as seductress which in turn perpetuates the myth of a lack of real sexuality to justify her responsibility for upholding sexual mores. Thomas uses a market analogy to female virtue: good women *keep* their bodies as capital to sell in matrimony for marriage and security, whereas bad women *trade* their bodies for excitement. One notes, of course, the familiar dichotomy. It is difficult, in this framework, to see how Thomas can make *any* moral distinctions, since morality seems to be merely good business sense. In fact, Thomas' yardstick is social harmony, necessitating *control.*

Thomas shows an insensitivity to real human relationships and needs. He also shows ignorance of economic hardships in his denial of economic factors in delinquency.

> An unattached woman has a tendency to become an adventuress not so much on economic as on psychological grounds. Life is rarely so hard that a young woman cannot earn her bread; but she cannot always live and have the stimulation she craves (Ibid.:241).

This is an amazing statement in an era of mass starvation and illness! He rejects economic causes as a possibility at all, denying its importance in criminal activity with as much certainty as Lombroso, Freud, Davis, Pollak and most other writers.

FREUD: "BEAUTY, CHARM AND SWEETNESS"

The Freudian theory of the position of women is grounded in explicit biological assumptions about their nature, expressed by the famous "Anatomy is Destiny." Built upon this foundation is a construction incorporating psychological and social-structural factors.

Freud himself sees women as anatomically inferior; they are destined to be wives and mothers, and this admittedly an inferior destiny as befits the inferior sex. The root of this inferiority is that women's *sex organs* are inferior to those of men, a fact *universally* recognized by children in the Freudian scheme. The girl assumes that she has lost a penis as punishment, is traumatized, and grows up envious and revengeful. The boy also sees the girl as having lost a penis, fears a similar punishment himself, and dreads the girl's envy and vengeance. Feminine traits can be traced to the inferior genitals themselves, or to women's inferiority complex arising from their response to them: women are exhibitionistic, narcissistic, and attempt to compensate for their lack of a penis by being well-dressed and physically beautiful. Women become mothers trying to replace the lost penis with a baby. Women are also masochistic, as Lombroso and Thomas have noted, because their *sexual* role is one of receptor, and their sexual pleasure consists of pain. This woman, Freud notes, is the *healthy* woman. In the familiar dichotomy, the men are aggressive and pain inflicting. Freud comments:

> The male pursues the female for the purposes of sexual union, seizes hold of her, and penetrates into her . . . by this you have precisely reduced the characteristic of masculinity to the factor of aggressiveness (Millett, 1970:189).

Freud, like Lombroso and Thomas, takes the notion of men's activity and women's inactivity and *reduces* it to the sexual level, seeing the sexual union itself through Victorian eyes; ladies don't move.

Women are also inferior in the sense that they are concerned with personal matters and have little social sense. Freud sees civilization as based on repression of the sex drive, where it is the duty of men to repress their strong instincts in order to get on with the worldly business of civilization. Women, on the other hand,

> have little sense of justice, and this is no doubt connected with the preponderance of envy in their mental life; for the demands of justice are a modification of envy; they lay down the conditions under which one is willing to part with it. We also say of women that their social interests are weaker than those of men and that their capacity for the sublimation of their instincts is less (1933:183).

Men are capable of sublimating their individual needs because they rationally perceive the Hobbesian conflict between those urges and social needs. Women are emotional and incapable of such an adjustment because of their innate inability to make such rational judgments. It is only fair then that they should have a marginal relation to production and property.

In this framework, the deviant woman is one who is attempting to be a *man.* She is aggressively rebellious, and her drive to accomplishment is the expression of her longing for a penis; this is a hopeless pursuit, of course, and she will only end up "neurotic." Thus the deviant woman should be treated and helped to *adjust* to her sex role. Here again, as in Thomas' writing, is the notion of individual accommodation that repudiates the possibility of social change.

In a Victorian fashion, Freud rationalizes women's oppression by glorifying their duties as wives and mothers:

> It is really a stillborn thought to send women into the struggle for existence exactly the same as men. If, for instance, I imagined my sweet gentle girl as a competitor, it would only end in my telling her, as I did seventeen months ago, that I am fond of her, and I implore her to withdraw from the strife into the calm, uncompetitive activity of my home . . . Nature has determined woman's destiny through beauty, charm and sweetness . . . in youth an adored darling, in mature years a loved wife (Jones 1961:117-118).

In speaking of femininity, Freud, like his forebearers, is speaking along racist and classist lines. Only upper and middle class women could possibly enjoy lives as sheltered darlings. Freud sets hegemonic standards of femininity for poor and Third World women.

It is important to understand Freudianism because it reduces categories of sexual ideology to explicit sexuality and makes these categories *scientific*. For the last fifty years, Freudianism has been a mainstay of sexist social theory. Kate Millett notes that Freud himself saw his work as stemming the tide of feminist revolution, which he constantly ridiculed:

> Coming as it did, at the peak of the sexual revolution, Freud's doctrine of penis envy is in fact a superbly timed accusation, enabling masculine sentiment to take the offensive again as it had not since the disappearance of overt misogyny when the pose of chivalry became fashionable (Millet 1970:189).

Freudian notions of the repression of sexual instincts, the sexual passivity of women, and the sanctity of the nuclear family are conservative not only in their contemporary context, but in the context of their own time. Hitler writes:

> For her [woman's] world is her husband, her family, her children and her home . . . The man upholds the nation as the woman upholds the family. The equal rights of women consist in the fact that in the realm of life determined for her by nature, she experience the high esteem that is her due. Woman and man represent quite different types of being. Reason is dominant in man . . . Feeling, in contrast, is much more stable than reason, and woman is the feeling, and therefore the stable, element (Ibid.:170).

One can mark the decline in the position of women after the 1920's through the use of various indices: by noting the progressively earlier age of marriage of women in the United States and the steady rise in the number of children born to them, culminating in the birth explosion of the late forties and fifties; by looking at the relative decline in the number of women scholars; and by seeing the failure to liberate women in the Soviet Union and the rise of fascist sexual ideology. Freudianism has had an unparalleled influence in the United States (and came at a key point to help swing the tide against the women's movement) to facilitate the return of women during the depression and postwar years to the home, out of an economy which had no room for them. Freud affected such writers on female deviance as Davis, Pollak and Konopka, who turn to concepts of sexual maladjustment and neurosis to explain women's criminality. Healthy women would now be seen as masochistic, passive and sexually indifferent. Criminal women would be seen as *sexual* misfits. Most importantly, *psychological* factors would be used to explain criminal activity, and social, economic and political factors would be ignored. Explanations would seek to be *universal*, and historical possibilities of change would be refuted.

DAVIS: "THE MOST CONVENIENT
SEXUAL OUTLET FOR ARMIES . . . "

Kingsley Davis' work on prostitution (1961) is still considered a classical analysis on the subject with a structural-functionalist perspective. It employs assumptions about "the organic nature of man" and woman, many of which can be traced to ideas proffered by Thomas and Freud.

Davis sees prostitution as a structural necessity whose roots lie in the *sexual* nature of men and women; for example, female humans, unlike primates, are sexually available year-round. He asserts that prostitution is *universal* in time and place, eliminating the possibilities of historical change and ignoring critical differences in the quality and quantity of prostitution in different societies. He maintains that there will always be a class of women who will be prostitutes, the familiar class of "bad" women. The reason for the universality of prostitution is that sexual *repression*, a concept stressed by Thomas and Freud, is essential to the functioning of society. Once again there is the notion of sublimating "natural" sex urges to the overall needs of society, namely social order. Davis notes that in our society sexuality is permitted only within the structure of the nuclear family, which is an institution of stability. He does not, however, analyze in depth the economic and social functions of the family, other than to say it is a bulwark of morality.

> The norms of every society tend to harness and control the sexual appetite, and one of the ways of doing this is to link the sexual act to some stable or potentially stable social relationship . . . Men dominate women in economic, sexual and familial relationships and consider them to some extent as sexual property, to be prohibited to other males. They therefore find promiscuity on the part of women repugnant (Ibid.:264).

Davis is linking the concept of prostitution to promiscuity, defining it as a *sexual* crime, and calling prostitutes sexual transgressors. Its origins, he claims, lie not in economic hardship, but in the marital restraints on sexuality. As long as men seek women, prostitutes will be in demand. One wonders why sex-seeking women have not created a class of male prostitutes.

Davis sees the only possibility of eliminating prostitution in the liberalization of sexual mores, although he is pessimistic about the likelihood of total elimination. In light of the contemporary American "sexual revolution" of commercial sex, which has surely created more prostitutes and semi-prostitutes rather than eliminating the phenomenon, and in considering the revolution in China where, despite a "puritanical" outlook on sexuality, prostitution has largely been eliminated through major economic and social change, the superficiality of Davis' approach becomes evident. Without dealing with root economic, social and political factors, one cannot analyze prostitution.

Davis shows Freudian pessimism about the nature of sexual repression:

> We can imagine a social system in which the motive for prostitution would be completely absent, but we cannot imagine that the system will ever come to pass. It would be a regime of absolute sexual freedom with intercourse practiced solely for pleasure by both parties. There would be no institutional control of sexual expression . . . All sexual desire would have to be mutually complementary . . . Since the basic causes of prostitution—the institutional control of sex, the unequal scale of attractiveness, and the presence of economic and social inequalities between classes and between males and females—are not likely to disappear, prostitution is not likely to disappear either (Ibid.:286).

By talking about "complementary desire," Davis is using a marketplace notion of sex: two attractive or unattractive people are drawn to each other and exchange sexual favors; people are placed on a scale of attractiveness and may be rejected by people above them on the scale; hence they (*men*) become frustrated and demand prostitutes. Women who become prostitutes do so for good pay *and* sexual pleasure. Thus one has a neat little system in which everyone benefits.

> Enabling a small number of women to take care of the needs of a large number of men, it is the most convenient sexual outlet for armies, for the legions of strangers, perverts and physically repulsive in our midst (Ibid.:288).

Prostitution "functions," therefore it must be good. Davis, like Thomas, is motivated by concerns of social order rather than by concerns of what the needs and desires of the women involved might be. He denies that the women involved are economically oppressed; they are on the streets through autonomous, *individual* choice.

> Some women physically enjoy the intercourse they sell. From a purely economic point of view, prostitution comes near the situation of getting something for nothing . . . Women's wages could scarcely be raised significantly without also raising men's. Men would then have more to spend on prostitution (Ibid.:277).

It is important to understand that, given a *sexual* interpretation of what is an *economic* crime, and given a refusal to consider widespread change (even equalization of wages, hardly a revolutionary act), Davis' conclusion is the logical technocratic solution.

In this framework, the deviant women are merely adjusting to their feminine role in an illegitimate fashion, as Thomas has theorized. They are *not* attempting to be rebels or to be "men," as Lombroso's and Freud's positions suggest. Although Davis sees the main difference between wives and prostitutes in a macrosocial sense as the difference merely between legal and illegal roles, in a personal sense he sees the women who *choose* prostitution as maladjusted and neurotic. However, given the universal necessity for prostitution, this analysis implies the necessity of having a perpetually ill and maladjusted class of women. Thus oppression is *built into* the system, and a healthy *system* makes for a sick *individual*. Here Davis is integrating Thomas' notions of social integration with Freudian perspectives on neurosis and maladjustment.

POLLAK: "A DIFFERENT ATTITUDE TOWARD VERACITY"

Otto Pollak's *The Criminality of Women* (1950) has had an outstanding influence on the field of women and crime, being the major work on the subject in the postwar years. Pollak advances the theory of "hidden" female crime to account for what he considers unreasonably low official rates for women.

A major reason for the existence of hidden crime, as he sees it, lies in the *nature* of women themselves. They are instigators rather than perpetrators of criminal activity. While Pollak admits that this role is partly a socially enforced one, he insists that women are inherently deceitful for *physiological* reasons.

> Man must achieve an erection in order to perform the sex act and will not be able to hide his failure. His lack of positive emotion in the sexual sphere must become overt to the partner, and pretense of sexual response is impossible for him, if it is lacking. Woman's body, however, permits such pretense to a certain degree and lack of orgasm does not prevent her ability to participate in the sex act (Ibid.:10).

Pollak *reduces* women's nature to the *sex act*, as Freud has done, and finds women inherently more capable of manipulation, accustomed to being sly, passive and passionless. As Thomas suggests, women can use sex for ulterior purposes. Furthermore, Pollak suggests that women are innately deceitful on yet another level:

> Our sex mores force women to conceal every four weeks the period of menstruation . . . They thus make concealment and misrepresentation in the eyes of women socially required and must condition them to a different attitude toward veracity than men (Ibid.:11).

Women's abilities at concealment thus allow them to successfully commit crimes in stealth.

Women are also vengeful. Menstruation, in the classic Freudian sense, seals their doomed hopes to become men and arouses women's desire for vengeance, especially during that time of the month. Thus Pollak offers new rationalizations to bolster old myths.

A second factor in hidden crime is the roles played by women which furnish them with opportunities as domestics, nurses, teachers and housewives to commit undetectable crimes. The *kinds* of crimes women commit reflect their nature: false accusation, for example, is an outgrowth of women's treachery, spite or fear and is a sign of neurosis; shoplifting can be traced in many cases to a special mental disease—kleptomania. Economic factors play a minor role; *sexual-psychological* factors account for female criminality. Crime in women is *personalized* and often accounted for by mental illness. Pollak notes:

> Robbery and burglary . . . are considered specifically male offenses since they represent the pursuit of monetary gain by overt action . . . Those cases of female robbery which seem to express a tendency toward masculinization comes from . . . [areas] where social conditions have favored the assumptions of male pursuits by women . . . The female offenders usually retain some trace of femininity, however, and even so glaring an example of masculinization as the 'Michigan Babes,' an all woman gang of robbers in Chicago, shows a typically feminine trait in the modus operandi (Ibid.:29).

Pollak is defining crimes with economic motives that employ overt action as *masculine*, and defining as *feminine* those crimes for *sexual* activity, such as luring men as baits. Thus he is using circular reasoning by saying that feminine crime is feminine. To fit women into the scheme and justify the statistics, he must invent the notion of hidden crime.

It is important to recognize that, to some extent, women *do* adapt to their enforced sexual roles and may be more likely to instigate, to use sexual traps, and to conform to all the other feminine role expectations. However, it is not accidental that theorists label women as conforming even when they are *not*; for example, by inventing sexual motives for what are clearly crimes of economic necessity, or by invoking "mental illness" such as kleptomania for shoplifting. It is difficult to separate the *theory* from the *reality,* since the reality of female crime is largely unknown. But it is not difficult to see that Pollak is using sexist terms and making sexist assumptions to advance theories of hidden female crime.

Pollak, then, sees criminal women as extending their sexual role, like Davis and Thomas, by using sexuality for ulterior purposes. He suggests that the condemnation of extramarital sex has "delivered men who engage in such conduct as practically helpless victims" (Ibid.:152) into the hands of women blackmailers, overlooking completely the possibility of men blackmailing women, which would seem more likely, given the greater taboo on sex for women and their greater risks of being punished.

The final factor that Pollak advances as a root cause of hidden crime is that of "chivalry" in the criminal justice system. Pollak uses Thomas' observation that women are differentially treated by the law, and carries it to a sweeping conclusion based on *cultural* analyses of men's feelings toward women.

> One of the outstanding concomitants of the existing inequality . . . is chivalry, and the general protective attitude of man toward woman . . . Men hate to accuse women and thus indirectly to send them to their punishment, police officers dislike to arrest them, district attorneys to prosecute them, judges and juries to find them guilty, and so on (Ibid.:151).

Pollak rejects the possibility of an actual discrepancy between crime rates for men and women; therefore, he must look for factors to expand the scope of female crime. He assumes that there is chivalry in the criminal justice system that is extended to the women who come in contact with it. Yet the women involved are likely to be poor and Third World women or white middle-class women who have stepped *outside* the definitions of femininity to become hippies or political rebels, and chivalry is *not* likely to be extended to them. Chivalry is a racist and classist concept founded on the notion of women as "ladies" which applies only to wealthy white women and ignores the double sexual standard. These "ladies," however, are the least likely women to ever come in contact with the criminal justice system in the first place.[4]

THE LEGACY OF SEXISM

A major purpose in tracing the development and interaction of ideas pertaining to sexual ideology based on implicit assumptions of the inherent nature of women throughout the works of Lombroso, Thomas, Freud, Davis and Pollak, is to clarify their positions in relation to writers in the field today. One can see the influence their ideas still have by looking at a number of contemporary theorists on female criminality. Illuminating examples can be found in Gisela Konopka's *Adolescent Girl in Conflict* (1966), Vedder and Somerville's *The Delinquent Girl* (1970) and Cowie, Cowie and Slater's *Delinquency in Girls* (1968). The ideas in these minor works have direct roots in those already traced in this paper.

Konopka justifies her decision to study delinquency in girls rather than in boys by noting girls' *influence* on boys in gang fights and on future generations as mothers. This is the notion of women as instigators of men and influencers on children. Konopka's main point is that delinquency in girls can be traced to a specific emotional response: loneliness.

> What I found in the girl in conflict was . . . loneliness accompanied by despair. Adolescent boys too often feel lonely and search for understanding and friends. Yet in general this does not seem to be the central core of their problems, not their most outspoken ache. While these girls also strive for independence, their need for dependence is unusually great (1966:40).

In this perspective, girls are driven to delinquency by an emotional problem—loneliness and dependency. There are *inherent* emotional differences between the sexes.

> Almost invariably her [the girl's] problems are deeply personalized. Whatever her offense—whether shoplifting, truancy or running away from home—it is usually accompanied by some disturbance or unfavorable behavior in the sexual area (Ibid.:4).

Here is the familiar resurrection of female personalism, emotionalism, and above all, *sexuality*—characteristics already described by Lombroso, Thomas and Freud. Konopka maintains:

> The delinquent girl suffers, like many boys, from lack of success, lack of opportunity. But her drive to success is never separated from her need for people, for interpersonal involvement (Ibid.:41).

Boys are "instrumental" and become delinquent if they are deprived of the chance for creative success. However, girls are "expressive" and happiest dealing with people as wives, mothers, teachers, nurses or psychologists. This perspective is drawn from the theory of delinquency as a result of blocked opportunity and from the instrumental/expressive sexual dualism developed by structural-functionalists. Thus female delinquency must be dealt with on this *psychological* level, using therapy geared to their needs as future wives and mothers. They should be *adjusted* and given *opportunities* to be pretty, sociable women.

The important point is to understand how Konopka analyzes the roots of girls' feelings. It is very possible that, given women's position, girls may be in fact more concerned with dependence and sociability. One's understanding of this, however, is based on an understanding of the historical position of women and the nature of their oppression. Konopka says:

> What are the reasons for this essential loneliness in girls? Some will be found in the nature of being an adolescent girl, in her biological makeup and her particular position in her culture and time (Ibid.).

Coming from a Freudian perspective, Konopka's emphasis on female emotions as cause for delinquency, which ignores economic and social factors, is questionable. She employs assumptions about the *physiological* and *psychological* nature of women that very well may have led her to see only those feelings in the first place. For example, she cites menstruation as a significant event in a girl's development. Thus Konopka is rooted firmly in the tradition of Freud and, apart from sympathy, contributes little that is new to the field.[5]

Vedder and Somerville (1970) account for female delinquency in a manner similar to that of Konopka. They also feel the need to justify their attention to girls by remarking that (while female delinquency may not pose as much of a problem as that of boys) because women raise families and are critical agents of socialization, it is worth taking the time to study and control them. Vedder and Somerville also stress the dependence of girls on boys and the instigatory role girls play in boys' activities.

Like Freud and Konopka, the authors view delinquency as blocked access or maladjustment to the normal feminine role. In a blatant statement that ignores the economic and social factors that result from racism and poverty, they attribute the high rates of delinquency among black girls to their lack of "healthy" feminine narcissism, *reducing* racism to a psychological problem in totally sexist and racist terms.

> The black girl is, in fact, the antithesis of the American beauty. However loved she may be by her mother, family and community, she has no real basis of female attractiveness on which to build a sound feminine narcissism . . . Perhaps the 'black is beautiful' movement will help the Negro girl to increase her femininity and personal satisfaction as a black woman (Ibid.:159-160).

Again the focus is on a lack of *sexual* opportunities for women, i.e., the Black woman is not Miss America. *Economic* offenses such as shoplifting are explained as outlets for *sexual* frustration. Since healthy women conform, the individual delinquents should be helped to adjust; the emphasis is on the "definition of the situation" rather than on the situation.

The answer lies in *therapy*, and racism and sexism become merely psychological problems.

> Special attention should be given to girls, taking into consideration their constitutional biological and psychological differences, and their social position in our male dominat-

ed culture. The female offender's goal, as any woman's, is a happy and successful marriage; therefore her self-image is dependent on the establishment of satisfactory relationships with the opposite sex. The double standard for sexual behavior on the part of the male and female must be recognized (Ibid.:153).

Like Konopka, and to some extent drawing on Thomas, the authors see female delinquents as extending femininity in an illegitimate fashion rather than rebelling against it. The assumptions made about women's goals and needs, including *biological* assumptions, lock women into a system from which there is no escape, whereby any behavior will be sexually interpreted and dealt with.

The resurgence of biological or physiological explanations of criminality in general has been noteworthy in the last several years, exemplified by the XYY chromosome controversy and the interest in brain wave in "violent" individuals.[6] In the case of women, biological explanations have *always* been prevalent; every writer has made assumptions about anatomy as destiny. Women are prey, in the literature, to cycles of reproduction, including menstruation, pregnancy, maternity and menopause; they experience emotional responses to these cycles that make them inclined to irrationality and potentially violent activity.

Cowie, Cowie and Slater (1968) propose a *chromosomal* explanation of female delinquency that hearkens back to the works of Lombroso and others such as Healy (1926), Edith Spaulding (1923) and the Gluecks (1934). They write:

The chromosomal difference between the sexes starts the individual on a divergent path, leading either in a masculine or feminine direction . . . It is possible that the methods of upbringing, differing somewhat for the two sexes, may play some part in increasing the angle of this divergence. (Ibid.:171).

This is the healthy, normal divergence for the sexes. The authors equate *masculinity* and *femininity* with *maleness* and *femaleness,* although contemporary feminists point out that the first categories are *social* and the latter ones *physical.*[7] What relationship exists between the two—how femaleness determines femininity—is dependent on the larger social structure. There is no question that a wide range of possibilities exist historically, and in a non-sexist society it is possible that "masculinity" and "femininity" would disappear, and that the sexes would differ only biologically, specifically by their sex organs. The authors, however, lack this understanding and assume an ahistorical sexist view of women, stressing the *universality* of femininity in the Freudian tradition, and of women's inferior role in the nuclear family.[8]

In this perspective, the female offender is *different* physiologically and psychologically from the "normal" girl.

The authors conclude, in the tradition of Lombroso, that female delin-quents are *masculine*. Examining girls for physical characteristics, they note:

> Markedly masculine traits in girl delinquents have been commented on . . . [as well as] the frequency of homosexual tendencies . . . Energy, aggressiveness, enterprise and the rebelliousness that drives the individual to break through conformist habits are thought of as being masculine . . . We can be sure that they have some physical basis (Ibid.:172).

The authors see crimes as a *rebellion* against sex roles rather than as a maladjusted expression of them. By defining rebellion as *masculine*, they are ascribing characteristics of masculinity to any female rebel. Like Lombroso, they spend time measuring heights, weights, and other *biological* features of female delinquents with other girls.

Crime defined as masculine seems to mean violent, overt crime, whereas "ladylike" crime usually refers to sexual violations and shoplifting. Women are neatly categorized no matter *which* kind of crime they commit: if they are violent, they are "masculine" and suffering from chromosomal deficiencies, penis envy, or atavisms. If they conform, they are manipula-tive, sexually maladjusted and promiscuous. The *economic* and *social* realities of crime—the fact that poor women commit crimes, and that most crimes for women are property offenses—are overlooked. Women's behavior must be *sexually* defined before it will be considered, for women count only in the sexual sphere. The theme of sexuality is a unifying thread in the various, often contradictory theories.

CONCLUSION

A good deal of the writing on women and crime being done at the present time is squarely in the tradition of the writers that have been discussed. The basic assumptions and technocratic concerns of these writers have produced work that is sexist, racist and classist; assumptions that have served to maintain a repressive ideology with its extensive apparatus of control. To do a new kind of research on women and crime—one that has feminist roots and a radical orientation—it is necessary to understand the assumptions made by the traditional writers and to break away from them. Work that focuses on human needs, rather than those of the state, will require new definitions of criminality, women, the individual and her/his relation to the state. It is beyond the scope of this paper to develop possible areas of study, but is is nonetheless imperative that this work be made a priority by women *and* men in the future.

Notes

[1] Quoted from the 1973 proposal for the Center for the Study and Reduction of violence prepared by Dr. Louis J. West, Director, Neuropsychiatric Institute, UCLA: "The question of violence in females will be examined from the point of view that females are more likely to commit acts of violence during the pre-menstrual and menstrual periods" (1973:43).

[2] I am indebted to Marion Goldman for introducing me to the notion of the dual morality based on assumptions of different sexuality for men and women.

[3] For a discussion of the possibilities of psychosurgery in behavior modification for "violence-prone" individuals, see Frank Ervin and Vernon Mark, *Violence and the Brain* (1970). For an eclectic view of this perspective on crime, see the proposal for the Center for the Study and Reduction of Violence (footnote 1).

[4] The concept of hidden crime is reiterated in Reckless and Kay's report to the President's Commission on Law Enforcement and the Administration of Justice. They note:

A large part of the infrequent officially acted upon involvement of women in crime can be traced to the masking effect of women's roles, effective practice on the part of women of deceit and indirection, their instigation of men to commit their crimes (the Lady MacBeth factor), and the unwillingness on the part of the public and law enforcement officials to hold women accountable for their deeds (the chivalry factor) (1967:13).

[5] Bertha Payak in "Understanding the Female Offender" (1963) stresses that women offenders have poor self-concepts, feelings of insecurity and dependency, are emotionally selfish and prey to irrationality during menstruation, pregnancy, and menopause (a good deal of their life!).

[6] See Theodore R. Sarbin and Jeffrey E. Miller, "Demonism Revisited: The XYY Cromosomal Anomaly," *Issues in Criminology* 5(2) (Summer 1970).

[7] Kate Millett (1970) notes that "sex is biological, gender psychological and therefore cultural . . . if the proper terms for sex are male and female, the corresponding terms for gender are masculine and feminine; these latter may be quite independent of biological sex" (*Ibid.*:30).

[8] Zelditch (1960), a structural-functionalist, writes that the nuclear family is an inevitability and that within it, women, the "expressive" sex, will inevitably be the domestics.

References

Bishop, Cecil. Women and Crime. London: Chatto and Windus, 1931.

Cowie, John, Valerie Cowie and Eliot Slater. Delinquency in Girls. London: Heinemann, 1968.

Davis, Kingsley. "Prostitution." Comtemporary Social Problems. Edited by Robert K. Merton and Robert A. Nisbet. New York: Harcourt Brace and Jovanovich, 1961. Originally published as "The Sociology of Prostitution." American Sociological Review 2(5) (October 1937).

Ervin, Frank and Vernon Mark. Violence and the Brain. New York: Harper and Row, 1970.

Fernald, Mabel, Mary Hayes and Almena Dawley. A Study of Women Delinquents in New York State. New York: Century Company, 1920.

Freud, Sigmund. New Introductory Lectures on Psychoanalysis. New York: W. W. Norton, 1933.

Glueck, Eleanor and Sheldon. Four Hundred Delinquent Women. New York: Alfred A. Knopf, 1934.

Healy, William and Augusta Bronner. Delinquents and Criminals: Their Making and Unmaking. New York: Macmillan and Company, 1926.

Hemming, James. Problems of Adolescent Girls. London: Heinemann, 1960.

Jones, Ernest. The Life and Works of Sigmund Freud. New York: Basic Books, 1961.

Konopka, Gisela. The Adolescent Girl in Conflict. Englewood Cliffs, New Jersey: Prentice-Hall, 1966.

Lombroso, Cesare. The Female Offender. (Translation). New York: Appleton, 1920. Originally published in 1903.

Millet, Kate. Sexual Politics. New York: Doubleday and Company, 1970.

Monahan, Florence. Women in Crime. New York: I. Washburn, 1941.

3

Females Under the Law: 'Protected' but Unequal

Gail Armstrong

The following selection is important because the author describes how men and women are not equal under the law. In both statutes and sentencing practices a double standard of morality exists, usually to women's disadvantage. As you read this chapter, notice that although in the administration of criminal law discrimination sometimes works in favor of women, it more often works against them so that women's sentences are frequently more severe than men's.

Armstrong provides many examples of the sexism thesis presented in the first essay in this section of the book. Her main point is that the sex of the offender is an important determinant of the length and type of punishment imposed on an individual after conviction for a crime. And that whatever the offense, the misbegotten motive for punishment is said to be either chivalry or special protectiveness where women are concerned.

Although not a part of Armstrong's argument, the following issue merits special attention: very few women in comparison to men are sentenced to prison terms. However, many more women are institutionalized in mental hospitals. According to Thomas Szaz, * a prominent psychiatrist, it is probably more harmful for a person to be locked up in a mental hospital with an indeterminate stay than to incarcerate someone in prison with a determinate sentence. Both mental hospitals and prisons are instruments of social control, conformity, and isolation of those who break laws—whether social or legal. Based on Armstrong's analysis of chivalry and special protection for women inherent in the criminal justice system's form of social control, how might the relationship between these two seemingly separate systems of social control, prisons and mental hospitals, be better understood?*

Sentencing is a crucial step in the processing of an offender through the criminal justice system. In some cases the sentencing judge may use discre-

Reprinted with permission of the National Council on Crime and Delinquency, from Gail Armstrong, "Females Under the Law—'Protected' but Unequal," *Crime & Delinquency*, April 1977, pp. 109-120.

* Thomas Szaz, *Ideology and Insanity: Essays on the Psychiatric Dehumanization of Man*, Garden City, N.Y.: Doubleday Anchor Original, 1970.

tion and choose from several modes of punishment. In other cases this discretionary power is pre-empted by the dictates of the state legislature. Both instances bear evidence of discrimination on the basis of the offender's sex. Women are sentenced both more severely and less severely than men are for the same offenses.

Some states have special sentencing provisions, enacted at the turn of the century to "protect" females, under which the length of a woman's sentence is determined not by the judge but by correctional authorities within the limits set by statute.[1] The result is denial of equal protection for women: under these statutes, female offenders often serve longer sentences than male offenders convicted of the same criminal conduct.[2]

Discrimination in favor of female offenders often occurs when judges have discretionary power. Many judges believe, erroneously, that women are better able than men to reform themselves[3] and that, though given to crimes of passion, they seldom possess the pervasive criminal tendencies that characterize male criminals.[4]

SENTENCING ADULT FEMALES

The Chivalry Factor

Our society is thought to have an especially protective attitude toward women,[5] and it is a widely held belief that women fare much better than men when the trial court has discretion. This selective application of the law is attributed to the "chivalry factor." Pollak states that traditional chivalry in the courtroom has led to acquittals that did not accord with the evidence but rather reflected our cultural attitudes toward women.[6] Compared with men, women are considered to be less liable to be detected, arrested, convicted, and committed, and those who are processed all the way through the criminal justice system are regarded as extraordinarily distasteful or dangerous: "Those who are ultimately sent to prison are the very worst of the total crop."[7]

"PROTECTIVE" STATUTES

In effect today are statutes which reflect the belief that something in the very nature of being a woman justifies her being incarcerated for a longer period than a man would be for the same offense.[8] Between 1869 and 1915, ten states (Indiana, Iowa, Maine, Massachusetts, Minnesota, New Jersey, New York, Ohio, Pennsylvania, and Wisconsin) enacted legislation that created separate facilities for convicted women and established the use of the indeterminate sentence for them, a logical consequence of the legislators' belief that women have psychological characteristics which make longer periods of incarceration necessary.[9] After 1915 three other states (Alabama, Arkansas, and California) enacted sentencing statutes applicable only to women and requiring indeterminate sentences. These statutes usually result in sentences more severe for women than for men guilty of the same offense. Thus there is an interim period during which the male defendant is either under consideration for parole or out on parole, whereas the female defendant remains "protected" in prison, where she is denied a great many fundamental rights.[10] For example, Iowa law allows women to be confined up to five years for a misdemeanor but, unless an exception is made in the statute defining the particular offense, limits that imprisonment of male misdemeanants to one year.[11] In Maine women between the ages of seventeen and forty can be sentenced to reformatories for up to three years even if the statutory maximum for the defense is less.[12]

Muncy Act

In Pennsylvania the Muncy Act (1913) required that all women over the age of sixteen who had been convicted of an offense punishable by more than one year in prison must be given a general sentence to the Muncy State Industrial Home for Women. The Muncy Act did not permit the trial judge to use discretion to impose a shorter maximum sentence than the maximum punishment prescribed by law for the offense or to fix a minimum sentence at the expiration of which the female prisoner would be eligible for parole. But he had discretionary power to make these decisions in the case of a male.[13]

Specifically, the Muncy Act discriminated against women in the following ways:

1. A woman could be sentenced to a term of three years even if the maximum was less; a man could not be sentenced over the maximum prescribed by law.

2. A woman was sentenced to the maximum legal penalty if convicted of a crime punishable by more than three years; a man could be sentenced to less than the maximum prescribed by law.

3. A woman could not receive a minimum sentence; not only could a man receive a minimum term but that term could not be more than half the maximum.

4. Under Pennsylvania law the authority to grant parole lies with the sentencing judge when the sentence is less than two years; it lies with the parole board when the sentence is two years or more. Since all sentences to Muncy were for at least three years, women imprisoned there came

under the jurisdiction of the parole board, which does not permit representation by counsel at its hearings.

5. Only if her offense was punishable by a sentence of one year or less could a woman serve the term in a county jail, but she was sent to Muncy, separated from relatives and friends, for the same kind of offense that would have sent a man to the county jail.[14] "Women sentenced under the Act actually spend more than 50 percent longer in jail than do men sentenced for like offenses. . . ."[15]

The philosophy upon which the Muncy Act was originally founded has been expressed as follows:

All delinquent women are sexually immoral and breed feeble-minded bastards; prolonged confinement deters delinquency and impedes sexual immorality; the conclusion drawn from this reasoning is that women should be given indefinite sentences.[16]

Many equal protection challenges to special sentencing statutes for women have failed because the courts concluded that, since women have a rehabilitative capacity different from men's, they *can* reasonably be sentenced differently. No case in court has ever *shown* that women take longer to be rehabilitated than men do![17]

Daniels

On May 3, 1966, Jane Daniels was convicted of robbery in Pennsylvania. The trial court sentenced her to one-to-four years in the Philadelphia County Prison. Thirty-one days later, the judge realized that the Muncy Act deprived him of the power to fix Daniels' term at less than the statutory maximum. He then sent her to the State Industrial Home for Women without fixing a minimum or maximum period of imprisonment. This allowed for the possibility that Daniels would serve ten years (the maximum for robbery) instead of her original maximum of four years.[18]

Theoretically, under the Muncy Act women received discriminatorily favorable treatment with regard to parole. Men were required to serve their minimum sentences before becoming eligible for parole, but women, because their sentences were indeterminate, were eligible for immediate parole. Under her original sentence, Daniels could have been paroled in one year, like a male sentenced to one-to-four years for the same offense.[19] However, under the parole policy of Muncy officials, she would not be paroled for at least three years.

Jane Daniels appealed.[20] The issue presented was the constitutionality of the Muncy Act—specifically, the differences of punishment imposed on male and female offenders convicted of the same offense. Unequal treatment, the United States Supreme Court has said, is permissible only when it is reasonable in the light of its purpose.[21]

Daniels was the first attack ever launched against the Muncy Act. All earlier attacks on similar statutes had failed.[22] Pre-*Daniels* opinions upheld sentencing schemes identical to the Muncy Act and indicated that the indeterminate sentence for female offenders was considered essential to a purpose of reform associated with treatment rather than punishment.[23] In 1946 the Maine Supreme Court, citing a legislative need to experiment with prison reform, upheld an unequal sentencing statute, which provided that women be incarcerated for potentially longer terms than men for identical offenses.[24]

The Pennsylvania Superior Court majority opinion ruled that there was a "rational basis" for the unequal treatment of women committed to Muncy, i.e., a reasonable connection between the classification by sex and the purpose of the legislation:

> The broad purpose of the legislation was to provide for the punishment and rehabilitation of prisoners. Different types of incarceration for the same crimes are regularly imposed both for classes of individuals (e.g., juveniles, sex offenders, recidivists, criminally insane), as well as among separate individuals where judicial discretion in imposing sentence may be allowed by the legislature. The only requirement for different classes of persons is that the class exhibits characteristics that justify the different treatment. . . . This court is of the opinion that the legislature reasonably could have concluded that indeterminate sentences should be imposed on women as a class, allowing the time of incarceration to be matched to the necessary treatment in order to provide more effective rehabilitation. Such a conclusion could be based on the physiological and psychological makeup of women, the type of crime committed by women, their relation to the criminal world, their roles in society, their unique vocational skills and pursuits, and their reaction as a class to imprisonment as well as the number and type of women who are sentenced to imprisonment rather than given suspended sentences. Such facts could have led the legislature to conclude that a different manner of punishment and rehabilitation was necessary for women sentenced to confinement. . . . [25]

The majority opinion justified discrimination on the basis of sex, not on the presumption that the Muncy facility provided effective treatment rather than punishment.

The Supreme Court of Pennsylvania unanimously reversed the Superior Court decision on July 1, 1968, saying that there is no difference between the sexes that justifies a shorter maximum sentence for men committing the same offenses as women. It did *not* altogether reject classification by sex.[26]

The inability of the women's reformatory system to offer its inmates a rehabilitative and curative experience—its failure to achieve the penological purposes that might have justified a special sentencing structure—may have been at the bottom of the state Supreme Court's willingness to strike down the sentencing provisions of the Muncy Act as violative of equal protection.[27]

Two weeks after the Pennsylvania Supreme Court handed down this decision, the legislature passed a revision of the Muncy Act. According to the new version, women would not necessarily receive longer maximum sentences than men but were still denied the right to have a minimum sentence set by the judge: consequently, they would remain in prison awaiting parole while men with fixed minimum sentences became eligible for parole.[28] Challenges to the 1968 amendment to the Muncy Act have been unsuccessful.[29]

Douglas

The *Douglas* case helped persuade the Supreme Court of Pennsylvania to permit an appeal from the superior court decision on *Daniels.* Daisy Douglas and Richard Johnson were convicted of aggravated robbery. Under the Muncy Act, Douglas was sentenced to Muncy for twenty years—the maximum legal penalty; Johnson was sentenced to three-to-ten years in the men's penitentiary. Statistics kept by the Pennsylvania Board of Probation and Parole showed that male parolees convicted of a second equally serious offense were rarely sentenced to the maximum. Douglas filed a petition under Pennsylvania's Post-Conviction Hearing Act, maintaining that her sentence was a denial of her Fourteenth Amendment rights. Her petition was dismissed but her case was consolidated with *Daniels* and was accepted for argument before the Supreme Court of Pennsylvania.[30]

Douglas provided convincing evidence of the discriminatory effect of the Muncy Act. Douglas and Johnson were co-defendants, jointly tried and convicted of the same offense. Johnson, unlike Douglas, had a serious criminal record. Johnson was eligible for parole after three years: under her indeterminate sentence Douglas was technically eligible for parole at any time but in practice would not be eligible for 3 1/2 years. The consolidated appeals of *Douglas* and *Daniels* were successfully argued. Both cases were remanded for resentencing.

Robinson

In Connecticut 38 year old Carrie Robinson pleaded guilty to breach of the peace and resisting arrest. Ordinarily these are misdemeanors carrying maximum terms of one year and six months respectively.[31] However, under a Connecticut statute,[32] women over sixteen who commit such misdemeanors were to be sentenced to an indefinite term not to exceed three years or to the offense maximum, if longer; the statute allowed women to be sentenced for longer terms than men for identical offenses. Robinson claimed that sentencing only women, not men, to indefinite sentences deprived them of equal protection.

The federal district court decision in *Robinson*[33] struck down the statute, finding it a violation of the equal protection clause of the Fourteenth Amendment. The state argued that the longer terms for women involved treatment and rehabilitation, not punishment; but the court followed the U.S. Supreme Court decision in *In re Gault*,[34] which stated that confinement by any other name is still confinement.

Like *Daniels*, *Robinson* did not reject all sex-based classifications. Some sex-based classifications, it said, are reasonable, e.g., limiting women's working hours. *Robinson* and *Daniels* emphasize that unequal deprivation of a *basic* civil right must be sustained by a valid justification.

Costello and Chambers

In New Jersey, males convicted on gambling charges get minimum-maximum terms in the state prison, and the judge can set the maximum; for identical offenses, females were sentenced (until 1973) to an indeterminate term of up to five years in the Correctional Institution for Women, and the judge had no discretion to lower the maximum.[36] The actual term served by the female offender was determined entirely by the institution's board of managers, while males earned earlier release through "good time" provisions or application to the state parole board.[37]

Mary Costello pleaded guilty in Camden County Court to gambling offenses. She was sentenced to an indeterminate term not to exceed five years at the New Jersey Correctional Institution for Women. For the same offense, a male would probably be sentenced to one-to-two years. Costello appealed, contending that her constitutional rights to equal protection under the law had been violated.[38]

Though New Jersey's sentencing scheme for women was similar to Pennsylvania's and Connecticut's (which had already been held unconstitutional[39]), it was deemed by the court in *Costello* not violative of the equal protection clause of the Fourteenth Amendment. The court cited cases in which sex-based discrimination in sentencing had been found constitutional, even though most of the statutes vindicated in those cases were no longer on the books.

In *State v. Chambers*[40] a composite of six cases (including *Costello*), each involving females who had been convicted of gambling offenses and had been given indeterminate sentences, the New Jersey Supreme Court held that disparate sentencing based on sex-based classifications violates the equal protection clause of the Fourteenth Amendment. Where a fundamental right of liberty is restrained in conjunction with a classification system based on sex, a state statute is unconstitutional unless a compelling state interest exists. The state's claim that females were better subjects for rehabilitation was insufficient to justify the infringement upon liberty.

Committing Juvenile Females

The Chivalry Factor

Many believe that female delinquents are not likely to be treated harshly when they come before the courts. Like their adult counterparts, female delinquents are considered to be the beneficiaries of chivalrous treatment. "Our police are inclined to treat unofficially all minor offenses of young girls in order to save them from the social stigma which follows an appearance in court."[41]

Enforcing the Double Standard

Most juvenile courts have broad discretionary powers vested in them by statutes that give them jurisdiction over a wide variety of juvenile activity. Theoretically, these statutes apply equally to males and females; actually, they are applied in accordance with our double standard of juvenile morality and lend themselves to discriminatory enforcement against females.[42]

Many of the young women who come into contact with the adjudicatory process are "turned in" by their parents or relatives rather than "arrested" by law enforcement officials. The juvenile court is very much concerned with obedience to familial demands. Because of the vastly different parental expectations regarding appropriate behavior for male and female children there is a corresponding differential response from the juvenile court toward male and female children. Females have a much narrower range of acceptable behavior.[43] For example, in the tradition that a woman's place is in the home, judges often decide that it is delinquent for a young woman, but not a young man, to return home at an "unreasonable" hour.[44]

Most male delinquency consists of statute violation. Most female delinquency involves violation of sex-role expectations *and* is more severely punished than male delinquency. There are basically five offenses that lead to commitment for the juvenile female: (1) running away, (2) incorrigibility, (3) sexual offenses, (4) probation violation, and (5) truancy. Although the official record may read differently, sexual misconduct usually underlies all of these female offenses.[45] A study of 252 young women committed to a correctional school for girls in Wisconsin during the early thirties said that "75.4 percent had records of sex irregularity. Over 40 percent of the total number had been promiscuous, and approximately 40 percent had a history of venereal disease. Sex delinquency was the most frequent offense."[46]

A few years ago in Connecticut a sixteen year old girl was sent to the State Farm for Women because her parents and the court agreed that she was "in danger of falling into habits of vice." The law under which she was committed was upheld on the grounds that her commitment was not punishment but a "protective safeguard."[47]

All girls brought into Family Court in New York, including those brought before the court for nonsexual offenses, are given vaginal smears to test for veneral disease. This procedure is terrifying for many young girls who have not engaged in sexual activity.[48]

Statistics

More than 50 percent of the girls—in contrast, only 20 percent of the boys—are institutionalized for "noncriminal" offenses. Because the offenses committed by girls are not very serious (over one-half are noncriminal) one would expect their dispositions to be shorter than those generally given to boys for criminal offenses. Actually, girls usually get longer dispositions than boys.[49] A 1958 study of 162 training schools throughout the United States showed that the average time served by a juvenile delinquent was 9.7 months. Separating the sexes, the study showed that the average for female delinquents was 12 months; for male delinquents, 9.3 months. In 1962 the overall average for both sexes was 9.5 months (10.8 months for females, 9.2 months for males). In 1964 the overall average declined to 9.3 months. Females averaged 10.7 months; males, 8.2 months.[50]

In 1964 nationwide statistics put the male-female ratio in juvenile institutions at 3 to 1. The male-female ratio for all juvenile offenses was 4 to 1; for major criminal offenses, 15.3 to 1. There were more juvenile females in institutions than the number of their offenses warranted. "The 'saving' or 'helping' of a girl often justifies more radical and severe 'treatment' than does the punishment of a male law violator."[51]

Statistics published by the Children's Bureau indicated that training schools serving only nonwhite children or only females keep a child for a longer period of time.[52]

Moral Statutes

Juvenile morals statutes are (1) unconstitutionally vague, (2) impermissibly overbroad because they inhibit constitutionally protected behavior, (3) unconstitutionally overbroad because they encourage selective enforcement against female juveniles according to a double standard of sexual morality, and (4) impermissible in that they punish a status.[53]

Most jurisdictions in the United States have statutes that allow a finding of juvenile delinquency when it is established that the defendant engaged in immoral conduct. Few distinctions are made between juveniles according to the grade of offense seriousness. Most jurisdictions lump them all together—all juveniles who break the law are delinquents. Kansas and

Illinois are the only states that do not send runaways to state reform schools.[54]

Morality statutes enable the states to place any juvenile under custody for almost any act for a period ranging from six months to eleven years. Vague delinquency provisions based on subjective determinations of "immorality" and unsupported predictions of future criminal conduct have no legal or practical justification. The due process clause of the Fourteenth Amendment requires that statutes provide fair warning. Delinquency statutes should be more precisely defined.[55]

Sex-Neutral Statutes

Courts have been reluctant to rule that juvenile morals statutes are unconstitutionally vague. According to the Texas juvenile morals statute, any child who "habitually so comports himself as to injure or endanger the morals of himself or others" can be adjudged a juvenile delinquent. Because our society believes that *female* sexual morals should be more restricted, such vague statutes will tend to enforce the double standard of morality. Sexual delinquency is the most common offense of female juveniles. Male juveniles are usually not adjudicated for such behavior and to this extent the vague language incorporated within sex-neutral juvenile morals statutes permits discriminatory enforcement of different sexual standards for males and females.[56]

Sexually Discriminatory Statutes

Juvenile court statutes that differentiate on their face between male and female juveniles fall into three categories:

1. Some juvenile statutes assume that females need more supervision than males and therefore establish higher jurisdictional age limits for females. At the same time, recognizing the earlier emotional maturity of females, many states with such statutes permit females to marry two or three years earlier than males. Jurisdictional statutes providing for higher age limits for females reflect the attitude that young men should be independent and that young women should graduate from parental supervision directly to marriage. These statutes enforce the double standard of morality.[57] Society is obsessed with the notion of protecting unmarried females from themselves.

Most states are moving toward a common jurisdictional age for both male and female juveniles.[58]

2. The juvenile court system is civil and its purported goal is rehabilitation. Delinquents within the custody of the court may be "treated" by any of several means defined in the disposition and confinement statutes of the

state juvenile court act. The integrity of the juvenile court judge determines whether these statutes are applied equally to males and females.[59]

Several states allow for discrepancies between the permissible length of confinement for female and male juveniles. In New York a female adjudged a "person in need of supervision" may be committed to the state training school to remain until the age of twenty. A male must be released by age eighteen.[60]

3. A few state legislatures have provided for special treatment of juvenile females. Until recently, Connecticut and Tennessee had provisions in their juvenile codes permitting institutional commitment of any female between certain ages who is leading a "vicious" or "criminal" life.[61] Now, only Tennessee allows juvenile courts to take custody of girls where they may not take charge of boys.[62]

PINS in New York State

The New York State Family Court Act provides:

> Persons in need of supervision means a male less than sixteen years of age and a female less than eighteen years of age who does not attend school in accordance with the provisions of part one of article sixty-five of the education law or who is incorrigible, ungovernable or habitually disobedient and beyond the lawful control of parent or other lawful authority.[63]
>
> Successive extensions [of the original placement] may be granted, but no placement may be made or continued under this section beyond the child's eighteenth birthday, if male, or twentieth birthday, if female.[64]

Under these provisions females are liable for two extra years of original liability and two extra years of placement. It is clear that these provisions deprive females of fundamental rights and liberties.

Court Tests

Courts have applied the equal protection clause to juveniles to invalidate sexually discriminatory juvenile statutes.[65] A statute that distinguishes between two or more classes of people is not always in violation of the equal protection clause of the Fourteenth Amendment. The state must establish that it has a compelling state interest which justifies the law and that the distinctions made by the law are necessary to further its purpose.[66]

The constitutional right to liberty is the major concern in cases challenging sexually discriminatory juvenile statutes. Juvenile laws that discriminate on the basis of sex do affect the liberty of juveniles. The imposition of longer confinement on one sex than on the other is no more permissible with juveniles than it is with adults.[67]

Sex-based discrimination, like racial discrimination, tends to create and perpetuate inferior status and second-class citizenship.[68] In 1972 the United States Supreme Court declared discrimination on the basis of sex to be a "suspect classification."[69]

Sentencing Provisions that Discriminate against Males

Dr. John MacDonald tells the following "apocryphal" story to illustrate "society's divergent attitudes toward the same behavior in males and females":

> If a man walking past an apartment stops to watch a woman undressing before the window, the man is arrested as a peeper. If a woman walking past an apartment stops to watch a man undressing before a window, the man is arrested as an exhibitionist.[70]

It would be a misrepresentation not to mention a few of the rare sentencing provisions that discriminate against males.

1. *Wark.* A male escapee from the Maine State Prison Farm received a longer sentence for his escape than a woman would have. He asserted that his Fourteenth Amendment rights had thus been violated. Denying his appeal in *Wark v. State,*[74] the court said:

> Viewing statutory provisions for punishment as in part a deterrent to criminal conduct, the legislature could logically and reasonably conclude that a more severe penalty should be imposed upon a male prisoner escaping from the State Prison than upon a woman confined at the "Reformatory" while serving a State Prison sentence who escapes from that institution. We conclude that a classification based on sex under these circumstances is neither arbitrary nor unreasonable but is a proper exercise of legislative discretion which in no way violates the constitutional right to equal protection of the law.[72]

2. *Assault under Arizona law.* Under an Arizona law, men are sentenced more severely than women when the victim of the crime is a woman. Arizona defines aggravated assault as an assault made by a male upon a female *or* by a person over age eighteen on a child under fifteen.[73] Under this law, if an adult female spits in the face of another adult female, she will probably be charged with simple assault and pay a $300 fine or serve up to three months. A male who commits the same offense can be charged with aggravated assault and be punished by imprisonment of one-to-five years and a fine of $100 to $200. North Carolina and Texas have similar assault statutes.[74]

3. *Oklahoma juvenile law.* Under Oklahoma juvenile court law, females who have been adjudged delinquent and have been institutionalized are discharged at age eighteen; males adjudged delinquent and institutionalized are discharged at age twenty-one.

THE EQUAL RIGHTS AMENDMENT

In Oklahoma male delinquents can be confined for a longer period than female delinquents; the reverse is true in New York State. How can the discrepancy between Oklahoma and New York juvenile court laws be rationally justified? Is there some factual difference between males in Oklahoma and males in New York? Or between males and females anywhere that justifies punishment more or less severe for one sex than for the other?

Such inconsistencies in our laws demonstrate the need for the proposed Twenty-Seventh Amendment to the U.S. Constitution—the Equal Rights Amendment.

Sexually discriminatory laws and the unequal application of many sex-neutral statutes coerce females to conform to society's conception of the female sex role. It does not make sense, however, to design training programs in domestication for women who have, by breaking the law, shown their reluctance to adjust to an inferior sex role. Yet institutions for women and girls offer no programs that teach independent trades. Confined females are trained as housekeepers, seamstresses, and waitresses.

Passage of the Equal Rights Amendment would render *any* discrimination on the basis of sex a "suspect classification." This would hold for juveniles as well as adults, for males as well as females. More comprehensive than an extension of the equal protection clause of the Fourteenth Amendment, the Equal Rights Amendment would be a mandate by the American people. But until that amendment is passed and goes into effect (two years after ratification), the equal protection approach should be rigorously pursued to challenge sexually discriminatory statutes.

CONCLUSION

Special sentencing statutes, sentencing judges, and society's conception of the female sex role are all responsible for the unjust sentencing of females. The disparate sentences received by males and females found guilty of the same offenses provide the most blatant evidence of this unequal treatment. Special sentencing statutes enacted at the turn of the century to "protect" women deny them their fundamental rights. The juvenile justice system enforces society's double standard of morality and severely sanctions only females for "sexual misconduct." These inconsistencies in the application of our laws and in our system of justice can be swiftly diminished and rendered unconstitutional with the passage of the proposed Twenty-Seventh Amendment to the U.S. Constitution. The Equal Rights Amendment can bring us all a *long* way.

Notes

1 Brown, Emerson, Falk, & Freedman, *The Equal Rights Amendment: A Constitutional Basis for Equal Rights for Women*, 80 Yale L.J. 871, 965 (1971).

2 Clements, *Sex and Sentencing*, 26 Sw. L.J. 890 (1972).

3 *Ibid.*

4 Baab & Furgeson, *Texas Sentencing Practices: A Statistical Study*, 45 Texas L. Rev. 471, 496-97 (1967).

5 W. Reckless, *The Crime Problem* 99 (4th ed. 1967).

6 O. Pollak, *The Criminality of Women* 4 (1950).

7 Kay & Schultz, *Divergence of Attitudes toward Constituted Authorities between Male and Female Felony Inmates*, in Interdisciplinary Problems in Criminology 209-16 (W. Reckless & C. Newman eds. 1967).

8 Temin, *Discriminatory Sentencing of Women Offenders: The Argument for the ERA in a Nutshell*, 11 Am. Crim. L. Rev. 355 (1973).

9 Clements, *supra* note 2, at 891.

10 Clements, *supra* note 2, at 901.

11 Iowa Code Ann. § 245.7 (1969).

12 Me. Rev. Stat. Ann. tit. 34. § 853-54 (Supp. 1972).

13 Pa. Stat. Ann. tit. 61, ch. 7 (1964).

14 Temin, *supra* note 8.

15 Brief for Appellee at 20-22. Commonwealth v. Daniels, 210 Pa. Super. 156, 232 A.2d 247 (1967).

16 *Id.* at 19.

17 Clements, *supra* note 2.

18 L. Kanowitz, *Women and the Law: The Unfinished Revolution* 167 (1969).

19 Gold, *Equal Protection for Juvenile Girls in Need of Supervision in New York State*, 17 N.Y.L.F. 570 (1971).

20 Commonwealth v. Daniels, 210 Pa. Super. 156, 232 A.2d 247 (1967).

21 Calloway, *Constitutional Law—Indeterminate Sentences for Women*, 22 Ark. L. Rev. 524 (1968).

22 State v. Heitman, 105 Kan. 136, 181 P. 630 (1919); *Ex parte* Dunkerton, 104 Kan. 481, 179 P. 347 (1919); Platt v. Commonwealth, 256 Mass. 539, 152 N.E. 914 (1926): *Ex parte* Brady, 116 Ohio St. 512, 157 N.E. 69 (1927); *Ex parte* Gosselin, 141 Me. 412. 44 A.2d 882 (1945), *cert.* denied sub. nom. Gosselin v. Kelley, 528 U.S. 817 (1946).

23 Note, *Equal Protection—Longer Sentences for Women than for Males Convicted of the Same Offenses Denies Equal Protection*, 82 Harv. L. Rev. 921 (1969).

24 Gosselin v. Kelley, *supra* note 22.

25 Commonwealth v. Daniels, *supra* note 20, 232 A.2d at 247, 251-52.

26 Commonwealth v. Daniels, 243 A.2d 400 (1968).

27 *Supra* note 23.

28 Temin, *supra* note 8.

29 Commonwealth v. Blum, 220 Pa. Super. 703. —— A.2d —— (1972); Commonwealth v. Piper, 221 Pa. Super. 187, 289 A.2d 193 (1972).

30 Commonwealth v. Daniels (II), 430 Pa. 642, 243 A.2d 400 (1968).

31 Gold, *supra* note 19.

32 Conn. Gen. Stat. Ann. ch. 309, § 17-360 (1960), as transferred, ch. 323, § 18-65 (Supp. 1972).

33 United States *ex rel.* Robinson v. York, 281 F. Supp. 8 (D. Conn. 1968).

34 387 U.S. 1 (1967).

35 Kanowitz, *op. cit. supra* note 18.

36 N.J. Stat. Ann. § 2A: 164-17 (1971); N.J. Stat. Ann. § 30: 4-155 (Supp. 1973).

37 Lillehaug, *Constitutional Law—Equal Protection-Sex Discrimination in Sentencing Criminal Offenders Is Unconstitutional,* 50 N. Dak. L. Rev. 359 (1974).

38 State v. Costello, 59 N.J. 334, 282 A.2d 748 (1971).

39 *See* notes 26 and 33 *supra* and accompanying text.

40 63 N.J. 287, 307 A.2d 78 (1973).

41 Pollak, *op. cit. supra* note 6.

42 Comment, *Juvenile Delinquency Laws: Juvenile Women and the Double Standard of Morality,* 19 U.C.L.A. L. Rev. 313 (1971).

43 Chesney-Lind, *Judicial Enforcement of the Female Sex Role: The Family Court and the Female Delinquent,* 8 Issues in Criminology 51 (1973).

44 *Supra* note 42.

45 C. Vedder & D. Somerville, *The Delinquent Girl,* 147 (1970).

46 Lumpkin, *Factors in the Commitment of Correctional School Girls in Wisconsin,* 37 Am. J. Sociology 222 (1931-32).

47 *To Be Minor and Female,* Ms., August 1972, at 74.

48 *Ibid.*

49 Gold, *supra* note 19.

50 W. Lunden, *Statistics on Delinquents and Delinquency* 258-59 (1964).

51 Chesney-Lind, *supra* note 43, at 57.

52 Children's Bureau, U.S. Dept. of Health, Education and Welfare, Statistical Series No. 81, Statistics on Public Institutions for Delinquent Children—1964, at 7 (1965).

53 *Supra* note 42.

54 Note, *An Aspect of the Texas Juvenile Delinquency Law—"Morals,"* 24 Sw. L.J. 698 (1970).

55 Note, *Statutory Vagueness in Juvenile Law: The Supreme Court and Mattiello v. Connecticut,* 118 U. Pa. L. Rev. 152 (1969).

56 *Supra* note 42.

57 Davis & Chaires, *Equal Protection for Juveniles: The Present Status of Sex-based Discrimination in Juvenile Court Laws,* 7 Ga. L. Rev. 494 (1973).

58 New York's Family Court Act is an exception; it has two provisions which subject females to the authority of the court for a longer period than males. *See* notes 63 and 64 *infra* and accompanying text.

59 Davis & Chaires, *supra* note 57.

60 *See* notes 63 and 64 *infra* and accompanying text.

61 Conn. Rev. Stat. § 2761 (1949); Tenn. Code Ann. § 37-440 (1955).

62 Davis & Chaires, *supra* note 57.

63 *N.Y. Judiciary-Family Court Act* § 712(b) (McKinney Supp. 1971).

64 *N.Y. Judiciary-Family Court Act* § 756(c) (McKinney Supp. 1963).

65 *E.g.,* Long v. Robinson, 316 F. Supp. 22 (D. Md. 1970): Lamb v. Brown, 456 F.2d 18 (10th Cir. 1972).

66 Davis & Chaires, *supra* note 57.

67 *Ibid.*

68 *Ibid.*

69 Frontiero v. Richardson, 41 U.S.L.W. 4609, 4613-14 (U.S. May 14, 1972).

70 J. MacDonald, *Psychiatry and the Criminal* 353 (3rd ed. 1976).

71 266 A.2d 62 (Me. 1970).

72 *Id.* at 65.

73 Ariz. Rev. Stat. Ann. § 13-245 (1972).

74 Note, *Sex Discrimination in the Criminal Law: The Effect of the E.R.A.* 11 Am. Crim. L. Rev. 469, 503 (1973).

75 Okla. Stat. Ann. tit. 10, § 1139(b) (Supp. 1973).

4

Guilty by Reason of Sex: Young Women and the Juvenile Justice System

Meda Chesney-Lind

This chapter is very useful for a full understanding of the treatment of women "offenders" because it deals with young girls who find themselves enmeshed in the juvenile justice system. Chesney-Lind gives considerable data which depicts the severe response of the system to girls charged with status offenses (acts which are not crimes if committed by adults, such as running away and disobedience, but are crimes if committed by those in a juvenile status— particularly girls).

The functions and purposes of status offenses for the society are carefully explained in this chapter. As a product of the court's history of extralegal paternalism, status offenses have involved the system in the maintenance of traditional family norms, which require a more restrictive role of greater obedience and chastity from females than males. Fully three-fourths of all girls in the criminal justice system are there for status offenses. The enforcement of status offenses has created a de facto double standard of juvenile justice in America. Like "good parents," police and court personnel tend to select for punishment girls whose behavior threatens parental authority and boys whose behavior is beyond that which can be excused as "boys will be boys."

The author provides a good summary of what little scholarly early work exists on female delinquency, work that Chesney-Lind describes as primarily descriptive, untheoretical, and non-critical. Most importantly, this article shows how such scholarly apathy contributed to gross distortions about female delinquency, did not lead to benign consequences, and allowed the judiciary to discriminate in its treatment against women and girls in the criminal justice system for nearly a century.

Recent research, often initiated by feminists, has faulted the traditional scholarly views that female delinquency, unlike male delinquency, is sexual and interpersonal in nature, that it is "treatable," and that differential socialization of male and female children is a significant cause in delinquency. The findings show, for example, that while females engage in far more delinquency (but less serious crimes than males) than is reported, they do not "specialize" in sexual or relational offenses; that police respond differently to females than they do to males; and that police are less likely to pick up a female suspected of a criminal offence and more likely to pick up a female than a male suspected of a sexual offence. The courts which receive one-third of all females from parental referral (but only one-tenth of all males from parental initiative) respond more severely to females than males, using institutionalization more often for women and providing harsher punishment. Finally, the numbers of women in detention are disproportionate to the numbers of arrested women, and females are incarcerated longer than males.

Chesney-Lind concludes by pointing to the need to challenge the juvenile justice system in the following ways: to deal forthrightly with the civil rights of young women who come into contact with the law, to confront the sexual double standard lying behind much of the protectionist rhetoric of courts and parents, to show how the philosophy of incarcerating young girls is not beneficial to them, and to develop more theoretical work focusing on "the relationship between official responses to female delinquency and other systems of sexual inequality."

Ask yourself what questions the harsher treatment of girls than boys raises about what happens to them as adults, either law-abiding or offenders. Since the data show that juvenile justice officials take more drastic action in response to girls' noncriminal actions than they do to either girls' or boys' criminal behavior, what does this say about social control in our society? Why does the molding of young girls into stereotypical "lady-like" behavior seem to be more important than deterring criminal behavior of boys—or even of girls? Finally, what do you think about Chesney-Lind's recommendations that challenge the criminal justice system and its treatment of female juveniles?

There has been increasing interest, of late, in the female delinquent and her older counterpart, the female criminal. While long overdue, much of this attention is less a product of a desire to redress a scholarly oversight than it is an attempt to discover the much sought after "dark side of female liberation." As a consequence, serious scholarly work on this issue has often been submerged by more opportunistic and hastily prepared tracts.[1]

This observation notwithstanding, the public interest in the female offender has had at least one positive consequence. It is now less fashionable for serious works on delinquency or crime to ignore women. Prior to the 1970s, it was more or less routine for delinquency researchers who were conducting rigorous studies or engaged in theory building to omit women from consideration. Sometimes this decision was accompanied with sheepish apologies, such as the following which appeared as a footnote in Hirschi's *Causes of Delinquency:*

> In the analysis which follows, "non-Negro" becomes "white," and the *girls disappear* (emphasis added) . . . Since girls have been neglected for too long by students of delinquency, the exclusion of them is difficult to justify. I hope to return to them soon.[2]

Another common justification for failing to include women in delinquency research was that because men and women were different, the study of that behavior was essentially the study of male delinquency. Cohen articulated this position when he argued that "people do not simply want to excel—they want to excel as a man or as a woman." It followed that the "problems of adjustment of men and women, of boys and girls, arise out of quite different circumstances and press for quite different solutions." In essence, Cohen felt that "the delinquent is a rogue male."[3]

This theoretical and empirical void has seriously hampered efforts to understand not only why, when, and how women deviate or commit delinquent offenses, but the equally important questions of why, when, and how the society responds to this behavior. Moreover, this pattern of neglect has permitted and encouraged theory building and research that is profoundly flawed by monosexism.[4] The failure of theories of deviance to account for the behavior (either conforming or rule violating) of over half of the population cannot, in the final analysis, be considered sound.

Recently, delinquency theorists have come to recognize this fact, and many are beginning the long neglected task of researching the issue of young women and delinquency.[5] The following sections will review not only these efforts, but also what might be called the "received tradition" in female delinquency. This review will reveal that the dearth of scholarly research in the past contributed to gross distortions of both the actual nature of female delinquency and also the official response to that behavior. Moreover, a review of the few rigorous studies of female delinquency and the treatment of women in the juvenile justice system will show that this scholarly apathy toward young women had anything but benign consequences.

SHE'S MORE TO BE PITIED THAN CENSURED

It goes without saying that in contrast to the vast body of work on male delinquency research on female delinquency is remarkably sparse.[6] The bulk of this literature is descriptive, untheoretical, non-critical, and not infrequently, self-congratulatory.

Because, as Smart has observed, young women are such perfect candidates for saving, protecting, and correcting,[7] they, unlike their older counterparts, have not often been the subjects of the studies which sought biological causes for their misbehavior.[8] Instead, early works on female delinquency were written by professional and amateur "childsavers" who, as the founders of the then fledgling family court system, had a vested interest in the repudiation of biological causes of delinquency in favor of those theories which suggested that environmental causes produced delinquency in otherwise innocent children. However, it is certainly not clear that this shift in attention, while appearing benign, actually benefitted young women. Historians of the early years of the juvenile court observe that the childsavers "were not indulgent sentimentalists" and, indeed, recommended increased imprisonment as a means of removing delinquents from corrupting influences and "immoral settings."[9] This is clearly seen in the earliest work on female delinquency which focused more on female reformatories or "training schools" than on the nature of youthful female misbehavior.

These works tended to encourage court intervention in the lives of young women and to promote incarceration as a solution to female delinquency.[10] A good example of this type of work was Reeves' *Training Schools for Delinquent Girls* published in 1928. Reeves' book was an extensive national survey of these institutions which she saw as settings in which delinquent young women, whom she called "the beneficiaries," could learn "self-expression," "freedom," and "outdoor life." Although Reeves does not admit that in her tour of these institutions she did find some severe problems of brutality, the book is replete with optimistic statements and pictures of happy young women engaged in exercise classes and outdoor theatre productions.[11] Other childsavers such as Margaret Reeves were enthusiastic about their ability to construct an environment superior to the young women's homes and were uncritical of their assumption that female defiance inevitably led to sexual immorality.

In this latter sense, both older and younger women shared a similar burden by being cast in the role of sexual deviants. The literature does, however, tend to take a different approach to the offender depending upon her age. If the woman is young, the work tends to focus on the need to protect her from the horrors of sexuality, pregnancy, and unwed motherhood. If she is an adult the literature tends to be both decidedly less forgiving and more voyeuristic.

A good example of what was to become the standard approach to the subject of young women in trouble with the law and one that supplied academic legitimacy to the assumption that female deviance was sexual is W. I. Thomas' *The Unadjusted Girl*. Based on his evaluation of case records drawn from the Girls' Protective Bureau and the Cook County Juvenile Court, the book is one of the first scholarly attempts to explore the source of female delinquent behavior. Since most of these cases involved young women taken into custody as a result of the "wholesale arrests of girls and women on the suspicion of venereal disease"[12] during World War I, it was not surprising that Thomas determined that nearly all female delinquency was an expression of sexual problems.

Initially, Thomas admits that the definition of young women as sexual property is culturally determined:

The role which a girl is expected to play in life is indicated to her by her family in a series of aesthetic-moral definitions of the situation. Civilized societies have endowed the young girl with a character of social sacredness. She is the subject of far-going idealization. "Virginity" and "purity" have an almost magical value.13

This awareness of the arbitrary emphasis placed on a young woman's sexuality sets Thomas apart from his contemporaries. He also determined that young women were not involved in sexual activity out of curiosity but rather, he felt, were encouraged to use sex as their "capital" to obtain other valued goods (clothing, money).14 Thomas does not condemn this arrangement but rather condemns a social class system which enables upper status women to sell themselves only once (for marriage) while poor women are forced to settle for less ("entertainment, affection and perhaps gifts").15

Thomas repeatedly debunks the notion that women are being punished for simple sexual experimentation:

> The cases which I have examined . . . show that sexual passion does not play an important role, for the girls usually become "wild" before the development of sexual desire, and their casual sexual relations do not usually awaken sex feeling.16

Nor is he hesitant about the source of the problem ("bad family" and "demoralization") and its solution—the family court:

> During the past decade some of these [family] courts have reached a high degree of elaboration and perfection. Their service has been very great in checking the beginnings of demoralization. The court is much wiser than the parents of children and incidently does much to influence home life.17

Thomas hoped that the family court would remedy the problems he detailed in the reformatories and he placed great hope in sensitive and enlightened casework.

Thomas' work in many ways sets the tone for the approach to family delinquency in the next half century. Subsequent researchers18 consistently echo the themes found in *The Unadjusted Girl,* albeit in less stilted language. That is to say, the authors make two critical assumptions: first, they assume that most female delinquency is either "sexual" or "relational" rather than criminal in nature; and second, they express the certainty that social intervention, administered by sensitive and informed individuals, can help young women with their problems.

Based almost without exception on labelled and/or incarcerated juvenile females (roughly three-quarters of whom were charged either directly or indirectly for sexual offenses), these authors rarely questioned the equity of the family court's exclusive preoccupation with female sexuality. Indeed, most were anxious to justify the situation:

> On first examination it would appear from these data that the court discriminates

heavily against the female sex offender, even though the offense that brings her to court is seldom, if ever, bizarre sex behavior characteristic of the male offender. Such an interpretation is, in our opinion, totally at variance with the facts. Training schools are more frequently needed for the promiscuous female for her own protection.[19]

[The] sexually delinquent girl violates the caring and protective attributes of her maternal role in a way which will harm her and her offspring for the remainder of her life.[20]

However, one of these authors (Konopka), critically commented about this situation, noting that "most girls find themselves confused because of the still prevailing double standard for boys and girls, and because of conflicting precepts which pronounce sex as healthy and good on the one hand and as base and sinful on the other."[21] None of these authors, however, recommend withdrawal of social service agencies from involvement in the non-criminal but sexual behavior of young women. In fact, some scholars, such as Vedder and Somerville, in their national review of female training schools are enthusiastic about the intervention:

While studying delinquent girls, we should keep this in mind; when you train a man you train one individual; when you train a woman, you train a family.[22]

The consistent theme in these works is how best to diagnose, treat, and keep young women, thereby protecting them from environments which might lure them back into sexual activity.

From these basic sources, it is accurate to say that until recently, the remaining literature on female delinquency fell into one of two general categories, both of which still made many of the assumptions of the major works previously described. The first category comprised numerous descriptive articles on the characteristics of labelled and/or incarcerated female youth, suggestions about treatment strategies for female delinquency, and literature on the social organization of female institutions.[23] The second category included a small number of sociological attempts to develop a coherent theory of female delinquency. Since these efforts have been few, the literature in this area is flawed by its intellectual isolation. In brief, those who elected to study female delinquency or criminality confronted an enormous task of theory building (since the vast bulk of the available theoretical literature was inapplicable to women). It is remarkable, for example, that while Cohen and others have acknowledged a deep intellectual debt to G.H. Grosser for his work, *Juvenile Delinquency and Contemporary American Sex Roles*, it remains today an unpublished Ph.D. dissertation.[24]

Generally, these works first assumed that young women in juvenile court populations across the country (most of whom were charged with sexual or relational offenses) were representative of the actual character of female delinquency, and then attempted to explain this phenomenon. The best works illustrative of this type are by Grosser[25] and Morris.[26] Grosser basically contended, and Cohen agreed, that the differential sex role socialization of males and females pushed women to achieve success through affiliation (marriage) while males were encouraged to achieve success through achievement. Female delinquency, which was assumed to be primarily relational and sexual, was both an extension and violation of the female subculture in the same way that aggressive and criminal behavior was a product of the male subculture.

Morris accepted the notion that female delinquency was deeply influenced by male and female socialization. She designed rigorous studies to explore differences between female and male delinquents as well as differences between these delinquents and non-delinquents. Morris attempted in her dissertation and two published papers[27] to develop a comprehensive theory of female delinquency which would explain both its sexual character and, in comparison to male delinquency, its smaller size.

To explain the smaller number of female delinquents, Morris argued that women experience both reduced access to illegitimate means and greater social disapproval of their delinquent acts than their male counterparts. To explain the predominance of relational offenses among women, she suggested that since "factors which interfere with reaching culturally defined success goals by legitimate means are most likely to lead to deviancy" and since these goals are different for males and females, the sources and character of delinquent behavior would, of necessity, be different. Obstacles to economic power and status would be most likely to lead to delinquency in males while obstacles to maintaining positive affective relationships would most likely produce delinquency in females.[28] In research testing this hypothesis, Morris found that female delinquents were more likely than a matched sample of non-delinquents to come from broken homes, to come from families with many family tensions, and to be rated low in personal appearance and grooming skills.

Other theorists have also argued that female delinquents are more sensitive to family disruption than either female non-delinquents or males, but the research on this is, by and large, unconvincing. As Shover and Norland observe in their review of the evidence on this point, "usually this assertion has been supported by research on officially adjudicated delinquents."[29] Since it is now known that young women are more often reported to the police by their parents than are young men, this might make it appear that family discord is a more important factor for females, even in the absence of any relationship between family problems and female delinquency.

Another of Morris' notions—that female delinquents experience frustration in the legitimate realization of female goals (i.e., dating and marriage)—has also not been directly confirmed or disproved. Sandhu and Allen concluded in their study of delinquent and non-delinquent girls that "delinquent girls showed significantly less commitment to marital goals, expressed less desire to marry, and perceived fewer obstacles in the fulfillment of their marital goals as compared to non-delinquent girls."[30]

Morris, in her dissertation, also had problems with this portion of her argument, reporting that her data failed to provide conclusive support for the notion that male delinquency is caused by "status" frustration while female delinquency is caused by "relational frustration," in part because delinquent females seemed to report low concern for both status and relational goals.[31]

On the other hand, in another examination of differential opportunity theory, Datesman, Scarpitti, and Stephenson[32] found some evidence that girls arrested for "public policy offenses" did have the lowest perception of opportunities among both non-delinquents and delinquent women. However, they cautioned that casuality is difficult to establish since sexual activity among young women in an environment which condemns such behavior, may cause girls to experience less success in obtaining dates. Finally, Morris and later Datesman et al. found strong evidence that the female delinquent enjoys significantly less subcultural support than her male counterpart, with both males and females being less tolerant of female delinquency.

All of these researchers make several assumptions which in retrospect seem simplistic. First, they assume that virtually all female delinquency is sexual or interpersonal in nature in contrast to male delinquency, which is more likely aggressive and criminal. Second, they assume that differential socialization of male and female children plays a significant role in the generation of sex differences.

Because of the widespread acceptance of these two points, it has always been assumed that young women who deviate from stereotypical feminine characteristics might become "more delinquent" since most delinquency was assumed to be expressive of "masculine" values and attributes. Yet one study which rigorously tested the relationship between self-reported delinquency and attachment to either feminine or masculine characteristics found surprising results. These researchers found that, if anything, masculine characteristics in women indirectly reduce the extent of their involvement in delinquent conduct. Surprisingly, too, was their finding that attachment to masculinity among males was more predictive of "status" (or "non-criminal," uniquely juvenile) offenses than either property or aggressive offenses.[33]

Clearly, recent research findings dispute the traditional scholarly view of female delinquency and call for a rigorous description of female delinquency uncluttered by simplistic and stereotypical notions of male and female behavior.

WHAT SHE REALLY DID

The efforts of Grosser and Morris were important attempts to explore the dynamics of female delinquency. Yet the frustration they and others report in confirming or disproving their hypotheses was no doubt a product of their own failure to question the "given" nature of female delinquency as almost exlusively "sexual" or "relational."

This characteristic of female delinquency was, in fact, being consistently eroded by studies of both detected and undetected male and female delinquency. These studies did not rely on court populations to determine the nature of female delinquency, but instead solicited from school children self-reported accounts of delinquent acts.

From one of the earliest such studies on the actual dimensions of delinquency came the message that while young women were engaging in delinquent behavior less frequently than males, there was evidence that official statistics were "under-reporting female delinquency" and also evidence that higher proportions of young males report sexual activity than did girls.[34] Subsequent studies continued to confirm that while young women tended to be involved in less frequent and less serious delinquent behavior than young men, they engaged in far more delinquency than official statistics indicated and they did not "specialize" in relational or sexual offenses.[35] As Gold summarized his findings:

> Discussions of girls' delinquency have emphasized the preponderance of running away, incorrigibility, and fornication among their offenses. For this reason, these offenses have come to be regarded as "girls' offenses" and their nature has provided the foundation for thinking about the causes for girls' delinquency. However, in the present data, running away, incorrigibility . . . and fornication account for only eight percent of girls' delinquent acts, and not much less of boys, six percent.[36]

A recent self-report study conducted by Weis[37] confirmed earlier findings that the volume of unreported female delinquency was substantial and also added another interesting perspective. Weis found that the oft-cited 1:6 ratio of male to female arrestees was twice as large as the mean ratio of 1:2.56 based on self-report data from participants in actual delinquent behavior. More importantly, Weis explored differences over time in the character and volume of self-reported delinquency to determine if, in fact, the women's movement had had any impact on the actual volume of female misbehavior. Comparing the findings of self-report studies conducted during 1960, 1964, 1968, and 1971, he showed that "the mean sex ratios across all delinquent acts and for theft and aggression items have not changed in the direction predicted by the 'liberation' theories for this time period."[38] He also noted that sex ratios across all offenses were "relatively stable for the decade contrary to the notion that they would get smaller."[39] Indeed, rates of violent behavior showed boys becoming more violent while girls became less violent.

Gold's own comparison of two national self-report studies for the periods of 1967 and 1972 confirms Weis' general finding with one important exception. Gold found that while girls in 1972 were reporting less larceny, property destruction and breaking and entering, "they reported greater use of marijuana and alcohol which increased their overall amount of reported delinquency."[40] These figures do not support the notion that dramatic changes in the level of female criminality have occurred as young women, presumably inspired by the women's movement, engaged in more "masculine" behaviors and thus became more delinquent. But how can these findings be reconciled with the dramatic percentage increases in female arrests that were seen in the early 1970s? For example, between 1960 and 1975 while arrests of adult females were up 60.2 percent, arrests of juvenile women increased a startling 253.9 percent.[41] In the area of violent crime, while Weis' data showed an actual decline in female violence during the 1960s, arrest data for that same period showed a 230.9 percent increase in the arrests of adolescent girls for violent offenses.[42]

To answer these questions, one must consider another neglected issue in the area of female delinquency. Until recently, there has been virtually no interest in those who officially label and process female delinquents. Further, little empirical work has been conducted on the disposition of female cases by these juvenile justice personnel. The following section will attempt to remedy this oversight by reviewing the research on the neglected side on the interaction which produces the social fact of female delinquency. Moreover, this information will illustrate that the failure to study this aspect of delinquency not only has obscured the character of female delinquency, but also has allowed the harsh punishment of these young women cast into the role of sexual delinquent to remain unnoticed and unchallenged.

DELINQUENT GIRLS IN COURT—REVISITED

Early in the history of the juvenile or family court a few alert citizens became concerned about the abandonment of minors' rights in the name of treatment, saving, and protection. One of the most insightful of these critical works, and one that has been unduly neglected, was Tappan's *Delinquent Girls in Court*. Stating that he was going to look at "what the courts do rather than what they say they do,"[43] Tappan evaluated several hundred cases in the Wayward Minor Court in New York City during the late 1930s and early 1940s. These cases caused Tappan to conclude that there were serious problems with a statute that brought young women into court simply for disobedience of parental commands or because they were in "danger of becoming morally depraved":[44]

> It is apparent that something more than willful disobedience to the parents' commands is necessary to confer jurisdiction, but the need to interpret the "danger of becoming morally depraved" imposes upon the court a legislative function of moralizing character. Is anything more implied than sexual misbehavior? If so, what? What is sexual misbehavior—in a legal sense—of the nonprostitute of 16, of 18, or of 20 when fornication is no offense under criminal law?[45]

Tappan's review of the functioning of the court also led him to caution against the wholesale abandonment of legal rules and procedures to accomplish social objectives. Noting that "the implications of judicial totalitarianism are written in history,"[46] Tappan observed that the structure of the Wayward Minor Court "entrusted unlimited discretion to the judge, reformer or clinician and his personal views of expedience."[47] Without any legal guidelines or rules of order, Tappan continued, "the fate of the defendant, the interest of society, the social objectives themselves, must hang by the tenuous thread of the wisdom and personality of the particular administrator."[48] Finally, he concluded with an insightful warning:

> The flood of facile recommendations from the impatient must, then, be carefully scrutinized to determine whether the gain that is promised by dilution or evasion of the established law is greater than the loss which it involves.[49]

It was unfortunate that for the next several decades Tappan's warning remained unheeded. Instead, students of juvenile delinquency assumed, often without any empirical evidence, that the court's treatment of young women was essentially chivalrous and benign.[50]

Because so few researchers studied the juvenile justice system (and those researchers who did included few females in their studies) researchers were frequently puzzled by their findings. For example, three comparative analyses of official treatment of male and female delinquents completed in the 1950s all expressed surprise and confusion about their findings. One study conducted by Terry entitled "Discrimination in the Handling of Juvenile Offenders by Social Control Agencies,"[51] revealed that the severity of sanctions was *not* positively related to the sex of the male offender, as the author had expected. Instead, Terry discovered that females were less likely than males to be released by police, and were more likely to be referred to a social or welfare agency. At the probation level, females were slightly less likely to be released and more likely to be placed under informal supervision. Finally juvenile court dispositions tended to be more severe for females: 76 percent of the females were institutionalized compared to 59 percent of the males.[52]

Another comparative study of differential treatment accorded juveniles on the basis of sex is provided by Cohn who studied the criteria for the Probation Officer's Recommendation to the Juvenile Court Judge. Cohn discovered that while females constituted only one-sixth of the population, they constituted nearly one-half of those recommended for institutionalization.[53]

Gibbons and Griswold[54] in their study of juvenile courts in Washington State also found that high rates of institutionalization of women. While they noted that young women were somewhat more likely than males to be dismissed from court jurisdiction, they found that among those cases not dismissed, proportionately twice as many females as males (25.8 percent versus 11.3 percent) were sent to institutions.[55] While Gibbons and Griswold did not comment on this finding, Cohn suggested that a possible explanation for this situation might be that the girls had committed offenses against either parental authority or public morality rather than acts against persons or property. She concluded that these were "acts which the probation officer generally considered products of social background and personality make-up beyond the range of effective probation treatment."[56] Cohn's rather terse discussion obscures more than it explains. Why, for example, are acts against parents and morality considered evidence of personal or social pathology? Moreover, why are young women charged with these non-criminal offenses not better candidates for probation than their male counterparts charged with criminal offenses?

It remained for several feminist researchers[57] to begin to fully explore the contradictions observed by prior research. As discussed in the next section, the feminists found that both the search for female sexual delinquency and the harsh official response to that behavior was built into the history and structure of America's juvenile justice system.

JUDICIAL PATERNALISM

Originally established in the late 1800s, the juvenile or family court has become a judicial body with broad powers over not only criminal youth but other groups of adolescents as well. Based on an assumption of the natural dependence of youth, the court's founders created a system charged with judging the guilt or innocence of those accused of criminal behavior and also with acting for or in place of the defendant's parents (*parens patriae*).

The intent of the founders' paternalism went far beyond a concern for removing the adolescent criminal from the horrors of the adult criminal justice system, as Platt notes:

Many of the childsavers' reforms were aimed at imposing sanctions on conduct unbecoming youth and disqualifying youth from the benefit of adult privileges. The childsavers were more concerned with restriction than liberation, with the protection of youth from moral weaknesses as well as from physical dangers. The austerity of the criminal law and criminal institutions were not their major target of their concern, nor were they especially interested in problems relating to "classical" crimes against person and property. Their central interest was in the normative behavior of youth—their recreation, leisure, education, outlook on life, attitudes to authority, family relationships, and personal morality.[58]

Other historians have taken a different perspective on the founders' interest in the morality and obedience of youth. Teitelbaum and Harris[59] argue that there was then, and remains today, a fundamental ambivalence in the courts' attitude toward children and their parents. The childsavers were anxious to involve themselves in an unprecedented intervention into a formerly private sphere—the family. In order to secure this power over the children of others, the court founders found it useful to borrow extensively from colonial laws regarding "stubborn" or "neglected" children. Rooted firmly in the notion that "parents were godly and children wicked," these laws supplied the childsavers with a legitimacy they readily embraced—that of strengthening the "endangered" family.[60]

Teitelbaum and Harris note, however, that most of the childsavers actually disagreed with the colonial precepts of child evil and instead, assumed that youth were basically innocent and either the child's parents or environment was morally suspect. Nonetheless, they may have resorted to colonial imagery to minimize "the pervasiveness of the intervention that marked nineteenth and twentieth century childsaving programs."[61] As they observe:

An effort to restore lost virtue seems less radical than one to create a new system for dealing with an ancient institution. It may also be that the colonial family, like the modern city, came to serve as a symbol for the general social order.[62]

Ultimately, the progressive or modern childsaving view (which encourages governmental intervention into the family to save the child from corrupting influences) and the puritan view of the sinfulness of children and the virtue of unquestioning obedience to parental commands are "fundamentally" incompatible. Nonetheless, both have existed in the court system since its inception. While at various times one view has held sway over the other, both bode ill for young women.

For example, Schlossman and Wallach[63] in their review of the attitudes toward female delinquency in the progressive era, note that early court records and writings of this period reveal a concern for the moral environment of youth which was riddled with stereotypes about women and girls, particularly immigrant women. Moreover, as has been noted, these court workers showed considerable enthusiasm for incarceration. During these early years young women were prosecuted almost exclusively for "immoral conduct," which according to Schlossman and Wallach, was "a very broad category that defined all sexual exploration as fundamentally perverse and predictive of future promiscuity, perhaps even prostitution."[64] And, more importantly, Schlossman and Wallach documented the court's harsh response to this non-criminal behavior. In Chicago they reported that between 1899 and 1909, of the juveniles who appeared in court, 59 percent of the young men and only 37 percent of the girls were placed on probation.[65] Conversely, one-half of the young women delinquents, but only one-fifth of the young men, were sent to reformatories.[66] In Milwaukee family court the same pattern obtained with twice as many young women as young men committed to institutions.[67]

This pattern is not purely of historical interest. Research by the author on court files of the Honolulu Family Court during 1930-1950 document the enthusiastic use of training schools for the treatment and protection of young women suspected of sexual activity. These years also witness a gradual shift in language as the court moved from the arrest of young women for "waywardness," "immorality," and "sexual delinquency," to the use of less explicit "status offenses." These uniquely juvenile offenses include: "running away from home," "ungovernability," "incorrigibility," being a "truant," in danger of becoming "morally depraved," or a "person (child, minor) in need of supervision." Obviously these offense categories invite substantial amounts of both parental and official discretion—and have been criticized for this reason.[69]

But more to the point, the function of these offense categories in female delinquency cases is to serve as "buffer charges" for suspected sexuality.[70] For example, Vedder and Somerville observe that between 75 and 85 percent of all young women arrested during the period of their study (1963) were taken into custody for what they called the "big five" (running away from home, incorrigibility, sexual offenses, probation violation, and truancy). However, they conclude that:

> The underlying vein in many of these cases is sexual misconduct by the girl delinquent. However, in most instances, the most innocuous charges of "running away," "incorrigibility," "ungovernability," and the like are used in the official record. It is for this reason that sexual offenses are in third place.[71]

Even if juvenile justice personnel are not themselves concerned about sexual misconduct, the uncritical acceptance of familial authority represented by these offense categories means that parents, who may well be anxious to control a daughter's sexuality, will bring her to court for behavior that they would ignore or endorse in their sons.[72]

The fact that young women continue to be more likely than their male counterparts to appear in juvenile court for offenses which represent violations of parental authority (often called "status offenses") rather than for violations of the law becomes significant. One recent study, for example, found that 75 percent of the females in the juvenile institutions were referred for non-criminal, status offenses.[73] In fact, it may be that young women who comprise only a quarter of the juvenile court population constitute a majority of those charged with these offenses.[74] Young men, on the other hand, are more likely to be adjudicated in the juvenile justice system for criminal offenses such as burglary, larceny and car theft.[75]

Given what is known about the dimensions of female delinquency from self-report studies, the difference between the offenses of males and females in court populations is puzzling. Self-report studies suggest that if juvenile courts sampled female deviance randomly, the court should have fewer females than males, but the females should be charged with roughly the same offenses as the males. Official court statistics consistently under-estimate the volume of female deviance, particularly criminal misbehavior, and over-estimate its sexual character. Because of this distortion it is reasonable to assume that some bias (either unofficial or official) is present within the juvenile justice system and functions to filter out those young women guilty of criminal offenses while retaining those women suspected of sexual misconduct.

Undoubtedly, parents constitute a major source of this bias as they are far more likely to refer their daughters than their sons to court. National data indicate that one-third of the young women but only one-tenth of the young men are referred to court by their parents.[76]

It may also be possible that other official referral sources abuse the status offense label as well. This is indicated by Kratcoski's[77] study of a Delaware family court. His research revealed that school officials were more likely to refer females than males to court. Police may also treat male and female suspects differently. One study of police-juvenile interactions indicates that this was a possibility. Monahan[78] found that police in Philadelphia were more likely to pick up a female than a male suspected of a sexual offense, equally likely to pick up a male and a female charged with runaway, and less likely to arrest a female suspected of criminal offense.

These data seem to explain a pattern discovered by an longitudinal study of delinquency in California. Elliot and Voss[79] queried high school students as to their own accounts of delinquent behavior and then checked official records for evidence of "police contact" (not necessarily official arrests). They found sizeable sex differentials in the frequency of police contact.

Comparing rates of unofficial and official delinquency, they noted that males were four times more likely to experience police contact for a serious offense. Their data showed that police contacts included only one percent of the serious offenses admitted by females and noted that this was "not simply a reflection of differential involvement in delinquency behavior on the part of males and females."[80] Instead they argued that "official records are biased in favor of girls."[81] To support this assertion they referred to data they had gathered on auto theft which showed a male-female self-report ratio of 2 to 1 and a ratio of police contacts of 26 to 1. Stating that "although females perceive themselves as partners in the theft of automobiles, apparently police officers apprehended only their male companions," they concluded that "there is serious sex bias in official police contact reports."[82] Unfortunately, Elliot and Voss were not able to study sexual offenses so that their data could not confirm Monahan's finding, but they did find evidence that young women who admitted to serious criminal offenses were not being apprehended by official agencies in the same numbers as their male counterparts.

In explanation of these findings, some have suggested that juvenile female misbehavior is scrutinized by law enforcement not for evidence of guilt or innocence but for evidence of sexual misconduct. A study conducted by Smith in Great Britain describes how this process, which might be called the "sexualization of female deviance," may be a significant source of the distortion between unofficial and official rates of female delinquency. Interviewing young women in a British family court (most of whom were referred for status offenses), Smith discovered that many respondents reported high rates of such typically male criminal acts as "deliberate property damage" (68%), gang fighting (63%), joy riding (60%), and breaking and entering (33%). To explain why the young women were not charged with these offenses, Smith cites interviews which indicated that "non-sexual offenses were overlooked in favor of sexual misbehavior"[83] by court officials:

> It's funny because once when I was down the cop shop for fighting, this woman saw the swastika on my arm and forgot all about what she was looking for. They never did nothing—just told me to stop fighting. But the woman cop, she kept on about the swastika and Hell's Angels. What a bad lot they were for a girl to go around with and how I had better stop going around with the Angels or else I'd get a really bad name for myself. Then she kept asking me if I'd had sex with any of 'em or taken drugs.[84]

Earlier research had indicated the existence of this pattern. All females admitted to Honolulu's family court during the 1950s, for example, were given physical examinations to determine whether the girls had had sexual contact. The findings of these exams were often added to the charges against the young woman.[85] Indeed, physical examinations of young women, conducted in search of venereal disease, pregnancy, or other substances, are routine in many jurisdictions despite the nature of the charge.[86] These examinations also serve to remind all women that any form of deviance may well be defined as evidence of sexual laxity.

Research suggests that once young women find themselves in the juvenile justice system, differential treatment may continue. Evidence suggests young women suspected of defiance to parental authority and/or sexual activity are retained while their sisters who are arrested or referred for criminal offenses are filtered out. Studies which examine police dispositions of arrest show some evidence of this pattern. One study, for example, found that police were more likely to recommend filing juvenile court petitions against young women for juvenile or status offense while they were more likely to recommend filing petitions against young men for criminal charges.[87] Goldman,[88] in his study of police dispositions, found that police referred a larger proportion of arrested females than males to court, but he felt that his sample size was too small to serve as conclusive proof of police bias against women. Terry[89] found in his study of an unnamed Midwestern town that police released fewer females than males, but that much of the observed difference was a product of a greater propensity to refer young women to social and welfare agencies. Neither he nor Goldman[90] controlled on offense. Finally, Chesney-Lind[91] found that among first offenders in Honolulu, police were more likely to refer a female than a male charged with a status offense to court (34% versus 22%) and further that female status offenders were significantly more likely than female criminal offenders to be referred to court.

Once in court, the pattern apparently continues with young women charged with status offenses receiving harsher punishment than their criminal counterparts. According to one observer, this results because the existence of status offenses invites "discretionary" application at every level of decision making and "allows parents, police, and juvenile court authorities, who ordinarily decide whether PINS proceedings should be initiated, to hold girls legally accountable for behavior—often sexual or in some way related to sex—that they would not consider serious if committed by boys."[92]

In one of the most thorough investigations of this phenomena, Datesman and Scarpitti[93] examined court dispositions of referrals for one Delaware family court and confirmed these findings. By controlling for offense, they found that at every stage of judicial decision making, from intake to institutionalization, female status offenders received the harshest sanctions. For example, 8 percent of the females whose first offense was a status offense were institutionalized compared to only 2 percent of the males

charged with felonies, less than 1 percent of the males charged with misdemeanors and 5 percent of the males charged with status offenses. For
repeat status offenders, females were six times more likely than their male
counterparts to be institutionalized.[94]

Two recent studies[95] have failed to find such marked discrimination in
judicial processing against females charged with status offenses, particularly when they are compared with males charged with status offenses.
While this is encouraging, there is an inherent danger in the comfort some
might draw from these studies. First, it is known that type of offense is
not unrelated to gender and that even when males and females are referred
for offenses which appear to fall into the same general "type" (i.e., status
offense) they are likely to represent different levels of severity. For example, studies of juvenile sex offenders conducted by Acheson and Williams
showed that while females were being incarcerated for heterosexual experimentation, males were typically incarcerated only for "bizarre sex
behavior."[96]

Second, and perhaps more important, neither of these studies disputes
that disproportionately large numbers of young women are charged with
these offenses or the fact that young people charged with these offenses
are more harshly sanctioned than their peers charged with criminal
offenses. For example, it is well known that women are held in detention
in disproportionate numbers in comparison to their arrest rates and that
they tend to be held longer than their male counterparts.[97] Also, the same
pattern appears in training school commitments. A recent survey of these
institutions revealed that "nearly half of all the females in state training
schools were status offenders. Results also show that young women have
longer average confinements than their male counterparts, even though the
vast majority of the males (82%) were criminal offenders."[98]

These patterns should not be taken, however, as evidence that nothing
is being done to remedy the abuses in the current application of the status
offender category. While efforts to extend due process rights to young
people charged with status offenses have been disappointing,[99] challenges
that status offenses are unconstitutionally vague have been more successful. Although in the case of State v. Mattiello[100] the conviction of a young
woman for "walking with a lascivious carriage" was upheld, two more
recent federal court decisions reflect different outcomes. In these cases
statutes which permitted officials to take young people in custody because
they were "in danger of leading an idle, dissolute, lewd or immoral life"
(Gonzalez v. Maillard),[101] or because they were "in danger of becoming
morally depraved" (Gesicki v. Oswald),[102] were found to be impermissibly
vague.

Efforts to extend these findings to other less explicitly sexual status
offense categories have been more discouraging, however. The constitu-

tionality of the "PINS" category in New York State was upheld in *Mercado v. Rockefeller*[103] in 1974 and Washington state's incorrigibility statute was upheld in *Blondheim v. State*[104] in 1975. In *Blondheim* the court was also asked to determine whether punishment for incorrigibility was "cruel and unusual punishment," since the law punished the "status" of incorrigibility; this argument was also rejected.[105]

Pressure for legislative reform of the court's broad jurisdiction over young people taken into custody for status offenses has been building in recent years, perhaps in response to the judiciary's reluctance to deal with this issue. The Juvenile Delinquency Prevention Act of 1974, which provides resources for states and communities to establish new programs for juvenile offenders, requires that states receiving funds must develop and implement plans to treat the status offender without recourse to juvenile detention or correctional facilities.[106]

While there were great hopes when this law was passed, it has become clear that the federal agency given the task of implementing the legislation, the Law Enforcement Assistance Administration (LEAA), was less than enthusiastic about the de-institutionalization provisions of the Act (hereafter referred to as the DSO provisions). A General Accounting Office report[107] to Congress on the agency's efforts to remove status offenders from secure facilities concluded that during certain administrations, the LEAA had actually "downplayed its importance and to some extent discourages states from carrying out the Federal requirements."[108]

The GAO report found monitoring systems to assess states' compliance with the law were lax or non-existent (only nine states had what the GAO thought was complete data), definitions of what constituted detention and correctional facilities were confused (children in jail, for example, were frequently not counted), and LEAA was apparently reluctant to take action against states which had taken federal monies while failing to implement the de-institutionalization of status offenders.

To be fair, much of this reluctance was a product of LEAA's recognition that the DSO provisions irritated virtually everyone. Juvenile court judges, the report continued, "often believe that status offenders are just as bad as delinquents and should be treated as such";[109] state officials identified this legislation as federal intrusion into their territory; and the general public defined efforts to de-institutionalize as "going soft on crime."

These problems notwithstanding, the criticisms of the family court system seem to be having some effect on official treatment of juveniles. Recent studies which have found less sex differentials in the official treatment of status offenders[110] may be pointing to a new awareness among court personnel that excesses of judicial paternalism may be inappropriate. More importantly, national figures show a decrease in the number of young women held in either detention or training schools. Between 1973 and 1977, for example, the number of women held in short-term facilities decreased by 36.3 percent (from 3779 to 2408), and the number of women held in long-term facilities decreased by nearly the same percentage (30.5 percent).[111] Nonetheless, more work remains to be done, particularly in view of recent efforts by such states as California and Louisiana, which had de-institutionalized status offenders, only to reinstate some form of incarceration.[112] In these states the strength of the opposition to DSO appears to come from those who see this legislation as a tentative step toward the withdrawal of judicial power from the enforcement of parental rights. The court founders' early compromise now appears as irony. The court is now confronted with angered parents who insist that it continue to bolster their flagging authority over rebellious children. Not surprising, many of the cases cited to support continued court involvement in the lives of youth involve a female runaway who refuses to remain in non-secure shelters.[113]

In more conservative states, such as Hawaii (which initially refused to participate in the Act because of the DSO requirements), strong opposition to de-institutionalization also comes from social workers, educators, and some judges who openly resent the loss of authority that the Act signals. For example, despite Hawaii's receipt of monies from the federal government, which requires that the state remove status offenders from detention facilities, the admission of young people charged with these status offenses (particularly young women) continues to increase.[114] These data from Hawaii caution against optimism that the Juvenile Delinquency Prevention Act will, in and of itself, remedy the abuses which have characterized juvenile court involvement with non-criminal youth, most of whom are females.

CHALLENGING SEXIST JUSTICE

Optimism about the fact that young women appear to be the indirect beneficiaries of the de-institutionalization movement cannot obscure one important fact. Differential treatment of juvenile females and males is so imbedded in the juvenile justice system that it may not disappear simply because the federal government places certain conditions on grants for juvenile delinquency prevention programs. Indeed, the lackluster enforcement of the DSO provisions to date (in addition to evidence that many states attempt to subvert the law's intent), the outright refusal of a number of states to participate in the Act, and most recently direct challenges to the intent of the Act by state legislatures and others to re-institute incarceration for some status offenders, all caution against optimism.

More efforts must be directed toward dealing with the issue of civil rights of young people and, particularly, the civil rights of young women who come into contact with the law. Because of the desire of many to "protect" these young women from their own sexuality, it will be necessary to confront the double standard which lies behind much of the protectionist rhetoric of court officials and parents. The notion that incarceration of children, particularly young women, is beneficial must be challenged. Indeed, the evidence on this point is all to the contrary.[115] New solutions to children in conflict with their parents must be sought, fought for, and supported financially.

Returning to the larger question about female delinquency—its causes, its characteristics, as well as the nature, efficacy, and fairness of the official responses to that behavior—it is clear that too little is known, and too much assumed, about the relationship of masculine and feminine characteristics to behavior which is labelled delinquent. What little is known suggests that common sense notions of the uni-dimensionality of sex role expections,[116] and their relationship to conformity and deviance are seriously flawed. More importantly, it is premature to suggest that recent changes in the types of offense for which women are being arrested are a product of the "women's liberation movement."[117] It is far more likely that changes in arrest rates are the result of new police orientations toward female suspects. Self-report data indicate that this would result in more arrests of women for serious offenses without any real change in female behavior.

With reference to the official processing of young women, more systematic research is needed to understand how the juvenile justice system is dealing with young women. It also seems clear, in view of the monetary significance of official statistics which include data on "law violators" or "status offenders," that it is folly to rely on these alone. Firsthand observation of judicial processing, similar to that conducted by Tappan,[118] is required to learn what is happening to young women in the juvenile justice system.

Finally, and perhaps most important, much theoretical work remains to be done to explore the relationship between official responses to female deviance and the other systems of sexual inequality.[119] The phenomenon of official agencies ignoring serious crimes committed by young women contrasted with the serious punishment of sexual expression must be linked to the other systems of sexual stratification. As the old silence about young women and the law permitted an injustice to be ignored, the new interest engendered by the women's movement should be harnessed to guarantee that the treatment of women, young or old, will never again be relegated to a footnote.

Notes

1 Two of the best known works which attempt to establish a link between the rising arrest rates of women and the women's liberation movement are Freda Adler's *Sisters in Crime* (New York: McGraw Hill, 1975) and Richard Deming's *Women: The New Criminals* (New York: Dell Publishing Co., 1977).

2 Travis Hirschi, *Causes of Delinquency* (Berkeley: University of California Press, 1969), pp. 35-36.

3 Albert K. Cohen, *Delinquent Boys* (Glencoe, Illinois: The Free Press, 1955). Similar assumptions can be found in more recent works as well. See Ira J. Silverman and Simon Dinitz, "Compulsive Masculinity and Delinquency," *Criminology* 11 (February 1974): 498-515.

4 Frances Herdensohn, "The Deviance of Women: A Critique and an Enquiry," *British Journal of Sociology* 11 (June 1968): 160-176.

5 See Susan K. Datesman, Frank R. Scarpitti, and Richard M. Stephenson, "Female Delinquency: An Application of Self and Opportunity Theories," *Journal of Research in Crime and Delinquency* (July, 1975): 107-122; Gary J. Jensen and Raymond Eve, "Sex Differences in Delinquency," *Criminology* 13 (February 1976): 427-448; Stephen Norland and Randall C. Wessell "Masculinity and Delinquency," paper presented at the Society for the Study of Social Problems Meetings, Boston, September 1979;

Neal Shover, Steven Norland, Jennifer James and William Thornton, "Gender Roles and Delinquency," *Social Forces* 58 (September 1979): 162-175; Neal Shover and Stephen Norland, "Sex Roles and Criminality: Science of Conventional Wisdom," *Sex Roles* 4 (January, 1978): 111-125.

6 For example, standard reviews of the serious literature on delinquency, such as that found in Roger Hood and Richard Sparks, *Key Issues in Criminology* (New York: McGraw Hill, 1970), mention only the "sex difference" in delinquency behavior.

7 Carol Smart, *Women, Crime and Criminology* (London: Routledge, Kegan and Paul, 1977), p. 37.

8 There have been three possible exceptions to this generalization: Sheldon and Eleanor Glueck, *Five Hundred Delinquent Women* (New York: Alfred A. Knopf, 1934); John Cowie, Valerie Cowie and Eliot Slater, *Delinquency in Girls* (Great Britain: Humanities Press, 1968); and Jensen and Eve, "Sex Differences," pp. 445-446.

9 Anthony Platt, *The Child Savers: The Invention of Delinquency* (Chicago: University of Chicago Press, 1969), p. 135.

10 Steven Schlossman and Stephanie Wallach, "The Crime of Precocious Sexuality: Female Juvenile Delinquency in the Progressive Era," *Harvard Educational Review* 48 (February, 1978) p. 67.

11 Margaret Reeves, *Training Schools for Delinquent Girls* (New York: Russell Sage Foundation, 1929), p. 46.

12 W. I. Thomas, *The Unadjusted Girl* (Boston: Little, Brown, and Co., 1928), p. v.

13 Ibid., p. 98.

14 Ibid., p. 109.

15 Ibid., p. 119.

16 Ibid., p. 109.

17 Ibid., p. 195.

18 The most influential of the works on female delinquency are undoubtedly the following: Gisela Konopka, *The Adolescent Girl in Conflict* (Englewood Cliffs: Prentice-Hall, Inc., 1966); *Family Dynamics and Female Sexual Delinquency*, Otto Pollak and Alfred S. Friedman, eds. (Palo Alto, California: Science and Behavior Books, Inc., 1969); and Clyde B. Vedder and Dora B. Somerville, *The Delinquent Girl* (Springfield: Charles C. Thomas, 1970).

19 J. D. Acheson and D. C. Williams, "A Study of Juvenile Sex Offenders," *American Journal of Psychiatry* 3 (1954), p. 370.

20 P. Blos, *On Adolescence: A Psycho-Analytic Interpretation* (New York: The Free Press, 1962).

21 Konopka, *Adolescent Girl in Conflict*, p. 126.

22 Vedder and Somerville, *Delinquent Girl*, p. viii.

23 See Marianne Felice and David Offord, "Girl Delinquency . . . A Review," *Corrective Psychiatry and Journal of Social Therapy* 17(2): 18-28, for a thorough review of this literature.

24 G. H. Grosser, *Juvenile Delinquency and Contemporary American Sex Roles* (unpublished Ph.D. dissertation, Harvard University, 1952). Several other important works, such as Marie Bertrand's *Self Image and Social Representations of Female Offenders* (Unpublished dissertation, University of California, Berkeley 1967), and Ruth R. Henhouse Morris' *A Comparison of Female and Male Delinquency* (unpublished Ph.D. dissertation, University of Michigan, 1963).

25 Grosser, *Juvenile Delinquency*.

26 Morris, *Female and Male Delinquency*.

27 Ruth Rittenhouse, "A Theory and Comparison of Female and Male Delinquency (unpublished Ph.D. dissertation, University of Michigan, 1963); Ruth R. Morrison "Female Delinquency and Relational Problems," *Social Forces* 43 (October 1964): 82-89; and Ruth Morris, "Attitudes Toward Delinquency by Delinquents, Non-Delinquents, and their Friends," *British Journal of Criminology* 5 (July 1965): 249-265.

28 Morris, "Female Delinquency."

29 Shover and Norland, "Sex Roles and Criminality," p. 121.

30 Harjit S. Sandhu and Donald E. Allen, "Female Delinquency: Goal Obstruction and Anomie," *Canadian Review of Sociology and Anthropology* 6 (1969), p. 109.

31 Cited in Rittenhouse, "A Theory and Comparison," p. 211.

32 Datesman, Scarpitti, and Stephenson, "Female Delinquency," pp. 107-122.

33 Norland and Wessel, "Masculinity and Delinquency," p. 12.

34 James F. Short, Jr. and F. Ivan Nye, "The Extent of Unrecorded Juvenile Delinquency: Tentative Conclusions," *Journal of Criminal Law, Criminology and Police Science* 49 (November-December, 1958), p. 100.

35 Ronald L. Akers, "Socioeconomic Status and Delinquent Behavior: A Retest," *Journal of Research in Crime and Delinquency* 1 (January 1964): 38-46; John P. Clark and Edward W. Haurek, "Age and Sex Roles of Adolescents and their Involvement in Misconduct: A Reappraisal," *Sociology and Social Research* 50 (1966): 496-508; Robert A. Dentler and Lawrence Monroe, "The Family and Early Adolescent Conformity and Deviance," *Marriage and Family Living* 23 (August 1961): 241-47; Datesman, Scarpitti and Stephenson, "Female Delinquency," pp. 107-122; D. Elliot and H. Voss, *Delinquency and Dropout* (Lexington, Mass.: Lexington Books, D.C. Heath and Company, 1974); Martin Gold and David J. Reimer, "Changing Patterns of Delinquent Behavior Among Americans 13 through 16 years old: 1967-72," *Crime and Delinquency Literature* 7 (December 1975): 483-517; Martin Gold, *Delinquent Behavior in an American City* (Belmont, Calif.: Brooks Cole, 1970); and Michael Hindelang, "Age, Sex and the Versatility of Delinquent Involvements," *Social Problems* 18 (Spring 1973): 522-535.

36 Gold, *Delinquent Behavior*, pp. 63-64.

37 Joseph G. Weis, "Liberation and Crime: The Invention of the New Female Criminal," *Crime and Social Justice* 6 (1976), p. 23.

38 Ibid., p. 24.

39 Ibid., p. 34.

40 Gold and Reimer, "Changing Patterns," p. 492

41 Steven Roberts, "Crime Rate of Women Up Sharply Over Men's," *New York Times* (June 13, 1971), 1-3.

42 Federal Bureau of Investigation, *Uniform Crime Reports* (Washington, D.C.: U.S. Department of Justice, 1976).

43 Paul Tappan, *Delinquent Girls in Court* (New York: Columbia University Press, 1947), 2.

44 Ibid., p. 32.

45 Ibid., p. 33.

46 Ibid.

47 Ibid.

48 Ibid.

49 Ibid., p. 22.

50 The development of the chivalry theory is well documented in Etta Anderson, "The Chivalrous Treatment of the Female Offender in the Arms of the Criminal Justice System: A Review of the Literature," *Social Problems* 23 (1976): 349-57.

51 Robert M. Terry, "Discrimination in the Handling of Juvenile Offenders by Social Control Agencies," *Becoming Delinquent,* Peter G. Garabedian and Donald C. Gibbons, eds., (Chicago: Aldine, 1970).

52 Ibid., p. 85.

53 Yona Cohn, "Criteria for the Probation Officers Recommendation to the Juvenile Court," *Becoming Delinquent* (unpublished paper), p. 193.

54 Don C. Gibbons and Manzer J. Griswold, "Sex Differences Among Delinquency Referrals, *Sociology and Social Research* 42 (1957).

55 Ibid., p. 109.

56 Cohn, "Criteria," p. 199.

57 The silence on the discriminatory treatment of women was broken almost simultaneously by women from many parts of the country. The earliest pieces on this phenomenon include: Meda Chesney-Lind, "Judicial Enforcement of the Female Sex Role: The Family Court and the Female Delinquent," *Issues in Criminology* 8 (Fall 1973): 51-70; Sarah Gold, "Equal Protection for Juvenile Girls in Need of Supervision in New York State," *New York Law Forum* 17 (1971): 570-598; Kristine Rogers, "For Her Own Protection," *Law and Society* 7 (1972); 223-246; Florence Rush, *"The Myth of Sexual Delinquency,"* *Women: A Journal of Liberation* 3 (1973): 38-40; Jean Strouse, "To Be Minor and Female," *Ms.* (August 1972): 70-75.

58 Platt, *Child Savers,* p. 199.

59 Lee E. Teitelbaum and Leslie J. Harris, "Some Historical Perspectives on Governmental Regulation of Children and Parents," *Beyond Control,* Lee E. Teitelbaum and Adam B. Gough, eds., (Cambridge, Mass.: Ballinger, 1977).

60 Ibid., p. 34.

61 Ibid.

62 Ibid.

63 Schlossman and Wallach, "Crime of Precocious Sexuality," pp. 65-94.

64 Ibid., pp. 72-73.

65 Ibid.

66 Ibid.

67 Ibid.

68 Meda Chesney-Lind, "Female Juvenile Delinquency in Hawaii," (unpublished M.A. thesis, Department of Sociology, 1971); and Meda Chesney-Lind, "Judicial Enforcement," 1973.

69 See Nora Klapmuts, "Children's Rights: The Legal Rights of Minors in Conflict with Law or Social Custom," *Crime and Delinquency Literature* (September 1972); Katheryn W. Burkhart, *The Child and the Law: Helping the Status Offender* (New York: Public Affairs Pamphlet, 1975); Milton G. Rector, "Jurisdiction Over Status Offenses Should be Removed from the Juvenile Court" (Hackansack, New Jersey: National Council on Crime and Delinquency, 1974); "The Dilemma of the 'Uniquely Juvenile Offender,'" *William and Mary Law Review,* 14 (Winter 1972): 386. Three critiques of the structure of the juvenile justice system are: Nicholas Kittrie, *The Right to Be Different* (Baltimore: John Hopkins Press, 1971); Orman Ketcham, "The Unfulfilled Promise of the American Juvenile Court," *Justice for the Child,* Margaret Rosenheim, ed.,

(New York: The Free Press, 1962); and F.A. Allen, *The Borderland of Criminal Justice* (Chicago: The University of Chicago Press, 1964).

70 Sarah Gold, "Equal Protection," p. 591.

71 Vedder and Somerville, *Delinquent Girl*, p. 147.

72 Families have always had different expectations and made different demands of male and female children. From their sons, parents expect achievement, aggressiveness, independence, but from their daughters obedience, passivity, and implicitly, chastity. The existence of the sexual double standard in patriarchial societies meant that while men were permitted and encouraged to experiment sexually prior to marriage, they demanded that their wives be virgins. Parents, in response to this reality, sought to guarantee the marriageability of their daughters by developing elaborate mechanisms of control over their behavior. This, it was hoped, would preserve if not their virginity then at least their reputation. A daughter who could not be married was of no value in these societies.

73 Rosemary Sarri and Robert Vinter, "Juvenile Justice and Injustice," *Resolution* 1 (Winter, 1975), p. 47.

74 Recent statistics cited by Andrew and Cohn, "Ungovernability: The Unjustifiable Jurisdiction," *The Yale Law Journal* 83 (June 1974): pp. 1383-1409, for the New York area indicate that young women comprise 62 percent of those charged with status or ungovernable offenses. In Hawaii, during 1976, young women constituted 55 percent of those charged with status offenses.

75 The most recent national data on this are provided in Children's Bureau, Department of Health, Education and Welfare, *Statistics on Public Institutions for Delinquent Children, 1965,* (Washington, D.C.: U.S. Government Printing Office, 1967). However, recent offense data from various jurisdictions indicate that the pattern persists.

76 Richard Flaste, "Is Juvenile Justice Tougher on Girls than Boys?" *New York Times* (September 6, 1977).

77 P. C. Kratcoski, "Differential Treatment of Boys and Girls by the Juvenile Justice System," *Child Welfare* 53, p. 19.

78 Thomas P. Monahan, "Police Dispositions of Juvenile Offenders," *Phylon* 31 (Summer, 1970), p. 134.

79 Elliot and Voss, *Delinquency and Dropout*, pp. 84-85.

80 Ibid., p. 87.

81 Ibid.

82 Ibid.

83 Lesley Shacklady Smith, "Sexist Assumptions and Female Delinquency," in *Women, Sexuality and Social Control,* Carol Smart and Barry Smart, eds., (London: Routledge, Kegan Paul, 1978), p. 83.

84 Cited in ibid.

85 Chesney-Lind, "Judicial Enforcement," p. 57.

86 See Meda Chesney-Lind, "Young Women in the Arms of the Law," in Lee H. Bowker, *Women, Crime and Criminal Justice* (Lexington, Mass.: Lexington Books, D.C. Heath and Co., 1978), for a review of the evidence on this point. It is interesting to note that one of the Jane Does involved in the highly publicized litigation against the Chicago police department for routine strip searches of women was a minor.

87 A. W. McEachern and Riva Banzer, "Factors Related to Disposition in Juvenile Police Contracts," *Juvenile Gangs in Context,* Malcolm Klein and Barbara Myerhoff, eds., (Englewood Cliffs: Prentice Hall, 1967).

88 Nathan Goldman, *Differential Selection of Juveniles for Court Appearance* (Hackensack, New Jersey: National Council on Crime and Delinquency, 1963), pp. 44-47.

89 Robert M. Terry, "Discrimination in the Handling of Juvenile Offenders by Social Control Agencies" in *Becoming Delinquent,* ed. Peter G. Garabedian and Don C. Gibbons (Chicago: Aldine Publishing Co., 1970), p. 78-92

90 Goldman, *Differential Selection of Juveniles.*

91 Meda Chesney-Lind, "Juvenile Delinquency: The Sexualization of Female Crime," *Psychology Today* (June 1974), p. 45.

92 Alan Sussman, "Sex-based Discrimination and the Pins Jurisdiction," *Beyond Control,* pp. 179-199.

93 Susan Datesman and Frank R. Scarpitti, "Unequal Protection for Males and Females in the Juvenile Court," Juvenile Delinquency, Theodore N. Ferdinand, ed., (Beverly Hills: Sage, 1977).

94 Ibid., p. 70.

95 Andrews and Cohn found that when comparing females and males brought in to a probation officer as a PINS case, males were slightly more likely to be referred to court (65 percent versus 57 percent) and, once in the court, slightly more likely to be adjudicated (53 percent compared to 43 percent). However, they noted that "when allegations of sexual activity are present, cases are sent to court at a rate higher than the norm." R. Hale Andrews, Jr. and Andrew H. Cohn, "PINS Processing in New York: An Evaluation," *Beyond Control.* Another researcher, after controlling for prior arrests, age, race, formality of the complaint, socio-economic status, family stability and detention status, found little difference in severity of disposition by sex. However, in his research, it is clear that controlling for "family stability" and "detention status" will certainly eliminate important differences in the treatment of female and male delinquents. See Lawrence Cohen, *Delinquency Dispositions: An Empirical Analysis of Processing Decisions in Three Juvenile Courts* (Washington, D.C.: U.S. Government Printing Office, 1975). Also, Cohen and James R. Kluegal, in two more recent papers, analyzed the same data and came to slightly different conclusions. Most notably, they found that sex of the offender does affect decision-making at both levels (intake and detention) with young women accused of "decorum" offenses (alcohol and drug referrals) penalized. Lawrence E. Cohen and James R. Kluegal, "Selecting Delinquents for Adjudication," *Journal of Research in Crime and Delinquency* (January 1979): 143-163; and Lawrence E. Cohen and James R. Kluegal, "The Detention Decision: A Study of the Impact of Social Characteristics and Legal Factors in Two Metropolitan Courts," *Social Forces* 58 (September 1979): 146-161. Also, in one of the two courts Cohen and Kluegal studied, female status offenders, in general, were more likely to be detained then their male counterparts. Cohen and Kluegal suggested that the likely explanation for these differences was the fact that "both courts operate on a double standard of behavior" reacting "more negatively toward females for moral reasons more often than males, and males for criminal reasons more often than females." Cohen and Kluegal, "The Detention Decision," p. 158.

96 Atcheson and Williams, "A Study of Juvenile Sex Offenders," p. 370. See also Albert J. Reiss, "Sex Offenses: The Marginal Status of the Adolescent," *Law and Contemporary Problems* 25 (1960), p. 316.

97 Donnell M. Pappenfort and Thomas M. Young, *Use of Secure Detention for Juveniles and Alternatives to Its Use* (Chicago: National Study of Juvenile Detention, The School of Social Service Administration, University of Chicago, 1977), p. 62. However, one study by Lawrence Cohen failed to find that young women were differentially detained once offense had been controlled. However, Cohen noted that young women charged with "deportment" offenses were detained more frequently than their male counterparts. Lawrence Cohen, *"Who Gets Detained?"* (Washington, D.C.: LEAA, 1975).

98 Female Offenders Resource Center, *Little Sisters and the Law* (Washington, D.C.: American Bar Association, 1977), p. 23.

99 See Linda Riback, "Juvenile Delinquency Laws: Juvenile Women and the Double Standard of Morality," *UCLA Law Review* 19 (1971): 313-321; and "The Dilemma of the 'Uniquely Juvenile Offender,'" *William and Mary Law Review* 14 (1972): 386-408.

100 4 Conn. 55, 225 A.2d 507 (App. Div. 1966).

101 Civil No. 50424 (N.D. Cal. 1972).

102 336 F. Supp. 371 (S.D.N.Y. 1971). The United States Supreme Court affirmed the Gesicki decision without opinion. 406 U.S. 913 (1972).

103 502 F.2d 666 (2nd Cir. 1974).

104 84 Wash.2d 874, 529 P.2d 1096 (1975).

105 See Rosemary Sarri, "Juvenile Law: How it Penalizes Females," *The Female Offender: An Anthology* (Lexington, Mass.: Lexington Books, D. C. Heath and Co., 1977) for a review of these and other cases as they relate to young women in the juvenile justice system.

106 42 U.S.C. § 5601-5751 (1977).

107 Comptroller General, General Accounting Office, *Removing Status Offenders from Secure Facilities: Federal Leadership and Guidance are Needed* (Washington, D.C.: General Accounting Office, June 5, 1978).

108 Ibid.

109 Ibid.

110 See Andrews and Cohn, "PINS Processing" and Cohen, *Delinquency Dispositions.*

111 Law Enforcement Assistance Administration, *Children in Custody: Advance Report of the 1977 Census of Public Facilities* (Washington, D.C.: U.S. Department of Justice, 1979).

112 On this see General Accounting Office, pp. 7-9.

113 Cited in ibid.

114 K. T. Lee and Elberta Usui, *Hale Ho'Omalu: Fiscal Year 1978-1979.* Mimeo report, Sept. 10, 1979. This report filed by the state agency with the task of monitoring compliance to the Act reveals that both numerically and proportionately, the admission of status offenders has increased; status offenders accounted for 51 percent of the population in 1976 but in 1978 that figure climbed to 56 percent and of those children held over eight days, 75 percent were status offenders. During the same period that these young people were being held in a detention facility that has received local publicity for repeated incidents of brutality, the family court in Hawaii was seeking national publicity for its federally funded "diversion" program. See Terry G. Wade, Teru L. Morton, Judith E. Lind, and Newton R. Ferris, "A Family Crisis Intervention Approach to Diversion from the Juvenile Justice System," *Juvenile Justice Journal* 28 (August 1977): 43-51.

115 For a summary of these studies, see Edwin M. Schur, *Radical Non-Intervention* (Englewood Cliffs: Prentice Hall, 1973).

116 Stephen Norland, Jennifer James, and Neal Shover, "Gender Role Expectations of Juveniles," *The Sociological Quarterly* 19 (Autumn 1978): 545-554.

117 See note 1 *supra.* For rebuttal of this argument, see Weis, "Liberation and Crime," p. 17-27.

118 Tappan, *Delinquent Girls.*

119 Meda Chesney-Lind, "Rediscovering Lilith: Misogyny and the 'New Female Criminal,'" forthcoming in *International Symposium on the Female Offender: Selected Papers,* Curt Griffiths and Marget Nance, eds. (Burnaby: Criminology Research Centre, Simon Fraser University).

5

The New Female Offender: Reality or Myth?

Carol Smart

Smart writes about the women's liberation movement. Unlike those whom she criticizes, the "emancipation theorists," Smart argues for an historical approach: in the 1880s, 1920s, 1950s, and most recently the late 1970s, she analyzes the alarm social analysts display concerning the "new" social problem of increasing female crime. This chapter is important because Smart explains that any single cause explanation of crime is inadequate and this includes the so-called "emancipation argument." Causation is complex since crime takes so many different forms. It is meaningless to even attempt to isolate out any particular single cause for all crimes committed by women. Smart makes the point that the women's movement is a social movement, the purpose of which is to improve the social, political, and economic conditions of women. She observes that the women's movement is itself the product of complex historical developments and has a variety of consequences. If there has been a change in the nature and amount of female criminality in recent years, Smart argues, explanations lie in a wide array of social factors (such as the increase in female poverty, the decline of the extended family, migration to urban areas, and rising standards of living) rather than turning solely to the women's movement.

Smart challenges some of the taken-for-granted assumptions that "emancipation theorists" have about the relationship between women's education and employment opportunities. Can you specify these? How do they affect her interpretation of the spurious relationship between the women's movement and crime causation. Finally, Smart argues that the women most likely to be directly affected by the women's movement are middle class, educated women. Yet those women and girls most likely to be vulnerable to arrest, police and social work intervention are working class, poor and minority women and girls. What does this say about the relationship "emancipation theorists" allege exists between the women's movement and crime?

The thesis that there is a relationship between the rate of crime committed by women and women's emancipation is not new to criminological litera-

British Journal of Criminology, vol. 19(1):50-59, 1979. Reprinted by permission of the publisher.

ture. Since Lombroso and Ferrero produced their study of female offenders in 1895 criminologists have periodically emphasized the social and moral implications of the trend away from traditional female roles towards more "liberated" conditions. On the one hand it has been argued that wage-earning mothers create latchkey children who become tomorrow's delinquents and social misfits, while on the other it has been maintained that women themselves become more criminally oriented because of their association with "masculine" values at work and their contact with opportunities for crime outside the home. Any change in women's social and economic position which lessens the strict division of labour between the sexes has therefore been viewed with considerable misgiving, whilst any reinforcement of the value of women's traditional, domestic role has been perceived as a stand against further social decline and disorder.

Whether the women's liberation movement is actually causing an increase in female criminality and giving rise to a new female criminal has rarely been questioned, however. On the contrary this thesis, in its various forms, has become so established that it appears to be self-evident and uncontroversial. One example of this position can be found in the Staff Report submitted to the U.S. National Commission on the Causes and Prevention of Violence, where it is stated that " . . . the 'emancipation' of females in our society over recent decades has decreased the differences in delinquency and criminality between boys and girls, men and women, as cultural differences between them have narrowed" (Mulvihill et al., 1969, p. 425). In this statement the causal relationship between an apparent emancipation of women and changes in criminal behaviour is not treated as problematic; it stands merely as a statement of the obvious. Similar assumptions are to be found in discussions of female criminality in the United Kingdom. For example, Hart has claimed that " . . . perhaps some of the problem is to do with uni-sex, the seeking by the girl for equality with the man, in every way, including violence. . . . No longer can you appeal to the girls, as in the past, on grounds of femininity, or of being feminine—that has no meaning at all. . . . . " (Hart, 1975, p. 7). It is therefore generally accepted that women's emancipation causes an increase in female crime and that women are in fact becoming more like men where crime is concerned, even though very little research has been carried out on this topic.

One of the few studies of this area is Adler's work, *Sisters in Crime: The Rise of the New Female Criminal.* Adler accepts the thesis that liberation increases female criminality; indeed female criminality is treated as an indication of the degree of liberation achieved by women. For Adler liberation in conventional areas is simply mirrored in illegal enterprises; she states: "The movement for full equality has a darker side which has been slighted even by the scientific community. . . . In the same way that women are demanding equal opportunity in fields of legitimate endeavor, a similar number of determined women are forcing their way into the world of major crimes" (Adler, 1975, p. 13). It is not entirely clear in Adler's work, however, whether she claims that the women's movement is inducing previously law-abiding women and girls to commit crimes because they are emulating men and that, implicitly, crime is some kind of epitome of male endeavour, or whether existing female "criminals" are turning to new, more masculine forms of crime such as robbery, burglary and organized crime. But more crucial to a critique of Adler is the fact that her entire thesis is based on a very scant observation of F.B.I. Uniform Crime figures between 1960 and 1972. She notes, for example, that between 1960 and 1972 there has been an increase of 277 percent in women arrested for robbery in the U.S.A. (for men it was an increase of 169 percent), while larceny increased by 303 percent for women (82 percent for men) and burglary increased by 168 percent for women (63 percent for men), and so on. She argues that these percentage increases reveal that female crime is increasing at a much faster rate than male crime. Similarly Adler outlines the statistical evidence relating to juvenile offenders and concludes not only that female juvenile delinquency is accelerating at a faster rate than male but also that the statistics are an indication of future patterns of adult female criminality.

There are two very elementary fallacies in these propositions, however; first, the comparison between two sets of percentage increases can be entirely misleading and, secondly, the assumption that the juvenile delinquency of today sets the pattern of adult crime for tomorrow is quite unwarranted. It is well known that juvenile delinquency and adult crime are quite different phenomena, involving largely different personnel, different motivations and different purposes. Yet on the basis of these two propositions Adler predicts dramatic increases in crime, particularly violent crime, by women. Furthermore Adler extends her analysis and prediction beyond the United States to Western Europe, New Zealand and even India. Ignoring cultural variations, different criminal codes and legal systems, different methods of collating statistics and different degrees of "emancipation" for women, she posits a universality to the thesis of the causal relationship between liberation and crime.

It is of course not unusual that a monocausal explanation of female criminality should be advanced, and the women's movement serves in this context as a convenient account for explaining what is actually a complex social phenomenon. In the past criminologists have proffered various explanations based on biological premises. Included amongst these has been the idea that the female offender is biologically abnormal, having too many male characteristics (Lombroso and Ferrero, 1895; Cowie et al., 1968), or the thesis that female criminality can be explained by an hormonal imbalance caused physiologically. Most of the explanations of female criminality have been essentially monocausal. Unlike the studies of male criminality which have moved on from the crude biologism of Lombroso to consider such factors as socio-economic class, subcultural membership, the effects of labelling and the actual constitution of our criminal laws, the few engaged in the study of female criminality still appear to be searching for one simple cause, in this case the women's movement.

In order to assess the proposition that there is a relationship between women's liberation and increases in female criminality there are two questions that need to be asked. First, what changes, if any, are occurring in the criminal behaviour of women and girls and, secondly, what relationship exists between socio-economic and political changes in the position, status and role of women and girls and a participation in crime? In dealing with the first question we need to look initially at official criminal statistics. Now it is well known that these official records are not a true representation of criminal behaviour; there are many omissions, an over-emphasis on certain types of offences and an under-representation of white-collar crime. In addition there are the influences of modifications in policing and prosecution policies and the effects of moral panics on particular crime rate figures. Indeed official statistics may tell us more about the law and its enforcement than about those people who come to be defined as offenders.

Yet in the current analyses of women's involvement in crime, official statistics have been crucial in building the case that female crime is on the increase, particularly violent crime, and that this has something to do with women's liberation. But official statistics do not speak for themselves; they require interpretation, and it is this interpretation that calls for examination. Most contemporary commentators on female criminality have restricted their observations to the last one or two decades. This is primarily because both in the United States and the United Kingdom the 1960s are perceived as crucial to the changing social position of women as it was during this period that the women's movement was revived. Official statistics for England and Wales show the following picture of women found guilty of indictable offences in all courts for the years 1965, 1970 and 1975 (see Table 1).

The total of all indictable offences by women has virtually doubled in the ten years from 1965 to 1975 and the greatest proportionate increase has been in violent offences against the person. Indeed between 1965 and 1975 there has been an increase of 225 percent in the numbers of women committing these offences, while offences against property with violence have increased by 149 percent and offences against property without violence by 66 percent. This compares somewhat alarmingly with the proportionate increase in indictable offences committed by males over the same period (see Table 2).

Table 2 indicates that it is particularly in the area of violence that female crime is increasing at a faster rate than male crime. But it is precisely with this type of interpretation that great care must be exercised. A 100 percent increase in anything sounds immense, when it is attached to crime it may appear horrifying, yet the absolute figures may be quite small. (For example, between 1965 and 1975 there has been an increase of 500 percent in murder by women; the absolute figure for 1965 was *one* and for 1975 it was *five*). It is also particularly misleading to compare proportionate increases in female crime with those in male crime because the absolute figures for the former are typically so small that an insignificant change distorts the percentage increase, while for the latter the figures are so large that massive changes are required before the percentage increase changes noticeably.

It is also quite misleading to present percentage increases in crimes for one decade only. This practice, by omission, implies that previous increases are less significant or even less rapid. This tends to collude with an ahistorical perspective which almost always treats crime as a contemporary problem and rarely as a recurring or even constant feature of social life. It is indeed astounding to find Lombroso in the 1890s, W. I. Thomas in the 1920s, Pollak in the 1950s and Adler in the 1970s all discussing a *new* social problem, namely the increase in female crime. A comparison with statistics from previous decades is therefore instructive (see Table 3).

Table 3 indicates that dramatic rises in female criminality are *not* a new phenomenon. Between 1935 and 1946 there was an increase of 365 percent in crimes against property with violence, while for the same period larceny increased by 68 percent. This latter figure of 68 percent relates very closely to the 66 percent increase in theft by women in the period 1965 to 1975. Remarkably, though, the increase in larceny by women between 1955 and 1965 is higher than either of these two figures; in fact the percentage increase between 1955 and 1965 was 127 percent. These figures and others in Table 3 indicate that there has not been a unilateral increase in female offences in general but that, on the contrary, there have been considerable fluctuations since the start of the Second World War. The period immediately following the war (1946 to 1955) is notable in that it shows a decrease in many offenses by women and a total decrease of 1.5 percent over all indictable offences. During this period there was, however, only a slight increase (14 percent) in the total of indictable offences by men. It would seem therefore that the early 1950s were a relatively "law-abiding" period for both men and women (or a particularly inefficient time for agencies of law enforcement). Interestingly, though, the totals of indictable offences for men and women between 1935 and 1946, 1955 and 1965, and 1965 and 1975, show women offenders to be increasing at an overall faster rate than men. Yet, with the exception of the period between 1946 and 1955, the figures for 1965 to 1975, the years of "emancipation" for women, show a slower percentage increase of women over men offenders for the whole period since before the Second World War. So although every decade except 1946 to 1955 shows women offenders to be increasing more rapidly than men this was much more the case between 1935 and 1946, 1955 and 1965, than between 1965 and 1975, the years during which the women's movement in Britain was revived.

It must be restated, however, that official criminal statistics, and particularly grand totals of indictable offences, are very clumsy (if not misleading) guides to actual criminal behaviour. For example, changes in the law, such as the Theft Act of 1968 or the Criminal Damage Act of 1971, have led to considerable modifications to total crime rate statistics. But nonetheless, given that much of the contemporary concern over current increases in female criminality is based on statistical evidence, it is useful to point out that such increases do *not* appear to be a modern phenomenon. It is also useful to keep in perspective that only a tiny proportion of all offenders are female. Table 4 shows the number of males and females found guilty of indictable offences per 100,000 of the male population and female population respectively from 1935 to 1975.

Moreover, Table 5 shows the extent to which the sex ratio of offenders as a percentage of all offenders has remained virtually constant. The belief in wholesale increases in female criminality is therefore not borne out by official statistics. Indeed the straightforward comparison between proportionate increases in male and female offenders can be totally misleading.

Further evidence on the question of changes and increases in female criminality can be gleaned from the growing number of self-report studies on juvenile delinquency. At present most of these are American studies (Wise, 1967; Weis, 1976; Morris, 1965) although there is a growing amount of information on Britain (Shacklady Smith, 1975; Campbell, 1977). Most of these studies agree that the official sex ratio for juvenile offences, which is usually placed at 7:1, is quite inaccurate, and claim a ratio of 2:1 is far more realistic. However, there are two issues that must be considered here. First, in what type of offences is there an overlap between boys' and girls' delinquency and secondly, are these re-evaluations of the sex ratio indicative of a recent change in delinquent behaviour by girls or are they retrospectively valid? The self-report studies indicate that girls commit all offences more than is generally appreciated, but the same can be said of boys. There is no reason to assume, without substantial evidence, that girls commit more "hidden" crimes than boys. The area of largest overlap between the sexes according to the self-report studies is in status offences; that is, where the activity is defined as an offence because of the age of the person committing it. Thus girls engage in entering pubs and drinking under age, gambling and smoking and using drugs as much as boys do. Interestingly, girls and boys both appear to engage in under-age sexual

Table 1   Indictable Offenses, All Courts: Women Found Guilty

Offence	1965	1970	1975
*Class I—offences against the person	857	1,338	2,785
Class II—offences against property with violence	1,073	2,022	2,677
Class III—offences against property without violence	28,262	37,437	46,910
Total of all indictable offences	31,011	42,681	60,356

Source: HMSO, Criminal Statistics, England and Wales.

* These classifications were modified in 1973. Class I has been divided into two groups, violence against the person and sexual offences. Class II is now burglary and robbery, two separate categories, and Class III is now theft and handling stolen goods (fraud is now included with forgery). For the purpose of this paper and to facilitate comparison across the years the old classifications are used. Totals include all indictable offences, not just those in classes I, II and III.

Table 2   Proportionate Increases in Indictable Offenses
by Males and Females between 1965-1975

Offence	Male	Female
	%	%
Class I	100	225
Class II	55	149
Class III	46	66
Grand total of all indictable offences	83	95

Source: HMSO, Criminal Statistics, England and Wales.

Table 3   Indictable Offenses: Persons Found Guilty
— % Increases and Decreases over Four Decades

Offence	1935-46		1946-55		1955-65		1965-75	
	M	F	M	F	M	F	M	F
	%		%		%		%	
Class I	70	94	108	(–)30*	102	111	100	225
Class II	199	365	74	97	176	129	55	149
Class III	32	68	(–)0·7	(–)5	84	127	46	66
Grand Total of all indictable offences	46	68	14	(–)1·5	103	121	83	95

Source: HMSO, Criminal Statistics, England and Wales.

* (–) indicates a percentage decrease. All other figures represent a percentage increase.

Table 4   Number of Males and Females Found Guilty
of Indictable Offenses Per 100,000
of the Male and Female Population Respectively

	1935	1940	1945	1950	1955	1960	1965	1970	1975
Male	370	428	512	553	502	747	971	1,423	1,694
Female	47	68	86	76	69	93	149	201	278

Source: HMSO, Criminal Statistics, England and Wales.

Table 5   Percentage of Persons Found Guilty of Indictable Offences:
Distribution by Sex

	1930	1950	1960	1970	1975
Male	89·0	86·0	88·0	87·0	85·0
Female	11·0	14·0	12·0	13·0	15·0

Source: HMSO, Criminal Statistics, England Wales.

intercourse to the same degree although this is nearly always treated officially as a female misdemeanour. Girls, however, admit to violence, theft, stealing cars and other typically "masculine" offences less often than boys. The self-report studies vary on how much overlap exists where these latter types of offences occur; however, this may be because Wise and Weis were both looking at middle-class delinquency while Campbell and Shacklady Smith fail to include a class dimension in their analyses. But it could equally be an indication of regional and cultural variation.

Campbell and Shacklady Smith indicate that boys and girls are similar in terms of the offences they commit, although frequency may vary. Neither of these studies implies, however, that this is due to recent changes in delinquent behaviour. On the contrary both authors argue that current distortions in the official picture of juvenile delinquency reflect traditional attitudes and preconceptions of female offenders. In particular Shacklady Smith (and also McRobbie and Garber, 1976) argue that most female juvenile delinquency involving property or violence has been ignored by male criminologists, creating an impression now that it is a new phenomenon, while the sexual (mis)behaviour of girls has been over-emphasised to such an extent that it has been traditionally assumed that all female delinquency is sexual in nature. (See also Chesney-Lind, 1973; Terry, 1970; and Cohn, 1970). There is therefore no evidence from these studies that "masculine" type juvenile offences by girls are a new or recent occurrence; on the contrary there is every indication that female juvenile delinquency has been "sexualized" because of prevailing double standards of morality and the desire to *protect* girls who are promiscuous (Smart, 1976).

In spite of the doubtful empirical basis for the current belief that female criminality is changing substantially, it is nonetheless achieving the status of a legitimate account of contemporary trends. The argument that this is *caused* by female emancipation is also gathering credence every time it is uttered, whether in academic journals or on the media. The emancipation argument is based on two premises. The first is that trends in female criminality are not just changing but that they are changing in a way significantly different from male criminality. Thus it is implied that an explanation dealing exclusively with women and girls is required rather than more general explanations that might be appropriate to either sex (e.g., changing social conditions, unemployment, law enforcement practices, or the influence of the media). The second premise is that increased legitimate opportunities, particularly those provided by leaving a traditional domestic role and going out to work, make way for increased illegitimate opportunities for women.

Now there are problems with both of these premises. The first premise assumes that official statistics and impressionistic media accounts of increasing female criminality are an unproblematic representation of reality.

The limitations of this premise have already been outlined. The second premise, namely that female emancipation is epitomized by better occupational opportunities for women, is equally unacceptable. The women's movement is not solely, or even primarily, concerned with equal opportunities at work or with encouraging women to adopt typically masculine work rules. It is therefore entirely misleading to conceptualize the women's movement solely in terms of a body responsible for improving wage-earning opportunities for women. But as this is the predominant view of the movement we need to discover to what extent occupational opportunities for women have improved and how this might provide further opportunity for crime.

Improvements in the labour market have so far affected mainly middle-class women; certain professions such as teaching and social work have a high number of women members, although they are rarely in the top grades. There has also been an expansion in clerical work over the past two decades which has mainly affected women. But as these developments are restricted to professional and white-collar work any consequent increases in illegitimate opportunities would presumably involve only white-collar crime rather than violence, burglary or robbery or other forms of non-white-collar criminal behaviour. It is therefore difficult to comprehend how contact with the labour market, for these women at least, can give rise to increases in crimes of violence or visible forms of larceny. If, however, this argument applies only to women who do manual work, then the assumption that legitimate occupational opportunities are improving becomes more controversial and the belief that such women are new to wage labour is misguided. Indeed working-class women have always worked outside the home; this is not an achievement of a relatively recent women's movement. As Konopka has argued: "The major point is that 'working women' are not the product of the emancipation movement at all, that occupations outside the home are nothing new to the laborer" (Konopka, 1966, p. 72).

In fact there is evidence that indicates a worsening occupational position for all women, but most especially working-class or coloured women. This is caused by the establishment of a dual labour market (Barron and Norris, 1977; Noblit and Burcart, 1976) in which certain people, because of their sexual, racial and class status, are confined to low-paid, routine, insecure, and unrewarding work or even to long spells of unemployment as a reserve army of labour that is superfluous in a declining economy. Rather than the picture of increased opportunities for all women, therefore, it may be more realistic to consider the effect of redundancy, unemployment or unfulfilling, low-paid work on women and girls. We need therefore to study these phenomena and particularly their impact on working-class girls (who are most vulnerable to arrest and police or social work intervention as well as to economic depressions) rather than the more diffuse influence of the women's movement, because such factors as unemployment or low pay are likely to have a more immediate influence on their lives. What impact the women's movement may have on female behaviour is unclear and is unlikely to be direct. Perceptions of the movement may be distorted by the media and will be differentially received according to class, race and religious factors. Moreover there is no evidence available yet to indicate whether girls who become officially defined as delinquent or women who are defined as criminal, accept, reject or are indifferent to the values of women's liberation.

The question of the influence of the women's movement on the behaviour of women in general must therefore still be treated as problematic. However, the existence of such a movement will not only affect the women to whom it is directed but will also influence the consciousness and perceptions of the police, social workers, magistrates, judges and others, who may well interpret female behaviour in the light of the belief that women are becoming more "liberated." As Shacklady Smith argues:

> Since deviant definitions are inevitably related to the social position of the group concerned, it follows that any real or perceived change in the economic and political position of women may lead to a redefinition of female criminality by the state and the media. It could well be argued that the recent increase in officially recorded violence among girls suggests that a change in definition rather than in behaviour *per se* has already taken place. (Shacklady Smith, 1975, p. 10).

The women's movement does not therefore affect only the consciousness and behaviour of women, but also the perceptions of women by significant defining agencies such as the police and the courts.

The current attempt to explain *apparent* changes and increases in female criminality in relation to the women's movement reveals a confused and simplistic understanding of the process of emancipation, its influence on consciousness and social institutions, and its location within and alongside other social and historical developments. It ignores that the movement itself is an outcome of social processes and forces which may themselves be more directly related to changes in criminal behaviour than a social movement intent on improving the position of women in society. Such explanations merely serve the purpose of strengthening reactionary forces that would deny women the right to overcome their subordinate, second-class status by arguing, implicitly and explicitly, that female emancipation produces a breakdown in the social order and gives rise to new dimensions of criminal behaviour.

References

Adler, F. Sisters in Crime: The Rise of the New Female Criminal. New York: McGraw Hill, 1975.

Barron, R.D. and Norris, G.M. "Sexual divisions and the dual labour market," in S. Allen and D. Barker (eds.), Dependence and Exploitation in Work and Marriage. London: Longmans, 1976.

Campbell, A. "What makes a girl turn to crime?" New Society, January 27, 1977, pp. 172-73.

Chesney-Lind, M. "Judicial enforcement of the female sex role: the family court and the female delinquent." Issues in Criminology, 8, 2, 1973.

Cowie, J., Cowie, V., and Slater, E. Delinquency in Girls. London: Heinemann, 1968.

Konopka, G. The Adolescent Girl in Conflict. New Jersey: Prentice-Hall, 1966.

Lombroso, D. and Ferrero, W. The Female Offender. London: Fisher Unwin, 1985.

McRobbie, A. and Garber, J. "Girls and subcultures: an exploration." Working Papers in Cultural Studies, 7/8, 1975.

Morris, R. "Attitudes towards delinquency by delinquents, nondelinquents and their friends." British Journal of Criminology, 5, 1965, pp. 249-265.

Mulvihill, D. et al. Crimes of Violence, 12. Washington: Government Printing Office, 1969.

Noblit, G. and Burcart, J. "Women and crime: 1960-1970." Social Science Quarterly, 56, 4, 1976.

Pollak, O. The Criminality of Women. New York: A.S. Barnes, 1961.

Shacklady Smith, L. "Female delinquency and social reaction." Unpublished paper presented at the University of Essex, Women and Deviancy Conference, Spring 1975.

Smart, C. Women, Crime and Criminology: A Feminist Critique. London: Routledge and Kegan Paul, 1976.

Terry, R.M. "Discrimination in the handling of juvenile offenders by social control agencies," in P.G. Garabedian and S.C. Gibbons (eds.), Becoming Delinquent. Chicago: Aldine Press.

Thomas, W.I. The Unadjusted Girl. New York: Harper and Row, 1970.

Weis, J.G. "Liberation and crime: the invention of the new female criminal." Crime and Social Justice, 6, Fall/Winter, 1976.

Wise, N. "Juvenile delinquency among middle class girls," in E. Vaz (ed.), Middle Class Juvenile Delinquency. New York: Harper and Row, 1967.

6

Trends in Female Crime: It's Still a Man's World

Darrell J. Steffensmeier

In this chapter the author provides an analysis of the nature and amount of crime by women. Steffensmeier uses national data collected by the Federal Bureau of Investigation between 1965 and 1980 (as well as other sources of evidence) to demonstrate that female crime is not changing so as to become more like the criminality of men.

Recall that Smart in the previous chapter discusses the relationship between the women's movement and women's crime, her point being that if there is a change, the cause is surely more complex than the women's movement. Now Steffensmeier reports that there really is not much change in women's criminality between the beginning of the current phase of the women's movement (mid-1960s) and today. Those changes which are observable are an increase in arrests in two categories: larceny (more specifically, shoplifting) and fraud— crimes women have long been committing. In fact, if larceny is treated as a non-serious crime instead of a serious offense as is currently done, argues Steffensmeier, sensational claims about dramatic changes in crimes by women are easily invalidated.

Rather, the data clearly show that U.S. women are not "catching up" with men in the commission of violent, serious or white-collar crimes. If this is the case, we should then ask why the women's movement has been blamed for recent rises in female crime and for the appearance of the "new female criminal" when, in fact, the situation is relatively unchanged from earlier times.

For generations, men were considered the primary perpetrators of most criminal activities. Now, this male dominance is beginning to change. The role of women in crime is responding to changes in sex roles and to the emergence of the contemporary Women's Movement. Women are fast becoming both feared and revered participants in the criminal world. The past decade and a half witnessed a marked change in patterns and levels of crime among American women. Or did it?

Most frequently, claims regarding the changing character of female

Reprinted from *USA Today*, September 1979. Copyright © 1979 by Society for the Advancement of Education.

crime are linked to the arrest statistics of the Uniform Crime Reports (UCR). Published by the FBI, these statistics are the only continuous national data available which give the number of arrests in a given year categorized by offense and which indicate whether the arrestee is male or female, adult or adolescent (i.e., whether under or over 18 year of age).

It is my purpose in this article to examine the FBI data as they relate to arrest patterns of *adult* females in the U.S. The focus is on adult women for two reasons: changes in sex roles and the contemporary Women's Movement are believed to be having a greater impact on adult rather than adolescent females and most of the claims regarding the changing character of female crime are made with respect to adult females. This concern with adult patterns notwithstanding, it is worth noting that arrest patterns of adolescent females generally parallel those of adult women.

These conclusions derived from analysis of the FBI data are contrary to the view depicted in the mass media and embraced by many social scientists. These data do *not* show that the criminal activities of women are becoming similar to men in either kind or degree. Rather, arrest gains of females are limited largely to two offense categories—larceny and fraud—and the gains in these two categories appear to be due to more females being arrested for traditional types of female offenses such as shoplifting and "bad check" passing (i.e., insufficient funds). American women are not catching up with males in the commission of violent, masculine, serious, or white-collar crimes.

To examine trends in female crime, let us begin by calculating male and female arrest rates per 100,000 adults (ages 18 through 59) for the years 1965 and 1980, for all the offense categories in the Uniform Crime Reports except forcible rape (a male crime) and prostitution (largely a female crime). (Since few crimes are committed by those over the age of 60, the rates were calculated on persons aged 18 through 59—that is, on the population at risk. The choice of 1965 as the starting point for this analysis was dictated by some changes in the collection of arrest data by the FBI. Beginning in 1963, the arrest volumes are provided for males and females under 18 years of age, as well as for males and females in the U.S. population as a whole. More importantly, beginning in 1965, the offenses of vandalism, arson, curfew violation, and runaways were added to the list of offense categories covered in the UCR. In addition, fraud and embezzlement are treated as separate categories, prior to 1965 having been combined into fraud/embezzlement. Also, arrest rates of both males and females began to rise around 1965). For both males and females, the size of the rates increase in some categories, decreased in others, and did not change in still others. Over all, the pattern of change was similar for both sexes, with large increases occurring only for the offenses of larceny, fraud, driving under the influence, and narcotic drug laws; and with decreases actually occurring in the categories of negligent manslaughter, sex offenses, gambling, offenses against family, liquor law violations, drunkenness, disorderly conduct, vagrancy, and suspicion.

The changes from category to category may reflect shifts over time in public attitudes and police practices, more than actual behaviors of arrested persons, either male or female. It seems likely that male and female arrest rates for drunkenness have declined sharply in response to growing pressures for decriminalization and alternative ways of handling drunk cases. In contrast, increasing public concern over alcohol-or-drug-impaired operation of motor vehicles has caused arrest rates to rise sharply in the offense category of "driving under the influence." Changes in official policy are also evident in the category of narcotic drug laws. From 1965 to 1973, arrest rates for drug offenses rose more rapidly than for any other offense, but have dropped off in recent years and will probably continue to do so in the years ahead with the increasing decriminalization of marijuana.

In any discussion of changing sex roles and their relation to female criminality, the central issue is whether or not sex differences in crime patterns diminish as men and women move toward greater equality in their rights and privileges. A related question is whether the Women's Movement has been a determinant of changes in female criminality. A major difficulty, however, in making comparisons over time between the sexes is the dramatic differences in initial arrest levels, since female arrest rates are so much smaller than those of males. The early arrest gains of females are partly a statistical artifact of low female starting points and rising rates for both sexes. (This article does not discuss changes in absolute differences in male/female arrest rates. It is worth noting, nonetheless, that in nearly all offense categories, absolute differences in arrest rates have become greater since 1965—that is, females have *lost* ground to males.) In this regard, female gains have been levelling off in the past five or six years and arrest rates of males continue to be considerably larger than those of females in all offense categories, except prostitution.

Notwithstanding the difficulty in comparing changes over time in male/female arrest patterns, the remainder of this article will examine whether the sex differential in arrest rates has been narrowing or widening since 1965. The sex differential is defined as the female proportion or share of all arrests, both male and female, in a specific offense category. Concerning burglary, for example, the arrest rate per 100,000 females was 11.4 in 1965 and 26.6 in 1980, while, among males, the rates were 283.3 in 1965 and 430.8 in 1980. The sex differential has narrowed slightly, i.e., females have gained on males since the female share of all persons arrested for burglary rose from 3 percent in 1965 to 5.8 percent in 1980. (As used here, the sex differential equals $\dfrac{\text{female rate}}{\text{male rate} + \text{female rate}} \times 100$. Specifically, for burglary, the sex differential in 1965 is 11.4 ÷ 283.3 + 11.4 × 100 = 3.9%. In 1980, the differential is 26.6 ÷ 430.8 + 26.6 × 100 = 5.8%.) A second example is aggravated assault: the female rate was 31.2 in 1965 versus 44.1 in 1980, while for males, the rates were 195.3 and 338.2, respectively. In this instance, the sex differential has widened, i.e., females have lost ground to males, since the female share of all arrests decreased from 13.8 percent in 1965 to 11.5 percent in 1980.

Despite the apparent narrowing of the sex differential for burglary and its widening for aggravated assault, the changes are so small in both instances, that, in ordinary statistical parlance, they would be considered insignificant, or simply negligible. Rather, in the case of both burglary and aggravated assault, we are safe in concluding that the sex differential has held constant over the past decade. Furthermore, this "holding constant" of the sex differential is the most common pattern in the UCR offense categories.

Male and female arrest rates for 1965-80 for burglary and aggravated assault, as well as for the categories of gambling and larceny, were chosen because the rates in these categories *typify* male/female arrest trends during the past decade and a half. First, as already noted, for burglary and aggravated assault, the rates have tended to rise, but the sex differential has held constant. Similar patterns exist in most of the remaining UCR categories. Specifically, there was a slight narrowing of the sex differential (female gain) in the offense categories of other assaults, driving under the influence, weapons, robbery, auto theft, and stolen property. Meanwhile, the sex differential widened slightly (female loss) for liquor laws, narcotic drugs, vandalism, arson, murder, and negligent manslaughter.

Second, there was a downward trend in the arrest rates of both sexes in a number of offense categories, with the sex differential gain holding constant. This pattern of arrest rates *dropping* for both males and females, with little change in the sex differential, occurred for the offenses of gambling, drunkenness, disorderly conduct, suspicion, sex offenses, and offenses against the family. Along with the patterns observed above, therefore, it is clear that in the majority of offense categories the sex differential has remained stable. Figures for this period also demonstrate the *parallel* changes in arrest rates of males and females over the past decade.

The final pattern in male/female arrest trends is shown in the arrest rates for larceny-theft. Although larceny rates have been rising rapidly for both sexes, the sex differential *has narrowed considerably*. The female share of all larceny arrests increased from 25.2 percent in 1965 to 33.4 percent in 1980. Similar patterns are found for fraud and, to a lesser extent, for forgery. The sex differential has also been narrowing for embezzlement, but *very few* females or males are arrested for embezzling and, therefore, arrests rates for embezzlement are of little significance in terms of overall male/female arrest trends.

Thus far, we have seen that the changes or shifts in arrests of females parallel those of males. To further determine whether new and diffferent patterns of criminality are occurring within the female population, the 27 offense categories of the UCR by the size of the arrest rates for the years 1965 and 1980 were rank-ordered for both males and females and then examined as to whether the ordering had shifted more for females than males.

Among both men and women, there have been shifts in seven offense categories: fraud, stolen property, and narcotic drugs rose in order, while the categories of gambling, suspicion, vagrancy, and sex offenses declined in rank order. This means that, of all persons arrested in 1980 versus 1965, a larger share of *both* male and female arrests were for narcotic drugs, and so on, whereas a smaller share of arrests were for gambling, etc. Two conclusions can be drawn from this rank-ordering of arrest rates. First, the distribution of offenses for which both males and females are arrested has remained fairly stable. Second, and most crucial, the shifts occurring in arrests of females are *not* greater than the shifts occurring among males. Relative to males, the profile of the female offender has not changed. The popular impression that there has been a drastic shift over the past decade in the kinds of crimes committed by women is simply not supported by the evidence.

TRENDS IN ARREST RATES
BY TYPE OF CRIME

So far, we have examined arrest rates for each individual offense category, but a more parsimonious approach in portraying trends is to group the offenses by types and then sum up or aggregate the arrest rates for each type. Let us examine four types: violent, masculine, serious, and petty property.

These were chosen so we can evaluate popular and scientific claims that women are increasingly engaging in crimes that have traditionally been the province of men. The relationship between female liberation and what is perceived as a new trend in female criminality hinges on the notion that, as women become increasingly involved in activities similar to those of men and as they attempt to emulate the male role, they will become more like men in terms of participation in crime. Female crime, therefore, represents a masculinization of female behavior.

Masculine and Violent Crimes

Masculine crimes are defined as offenses involving physical strength, elements of coercion and confrontation with victim, and/or specialized skills. The nine offenses we categorized as masculine are listed at the bottom of Table 1, which shows that the aggregated arrest rates for masculine type crimes increased somewhat from 1965 to 1980 for both males and females, but the sex differential held constant—8.2 percent in 1965, compared to 10.5 percent in 1980. The table also provides a comparison of the percentage which arrests for masculine type offenses comprise of all male arrests and all female arrests. Of all males arrested, the percentage of arrests which are for masculine crimes increased 3.8 percent (16.2 percent minus 12.4 percent) from 1965 to 1980, while for females the increase was 0.7 percent (10.4 percent minus 9.7 percent). In sum, the small increases in arrests for masculine type crimes were nearly identical for males and females.

If we separate from the masculine crimes those offenses which also can be categorized as violent offenses—murder, aggravated assault, other assaults, vagrancy, possession of weapons, robbery—we again find parallel changes between the sexes. The sex differential has not changed and the percentage of all arrests which are for violent crimes increased only slightly among males and females. The percentage of all female arrests which were for violent crimes was 7.8 percent in 1965, compared to 8.4 percent in 1980, while, for males, it was 8.1 percent in 1965 and 11.5 percent in 1980. For both masculine and violent type crimes, then, females have not gained ground on males, nor has there been a shift toward greater commission of these offenses on the part of females.

Female Increases in Serious Crimes

The term "serious crime" usually refers to the seven Index or Type 1 offenses of the UCR—homicide, forcible rape, aggravated assault, robbery, burglary, larceny-theft, and auto theft. It is frequently claimed that the proportion of women arrested for serious crimes has been increasing dramatically and that the increase has been greater among females than males. It will be seen, however, that, while these claims have some validity, they are misleading and illusory. The increase in arrests of women for serious crimes is almost entirely due to more women being arrested for larceny and, more specifically, to greater numbers of women being arrested for shoplifting.

Leaving out forcible rape for our analysis, the data in Table 1 show that females indeed have gained ground compared to males in arrests for serious crimes. The sex differential has narrowed considerably, going from 14.7 percent in 1965 to 19.3 percent in 1980. Also, the increase in percent of all arrests which were for serious crimes was greater for females than males. In 1980, a hefty 24.5 percent of all female arrests were for serious crimes, compared to only 15 percent in 1965. For males, arrests for serious crimes increased more modestly, going from 9.9 percent in 1965 to 16.8 percent in 1980.

Table 1   *Aggregated Arrest Rates per 100,000 Male and Female Adults for Masculine, Violent, Serious, and Petty Property Types of Crime, 1965 and 1976*

Type of Crime	Male Rate	Female Rate	%FC	AD	% of All Male Arrests	% of All Female Arrests
Violent[1]						
1965	909.1	99.7	9.9	809.4	8.1	7.8
1976/1980	1302.9	153.3	10. 5	1149.6	11.5	8.4
Masculine[2]						
1965	1388.3	124.1	8.2	1264.2	12.4	9.7
1976/1980	1835.8	192.9	10.5	1642.9	16.2	10.4
Serious[3]						
1965	1109.8	191.9	14.7	920.6	9.9	15.0
1976/1980	1907.2	455.4	19.3	1451.8	16.8	24.5
Serious Without Larceny						
1965	707.9	56.3	7.4	764.2	6.3	4.4
1976/1980	1065.0	95.1	8.2	969.9	9.4	5.2
Petty Property[4]						
1965	607.7	183.5	23.2	424.2	5.4	14.4
1976/1980	1185.8	576.0	32.7	609.8	10.5	31.0
Embezzlement & Forgery						
1965	88.5	19.0	17.7	69.5	0.8	1.5
1976/1980	84.4	36.5	30.2	49.9	0.8	2.0

[1] Violent crimes are: murder, aggravated assault, other assaults, weapons, and robbery.

[2] Masculine crimes are: murder, other assaults, weapons, robbery, burglary, auto theft, vandalism, arson, and aggravated assault.

[3] Serious crimes are: murder, robbery, aggravated assault, burglary, larceny-theft, and auto theft.

[4] Petty property crimes are: larceny-theft, fraud, forgery, and embezzlement.

To define larceny as a serious crime and include it with such offenses as murder, robbery, and so on, however, is to use the term "serious" in a rather shortsighted and nondiscriminating fashion. Many arrests for larceny are for shoplifting of items of small monetary value and, therefore are nonserious compared to other index offenses (e.g., murder, robbery), and are not regarded as very serious in the opinion of the general public. In addition, as used in the UCR, arrests for larceny include both petty (less than $50) and grand ($50 and over) thefts.

A variety of studies have shown that the majority of arrests of females for larceny are for shoplifting, that most arrests for shoplifting are for petty theft, and that the increase in arrests of females for larceny is due largely to greater numbers of females being arrested for shoplifting.

Treating larceny, in fact, as a nonserious offense, the data in the table reveal a much different picture of trends in serious crimes when larceny is omitted than when it is included in the aggregated arrest rates. Now, the sex differential is unchanged (7.4 percent in 1965 versus 8.2 percent in 1980) and, from 1965 to 1980, the percent of all female arrests which were for serious crimes (without larceny) shows no increase (4.4 percent versus 5.2 percent). Without larceny, therefore, the data on serious crimes contradict the sensational claims about dramatic changes in the kinds of crimes committed by females.

Petty Property Crimes

In addition to larceny, females have made gains in the offense categories of fraud and, to a lesser extent, in forgery and embezzlement. Contrary to the view of many analysts of female crime who refer to these as white-collar or occupational crimes, these offenses are more accurately classified as petty theft or property crimes and can be viewed as traditionally "feminine" crimes. Larceny also can be classified as a petty property crime.

These four offenses represent extensions of female role activities, rather than new role patterns. None of these offenses requires particularly masculine attributes, such as use of force or confrontation with the victim. Each of these crimes, with the exception of embezzlement, fits well into the everyday round of activities in which women engage, especially their role of buying most family necessities and paying family bills.

The available research indicates that most arrests of women for larceny are for shoplifting and arrests for fraud involve passing "bad checks," credit card fraud, fraudulent theft of services, and small con games. Women are not being arrested for fraud which are occupationally related or which tend to be real white-collar crimes, such as false advertising, product defects, and so on. Forgery is also a crime that is consistent with female sex roles and fits into the everyday round of activities in which women engage, especially since the skills and techniques required for forging credit cards, checks, etc., are learned in the normal process of growing up. It is the case that those arrested for forgery tend to be amateurs, or "naive forgers."

Contrary to widespread assumptions, the person arrested for embezzlement is usually more a petty thief than a white-collar offender. Most arrestees for embezzlement are not persons of high social standing and responsibility who commit a crime in the course of their occupation and which involves large sums of money. Rather, the typical embezzler is the trusted clerk, cashier, or secretary who takes his/her employer's money and the amount taken is usually small.

More importantly, while the sex differential has narrowed for forgery and embezzlement, these offenses account for a very small proportion of all female arrests (same is true of males). The table shows first the aggregated rates for the four petty property crimes, then shows the rates for forgery and embezzlement. With the four offenses together, the changes in petty property crimes are greater than in any of the other types of crime. The sex differential narrowed from 23.3 percent in 1965 to 32.7 percent in 1980. Even more dramatic, the percentage of all female arrests which were for petty theft crimes rose from 14.4 percent to 31.0 percent over the 1965 to 1980 period, while, for males, the increase was from 5.4 percent to 10.5 percent.

If the aggregated arrest rates included only forgery and embezzlement, it is clear that these offenses account for a small proportion of all female arrests in both 1965 (1.5 percent) and in 1980 (20 percent). Treated separately, in 1980, only .3 percent of all female arrests were for embezzlement, while for forgery it was 1.7 percent. Forgery and particularly, embezzlement, therefore, are relatively insignificant in terms of overall female arrests trends.

Female Gains Limited to Larceny and Fraud

It is the offense categories of fraud and of larceny, in particular, that are almost entirely responsible for change in patterns of female arrests. The sex differential has narrowed considerably since 1965, going from 19.8 percent to 40.9 percent for fraud and from 25.2 percent to 30.4 percent for larceny. In addition, more so than for males, a sizable portion of female arrest gains are due to the rise in arrest rates for these two offenses. Larceny accounted for 10.6 percent of all adult female arrests in 1965 versus a hefty 19.4 percent in 1980, while the percentage of fraud arrests rose from 2.3 percent in 1965 to 9.6 percent in 1980. These arrest gains of females notwithstanding, petty thefts and frauds are the kinds of crimes that women have always committed. Therefore, even though women are making gains compared to men, they are not committing new types of crimes. More women are being arrested for traditional types of female crime.

Some of the increase in arrests for larceny and fraud, of course, may be due to changes in official policies, which have had a differential effect on male and female arrest trends. In recent years, there have been improvements in store surveillance methods and a greater willingness by store officials to prosecute apprehended shoplifters. This would tend to increase female more than male arrests for larceny, since males are more likely to commit larcenies other than shoplifting. Similarly, "crackdowns" on welfare and related kinds of fraud, the trend toward computerized record-keeping systems, and other improvements in detecting fraud and "fraud recidivists" (e.g., "bad check" writers) would tend to increase female more than male arrests for fraud.

It is also possible that, with the Women's Movement, changes in attitudes toward female suspects have occurred. ("If it's equality these women want, we'll see that they get it.") If, indeed, this attitude is reflected in official behavior, then we would expect less preferential treatment of women in the criminal justice system. Some of the increase in arrests of females could be accounted for by these changes in official policies.

The increase in arrests of females for larceny and fraud probably also reflects market consumption trends and the worsening economic position of many females in the U.S. The opportunities for petty theft have increased as a result of greater reliance on self-service marketing and credit card purchasing. In addition, a number of economic and demographic factors have pushed more women into handling family finances and market place activities. The economic necessity of females to support themselves and their offspring is greatest among lower-class and minority women, who are most likely to be affected by generally deteriorating economic conditions. The economic position of "Third World" women has worsened in recent years because of increases in illegitimacy, in divorce, and in female-head households and because an inflationary and somewhat depressed U.S. economy has hit the poorer segments of society hardest. In fact, over the past 10-15 years, poverty has become more and more a female problem.

The contemporary Women's Movement of the late 1960's and early 1970's has been linked to changing patterns of female crime. So far, however, we have seen that female arrest patterns have changed very little over the past decade and that whatever changes have occurred appear to be due to changing law enforcement practices, market consumption trends, and the worsening economic position of many females in the U.S., rather than to women's liberation or changing sex roles.

To check the effects of the Women's Movement on female crime, let us examine male/female arrest rates throughout the 1965-80 period, in particular the rates for the pre- versus post-1970 periods, since it is generally assumed that the Women's Movement began in the late 1960's and, therefore, its effects on female crime would be most obvious after 1970. Analysis reveals that whatever changes were occurring began prior to the spread of the Women's Movement. Specifically changes in the sex differential were generally similar before, during, and after the rise of the Women's Movement.

To sum up, no shift is apparent in the pattern of female arrests after the appearance of the Women's Movement. The movement appears to have had a greater impact on changing the image of the female offender than on the level or types of criminal behavior that she is likely to commit.

The trends in arrest rates of adult women in the U.S. are consistent with traditional sex role expectations, behaviors, and opportunities. Indeed, it would be surprising if substantial changes have been occurring in the illegitimate activities of women, for, contrary to what is commonly believed, a great deal of evidence is accumulating which shows that the economic and social position of women in American society has changed very little in the past decade and that today's female has not achieved a "liberated" position. The traditional sex roles of wife-mother and sex object have remained remarkably stable. The female's status remains a deprived one and her identity continues to be defined in terms of relationships with men. As social psychologist Shirley Weitz noted recently, while female roles may have become more flexible, male roles have changed little, if at all. "The sex roles system has not changed much though the climate may favor more individual latitude than before. By and large, in our society, sex role standards and patterns have successfully withstood attempts at change."[1]

Traditional sex roles persist in the world of work, despite some token gains by females. Recent labor force statistics reveal that women continue to be concentrated in "pink-collar" jobs—teaching, clerical, and retail sales work. Women are virtually excluded from management and from industrial and service occupations that require high levels of technical or mechanical skills. Most crucially, women are not increasing their participation in occupations such as truck driver, warehouse worker, delivery person, dockworker, carpenter, mechanic, and so on that would provide opportunities for theft, drug dealing, fencing, and other illegitimate activities, or that would provide the specialized tools, skills (e.g., mechanical), etc., conducive to criminal activities. Thus, the barriers are not coming down in legitimate occupational categories which would provide opportunities for criminal activities and thereby would lead to increased crime among females.

Most importantly, perhaps, relative to women in the past, women today are just as limited by male constrictions on their roles and male leadership in the illegal market place as they are in the legal one. Autobiographical and case history studies of professional and street criminals indicate that women continue to have limited access to criminal subcultures and the criminal underworld. In fact, traditional sex role attitudes and the structure of sexism appear to be more pervasive within the arena of crime than "above ground."

FUTURE PROSPECTS

The findings from the FBI's Uniform Crime Reports, when examined carefully, do not support widespread beliefs about female crime. Evidence from other sources on crime trends also show little or no change in female crime relative to male crime over the past two decades. We single out the major sources: (1) Data from the National Crime Survey on victim's perception of the offender's sex shows that during the 1970's sex differences held stable for crimes such as robbery, burglary, auto theft, and assault, and only small gains for larceny. Shoplifting is not included in the larceny category in the National Crime Survey.[2] (2) Self-report studies of delinquency over the last two decades show sex differences in admitted delinquencies to be generally stable, the major exceptions being small female gains in petty larceny and in marijuana use.[3] Further documentation comes from the National Youth Survey, the best source of trend data by far on sex differences in reported delinquency: "Reports from representative samples of American adolescents, spanning a decade or more (from '67 to '72 to '77) indicate increased delinquent involvement in certain delinquent acts (alcohol and drug use) in males and females but *stable sex differences in delinquency*"[4] (emphasis added). Moreover, studies of gang delinquency also reveal little change in female delinquency. Walter Miller specifically observes that "despite claims by some that criminality of females, either in general or in connection with gang activity, is both more prevalent and violent than in the past, what data were available did not provide much support to such claims."[5] Elsewhere he adds that "stories told about the nature of female participation in gang activities (weapons carriers, decoys for ambush killings, participants in individual or gang fighting) do not differ significantly from those told in the past . . . the part played by females did not represent a particularly serious aspect of current gang problems."

Indeed, contrary to much current rhetoric and sometimes paranoia, the effects of "women's liberation" are not necessarily in a one-sided, criminogenic direction. Rather than "increasing the opportunities and propensities that women have for committing crimes,"[6] for example, more women in the paid workplace may in fact have the opposite effect. Work not only may lessen temptations toward crime by assuring a steady income but also for many women their working is indicative of upward mobility, and upwardly mobile persons tend to be more conforming. Also, the new work roles have not freed women from traditional domestic ones so they have little time and energy for criminal enterprise.

Finally, what about the future? We should expect to see in the foreseeable future little change in the nature and extent of female criminality. At least in the illegitimate sphere, the aspirations, expectations, and experiences of women are not apt to move beyond traditional roles.

Notes

[1] Shirley Weitz, *Sex Roles: Biological, Psychological, and Social Foundations* (New York: Oxford University Press, 1977), p. 4.

[2] See Michael Hindelang, "Sex Differences in Criminal Activity," *Social Problems*, 1979 (27): 143-156.

[3] See Darrell Steffensmeier and Renee Hoffman Steffensmeier, "Trends in Female Delinquency: An Examination of Arrest, Juvenile Court, Self-Report and Field Data," *Criminology*, 1980 (8): 62-85.

[4] See Rachelle Canter, "Sex Differences in Self-Report Delinquency," Forthcoming in *Criminology*.

[5] See Walter Miller, *Violence by Youth Gangs and Youth Groups as a Crime Problem in Major American Cities*, U.S. Department of Justice, Washington, D.C. 1975, pp. 23-24.

[6] See Rita James Simon, *The Contemporary Woman and Crime*, Washington, D.C., National Institute of Mental Health, 1975, pp. 3, 4.

7

Sex Role Stereotypes and Justice for Women

Clarice Feinman

While continuing to provide evidence against the "emancipation theory," this chapter represents the first in a series of chapters on women in prison. Its historical perspective allows us to see how earlier sex role stereotypes continue to affect what happens to women in prison today. A stereotype is a fixed mental impression. If sex roles are stereotyped, it means that some people have a set idea of how women (or men) should behave and that makes the stereotype virtually unchangeable. Hence Feinman discusses what happens to women offenders once they are sentenced to jail or prison and are made to conform to their keepers' stereotypes of what a woman should be. She argues that because of sex role stereotyping, justice is denied and continues to be denied for women. These stereotypes are a fundamental reason why so little is known about the causes of female criminality and the types of women found in prisons. This chapter is important because it also explains how sex role stereotyping has adversely affected women after release from incarceration in terms of their ability to cope and be law-abiding.

The chapter contains a brief but relevant historical account of reformers of women offenders in the state of New York. Such historical analysis is infrequently provided but is essential in an understanding of how women are treated as offenders in society. It raises many questions about the state's role in sanctioning offenders and the purposes of punishment historically. Another key section of this chapter discusses the fact that it is predominantly poor and working class women who are incarcerated and the middle and upper class women who are imposing their own middle class standards of proper conduct on inmates. Ironically, while higher class women's organizations have historically played a major role in improving conditions facing poorer and minority women in prison, they simultaneously have perpetuated sexist stereotypes. Thus, not only did reform and work training programs in the 19th century try to turn incarcerated women into "perfect ladies," but in so doing, they ended up training women to be maids for middle and upper class women. Today, while "wife and mother" continue to be held out as the "proper role" for imprisoned women, the 19th century "servant-housekeeper" roles have been replaced by the 20th century "waitress-typist" roles.

Feinman's analysis ties in with one of the overarching themes in the book—that class

Reprinted with permission of the National Council on Crime and Delinquency, from Clarice Feinmen, "Sex Role Stereotypes and Justice for Women," *Crime & Delinquency*, January 1979, pp. 87-94.

is a key factor to be taken into account in understanding offenders, how and if they are both labeled and punished and how the system responds to them after they are categorized as offenders.

Since the development of the modern prison system 200 years ago, obvious physical improvements in the housing and supervision of incarcerated women have been made. We no longer herd convicted women into attics or sections of male institutions or subject them to virtually unrestrained abuse by male guards.[1] Today, both the federal government and most states have separate penal institutions for women, supervised by other women. However, separate does not necessarily imply equal or just.

Regardless of the changes in the physical treatment of female offenders, three main facts stand out throughout the history of women in jail and prison. First, the treatment of incarcerated women reflects the sex role stereotypes which society has relegated to women. Second, although women have played a major role in improving the conditions of incarceration, they have perpetuated those role stereotypes. Third, sex role stereotypes have significantly affected the exoffenders' opportunity to succeed in the community after release.

These three factors have intruded—and they continue to intrude—on the treatment of women in prison and their reception in the community following release. That the problem is as much contemporary as it is historical is a conclusion that will be illustrated by a discussion of programming and problems affecting inmates in the New York City Correctional Institution for Women.

SEXUAL STEREOTYPING:
THE CONSEQUENCES OF DEVIATION

Coinciding with the advent of the modern American prison system in 1790 was the development of the "cult of true womanhood,"[2] wherein the ideal woman was defined as the wife and mother in the home. Women were expected to be pious, pure, submissive, and oriented toward the family. Historians Barbara Welter and David B. Davis have both cited this American obsession with women's role in society, which reached its first peak in the period between 1820 and 1860,[3] a time when the United States experienced significant political, econimic, social, and territorial changes. In addition, the first women's rights movement was organized during this period. Fearful for the strength and security of the nation, religious, political, and literary spokesmen pointed to true womanhood as the only constant in a rapidly changing society. Since that time, these sex roles, steeped in religious and moral values, have had a decisive impact on the manner in which nonconforming women have been defined and treated. The deification of the spiritually pure wife/mother brought demands for laws to punish the nonconforming woman as unnatural, as the symbol of sin.[4] Thus, in the first half of the nineteenth century, those female offenders who had "fallen" from their naturally pure state were viewed as more depraved than their male counterparts; as such, they were dealt with more harshly while incarcerated. Moreover, they continued to carry the stigma imposed upon them by an unforgiving society when they left prison.[5]

The special threat presented by delinquent women stemmed from the popular conviction that women were generally passive and domestic—unlike men, who were naturally aggressive. Women who went against their natural tendencies were considered to be "monster[s],"[6] the "embodiment of the evil principle,"[7] and unable to distinguish right from wrong. An experiment such as the penitentiary movement could have no effect on these creatures, for redemption was clearly out of the question. The result was that female criminals were simply removed from public view. Women were crowded together into small, unsanitary, poorly ventilated quarters in male institutions such as Auburn and Sing Sing. There they were subjected to the demands of male guards.[8] Under this "policy of calculated neglect,"[9] women were flogged, sometimes impregnated, and they often died from the abuse. The horrible conditions in Auburn and Sing Sing impelled B. C. Smith, chaplain at Auburn Prison during the 1820s, to state that to be a woman in prison was "worse than death."[10]

In 1828, De Witt Clinton, governor of New York, recommended to the state legislature that a separate penitentiary be built for women. In rejecting the proposal, members of the legislature expressed fear that, when released, the women would corrupt the morals and contaminate the young men in the vicinity of the institution.[11] Even the exposure of the unbearable conditions at Auburn and Sing Sing failed to temper the views of these opponents to reform.[12]

FEMALE REFORMERS:
PERPETUATION OF THE STEREOTYPE

In 1830, despite public hostility toward the project, a group of middle- and upper-class women, motivated by religious impulses and aiming to reform their fallen sisters, established a home for delinquent women. The Magdalen Society of New York City opened the Magdalen Home to serve female offenders who manifested a desire to repent and assume their proper role. The home provided vocational training in the domestic arts for those women who gave "evidence that true womanhood [was] really retur-ning"[13] and secured employment for them as domestics in good Christian families.[14] In 1845, the Women's Prison Association of New York City opened the Issac T. Hopper Home, which operated according to the princi-ple that delinquent females could be redeemed if separated from men and guided by virtuous women. Pregnant women, alcoholics, and narcotics addicts could not live or receive help at the home. Those who did qualify received medical care and vocational training in traditional skills. If re-deemed, they too were placed as domestic workers in respectable Christian homes.[15]

Throughout the nineteenth century, women continued to lead the efforts to reform delinquent women and to improve the conditions of their incarceration. While these reformers were unusual in assuming an aggres-sive role,[16] their fundamental approval of their own social positions and their deeply embedded religious and moral values resulted in a perpetua-tion of those very stereotypical sex roles that imposed restrictions on them.

During the years between 1870 and 1930, prevailing attitudes toward the female offender began to change, partly because of these women in-volved in penal reform. Errant women were no longer castigated as generi-cally depraved but were seen as the victims of male lust and imposed sex roles which afforded women few opportunities to work and earn an ade-quate wage. Many reformers at the end of the nineteenth century consid-ered themselves morally superior to men and therefore singularly capable of uplifting their fallen sisters, and they crusaded for separate, wholly female penal institutions as the only means of uplifting the poor unfortu-nate fallen women. With separate institutions came careers and employ-ment for a number of these reformers, who became professionals in female correction and penology—a field in which they did not compete with men or threaten the stereotypical sex role structure.[17]

One would have hoped that these reformers would develop an icono-clastic approach to correction and provide alternatives to stereotypical sex roles. But education and career orientation notwithstanding, the time had not yet come for a break with traditional values. Female administrators established an atmosphere that simulated a homelike environment, with a mother-child relationship between matron and inmate. Inmates were taught to be good homemakers and were prepared for their proper role in society.[18]

The assumption that women were naturally passive, and thus less dan-gerous then their male counterparts in prison, did give female administra-tors one advantage—that of being free to experiment with programs and innovations. Some of these innovations later became part of the institu-tional programming in men's prisons. Elizabeth Farnham, head matron of the women's division at Sing Sing in 1844, introduced educational classes, a library, and art and music programs. She attempted to simulate a home-like atmosphere by decorating the women's quarters with flowers, pictures, and lamps.[19] Dr. Katherine B. Davis, the first superintendent at the New York State Reformatory for Women at Bedford Hills, introduced in 1901 a formal school program, vocational training, and recreation. She also developed a research project to study career patterns of female prisoners.[20]

As effective as they were, the administrators could not convince the public to accept the exoffender into the community. Yet, ironically, while women's roles in the community were severely restricted, society did continue to accept the exoffenders as servants working for upright Christian families.[21]

THE SITUATION TODAY

These historic factors continue to affect female offenders. First, the treatment of incarcerated women today still reflects the sex role stereotyping. Second, although women have played a major role in improving conditions in institutions for female offenders, they have perpetuated those role stereotypes. And third, sex role stereotypes continue to affect the ex-offenders' opportunity to succeed in the community. This is a conclusion based largely upon the writer's firsthand experience as the project director of a rehabilitation program in the New York City Correctional Institution for Women.

In 1929, the New York City Department of Correction attempted to explain the increase in the number of imprisoned women by stating:

> It is possible, of course, that the comparative emancipation of woman, her greater participation in commercial and political affairs and the tendency towards greater sexual freedom may be playing their part in bringing about this situation.[22]

Recent statements concerning the reported rise in the crime rate among women continue in the same vein. In 1975, Rita J. Simon wrote:

> As women's opportunities to commit crimes increase, so will their deviant behavior, and the types of crimes they commit will much more closely resemble those committed by men.[23]

Simon's thesis is supported by Freda Adler who contends that, as cultural restraints disappear because of the women's rights movement, women will enter the criminal arena on an equal footing with men.[24] According to the New York City Department of Correction, Simon, and Adler, the emancipation of women leads to increased criminality and incarceration. Thus, the myth that the emancipation of women from the traditional roles of wife and mother will lead to increased criminality finds continued support. Wife and mother remain the socially acceptable roles. The perpetuation of the myth has contributed to society's fears and misunderstanding by equating equal rights and opportunity for women with delinquent behavior. (As in the first peak period of the "cult of true womanhood," the statements by the New York Department of Correction, Simon, and Adler have been made during a time of unusual domestic insecurity characterized by major political, economic, and social changes as well as an organized movement fighting to increase the rights of women. The second peak period of the American obsession with women's role in society—the resurgence of the "cult of true womanhood"—occurred in the 1920s after women won the right to vote. We are presently in a third peak period.)

Yet the myth denies some basic historical facts. Poor women have always been overrepresented in penal institutions. From 1932, when the first jail for women opened in New York City, to the present, the jail population has been predominantly poor, uneducated, and unskilled. When employed, these women have worked in factories or as domestics or waitresses.[25] Incarcerated women in New York City are neither emancipated nor are they participants in the women's movement; rather, these women are victims of denied economic opportunities. In 1976, the superintendent of the New York Correctional Institution for Women, Essie O. Murph, called them "the bottom of the barrel."[26]

The role of middle- and upper-class women in determining treatment also remains relatively unchanged since the nineteenth century. Because of their own backgrounds, they continue to perpetuate the concept that the woman's proper role is wife and mother. Staff in the New York City Correctional Institution for Women attempt to establish a homelike environment in the jail with flowers, pictures, and draperies; and inmates are taught domestic skills. Treatment is oriented toward exposing the female offender to an "acceptable" lifestyle and to values deemed desirable. Rehabilitation means instilling in offenders "certain standards of sexual morality and sobriety and preparing them for their duties as mothers and homemakers."[27]

Like her predecessors, the present superintendent perpetuates the stereotypical sex role by referring to the institution as a home and insisting that each inmate act and dress as befits a "lady." In 1970, superintendent Murph said, "We're a lot like a family here. . . . This is a home for most of them."[28] Until recently, detained women were not permitted to wear slacks, and Murph strongly disapproves of slacks worn by civilian female personnel.[29] She does not consider such apparel "ladylike."[30]

Other women's organizations seeking to bring about improvement for the female offender also maintain traditional expectations. Since 1955, the Women's Prison Association, the Friendly Visitors, and the New York City

Junior League have offered the incarcerated women in New York City the choice of training programs, but all are premised on the traditional societal attitudes and cultural role expectations for women.[31] In the nineteenth century it was servant-housekeeper; in the twentieth century, waitress-typist. Members of those organizations may have supported the women's movement, but few if any ever brought the ideas into the jails.

Any attempts to establish training programs in jail which could prepare the women for skilled, well-paying jobs have met with failure. Companies such as New York Telephone and IBM explained that it was not economical to bring in machines and an instructor for the few eligible women; apparently, these companies did not consider the possibility of permitting the women to continue the program of study after their release from jail.[32] Government policy makers have been unwilling to allocate money for training programs for women on the premise that women do not support themselves or their families. But in 1970, approximately 70 percent of the inmates were single workers with full responsibility for support of their families.[33]

While female superintendents are still allowed a greater range of experimentation than is permitted in male facilities, neither the administrators nor the volunteers employed in special programs have managed to overcome social hostility toward the offenders. Inmates leaving penal institutions today still face a hostile society in which jobs, housing, and training programs are either nonexistent or of poor quality.

To be fair, the fault is not entirely with prison administrators. In some cases, female offenders have refused training in nontraditional fields even though wages would be high.[34] Many of these women leave jail only to go back on the welfare rolls and back to their old way of life.

A WARNING

There are inherent dangers in the myth that the emancipation of women leads to criminal behavior. First, it misdirects and confuses investigation into the causes of female crime. Second, it denies the reality that many wives and mothers—as well as single women—have worked outside the home. Finally, and most important, it denies the fact that our jails and prisons are populated largely by poor women. In so doing, it obviates the need to seek the real reasons for this situation.

Notes

1 David W. Lewis, *From Newgate to Dannemora: The Rise of the Penitentiary in New York, 1796-1848* (Ithaca, N.Y.: Cornell University Press, 1965) pp. 73-75, 162-63.

2 Barbara Welter, "The Cult of True Womanhood: 1820-1860," in *Our American Sisters: Women in American Life and Thought,* Jean E. Friedman and William G. Shade, eds. (Boston: Allyn and Bacon, 1973), pp. 96-123; and Andrew Sinclair, "Ladies, Not Women," in *The Woman Question in American History,* Barbara Welter, ed. (Hinsdale, Ill.: Dryden Press, 1973), pp. 66-67.

3 Welter, "The Cult of True Womanhood," pp. 96-123; and David B. Davis, *Homicide in American Fiction, 1789-1860: A Study in Social Values* (Ithaca, N.Y.: Cornell University Press, 1957), pp. xiii, 148.

4 Robert E. Reigel, *American Women* (Rutherford, N.J.: Fairleigh Dickinson University Press, 1970), p. 58; and Davis, *Homicide in American Fiction,* pp. 154-55.

5 Estelle B. Freedman, "Their Sisters' Keepers: An Historical Perspective on Female Correctional Institutions in the United States: 1870-1900," *Feminist Studies,* vol. 2, no. 1 (1974), pp. 78-79.

6 Caesar Lombroso and William Ferrero, *The Female Offender* (New York: Philosophical Library, 1958), p. 152.

7 Davis, *Homicide in American Fiction,* p. 177.

8 Lewis, *From Newgate to Dannemora,* pp. 94-95, 162.

9 *Ibid.,* p. 163.

10 *Ibid.,* p. 164.

11 *Ibid.,* pp. 164-65.

12 *Ibid.,* p. 143.

13 John F. Richmond, *New York and Its Institutions, 1609-1872* (New York: E. B. Treat, 1972), p. 319.

14 *Ibid.,* pp. 317-19.

15 *Ibid.,* pp. 457-58; and Freedman, "Their Sisters' Keepers," pp. 79-80.

16 Allen F. Davis, *Spearheads for Reform: The Social Settlements and the Progressive Movement 1890-1914* (New York: Oxford University Press, 1967); and Page Smith, *Daughters of the Promised Land* (Boston: Little, Brown, 1970), pp. 255-58.

17 Freedman, "Their Sisters' Keepers," pp. 77-78; and Robert W. Smuts, *Women and Work in America* (New York: Schocken Books, 1971), pp. 112-13, 119.

18 Philip Klein, *Prison Methods in New York State* (New York: Columbia University Press, 1920), pp. 105-06; and *Ibid.,* p. 88.

19 Lewis, *From Newgate to Dannemora,* pp. 238-41.

20 Blake McKelvey, *American Prisons: A Study in American Social History Prior to 1915* (Chicago: University of Chicago Press, 1936), p. 214.

21 Richmond, *New York and Its Institutions,* pp. 319, 457-58; Freedman, "Their Sisters' Keepers," pp. 79-80; and Klein, *Prison Methods in New York State,* p. 324.

22 The City of New York, Department of Correction, *Annual Report,* 1929, pp. 13-14.

23 Rita J. Simon, *The Contemporary Woman and Crime,* Crime and Delinquency Issues (Rockville, Md.: National Institute of Mental Health, Center for Studies of Crime and Delinquency, 1975), p. 48.

24 Freda Adler, "The Rise of the Female Crook," *Psychology Today,* November 1975, pp. 42, 46-47, 112-14.

25 The City of New York, Department of Correction, *Annual Report,* 1931, pp. 103, 114, 117, 121, 129, 132-33; *Annual Report,* 1955, p. xxvii; and New York City Correctional Institution for Women, "Inmate Demographic Profile, March 1975—December 1975," in Women's Development Unit Project, *Annual Report, January 1, 1975—April 9, 1976,* p. 18, Appendix H.

26 Interview with Essie O. Murph, Superintendent, New York City Correctional Institution for Women, Jan. 16, 1976.

27 Rose Giallombardo, *Society of Women: A Study of Women's Prisons* (New York: John Wiley, 1966), p. 7.

28 Kathryn W. Burkhart, *Women in Prison* (Garden City, N.Y.: Doubleday, 1973), p. 137.

29 One of the major reasons for Superintendent Murph's prohibition of slacks was her contention that these would be used as a form of role identification for potential homosexual liaisons among female inmates. In March 1977, the Legal Aid Society of New York won its dress-code case brought on behalf of detained prisoners against Superintendent Murph. Thereafter, detained women were permitted to wear slacks. To prevent jealousy or conflict between detained and sentenced women, Superintendent Murph had uniform slacks supplied to the sentenced women.

30 Murph interview.

31 Women's Prison Association, "Profile, Open Door Project," 1974; and City of New York, Department of Correction, *Annual Report, 1960*, p. 49.

32 Murph interview.

33 *Ibid.;* and New York City Correctional Institution for Women, p. 18.

34 *Ibid.*

8

National Study of Women's Correctional Programs

Ruth M. Glick and Virginia V. Neto

The sex stereotyping consequences of the historical analysis presented in the previous chapter by Feinman are verified by Glick and Neto in their report on the first (and only) national study of incarcerated women offenders. This study covers women in state prisons, county jails, and community-based programs in fourteen states; inmates with long and short sentences as well as inmates not yet convicted but awaiting trial in a county jail are included in the discussion.

Data is presented on inmate characteristics such as age, ethnicity, education, employment history, marital status, and the number of children the women have. It is important to remember that the proportion of women prisoners in local jails and in prisons is small. About six percent of all jail prisoners are women and this figure has remained relatively constant, although the percentage of women in federal and state prisons has been increasing in the last decade—from four to six percent in federal prisons and from three to four percent in state prisons. For incarcerated girls, however, the figures are different. Almost one-fourth (23 percent) of all delinquents in detention are girls. Incarcerated women are young, generally under 30 years of age, most (80 percent) are without male partners at the time of incarceration, three-fourths have children and 70 percent are single workers with full responsibility for the support of their families. Ninety percent have worked at some time, but with poor education and limited job opportunities, one-half have had to receive welfare at one time or another.

The authors also examine in detail the conditions of the jails and prisons in which the women are imprisoned. They report that most institutions are inadequate, that very little job training is available, that preparation for release to the community is neglected (and that which exists is sex stereotyped), and that only limited medical services are to be found. Moreover, as badly as felons in prison are served by programs and services, Glick and Neto point out that less serious offenders (misdemeanants and women awaiting trial) were even

Prepared under Grant Number 74-NI-99-0052 from the National Institute of Law Enforcement and Criminal Justice, Law Enforcement Assistance Administration, U.S. Department of Justice, under the Omnibus Crime Control and Safe Streets Act of 1968, as amended. Points of view or opinions stated in this document are those of the authors and do not necessarily represent the official position or policies of the U.S. Department of Justice.

worse off. For them incarceration in jails means living under tight security with the least program opportunities.

The findings reported in this chapter are particularly interesting because they give a profile of incarcerated women based on firsthand information collected by the researchers. One very important finding is the overrepresentation of black women and poor women in the jails and prisons. For example, while just under 12 percent the U.S. population, blacks comprise half of the women prisoners. This fact helps substantiate several themes running through this volume which emphasize the need to take into account race and class in studying the criminal justice system and the women who get in trouble with the law.

INTRODUCTION

Background

Women offenders account for only a small proportion of all persons arrested and convicted of crimes. Because their number is small and their crimes generally less threatening to society, they have been easy to ignore, both by society itself and the criminal justice system in particular.

Research on the female offender has been minimal, both in terms of the characteristics of the offender population and the conditions of her incarceration. Much of what has been done is outdated.[1] Very few carefully designed studies exist that provide useful empirical data for planning meaningful programs and services for the convicted female offender. The few studies that do include demographic information on the offender population are often not readily comparable because of differences in definitions or lack of consistency in collecting information from one study to another.[2]

Although research on the female offender has been extremely limited, numerous books and articles have appeared in the last few years that present virtually the same unsubstantiated impressions of both the individual offender and the programs available to her in the correctional setting.[3] Quotes often appear out of context,[4] and the caveats and concerns of the original work are often ignored, (a condition that exists even when the original work is beyond reproach).

This lack of data is a problem that has been with us for a long time, and no one seems to have been unduly concerned. Why, now, a study of the female offender?

The changes that are affecting our entire society have begun to be felt even inside the walls of the most hidden of all institutions—the prison. Concern over legal and human rights has spread to include the rights of inmates, both male and female, (often as an aftermath of riots and disturbances by the inmates themselves).[5]

Special concern for the female offender has surfaced in recent years, largely due to growing public awareness of the changing role of women in society. This spotlight on women's roles has led some people to blame (or credit) the women's movement for the rising crime rate among women. Whether or not this is true is a matter of considerable conjecture. What is certain, however, is that the women's movement has helped to focus attention on the way women are treated by our criminal justice system. And this spotlight on treatment of the woman offender has stimulated demands for reform of the justice system.[6]

It is important to note that many of these demands for reform have come from outside the criminal justice system, often from groups with widely divergent interests and concerns. This often means that many new proposals for reform are acted upon simultaneously although they may conflict with one another, and often when they are greatly at odds with the philosophy of the existing system. In effect, this means that model programs are frequently superimposed on a system whose basic purpose is antithetical to the goals of the model, and this lack of consistency dooms the projects to failure. For example, model counseling programs which utilize such techniques as Transactional Analysis can fail miserably because the participants are unable to utilize their new communication skills in their interactions with staff who have not been trained in Transactional Analysis.

In the past, much of the thinking about women offenders drew heavily on the assumptions about women generally that have dominated the literature in psychology, psychiatry, medicine, and other disciplines.[7] Many of these assumptions were variations on the Freudian theme that "anatomy is destiny." Women were defined primarily in terms of their biological and physiological make-up, and their childbearing and childrearing functions became the basis for characterizing women as warm, nurturing, passive, and dependent. These were considered the characterisitics of the "normal" or "good" woman.[8]

Conversely, women who failed to conform to society's expectations were labeled as "deviant" or "bad" and were presumed to be acting in response to the frustrations and the limitations imposed by their biological make-up, rebelling against their natural feminine roles.

The failures of such theoretical constructs were perhaps most apparent in efforts to ascribe these characteristics to women who were not white and middle class, since these standards of femininity and of appropriate female behavior were defined largely in terms of an idealized norm that reflected dominant white, middle class, male values. In those terms, a woman's primary role was seen as providing the life-support systems for her spouse, the assumptions being: that all women would marry, all marriages would remain intact, all wives would bear children, and all males could and would provide adequately for the needs of their families.

Theories of female criminality that link deviant behavior to a rejection of the female role fail to account for the large number of women for whom this idealized role was neither possible nor desirable. The implicit belief behind any theory that links female criminality with a rejection of the female role is an assumption that a rejection of one role means the desire to assume the opposite role, in this case to be "one of the boys."[9]

Many of these same assumptions are behind some of the current explanations of the rising female arrest rate. The media, among others, drawing heavily on the statistics in the *Uniform Crime Report*, assert that the apparent sharp increase in the female arrest rate is "the dark side of women's liberation."[10] Thus, the thinking goes, as women become liberated from traditional roles and enter the work force in greater number, they will become more like men in terms of participation in crime.[11] Since crime is viewed as a predominantly male stronghold, it is assumed that as women become more like men, the crime rate for women will rise until it equals that of men. There are several issues that must be considered in attempting to understand this line of reasoning. In the first place, one must question whether a causal relationship exists between any two or more social phenomena which occur within the same relative time frame. It is true that the women's liberation movement and the increase in arrests for females have occurred during the last ten or so years. However, during that same time frame we have seen several major and minor social upheavals—the war in Vietnam, the recession, Watergate, drugs, etc. It is virtually impossible to single out the women's liberation movement as *the* cause of the rise in female crime.[12]

A second issue that needs some clarification is the link between the women's liberation movement and women working outside the home. For most people, both males and females, work is dictated by economic necessity. Only a fortunate few have the luxury of working because they want to work, and because they like what they are doing. Most women work because they need the money.

Liberation is another matter entirely. It has legal, medical, and social ramifications that go well beyond the world of work. Liberation means having a choice regarding whether and when to have children; getting married, staying married or not getting married at all; owning property and credit cards, and then, accepting responsibility for these decisions.

In part, of course, all of those choices have economic ramifications, but economic self-sufficiency is only one of many facets of liberation.

The importance of all of the assumptions about the causes of crime (for both males and females) is that these assumptions form the ideological underpinnings for the development of programs and services that are designed to correct or cure the presumed deficiency in the individual. Nagel[13] summarizes the history of correctional philosophy as the shift from "supernatural" to "psychological" to "social" forces as the cause(s) of crime. And both prison architecture and programs reflect these changes in philosophy.

The history of women's programs shows an early shift from punishment to treatment, when in the late 19th century, social reformers urged the establishment of separate institutions for women. These new prisons were called reformatories and were intended to help women learn to accept appropriate female role behavior, which as Giallombardo[14] notes, meant "instilling certain standards of sexual morality and sobriety, and fitting them for their duties as mothers and homemakers."

Even the style of architecture of these institutions was designed to enhance this image. Small, home-like cottages with individual rooms were built to replace the monolithic penal structures that were the style for men. The programs reflected the emphasis on domestic skills, including sewing, laundry, cooking and institutional maintenance, as well as teaching lady-like behavior and good manners.[15]

Correctional programs for the female offender are still heavily steeped in the myths of appropriate female behavior and traditional sex roles. Eyman[16] as recently as 1971 suggests that a useful vocational program for females in prison might be in the dairy industry. She says:

> Dairymen are turning to women to help ease the labor shortage. Those dairymen who have tried women in milking operations are pleased with the results. *Women are proving to be better milkers than men and understand the problems of swollen udders, mastitis, and other mammary infections.* [Emphasis added.]

It seems clear that we need a different approach to planning and implementing programs for the female offender, an approach based on an accurate profile of the offender as well as a more realistic assessment of her needs. It is not enough to develop programs based on presumed causes of crime, nor in terms of how the female offender may differ from her male counterpart. A more promising approach is to focus on the female offender as a woman, and examine how her needs relate to those of other women on the outside.

Our study of women's prisons and jails revealed both great similarities and significant regional and local differences in the delivery and organization of programs and services for women, as well as the rationale behind them. We were, however, struck by the fact that certain trends and new directions in programs seemed to be gaining an almost unquestioned acceptance, even though many of these programs lacked any sound empirical underpinnings. In fact, many of the new programs are based on the same assumptions as the programs that preceded them.

It should be noted that the major impetus for a large number of these innovations was the federal funding that made them possible. Federally funded programs have generally been developed in response to a variety of pressures and an assessment of needs at a national level. Unfortunately, this assessment at the national level does not always accurately reflect local conditions and needs. The result is that model programs developed in one locale may fail miserably when transplanted to another, often alien environment.

National statistics are unquestionably important for long-range planning and analyzing population trends; however, for successful program planning, we need to know more about both the population and the community at the local level.

Obviously there are many changes that can and should be made in the criminal justice process that do not depend on the results of research but are dictated, rather, by human decency and a desire for justice.

Programs and services, however, fall into a different category. Without specific information about the client group to be served, such programs are often ill-conceived and consequently doomed to failure. In order to guard against such failures and eventual disillusionment, we need to develop a systematic and comprehensive model for program planners that includes an on-going analysis of the characteristics and needs of the population, where research is recognized as an important planning tool and not an end in itself.

SUMMARY OF FINDINGS

The National Study of Women's Correctional Programs was funded by Law Enforcement Assistance Administration to conduct the first comprehensive examination of programs and services provided for women in correctional institutions, as well as to develop a demographic portrait of the incarcerated woman offender. Sixteen state prisons, 46 county jails and 36 community-based programs, were studied in 14 states. Data came from several sources: administrators, staff, consultant observations, and an inmate questionnaire administered to 1,607 inmates representing 6,466 incarcerated women.

In most states, unsentenced women and sentenced misdemeanants were held in county jails, while convicted felons served their sentences in state prisons. In Massachusetts, however, unsentenced women and misdemeanants were detained in the state prison; in four states women served misdemeanant sentences of one year or less in the state prison.

Institutions tended to reflect the political climate and socio-economic conditions of the state or local community. Inmates also reflected state differences, especially in terms of their ethnic distribution, educational level, and even their offenses.

Institutional Profiles

Location: Prisons for women are less remote than they once were, primarily because surrounding communities have expanded, making more services available within these communities. However, many prisons continue to be remote from inmates' families and not readily accessible by public transportation.

Most of the jails are located in urban areas close to public transportation, facilitating family visits, but only a few jails utilize the many services available in the larger community.

Community-based programs were most accessible to families and community services.

The capacity of women's institutions ranged from 16 in the Minnesota Property Offender Program to 979 in the Sybil Brand Institute, Los Angeles County. In almost all institutions capacity exceeded the actual inmate population.

Security: Only one women's prison was classified as maximum security, but 27 of 41 jail units were classified minimum.

Physical Adequacy: Four types of design for women's prisons were identified: the campus, the complex, single building, and cottage. Most jail sections for women occupied all or part of a floor of the main jail, some occupied a separate building. Community-based programs for women were usually operated in large private residences.

Space and condition were important interrelated factors in the physical adequacy of an institution. On a Physical Adequacy Index, community-based programs scored highest, followed by prisons and lastly jails.

Although three out of four prisons provided individual cells or rooms for inmates, only 9 of 57 jails used individual cells as the primary housing unit. Despite the single cell trend for women inmates, the majority of incarcerated women were housed in multiple cells and dormitories.

The physical adequacy of an institution was directly related to program richness. The more adequate a physical facility the broader the range of services provided in institutional programs. It is unlikely that a program can be maintained in an institution unless space is allocated, furnished and supplied for that specific program.

Social Environment: The physical settings in institutions ranged from strictly penal (concrete floors, steel bars, etc.) to simply institutional, similar to colleges and other group accommodations in the community. Ratings on this dimension were combined into a normalization index.

Community-based programs ranked much higher on normalization than prisons which, in turn, were more normalized than jails.

Normalization was positively correlated with Physical Adequacy in both prisons and jails. The more adequate the institution the more likely it would have a normalized atmosphere.

The Inmate Autonomy Index measured the degree to which inmates made day-to-day decisions affecting their institutional life.

Inmate autonomy within the institution was lowest in jails and about equal in prisons and community-based programs. However, most community-based programs, especially work-release centers and halfway houses, offered more autonomy to inmates in the community itself.

Was inmate autonomy related to a normalized atmosphere? Yes, but normalization in an institution had to increase substantially before inmate autonomy increased.

Administration: Between March 1975 and March 1976 the superintendent was replaced in 8 of the 14 major state prisons for women. Only 3 of the 14 prisons had had a stable administration for several years or more.

Institutional goals as stated by administrators varied by type of institution. Prison administrators usually espoused treatment and rehabilitation goals; jail administrators were primarily oriented toward custody; community program directors saw reintegration of the offender as their primary goal.

Intake-Transition to Institutional Life: Many prisons and a few large jails maintained separate units where new inmates were housed for a few days to five weeks.

Most prisons conducted some form of orientation for new inmates, but most jails did not. Orientation might be a fairly informal process or an organized series of lectures and activities dealing with all aspects of the institution.

While a general classification scheme was used in many jails, formal classification was rare. Most prisons used a formal classification process which included medical exams, educational, vocational and psychological testing. Classification was primarily a management tool for assigning the inmate to housing, jobs and programs as well as security status.

Intake criteria in community-based programs were usually exclusionary. Certain kinds of clients were not accepted, often resulting in the selection of the best risks for the program.

Counseling and Treatment: Treatment in correctional institutions was conspicuous by its absence. Treatment staff, such as psychiatrists and psychologists, were most often involved in intake testing, court ordered examinations, and in the case of psychiatrists, prescribing medication. Counseling was often a duty of correctional officers, who were not necessarily trained and whose primary role was custodial.

Group sessions were more often unit management meetings than group therapy. On-going individual therapy was rare. Ten percent of women prisoners indicated that group sessions were helpful to them while in prison, and eight percent felt that these sessions would be helpful to them even after their release.

Counseling was a more integral part of community-based programs. Therapeutic communities for drug users were the most treatment-intense, while other community programs focused more on reality therapy and survival skills training.

Health Care: Most prisons provided intake examinations, routine medical care, and limited dental care. In some large jails medical examinations were given to women, but most jails did no medical screening; medical staff spent most of their time on the men's units and came to the women's side for sick call, pill call, or only on request. Emergency care was usually available in-house in prisons, but most jails utilized community hospitals for emergency care. Prenatal care was usually available within the prison, but babies were delivered in a local hospital.

What were the most common medical problems of women inmates? According to medical staff, gynecological problems and "nerves" were most common. The most frequent chronic diseases reported were diabetes, hypertension and drug addiction or alcoholism.

A majority of institutions dispensed pain medications and tranquilizers or mood elevators to inmates. The proportion of inmates receiving tranquilizers or mood elevators ranged from 0 percent to 98 percent. It appears that tranquilizers may be used instead of programs to help maintain control in an institutional setting.

Education and Training: Educational programs, which were found in all prisons and most large jails, usually offered remedial education, G.E.D. preparation, and sometimes junior college classes. Many jails housed so few sentenced women that educational programs were not economically feasible, although such programs might be available on the male side of the jail.

What were the educational needs of women inmates? Only fourteen percent of the inmates, usually older women, had not gone beyond eighth grade. The largest group (45 percent) had not completed high school. Thus, six out of ten women would theoretically be candidates for remedial education and/or G.E.D. preparation. At the same time, 40 percent of the inmates had a high school education or better and might best be served by college classes, adult education, or training.

Since educational level varied greatly from one state to another, the educational profile in a given institution sometimes revealed a predominance of inmates at one end of the spectrum or the other.

Vocational training in prisons and a few large jails concentrated on traditional areas of cosmetology, clerical skills, and food services. Data from the inmates themselves indicated that 43 percent of them had received prior training most often in clerical skills, cosmetology, or para-medical occupations. For the future, the inmates were most interested in clerical jobs, para-professional jobs (often medical), and professional or managerial jobs (perhaps unrealistically). Only three percent of the women aspired to work in traditional male jobs in the skilled trades.

In the Minnesota and Washington prisons training release programs enabled women to select and take training in the community with two obvious advantages: (1) individualization of training, and (2) no costly in-house capital outlay.

In terms of the inmate's future, both inmates and staff placed the most value on educational programs; inmates also indicated that education was very valuable to them during incarceration.

Work Assignments: In prisons work was an inmate's duty; in jails it was a privilege, usually reserved for sentenced women in trustee status. Work assignments were primarily oriented toward institutional maintenance, with little consideration given to on-the-job training or carry-over into the community. Work supervisors indicated that women preferred clerical jobs, but only ten percent of the jobs available were clerical. This directly relates to training needs and aspirations of inmates. Pay was usually mini-mal or non-existent, although one small program in Minnesota paid wages of $1.00 per hour.

Work-release programs for women were extremely rare, involving only two percent of the total prison inmates and one percent of jail inmates.

Considering the positive attitudes toward work expressed by the in-mates, their prior work experience and training, and their aspirations, it appears that institutional work could become a more significant program area.

Religion: Religious programs were available in almost all institutions and often involved community clergy and church volunteers. The chaplain was sometimes the primary "counselor" available to inmates. Religion was most often mentioned by women in prison as most worthwhile during their incarceration. In many jails religion was the only program offered.

Recreation: The opportunity for physical exercise was often limited and sometimes non-existent for women in jail. In prisons, where indoor and outdoor space was usually available, exercise and sports were also avail-able, but without regularly scheduled activities and recreational leaders, it appeared that many women did not participate. In fact, a higher proportion of jail than prison inmates felt that recreation was the most worthwhile program; perhaps, in part, because of their closer confinement, recreation was the only program which enabled women in jail to leave the cell area.

Community-Based Programs: In the study states, for every ten women in prison or jail there was one women in a community-based program. There were three basic types of programs: halfway houses, work-release centers, and treatment programs for drug abusers or alcoholics. Most programs took a reality approach, emphasizing jobs and survival skills; however, therapeutic communities for drug offenders emphasized changing the client through intensive therapeutic techniques.

PROFILE OF INCARCERATED WOMEN

Age: Incarcerated women are young; two-thirds were under 30 years of age. The median age of unsentenced women and misdemeanants was 24 years; the median age of felons was 27 years. Girls under 18 years were usually not found in adult institutions.

Ethnic Group: While Blacks comprised only 10 percent of the adult female population in the study states, 50 percent of the incarcerated women were black. Indians were also over-represented, but the proportion of Hispanic women (Puerto Ricans in New York and Mexicans in Texas and California) appeared similar to that in the general population.

Education: Although incarcerated women tended to be less educated than women as a whole, their educational level related directly to the state-wide median. In states where the median grade level completed by adult women is lower than for the country as a whole, inmates also had less education than inmates from other regions of the country.

Educational level was significantly related to ethnic group. Whites and Indians were better educated, followed by Blacks, with Hispanics notably behind the other groups.

Marital Status: At the time of their incarceration, 27 percent of the women were single, 19 percent were non-married but living with a man, 20 percent were married, 28 percent were separated or divorced, and 7 percent were widowed.

Although 60 percent of the women had been married at least once, only 10 percent of all inmates had actually been living with a husband prior to incarceration.

About one-third of the women had been involved in serial relationships including at least one marriage plus other non-marital living arrangements.

Children: Only 56 percent of the women had dependent children living at home prior to incarceration, although 73 percent of the women had actually borne children. The average number of children per inmate mother was 2.48, compared to 2.18 reported by the census for all families with children in 1973.

Who took care of the children while their mothers were incarcerated? It did not appear that children of incarcerated women were bound for foster homes. In 85 percent of the cases, the woman's parents or other relatives took the children; however, husbands provided only 10 percent of all child care arrangements. Ethnic differences in child care were significant, with Whites and Indians relying more on husbands and on non-relatives, including agencies.

Childhood: Half of the women came from two-parent homes; 31 percent lived with mother only; 3 percent with father only; and 4 percent lived with non-relatives, sometimes in foster homes but rarely in institutions.

Welfare: Over half (56 percent) of the women had received welfare during their adult lives and one-third had received welfare during childhood. The welfare pattern of each state was mirrored in the proportion of inmates who had been on welfare, ranging from a low of 35 percent in Georgia to a high of 76 percent in Minnesota.

Work: Almost all of the women had worked at some time in their lives; 40 percent had worked in the two months prior to incarceration. Whether or not a woman worked had no bearing on the type of crime she committed. This finding contradicts the opportunity theory of crime which postulates a link between increased participation in the labor force and a rise in crime.

Attitudes: On 26 attitudinal items, the women scored higher than expected on self-esteem. They expressed a desire to work and felt that working was an appropriate female role. However, they supported traditional sex roles, feeling that it is important for women to have children and for men to be the hard workers and primary support of the family. Although the inmates indicated that non-traditional jobs for women are all right, they strongly endorsed high status, white collar jobs.

Offense: Misdemeanants serving one year or less had been convicted in the following proportions: 41 percent for property crimes (shoplifting, forgery, fraud); 20 percent for drug offenses; and 11 percent for violent crimes (usually assault, battery, or armed robbery).

Convicted felons were serving one year or more: 43 percent for violent crimes (murder, armed robbery); 29 percent for property crimes (forgery, fraud, some larceny); 22 percent for drug offenses.

Most unsentenced women had been charged with the following felony-type offenses: 30 percent for violent crimes; 22 percent drug offenses; and 14 percent forgery or fraud.

Arrests: Most arrests do not result in incarceration. In 1973, 56 percent of all arrests of women were for misdemeanors such as drunkenness, drunk driving, disorderly conduct, but only 18 percent of the misdemeanants were in jail for this type of offense, 13 percent of the unsentenced women, and 4 percent of the felons. For violent crimes the reverse was true. Only 7 percent of female arrests were for violent offenses, but 43 percent of the felons serving prison sentences had been convicted of violent crimes.

The arrest and offense data highlight the differences between states and between areas within a state in the criminal climate and in the response of the criminal justice system.

Offense History: Nearly one-third of the women had been arrested for the first time at age 17 or younger. Another 49 percent were first arrested between ages 18 and 24. Almost one-third of the women had spent time in juvenile institutions.

Property offenders were most often recidivists; murderers were most likely to be first offenders. The women with the most extensive involvement with the criminal justice system were the habitual offenders—prostitutes, drug offenders and petty thieves.

Offense and Type of Incarceration: It is ironic that less serious offenders (sentenced misdemeanants) usually serve their time in jails under the tightest security with minimal program opportunities. The same is true of women awaiting trial who supposedly are innocent until proven guilty. So little was happening in jails with less than 100 women that the program section of this report does not even deal with these institutions. After one acknowledges the shorter time being served and the economic constraints of local jails, one is still faced with the problem of improving jail conditions for women.

This is not to imply that felons in prison were that well off—only by contrast. Conditions varied greatly from one state to another and even within an institution, inmates participated in programs in varying degrees.

Notes

[1] Marilyn Haft notes that "[t]he most recent comprehensive study of correctional facilities for women is J. Lekkerkerker, "Reformatories for Women in the United States (1931)." See footnote 1a in "Women in Prison," *Prisoners' Rights Sourcebook,* edited by Michele G. Hermann and Marilyn G. Haft (New York: Clark Boardman, 1973) p. 352.

[2] For example, the sections on work experience in a number of articles are not at all comparable. Not only are the listed jobs different, but the time frame for recording prior work experience is different in each article. This is not to say that the information, per se, is incorrect, but simply to underscore the problem of comparing or combining data from multiple sources. See Rose Giallombardo, *The Seasonless World: A Study of a Women's Prison,* University Microfilms, Ann Arbor, Michigan (Ph.D. Dissertation, 1965), p. 103; Omar Hendrix, *A Study in Neglect,* Women's Prison Association, New York, 1972, p. 21; Carol Spencer and John Berecochea, "Vocational Training at the California Institution for Women," Department of

Corrections, California, January 1971, p. 3; "Study of Female Offenders," Department of Social and Health Services, State of Washington Research Report, Vol. 3, No. 18, April 1971.

3 It is illuminating to examine the footnotes in some recent articles to see how many of them rely on journalistic accounts and personal descriptive narratives as documentation of the characteristics of the female offender and conditions in prisons and jails.

4 For example, several authors of articles refer to data from Margery Velimesis' *Report on the Survey of 41 Pennsylvania County Court and Correctional Services for Women and Girl Offenders,* 1969. Helen Gibson's article, "Women's Prisons: Laboratories for Penal Reform," Wisconsin Law Review, 1973, p. 224, quotes Velimesis as follows: "[she] found that 80 percent of all the women in jail or prison had children to support." Richard Palmer's article, "The Prisoner-Mother and Her Child," Capital University Law Review, Vol. 1, No. 1, p. 127, says Velimesis' data "showed that 60-70% [of the women surveyed] were not married, but that 80% *of these unmarried women had children"* (our emphasis). Interestingly, Velimesis' original report does not contain the data from which either of these figures could be derived.

5 Although riots at male institutions are generally more visible to the public, the fact is that "disturbances" (as the media like to say) have occurred in several women's prisons during the last 18 months.

6 Ann Grogan, "Women Locked Up: Feminist Perspectives and Alternatives," text of Keynote address at Conference of Women in Prison, Denver, Colorado, January 18, 1975.

7 The most comprehensive review of the early literature on female criminality appears in Dorie Klien's article, "The Etiology of Female Crime: A Review of the Literature," *Issues In Criminology,* Vol. 8, No. 2, Fall 1973, pp. 3-30.

8 *Ibid.,* p. 17.

9 See Dale Hoffman-Bustamante, "The Nature of Female Criminality," *Issues In Criminology,* Vol. 8, No. 2, Fall 1973, pp. 117-136, for a discussion of the relationship between specific crimes and differential role expectations.

10 Daniel Green, "Crime Takes a Female Turn," *National Observer,* October 5, 1974. Also note that since August, 1974 to the present writing, similar statements linking liberation and crime have appeared in *The New York Times* (March 14, 1976); *The San Francisco Chronicle* (January 30, 1976); and *The Los Angeles Times* (February 27, 1976). Articles on the same subject have appeared in *Newsweek* (January 26, 1975) and *Oui* (April 1975).

11 Freda Adler, *Sisters in Crime* (New York: McGraw-Hill, 1975).

12 One must also note that the rise in *crime* is not absolutely accurate either. What is being reported is a rise in *arrests.*

13 William Nagel, *The New Red Barn: A Critical Look at the Modern American Prison,* (New York: Walker and Co., 1973).

14 Giallombardo, *op. cit.,* p. 11.

15 *Ibid.* It is interesting to note also that many of these early programs still survive despite the many changes that have occurred in society. Perhaps one of the most universal of all of these notions is reflected in the prison rules and regulations for females that punish "unlady-like" or abusive language.

16 Joy Eyman, *Prisons for Women* (Springfield, IL: Charles C. Thomas, 1971) p. 60.

9

You Can't Be a Mother and Be in Prison . . . Can You? Impacts of the Mother-Child Separation

Phyllis Jo Baunach

It has been documented that prisons pay little if any attention to incarcerated women's physical and emotional health. This chapter focuses on one of these areas: the reality of many incarcerated women's biological and social roles as mothers. Since the age of incarceration and biological reproductivity overlap so greatly, not only do about two-thirds of all incarcerated women have children outside prison, but a substantial proportion of women are pregnant on entrance to prison.

This chapter focuses particularly on women who are separated from their children as a result of incarceration. As with women inmates in general, inmate-mothers are low-skilled, poor yet the head of a household, fairly young, and often black. Of particular interest is the discussion of the grief women prisoners experience because of their separation from their children and the discussion of the difficulties of returning to the parent role after release. The author points out that inmate-mothers face all the hurdles other released inmates face in staying crime-free plus the additional burden of child care. The lack of adequate means to maintain relations between incarcerated mothers and their children is contradictory at best: on the one hand the image of the "good mother" is held out as the role they should strive for; on the other hand, they are twice punished, first for their offense and second by being unable to be with or adequately provide for their children. Program recommendations for reuniting inmates with their children are suggested. The chapter also raises some hard questions about role expectations for the woman prisoner who is a mother; often she is judged to be unworthy to be a mother by others once arrested and her children are taken from her custody, while in other cases those judging her emphasize her guilt in causing her children

The study by Baunach (1979) was supported by Order Number 8-0754-J-LEAA awarded by the Law Enforcement Assistance Administration, U.S. Department of Justice, under the Omnibus Crime Control and Safe Streets Act of 1968, as amended. Points of view or opinions stated in this document are those of the author and do not necessarily represent the official position or policies of the U.S. Department of Justice, the Law Enforcement Assistance Administration, or the National Institute of Justice.

The author would like to thank Jean Magnotto for her efficient and careful typing services and the University of Maryland Computer Science Center for providing facilities for the data analysis.

to be separated from her. And yet the author's data shows that inmate-mothers are generally sensitive to their children's needs and on the whole honest with them about their imprisonment when given the opportunity to tell their children themselves what has happened.

INTRODUCTION

Anecodotal and limited statistical information indicate that a large proportion of incarcerated women are mothers[1] and that one of the greatest concerns of these women is their children (Ward and Kassebaum, 1965; Murton and Baunach, 1973, Baunach and Murton, 1973; Glick and Neto, 1977; Baunach, 1979; Stanton, 1980). Although experimental research in this area is sparse, there have been a number of descriptive studies outlining the characteristics of these women, their general feelings about the separation (Bonfanti, et al., 1974; DuBose, 1975; Lundberg, et al., 1975; McGowan and Blumenthal, 1978; Baunach, 1979), and the problems of coordinating agency services to meet the needs of inmate-mothers and their children (Zalba, 1964; McGowan and Blumenthal, 1978). This chapter will discuss some of the important issues regarding the separation, including the psychological effects of the separation, explaining mother's absence, custody issues, and problems in visitation, and will suggest a direction that emphasizes the involvement of inmate-mothers in developing a sense of parental responsibility.

A PROFILE OF INCARCERATED MOTHERS

Incarcerated mothers tend to be black more often than white (like the general prison population which reflects the racism of our society), under 35 years old, most likely divorced or never married and, like most incarcerated women, poorly educated and poorly skilled. Given this generally low level of skills, education and status, it is not surprising that they had little choice in the selection of job options. Those women who worked usually held jobs most closely associated with traditionally feminine roles (i.e., waitress, cook, or secretary) with average wages of $2-$3 an hour or $6,000-$9,000 a year (Baunach, 1979 and 1981b).

Most incarcerated mothers have between two or three children and many have children under 13 years of age (Zalba, 1964; Bonfanti, et al., 1974; McGowan and Blumenthal, 1978; Baunach, 1979). Well over half of the inmate-mothers lived with their children prior to arrest.[2] In addition, Baunach (1979) found that about 62 percent of the 283 children in her study had not been separated from their mothers because of incarceration in the past. These findings suggest that up until the mother's incarceration, most of the children had been living with their mothers on a continuous basis and that the current incarceration was the first major change for them. However, little is known about the nature or quality of the mother-child relationship prior to the mother's arrest or about the veracity of the mother's self-reports, as few studies have interviewed caretakers or other relatives or children systematically.[3] Moreover, a substantial proportion of inmate-mothers reportedly plan to reunite with children following release from prison and thus regard the separation as only temporary.[4]

During incarceration caretakers for children are usually relatives. If relatives are unavailable or unsuitable, children may be put up for adoption or placed in foster care. Foster care placement, however, is used infrequently.[5] Yet decisions to place children may be made without involving inmate-mothers in the process. The net effect of intervention by authorities who "know what is best" for the child's welfare may be traumatic for both mother and child. For instance, O'Brien (1974) noted that an inmate in Washington state had procured placement for her eight children with members of her congregation. Despite the inmate's efforts, and the help of her Christian friends, a young social worker decided that the children should be placed elsewhere. The inmate objected, stating that her children would be happier with friends than with strangers and responded, "They're not like kittens where you give half the litter away."

Impacts of the Separation

Psychological Impacts

Perhaps one of the most important impacts of the separation from their children is the emotional stress experienced by inmate-mothers. Many mothers feel conflict and guilt because their own behavior has resulted in the separation. Often this anxiety and guilt is expressed in terms of dissatisfaction with current caretakers of the children. This seems to be especially true if the mother was not involved in determining the child's placement (Lundberg, et al., 1975, Baunach, 1979 and 1981b).

Moreover, for many women with drug problems, incarceration may be the first time they are "down" and have an opportunity to consider the effects of their behavior upon both themselves and their children. These women wonder how they will remain "clean" once released and reunited with their children. Other women become bitter and angry at "the system" because they pled guilty believing they would be placed on probation or because they feel that they have been convicted unfairly. These women tend to blame others for their plight and to minimize their own behavior (Baunach, 1979).

For many mothers, the psychological repercussions may be analagous to those resulting from other forms of loss, such as death or divorce. The grief response emitted by inmate-mothers may be characterized by emptiness, helplessness, anger and bitterness, guilt, and fear of loss or rejection. Imprisonment may, in fact, make it difficult to work through this loss. In a prison setting the means to express grief freely, support for confidentiality, and learning to cope with the situation are minimal. Instead, women tend to be pressured to suspend emotional involvement in order to complete their prison terms successfully. Consequently, upon release, mothers may foresee little or no difficulty in reuniting with children. Their assessment of the situation, however, may be unrealistic given the complexity of the emotions involved.

At the time of the reunion a crucial issue may be the extent to which both mother and child have internalized their defenses. In the absence of resolving or working through the grief associated with the separation, the mother-child relationship might be jeopardized. Children are much more vulnerable than adults and thus may be subject to more severe disturbances as a result of the loss. Thus, the mother's resolution of the grief may be a significant factor in maintaining a healthy reunion and relationship with the child (Lundberg, et al., 1975). In the sterile prison world devoid of real intimacy or supportive relationships, this resolution may be nearly impossible.

Related to the sense of loss faced by inmate-mothers are the fear of overall inadequacy as a mother and the fear of being unable to re-adjust to living with children upon release. In her study Baunach (1979) asked mothers to indicate as many problems as they thought they might encounter in re-adjusting to living with their children after release.

About 20 percent of the 138 mothers foresaw no difficulties in the re-adjustment. These women felt secure in their current relationships with children and confident in their abilities as mothers despite the separation. In addition, many of these women had left infants or very young children and anticipated a short separation. Therefore, they perceived that there would be a minimum of difficulty in reestablishing relationships with their children.

Two major types of problems were mentioned: problems of children readjusting to mothers ("Children's Problems") and problems of mothers in readjusting to children ("Mothers' Problems"). Children's Problems accounted for about 36 percent of the problems mentioned and Mothers' Problems for the remaining 64 percent. Mothers thus felt that they would have more difficulty than their children in readjusting after release.

With respect to Children's Problems, mothers thought children might not know them, respect them, or want to live with them in the future. Some mothers worried that children would reject them outright because they had been in prison or because they had been away for so long. On the other hand, many mothers worried that children would be more dependent on them than they had been prior to the separation. These mothers felt that children might want them around constantly and may be reluctant to let them leave the house to go to work or shopping for fear that they might not return. Some mothers noted that even during visits children watched them or followed them around constantly.

With respect to Mothers' Problems, some women questioned their own adequacy as parents. By far the largest proportion of problems mentioned related to discipline. Slightly more than one-third of the mothers cited discipline as a possible source of difficulty. This difficulty was expressed in one of two ways. On one hand, mothers felt that children were becoming used to discipline techniques that they had not used and would have difficulty in re-adjusting to a different means of discipline. For example, grandparents often were seen as more lax in their approach. They would not enforce rules as mothers thought they should or they would allow privileges mothers did not permit. On the other hand, some mothers questioned their ability initially to handle discipline problems. They pointed out that children would test them at first to see how much they could "get away with" and that they would have to learn to handle these situations all over again.

In addition, many mothers said they might not know how to relate to children. Most of these women had been incarcerated for two or more years and had had minimal contact through visits. During this time children would have changed considerably and they would have to learn to communicate with them anew.

Other anticipated Mothers' Problems focused on more practical matters such as regaining custody, relocating children or finding housing. Mothers who reported that regaining custody or relocating children would be problems feared that caretakers would be unwilling to return the children. A few mothers, mainly those whose children were living with foster parents, had little or no idea where the children were located or how to contact them either during or following incarceration.

Still other mothers felt that they could not compete with middle class foster mothers who were able to provide more "creature comforts" and who had a great deal more confidence and perhaps more experience as mothers. As one inmate put it, "I can't compete with all that she can give my son, so why try? I know I'll lose him."

Explaining Mother's Absence

Perceptions of Where Mother Is Now

When mothers are incarcerated, children may or may not learn from them where they are and why they are there. Unless they are very young, however, children apparently understand that mothers may go away because they have done something bad. Baunach (1979), for instance, found that about two-thirds of the mothers in her study said that their children knew that they were in prison, or as some women put it, "in jail" or "a place to be punished." Less than 10 percent of the mothers said their children believed they were away at work, school or college, in a hospital or visiting relatives. About 21 percent of the mothers said that they did not know where their children thought they were as they never had a chance to talk with their children following arrest. When their children had been placed, mothers were not sure what information caretakers had provided about their absence.

Two mothers said their children had definite but inaccurate ideas about their absence. One mother said her only child, a young son, believed the institution was her home. She had been incarcerated ever since he was born and he visited her regularly each week in prison. Therefore, as she put it, "He thinks this is where mothers are supposed to live." Another mother noted that her two ex-husbands told each of her two children that she was dead. This mother was particularly upset as she had been trying in vain to write to the children but they never received the letters.

Who Told Children

The circumstances under which mothers are arrested as well as their attitudes and relationship with children dictate whether or not they have or take advantage of an opportunity to explain to children what has happened. About half of the mothers in Baunach's study (1979) told their children themselves that they were in prison. Most of them had explained at the time of arrest or prior to imprisonment that they were going away because they were bad. Some mothers, however, said that they found it difficult initially to tell their children that they would be in prison as they were trying to accept this fact for themselves. These mothers, often imprisoned for the first time, waited until after incarceration to explain their absence and frequently did not broach the subject until children raised questions first. A few mothers commented that in the interim, well-intentioned relatives had told the children that they were visiting friends or on vacation. Upon discovering this ruse the mothers were angry and told the children the truth. One woman noted, "My mother told her I was away on vacation. She thought that was the best thing to do because [my daughter] is so young. When I found that out I got mad. I wanted her to know the truth so I told her myself."

Less frequently (18 percent), mothers said that other relatives or caretakers had explained the absence and that they concurred. Some of these women said that they had not seen their children following arrest and had not had an opportunity to explain their absence. Consequently, caretakers provided an explanation and mothers went along with it, despite its veracity.

Still other mothers (12 percent) said their children found out for themselves before anyone had explained the situation to them. Some of these children were at the scene of the crime and realized what had happened. Other children were with their mothers at the time of arrest or visited them in jail and knew that their mothers would have to be away although they may not have understood the reasons.

About 18 percent of the mothers said they did not know who explained their absence to the children. They thought that caretakers probably had told the children but they were not sure what information had been conveyed. These mothers expressed the most concern as they were afraid their children would be given an erroneous impression or that they would not understand what had happened. Many of these mothers wanted the chance to explain their absence to the children for themselves.

Reasons to Explain the Absence

Given the opportunity, mothers generally tend to tell older children the truth. In her study Baunach (1979) found that about 54 percent of the mothers said they told their children the truth about their imprisonment because they wanted the children to know at the outset why they were leaving. Some mothers feared children would otherwise learn the truth elsewhere and might lose respect for them.

Mothers often said children were capable of understanding the real reason for their absence and had a right to know the truth. One mother said, "Why lie? They'll find out soon or later from somebody and I'd rather it be from me than the neighbor's kids or some stranger." Another mother commented:

> I have had a straight relationship with my children from jump street. Why should I start telling them stories about my life now? Besides, if they're going to visit me here it would be very hard for me to tell them why I can't come home with them unless I lay it on the line.

On the other hand, mothers with very young children (i.e., under two years old) had not told them they were going to prison because they felt these children were too young to understand. Many of these mothers said that as the children got older, they wanted to explain what had happened, especially if the children asked.

A small proportion of the mothers (8 percent) felt that regardless of their age, children might be more upset if they knew mother was in prison. Some of these women argued that telling children they were in prison would simply burden their minds with unnecessary pressures and misunderstandings. A frequent comment along this line was: "They don't need to know. They've gone through enough already with me just being away. Someday I'll probably tell them all about it."

Taken together, these data suggest that mothers generally want to be honest with their children in telling them realistically that they are imprisoned. Mothers express concern that children may turn away from them if they learn the truth from others. This orientation is particularly true of women with older children. Mothers frequently remark that they want their own incarceration to serve as an indication of what children could expect if they break the law. In this respect many mothers often express guilt and shame or anger at themselves for their involvement in crime. Mothers convicted of property crimes often point out that had they considered the potential consequences of their behavior they would have acted differently. Mothers involved in person offenses may express similar feelings but say that the offense itself happened so fast that it had been unavoidable (Baunach, 1979).

Legal Custody

Whether or not an inmate-mother *should* retain or relinquish her parental rights to her child(ren) during or following incarceration involves both moral and legal decisions which in some ways may overlap. From a legal perspective, Palmer (1972) argued that incarceration, per se, does not provide adequate evidence that a parent is unfit. Rather, he suggested that the courts should consider additional factors, such as the woman's relationship to the offspring prior to incarceration and the casual relationship between the criminal act and the mother's ability to perform her parental role. With these points in mind, judges would be better able to determine the mother's parental fitness and to decide whether or not the child(ren) should be placed in her custody after her release.

A further argument raised along these lines is that legislative guidelines limit the extent to which the courts may modify their procedures for deciding parental fitness. Guidelines currently consider the best interests of the child(ren), but simultaneously treat the issue of parental fitness inequitably. Established standards such as non-support, child abuse, neglect, desertion, drunkenness, adultery, mental illness, and incarceration have been regarded as manifestations of the abandonment of parental responsibilities and their justification for the termination of parental rights. However, these interpretations are erroneous and a reassessment of the standards is required.

The court's consideration of a mother's criminal act and subsequent incarceration as voluntary relinquishment of her parental rights was decided in *In re Jameson* (1967). In this case, the court held that the mother knew prior to committing the act that she would be incarcerated for it if convicted. Palmer challenged this justification as illogical, since the woman's intention may have been to obtain money or food with *no intention* of getting caught. Furthermore, he noted, if she wished to abandon her child, the woman could have probably devised alternative means which would not have been detrimental or discomforting to herself. This is an important point and leaves one to wonder why the court seems to attribute such masochistic motives to the mother.

The author suggested that imprisonment in and of itself does not constitute abandonment. Rather, additional factors, such as parental neglect and withholding affection, should be used to substantiate claims of abandonment. Given this background, Palmer recommended legislative reform, such as allowing an inmate to live with her children (under two years old) in prison, in conditions conducive to a positive interaction; devising "mother release" programs to enable inmate-mothers to stay with their children in the community; and reforming visitation practices to allow for more relaxed visits in less security-oriented surroundings.

A few states have legislation allowing children under two years old to live with their mothers in prison; however, this practice is not currently used on a regular basis. Although current research does not specifically address why this is so, from a practical standpoint it may be difficult to provide housing, clothing, food, and adequate medical care for infants. Moreover, the long-range impacts of the prison on a child's growth and development are unknown.

In this regard, a California law suit regarding an inmate-mother's right to have her children live with her in prison was denied in court. Arguments raised included the effects that the prison environment and procedures could have on the child and the potential effects of the child's presence on the prison and other inmates.

Baunach's study (1979) includes data on the effects of having children in an institutional setting for short periods of time (i.e., all day or overnight). Preliminary analyses show that regardless of whether they have children of their own, women in prison tend to respond favorably to the presence of children. Many women indicated that they try to "clean up their language and behavior" when children are present, and enjoy watching or playing with children. In addition, there were no serious incidents regarding children since the program began in the women's prisons in Washington State and Kentucky. However, to date, there has been no research on the effects on the children of living in a prison with mothers for short or long periods of time.

On the other hand, within recent years there has been growing concern for the legal rights and rehabilitative needs of inmate-mothers and children. In 1978 Terry Moore, a young first offender at the Florida Correctional Institution for Women, gave birth to a baby whose father was a prison guard. Until she was released a few months later, Ms. Moore fought and won the right to have her baby stay with her in the prison. More recently, a brief *New York Times* (1981: 49) article noted that a Florida Circuit Court judge declared that "an infant should remain with his mother if possible" and ordered the Florida State Prison Correctional Institution for Women to provide a joint cell for an inmate-mother and her newborn son. This case was apparently the first test of a Florida law allowing judges to decide the best interests of both mother and child when mothers are imprisoned. In June, 1980 there were reportedly nine mothers and ten babies ranging in age from four weeks to a year living in a nursery cottage. The mothers' work assignment was mainly the care of their children. The article further noted, however, that prison authorities were attempting to phase out the program "by attrition" under a revised state law that provides the courts less latitude in determining cases where mothers are imprisoned.

With respect to retaining legal custody, Baunach (1979) found that about half of the 283 children were in the custody of their incarcerated mothers at the time of the study. The remaining children were mainly in the custody of relatives.

For a small proportion of the children (16 percent), mothers reported that they were forced to give up custody at the time of arrest or prior to incarceration. Mothers that responded in this manner said that the state, their own mothers, or an ex-husband forced them to relinquish custody. For slightly more than a quarter of the children, mothers said they voluntarily relinquished custody temporarily for the child's benefit. They noted that caretakers on the outside would be better able to obtain medical, dental, or other services for the children as the legal guardian. Although most of these mothers intended to regain custody upon release, they feared that it would be difficult because of their felony convictions.

Visitation

Although varying among institutions, visitation policies and procedures determine the extent to which a woman can maintain contact with her children. Sometimes this contact is minimal. For example, the Washington, D.C. Citizen's Council issued a report in 1972 which noted, among other things, that women at the Washington, D.C. Detention Center had only two one-hour visits each week. Moreover, there had been no other provisions made for the mothers, who comprised some 86 percent of the inmate population, to visit with their children (Murton and Baunach, 1973:6).

Some institutions allow for increased visiting and telephone contact as women earn additional privileges during incarceration. Yet, the extent of visiting may be limited. Baunach (1979) reported that more than half of the children in her study visited with mothers irregularly or not at all. Similarly, McGowan and Blumenthal (1978) found that although 80 percent of the children in their study had "regular contact" with mothers, these contacts often were as few as once a month or less. Besides institutional policies, limitations to visiting may include transportation costs and distances, caretakers' opposition to children visiting, or less frequently, mothers' desire not to see children during incarceration. Mothers not wishing to see their children most often indicate that either they do not want children to know they are incarcerated or they do not know how to explain the fact that they cannot go home with the children when the visit ends. The impacts of limited visitation and direct contact with children are despondency, feelings of inadequacy, and fear of permanent loss of children. In Baunach's study (1979), these feelings were often manifested by mothers crying while discussing their children during the interviews.

CONCLUSIONS AND FUTURE DIRECTIONS

Parental responsibility entails making decisions about children's welfare. Perhaps the greatest input inmate-mothers have is in determining the placement of children prior to incarceration. Although inmate-mothers involved in these decisions tend to feel more satisfied with placements and subsequent care for children, the sense of loss, guilt, shame, despondency, and conflict are nonetheless quite common among these women. Beyond peripheral involvement during visits, the parental role is not allowed to be more than negligible during incarceration. Moreover, prison environments, which foster dependency, are not conducive to the development of a sense of responsibility for oneself or for children. As many inmate-mothers so aptly put it: "You can't be a mother and be in prison."

Yet, some studies suggest that despite these feelings of inadequacy and institutional conditions, inmate-mothers attempt to maintain some semblance of the mother role (Lundberg, et al., 1975; Baunach, 1979). They often retain legal custody, explain their absence directly to their children (when possible), lived with children prior to incarceration, and plan to reunite with them after release. In this respect, children are important to incarcerated mothers: a majority of these mothers apparently want to develop a sense of responsibility as parents. Perhaps one of the greatest impacts of the separation is to heighten this interest in children.

It must be noted that the sincerity of this interest in children has been questioned. Although studies in this area almost uniformly report that inmate-mothers are worried about their children, there are many instances in which incarcerated mothers express grave concern for their children during incarceration. Yet once released, they return to old habits and criminal patterns, are rearrested and reincarcerated. If these women truly cared for their children, the argument goes, then they would not revert to crime a second or third time. Hence, the cry of "My children, my children" among incarcerated mothers is sometimes seen as a ruse for leniency from the parole board and other correctional authorities.

The extent of this response among inmate-mothers is unknown, however. To date, no one has documented the problems and reactions of inmate-mothers following release. In fact, the extent to and success with which these women actually reunite with children is as yet undetermined. However, in assessing the "success" of reunions, one must consider the nature of the problems encountered. Despite the fact that these mothers may indeed want to resume parental responsibilities, the fact is that they must juggle these responsibilities for one or more children on their own along with obtaining stable employment, schooling, finding housing, and other parole requirements. Inmate-mothers, especially if they belong to a minority ethnic group, face two additional stigmas upon release that male offenders do not. Besides the problems associated with their race, criminal record and lack of skills or education, released inmate-mothers face the problems of being a woman and resuming sole care for their children after an extended absence. Perhaps more out of sheer frustration or an inability to cope with the situation than out of lack of concern for children, some of these women may revert to crime. The conditions under which inmate-mothers "successfully" reunite with children are, therefore, significant foci for future research efforts.

In any case, parental responsibility begins with an implicit acceptance of the role as mother. For some inmate-mothers, as for some women in general, shouldering the responsibility of children may make it more difficult to deal with their own problems. Thus inmate-mothers should be encouraged to decide for themselves whether they want to be involved with their children during and following incarceration. Many women feel that unless they want to be with their children, they will be viewed as "bad mothers" by those around them. In fact, many of these women may feel insecure in this role and unable to handle the responsibilities adequately. Other women may not really want to be mothers upon release but feel compelled by social pressure to behave otherwise.

Once an inmate-mother has decided she will resume parental responsibilities following release, she must be able to maintain contact and to develop parenting skills. If a mother plans to reunite with her children upon release (as most apparently do), unless she is given the chance to interact with her children continuously, she will not be able to determine if she really wants to be a mother or is able to handle the problems of discipline, demands by or even routine care for her children. Parenting entails far more than simply showing off a child to others or sitting together during regular visiting hours.

Some states (i.e., California, Kentucky, Minnesota, Nebraska, New

York, Tennessee and Washington State) provide parenting programs or allow children to stay overnight with mothers in prison. Although a step in the right direction, these programs do not go far enough. Day-long, overnight, or weekend visitation still do not allow enough time for the glamour of the initial reunion to wear off. Moreover, out of necessity, these programs are carried out in security-oriented prison settings and therefore subject to all of the problems and limitations associated with programs in these settings.

There is a need for alternative programs, perhaps in the community, which house mothers and children together. One of the key aspects of this approach is the voluntary involvement of inmate-mothers in the development, implementation, and operations of the programs. Adherence to the medical model that suggests that offenders are "sick and must be cured" prior to release means that things must be done *to* or *for* the offender rather than *with* her. However, this antiquated model is antithetical to the development of a sense of responsibility among inmate-mothers. Involvement in the decision-making process means that inmate-mothers themselves are given the opportunity to determine the focus and direction of the program. Elsewhere this has been referred to as the "goal of empowerment" (Rafter and Natalizia, 1981:94) or as participatory management (Murton, 1975; Baunach, 1981a).

In order to have a vested interest in the program, inmate-mothers must participate in determining the selection criteria and process, the nature and directions of the program, rules and disciplinary procedures, and for themselves, whether or not they want to participate. Moreover, as part of the selection, each inmate-mother should be involved with staff and child care case workers in deciding whether the current situation, possible impacts on or welfare of their children, would be enhanced or threatened by their participation in the program. This type of involvement prior to actual program participation would give inmate-mothers a chance to make responsible decisions as parents.

Optimally, an environment that is less security-oriented, encourages independence and growth, and provides access to community resources would enable both mothers and children to test one another and to learn their own strengths and weaknesses (with some supervision if they request it). This type of program would foster the development of a sense of responsibility and assist inmate-mothers to plan more realistically for themselves and their children after release.

Notes

[1] The proportion of incarcerated women reportedly having dependent children 18 years or younger generally ranges between 56% and 68%. For example, in their study of homosexuality among incarcerated women at the California Correctional Institution for Women, Ward and Kassebaum (1965) reported that 68% of the women were mothers. Similarly, Bonfanti, et al., (1974) found 68% of the women in the Louisiana Correctional Institution for Women were mothers. Glick and Neto (1977) noted 56.3% of their 1,607 incarcerated women in 14 states were mothers. McGowan and Blumenthal (1976) reported 67.1% and Baunach (1981) found that 66.9% of the imprisoned women in Kentucky and Washington state were mothers.

[2] For instance, Bonfanti, et al., (1974) reported 66%, Lundberg, et al., (1975) found 74%, McGowan and Blumenthal (1978) noted 75% of their national sample and Baunach (1979) found that 74% of the inmate-mothers in her sample had lived with children prior to arrest.

[3] Studies by LaPoint (1979) and Stanton (1980) include some information about mothers or children obtained by interviews with caretakers and relatives.

[4] Zalba (1964) found that 34% of the mothers in her study planned immediate reunions and another 27% planned reunions after a period of adjustment. Bonfanti, et al., (1974) found that nearly two-thirds of the mothers planned reunions. McGowan and Blumenthal (1978) found 78.2% of their national sample and 92.5% of their sample of sentenced women at the New York Correctional Institutions for Women planned to re-establish homes for children following release. Baunach (1979) reported that 89% planned reunions with children.

[5] McGowan and Blumenthal (1978) reported 76%, Baunach (1979) found 82% and Stanton (1980) noted that 77% of the caretakers for children during mothers' incarceration were relatives. On the other hand, McGowan and Blumenthal (1978) found 12%, Baunach (1979) reported 7% and Stanton (1980) indicated that only 10% of the caretakers were foster parents.

References

"Babies in prison." New York Times 130, 44,979 (Sunday, June 14):49, 1981.

Baunach, P.J. "Participatory management: restructuring the prison environment," in D. Fogel and J. Hudson (eds.), Justice as Fairness. Cincinnati: Anderson Publishing Co., 1981a.

_____ "Mothers in prison: perspectives on the separation from their children." Presented at the Academy of Criminal Justice Sciences Conference, Philadelphia, Pennsylvania, 1981b.

_____. "The separation of inmate-mothers from their children." Draft final report submitted to the National Institute of Justice, 1979.

_____ and T.O. Murton. "Women in prison: an awakening minority. Crime and Corrections 1, 2 (Fall):4-12, 1973.

Bonfanti, M., S. Felder, M. Loesch, and N. Vincent. "Enactment and perception of maternal role of incarcerated mothers." Masters Thesis. Baton Rouge: Louisiana State University, 1974.

Dubose, D. "Problems of children whose mothers are imprisoned." New York: Institute of Women's Wrongs, 1975.

Glick, R. and V. Neto. National Study of Women's Correctional Programs. Washington, D.C.: U.S. Government Printing Office, 1979.

Lapoint, V. "Child development during maternal separation: via incarceration." NIMH Project #76-NM-143 in progress, 1977.

Lundberg, D., A. Sheckley, and T. Vuelkar. "An exploration of the feelings and attitudes of women separated from their children due to incarceration." Masters Thesis. Portland: Portland State University, 1975.

McGowan, B. and K. Blumenthal. Why Punish the Children: A Study of Children of Women Prisoners. Hackensack: National Council on Crime and Delinquency, 1978.

Murton, T.O. Shared Decision-Making as a Treatment Technique in Prison Management. Minneapolis: The Murton Foundation for Criminal Justice, Inc., 1975.

————— and P.J. Baunach. "Women in prison." The Freeworld Times 2 (June-July), 1973.

O'Brien, L. "Women in prison." The Freeworld Times 3 (March), 1974.

Palmer, D. "The prisoner-mother and her child." Capital University Law Review 1, 1:127-144, 1972.

Rafter, N. and E. Natalizia. "Marxist feminism: implications for criminal justice." Crime and Delinquency 27, 1 (January): 81-98, 1981.

Stanton, A. When Mothers Go To Jail. Lexington: D.C. Heath and Company, 1980.

Ward, D. and G. Kasserbaum. Women's Prison. Chicago: Aldine, 1965.

Zalba, S. Women Prisoners and Their Families. Sacramento: State of California Department of Social Welfare and Department of Corrections, 1964.

10

Women Prisoners and the Law: Which Way Will the Pendulum Swing?

Geoffrey P. Alpert

In this chapter Alpert points out that historically women offenders have been less likely than men to use the courts to secure relief from harsh prison conditions. He speculates on the reasons for this, suggesting that they undoubtedly have less access to legal services and that the structure and nature of the atmosphere in women's jails and prisons are such that women are treated as dependent and child-like, which reduces the likelihood of their turning to the courts. As you read this chapter, pay attention to the other reasons Alpert suggests that also limit women's ability to use the minimally available legal services in comparison to men.

Several amendments to the Constitution which pertain to the treatment of prisoners are discussed, including the 8th Amendment, the right of citizens to be free of cruel and unusual punishment, and the Equal Protection Clause through which women inmates might seek parity with men prisoners. Alpert concludes with a discussion of the possible directions of litigation in the coming decade. He explains how Title VII of the Civil Rights Act of 1964 could be used by women inmates in arguing their case for obtaining job training equal to that available to male inmates. This is an important area as was demonstrated earlier in this section in which Glick and Neto described how women are short-changed in training programs and work release opportunities. Finally, the chapter takes a look at the potential of an Equal Rights Amendment for women prisoners.

> The study of history is useful to the historian by teaching him his ignorance of women . . . The woman who is known only through a man is known wrong.
>
> Henry Brooks Adams *The Education of Henry Adams*

Reprinted with permission from Pergamon Press, 1981. To be published in a future issue of *Journal of Criminal Justice*. Appreciation is expressed to E. Muhammed Caleb, Harry Allen, and Ron Huff for comments on an earlier draft of this manuscript, presented at the 1980 Annual Meeting of the American Society of Criminology, San Francisco.

INTRODUCTION

Female offenders have been incarcerated in American prisons since the late 18th century. Although incarceration was for the expressed purpose of reform, it is reported that women, and often their children, were placed together with male prisoners in facilities criticized for their poor conditions (Comment, 1973). Even when prisons were successfully segregated by sex, women prisoners were supervised by male guards who often took sexual liberties with the prisoners (Hermann and Haft, 1973). In addition, prison administrators were reluctant to segregate the prisons as they did not want to lose the domestic help which the women provided (Hermann and Haft, 1973). It was not until 1873 that Indiana opened the first women's prison. Currently, each state either has facilities for women prisoners or contracts with other states to house them.

Interest in women prisoners has risen significantly during the past several years as evidenced by a major increase in the legal, sociological, and psychological literature. Women have consistently comprised about four percent of the total prison population, but until recently have received less than a proportionate share of attention (Adler and Simon, 1979). In the past women offenders have been rather passive, both in their institutional behavior and in the exercise of their legal rights. Recently, however, this passivity has diminished; a number of disturbances in women's prisons has taken place, and there has been an increase of women inmates' activity in prisoners' rights issues (Fabian, 1979).

In the 1980s, women's prisons have an opportunity to change drastically and a great deal of change could come through litigation. The purpose of this chapter is to review this last avenue of change: litigation.

LITIGATION

Prisoner litigation is a recent phenomenon. The history of prisons includes a judicial 'hands-off' doctrine by which the courts limited their own power to supervise prison administration and ability to interfere with daily rules or regulations (Palmer, 1977). In the late 1960s there was a demise of this hands-off doctrine, and correctional administrators increasingly were being held responsible for justification of restrictive regulations. In the 1980s the interests of the Court may return to a hands-off approach, but for the immediate future, legal remedies are readily available.

Although legal precedents are seemingly available to argue women prisoners' rights issues, several barriers remain in place: first, the actual precedents; second, access to the courts; and third, inclination to set the legal machinery in motion.

LEGAL PRECEDENT

When the Supreme Court paved the way for lower courts to remove the hands-off doctrine, nothing was said about the sex of the petitioner. In other words, both male and female prisoners were theoretically provided with an avenue to secure their constitutional rights, and therefore challenge the status of confinement. However, these issues are clouded by case law and corresponding differences between male and female prisoners (Fabian, 1979).

It was the Attica riot in September, 1971 that sparked a revolution in corrections which focused public attention on prisoners and prisons throughout the country (Oxberger, 1973 and Note, 1977). In fact, the Attica incident gave impetus for inmates from various prisons to file law suits with the hope of improving their conditions (Singer, 1972). Even though hundreds of petitions were filed, only a handful were filed by or on behalf of women prisoners. Consequently, the majority of the positive results of this litigation left virtually untouched the fate of women prisoners (Herman and Haft, 1973). Even the numerous class actions filed by male prisoners were brought against specific institutions and therefore did not extend to women prisoners. Since women prisoners historically have been reluctant to file law suits themselves, their specific problems continued to go relatively unnoticed (Alpert, 1978). Even when a female prisoner decides to break the mold and litigate, it is often difficult to gain access to the courts.

ACCESS TO THE COURTS

Providing women prisoners access to the courts is a noteworthy service, but the value of this or any other service depends on the extent to which it is used and by whom. Several states provide prisoners with legal assistance and all states must allow reasonable access to the courts (Alpert and Miller, 1978). In many states, however, women prisoners are left with the short end of the stick, with minimal services, while the more vocal and litigious males are provided with a disproportionate share of the services. There is a push to equalize the provision of services, but it is unknown when the women prisoners will receive the attention they deserve (Fabian, 1979).

USING THE COURTS

Having a legal problem does not necessarily mean that an individual will seek a remedy in court. Prisoners often try to solve their own problems or seek alternative solutions before going to court. In some cases administrative actions such as an inmate advocacy system, grievance committee, resident council, ombudsman, negotiated settlement, or other non-judicial action can resolve questions or problems. In other cases prisoners simply do not trust lawyers or courts and will avoid them at all costs.

Perhaps it is the nature of the women's prison and the attitudes and values it fosters that affects prisoners' behavior. We know something about the overriding influences of being incarcerated (Thomas and Petersen, 1977), and the psychological decision to invoke the legal process is a difficult one. Yet professional assistance can alleviate the problems of filing *pro se, in forma pauperis.*

It is a long road to the Courthouse both mentally and physically, but once there, positive consequences are likely to follow. However, the legal theory one chooses can determine the outcome of the case (Potts and Bronstein, 1976).

LEGAL THEORIES

Prisoners have been granted the ability to use the First, Fourth, Fifth, Sixth and Eighth Amendments to challenge prison policies. First Amendment cases include freedom of communication, access to the courts, right to receive and read materials, religion, freedom of expression, visitation, associations, dress, and hygiene. Fourth Amendment issues deal with search and seizure. Fifth Amendment claims include due process, discipline, classification, and parole. The Sixth Amendment defines the right to counsel, and Eighth Amendment cases involve cruel and unusual punishment. John Palmer (1977) has written the most comprehensive, up-to-date casebook on prisoners' rights, and has analyzed prisoners' legal status. Sharon Fabian (1979) has done a similar study of women prisoners, without the casebook addition, and reports that most prison litigation for women has involved the use of the Equal Protection Clause, the Eighth Amendment and the Civil Rights Act of 1871.[1] Because these theories are the most frequently used by women litigants, their use and the use of several theories which may be used in the future will be the focus of this chapter.

Figure 1   *Legal Theories for Women Prisoners*

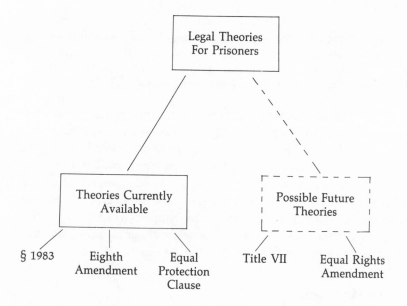

Figure 1 displays the legal theories that deserve description and analysis. The first set of theories, Section 1983 of the Civil Rights Act of 1871, the Eighth Amendment, and the Equal Protection Clause, are available to men and women prisoners, but close scrutiny of the petitioners reveals a disproportionately low representation of women.

THEORIES CURRENTLY AVAILABLE

Section 1983 Claims

The United States Supreme Court ruled in *Cooper v. Pate* [2] that prison inmates were entitled to bring suit against prison officials under the Civil Rights Act of 1871 which states that:

> Every person, who under color of any statute, ordinance, regulation, custom or usage, of any State or Territory, subjects, or causes to be subject, any citizen of the United States or any other person with the jurisdiction thereof to the deprivation of any rights, privileges, or immunities secured by the constitution and laws shall be liable to the party injured in an action at law, suit in equity, or other proper proceeding for redress.

Under this Act, prisoners, like other citizens, may sue state and local officials to redress the deprivations of federal constitutional rights. Specifically, the Court in *Preiser v. Rodriguez* [3] stated:

> [F]or state prisoners, eating, sleeping dressing, washing, working and playing are all done under the watchful eye of the state . . . what for a private citizen would be a dispute with his landlord, with his employer, with his tailor, with his neighbor or with his banker becomes for the prisoner, a dispute with the state.

Section 1983 claims can cover almost every area of prison life. Since it has such a broad spectrum of coverage, its access and use are relatively complex. An excellent discussion of prisoners' use of § 1983 and an analysis of hundreds of cases has been compiled in a University of Richmond Law Review Note (1977). More recently, William Turner has completed an empirical study of prisoner 1983 suits in federal court (Turner, 1979). His study represents a landmark analysis of what happens when prisoners sue. Although this is the most active avenue of relief for all prisoners, men prisoners continue to sue at a disproportionate rate.[4]

The Eighth Amendment

Under the protections of the Eighth Amendment, prisoners have an absolute right to be free from cruel and unusual punishment. Although it is a relatively easy matter to state these rights in theory, it is much more difficult to pursuade the courts to act on a specific situation.[5] The Eighth Amendment protects citizens' rights to human decency. It contains a "basic prohibition against inhumane treatment" protecting "nothing less than the dignity of man." The Amendment was structured to assure that the state's punishment power be exercised only within the limits of a civilized society.[6]

In 1980 there are three principal tests that are applied to the Eighth Amendment: (1) the punishment in question must not shock the collective conscience of our society; (2) the punishment must not be unnecessarily cruel; and (3) the punishment must not go beyond the legitimate goals of the state. These rather vague guidelines have given courts the power to rule on various prison conditions brought to their attention. Among specific practices held to violate the Eighth Amendment are overcrowding, physical abuse by guards and/or other inmates, certain forms of solitary confinement, most forms of corporal punishment, and inadequate medical treatment, diet, and recreation, among others (Comment, 1979).[7] As with § 1983 claims, women prisoners are underrepresented in Eighth Amendment claims.

The Equal Protection Clause

Litigation in this category includes an individual or group of individuals seeking treatment equal to that of another individual or group. While there are many cases of men prisoners seeking treatment similar to that of other men prisoners (Palmer, 1977), the more interesting use of the Equal Protection Clause as it relates to women prisoners is in pursuing parity with male prisoners in various substantive areas (DeCrow, 1974). Under this clause of the United States Constitution, women prisoners *should* be entitled to the same benefits and responsible for the same duties as male prisoners. A note in the Yale Law Journal (1973) agrees with this theory but claims that in actuality, women prisoners are not provided equal protection or due process, and in fact receive only minimal, token treatment and training.

Although the United States Supreme Court has never ruled directly on this issue, in *Reed v. Reed,*[8] and again in *Craig v. Boren,*[9] the Court has declared that sexual discrimination "must be reasonable, not arbitrary." Women prisoners may now use this clause to require states to justify any treatment different from that which is provided men prisoners. The exact meaning of what is 'reasonable' remains in the discretion of the Court. For example, maintenance of order, security, rehabilitation, fiscal responsibility and/or administrative efficiency are valid and reasonable justifications for *not* granting equal treatment of male and female prisoners (Note, 1973a and Ruback, 1975).[10] The Court has basically ruled that the small number of women prisoners does not warrant the degree of expenditure that would be required to assure parity of services and programs with men prisoners. However, the *Reed* standard can be applied when it is relatively inexpensive to duplicate services. Since the evidence from integrated prisons is not conclusive, inferences from these experiences cannot be drawn (Applebome, 1979). As it stands today, the Equal Protection Clause provides partial equality for women prisoners when the state has no justification for differential treatment. But it will remain only a partial shelter until a majority of the Supreme Court Justices agree that sex is a suspect class, worthy of full and complete recognition. If this standard should ever be more widely adopted, the state's justifications for *not* granting equal protection would be eroded.

POSSIBLE FUTURE THEORIES

Title VII

The Civil Rights Act of 1964 was intended "to achieve equality of employment opportunities."[11] It has been argued that because women prisoners do not have the same access to employment and training opportunities as men prisoners, Title VII might offer a remedy for achieving parity. Singer (1973) provides evidence and argues that prisoners would be covered under the Act. But since this issue has never been tested, Title VII will remain a theoretical avenue for prisoners until it is properly brought before the Equal Opportunity Commission or the Supreme Court. The major issue to be argued is the status of the prisoner as an employee. The Act leaves this status vague and only defines an employee as one who is employed by an employer. Is a prisoner employed? There are several different situations which must be analyzed. First, involuntary, in-prison work activities which are performed for the benefit of the state, and second, voluntary in-prison work performed for the prisoner's benefit, including pay, privileges, good time, etc. This question becomes more complex when one considers a third category, prison industries, work release or other outside labor contracts for which the prisoner receives compensation, pays taxes, etc.[12]

Unfortunately, there are also hurdles other than the employee-employer status question. The state may argue from purely economic criteria and the Equal Protection Clause that Title VII should not be applied to women prisoners. Perhaps the fatal blow to a Title VII remedy is the creation of the woman prisoner as an aggrieved party. Such a construction is necessary for this theory to work, but it may imply that a prison experience be a positive influence on post-release behavior. While this may not be a legal obligation, it is possible to argue that one is more employable after release than before release.[13] The hurdles are not insurmountable and a clever attorney with the right "facts" might be able to argue successfully that Title VII has an affirmative duty to provide job opportunity and training for women prisoners equal to those provided for men prisoners. An unexpected result might be the curtailment of programs in men's prisons, but that is a question of interpretation which is left up to the courts.

Equal Rights Amendment[14]

The proposed Equal Rights Amendment (E.R.A.) has enjoyed a lively and controversial life. In 1971 the Amendment was passed by both Houses, and seven years later when it looked as though it might die before ratification, Congress passed a three-year extension; thus, the Amendment has until March, 1982 before it must be ratified. The text in Section 1 of the proposed Amendment could remedy sex discrimination which still exists in our laws. The Section reads in part:

> Equality of rights under the law shall not be denied or abridged by the United States or any state on account of sex.

The effect of passage of the E.R.A. on women prisoners would depend solely upon the standard the Supreme Court would use in interpreting it. On the one hand, the Court could adopt one of the traditional tests which would seek to balance state interests and individual rights. These tests include the rational relation test and the strict scrutiny test.[15] On the other hand, the Court could adopt an absolutist interpretation of the E.R.A., making all differentiation by sex illegal, regardless of whether it is reasonable, beneficial, or justified. The most probable interpretation for what Courts have termed "quasi-suspect" classifications is somewhere in between the traditional tests and holds that any discrimination must be *substantially* related to important government objectives.[16] It appears that the preferred test will be this *substantial relation* test and women prisoners' rights will depend upon: (1) whether the courts accord a separate status to women prisoners; and (2) whether the states' actions are substantially related to important government objectives.

Adoption of the Amendment could mean that superior services received by men might be extended to women, but cases in which women prisoners receive the better treatment, cost and size restrictions could prohibit their extention to men prisoners. The administration of women's prisons could be run by either a "reasonableness" standard or a "fully integrated" standard.[17] In fact, it may be that the quality of all services would be reduced to the lowest common practice. Unfortunately, we can only discuss the effects on prisoners of the E.R.A. in hypothetical terms.

CONCLUSION

What we know about women's prisons and female inmates stems mostly from our knowledge of men's prisons and male prisoners (Note, 1973b). We must continue to study women's prisons and female inmates to gain knowledge of their particular and unique situations. Specifically, we need to investigate female prisoners' legal needs and remedies.

Women prisoners have the ability to litigate under a variety of legal theories. Five theories have been discussed which may provide significantly different results for men and women prisoners, or which may be available to women prisoners only. The first three, §1983, the Eighth Amendment, and the Equal Protection Clause, are available and currently used to challenge conditions in prison. If Title VII were made available to women prisoners and the Equal Rights Amendment ratified, two more legal theories could be used to gain relief. But will there be a rebirth of the hands-off doctrine, and will the pendulum swing back toward judicial non-intervention? An analysis of the latest federal court cases points toward a more conservative trend which could limit the ever-growing array of prisoners' rights. The nature and extent of these limitations can only be defined by the courts.

Most recently, the Supreme Court upheld the general conditions of the new federal jail in New York City. In *Bell v. Wolfish*[18] the Court upheld specific practices, including the housing of two prisoners in a room designed for one, visual searches of body cavities after contact visits, and a prohibition of certain books. Although this decision involved pretrial detainees, and not convicted felons, it required a showing of an intent to punish or that a challenged condition was arbitrary or served no purpose. *Wolfish* is a step backwards for the courts and may turn out to be an isolated case, or it may have set the tone for the 1980s; only time will tell. Regardless, there will be new challenges under existing theories as well as the attempt to secure new theories which will keep the prisoners' rights movement alive. And women should receive their fair share of the benefits, but only after fighting for what belongs to them.

Notes

1 42 U.S.C. § 1983.

2 378 U.S. 546 (1964).

3 411 U.S. 475, 492 (1973).

4 An analysis of the situation may reveal that women's prisons are more livable and less open to injunctive or compensatory relief.

5 In 1910 the Supreme Court in *Weems v. United States* (1910) held that the Eighth Amendment protections are not tied to a particular theory or a point in time.

6 *Trop v. Dulles,* 356 U.S. 86 (1958).

7 Most recently, a federal district court in Alabama added a new element in Eighth Amendment law by holding that the entire Alabama prison system was in violation as it constituted cruel and unusual punishment. See *Pugh v. Locke,* 406 F. Supp. 318 (M.D. Ala. 1976), *aff'd in substance, sub nom., Newman v. Alabama,* 599 F.2d 283 (5th Cir. 1977), *cert. den. in relevant part, sub nom., Alabama v. Pugh,* 98 S. Ct. 3057 (1978).

8 404 U.S. 71 (1971).

9 429 U.S. 190 (1976).

10 These reasons have been used to keep prisons racially segregated.

11 The Equal Employment Opportunity Act of 1972, U.S.C. §§ 2000e to 2000e-17 (Supp. II, 1973) (amending Civil Rights Act of 1964, Title VII, 42 U.S.C. §§ 2000e to 2000e-15 (1970)).

12 The Wage and Hour Division of the U.S. Department of Labor has issued an opinion that "a prison inmate who is required to work by or who does work for the prison within the confines of the institution while serving a sentence is *not* an employee within the meaning of the Fair Labor Standards Act." Cited in Fabian (1979). While this opinion is an influential one, it is open to challenge. In fact, prisoners' unions have sought to obtain recognition of prisoners who work for the State as "employees."

13 This may not be a traditional legal premise, but it is true that one is easier to employ when free than when incarcerated.

14 For a discussion of the E.R.A., see Conlin, 1975 and Brown et el., 1975.

15 In the "rational relation test" the Court determines the reasonableness of a *suspect*

classification by deciding whether the classification itself is a rational one, such as whether it bears a rational relationship to a proper governmental purpose. The "strict scrutiny test" is applied in situations which are thought to be violations of specific fundamental rights. For example, the "strict scrutiny" or "compelling state interest test" can be applied to state action that penalizes or unduly burdens fundamental rights.

16 See *Craig v. Boren, supra* n. 9.

17 Many pro-E.R.A. groups are hoping that courts will accept the analogy of sex and race discrimination. To their dismay, a separate but equal standard might be rejected and a fully integrated society may be required.

18 99 S. Ct. 1861 (1979).

References

Adler F. and R. Simon. The Criminality of Deviant Women. Dallas: Houghton Mifflin Co., 1979.

Alpert, G. "Prisoners' right of access to courts: planning for legal aid." 51 Wash. Law Rev. 653 (July), 1976.

————. The determinants of prisoners' decisions to seek legal aid." 4 New England J. on Prison Law 309 (Spring), 1978.

————, and N. Miller. "Legal delivery systems to prisoners." 4 The Justice System Journal 9 (Fall), 1978.

Applebome, P. "Life and love in a coed prison." 7 Student Lawyer 20 (February), 1979.

Brown, B., T. Emerson, G. Folk, and A. Freeman. "The equal rights amendment: a constitutional basis for equal rights for women." 80 Yale Law J. 871 (April), 1971.

Christianson, S. "Corrections law development: how unions affect prison administration." 15 Crim. Law Bul. 238 (May-June), 1979.

Comment. "Women's prisons: laboratories for penal reform." 1 Wisc. Law Rev. 210, 1973.

Comment. "Eighth amendment challenges to conditions of confinement: state prison reform by federal judicial decree." 18 Washburn Law J. 288 (Winter), 1975.

Conlin, J. "Equal protection versus equal rights amendment—where are we now?" 24 Drake Law Rev. 259 (Winter), 1975.

DeCrow, K. Sexist Justice. New York: Vintage Books, 1974.

Fabian, S. "Toward the best interests of women prisoners: is the system working?" 6 New England J. on Prison Law (Fall), 1979.

Hermann, M. and M. Haft. Prisoners' Rights Sourcebook. New York: Clark Boardman Co., 1973.

Noblit, G. and G. Alpert. "Advocacy and rehabilitation in womens' prisons." 2 Law and Policy Quarterly (April), 1979.

Note. "Sex discrimination in the criminal law: the effect of the equal rights amendment." 11 Am. Crim. Law Rev. (Winter), 1973a.

Note. "The sexual segregation of American prisons." 82 Yale Law J. (May), 1973b.

Note. "A review of prisoners' rights litigation under 42 U.S.C. § 1983." 11 Rich. Law Rev. 4, 1977.

Oxberger, R. "Revolution in corrections." 22 Drake Law Rev. (January), 1973.

Palmer, J. Constitutional Rights of Prisoners. Cincinnati: Anderson Publishing Co., 1977.

Potts, J. and A. Bronstein. Prisoners' Self-Help Litigation Manual. Lexington, MA: Lexington Books, 1976.

Ruback, P. "The sexually integrated prison: a legal and policy evaluation." 3 Am. J. of Crim. Law 3, 1975.

Singer, L. "Women in the correctional process." 11 Am Crim. Law Rev. 2, 1973.

Thomas, C. and D. Petersen. Prison Organization and Inmate Subcultures. Indianapolis: Bobbs-Merrill Co., 1977.

Turner, W. "When prisoners sue: a study of prisoner § 1983 suits in federal court." 92 Harv. Law Rev. (January), 1979.

PART 2

Women Victims of Crime

Introduction

Andrew Karmen

The subject of this section, how and why women are victimized by men, is surrounded by controversy. In the process of examining the issues and reviewing the data, only the strongest arguments and clearest examples will be presented to support these five themes:

— that sexual harassment, wife-beating, and rape are at the center of a heavy crime burden which falls most directly on women with social disadvantages due to their class, race, or marital status;
— that the criminal justice system and related social service agencies are not effectively protecting or assisting victimized women;
— that an additional source of trouble for victimized women is the widespread ideology which blames them for their misfortunes;
— that the fundamental institutions upon which this social system is built are the root causes of the crime problem women face;
— that victimized women and their support groups are becoming an important force within a movement that is making significant progress in the struggle for social justice.

VICTIMIZATION AS AN ADDITIONAL BURDEN

According to public opinion polls, women in the United States are becoming increasingly concerned about their safety, they are much more worried about the crime problem than men, and they take more precautions to avoid trouble (Riger, Gordon, and Le Bailly, 1978). Yet crime statistics compiled from reports received by the police and from surveys of thousands of households across the country show that men are much more likely than women to be the victims of most serious crimes. This apparent lack of correspondance between the high level of fear among women and the relatively low level of actual incidents has been explained in several ways. Inordinate concern about crime has been attributed (1) to the presumably widespread personality traits of passivity and dependence (which stimulate fears) that girls develop during their sex-role socialization; (2) to the relative lack of strength and experience in self-defense of girls and women; and (3) to the effectiveness of precautions which lower exposure to risks while at the same time heighten the awareness of threats and dangers.

But there are different explanations as well. Women are very worried about crime because there is a growing tide of victimization and violence directed against them and their families; there is a heightened consciousness about the different forms these attacks can take; and there is a whole spectrum of male versus female criminality that nearly exclusively burdens girls and women—sexual harassment at work (only recognized recently as an offense), purse snatchings in the street, beatings at home, and rapes by acquaintances, even intimates, as well as strangers.

These acts of hostility and intimidation, which have an unmistakable character of male antagonism directed at the "opposite sex," are disturbingly routine and probably shape women's fears more than the highly publicized rampages of a notorious woman-hating "Jack the Ripper," "Boston Strangler," or "Son of Sam." It is the common, familiar incidents which hold back the progress of women and bolster the status quo of gross inequality between the sexes.

Victimization is just another problem women face that can mar everyday life or thwart long-range plans, something else that can suddenly "go wrong," along with unexpected lay-offs, accidents, illnesses, or unwanted pregnancies. Although crime, especially street crime, bothers everyone, the impact is felt most acutely by those who are already afflicted by other social handicaps and economic hardships. But this is not surprising. Security—avoiding, deflecting, or repelling criminal attack—is and always has been one of the most prized privileges of the wealthy and powerful. The problems posed by criminals, like other social problems, e.g., unemployment, inadequate health care, inferior schooling, and pollution, fall heaviest on low income persons rather than on the affluent; minorities more than the white majority; non-married individuals more than married couples; younger people more than middle-aged adults; and city dwellers more than suburban or rural folk. Taking these other variables into account, some categories of women face much higher risks than opposite categories of men.

Robbery and Purse Snatching

Robbery is a frightening street crime involving confrontation, intimidation, and sometimes assault, usually by a stranger. Nationwide, men are the victims twice as often as women. But women, especially older women, were the favored targets of robbers who accosted victims in streets, alleys, elevators, and hallways (Conklin, 1972; Aceituno and Matchett, 1973).

Purse snatchings carried out through confrontations, with threats and force, are classified as robberies; otherwise, these thefts are categorized as personal larcenies with contact. Only about 40 percent of all purse snatchings are reported to the police. Of those which are personal larcenies, black and hispanic women outnumbered white victims by a ratio of 2 or even 3 to 1. Divorced or separated women lost their handbags to thieves and robbers five times as often as married women. The pocketbooks of the very poorest women (with incomes of less than $3000 a year) were snatched more than three times as frequently as those of the more affluent (with incomes of over $25,000 a year) (U.S. Bureau of Justice Statistics, 1978).

Sexual Harassment at Work

The majority of working women have experienced repeated unwanted, objectionable, and offensive sexually oriented comments, looks, suggestions, or physical contacts (squeezes, pats, pinches, embraces) on the job from male colleagues and supervisors, according to recent surveys seeking to establish the scope of sexual harassment (WWUI, 1975 and Safran, 1976). Although most of the victims ignored or endured the incidents rather than complained about them, the overwhelming response was that such unwelcomed advances constituted a serious problem. Sexual harassment victims frequently felt diminished ambition in their careers, decreased job satisfaction, and impaired work performance, as well as embarrassment, guilt, and anger.

Although women of all ages, in all lines of work and of varying marital status reported incidents of harassment, one pattern stood out: women in the lower paid, less prestigious jobs tended to be subjected to the more severe forms of harassment that involved physical contact, whereas women in more desirable occupations generally encountered mostly verbal abuse.

Wife-Beating

Spouse abuse has been a serious and widespread problem throughout history, but only recently has it received the attention it merits. Cases in which the wife is battered by the husband are estimated to total between 1.8 million (Straus, 1978) and 3.5 million (Weiss, 1980a) a year.

Wife-beating is probably the most common form of violence in the U.S. and in the world. According to a nationwide victimization survey, husbands or ex-husbands were responsible for about 16 percent of all the assaults experienced by married women, 28 percent of the attacks on divorced women, and 55 percent of the beatings of separated women. Spouse abuse was not associated with race but was correlated with class:

poor women were beaten much more often by their mates than middle-income or affluent women. Domestic violence incidents were more likely than other types of assaults to result in injuries which required medical attention and loss of work time. A little more than half of all cases of family violence were reported by the female victims to the authorities (Gaquin, 1978).

Rape

Rapes and related sexual assaults are acts of violence in which desires for power (to dominate, subordinate, control) and feelings of hostility (contempt, anger) are vented on the victims, transforming them from persons into objects, and often plunging them into a "rape crisis syndrome." The initial acute phase which follows a sexual attack lasts about two or three weeks and is marked by sleeplessness, nausea, tension headaches, fear, fury, embarrassment, and self-recrimination. The second phase of personality reorganization can last much longer, producing nightmares, defensive reactions, phobias, and strains in the victim's sex life and her relationships with men in general (Burgess and Holmstrom, 1977).

Only about one half of all rapes are reported to the authorities. The reasons given by victims, in order of importance, for non-reporting were: fear of retaliation, especially if the offender was known to the victim; fear of hospital, police, and court procedures during which the victim's version of the events will be challenged and her charges disbelieved; fears of teenagers about their parents' negative reactions; fears about the unsupportive or violent and vengeful reactions of husbands or boyfriends; and feelings of embarrassment and self-blame which lead the victim to assume she has no legal recourse (Belden, 1979).

For every completed rape there are more than two attempted rapes in which the victim is able to thwart the attacker's aims. Nationwide, between one and two females for every 1000 in the population are raped or are the victims of an attempted rape every year. But the risks of rape vary greatly by age, race, marital status, and income. The greatest dangers are faced by 16 to 24 year olds, who are three times more likely to be singled out for attack than women or girls of other ages. Black women are between two and three times more likely to be raped than white women. Separated and divorced women are victimized twelve times as often as married women; women who were never married face six times the risk as married women. The desperately poor (with incomes of $3000 or less) are raped four times as often as middle-income and affluent women (U.S. Bureau of Justice Statistics, 1978). The profile of the most frequent rape victim is therefore a young woman, divorced or separated, black, and poverty stricken.

Except for a brief interlude in the late 1940s, the trend in rape statistics has been upward ever since the FBI began compiling reports from the nation's police departments in 1933. The rate of increase for incidents of rape has been greater than for the other crimes of violence, murder, robbery, assault, which have also been on the rise in recent decades (Bowker, 1978; 1981).

THE CRIMINAL JUSTICE SYSTEM
AS PART OF THE PROBLEM

There is a long-standing controversy over how the criminal justice system is supposed to function as opposed to how it actually works. Officially, the criminal justice system's mandate is to provide equal protection under the law and to safeguard the lives, rights, and property of all citizens. But in reality the police departments, prosecutorial divisions, regulatory agencies, judicial bodies, and prison systems consistently act in the interests of the wealthy and powerful to the detriment of other classes and groups. For example, throughout U.S. history, racial minorities have found the criminal justice system to be an obstacle to their advancement in their struggle for equality. Even today, the system fails to deliver its promised services to victims of racism, whether Ku Klux Klan terrorism or more subtle discrimination in the form of real estate blockbusting and bank and insurance company redlining. In a parallel manner, victimized women demanding their rights to be protected against sexism in its many guises have discovered that the criminal justice system is often part of the problem rather than the solution. Victims of sexual harassment, wife-beating, and rape find that instead of being treated with care they must battle the men at the helm of the criminal justice system over priorities, policies, and practices.

A critical evaluation of the laws prohibiting rape reveals that they are not intended, and never functioned, to guarantee the physical integrity, peace of mind, and freedom of movement of women. The choice of words like "ravaged" and "despoiled" in earlier legal codes to describe the condition of rape victims reflected very clearly and frankly the judgments men made about women as the property of their husbands or fathers who lost market value if they were "violated." Contemporary rape laws reinforce traditional outlooks about sexual mores, standards of conduct, and appropriate sex-based roles (Le Grande, 1973:921).

Rape victims today frequently complain that they are mistreated by representatives of the criminal justice system; they receive what victimologists call "a second wound." Detectives and prosecutors often act as if the victim is lying unless she can establish her credibility as an effective com-

plaining witness. Judges and juries must be convinced of her total innocence of any complicity and of her good character and reputation before
they are willing to consider her charges against the defendant. Since many
victims are reluctant to put themselves on trial, and undergo polygraph
tests, harsh interrogation, and demeaning cross examinations by defense
attorneys in court, many sexual assaults go unreported or unprosecuted.
These victims are then castigated for letting dangerous rapists roam free
to strike again; yet the motives of those women who come forward and
identify themselves and their assailants are immediately suspect.

The criminal justice system puts battered women into a similar bind.
Those who fail to invite the authorities to invade the sanctity of their home
are dismissed for being unwilling to change or to leave an unhealthy
relationship in order to accept help; but victims who press charges and vow
never to return to their wife-beating husbands are open to condemnation
for "breaking up the family." Police who respond to domestic disturbance
calls tend to take the man's side, urge on-the-spot-reconciliation, and
discourage the victim from having the offender arrested. Prosecutors pressure victims to drop charges or to take matters to family court. And the
sad fact is that, because the police and the courts fail to enforce protection
and vacate orders, repeated beatings occur.

Sexual harassment victims are not just transferred, denied promotions,
or demoted, they are usually fired or driven to quit for making complaints
or rejecting advances and ultimatums. Only after the damage is done can
they seek help in the form of unemployment insurance benefits or lawsuits
in federal court for compensation and reinstatement. But the burden is on
the victims to prove that they lost their jobs for "good cause" and that the
harassment is the sex-based discrimination as prohibited by the 1964 Civil
Rights Act (Evans, 1978). The odds are also against the victims because
regulatory and judicial bodies are reluctant to challenge managerial authority over workplace relationships. Here too, a dilemma arises for victims. If they do not complain, they suffer humiliation and downward
mobility; if they do make an issue out of their on-the-job experiences, they
can be labeled "troublemakers," which also undermines their careers.

These institutionalized anti-female biases in the workings of the criminal justice system push harassment, wife-beating, and rape victims in the
direction of dealing with public issues as if they were private matters best
coped with through personal solutions. At the same time, the ineffective-
ness of the criminal justice system as a means of protecting the safety and
rights of females encourages the impression too many offenders have that
it is "open season" on girls and women. As a result, for all three of these
crimes there is a high degree of non-reporting, a low rate of arrests, a high
rate of dropped charges, a low rate of prosecutions, an even lower rate of

convictions, and a tendency to stigmatize the victim and exonerate the man found guilty through a light sentence.

But crime victims and their allies are trying to reform some of the most abusive practices of the criminal justice system. For example, greater sensitivity for the rights of rape victims has led to the imposition of strict limits on the circumstances under which testimony and evidence about the woman's past sexual conduct are admissable in most state and all federal trials. Greater concern about the rape victim's ordeal has inspired improvements in police investigation practices and hospital emergency room procedures. More rape victims are suing their attackers in civil court for monetary damages for pain and suffering in addition to prosecuting them in criminal court.

Battered women and their support groups have sued police departments in civil court to force them to take the crime more seriously and to train their officers to respond more effectively. State laws have been reformed to make emergency protective orders more obtainable and enforceable and to permit victims to seek reparations from their estranged mates.

Sexual harassment victims and their advocates are pressuring government agencies such as the federal Equal Employment Opportunity Commission, state Fair Employment Practices Offices, and municipal Human Rights Commissions to develop guidelines, rules, grievance mechanisms, and due process procedures to provide victims with more remedies. They are also seeking greater contract protections through their trade unions.

Some of these efforts to make the criminal justice system and ancillary agencies more responsive to the needs of crime victims have provoked backlashes. For example, at a Senate hearing about sexual harassment of federal employees, ultra-conservative, anti-feminist organizer Phyllis Schlafly argued that there really is not much of a problem, and that new remedies permit unscrupulous individuals to file mischievous claims that penalize innocent employers. She asserted that virtuous women are seldom accosted by unwelcomed sexual propositions because men hardly ever ask sexual favors of women from whom the certain answer is "No!", and therefore the women must have been asking for such responses, perhaps by communicating secret desires through their body language (New York Times, 1981:22). Similarly, the arch-conservative, religiously fundamentalist Moral Majority organization led a successful lobbying drive in Congress to kill what they considered to be an "anti-family" legislative proposal—a bill to allocate federal funds to help pay for emergency shelters for battered women and their children who fled from their violent mates (Weiss, 1980b:2719).

The common denominator in both these reactions to the initiatives to help victimized women is the belief that in some manner and to some degree the injured parties are undeserving of help—in fact, they are partly to blame.

THE MISTAKEN BELIEF THAT
THE VICTIM IS USUALLY TO BLAME

The possibility of victim-blaming inevitably arises whenever the causes of crime are examined, aggravating factors identified, and actual incidents reconstructed. Victim-blaming is a particularly familiar practice which is often invoked to explain why women are victimized, e.g., see Sokoloff, 1980, in terms of occupational victimization, although the same logic is applied to many other crimes such as auto theft (Karmen, 1979).

In certain incidents victims may share some responsibility with offenders for crimes if through carelessness they make the criminals' tasks easier (facilitation); if they single themselves out for trouble by acting in a rash manner (precipitation); and worst of all, if they incite otherwise law-abiding people to attack them (provocation).

The trouble with victim-blaming, though, is that the exception tends to be mistaken for the rule. Almost automatically the charge is voiced that there is something "wrong" with the victim, that the problem lies in her attitudes or her behavior. The burden of responsibility is shifted from the offenders, and the social system that produces them, to the injured parties; they have to prove that they are "bona fide" victims before they are considered deserving of aid.

Just as the threat of punishment is intended to make would-be criminals "think twice" before breaking the law, the public humiliation caused by victim-blaming forces would-be victims to "think twice" and take precautions. Victim-blamers feel they can prevent incidents by compelling victims to behave "properly" since it has proven so difficult to curtail the lawlessness of offenders.

For cases of sexual harassment at work, victim-blaming takes two forms: (1) faulting women for imagining insults and affronts where none exist (women who complain are said to be "super-sensitive" and guilty of "overreacting" to bouts of good-natured teasing and to affectionate pats and squeezes that other women would find complimentary, even enjoyable); and (2) condemning women for instigating trouble in the office or on the assembly line by flirting with their co-workers or bosses, and using their sex appeal to advance their careers.

When the crime is wife-beating, it is usually the battered woman who is blamed for transforming her mild-mannered husband into a raving brute. Either she is responsible because of her nagging or belittling of him (especially when he is beset by financial problems), or she is at fault because of her playing the role of the "perfect victim" by being submissive. Such wives are also often accused of harboring deepseated masochistic tendencies, feeding on guilt, savoring punishment, and gaining satisfaction from pain.

Victim-blaming arguments are the prime causes of the traditional misconceptions about rapes. The "personal accountability doctrine" demands of the victims that they review their own behavior before, during, and after the assault to figure out what they said, did, or even wore that brought about their own downfall. In the quest for evidence of shared responsibility, no stone is left unturned. The motives of the victims for reporting the crimes are scrutinized as thoroughly as the motives of the offenders for committing the assaults. It is alleged that some women secretly desire to be ravished, overpowered, and manhandled, despite their protestations to the contrary. Adolescent girls, for example, are blamed for being foolhardy, even willing victims who blithely enter into risky situations permeated with sexual overtones and fraught with danger, such as hitchhiking rides with strange men or drinking heavily and acting seductively in the company of a casual acquaintance. Victim-blaming explanations for rape are especially misleading because they portray the act as one of sexuality, lust, or passion, rather than an outburst of violence, aggression, domination, hostility, and humiliation (Schwendinger and Schwendinger, 1974).

Sexual harassment, wife-beating, and rape are all crimes in which male offenders try to exert control over female victims. But victim-blaming de-politicizes and personalizes acts which are inherently connected to the distribution of power and the legitimacy of authority, and thereby obscures the sources and consequences of crimes against women. Although individual offenders may not be consciously aware of the long-term consequences of their aggressive acts, sexual crimes make their victims feel more powerless and dependent than they did before, more at the mercy of men for support and protection, more subordinate, more oppressed, more ripe for exploitation, and more in need of empowerment and liberation. Certainly, stifling precautions and unfair blame are what these women need least.

THE INSTITUTIONAL SOURCES
OF CRIMES AGAINST WOMEN

"Institutional analysis" is an alternative to criminal-blaming and victim-blaming. This approach to examining and explaining crime arises from the fundamental principle of sociology that people are to a large extent products of their environments and that their beliefs and behaviors are profoundly shaped by social forces beyond the ability of any single person to escape or control. Individual responsibility and personal accountability do exist, but only within the context of a larger social, economic, political, and cultural framework. Criminals as well as victims are created by the ways certain key social institutions are organized.

Criminal-blamers and victim-blamers take a nearsighted view of the problem of crime and "solutions," focusing entirely on the leading actors in the drama while totally ignoring the social structure. Although the details of the crime are important, and the motives and responses of both parties need to be reconstructed, such a limited, interactionist approach fails to grasp larger patterns, trends, and themes. Instead of putting either the criminal or the victim on "trial," an institutional analysis proceeds by questioning whether the offender's actions were genuinely "deviant" (highly unusual and in violation of prevailing norms) and by asking whether certain social, economic, or political arrangements, rules, and relationships could be responsible for the crime. An institutional analysis in search of the causes of crimes against women must probe power structures, codes of conduct, child-raising practices, sources of tension and conflict, rights of ownership to wealth and income, competing social movements and interest groups, and the determinants of class, race, and sex-based discrimination. Such an analysis recognizes the necessity to challenge what exists and to see if the quality of life can be improved.

An institutional analysis of sexual harassment at work recognizes, for instance, that given the widespread occurrence of this type of abuse, offenders must be average males rather than isolated deviants. Such an analysis also examines the consequences of sexual harassment to explain its occurrence. Sexual abuse in the workplace wears down its victims and interferes with their job performance, and thus ultimately undermines the economic security of female workers. It maintains job segregation by sex; women who break out from "women's work" and enter non-traditional job areas are often sexually harassed back out by co-workers and supervisors. In short, sexual harassment is caused by the inequality between employers and workers, and the inequality between men and women. This type of abuse can be seen, then, as a mechanism of group control of women by men aimed at driving victims out of desirable jobs (Farley, 1979).

Another way to explain sexual harassment from an institutional perspective is to focus on the consequences of male expectations regarding the "female role." Men who were raised to believe that a woman's place is in the home find women at work a disturbing challenge to their stereotypes and react aggressively to remind the victims of their "proper" place in life. Their propositions and passes are symbolic warnings to females that they are encroaching on male preserves, that they are entering a "man's world" at their peril. A related explanation centers on the fact that most men cannot fulfill their dreams of material success, and exercise little if any genuine control over their work. Out of frustration, these men turn to harassment to compensate for their feelings of powerlessness on the job. They try to offset the damage to their self-assurance of maleness in one realm by a "manly" performance in another arena—badgering women (AASC, 1981).

An institutional analysis of wife-beating within marriage proceeds from a recognition that both the battered woman and her violent mate are victims of an inequitable set of roles which places the two of them on a collision course. The division of domestic labor into dominant and submissive roles, with male perogatives and female duties within the traditional patriarchal family simply invites abuse when the "head of the household" feels threatened. Protectors and providers too easily can transform into tyrants and victimizers; dependents are ready-made victims and tempting targets for displaced aggression and misplaced blame. In a society controlled by giant corporations and huge government bureaucracies, most men wield no real political or economic clout. But the patriarchal system bestows upon all males special rights and privileges which can be exercised within the family as a source of power. Domination over one's wife and children is offered to men as a substitute for real autonomy (Schechter, 1979).

Wife-beating represents a desperate and extreme, but until recently permissible and not deviant, attempt by a husband to maintain his "rightful" authority over his wife, and "discipline" her as he sees fit. Although this privilege is no longer granted to a husband by law, a cultural legacy supporting male dominance remains. It is best expressed in the marriage vows, sanctioned by religion and the state, that a wife should "love, honor, and obey" her husband; that is, care for him, look up to him, and do as he commands or else he will use his "hitting license" (Straus, 1978; Dobash and Dobash, 1977).

Rapes and other sexual assaults are not solely the deeds of psychopathic strangers. When acquaintance rapes are taken into account, these sex crimes can be considered as exaggerated forms of typical male-female interactions. Raping is an outgrowth of "normal" and culturally approved patterns of behavior, which emanate from the deeply entrenched sexism that pervades everyday life. Rapes and other sexual assaults are acts of violence, terror, and conquest more than they are crimes of lust, passion, and desire. They represent gestures of disdain, even hatred, certainly not love (Russell, 1975).

Male supremacy is maintained in part by the ideology of male chauvinism. Located within this set of beliefs is the cult of male virility with its myths, values, and expectations which justify the treatment of females with contempt. The drive for success, the emphasis on winning, the urge to control, and the willingness to command respect through force are all regarded as strictly masculine traits and as unquestionable virtues. Men who freely exude independence from female "entanglements," toughness towards challengers, and aggression towards opponents are looked upon as super-masculine. An important facet of their sense of self, and of the average male's feelings of achievement, is derived from the sexual conquest of females. Females are viewed as objects to be cynically manipulated and exploited, and femininity is caricatured as weakness, passivity, dependency, vulnerability, and subservience. In male supremacist thinking, masculine qualities are the highest ideals while feminine traits are pitiful, even despicable handicaps more deserving of violation than chivalrous protection. Females, as the "opposite sex," become defined as legitimate targets for scorn and wrath because of their "otherness" (Hills, 1980).

In a society based on the pursuit of profit, sexual satisfaction has become a commodity to be bought and sold. Women are put in the role of sellers, and males act as eager consumers. Men of wealth and power can use subtle coercion to get what they want, although they have been known to resort to force. But most arrested rapists are drawn from the ranks of those males (usually young, often poor) who do not have much purchasing power in the sexual marketplace. They believe they have a right to take what females are unwilling to share with them. To retaliate, these males defy convention and employ violence to show their disdain for the entire barter system and their lowly place within its hierarchial structure (Clark and Lewis, 1978).

When seen within a power and conflict perspective, each rape is another skirmish in the "battle of the sexes" surrounding the rise or fall of male supremacy. Rapes are terrorist acts and rapists are the shock troops in behalf of patriarchy. These violent victimizations serve, as other crimes against women, to remind them of their "appropriate" place in society—beneath men—just as the lynchings of blacks by whites in the south carried the message "accept your lot in life—don't step out of line." Whether rapes are random incidents of indiscriminate misogyny or selective reprisals directed at "uppity females," these crimes underscore how important it is that women struggle for self-determination beyond the "safety" of the home and the protection of law-abiding men (Brownmiller, 1975).

CRIME VICTIMS AS PART OF THE MOVEMENT FOR SOCIAL JUSTICE

It is widely conceded that the current levels of aggression directed by men against women are intolerable. But three very different courses of action are often proposed: (1) to place major emphasis on identifying, capturing, and convicting violators, so they can be rehabilitated and returned to society; (2) to focus the primary thrust of victimization prevention towards educating the targets themselves so they will not facilitate, precipitate, or provoke crimes in the future; and (3) to concentrate on empowering the victims so that, acting in their own behalf, they can effectively uproot the institutional sources of male dominance and economic insecurity which seem to instigate men to victimize women.

The first strategy is unlikely to succeed because it is based on the mistaken assumption that the offenders are deviants who need treatment while the institutions of society are sound and essentially blameless. The second strategy dramatizes the unfair one-sidedness of its victim-blaming premises. The entire burden of change falls on the victims themselves. Since getting into trouble is presumed to be the victim's fault, then preventing incidents is also her responsibility. Victim-blamers instruct women that it is their obligation to safeguard their own security and cut the risks they face. Their well-intentioned tips and pointers invariably place severe restrictions on women's activities just at a time when feminists are revealing how circumscribed the options and life-chances of girls and women already are.

To shield themselves from sexual harassment, women are advised to adopt a cool guarded manner, learn to ignore remarks, discourage advances and avoid carefully set "traps." They are told to dress modestly and to behave in a way that cannot be misinterpreted as seductive.

To reduce the dangers of being beaten, wives are counseled to accomodate themselves to their husbands' demands and practice expressing their own wishes in non-threatening, non-antagonistic ways.

Thus, victim-blamers emphasize the importance of internalizing a long list of commonsense "do's and don't's" in order to minimize the dangers of rape. Exposure to situations of extreme vulnerability and to untrustworthy men must be avoided at all costs, even if it means that the potential victims must forego the freedom of movement that men take for granted.

As long as sexual harassment, wife-beating, and rape remain acute problems, taking precautions can reduce risks. But victimization prevention strategies may just deflect offenders from well-prepared and privileged potential victims to unprepared and disadvantaged female targets. Genuine crime-prevention strategies can only be based on an analysis of the institutions responsible for the problems and on a willingness to fundamentally restructure the arrangements, roles, rules, and ideologies that goad offenders into action. Victims and their support groups must take the lead in initiating these charges.

The most conscious and consistent champions of the female crime-victims' cause have been feminists in the women's liberation movement.

They have forced the public to confront the long-neglected issues of harassment, battering, and rape through the vehicles of "speak-outs," where victims come forward and testify, conferences, rallies, and demonstrations in support of women who fought back and got in legal trouble for their retaliatory violence. Convinced that "the personal is political," these groups have helped victims realize that what appear as private troubles are really concrete manifestations of larger social problems that burden millions of others and require sustained unified actions to correct.

Women's groups have adopted a strategy of empowering the victims (PREAP, 1976 and Rose, 1977) as the best short-run defense so that they will be less vulnerable to exploitation and attack in the future. A first step is to restore their self-confidence and to transform their self-destructive guilt feelings into more positive energy by thoroughly rejecting the ideology of victim-blaming. Instead of asking the victims to adjust, adapt, or even acquiesce, women are encouraged to shed any "victim mentality" or "learned helplessness" they may have developed (Walker, 1978). Women are currently engaged in assertiveness training workshops, self-defense drills, and marches to "Take Back the Night" (to be able to walk about after dark in safety, free from harassment). Rather than abandon the victims to whatever private resources they may be able to draw upon, pro-victim advocates have also put pressure on criminal justice agencies to meet their obligations and to be more responsive to their clients. To fill in the gaps in the existing social service system, alternative institutions and self-help projects have been initiated—support groups for harassed workers, refuges for battered women and their children, and crisis centers to help rape victims at the time of their greatest needs.

Men have been enlisted into the fight to stop the victimization of women. Groups of batterers and groups of prisoners convicted of rape are being engaged in consciousness-raising groups focusing on the limitations sexist ideology places on the development of men as well as women. A new generation of parents are raising their children to transcend the confines of rigid sex-based roles. In particular, alternative models of masculinity that do not rest on the subjugation of females as a sign of manhood are the subject of experimentation. These new visions of equality and authentic individuality reject the misogynistic elements of the old definitions embedded in such diverse settings as orthodox religious teachings, sexist fairy tales and toys, and traditional child-rearing practices. And of course, the liberation of women requires their emancipation from total responsibility for housework and childcare, and their full participation in the construction of an economy free from exploitation.

There is a growing movement for change, dedicated to reducing the victimization of women, especially in the forms of sexual harassment, wife-beating, and rape. Male dominance and economic injustice have been identified as the root causes of these crimes and related social problems. Despite the current wave of violence and the emergence of a backlash, there are unmistakeable signs that the tide is turning.

Are women the "weaker sex," are they victimized simply because they are easy targets for sexual abuse and discriminatory practices? Or are they victims of a society that has fostered stereotypical notions of what a woman "should be"—and should remain? The chapters that follow in Part 2 represent a number of perspectives on female victimization, with a special emphasis on the causes and consequences of crimes against women. In addition, many of the chapters discuss efforts to eliminate both the blatant acts of aggression committed against women and the more subtle "crimes" which serve to maintain a male-dominated society.

How the criminal justice system is part of the problem for battered women is analyzed by Dorie Klein and Del Martin; rape victims are discussed in the selections by Klein, Gerald Robin, and Susan Griffin; prostitutes are the topic of discussion in Jennifer James' and Dorothy Bracey's chapters; incestuously assaulted girls are the subjects of Sandra Butler's chapter; the problem of pornographic violence against all women is Irene Diamond's subject in Chapter 18; and employed women who are sexually harassed on the job is the focus of Chapter 19 by Catharine MacKinnon.

Dorie Klein, Del Martin, and Susan Griffin delve deeply into the intimate connections between patriarchy, economic exploitation, and crime. Catharine MacKinnon touches on these issues when she argues that "[w]omen who protest sexual harassment at work are resisting economically enforced sexual exploitation." Keep this in mind when in the next section of this sourcebook, Part 3, sexual harassment of women employed by the criminal justice system is explicitly discussed by Cheryl Bowser Peterson and implicitly referred to in other readings.

References

AASC (Alliance Against Sexual Coercion) "Sexual harassment and coercion: violence against women." Aegis (March-April): 18-19, 1981.

Aceituno, T. and M. Matchett. "Street robbery victims in Oakland." University of California, Davis: The Center on Administration of Criminal Justice, 1973.

Belden, L. "Why women do not report sexual assault." Aegis (Sept.-Oct.): 38-43, 1979.

Bowker, L. Women, Crime and The Criminal Justice System. Lexington, MA: Lexington Books, 1978.

_____. Women and Crime in America. New York: MacMillan, 1981.

Brownmiller, S. Against Our Will. New York: Simon and Schuster, 1975.

Bularzik, M. "Sexual harassment at the workplace: historical notes." 12 Radical America 4:25-44, 1978.

Burgess, A. and L. Holmstrom. "Rape trauma syndrome," in D. Chappell, R. Geis, and G. Geis (eds.), Forcible Rape—The Crime, The Victim, and The Offender. New York: Columbia University Press, 1977.

Clark, L. and D. Lewis. Rape: The Price of Coercive Sexuality. Toronto: The Woman's Press, 1978.

Conklin, J. Robbery and the Criminal Justice System. New York: J.B. Lippincott, 1972.

Dobash, R.E. and R.P. Dobash. "Love, honor and obey: institutional ideologies and the struggle for battered women." 1 Contemporary Crises (June-July): 403-415, 1977.

Editors, New York Times. "The mud slinger." The New York Times, (April 26, Sec. 4): 22E, 1981.

Evans, L. "Sexual harassment: women's hidden occupational hazard," in J. Chapman and M. Gates (eds.), The Victimization of Women. Beverly Hills: Sage, 1978.

Farley, L. "Response to sexual shakedown review." Aegis (Jan.-Feb.): 24-25, 1979.

Gaquin, D. "Spouse abuse—data from the national crime survey." 2 Victimology 3: 632-634, 1978.

Hammer House. "Combat sexual harassment on the job." Aegis (May-June): 24-28, 1979.

Hills, S. Demystifying Social Deviance. New York: McGraw Hill, 1980.

Karmen, A. "Victim facilitation: the case of auto theft." 4 Victimology 4: 361-370, 1979.

Le Grande, C. "Rape and rape laws: sexism in society and the law." 61 Calif. Law Rev., 1973.

PREAP (Prison Research Education Action Program). Instead of Prisons. Geneseo, New York: PREAP, 1976.

Riger, S., M. Gordon, and R. Le Bailly. "Women's fear of crime: from blaming to restricting the victim." 3 Victimology 4: 274-284, 1978.

Rose, V. "Rape as a social problem: a by-product of the feminist movement." 25 Social Problems (October): 75-89, 1977.

Russell, D. The Politics of Rape. New York: Stein and Day, 1975.

Safran, C. "What men do to women on the job: a shocking look at sexual harassment." 148 Redbook Magazine 149 (November): 217-223, 1976.

Schechter, S. "Towards an analysis of the persistence of violence against women in the home." Aegis (July-August): 46-56, 1979.

Schwendinger, H. and J. Schwendinger. "Rape myths: in legal, theoretical and everyday practice." 1 Crime and Social Justice (Spring-Summer): 18-26, 1974.

Sokoloff, N.J. Between Money and Love: The Dialectics of Women's Home and Market Work. New York: Praeger, 1980.

Straus, M. "Wife-beating: how common and why? 2 Victimology, 1978.

U.S. Department of Justice, Bureau of Justice Statistics. Criminal Victimization in the United States, 1978: A National Crime Survey Report. Washington, D.C.: Government Printing Office, 1980.

Walker, L. Battered Women. New York: Harper & Row, 1978.

Weiss, L. "Senate passes domestic violence bill, 46-41." Congressional Quarterly Weekly Report, September 13, 2718, 1980a.

_____. "Moral majority leads lobby blitz on bill." Congressional Quarterly Report, September 13, 2719, 1980b.

WWUI (Working Women United Institute). Sexual Harassment on the Job: Results of a Preliminary Survey. Ithaca, New York, 1975.

11

Violence Against Women: Some Considerations Regarding Its Causes and Its Elimination

Dorie Klein

In this chapter Klein deals with several overriding issues concerning violence against women—its causes and some possible remedies. She identifies violence against women as an outcome of both social structural and ideological conditions of male dominance. In her definition of crimes against women Klein argues that such crimes are both politically defined and depend on the particular historical relationships that exist between men and women. For example, it was not until 1870 that the use of birth control or the decision to have an abortion was declared a crime by women. Another example would be women condemned as witches were often healers of the poor; and the violence committed against both witches and midwives (often one and the same person) was often done in both Europe and the U.S. as men took over legal control and economic monopoly of medicine in the 19th century. Today, on the other hand, with exposure by the women's movement, age-old violence against women, wife battering, incestuous attacks of young girls by fathers or father substitutes, rape in general as well as rape of wives by husbands, are all beginning to be defined as crimes against women not to be tolerated by society. In short, crimes against women vary over time and are determined by economic, political, and social circumstances of a particular period in time.

In her definition of violence against women, Klein identifies three specific areas of activity in which men dominate women and through which women are directly victimized by institutionalized male control: (1) childbearing (involuntary childbearing, forced sterilization, surgical mutilation—hysterectomies, unsafe contraception), (2) sexual activity (rape, need of a male escort on the streets late at night, advertising that promotes women as sexual objects for men), and (3) nurturance.

Klein picks up on several themes alluded to by Karmen in the introduction to this section. First, Klein distinguishes between blaming the individual woman for the violence that befalls her and the need to reorganize the entire social structure that puts women in the position to be victimized. Second, she argues we must understand and differentiate both

Reprinted with permission of the National Council on Crime and Delinquency, from Dorie Klein, "Violence against Women: Some Considerations Regarding Its Causes and Its Elimination," *Crime & Delinquency*, January 1981, pp. 64-80.

individual and systemic forms of violence against women: the individual experience of the brutality of rape as well as the underlying social organization of society that both condones and encourages rape of women by men in general. Finally, Klein argues that the criminal justice system sees only extreme and relatively infrequent forms of violence against women— rape, incest, wife battering, murder, etc., but that these crimes represent only the "tip of the iceberg." Such an approach to violence against women by the criminal justice system, according to Klein, both obscures and legitimates more subtle and pervasive daily abuse of women.

In evaluating Klein's arguments readers might direct their attention to the following questions: What is the difference between a legal crime against women and the more informal, yet pervasive and continual, daily violence against women? Why are some of these abuses against women defined as crimes while others are not? What are the social processes through which abuses of women are or are not labeled as crimes? What do you think of her concern about the inherent limitations of a male-dominated, profit-oriented social structure in reforming its sexist ideology and practices? Is it the commitment to the present capitalist economic order, as she argues, that in large part makes genuine social change to eliminate violence against women unlikely? What do you think about her argument that too much of the recent concern with violence against women shown by criminal justice practitioners and scholars is with increased policing or regulation of individuals rather than with a basic reordering of society—in terms of class, sex, and race?

In the past few years many of us have come to recognize that women and girls are severely victimized by certain acts of violence that are committed overwhelmingly by men, such as rape, wife battering, sexual molestation, marital rape. Although violence and abuse have been no strangers to most dominated groups, in tracing the female experience through history and across cultures, one notices that women have often been injured *as women:* as childbearers, sexual objects for men, and nurturers. The focus of this discussion will be twofold: to locate this violence theoretically in women's experience in male-dominated society and to identify issues relevant to criminal justice practitioners and scholars.

The violence against women that comes to the attention of criminal justice agents is usually extreme and relatively infrequent: stranger-to-stranger rapes, the most severe beatings of wives and lovers, brutal and fatal assaults on women in the streets and public places. It is not that these incidents do not threaten women's everyday lives in a direct way. Rather, what is important here is that these comparatively rare events obscure the subtler and more pervasive forms of abuse of women which are woven into the fabric of our society. It is easy for many of us to dismiss individual acts of brutality as outside most people's daily experience, to attribute them to a handful of disturbed men—a comforting thought both for women as potential victims and for men as suspected culprits. It is also easy to overlook the relationship between these acts of "sociopathy" and more widely shared (albeit sometimes subterranean) beliefs and behaviors that degrade women.

In light of this, the discussion here will focus not only on the most flagrant and well-known examples of individual abuses. It will also encompass, at least in passing fashion, more systemic violations of women. Of the many facets of sexism, it is difficult to know where to draw the line separating what is from what is not violence, particularly once one recognizes the interconnections among economic exploitation, political domination, and psychological oppression. One thing leads to another. Many counselors of battered women, for example, consider a woman to be the victim of battering if she has been psychologically tormented, even if no physical force has been used. In terms of suffering, becoming vulnerable to further victimization, and inability to resist, such a broad definition of battering is justified in the counselors' experience. What is more important than drawing fine lines about physical force is to understand the specificity of its character and the reasons why its appropriate targets are female. It is not by chance that females are the usual objects of child molestation, spouse abuse, rape, pornography, and sexual harassment. Physical force backs up all subordination. Women experience individual violation as one end of the continuum rather than as an anomaly; since they are economically and psychologically ill-equipped to stop it, misogynistic abuse is latently encouraged in a society which formally disapproves of it.

Among these misogynistic behaviors, which of them are condemned and which go silently condoned is less a function of their innate harmfulness than of changing patterns of gender, class, and racial domination and the strength of resistance, which affect the behaviors in themselves and the legal definitions of those behaviors as crimes.[1] The criminal law and its enforcement are complex phenomena which reflect dominant economic exigencies and their ideological supports, as well as ongoing concessions to political demands and expedient interests. Wife beating illustrates this: A traditional male marital right under patriarchy is now being challenged behaviorally and redefined as illegal in the face of women's wage labor, changing family relations, and feminist activity. The criminal law forbids wife beating not as a manifestation of sexism, however, but as socially disruptive individual violence; in addition, its scope is restricted to those men vulnerable to identification by virtue of their class and race. Furthermore, it is not always a question of getting the law to broaden its coverage of violence against women. In many areas the law *itself* constitutes the harm. Abortion restrictions are an example of this; given present statutes, access to abortion reflects the differential privileges of class. In still other instances the harm is embedded in ubiquitous social practices lying beyond the realm of law. Advertising, for example, invokes sexist imagery in the legal pursuit of profit; the degradation of women involved is incidental, although not accidental. Still, given sufficient political pressure, law can bend to accommodate demands for equity, if not liberation. It is therefore essential to analyze crimes against women as forms of sexism, transcending gender-neutral and individualized legal definitions.

I have mentioned that women are victimized in their gender-specific duties as childbearers, sexual objects, and nurturers. These roles find their dim prehistoric origins in women's biology, but they are continuously being recreated socially. While women's childbearing may tend to confine them to domestic tasks in less developed societies, the range of activities they perform and the levels of political and economic power they attain in diverse cultures vary so tremendously as to suggest that humans are more socially malleable than they are physiologically or psychologically determined. Looking at it from the other side, the persistence of male domination in our society, where the level of technology and organization of production have surely eliminated the necessity for a division of labor according to gender, indicates that something is going on beyond biological necessity or social convenience. Finally, the pervasiveness and intensity of the victimization of women today do not lead us to predict the automatic withering away of sexism as a relic of the past. Women's subordination is actually intertwined in a thousand different ways with contemporary economic structures and practices. Without denying either sexism's predating of capitalism or its capacity to outlive capitalism, it is fair to say that the patriarchal family, the private accumulation of surplus wealth, and the rise of the modern state have developed more in accommodation than in contradiction to one another.[2] Violence against women thus takes historically specific forms.

The point is to make sense out of this rather than to catalog centuries of horrors. The world is not one undifferentiated patriarchy where women are fair game for whatever brutalities men may choose to inflict for their own power or amusement.[3] This would insult both women, who are not simply the helpless victims of history, and men, most of whom do not necessarily approve of or voluntarily engage in abuse of women. Not all men have the individual power to place women at their command—in fact, hardly any do—and most women actively fight back in myriad ways against their own victimization. The point of analysis should be to make this struggle as effective as possible.

CRIMES AGAINST CHILDBEARERS

The aspect of women's victimization to be addressed first arises from their place in reproduction. The control of women's reproductive capacity is a primary and causal aspect of sexism. The organization of reproduction, like the organization of production, is a determining feature of any society, and what we think of as personal life is neither private nor apolitical. When and how to have and not to have children is not left to the individual, appearances notwithstanding. As potential or real mothers, women find themselves confronted by stringent laws, restrictve institutions, and powerful ideologies of motherhood. With the historical transformation of production from pre-capitalist agrarian to capitalist industrial forms, the home gradually lost much of its productive character and became a more narrowly focused center of reproduction. As a consequence, most women were even more isolated from public, economic and political institutions and confined to their separate domestic sphere, although their experiences varied tremendously by class and culture. The emphasis on and control over childbearing intensified.

In early ninteenth century America, birth control and abortion—surprisingly safe and effective for this time—were widely practiced, generally legal, and tolerated by organized religion. Birth control paraphernalia were outlawed in the 1870s by the Comstock Act, which prohibited the sending of obscene materials through the United States mail. During the latter half of the 1800s states passed laws against abortion, in 1869 the Catholic Church banned it as a sin, and medical practitioners campaigned against it as a wide-spread social evil.[4] Of course, women did not stop having abortions or practicing birth control. What did happen was that abortion became far more dangerous, expensive, difficult to obtain, and accessible only to the privileged and knowledgeable. Women have since resorted in desperation to coat hangers, vacuum cleaners, and purgatives—ironic, since the early medical campaign was ostensibly aimed at ending dangerous abortions and since legal surgery was meanwhile becoming safer and more reliable. The technology and availability of birth control as well have been hampered by legal restriction, accompanied by religious and moral injunctions. Women give birth against their will, find their experience of sexuality twisted by fear of pregnancy, and depend upon dangerous devices and chemicals. The stories of fatal intrauterine devices, untested birth control pills, and carcinogenic morning-after pills are well known, as are the lack of good contraceptives for men, the continued inaccessibility of birth control for juveniles, and the ongoing attempts to restrict and outlaw funding for abortions.

In seeming contradiction, at the same time as women's right not to have children has been severely curtailed, the right of some women to have children has been attacked. During the early twentieth century a number of states passed laws for compulsory sterilization of persons deemed unfit, such as mental patients, criminal offenders, and the mentally retarded. Today women receiving welfare and women patients in public hospitals are often sterilized without their consent. This affects mostly "surplus" poor and minority women. One-third of Puerto Rico's female population, for example, has been sterilized.[5] Overseas, the United States Agency for International Development and private foundations encourage population reduction in the underdeveloped world, often by drastic methods. Women's reproductive capacity is thus subject to state control in both directions, forced fertility and coerced childlessness, as part of varying efforts to regulate the population and particular sectors within it to suit economic and political strategies of rule.

Childbirth itself has become subject to the hegemony of male experts. At the end of the nineteenth century, ambitious American medical practitioners developed an elaborate gynecology and drove the traditional female midwife out of business.[6] She was attacked as dirty, foreign, and déclassé. Scholars note, however, that the early "regular" gynecologists were nothing to write home about insofar as cleanliness was concerned. Surgery on the ovaries, clitoris, and uterus was routinely done, and without anesthesia, for no compelling medical reason, as continues to be true today for many hysterectomies. The point of much of the early gynecology was to bully middle-class women into having children. One historian, for example, has probed the career of Marion Sims, known as the father of American gynecology, who rose from obscure beginnings as a surgeon experimenting on black female slaves, bought expressly for that purpose, to be doctor to New York society and eventually to the Empress of France:

> Sims could not construe therapeutic action apart from preparation for pregnancy. So he demanded a 35-year old woman become pregnant in exchange for a cure of general pain and trouble in her reproductive tract. . . . "Notwithstanding her feeble state of health and length of time since the birth of her last child [he wrote], conception occurred after the operation. . . . But I am constrained to say that the pregnancy produced no good effect either constitutionally or locally."[7]

These women and the generations who followed them into dangerous operations and involuntary childbearing are as much the victims of violence as the woman raped in the street by a stranger. This is a violence sanctioned by the state and shaped by professionals, studied in the history of science rather than in the annals of crime. Individuals have suffered physically while their contemporaries have experienced the psychological abuse of the degradation of women and the cult of motherhood. All women find their control over a major part of their lives, the bearing of children, threatened by the tyranny of a well-paid expertise in service to

economic and political power. The weight of legal tradition, medical opinion, and profitable enterprise has been amassed against women's interests
in these matters. Hegemonic notions of women as mothers—anatomy as
destiny—rule our consciousness, reinforcing female subordination in general. As the United States Supreme Court noted, in the landmark ruling of
Muller v. Oregon in which "protective legislation" for women at work was
upheld,

> That women's physical structure and the performance of maternal functions place her
> at a disadvantage in the struggle for subsistence is obvious. This is especially true when
> the burdens of motherhood are upon her. . . . By abundant testimony of the medical
> fraternity . . . healthy mothers are essential to vigorous offspring, [and] the physical
> well-being of woman becomes an object of public interest and care in order to preserve
> the strength and vigor of the race.[8]

Today women are fighting for the simplest and most basic rights of
physical self-determination: access to abortion, choice over childbearing,
safe contraception, swift and humane medical attention. All these will
remain tenuous privileges, confined to those with economic resources and
personal determination, until women are no longer policed for bearing
children.

SEXUAL ABUSE

Women are victimized not only as childbearers, but also as sexual objects
for men. Women were once called "The Sex"; *sex* referred both to "the
other sex" and to sexual intercourse. (Today many have begun to substitute the term *gender* to describe the male/female distinction, and I am
following this practice.) The linking of sexuality and femininity is an
ancient one: the Christian condemnation of sex was also a denunciation of
women as evil with lust and redeemable only by motherhood, preferably
a virginal one. Like procreation, sex is no individually determined matter.
The same historical forces which shape parenthood act upon our erotic
choices. Although mystified as a natural drive, sex is socially defined.[9]
    The last one and one-half centuries have seen the rise of a powerful
double standard of sexuality both for the genders and for different classes
of women, and an equally impressive and contradictory marketing of
sexuality as a universal and egalitarian commodity, "an offer you can't
refuse." Each of these movements contributes in its own way to the victimization of women. The historical origins of the first lie in women's status
as the property of men under patriarchy. Women are not an undifferentiated mass, of course; their experiences have varied along class and ethnic
lines. The protection of "good" women in the Victorian era led to the

creation of a complementary class of "bad" women: virgins and whores, ladies and tramps. Emma Goldman noted drily that it was often a question of whether one was selling oneself sexually (and trading one's labor in exchange for support) to one man or to several that made the crucial difference. The gradation of sanctions survives today in the double standard of morality for women and men; in the different treatment accorded women by marital status, social class, race, age, and "virtue"; and in the "Catch 22" of blame both for women who appease men and for women who do not (harlots and hags, bitches and bags).

Traditional patriarchy, the rule of the father and husband, has been absorbed by the rule of the modern state, medicine, and public institutions. At the same time, people's experiences of their sexual needs are in flux, reflecting new material conditions of fulfillment and new ideologies. Recently there has been a tendency in advanced capitalist societies toward formal egalitarianism in sexual relations between women and men—which has not deeply affected the proscriptions on girls' sexuality, lesbianism, homosexuality, sex among the old, adult celibacy, interracial sex, and group sexuality, one must add. Behind this "sexual revolution" lies the commercialization of sex itself, the marketing of one's body and soul in personal relationships. We have long been used to having to sell our labor and buy our leisure—and under conditions over which we have little control and in which we expect to be exploited—and now this proletarianization of work and marketing of play permeate our forms of intimacy. These changes in sexuality have not eroded sexism or the sexual abuse of women. They have not even wiped out the old double standards, but have simply added to the burden of demands on women. The continued and ever wider-ranging sexual selling and stealing, once confined to women who were not "ladies" and now increasingly generalized, are evidenced in pornography and media exploitation, prostitution, child molestation, rape, and sexual harassment of women wage workers.

The reason why women "take" such abuse, from ogling on the street to so-called date rapes, has to do with the gender domination that pervades their every moment of existence. The violent episodes are not a sharp break from their everyday experience, but one extreme. Can one, for example, distinguish overt sexual harassment at work from having to flirt with the customers, wear provocative clothes, make the coffee, watch oneself be paid less than a man, be passed over for promotion, and be fired summarily as one grows older and less valuable as decoration?

The phenomenon of rape illustrates the most brutal use of sex to dominate women. Rape is admittedly one of the most serious of the officially defined crimes of violence, yet it is underreported, infrequently cleared, and rarely successfully prosecuted. Of rapes known to victimization surveys in the United States *as revealed by the victim herself* (women are unlikely to reveal forced sex with friends, lovers, escorts, and spouses), only half were reported to the police. And in 1976 only about half of those reported resulted in an arrest—a clearance rate not much better than that for aggravated assault, which is a much more widespread offense and hence supposedly more difficult to clear. While it is difficult to know whether the longitudinal increases reflect changing incidence, changing rates of reporting, or the changing character of much rape, rapes known to the police have tripled since 1960. (It should be remembered, however, that all reported crimes of violence save murder have increased comparably during this period.)[10] It is certainly evident that easing sexual standards has not at all discouraged rape, as male scholars had prophesied. Rather, as feminists have pointed out, much of the ideology of the male-oriented sexual revolution glorifies rape. The macho "stud" subdues haughty "bitch" and submissive "chick" alike; pornography and advertising amass fortunes by displaying and dismembering women's bodies. The myth that men rape because of overwhelming sexual drive, goaded to it by women who provoke or secretly desire rape, lives on. Recent criminological trends toward victimology and interactional analysis of crime reinforce this victim-blaming tendency regarding women.[11]

One must understand that at bottom rape is not an erotic act at all. It is an act of violent domination, cloaking hatred and fear. Former GIs in Vietnam have testified about the rape of Vietnamese women:

> I saw one case where a woman was shot by a sniper, one of our snipers. When we got to her she was asking for water. And the lieutenant said to kill her. So he ripped off her clothes, they stabbed her in both breasts, they spread her eagle and shoved an E tool [entrenching] up her vagina, and she was still asking for water, And then they took that out and used a tree limb and then she was shot.[12]

In our own cities women show a realistic fear of physical victimization. Recent polls by the National Opinion Research Center indicate that over 60 percent of all women are afraid to walk in their neighborhoods at night, in contrast to less than 25 percent of all men. The fear of victimization is highest among the poor, minorities, and the elderly. When asked by a media poll, almost half the women indicated that they worried "a lot" about rape.[13] In her classic piece on the subject, Susan Griffin describes how fear of rape serves a de facto protection racket akin to organized crime's, whereby men protect "their" women against the abuse of other men.[14] All women are obliged to avoid public places at night, isolated areas, and conspicuous states of singlehood. Essentially women are under house arrest, their activities constrained by what is dismissed as a brutal fact of life.[15] This protection racket, and the simultaneous selling of women by means ranging from the Dallas Cowgirls to *Deep Throat,* underhandedly promotes rape by objectifying female sexuality and glorifying male power. That this reinforces the domination of women in all aspects of their lives was an early and profound perception of the feminist movement.

Male physical power over women, or the illusion of power, is nonetheless a minimal compensation for the lack of power over the rest of one's life. Some men resort to rape and other personal violence against the only targets accessible, the only ones with even less autonomy. (One must also remember that men with more power and money may engage in more acceptable or covert rapes, which they can successfully cover up, not to mention the institutional violence that they may direct in more impersonal fashion.) Thus sexual warfare often becomes a stand-in for class and racial conflict by transforming these resentments into misogyny. One man recalls,

> I met a girl at a party and I considered her snobbish and phony. She latched onto me at the party and we laughed and had a good time and went somewhere else. She was an attractive women in her thirties, but she irritated me. When I took her home to her apartment she was telling me good night and I raped her. I didn't really feel the urge. As a matter of fact, I had a hell of a time getting an erection. Once again, I'd had quite a bit of booze. But I forced myself to do it to prove a point to her, to prove that she wasn't as big as she thought she was.[16]

The crucial point is not that men are frustrated and take it out on the next person. It is that men are structurally and psychologically accustomed to taking it out on women. It is women who are supposed to take care of men's sexual (and other) needs—are targets, refuges, and symbols for men.

How convenient this turns out to be for bolstering existing class divisions! Men's sexual privileges over women have a long-run material cost to us all, since sexism not only directly keeps women in their place, but indirectly helps keep most men in *their* place too.

NURTURERS AND SCAPEGOATS

The third and last aspect of women's victimization to be addressed is their abuse as nurturers. The infinite task of emotional and physical support of men, children, the aged, and infirm—as well as themselves—is part of women's work, which was strengthened by the division between job and family and by the increasing impersonality of the former under capitalism. Mythically connected to both childbearing and sexuality, nurturing is part and parcel of what is involved in most of the female occupations: wife, mother, daughter, nurse, schoolteacher, secretary, social worker, domestic, waitress. The reinforcement of nurturance is behind the classic definitions of the feminine personality as passive, emotional, and empathetic. (These qualities are also related to ideal female sexual objects and childbearers.) The expectation of nurturance also justifies the deliberate confusion of women as biological childbearers with women as "natural" child rearers.[17] Similar myths of female biology or psychology justify the prescription of wifely duties. Traditional ideology had women receiving economic support in exchange for nurturance. The contemporary realities of most women's wage labor—and the historical realities of much female wage and slave labor—demonstrate that nurturance is often done for free, is a triple burden of working, "wifing," and "mothering."

Today much nurturance, like sexuality (and tomorrow childbearing?), is being made into a commodity. What you cannot get free from your wife or mother, if you have one, you purchase, be it meals, day care, or therapy. (It is still mostly women who perform the services, although it is usually men who own the companies that make the money. It is true, of course, that upper- and middle-class women have long had maids, cooks, slaves, and cleaning women to do their domestic labor for them.) The emotional, as opposed to purely material, aspect of nurturance largely remains for women to cope with within the family; in fact, this aspect grows stronger as the economic independence of the family shrinks. Like the sexual revolution, the marketing of nurturance imposes additional demands on women rather than lightening the burdens of patriarchy. The material and emotional realities of work and intimacy are increasingly fragmented: witness the contradictory standards of soft femininity and those of the labor market for hard independence. One is expected to "dress for success" in the daytime and "turn into a woman" at night.[18]

The nurturer becomes the scapegoat when things go awry. In one historical instance in Europe from the fourteenth to seventeenth centuries, the persecution of female lay healers, otherwise called witches and midwives, was undertaken jointly by ambitious physicians, church theologians, and state officials. It is estimated that thousands to millions of women were burned alive in Europe, following confessions extracted by such tortures as being pricked with needles (to find the mark of the devil) and being submerged in water while tied up (to see whether one drowned like an ordinary person or floated like a witch). Witches were scapegoated as healers, for their sexuality, and for their gender, one and the same thing to persecutors. Scholars note that the witch hunts diverted mass resentment over plague and social upheaval onto a powerless group of women. "Good" witches known for cures and kindness were targeted along with those accused of evil; in fact, successful unauthorized healing sealed one's fate.[19]

The persecution of witches, faintly echoed and followed by the outlawing of midwives in this country, also speeded male control of medicine. Suppressing female healers among the poor went hand-in-hand with establishing church-blessed state-sanctioned male doctors accessible only to the rich—a dubious privilege, given medical techniques at the time. Caring for the sick had been an integral part of woman's work within the family, and women had acquired great skill and a passed-on body of knowledge. But with the relegation of women to the subordinate nurturing role of nurse (and patient par excellence), definitions of what constituted good nurturing were increasingly monopolized by male expertise. This professional monopoly was based less on empirical merit than on social power; like theology before it, medical science is a system of belief that has triumphed at the expense of women.[20] The official identifying and killing of witches has been attributed by science to mass hysteria and written up as a curiosity of psychology. It remained for recent feminist and libertarian scholarship to uncover it as genocide of horrifying proportions.

A contemporary instance of abuse of women as nurturers, and the last example of victimization to be discussed, is the battering of wives, which doubtless surpasses witch hunting in numbers of victims.[21] One may trace the practice of men "disciplining" their wives to women's chattel-like condition under patriarchy; the rule of thumb in English common law referred to men's traditional right to hit their wives with a stick no thicker than their thumb. Formal mild legal modifications apparently had little impact on actual behavior, with male familial violence surviving and perhaps even exacerbated by the decline in male familial authority. With the influence of new bourgeois moral and legal standards of family conduct among all classes and increased emphasis on individual rights, wife beating did retreat underground.[22] Only recently has it returned to public view, thanks to feminist activists.

Contemporary United States studies estimate that violence may occur in up to half of all intimate relationships, with women receiving the brunt of the abuse.[23] The evidence of household surveys and the testimony of shelters are now being added to statistics collected by the police, who have long been aware that domestic disturbance calls are among the most common and most dangerous. Difficulties in estimating rates spring from different definitions as well as from the mask of privacy and from problems with the reliability and accuracy of responses. (For example, one criticized survey found "husband battering" to be as prevalent as wife beating by using sufficiently broad definitions of violence, so that slapping with a shoe ranked equally with bludgeoning with a lamp.[24])

The origins of wife beating lie not only in patriarchal rights of discipline, but also in contemporary expectations of female nurturance. Women commonly tell stories of being beaten for burning the toast, coming home late, talking to another man (or woman), and so on. More subtly, they are abused for failing to give the constant emotional attention that men may expect and are themselves socially inept at giving or getting others besides

their wives to give. Again, the point is not so much that men are emotionally inadequate and likely to resort to violence as it is that women are
expected to compensate and thus become the scapegoats when things go
wrong. One of Lenore Walker's battered respondents recalls,

> After we got married, every little thing would set him off. It seemed he needed extra
> special loving at all times and I kept throwing hurdles because I wasn't doing that.
> Evidently that was causing him to be very upset. I always got the impression that I
> wasn't loving enough, giving enough, that there was something defective in my
> character as far as giving love. That's basically the message he gave to me.25

It is not surprising that women often blame themselves when their
husbands beat them. Social scientists blame them as well; one study by
psychologists in the 1960s, for example, characterizes beaten wives as
"aggressive, masculine and sexually frigid" women who "castrate" their
husbands.26 Officials are usually skeptical toward the woman: suspicious
of her for provoking the abuse, contemptuous of her for staying in an
abusive situation, and equally, though contradictorily, disbelieving of her
complaints of abuse in the first place. As with rape, victimology and
interactional analyses tend to diffuse responsibility for the violence and
defuse the reality of unequal power between the genders. Del Martin
illustrates this with a letter from a woman battered by her husband:

> For most of my married life I have been beaten. . . . Early in our marriage I went to
> a clergyman, who, after a few visits, told me that my husband meant no real harm,
> that he was just confused and felt insecure. I was encouraged to be more toler-
> ant. . . . Next time I turned to a doctor. I was given little pills to relax me and told to
> take things a little easier. I was just too nervous. . . . I turned to a professional family
> guidance agency. I was told there that my husband needed help and that I should find
> a way to control the incidents. I couldn't control the incidents—that was the whole
> point of my seeking help. At the agency I found I had to defend myself against the
> suspicion that I wanted to be hit, that I invited the beatings. I called the police one
> time. They not only did not respond to the call, they called several hours later to ask
> if things had "settled down." I could have been dead by then! I have nowhere to go
> if it happens again. No one wants to take in a woman with four children.27

Encouraged by this social tolerance, wife beating also is a response to
the new tensions of contemporary marriage. Although women are certainly the victims of most domestic violence, it is questionable whether men
are the victors. The necessities of women's increasing participation in wage
labor, women's freedom from constant childbearing, and tendencies toward equal legal rights challenge patriarchal authority. Yet conditions
supporting egalitarian intimacy do not exist. Lillian Breslow Rubin's study
of working-class families explores the gaps between dissatisfied spouses.
A postal clerk in his early thirties, married nine years and father of three,
talks about his wife:

> She was too busy running off at the mouth—you know, nagging—to listen to any-
> thing. I just got mad and I'd take off, go out with the guys and have a few beers or
> something. When I'd get back things would be even worse. Sometimes I'd feel like
> hitting her just to shut her up. . . . Did she think I didn't care about not making enough
> money to take care of my family?[28]

The displacement of blame onto women for things perceived as individual failures rather than as social injuries—inadequate income, accidental pregnancies, unsatisfying work and leisure—makes it all the more
difficult to move beyond guilt into resistance. As long as families remain
microcosms of male domination and deposits for the injuries of class and
racial domination, they will absorb social ills, converting the energies into
personal and painful battles between women and men, thinly concealed by
veneers of domestic harmony and romantic love. At the same time, marriage does not exist in a vacuum; it cannot be a refuge of mutual concern
and perfect equality in a society torn by sexism and exploitation. The
complex and unbreakable link between the personal and the political has
been a central and potentially revolutionary theme of contemporary feminism.

TOWARD ELIMINATION

> In the bourgeois mind for which the ways of capitalism are ahistorical, inevitable and
> eternal, this conflict appears either as essentially a tragedy in which the liberation of
> women is an obscure and religious affair, or the sex-war is presented as a timeless
> comedy. . . . In fact the particular manner in which women are oppressed within the
> family in capitalism is an historical aspect of one form of society. . . . The organization
> of production within capitalism creates a separate and segmented vision of life which
> continually restricts consciousness of alternatives. People perceive themselves in op-
> position to one another.[29]

Both sexism and violence are often seen by most of us as at some level
inevitable, so ubiquitous are they. Whether one attributes violence to
"sociopathic" individuals, "natural" male human aggression, or generally
"sick society," whether one views gender domination as biological or
psychological or purely social in origin, it is difficult to envision a society
free of both. Much of the recent concern with violence against women that
has been shown by criminal justice practitioners and scholars, for example,
is with its effective regulation rather than its elimination, with the policing
of individuals rather than with the reordering of society.

The preceding discussion of the root causes of violence against women
has been intended to show both the total systemic gender domination from
which it arises and the historical specificity of its character, definition, and
etiology. On the one hand, the elimination of gender domination being a

prerequisite for eliminating women's victimization, significant change does require a radical reordering of society and is therefore unlikely to come about automatically or in piecemeal reform. On the other hand, the relationships between women and men, the separation of family and workplace, and the ideological supports for and challenges to sexism are continuously changing and changeable, at both the individual and societal levels. In considering the role of criminal justice, we need to move beyond examinations of policing and institutional responses to individuals and toward strategies for eliminating both violence *and* policing.

The new feminist drive against violence against women has gathered considerable strength and has challenged old criminal justice practices. The ill treatment afforded victims of rape and battering by police and prosecutors has been documented. Women have successfully organized rape relief and shelter organizations to support victims and pressure service-delivering institutions to respond. Efforts are under way to redefine statutes on rape, marital rape, wife battering, pornography, child molestation, and incest to enable prosecution of offenders and develop recourse for victims.[30] Female rights to birth control, abortion, voluntary sterilization, and sensitive gynecological care are being defined and demanded by activist groups with mass support. These developments are important to the movement for equality and justice for women; as such they are heartening in their success and worth fighting for. The attacks on them by conservative antifeminist forces underscore the fragility of the mildest of gains and make defense of them imperative. These gains are not due solely to the women's movement, which itself did not appear in a vacuum. Women's mass entry into the wage labor market, the continuous breakdown of the family into more and more autonomous individuals dependent on the market and the state for sustenance, and the requisite contractual equality of the genders are powerful impersonal forces in themselves. Although giving rise to feminism and creating long-run opportunities for liberation, in the short run many of these forces merely exacerbate the exploitation and isolation of women and men. This is made clear by the sexual revolution and by the transformation of nurturance into a marketable commodity. With respect to the cause of liberation, these forces are neither inherently progressive nor regressive; they will take their shape from how they are handled.

Current efforts to strengthen rape enforcement, expand definitions of marital rape and battering, enforce antipornography statutes, and intervene on behalf of abused family members should consequently be weighed for their immediate and long-range implications. The history of failed or warped criminal justice reform, from the juvenile court to Prohibition, argues against unquestioning dependence on the criminal law to achieve desired social ends. First, sympathetic attention to victims and efforts to convict individual perpetrators can achieve only so much by themselves; it is difficult to imagine rehabilitating or deterring a rapist in a society that thoroughly degrades women and promotes rape. Second, many of the reforms proposed by feminists that are winning official recognition and funding are not necessarily desirable, aside from the question of their effectiveness. The criminal justice system is not a class-, race-, or gender-neutral object manipulable at will by sufficiently strong feminist interests. (The feminist movement is also not neutral with respect to class or race, but that is a different discussion.) Although open to political bargaining, the predominant determinants of the system's character remain the protection of economic order and ideological legitimacy. These priorities, and the class, race, and gender biases which express them, are therefore built into the very conceptualization, definitions, and enforcement of the criminal law.[31] Laws against pornography, for example, have as their criteria the explicitness of sexuality rather than the harmfulness to women, and touch the small-time purveyors of sleaze rather than mass promoters and advertisers. If rigorously enforced, as some feminists argue for, would they not simply drive stag movies underground and leave "Charlie's Angels" untouched? And would there not be the threat of their being used against feminist materials on sex? The potential for discrimination, which we have long seen in the differential treatment of rapists by race and which is now being reproduced in the differential identification of wife batterers by class, exists also in the feminist-supported movement to root out child abusers, with welfare families, gay parents, and single mothers the most vulnerable to state intervention. The history of "policing the family" through casework and detention is one of continuing struggle between agents of the official morality and members of working-class, immigrant, and minority communities.[32]

Finally, the power of the state, medicine, and welfare institutions grows as the patriarch's declines, as the professionalization of medicine and state control over reproduction make evident. Individual male victimization of women does, of course, go on. Yet the declining authority of the patriarch in an economic world out of his control means that the state takes on the job of regulating families to maintain their viability. This may include concessions of formal equality to women, which of course is not the same thing as commitment to their liberation. This transformed base of gender domination should not lead us to demands for "radical nonintervention" or laissez faire, those dreams of the privileged of today for an even more privileged yesterday. Instead, the forms of state intervention demanded must redistribute power to women rather than to the state or back to individual men.

At present, criminal justice intervention with both victims and offenders has structural features that inherently strengthen the material and ideological supports of sexism. There is a rigid hierarchical bureaucracy funded and directed from above, which excludes participation by the poor and female, and makes agencies accountable to priorities of the governing elite. At the individual level there is a careful separation between the passive and often unwilling client and the professional agent or counselor who provides prepackaged services or thinly disguised commands. Choice, autonomy, and exchange among peers are usually impossible. Finally, there is an isolation of personal problems as fragments rooted in individuals' psychological deficiencies, even though in reality these problems are being addressed only because they threaten the social order. By precluding a holistic understanding of the relation between the individual and the social structure, not only effective social change but also effective individual change is made more difficult.

Viable solutions will emerge out of practice and not out of speculative theory. The recent establishment of rape relief groups, abused women's shelters, women's health clinics, feminist advertising boycotts, and marches against pornography are examples. The analysis of the systemic causes of violence against women will, it is hoped, be of use in the development of programs for its elimination. This will require forms of intervention that collectively and democratically emerge from people's concerns; that involve active commitment by and among (female) victims, (male) offenders, and interveners; and that recognize the dialectic between our individual experiences and political solutions. A fundamental redefinition of what constitutes crime and violence, their causes, and correction is necessarily part of what eventually needs to be done. In the meantime, judgment with respect to the value of reforms—whether they advance women's livelihood and autonomy or whether they deliver illusory gains which in the end serve systemic needs for order—will be made in the daily lives of women experiencing violence.

Notes

[1] For the observation that legal crimes should not be assumed to be congruent with universally agreed upon harms, see Herman Schwendinger and Julia Schwendinger, "Defenders of Order or Guardians of Human Rights?" *Issues in Criminology*, Summer 1970, pp. 123-57.

[2] For the insight that women's subordination is tied to the rise of surplus wealth and the state, see Frederick Engels, *The Origin of the Family, Private Property and the State* (1884, New York: International Publishers, 1970).

[3] For an example of the "catalog of horrors" approach to which I refer, see Susan Brownmiller, *Against Our Will: Men, Women and Rape* (New York: Simon & Schuster, 1975).

[4] See Linda Gordon, *Women's Body, Women's Right: A Social History of Birth Control in America* (New York: Penquin, 1977).

[5] *Ibid.*

6 See Barbara Ehrenreich and Deirdre English, *For Her Own Good: 150 Years of the Experts' Advice to Women* (New York: Anchor, 1979).

7 G.J. Barker-Benfield, *The Horrors of the Half-Known Life: Male Attitudes toward Women and Sexuality in Nineteenth-Century America* (New York: Harper Colophon, 1976), pp. 111-12.

8 Karen DeCrow, *Sexist Justice* (New York: Vintage, 1975), p. 46.

9 For the classic discussion of women as "the other," see Simone de Beauvoir, *The Second Sex* (New York: Knopf, 1953); on the social basis of sexuality, see Michel Foucault, *The History of Sexuality* (New York: Random House, 1978).

10 U.S. Department of Justice, *Sourcebook of Criminal Justice Statistics 1978* (Washington, D.C.: Govt. Printing Office, 1979), pp. 362-63, 433, and 478.

11 Julia Schwendinger and Herman Schwendinger, "Rape Myths: In Legal, Theoretical and Everyday Practice," *Crime and Social Justice*, Spring 1974, pp. 18-26; Kurt Weis and Sandra Borges, "Victimology and Rape: The Case of the Legitimate Victim," *Issues in Criminology*, Fall 1973, pp. 71-115.

12 Arlene Eisen Bergman, *Women of Vietnam* (San Francisco: People's Press, 1974), p. 69.

13 Dept. of Justice, *Sourcebook*, pp. 288-89.

14 Susan Griffin, "Rape: The All-American Crime," *Ramparts*, September 1971, pp. 26-35.

15 While working on this piece, this was brought home to me while uneasily writing in my office on campus alone late at night. (Fortunately, I have a large dog which accompanied me.) In a telling incident, in the wake of a rape on one campus, feminists posted a notice to curfew all male students—to their fury. The "natural" response would be to curfew the women!

16 Diane Russell, *The Politics of Rape: The Victim's Perspective* (New York: Stein and Day, 1975), p. 253.

17 On the question of who "parents," see Nancy Chodorow, *The Reproduction of Mothering: Psychoanalysis and the Sociology of Gender* (Berkeley: University of California, 1978).

18 It is the false choice presented by the ruling ideology—success in the workplace along masculine lines versus success as a family woman—which dominates most of the media debates between anti-feminists and liberal feminists. Not only does this present a class-based and individualistic model of liberation, but most important, it restricts our vision of other possibilities.

19 On the significance of witch hunts, see Thomas Szasz, *The Manufacture of Madness* (New York: Harper & Row, 1970).

20 See Barbara Ehrenreich and Deirdre English, *Witches, Midwives and Nurses* (Old Westbury, NY: Feminist Press, 1973).

21 The term *wife beating* will be used here to emphasize the unequal social relationship of marriage, or an unmarried variant of it, as a determining feature. This is in contrast to the more gender-neutral "domestic violence" or "spouse abuse," and also different from "women beating," which emphasizes biological gender.

22 For a historical discussion, see Margaret May, "Violence in the Family: An Historical Perspective," in *Violence and the Family*, J.P. Martin, ed. (Chichester, England: Wiley and Sons, 1978), pp. 135-67.

23 For an overview, see Dorie Klein, "Can This Marriage Be Saved? Battery and Sheltering," *Crime and Social Justice*, Winter 1979, pp. 19-33.

24 Suzanne Steinmetz, "Physical Violence between Spouses," in *Battered Women: A Psychosociological Study of Domestic Violence*, Maria Roy, ed. (New York: Van Nostrand Reinhold, 1977), pp. 63-72.

25 Lenore Walker, *The Battered Woman* (New York: Harper & Row, 1979), p. 84.

26 John Snell, Richard Rosenwald, and Ames Robey, "The Wifebeater's Wife," *Archives of General Psychiatry*, August 1964, pp. 107-12.

27 Del Martin, *Battered Wives* (New York: Pocket Books, 1977), pp. 2-3.

28 Lillian Breslow Rubin, *Worlds of Pain: Life in the Working-Class Family* (New York: Basic Books, 1976), p. 77.

29 Sheila Rowbotham, *Woman's Consciousness, Man's World* (New York: Penguin, 1973), p. 57.

30 For an overview of the movement against battering, see Klein, "Can This Marriage Be Saved?" For rape, see Vicki NcNickle Rose, "Rape as a Social Problem: A Byproduct of the Feminist Movement," *Social Problems,* October 1977, pp. 75-89.

31 On ideological hegemony, see Antonio Gramsci, *Selections from the Prison Notebooks 1947* (New York: International Publishers, 1971). On law, see Evgeny Pashukanis, *Law and Marxism: A General Theory* (1929, London: Ink Links, 1978).

32 The phrase "policing the family" is from Jacques Donzelot, *The Policing of Families* (New York: Pantheon, 1979).

12

Rape: The All-American Crime

Susan Griffin

In the last chapter Klein provided a theoretical analysis of the forms that violence takes against women in our society and suggested several causes of and solutions to eliminate their victimization. In this chapter Griffin examines in detail one of these crimes, rape, which Klein labels one of the most brutal uses of sex to dominate women.

Published in 1971, Griffin's chapter stands as a classic contribution to the field—as one of the earliest and most widely published articles to talk about rape as an act of violence against women, not an act of sex. This chapter by Griffin is important because the author systematically refutes six well-known, long-standing myths about rape. In so doing, she exposes much of the racism as well as the sexism that underlies these misogynistic myths. Moreover, she takes an historical approach to the issue of rape and suggests that rape has always been understood as a crime of one man against another man's property—his woman. The fact that a human being, a woman, was brutally victimized, was not the issue before the law.

In the process of exposing the fallacies underlying rape myths, Griffin cites studies and data, both anecdotal and statistical. Researchers have available national data on violent crime from only two sources. The Uniform Crime Reports (UCR), which consist of crimes known to the police is one source; the other is the National Crime Survey (NCS). Often referred to as victimization studies, the National Crime Surveys are conducted by the Census Bureau and consist of information compiled from personal interviews with citizens. At the time Griffin wrote, she had access to the first source, the UCR data only, since the National Crime Surveys were just getting under way.

As you read Griffin's account of the myths, ask yourself if you ever believed any of them. The author exposes chivalry with a considerable range of documentation: classical literature, scholarly studies, both sociological and anthropological, law journal material, and autobiography to make her point that chivalry is a male "protection racket." Her final conclusion about rape is that it is inseparable from our patriarchal society. Answers to reducing the crime or actually eliminating it, she convincingly argues, will occur only when patriarchy ends. Compare Griffin's analysis of crimes against women with that of Klein's in the previous chapter. What are the similarities and differences in their understanding of the causes of crimes against women in our society? Which of the two arguments do you find most useful in understanding how women are victimized today?

Reprinted with permission. *Ramparts,* vol. 10, no. 3, September 1971.

I

I have never been free of the fear of rape. From a very early age I, like most women, have thought of rape as a part of my natural environment— something to be feared and prayed against like fire or lightning. I never asked why men raped; I simply thought it one of the many mysteries of human nature.

I was, however, curious enough about the violent side of humanity to read every crime magazine I was able to ferret away from my grandfather. Each issue featured at least one "sex crime," with pictures of a victim, usually in a pearl necklace, and of the ditch or the orchard where her body was found. I was never certain why the victims were always women, nor what the motives of the murderer were, but I did guess that the world was not a safe place for women. I observed that my grandmother was meticulous about locks, and quick to draw the shades before anyone removed so much as a shoe. I sensed that danger lurked outside.

At the age of eight, my suspicions were confirmed. My grandmother took me to the back of the house where the men wouldn't hear, and told me that strange men wanted to do harm to little girls. I learned not to walk on dark streets, not to talk to strangers, or get into strange cars, to lock doors, and to be modest. She never explained why a man would want to harm a little girl, and I never asked.

If I thought for a while that my grandmother's fears were imaginary, the illusion was brief. That year, on the way home from school, a schoolmate a few years older than I tried to rape me. Later, in an obscure aisle of the local library (while I was reading *Freddy the Pig*) I turned to discover a man exposing himself. Then, the friendly man around the corner was arrested for child molesting.

My initiation to sexuality was typical. Every woman has similar stories to tell—the first man who attacked her may have been a neighbor, a family friend, an uncle, her doctor, or perhaps her own father. And women who grow up in New York City always have tales about the subway.

But though rape and the fear of rape are a daily part of every woman's consciousness, the subject is so rarely discussed by that unofficial staff of male intellectuals (who write the books which study seemingly every other form of male activity) that one begins to suspect a conspiracy of silence. And indeed, the obscurity of rape in print exists in marked contrast to the frequency of rape in reality, for *forcible rape is the most frequently committed violent crime in America today.* The Federal Bureau of Investigation classes three crimes as violent: murder, aggravated assault and forcible rape. In 1968, 31,060 rapes were *reported.* According to the FBI and independent criminologists, however, to approach accuracy this figure must be multiplied by at least a factor of ten to compensate for the fact that most rapes are not reported; when these compensatory mathematics are used, there are more rapes committed than aggravated assaults and homicides.

When I asked Berkeley, California's Police Inspector in charge of rape investigation if he knew why men rape women, he replied that he had not spoken with "these people and delved into what really makes them tick, because that really isn't my job. . . . " However, when I asked him how a woman might prevent being raped, he was not so reticent, "I wouldn't advise any female to go walking around alone at night . . . and she should lock her car at all times." The Inspector illustrated his warning with a grisly story about a man who lay in wait for women in the back seats of their cars, while they were shopping in a local supermarket. This man eventually murdered one of his rape victims. "Always lock your car," the Inspector repeated, and then added, without a hint of irony, "Of course, you don't have to be paranoid about this type of thing."

The Inspector wondered why I wanted to write about rape. Like most men he did not understand the urgency of the topic, for, after all, men are not raped. But like most women I had spent considerable time speculating on the true nature of the rapist. When I was very young, my image of the "sexual offender" was a nighmarish amalgamation of the bogey man and Captain Hook: he wore a black cape, and he cackled. As I matured, so did my image of the rapist. Born into the psychoanalytic age, I tried to "understand" the rapist. Rape, I came to believe, was only one of many unfortunate evils produced by sexual repression. Reasoning by tautology, I concluded that any man who would rape a woman must be out of his mind.

Yet, though the theory that rapists are insane is a popular one, this belief has no basis in fact. According to Professor Menachem Amir's study of 646 rape cases in Philadelphia, *Patterns in Forcible Rape*, men who rape are not abnormal. Amir writes, "Studies indicate that sex offenders do not constitute a unique or psychopathological type; nor are they, as a group invariably more disturbed than the control groups to which they are compared." Alan Taylor, a parole officer who has worked with rapists in the prison facilities at San Luis Obispo, California, stated the question in plainer language, "Those men were the most normal men there. They had a lot of hang-ups, but they were the same hang-ups as men walking out on the street."

Another canon in the apologetics of rape is that, if it were not for learned social controls, all men would rape. Rape is held to be natural behavior, and not to rape must be learned. But in truth rape is not universal to the human species. Moreover, studies of rape in our culture reveal that, far from being impulsive behavior, most rape is planned. Professor Amir's study reveals that in cases of group rape (the "gangbang" of masculine slang) 90 percent of the rapes were planned; in pair rapes, 83 percent of the rapes were planned; and in single rapes, 58 percent were planned. These figures should significantly discredit the image of the rapist as a man who is suddently overcome by sexual needs society does not allow him to fulfill.

Far from the social control of rape being learned, comparisons with other cultures lead one to suspect that, in our society, it is rape itself that is learned. (The fact that rape is against the law should not be considered proof that rape is not in fact encouraged as part of our culture.)

This culture's concept of rape as an illegal, but still understandable, form of behavior is not a universal one. In her study *Sex and Temperament,* Margaret Mead describes a society that does not share our views. The Arapesh do not " . . . have any conception of the male nature that might make rape understandable to them." Indeed our interpretation of rape is a product of our conception of the nature of male sexuality. A common retort to the question, why don't women rape men, is the myth that men have greater sexual needs, that their sexuality is more urgent than women's. And it is the nature of human beings to want to live up to what is expected of them.

And this same culture which expects aggression from the male expects passivity from the female. Conveniently, the companion myth about the nature of female sexuality is that all women secretly want to be raped. Lurking beneath her modest female exterior is a subconscious desire to be ravished. The following description of a stag movie, written by Brenda Starr in Los Angeles' underground paper, *Everywoman,* typifies this male fantasy. The movie "showed a woman in her underclothes reading on her bed. She is interrupted by a rapist with a knife. He immediately wins her over with his charm and they get busy sucking and fucking." An advertisement in the *Berkeley Barb* reads, "Now as all women know from their daydreams, rape has a lot of advantages. Best of all it's so simple. No preparation necessary, no planning ahead of time, no wondering if you should or shouldn't: just whang! bang!" Thanks to Masters and Johnson even the scientific canon recognizes that for the female, "whang! bang!" can scarcely be described as pleasurable.

Still, the male psyche persists in believing that, protestations and struggles to the contrary, deep inside her mysterious feminine soul, the female victim has wished for her own fate. A young woman who was raped by the husband of a friend said that days after the incident the man returned to her home, pounded on the door and screamed to her. "Jane, Jane. You loved it. You know you loved it."

The theory that women like being raped extends itself by deduction into the proposition that most or much of rape is provoked by the victim. But this too is only myth. Though provocation, considered a mitigating factor in a court of law, may consist of only "a gesture," according to the Federal

Commission on Crimes of Violence, only 4 percent of reported rapes involved any precipitative behavior by the woman.

The notion that rape is enjoyed by the victim is also convenient for the man who, though he would not commit forcible rape, enjoys the idea of its existence, as if rape confirms that enormous sexual potency which he secretly knows to be his own. It is for the pleasure of the armchair rapist that detailed accounts of violent rapes exist in the media. Indeed, many men appear to take sexual pleasure from nearly all forms of violence. Whatever the motivation, male sexuality and violence in our culture seem to be inseparable. . . .

In a recent fictional treatment of the Manson case, Frank Conroy writes of his vicarious titillation when describing the murders to his wife:

> "Every single person there was killed." She didn't move. "It sounds like there was torture," I said. As the words left my mouth I knew there was no need to say them to frighten her into believing that she needed me for protection.

The pleasure he feels as his wife's protector is inextricably mixed with pleasure in the violence itself. Conroy writes, "I was excited by the killings, as one is excited by catastrophe on a grand scale, as one is alert to pre-echoes of unknown changes, hints of unrevealed secrets, rumblings of chaos. . . . "

The attraction of the male in our culture to violence and death is a tradition Manson and his admirers are carrying on with tireless avidity (even presuming Manson's innocence, he dreams of the purification of fire and destruction). It was Malraux in his *Anti-Memoirs* who said that, for the male, facing death was *the* illuminating experience analogous to childbirth for the female. Certainly our culture does glorify war and shroud the agonies of the gunfighter in veils of mystery.

And in the spectrum of male behavior, rape, the perfect combination of sex and violence, is the pen-ultimate act. Erotic pleasure cannot be separated from culture, and in our culture male eroticism is wedded to power. Not only should a man be taller and stronger than a female in the perfect love-match, but he must also demonstrate his superior strength in gestures of dominance which are perceived as amorous. Though the law attempts to make a clear division between rape and sexual intercourse, in fact the courts find it difficult to distinguish between a case where the decision to copulate was mutual and one where a man forced himself upon his partner.

The scenario is even further complicated by the expectation that, not only does a woman mean "yes" when she says "no," but that a really decent woman ought to begin by saying "no," and then be led down the primrose path to acquiescence. Ovid, the author of Western Civilization's most celebrated sex-manual, makes this expectation perfectly clear:

. . . and when I beg you to say "yes," say "no." Then let me lie outside your bolted
door. . . . So Love grows strong. . . .

That the basic elements of rape are involved in all heterosexual relationships may explain why men often identify with the offender in this crime.
But to regard the rapist as the victim, a man driven by his inherent sexual
needs to take what will not be given him, reveals a basic ignorance of
sexual politics. For in our culture heterosexual love finds an erotic expression through male dominance and female submission. A man who derives
pleasure from raping a woman clearly must enjoy force and dominance as
much or more than the simple pleasures of the flesh. Coitus cannot be
experienced in isolation. The weather, the state of the nation, the level of
sugar in the blood—all will affect a man's ability to achieve an orgasm. If
a man can achieve sexual pleasure after terrorizing and humiliating the
object of his passion, and in fact while inflicting pain upon her, one must
assume he derives pleasure directly from terrorizing, humiliating and
harming a woman. According to Amir's study of forcible rape, on a statistical average the man who has been convicted of rape was found to have
a normal sexual personality, tending to be different from the normal,
well-adjusted male only in having a greater tendency to express violence
and rage.

And if the professional rapist is to be separated from the average dominant heterosexual, it may be mainly a quantitative difference. For the
existence of rape as an index to masculinity is not entirely metaphorical.
Though this measure of masculinity seems to be more publicly exhibited
among "bad boys" or aging bikers who practice sexual initiation through
group rape, in fact, "good boys" engage in the same rites to prove their
manhood. In Stockton, a small town in California which epitomizes silent-
majority America, a bachelor party was given last summer for a young man
about to be married. A woman was hired to dance "topless" for the amusement of the guests. At the high point of the evening the bridegroom-to-be
dragged the woman into a bedroom. No move was made by any of his
companions to stop what was clearly going to be an attempted rape. Far
from it. As the woman described, "I tried to keep him away—told him of
my Herpes Genitalis, et cetera, but he couldn't face the guys if he didn't
screw me." After the bridegroom had finished raping the woman and
returned with her to the party, far from chastising him, his friends heckled
the woman and covered her with wine.

It was fortunate for the dancer that the bridegroom's friends did not
follow him into the bedroom for, though one might suppose that in group
rape, since the victim is outnumbered, less force would be inflicted on her,
in fact, Amir's studies indicate, "the most excessive degrees of violence
occurred in group rape." Far from discouraging violence, the presence of

other men may in fact encourage sadism, and even cause the behavior. In an unpublished study of group rape by Gilbert Geis and Duncan Chappell, the authors refer to a study by W. H. Blanchard which relates, "The leader of the male group . . . apparently precipitated and maintained the activity, despite misgivings, because of a need to fulfill the role that the other two men had assigned to him. 'I was scared when it began to happen,' he says. 'I wanted to leave but I didn't want to say it to the other guys—you know—that I was scared.' "

Thus it becomes clear that not only does our culture teach men the rudiments of rape, but society, or more specifically other men, encourage the practice of it.

II

Every man I meet wants to protect me. Can't figure out what from.—Mae West

If a male society rewards aggressive, domineering sexual behavior, it contains within itself a sexual schizophrenia. For the masculine man is also expected to prove his mettle as a protector of women. To the naive eye, this dichotomy implies that men fall into one of two categories: those who rape and those who protect. In fact, life does not prove so simple. In a study euphemistically entitled "Sex Aggression by College Men," it was discovered that men who believe in a double standard of morality for men and women, who in fact believe most fervently in the ultimate value of virginity, are more liable to commit "this aggressive variety of sexual exploitation."

(At this point in our narrative it should come as no surprise that Sir Thomas Malory, creator of that classic tale of chivalry, *The Knights of the Round Table*, was himself arrested and found guilty for repeated incidents of rape.)

In the system of chivalry, men protect women against men. This is not unlike the protection relationship which the mafia established with small business in the early part of this century. Indeed, chivalry is an age-old protection racket which depends for its existence on rape.

According to the male mythology which defines and perpetuates rape, it is an animal instinct inherent in the male. The story goes that sometime in our prehistorical past, the male, more hirsute and burly than today's counterparts, roamed about an uncivilized landscape until he found a desirable female. (Oddly enough, this female is *not* pictured as more muscular than the modern woman.) Her mate does not bother with courtship. He simply grabs her by the hair and drags her to the closest cave. Presumably, one of the major advantages of modern civilization for the female has been the civilizing of the male. We call it chivalry.

But women do not get chivalry for free. According to the logic of sexual politics, we too have to civilize our behavior. (Enter chastity. Enter virginity. Enter monogamy.) For the female, civilized behavior means chastity before marriage and faithfulness within it. Chivalrous behavior in the male is supposed to protect that chastity from involuntary defilement. The fly in the ointment of this otherwise peaceful system is the fallen woman. She does not behave. And therefore she does not deserve protection. Or, to use another argument, a major tenet of the same value system: what has once been defiled cannot again be violated. One begins to suspect that it is the behavior of the fallen woman, and not that of the male, that civilization aims to control.

The assumption that a woman who does not respect the double standard deserves whatever she gets (or at the very least "asks for it") operates in the courts today. While in some states a man's previous rape convictions are not considered admissible evidence, the sexual reputation of the rape victim is considered a crucial element of the facts upon which the court must decide innocence or guilt.

The court's respect for the double standard manifested itself particularly clearly in the case of the *People v. Jerry Plotkin.* Mr. Plotkin, a 36-year-old jeweler, was tried for rape last spring in a San Francisco Superior Court. According to the woman who brought the charges, Plotkin, along with three other men, forced her at gunpoint to enter a car one night in October, 1970. She was taken to Mr. Plotkin's fashionable apartment where he and the three other men first raped her and then, in the delicate language of the *S.F. Chronicle,* "subjected her to perverted sex acts." She was, she said, set free in the morning with the warning that she would be killed if she spoke to anyone about the event. She did report the incident to the police who then searched Plotkin's apartment and discovered a long list of names of women. Her name was on the list and had been crossed out.

In addition to the woman's account of her abduction and rape, the prosecution submitted four of Plotkin's address books containing the names of hundreds of women. Plotkin claimed he did not know all of the women since some of the names had been given to him by friends and he had not yet called on them. Several women, however, did testify in court that Plotkin had, to cite the *Chronicle,* "lured them up to his apartment under one pretext or another, and forced his sexual attentions on them."

Plotkin's defense rested on two premises. First, through his own testimony Plotkin established a reputation for himself as a sexual libertine who frequently picked up girls in bars and took them to his house where sexual relations often took place. He was the Playboy. He claimed that the accusation of rape, therefore, was false—this incident had simply been one of many casual sexual relationships, the victim one of many playmates. The second premise of the defense was that his accuser was also a sexual libertine. However, the picture created of the young woman (fully 13 years younger than Plotkin) was not akin to the light-hearted, gay-bachelor image projected by the defendant. On the contrary, the day after the defense cross-examined the woman, the *Chronicle* printed a story headlined, "Grueling Day for Rape Case Victim." (A leaflet passed out by women in front of the courtroom was more succinct: "Rape was committed by four men in a private apartment in October; on Thursday, it was done by a judge and lawyer in a public courtroom.")

Through skillful questioning fraught with innuendo, Plotkin's defense attorney James Martin MacInnis portrayed the young woman as a licentious opportunist and unfit mother. MacInnis began by asking the young woman (then employed as a secretary) whether or not it was true that she was "familiar with liquor" and had worked as a "cocktail waitress." The young woman replied (the *Chronicle* wrote "admitted") that she had worked once or twice as a cocktail waitress. The attorney then asked if she had worked as a secretary in the financial district but had "left that employment after it was discovered that you had sexual intercourse on a couch in the office." The woman replied, "That is a lie. I left because I didn't like working in a one-girl office. It was too lonely." Then the defense asked if, while working as an attendant at a health club, "you were accused of having a sexual affair with a man?" Again the woman denied the story, "I was never accused of that."

Plotkin's attorney then sought to establish that his client's accuser was living with a married man. She responded that the man was separated from his wife. Finally he told the court that she had "spent the night" with another man who lived in the same building.

At this point in the testimony the woman asked Plotkin's defense attorney, "Am I on trial? . . . It is embarrassing and personal to admit these things to all these people. . . . I did not commit a crime. I am a human being." The lawyer, true to the chivalry of his class, apologized and immediately resumed questioning her, turning his attention to her children. (She is divorced, and the children at the time of the trial were in a foster home.) "Isn't it true that your two children have a sex game in which one gets on top of another and they—" "That is a lie!" the young woman interrupted him. She ended her testimony by explaining, "They are wonderful children. They are not perverted."

The jury, divided in favor of acquittal ten to two, asked the court stenographer to read the woman's testimony back to them. After this reading, the Superior Court acquitted the defendant of both the charges of rape and kidnapping.

According to the double standard a woman who has had sexual intercourse out of wedlock cannot be raped. Rape is not only a crime of aggression against the body; it is a transgression against chastity as defined by men. When a woman is forced into a sexual relationship, she has, according to the male ethos, been violated. But she is also defiled if she does not behave according to the double standard, by maintaining her chastity, or confining her sexual activities to a monogamous relationship.

One should not assume, however, that a woman can avoid the possibility of rape simply by behaving. Though myth would have it that mainly "bad girls" are raped, this theory has no basis in fact. Available statistics would lead one to believe that a safer course is promiscuity. In a study of rape done in the District of Columbia, it was found that 82 percent of the rape victims had a "good reputation." Even the Police Inspector's advice to stay off the streets is rather useless, for almost half of reported rapes occur in the home of the victim and are committed by a man she has never before seen. Like indiscriminate terrorism, rape can happen to any woman, and few women are ever without this knowledge.

But the courts and the police, both dominated by white males, continue to suspect the rape victim, *sui generis*, of provoking or asking for her own assault. According to Amir's study, the police tend to believe that a woman without a good reputation cannot be raped. The rape victim is usually submitted to countless questions about her own sexual mores and behavior by the police investigator. This preoccupation is partially justified by the legal requirements for prosecution in a rape case. The rape victim must have been penetrated, and she must have made it clear to her assailant that she did not want penetration (unless of course she is unconscious). A refusal to accompany a man to some isolated place to allow him to touch her does not in the eyes of the court, constitute rape. She must have said "no" at the crucial genital moment. And the rape victim, to qualify as such, must also have put up a physical struggle—unless she can prove that to do so would have been to endanger her life.

But the zealous interest the police frequently exhibit in the physical details of a rape case is only partially explained by the requirements of the court. A woman who was raped in Berkeley was asked to tell the story of her rape four different times "right out in the street," while her assailant was escaping. She was then required to submit to a pelvic examination to prove that penetration had taken place. Later, she was taken to the police station where she was asked the same questions again: "Were you forced?" "Did he penetrate?" "Are you sure your life was in danger and you had no other choice?" This woman had been pulled off the street by a man who held a 10-inch knife at her throat and forcibly raped her. She was raped at midnight and was not able to return to her home until five in the morning. Police contacted her twice again in the next week, once by telephone at two in the morning and once at four in the morning. In her words, "The rape was probably the least traumatic incident of the whole evening. If I'm ever raped again, . . . I wouldn't report it to the police because of all the degradation. . . . "

If white women are subjected to unnecessary and often hostile questioning after having been raped, third world women are often not believed at all. According to the white male ethos (which is not only sexist but racist), third world women are defined from birth as "impure." Thus the white male is provided with a pool of women who are fair game for sexual imperialism. Third world women frequently do not report rape and for good reason. When blues singer Billie Holliday was 10 years old, she was taken off to a local house by a neighbor and raped. Her mother brought the police to rescue her, and she was taken to the local police station crying and bleeding:

> When we got there, instead of treating me and Mom like somebody who called the cops for help, they treated me like I'd killed somebody. . . . I guess they had me figured for having enticed this old goat into the whorehouse. . . . All I know for sure is they threw me into a cell . . . a fat white matron . . . saw I was still bleeding, she felt sorry for me and gave me a couple glasses of milk. But nobody else did anything for me except give me filthy looks and snicker to themselves.
>
> After a couple of days in a cell they dragged me into a court. Mr. Dick got sentenced to five years. They sentenced me to a Catholic institution.

Clearly the white man's chivalry is aimed only to protect the chastity of "his" women.

As a final irony, that same system of sexual values from which chivalry is derived has also provided womankind with an unwritten code of behavior, called femininity, which makes a feminine woman the perfect victim of sexual aggression. If being chaste does not ward off the possibility of assault, being feminine certainly increases the chances that it will succeed. To be submissive is to defer to masculine strength; is to lack muscular development or any interest in defending oneself; is to let doors be opened, to have one's arm held when crossing the street. To be feminine is to wear shoes which make it difficult to run; skirts which inhibit one's stride; underclothes which inhibit the circulation. Is it not an intriguing observation that those very clothes which are thought to be flattering to the female and attractive to the male are those which make it impossible for a woman to defend herself against aggression?

Each girl as she grows into womanhood is taught fear. Fear is the form in which the female internalizes both chivalry and the double standard. Since, biologically speaking, women in fact have the same if not greater potential for sexual expression as do men, the woman who is taught that she must behave differently from a man must also learn to distrust her own carnality. She must deny her own feelings and learn not to act from them. She fears herself. This is the essence of passivity, and of course, a woman's passivity is not simply sexual but functions to cripple her from self-expression in every area of her life.

Passivity itself prevents a woman from ever considering her own potential for self-defense and forces her to look to men for protection. The woman is taught fear, but this time fear of the other; and yet her only relief from this fear is to seek out the other. Moreover, the passive woman is taught to regard herself as impotent, unable to act, unable even to perceive, in no way self-sufficient, and, finally, as the object and not the subject of human behavior. It is in this sense that a woman is deprived of the status of a human being. She is not free to be.

III

Since Ibsen's Nora slammed the door on her patriarchal husband, woman's attempt to be free has been more or less fashionable. In this 19th century portrait of a woman leaving her marriage, Nora tells her husband, "Our home has been nothing but a playroom. I have been your doll-wife just as at home I was papa's doll-child." And, at least on the stage, "The Doll's House" crumbled, leaving audiences with hope for the fate of the modern woman. And today, as in the past, womankind has not lacked examples of liberated women to emulate: Emma Goldman, Greta Garbo, and Isadora Duncan all denounced marriage and the double standard, and believed their right to freedom included sexual independence; but still their example has not affected the lives of millions of women who continue to marry, divorce and remarry, living out their lives dependent on the status and economic power of men. Patriarchy still holds the average woman prisoner not because she lacks the courage of an Isadora Duncan, but because the material conditions of her life prevent her from being anything but an object.

In the *Elementary Structures of Kinship*, Claude Levi-Strauss gives to marriage this universal description: "It is always a system of exchange that we find at the origin of the rules of marriage." In this sytem of exchange, a woman is the "most precious possession." Levi-Strauss continues that the custom of including women as booty in the marketplace is still so general that "a whole volume would not be sufficient to enumerate instances of it." Levi-Strauss makes it clear that he does not exclude Western Civilization from his definition of "universal" and cites examples from modern wedding ceremonies. (The marriage ceremony is still one in which the husband and wife become one, and "that one is the husband.")

The legal proscription against rape reflects this possessory view of women. An article in the 1952-53 *Yale Law Journal* describes the legal rationale behind laws against rape: "In our society sexual taboos, often enacted into law, buttress a system of monogamy based upon the law of 'free bargaining' of the potential spouses. Within this process the woman's power to withhold or grant sexual access is an important bargaining weapon." Presumably then, laws against rape are intended to protect the right of a woman, not for physical self-determination, but for physical "bargaining." The article goes on to explain explicitly why the preservation of the bodies of women is important to men:

> The consent standard in our society does more than protect a significant item of social currency for women; it fosters, and is in turn bolstered by, a masculine pride in the exclusive possession of a sexual object. The consent of a woman to sexual intercourse awards the man a privilege of bodily access, a personal "prize" whose value is enhanced by sole ownership. An additional reason for the man's condemnation of rape may be found in the threat to his status from a decrease in the "value" of his sexual possession which would result from forcible violation.

The passage concludes by making clear whose interest the law is designed to protect. "The man responds to this undercutting of his status as *possessor* of the girl with hostility toward the rapist; no other restitution device is available. The law of rape provides an orderly outlet for his vengeance." Presumably the female victim in any case will have been sufficiently socialized so as not to consciously feel any strong need for vengeance. If she does feel this need, society does not speak to it.

The laws against rape exist to protect rights of the male as possessor of the female body, and not the right of the female over her own body. Even without this enlightening passage from the *Yale Law Review*, the laws themselves are clear: In no state can a man be accused of raping his wife. How can any man steal what already belongs to him? It is in the sense of rape as theft of another man's property that Kate Millett writes, "Traditionally rape has been viewed as an offense one male commits against another—a matter of abusing his woman." In raping another man's woman, a man may aggrandize his own manhood and concurrently reduce that of another man. Thus a man's honor is not subject directly to rape, but only indirectly, through "his" woman.

If the basic social unit is the family, in which the woman is a possession of her husband, the super-structure of society is a male hierarchy, in which men dominate other men (or patriarchal families dominate other patriarchal families). And it is no small irony that, while the very social fabric of our male-dominated culture denies women equal access to political, economic and legal power, the literature, myth and humor of our culture depicts women not only as the power behind the throne, but the real source of the oppression of men. The religious version of this fairy tale blames Eve for both carnality and eating of the tree of knowledge, at the same time makng her gullible to the obvious devices of a serpent. Adam, of course, is merely the trusting victim of love. Certainly this is a biased story. But no more biased than the one television audiences receive today from the latest slick comedians. Through a media which is owned by men, censored by a State dominated by men, all the evils of this social system which make a man's life unpleasant are blamed upon "the wife." The theory is: were it not for the female who waits and plots to "trap" the male into marriage, modern man would be able to achieve Olympian freedom. She is made the scapegoat for a system which is in fact run by men.

Nowhere is this more clear than in the white racist use of the concept of white womanhood. The white male's open rape of black women, coupled with his overweening concern for the chastity and protection of his wife and daughters, represents an extreme of sexist and racist hypocrisy. While on the one hand she was held up as the standard for purity and virtue, on the other the Southern white woman was never asked if she wanted to be on a pedestal, and in fact any deviance from the male-defined standards for white womanhood was treated severely. (It is a powerful commentary on American racism that the historical role of Blacks as slaves, and thus possessions without power, has robbed black women of legal and economic protection through marriage. Thus black women in Southern society and in the ghettoes of the North have long been easy game for white rapists.) The fear that black men would rape white women was, and is, classic paranoia. Quoting from Ann Breen's unpublished study of racism and sexism in the South *"The New South: White Man's Country,"* Frederick Douglass legitimately points out that, had the black man wished to rape white women, he had ample opportunity to do so during the civil war when white women, the wives, sisters, daughters and mothers of the rebels, were left in the care of Blacks. But yet not a single act of rape was committed during this time. The Ku Klux Klan, who tarred and feathered black men and lynched them in the honor of the purity of white womanhood, also applied tar and feathers to a Southern white woman accused of bigamy, which leads one to suspect that Southern white men were not so much outraged at the violation of the woman as a person, in the few instances where rape was actually committed by black men, but at the violation of his property rights. In the situation where a black man was found to be having sexual relations with a white woman, the white woman could exercise skin-privilege, and claim that she had been raped, in which case the black man was lynched. But if she did not claim rape, she herself was subject to lynching.

In constructing the myth of white womanhood so as to justify the lynching and oppression of black men and women, the white male has created a convenient symbol of his own power which has resulted in black hostility toward the white "bitch," accompanied by an unreasonable fear on the part of many white women of the black rapist. Moreover, it is not surprising that after being told for two centuries that he wants to rape white women, occasionally a black man does actually commit that act. But it is crucial to note that the frequency of this practice is outrageously exaggerated in the white mythos. Ninety percent of reported rape is intra- not inter-racial.

In *Soul on Ice*, Eldridge Cleaver has described the mixing of a rage against white power with the internalized sexism of a black man raping a white woman. "Somehow I arrived at the conclusion that, as a matter of principle, it was of paramount importance for me to have an antagonistic, ruthless attitude toward white women. . . . Rape was an insurrectionary act. It delighted me that I was defying and trampling upon the white man's law, upon his system of values and that I was defiling his women—and this point, I believe, was the most satisfying to me because I was very resentful over the historical fact of how the white man has used the black woman." Thus a black man uses white women to take out his rage against white men. But in fact, whenever a rape of a white woman by a black man does take place, it is again the white man who benefits. First, the act itself terrorizes the white woman and makes her more dependent on the white male for protection. Then, if the woman prosecutes her attacker, the white man is afforded legal opportunity to exercise overt racism. Of course, the knowledge of the rape helps to perpetuate two myths which are beneficial to white male rule—the bestiality of the black man and the desirability of white women. Finally, the white man surely benefits because he himself is not the object of attack—he has been allowed to stay in power.

Indeed, the existence of rape in any form is beneficial to the ruling class of white males. For rape is a kind of terrorism which severely limits the freedom of women and makes women dependent on men. Moreover, in the act of rape, the rage that one man may harbor toward another higher in the male hierarchy can be deflected toward a female scapegoat. For every man there is always someone lower on the social scale on whom he can take out his aggressions. And that is any woman alive.

This oppressive attitude towards women finds its institutionalization in the traditional family. For it is assumed that a man "wears the pants" in his family—he exercises the option of rule whenever he so chooses. Not that he makes all the decisions—clearly women make most of the important day-to-day decisions in a family. But when a conflict of interest arises, it is the man's interest which will prevail. His word, in itself, is more powerful. He lords it over his wife in the same way his boss lords it over him, so that the very process of exercising his power becomes as important an act as obtaining whatever it is his power can get for him. This notion of power is key to the male ego in this culture, for the two acceptable measures of masculinity are a man's power over women and his power over other men. A man may boast to his friends that "I have 20 men working for me." It is also aggrandizement of his ego if he has the financial power to clothe his wife in furs and jewels. And, if a man lacks the wherewithal to acquire such power, he can always express his rage through equally masculine activities—rape and theft. Since male society defines the female as a possession, it is not surprising that the felony most often committed together with rape is theft. As the following classic tale of rape points out, the elements of theft, violence and forced sexual relations merge into an indistinguishable whole.

The woman who told this story was acquainted with the man who tried to rape her. When the man learned that she was going to be staying alone for the weekend, he began early in the day a polite campaign to get her to go out with him. When she continued to refuse his request, his chival-rous mask dropped away:

"I had locked all the doors because I was afraid, and I don't know how he got in; it was probably through the screen door. When I woke up, he was shaking my leg. His eyes were red, and I knew he had been drinking or smoking. I thought I would try to talk my way out of it. He started by saying that he wanted to sleep with me, and then he got angrier and angrier, until he started to say, 'I want —,' 'I want —.' Then, I got scared and tried to push him away. That's when he started to force himself on me. It was awful. It was the most humiliating, terrible feeling. He was forcing my legs apart and ripping my clothes off. And it was painful. I did fight him—he was slightly drunk and I was able to keep him away. I had taken judo a few years back, but I was afraid to throw a chop for fear that he'd kill me. I could see he was getting more and more violent. I was thinking wildly of some way to get out of this alive, and then I said to him, 'Do you want money? I'll give you money.' We had money but I was also thinking that if I got to the back room I could telephone the police—as if the police would have even helped. It was a stupid thing to think of because obviously he would follow me. And he did. When he saw me pick up the phone, he tried to tie the cord around my neck. I screamed at him that I did have the money in another room, that I was going to call the police because I was scared, but that I would never tell anybody what happened. It would be an absolute secret. He said, okay, and I went to get the money. But when he got it, all of a sudden he got this crazy look in his eye and he said to me, 'Now I'm going to kill you.' Then I started saying my prayers. I knew there was nothing I could do. He started to hit me—I still wasn't sure if he wanted to rape me at this point—or just to kill me. He was hurting me, but hadn't yet gotten me into a strangle-hold, because he was still drunk and off balance. Somehow we pushed into the kitchen where I kept looking at this big knife. But I didn't pick it up. Somehow, no matter how much I hated him at that moment, I still couldn't imagine putting the knife in his flesh, and then I was afraid he would grab it and stick it into me. Then he was hitting me again and somehow we pushed through the back door of the kitchen and onto the porch steps. We fell down the steps and that's when he started to strangle me. He was on top of me. He just went on and on until finally I lost consciousness. I did scream, though my screams sounded like whispers to me. But what happened was that a cab driver happened by and frightened him away. The cab driver revived me—I was out only a minute at the most. And then I ran across the street and I grabbed the woman who was our neighbor and screamed at her, 'Am I alive? Am I still alive?' "

Rape is an act of aggression in which the victim is denied her self-determination. It is an act of violence which, if not actually followed by beatings or murder, nevertheless always carries with it the threat of death. And finally, rape is a form of mass terrorism, for the victims of rape are chosen indiscriminately, but the propagandists for male supremacy broadcast that it is women who cause rape by being unchaste or in the wrong place at the wrong time—in essence, by behaving as though they were free.

The threat of rape is used to deny women employment. (In California, the Berkeley Public Library, until pushed by the Federal Employment Practices Commission, refused to hire female shelvers because of perverted men in the stacks.) The fear of rape keeps women off the streets at night. Keeps women at home. Keeps women passive and modest for fear that they be thought provocative.

It is part of human dignity to be able to defend oneself, and women are learning. Some women have learned karate; some to shoot guns. And yet we will not be free until the threat of rape and the atmosphere of violence is ended, and to end that the nature of male behavior must change.

But rape is not an isolated act that can be rooted out from patriarchy without ending patriarchy itself. The same men and power structure who victimize women are engaged in the act of raping Vietnam, raping black people and the very earth we live upon. Rape is a classic act of domination where, in the words of Kate Millett, "the emotions of hatred, contempt, and the desire to break or violate personality," takes place. This breaking of the personality characterizes modern life itself. No simple reforms can eliminate rape. As the symbolic expression of the white male hierarchy, rape is the quintessential act of our civilization, one which, Valerie Solanis warns, is in danger of "humping itself to death."

13

Forcible Rape: Institutionalized Sexism in the Criminal Justice System

Gerald D. Robin

In this chapter Robin discusses rape in the context of the criminal justice system, with the focus of his discussion on obtaining rape convictions. He makes it clear that rape is a unique crime in the manner in which its victims are dealt with by the criminal justice system. He documents for the reader the frequently inhumane treatment that rape victims receive from the system. Raped women are subjected to an institutionalized sexism that begins with their treatment by the police, continues through a male-dominated criminal justice system influenced by pseudo-scientific notions of victim precipitation, and ends with the systematic acquittal of many de facto guilty rapists. Once again, women are all too often wrongly blamed for their own victimization by men. The codification of sexism centers in the legal elements involved in proving guilt and obtaining convictions. In effect, the law's focus on corroboration, consent (i.e., the raped woman resisted, did not consent), and character has established a standard of proof in rape cases that is more stringent than "beyond a reasonable doubt."

This chapter underscores the institutional nature of sexism in the criminal justice system. It is Robin's contention that the poor handling of the crime of rape and the victim is due to the fact that the victim is always a woman and the accused is always a man. Moreover the criminal justice system appears to be more concerned with the threat of false accusation against the rapist (which, in fact, is extremely rare), than the brutal fact that a woman was raped!

Robin goes on to discuss reform measures—the emergence of rape crisis centers and changes in the rape law—all of which have been heavily influenced by the women's liberation movement. He ends on a pessimistic note with one prosecutor's assessment that meaningful change in rape laws has yet to be made despite claims to the contrary.

Reprinted with permission of the National Council on Crime and Delinquency, from Gerald D. Robin, "Forcible Rape: Institutionalized Sexism in the Criminal Justice System," *Crime & Delinquency*, April 1977, pp. 136-53.

Since rape is more an act of assault than of sex, the resisting woman runs the risk of being crippled, blinded, disfigured, paralyzed, mutiliated, or murdered. The fear of being raped—which every woman knows—has made women, collectively, the largest group of prisoners in America, sentenced to lifelong deprivation of liberty by the frightening reality of sexual assault and by a sexist society and criminal justice system which require that the victim first establish *her* innocence before the rapist can be convicted. The punishment imposed upon all women as potential victims of rape exceeds that given to convicted rapists. Every woman—not only the young, physically attractive adult whom normal men might ordinarily find most sexually desirable—is a potential victim of rape. When a 25-year-old addict who broke into a building and raped an elderly woman was asked, "Why did you rape such an old woman?" his response was, "Because she was there." After each of three previous random rapes, he said, "I apologized to the woman, said I was sorry and didn't know why I did it."[1]

Among crimes of violence, rape may be the one least often reported to authorities. According to Uniform Crime Reports, 56,000 women were raped in 1975.[2] Victimization surveys, however, place the actual incidence of rapes at almost four times the number reported to the police.[3] And the FBI estimates that for each rape which comes to official attention, ten do not.[4] Despite its low reportability, rape statistics have risen sharply and continuously since 1968.[5] What these statistics mean to women living in urban areas is that, by the most conservative estimates, one in ten will, at one time or another, be confronted by a rapist. If the true incidence of rape is as high as some believe, the average female city-dweller can expect to be raped sooner or later.[6]

Raped women are reluctant to report the crime because of the male chauvinism built into the rape laws; the ordeal accompanying prosecution; their sexist treatment by police, prosecutor, court, and jury; and the "legal technicalities" that authorize invasion of their privacy. With respect to the latter, raped women recently suffered a major defeat in their desire to avoid personal identification as victims by the mass media. The case originated in Georgia, which had a statute prohibiting newspaper identification of rape victims. A seventeen-year-old woman was raped—and murdered— by five young men, who pleaded guilty to the sexual attack. A television report disclosed the identity of the victim in a news account of the trial. Her father sued the station owners for damages, charging invasion of his family's privacy. The company moved to have the case dismissed on the grounds that the Georgia statute was a violation of the First Amendment to the Constitution. Freedom of the press is explicitly guaranteed in the First Amendment, whereas the right to privacy has achieved Constitutional protection much more recently through a series of judicial opinions. The issue was resolved by the U.S. Supreme Court in March 1975. The Court decided that the First Amendment came first, thus legalizing the continued indignities and social stigma raped women are exposed to even after trial.[7]

All too frequently the outcome of a rape trial is acquittal of a clearly guilty assailant. The consequences of the woman's public exposure are family shame and, possibly, a "damaged goods" reaction from her husband which may lead to divorce because of her marital "infidelity." Though asserting that innocent women can be raped, a well-known sociologist who is an expert in victimology and *intellectually* sympathetic to the plight of raped women nonetheless concedes, "If my wife were raped, I don't know how I could forgive her. Even though I am wrong."[8]

At common law, rape was defined as unlawful carnal knowledge of a woman not one's wife (intercourse), committed forcibly and without her consent,[9] and, because it was considered a heinous offense, punishable by death and by both castrating the offender and removing his eyes. The latter penalties have been virtually eliminated. However, the basic common law definition has become the statutory standard for forcible rape, one of the few remaining crimes which the penal codes consistently make punishable by death, life imprisonment, or the equivalent of permanent incapacitation (a prison term of twenty to thirty years).[10]

Among serious offenses, rape is unique in that distinctly *human* factors have established the legal elements of the crime, which must be proved beyond a reasonable doubt. These human factors discourage victims from reporting the crime to the police and make conviction especially difficult. They include a sexist society, the historical role of women as "property," obsolete rape laws, stereotyped legal notions of how women should act when they are being forcibly attacked, and an unreasonable concern for the rights of the accused. Convicting the rapist requires corroboration and proof of the victim's resistance and good character.[11]

CORROBORATION

Corroboration is confirmation (a) that the event occurred and is thus not a complete fabrication, (b) that the defendant has been identified as the rapist, (c) that there was actual "penetration" of the woman, and (d) that force was present and "consent" was absent. The amount and type of corroborative evidence required by law to reliably establish occurrence of the event and identity of the rapist vary. Some states require innocent third-party eyewitness corroboration; others accept as corroboration of the rape and the rapist's identity testimony of a third party to whom the victim reported the crime shortly after its commission. The law's concern for trustworthy identification of suspects in general is based on the legal presumption of innocence. With respect to forcible rape in particular, insistence upon accuracy of identification is heightened by the severe penalties attaching to the offense, the extreme social stigma associated with the charge itself, psychological experiments showing the unreliability of eyewitness identification, and a history of erroneous "proof of identification" which has sent innocent men to their deaths.[12]

The highly emotional and distraught state of the woman in a rape situation makes mistaken identity possible; this is especially true when brutality and sexual indignities accompany the rape. Yet, these very features—the intensity of the experience and its traumatic impact—heighten the victim's sensitivity to the rapist's identity. Other factors support the presumption of reliable identification by the victim: as often as not, victim and rapist are not complete strangers to each other, the rape occurs in the woman's place, and the woman submits rather than resisting or fighting.[13] In addition, no rape is so instantaneous or rapidly consummated that the woman has no opportunity to observe her assailant. It takes time for the woman to disrobe or for the rapist to tear her clothes off. The sexual encounter is one in which the male may extend his physical pleasure—encompassing a period before, during, and after intercourse. A woman about to be raped may attempt to talk the man out of it.[14] Under these conditions, she certainly has far greater natural inclination, motivation, and opportunity to observe the identity of her attacker than does a victim of other direct-contact crimes. The pervasive sensitivity to sex in American society, the conditioning of women to their role as sex-objects and to the bestiality of all men, their intuitive awareness of sexual motifs in contacts with men—these factors make it unlikely that the rape victim would be so disoriented as to misperceive her assailant. These considerations raise the question of why, in practice, corroboration of identification in rape cases should be any more at issue than in other crimes, such as robbery.

Most jurisdictions do not formally require corroboration of the rape and the rapist's identity; however, the reality of persuading a jury to convict on a possibly capital offense requires that proof of both be corroborated.[15] The prosecutor must be prepared to establish corroboration at trial. Therefore, his interviews with the victim beforehand may involve searching questions about her assailant's features, face, penis and its placement, her position and reaction, her opportunity to observe, lighting and location, time spent together, and time of complaint to authorities.[16] Though necessary in preparation for her testimony in open court, such questioning makes the raped woman feel more like the criminal than the victim.

Recent Supreme Court decisions[17] have sensitized the prosecutor of a rape case to the need for solid corroboration of identification. Thus, "intimate" interrogation of raped women by police and prosecution is required in their own interest, to bring the offender to justice; the need for corroboration takes precedence over embarrassment and humiliation of the victims. The refusal of citizens who observe sexual assaults to become involved as witnesses makes successful prosecution all the more frustrating and unpredictable.[18]

Penetration is an essential legal element of rape. Intercourse need not be completed: the slightest entrance of the penis to the *labia majora* is "penetration."[19] When required, corroboration of penetration may come from (1) medical evidence and testimony, (2) evidence of breaking and entering the woman's apartment, (3) the condition of her clothing, (4) injuries sustained, (5) her emotional state, (6) opportunity of the accused, (7) his conduct when arrested, (8) semen or blood on either's clothing, (9) promptness of reporting the crime to friends or authorities, and (10) absence of motive to falsify.[20] Medical and scientific corroboration would be the most indisputable evidence of penetration. For example, hair in the vaginal area can be analyzed by race and body location and compared microscopically with the defendant's. A serological test, conducted by applying benzidine to the penis, may indicate the presence of blood.[21]

Despite the prosecutor's access to scientific corroboration of penetration, its availability is not always utilized by the police and sensitive, intelligent interrogation still remains the standard fact-finding technique. An important function of police questioning in rape cases is to prepare the woman for aggressive cross-exmination by defense counsel and "to make sure that the woman is not petrified, embarrassed, or driven to tears on the stand."[22] It is doubtful, however, whether police interrogation is restricted to this purpose and the collection of necessary corroborative evidence. A male-dominated cultural arrogance that "some girls rape awful easy" and many "say no no when there's yes yes in their eyes"[23] is the popular image associated with the crime. Male prisoners who are homosexually raped are probably the only men in our society who can fully appreciate the fear and trauma of rape.

Questions and comments like the following made by police to rape victims suggest a voyeurism and callousness which discourage victims from reporting the offense: How many orgasms did you have? I know why you got raped. How big was he? Was he good looking? What were you thinking about while he was doing it? Weren't you a little cold in that miniskirt, Sweetie? Well, why were you out so late? Don't you ever wear a bra?[24] Many a victim—in tattered clothes, sobbing, shaking with fear, and suffering from visible bruises—is exposed to such interrogation by police and detectives in a local police precinct immediately after reporting the attack.[25] Such treatment led one victim to conclude that while the rape was bad enough, the police interrogation was six times worse![26]

Dr. Cynthia Cooke, a gynecologist and chief of Adolescent Clinics at Philadelphia General Hospital, supervised examination of raped victims for several years; she believes that by the time the women are through being questioned by the police, they have been doubly assaulted. Addressing a seminar of police personnel, she said: "Police brutalization of the victim is responsible for the failure of women to report the crime of rape. You, with your inept questioning, rape the woman psychologically and, with your lack of understanding, are responsible for many instances of severe emotional damage and psychological trauma."[27]

In addition, the police have been accused of discouraging women from reporting rape through discrimination and a double standard of justice reflecting the "slum sex code," dismissing a complaint if the victim is alone when she makes it, is suspected of being promiscuous, or is black.[28] Rape Crisis Center members say that police in effect have complete discretion in deciding whether to accept the woman's complaint of the crime, and even when they grudgingly do so they neglect working on cases which they believe are unsubstantiated.[29] An interesting study of police screening of rape claims found that they disbelieved black rape complainants more often than white victims and therefore dismissed some allegations as unfounded.[30] As a further indication of heightened police suspicion toward the validity of rape complaints, the proportion of index offenses considered "unfounded" by them ranged from 2 per cent of the larcenies to 18 per cent of the forcible rapes.[31]

Equally discouraging to women are the attitudes of prosecutors who refer to the raped woman as "a silly bitch" and brazenly ask the victim of a brutal gang rape whether she enjoyed forced anal intercourse, and judges conducting rape trials who remark that "boys will be boys." Incredibly, one judge stated for the record that he himself could not conceptualize how a truly innocent woman could allow herself to be raped: unless there is evidence of extensive physical trauma, "a hostile vagina will not admit a penis." In this regard, a study of thirty-eight Philadelphia judges involved in trying rape cases revealed how their personal attitudes toward the victim would affect their interpretation of evidence and ultimately the question of the rapist's guilt. Rape according to the law may not be rape according to the judges, who define it as "assault with failure to please, friendly rape, breach of contract, and felonious gallantry." One interviewed judge commented that "With the Negro community you really have to redefine the term rape. You never know about them." Delay by the victim in reporting the crime to the police out of fear, shame, or anxiety over how she will be treated by officials was viewed by some judges as an indication that the event was fabricated by a lying and perhaps vindictive woman.[32]

Various approaches have been suggested to encourage greater reporting of the crime, to insure continued cooperation by the complainant, and to reduce her embarrassment by criminal justice personnel. The founder of the Chicago North Side Rape Crisis Line has urged that police and prosecutors be sensitized to the impact of forcible rape upon the victim and that each group receive special training in gathering evidence and case preparation.[33] As part of their sensitivity training, police recruits at the Northern Virginia Police Academy watch a team of psychologists, as victim and attacker, simulate a rape scene, which is then discussed with the recruits.[34] Increasingly, civilian police personnel and policewomen are being used to conduct the interrogation and investigation in rape cases. The Law Enforcement Assistance Administration has become active in funding a variety of projects intended to alleviate the problems of rape victims in the arms of the law. The Denver Rape Reduction Project was awarded $86,000 from LEAA to reduce the trauma associated with processing rape cases and to encourage prosecution. A $250,000 LEAA grant was awarded to the Center for Women's Policy Studies to develop model programs for more adequately responding to the needs of rape victims and to marshal community resources.[35]

Rape Crisis Centers may be the criminal justice system's most effective and promising means of humanizing the treatment of victims. Largely a product of the women's liberation movement, these centers provide information, referral services, temporary shelter, emotional support, and counseling when victims are most in need of such assistance and understanding—often extending through the re-adjustment period after the trial is over. The centers are operated by women who have been sexually assaulted themselves, volunteers, practitioners from the helping professions, "ordinary housewives," and even former policewomen. Crisis center staff may accompany the victim in reporting the offense and be present during interrogation. Their presence during questioning by the police and the prosecutor and in court increases victim rapport with the authorities and encourages humane and dignified treatment, and their continued support in preparation for the trial also reduces the need to use immediate police interrogation as a testing-ground for the victim's stamina later. Grueling police interrogation on the heels of a sexual assault is a questionable procedure for preparing the rape victim for her day in court several months away. Given the slowness with which offenders are brought to trial, there is ample and more appropriate time to attend to this legitimate need of the system. Also, the screening function performed by rape crisis centers may moderate the intimacy of police questions directed to corroboration and complainant credibility. At the least, it would serve to postpone such questioning until the victim is more composed and better able to communicate the facts of the event objectively. Finally, the continued assistance provided by rape crisis centers—especially after conviction or acquittal, when the system has disposed of the case and dropped its interest in the victim—is crucial in helping raped women recover from the effects of the experience. Indeed, we have just begun to consider the long-range effects of being raped. A study of ninety-two adult rape victims who were treated in the emergency ward of the Boston City Hospital revealed a "rape trauma syndrome" that included tension headaches, fatigue, sleep pattern disturbances, self-guilt, and a pervasive, generalized fear—fear of physical violence, of death, and of resuming sexual activity with husband or boy-friend.[36] Intense guilt and self-blame was a common reaction of the victims—a pathetic "tribute" to a sexist society, sexist rape laws, and sexist treatment by a criminal justice system that has collectively succeeded in convincing some women that they had "precipitated" their own victimization.[37]

The Rape Victim Advocate Program in Portland, Oregon, incorporates the major features and functions of rape crisis centers. Funded by a $124,132 grant from the LEAA, the program encourages women to report rapes by easing the emotional strains that accompany a call to the police, investigation, and prosecution. Before it was established, raped women were forced to submit immediately to humiliating questions by the police. Intimate clinical examinations were conducted in a screened-off section of the booking room, the area in the police station reserved for fingerprinting and photographing the criminal! Under the new program, the victim receives immediate counseling, is given a physical examination at a private hospital, and, after the trial, is given follow-up counseling if necessary. The director and her staff are available twenty-four hours a day to aid the rape victim. Ordinarily, when a rape is reported the advocate will meet the police and the woman at the hospital, remain with her during the examination and interviews, accompany her home afterward, and return whenever the victim needs advice and comfort. Since the program started, rape arrests have more than tripled.[38]

RESISTANCE

The most problematic legal element in rape is that it be committed "without the consent" of the woman. The more stringent statutes and case law require the victim to prove to the judge or jury that she risked or sustained injury resisting an attack which placed her in fear of immediate death or serious bodily harm. Anything less than convincing physical resistance by the woman makes her submission "consensual."[39] In a leading decision on the meaning of "utmost resistance," the Wisconsin Supreme Court said the phrase requires "the most vehement exercise of every physical means or faculty within the woman's power to resist the penetration of her person, and this must be shown to persist until the offense is consummated," and it overturned the rapist's conviction in that case because the victim, facing a larger and stronger combatant, had simply tried to escape. The court ruled that "resistance is opposing force to force, not retreating from force."

The court's standard of "utmost resistance" was illustrated in a subsequent rape case, in which the victim, a "mild, timid, socially inexperienced female," was beaten and choked. As recently as 1968 the same judicial body, reversing a rapist's conviction, found that the intercourse was consensual because the woman was not hysterical during or after the act.[40] Such cases and law account for one rape victim's observation that a woman must be " 'bruised, bloody, and damned near dead' in order for the activity to be considered not consensual."[41]

The major stumbling block in conviction for rape is the difficulty of proving that the intercourse occurred "without the consent" of the woman —the thin legal line separating rape from seduction. The absence of physical force by the man and the woman's failure to struggle and resist were responsible for a Manhattan judge's ruling that "conquest by con job" was seduction and not rape. The incident which resulted in dismissing the charges against Martin Evans, a 36-year-old cable-TV interviewer accused of luring a college girl to his apartment and attacking her, occurred on July 15, 1974. On that day he befriended a twenty-year-old Wellesley College sophomore at La Guardia Airport. Posing as a psychologist named Dr. Martin Sage, he explained to the young woman that he was a famous scientist doing research on women and the singles scene. She accepted Martin's offer to drive her to Manhattan, where she was to take a train to see about a summer job caring for disturbed children. Once in the city, he persuaded her to join him for conversation and a drink at his Lincoln Towers apartment. When she asked him why toys and a crib were in one of the rooms, he continued his impersonation by explaining that the "equipment" was used to encourage his patients to associate freely about their childhood experiences and feelings. Subsequently, she testified in court, Evans grabbed her, pulled her over to the bed, pushed her down, and raped her. Upon arrest, Evans admitted to the police that he "played games on girls' heads."

At the end of the four-day trial, Justice Greenfield acquitted Evans of rape because there was insufficient evidence to show that the intercourse occurred "without the consent" of the woman: Evans had not used physical force or threats and she had not actively resisted or struggled. The judge accepted the young woman's testimony as essentially credible and described her as a "naive, gullible, and unworldly girl who was unacquainted with New York and its sophisticated ways." Nonetheless, the court found that sexual conquest by deception, impersonation, and application of psychological techniques is not rape.

The question in this case is whether the sexual conquest by a predatory male of a resisting female constitutes rape or seduction. It is a fact that since before the dawn of history men with clubs have grabbed women, willingly or unwillingly, by their hair, to have their way with them.

As we have become more civilized, we have come to condemn the more overt, aggressive, and outrageous behavior of some men toward women and labeled it rape. At the same time, we recognize there are situations which do not deserve the extreme penalty, in which the male objective was achieved through charm, guile, protestations of love, promises, and even deceit—where force was not employed to overcome reluctance.

The taint of judicial sexism in the opinion was revealed in the court's concluding observation in its ten-page decision: "Bachelors and other men on the make, fear not. It is still not illegal to feed a girl a line," and Evans agreed: "I seduce. I don't rape." Ironically, Evans *was* found guilty of using an apartment without the *owner's consent*. In 1975 a charge against him for raping a minor was dismissed because the complainant refused to appear.[42]

The law's insistence that rape victims violently engage their molesters in order to prove force and nonconsent is questionable on three counts:

1. It is based upon misconceptions about the realities of rape and rapists and the way normal women respond under the circumstances. Many of these erroneous expectations reflect a sexist view of gallantry which has been incorporated into the law of rape and into the decisions of juries.

2. Nonresistance is not the equivalent of consent: robbery victims who do not put up a fight are not said to have *consented* to the crime. Nor is a motorist who sees his car being stolen and calls the police rather than aggressively pursuing the thieves presumed to have consented to auto theft. The absence of resistance does not establish the element of consent.

3. "Utmost resistance" to rape is the quickest way to intensify the offense to first-degree murder. Physical resistance to *any* assault simply escalates the level of violence used by the assailant. One woman who "successfully" resisted required 120 stitches on her face—a high price to pay for "utmost resistance." Commenting on this case, the detective involved said:

We've been looking for this guy for a long time. Two years ago we picked him up for attempted rape, and it was a throw-out in court; no corroboration. Now we have this poor woman, who fought like hell and didn't get raped. The guy has been indicted for assault in the first degree. She's scarred for life. And you know what she says now? She says she wishes she hadn't fought, and maybe he wouldn't have cut her up the horrible way he did.[43]

Police files are replete with accounts of dead robbery victims who refused to "consent." The victims of violent crimes and dangerous offenders—whether they are armed or not—increase their chance of being severely injured when they physically resist; even "verbal" resistance may be a trigger to fatal force. The psychotic brutality of some rapists and their threats of retaliation deter women not only from resisting but from reporting the crime at all. Law enforcement personnel routinely advise victims not to resist when in a potentially dangerous situation.

Taking a different position concerning the appropriate response by a potential victim, a recent article notes that being raped, though traumatic, is not a fate worse than death. While endorsing resistance, the article offers this caveat: "A half-hearted struggle is worse than none at all; you must be prepared to hurt your attacker, and to get hurt yourself."[44] As we have seen, however, many women submit to rape to avoid the possibility of being seriously physically injured; others—like the woman whose resistance was rewarded by 120 facial stitches—wishes that they had "taken it lying down." The fear of rape *as* a fate worse than death is being commercially exploited by the karate business. Women's Martial Arts Center's course in "Street Technique" includes exercises, pummeling a punching bag, and practice-fighting with rubber knives. Its effectiveness in preventing rape and escaping unharmed may be as limited as karate and judo in discouraging muggers.[45]

Recommending that a victim's best strategy is to resist and to refuse to be intimidated by her assailant, a clinical psychologist presents comparative data from twenty raped victims and sixteen who successfully resisted their attackers.[46] The data suggest that the "emotionally healthy resisters" were more socially flexible than the submitters, were more likely to understand other points of view ("including the rapist's"), were less anxious and less depressed, and had fewer symptoms of stress after the attempted rape—in short, they had stronger personalities than the submitters. The woman with 120 stitches would probably have been classified as an emotionally *very* healthy resister. Now that this "successful" victim who avoided being raped is permanently disfigured as a result of misjudging when to resist, one wonders how emotionally healthy she is.

CHARACTER AND REPUTATION

In most jurisdictions, evidence of the victim's character and reputation is admissible at trial as part of the issue of consent.[47] Character evidence is not directly concerned with "resistance" as discussed above; rather, it lets the jury decide whether the victim is the "type of person" who would have willingly had intercourse with the defendant on the occasion in question. This source of evidence can be very damaging to the prosecutor. It may be relatively easy for the defense, through character evidence, to create a reasonable doubt about "absence of consent"; by contrast, it is difficult for the prosecutor to establish the victim's character and reputation as so impeccable that absence of consent can be presumed by the jury. The fact that it is the *victim's* character and not the defendant's which is at issue favors acquittal. Any defense evidence illustrating questionable or immoral conduct by the complainant may cause the jury to doubt her credibility and can destroy the prosecutor's case no matter how well founded it is.

Male jurors are very unsympathetic to the prosecution in cases where the rape victim is "unchaste," had prior sexual relations with the accused, or even only had prior acquaintance with him. Given these conditions, they may identify with the male defendant and infer consent and lack of resistance by the woman. Female jurors may find it even more difficult to give rape victims with bad reputations the benefit of a doubt. Thus women with illegitimate children and prostitutes have little chance of securing convictions of men who raped them. Simply referring to the victim as a prostitute or as sexually "liberated" may be enough to exonerate the accused, even if brutality was involved.[48] It would seem that, to satisfy the nonconsensual element in rape, such a victim must be murdered by the rapist.

REASONS FOR STRINGENT REQUIREMENT OF PROOF

Psychiatrists and medical authorities have emphasized that false accusations of rape stem from the fantasies of normal and abnormal women. Manfred Guttmacher has noted that "women frequently have fantasies of being raped," and Karl Menninger believes that such fantasies may be universal. Their concern is that "these fantasies are all too easily translated into actual belief and memory falsification. It is fairly certain that many innocent men have gone to prison on the plausible tale of some innocent looking girl because the orthodox rules of evidence . . . did not permit adequate probing of her veracity."[49] Though Wigmore, an oft-quoted and influential legal scholar, strongly endorses the imaginary quality of rape and its relationship to false accusation, he is unable to provide a single example of a false conviction; instead, he relies upon five case histories of mentally ill females who made false sexual charges, none of which resulted in conviction of the accused.[50] Such exaggerated concern over female "sexual" exploitation of innocent men by rape-fantasizing women making false accusations makes one wonder *who* is doing the fantasizing. Nonetheless, the attitude that juries in rape cases are especially prone to convict upon false accusation has found its way into the statutes and case law.

That female fantasies of rape may lead to false accusation and even conviction in isolated instances is undeniable.[51] However, the general "theories" about them are too weak to justify skepticism toward the rape victim's credibility which exceeds the standard presumption-of-innocence rule applied to defendants in all crimes. The threat of false accusations, of course, may stem from more practical considerations: resentment or revenge, pregnancy, inducement to marriage, etc. Regardless of motivation, it is the function of the court and jury to acquit or convict on the merits of the case. Accordingly, written and unwritten law which in effect recognizes a presumption of consent that must be refuted at trial by the prosecution is unduly harsh and unfair, both to the victim and to society.

A second reason for the stringent elements of proof is the assumed ease with which the charge of rape may be made, the stigma associated with the accusation alone, and the severe penalties available upon conviction. Stringent proof is intended to discourage easily made false accusations, which result in severe social and legal punishment. However, women who act out their rape fantasies by false accusation would not be discouraged from doing so by such requirements, nor would more normal women be motivated to false reporting by the compelling emotions of love, hate, and security. Those who *would* be most discouraged from reporting the crime because of the ordeal associated with the harsh elements of proof are the innocent and actual victims of rape.

Third, it is assumed that the jury will have a natural sympathy toward the victim, which would prejudice them against the defendant and thus make a fair trial impossible. To guard against the tendency of jurors to convict without adequate evidence, the law makes proof of rape especially rigorous. But we have already seen how male-dominated juries tend to identify with the defendant and how female jurors give him the benefit of a doubt if the victim's character or reputation is questionable.

The most ambitious study ever conducted on jury decision-making revealed the comparative leniency of the defendants' legal peers.[52] Kalven and Zeisel divided the rapes they studied—all of which were restricted to those tried by juries—into aggravated and simple rape. In aggravated rape there was violence, the parties were strangers to each other, and there was more than one assailant; simple rape consisted of the remainder of the cases. They found that in 12 per cent of the aggravated rape cases the jury acquitted when the trial judge, had the decision been left to him, would have convicted. The decisions of the jury in simple rape are more relevant to the consent issue. Because corroboration of absence of consent was not obvious in these cases, the jury has the discretion and opportunity to be influenced in its verdict by many other factors. Here, the jury acquitted 60 per cent of the simple rape defendants whom the judge would have found guilty.[53]

The elements of proof in rape—particularly the core requirement of "absence of consent" and its interpretation—may facilitate convicting the innocent and acquitting the guilty. The availability of these "legal technicalities" permits jurors to reach verdicts which conceal racial prejudice.

Such legally aided exploitation of race prejudice contributes to the victimization of both black and white defendants: studies of rape show that it is intraracial and *Uniform Crime Reports* displays its increase. Legal reform of rape laws, especially of utmost-resistance consent elements, would reduce miscarriages of justice and increase deterrence. Effective revision of the consent element in rape could prevent jurors from using utmost-resistance standards as a legal escape hatch to permit, conceal, and dignify racially motivated decisions.

Fourth, a sexist American society may have contributed subtly to the stringent requirements of proof of rape. Historically, women were legally viewed as the property of men and as deficient in the faculty of "reason"— giving rise to the notion that rape charges can be too easily and frivolously made by this basically irresponsible and irrational subsegment of society. Their earlier status as the chattel of their spouses may sustain contemporary rape statutes which do not recognize rape of wives by their husbands. The language of the law further reflects this sexist performance for male rationality in the yardstick of "the reasonable *man.*" It is not coincidental that rape is the only crime which by definition can be committed only by males against females. Such identification implies and reflects a cultural suspiciousness toward women as "provocateurs" in any sexual encounter with men. The crime of rape is also unique in shifting the *mens rea* element from the defendant to the victim. These legal biases have been exploited by male police officers, male prosecutors, male judges, male legislators, and male psychiatrists to justify an unrealistically high level of proof in rape cases.

Finally, social science research has reinforced support for stringent rape law by focusing upon the role played by victims of homicide and forcible rape in "precipitating" their own deaths and sexual assaults. The concept and contribution of victim-precipitation to violent crime was introduced by criminologist Marvin Wolfgang in his distinguished study, *Patterns of Criminal Homicide.* Wolfgang analyzed all criminal homicides listed in the Philadelphia police records in the five years 1948-1952. His work was a groundbreaking attempt to explore the social and behavioral relationship between victim and offender in the most violent and intensely personal of all crimes. A major finding was that in 26 per cent of the 588 cases of criminal homicide, the *victim* was the first to resort to physical violence— e.g., to display or use a deadly weapon, or to strike a blow in an argument: a drunken husband beating his wife gave her a butcher knife and challenged her to use it on him; she did. Wolfgang coined the term "victim-precipitation" to describe those situations in which the victim's direct, immediate, and positive action leads to his own death.

M. Amir, a student of Wolfgang, applied the concept of victim-precipitation to his examination of 646 cases of rape recorded by the Philadelphia

Police Department in 1958 and 1960. Unlike Wolfgang's work—where the police files made it possible to clearly operationalize the concept—there was no objective way for Amir to identify cases of "victim-precipitated" rape.[54] This limitation was reflected in Amir's all-embracing definition of victim-precipitated rape: (a) situations where the woman actually or *apparently* agreed to intercourse "but retracted before the actual act or did not react strongly enough when the suggestion was first made by the offender" and (b) risky or vulnerable situations "marred with sexuality"—e.g., the woman uses indecent language and makes gestures that can be interpreted by the man as an invitation to sexual relations. Thus, where the woman aroused the defendant without intention of intercourse, agreed to have a drink or go for a ride with a stranger, or didn't resist her assailant's sexual advances strongly enough, victim-precipitation was considered present.[55] Using this ambiguous definition, Amir identified 19 per cent of the 646 cases as victim-precipitated rape.[56] The effect of this theory lends scientific credibility to the myth that women are responsible for the crime ("they asked for it") and want to be forcibly raped, and it mitigates the guilt of the defendant at trial.

Although the law does not recognize precipitation, provocation, and seduction as mitigating factors in rape, jurors do. While the law recognizes only the issue of consent at the moment of intercourse, jurors recognize contributory provocation by the victim and are moved to leniency toward the defendant; while victim-precipitation is not a valid legal defense against a charge of forcible rape, jurors are influenced by it in *their* definition of the crime and in their verdicts.[57] If required to choose between total acquittal and conviction as charged in situations described under victim-precipitated rape, the jury will probably acquit.[58] Thus, the administration of justice may be determined more by the *human* elements that influence jurors than by the legal elements that define the offense.

Several reasons have been mentioned which discourage raped women from reporting the crime to the authorities, not the least of which is their treatment by the police themselves. In this connection, the most direct and practical response to encourage greater reporting of rape has been the use of policewomen to conduct the initial interrogation and follow-up investigation. The New York Police Department, for example, has a seven-women Rape Analysis & Investigation Squad and a special telephone number for women who are too embarrassed to report sexual assaults to policemen.[59] Desirable as they are, such measures are limited inducements to reporting the offense and going through the ordeal of prosecution and trial. The major determinants of victim participation in the administration of justice are the legal elements which define the offense, the barriers they present to conviction, and the unnecessary "invasion of privacy" permitted by rape laws. The most effective, equitable, and ambitious incentives to report rape are contained in the efforts, primarily by women's liberation groups and feminists, to reform rape laws.

REFORM OF RAPE LAW

Reform of rape laws has involved changes in the legal elements of proof and in establishing different degrees of the offense. The two are closely related.

Changes in Legal Elements of Proof

Changes in the legal elements of proof have focused upon corroboration. So far, eighteen states have provided that before evidence of the woman's past sexual conduct may be presented to a jury, its relevance must first be determined by the judge. New York formerly required corroboration of identity of the rapist, penetration, and force and lack of consent. Corroboration of only the last of these three elements is required under the new law, which went into effect March 1974. A 16 per cent increase in reported rapes after this legislation has been credited to greater willingness of victims to file complaints.[60] Until 1974, Connecticut and Ohio required that the occurrence of the sexual encounter be corroborated by medical evidence or by witnesses. These corroboration requirements have been revoked, putting the rape victim's testimony on a par with that of a robbery victim.[61]

Legislative changes in rape laws were adopted or approved in ten states in 1974, and legislation was pending in at least twelve more. Some of these amendments—e.g., requiring that rape victims be examined by female police personnel and protecting separated women from their husbands— do not apply strictly to the legal elements of proof. Among those that do, changes in disclosing at trial the victim's previous sexual history (bearing on consent) are the most likely to increase convictions. California and Michigan have passed the most liberal "sexual chastity amendments." In California it was an intentional reform measure to control, through facilitating convictions, the 120 per cent increase in reported rapes from 1960 to 1972. That state's new law has all but prohibited trial evidence on the previous sexual conduct of the victim.[62] In Iowa, the victim's sexual experience with other men which occurred more than a year before the rape is excluded from trial testimony.[63] Florida law permits the judge to determine in closed hearing, before it can be introduced at trial, that sexual chastity material is pertinent. Other states have passed, or are expected to pass, similar legislation to limit defense introduction of the victim's prior sexual behavior. The model legislation for much of the revised rape law is the Michigan statute that went into effect in April 1975. Michigan's new law incorporates the crime of rape into the more generic offense category of "criminal sexual conduct," drops the corroboration requirement, and prohibits cross-examination concerning the victim's prior sexual experiences unless they are absolutely relevant. It is also rigorously nonsexist: it provides that a woman can be charged with raping a man—e.g., by using a weapon to force him to perform sexual acts with her. The model legislation encompasses homosexual rape and establishes a procedure under which legally separated husbands can be charged with raping their wives.[64]

Degrees of Offense

Closely related to the reasons for revising the legal requirements of proof is the increasing statutory recognition of degrees of the offense. The standard being adopted is that of the Model Penal Code: (a) A man is guilty of "gross sexual imposition" if he compels the woman "to submit by any threat that would prevent resistance by a woman of ordinary resolution," a *third-degree* felony punishable by a minimum term of one to two years and a maximum term of five years. (b) An act in which a male compels a female to submit to sexual intercourse "by force or by threat of imminent death, serious bodily injury, extreme pain or kidnapping" is defined as rape and a felony in the *second degree,* punishable by a minimum prison term of one to three years and a maximum term of ten years. (c) Where the man actually inflicts serious bodily injury to the woman, he is guilty of rape and a felony in the *first degree,* carrying a minimum of one to ten years and a maximum sentence of life.[65]

The Model Penal Code's recommendations do not go so far as to redefine rape basically as an *assaultive* rather than a *sexual* offense—a major objective and rallying point of women's rights advocates. Some states do and others are moving in this direction. A task force of the Connecticut Commission on the Status of Women has drafted legislation to replace its state's lengthy list of sex crimes by a single category of sexual *assault,* recognizing four degrees thereof.[66] The National Organization of Women's Task Force on Rape has endorsed the "staircasing" of sexual offenses, such as that achieved in Michigan, which recognizes four degrees of criminal sexual conduct, depending on the specific circumstances of the assault. Making rape part of the criminal category of assault shifts attention from the role of the victim to the culpability of the offender. The criminal justice system has a clear responsibility to intervene when violence enters the picture. Thus, husbands who sexually *force* themselves upon their wives would be more subject to prosecution and conviction, as assailants if not rapists. Whether the contemporary reform of rape laws focuses upon rape as an act of violence rather than sex is incidental to the objectives of rape law reform: to encourage victims to report the sexual attack, to convict the guilty, and to assure equitable punishment.

Juries reluctant to convict for single-category rape need no longer choose between the extreme options of acquittal or conviction. Evidence that might be just short of convincing a jury beyond a reasonable doubt that the defendant was guilty of rape as traditionally defined can fairly convict on a lesser-related count, and, because of the lower penalties and clearer guidelines on determining when the defendant is guilty of the most serious form of this crime, a jury might be more willing to convict for first-degree felony rape. Where a jury would acquit the defendant despite the evidence rather than subject him to the social stigma attaching to "rape," it can convict him of "gross sexual imposition." At the least, different degrees of rape would partly compensate for the perhaps inevitable tendency of juries and society to consider assumption-of-risk and victim-precipitation as evidence of the woman's guilt. Scaling the crime would make it harder for juries to be improperly influenced by consent, corroboration, and reputation even where these legal elements of proof have been revoked or liberalized.

The reform of rape laws and revision of the rules of evidence are not without their critics. Some see changes in procedures like the sexual-chastity prohibition as clouding the law of evidence. Others have expressed concern that rape law reforms motivated by stricter prosecution and more convictions threaten the basic principle of presumption of innocence. Perhaps the fairest assessment and conclusion has come from a New York assistant district attorney:

"The law is not really changing. It is simply serving as a balance. Scepticism toward women was built into the laws but it wasn't necessary, since it already existed in the police, the jury, the judges, even the D.A.'s office. What we're getting now is just long-needed rebalancing."[67]

Notes

[1] *A.M. America,* TV program, Channel 8, May 8, 1975. Based on interview with director of South Florida State Hospital.

[2] *UCR,* 1975, p. 11.

[3] President's Commission on Law Enforcement and Administration of Justice, *The Challenge of Crime in a Free Society* (Washington, D.C.: U.S. Govt. Printing Office, 1967), p. 21, Table 4.

[4] Carole Wade Offir, "Rape: Don't Take It Lying Down," *Psychology Today,* January 1975, p. 73.

[5] Based upon *UCR,* 1975, p. 11, and James Selkin, "Rape," *Psychology Today,* January 1975, p. 72, Chart I.

6 These are figures I have interpolated from rape statistics in Los Angeles reported in Selkin, *supra* note 5.

7 95 S. Ct. 1029 (1975); *New York Times*, Dec. 15, 1974, pp. 11, and March 4, 1975, pp. 1, 15.

8 S. Schafer, quoted in Kurt Weis and Sandra S. Borges, "Victimology and Rape: The Case of the Legitimate Victim," *Issues in Criminology*, Fall 1973, p. 105.

9 Code of Alabama, Recompleted 1958, Title, 14-18, p. 286.

10 Of the 162 persons executed in South Carolina between 1930 and 1973, 127 were blacks convicted of rape or murder. In Arkansas, four of the eleven men on Death Row in a recent year were blacks convicted of raping white women. "Death Row: The Final Ghetto," *National Observer*, Nov. 9, 1974, p. 12.

11 Richard A. Hibey, "The Trial of a Rape Case: An Advocate's Analysis of Corroboration, Consent, and Character," *American Criminal Law Review*, Winter 1973, pp. 309-34.

12 Elizabeth Loftus, "Reconstructing Memory: The Incredible Eyewitness," *Psychology Today*, December 1974, pp. 117-19. See also Edwin Borchard, *Convicting the Innocent* (Hamden, Conn.: Archon, 1961).

13 Menachem Amir, "Victim Precipitated Forcible Rape," *Journal of Criminal Law, Criminology and Police Science*, December 1967, Table 1, pp. 498-500.

14 Mary Meyer, "Rape: The Victim's Point of View," *Police Law Quarterly*, April 1974, p. 42.

15 Hibey, *supra* note 11, pp. 313-16.

16 *Id.*, p. 313.

17 United States v. Wade, 388 U.S. 218, 18 L. Ed. 2d 1149, 87 S. Ct. 1926 (1967).

18 Ironically, this "bad Samaritan" attitude may be a reasonable precaution against *being* raped: a Denver study found that one-fourth of women sexually assaulted by strangers were responding to the *rapists'* false request for help. Selkin, *supra* note 5, p. 72.

19 Hibey, *supra* note 11, p. 312 at note 9.

20 *Id.*, p. 320.

21 Such an involuntary physical intrusion into the defendant's person apparently does not violate Fifth Amendment constitutional rights against self-incrimination. In the guideline case, an intoxicated man refused to take a "breathalizer" test from the police and a sample of his blood was later taken involuntarily. The Supreme Court ruled in 1966 that there was no evidence of "testimonial compulsion" and that a defendant's body is a source of physical evidence which may be used against him. *Id.*, pp. 320-21, at note 44

22 "The Victim in a Forcible Rape Case: A Feminist View," *American Criminal Law Review*, Winter 1973, p. 351 (hereafter cited as "The Victim").

23 S. Rosenblatt, *Justice Denied* (Los Angeles: Nash, 1971), p. 36.

24 "The Victim," *supra* note 22, p. 348; "Victim or Criminal," *Human Behavior*, June 1974, p. 53; "Rape," *Encore*, Feb. 17, 1975, p. 20.

25 "Victim or Criminal," *supra* note 24.

26 "The Victim," *supra* note 22, p. 348.

27 "Victim or Criminal," *supra* note 24.

28 "The Victim," *supra* note 22, pp. 343, 348.

29 *Id.*, p. 348.

30 "Police Discretion and the Judgment that a Crime Has Been Committed—Rape in Philadelphia," *University of Pennsylvania Law Review*, 1968, p. 277.

31 Gwynn Nettler, *Explaining Crime* (New York: McGraw-Hill, 1974), p. 45.

32 Carol Bohmer, "Judicial Attitudes toward Rape Victims," *Judicature*, February 1974, pp. 303-07.

33 Meyer, *supra* note 14, p. 43.

34 "Rape Alert," *Newsweek*, Nov. 10, 1975, p. 71.

35 *Behavior Today: The Professionals' Newsletter*, May 27, 1974, p. 147. The Center's 600-page

report, released in November 1975, described the treatment of rape victims at the hands of the criminal justice system as indifferent at best and demeaning at worst. Specific abuses cited included the following: inhospitable attitudes by hospitals with respect to accepting and treating rape cases; the reluctance of doctors to testify in rape cases and to prepare thorough reports which could be used as incriminating evidence; inadequate police facilities to identify rapists who are recidivists or to aid in victim identification of their assailants; assigning the least experienced assistants to prosecute rape defendants and frequently changing prosecutors as the case approaches trial; and excessive emphasis on questioning the credibility of the rape victim at trial. Barbara J. Katz, "Society Hit on Response to Rape," *National Observer*, Nov. 8, 1975, p. 3.

36 Ann Wolbert Burgess and Lynda Lytle Holmstrom, "Rape Trauma Syndrome," *American Journal of Psychiatry*, September 1974, pp. 981-86.

37 *Id.*, p. 983. Of 1,070 questionnaires voluntarily submitted to *Viva* by purportedly raped women, half reported suffering a marked loss of trust in male-female relationships. Significant proportions reported nightmares, hostility toward men and other adverse effects on their sexuality, loss of self-respect, and suicidal impulses. Impairment of sexuality by the crime was reported by 41 per cent of the women whose rapists were not convicted, but by only 27 per cent of those whose rapists were convicted. Pauline B. Bart, "Rape Doesn't End with a Kiss," *Viva*, June 1975, pp. 41-42.

38 Harl Haas, "Upgrading Rape Investigations," *National Observer*, May 17, 1975, p. 5.

39 Sybil Landau, "Rape: The Victim as Defendant," *Trial*, July-August 1974, p. 20.

40 *Id.*, pp. 21-22.

41 "The Victim," *supra* note 22, p. 347.

42 379 N.Y.S.2d 912 (1975); *New York Times*, May 31, 1975, p. 31; "Rape and Consent," *Time*, May 12, 1975, p. 55.

43 "The Victim," *supra* note 22, pp. 346-47.

44 Offir, *supra* note 4, p. 73.

45 "Smile and Give the Mugger Your Money," *New Haven Journal-Courier*, Jan. 1, 1975, p. 33.

46 Selkin, *supra* note 5, p. 70 ff.

47 Hibey, *supra* note 11, p. 325.

48 "The Victim," *supra* note 22, pp. 343-44.

49 Hibey, *supra* note 11, p. 327.

50 "The Victim," *supra* note 22, pp. 336-37 at note 8.

51 According to Robert Kasanof, former head of the New York Legal Aid Society, "Rape remains a crime that is particularly susceptible to false accusation. That is the universal experience starting with Potiphar's Wife, running through the Scottsboro boys, up to the experience of most practicing lawyers today." "Rape Alert," *supra* note 34, p. 77.

52 Harry Kalven and Hans Zeisel, *The American Jury* (Boston: Little, Brown, 1966).

53 "The Victim," *supra* note 22, p. 342.

54 Amir, *supra* note 13, p. 495.

55 "The Victim," *supra* note 22, p. 339.

56 Amir, *supra* note 13, p. 496.

57 "The Victim," *supra* note 22, pp. 339, 341.

58 Kalven and Zeisel, *op. cit. supra* note 52.

59 *New York Times*, March 22, 1973.

60 *New York Times*, Oct. 24, 1974, p. 13; June 3, 1975, p. 37; April 29, 1975, p. 31.

61 *New York Times*, Dec. 1, 1974, Sec. E, p. 10.

62 Two exceptions: (a) where the prosecutor or the victim maintains that she was a virgin, the defendant can introduce evidence to rebut; (b) if there is evidence that the victim lied on the stand, the defense can introduce evidence attacking her credibility. *Sacramento Bee*, Aug. 23, 1974.

[63] *New York Times*, Dec. 1, 1974, p. 10; Gerald J. Szumski, "A New Law Shields Rape Victims' Private Lives," *National Observer*, May 25, 1974, p. 15.

[64] "Rape Alert," *supra* note 34, pp. 76-77.

[65] *Model Penal Code*, Proposed Official Draft (Philadelphia: American Law Institute, July 30, 1962), pp. 97, 142-43.

[66] *Hartford Courant*, Dec. 21, 1974, p. 8.

[67] *New York Times*, Dec. 1, 1974.

14

Battered Women: Society's Problem

Del Martin

This chapter provides a comprehensive examination of the problems associated with battered women. Del Martin is an outspoken feminist. Her brief history of marriage introduces the reader to a basic cause of wife battering: the socially structured economic dependence of women on men in marriage. She documents the problems women have in getting the police to respond to the seriousness of their complaints about their husband's brutality and the consequences of this lack of response for the women. In addition to the failures of the legal system, she continues by documenting the serious inadequacies of the social services systems in assisting battered women. In so doing she reiterates a point made by Klein in Chapter 11 that mental health professionals frequently continue the harmful practice of blaming the victim—as does much of the legal and political system.

This chapter emphasizes a point made throughout this book: that in studying the relationship between women and crime in any particular area, we must take into account social structural variables surrounding the specific phenomenon—in this case, wife battering. According to Martin, this means examining those institutions that structurally create the conditions for women's subservience to men: the organization and history of marriage; the organization of the economy which structures preferred jobs and better wages for men; the organization of legal and religious systems that structure men as the "head of the family"; the system of sex role socialization of boys and girls that encourages male supremacist relations between men and women, as well as a set of values that associates aggression and violence with masculinity: in short, the organization of the secondary status of women in each and every institution in our society. As Martin says, "When studying wife beating, the institutional history of marriage, the lack of effective sanctions by social agencies, and the general status of women (in our society) must be taken into account." This is one example of what is meant by taking into account social structural variables. The analysis must ask what is it about the institutions in society, the way in which they are organized to benefit one group (men) at the expense of another group (women), about the values held, about the history of certain relationships and traditions, that have a direct bearing on the issue (in this case wife battering) under examination.

Reprinted from "Battered Women: Society's Problem" by Del Martin, pp. 111-141, in *The Victimization of Women,* J.R. Chapman and M. Gates (eds.), © 1978 Sage Publications, Beverly Hills, by permission of the publisher.

Martin reminds the reader of a key issue that tends to be forgotten in the heat of most discussions on the issue: that despite the tendency for researchers, therapists, and law enforcers to look for ways to vindicate or excuse the assailant/husband in woman beating, there is never any justification for even a "little" violence. "No matter what she may have said or done, no woman deserves to be beaten."

Martin's contribution is manifold in this chapter. Not only does she describe and analyze the problem of woman battering; she goes on to explain the strengths and weaknesses of current programs attempting to deal with battered women and their families and makes important suggestions for change in the immediate future.

Wife beating is a complex problem that involves much more than the act itself or the personal interaction between a husband and his wife, despite what many prefer to believe. It is a social problem of vast proportions with its roots in historical attitudes toward women and the institution of marriage. The socialization of women and men in our society and the assignment of women to inferior roles that keep them economically dependent make women vulnerable to abuse by the men with whom they live. This victimization of women, who are married to or who live in quasilegal relationships with men, is reinforced by law enforcement, social service agencies, mental health professions, educational institutions, and the economy. Protections, legal or otherwise, to which a wife may resort when she has been brutalized or her life threatened, are more theoretical than practical. In application they are virtually nonexistent because they are geared to protect the marriage, not its victims. Any solution to family violence must address the values and the structure of the society that permits and thus perpetuates crimes against women. Clinical approaches cannot be effective unless pervasive social attitudes and the institutions that now give tacit approval to the practice of wife beating are drastically changed.

Wife abuse is not just slapping or shoving—it is described (Gayford, 1975; Gelles, 1972; Eisenberg and Micklow, 1974) as punching with fists, choking, kicking, knifing, slamming the victim against the wall, throwing her to the floor, or shoving her down the stairs. Beatings can last anywhere from a few minutes to over an hour. Threats of violence—punching holes in the wall, breaking down doors, and wielding a gun—can be as frightening and intimidating as actual physical attack.

The reluctance of society to recognize the prevalence of violence in marriage and to interfere with the privacy of the family is best illustrated by the inability to obtain data on the incidence of marital violence. Obvious sources like the police, attendants in hospital emergency rooms, the district attorney, private physicians, the courts, social workers, family service counselors, and other mental health professionals do not keep such records.

The FBI believes that marital violence is the most unreported crime, probably ten times more unreported than the crime of rape (Durbin, 1974: 64). From the pockets of evidence available and the educated guesses of experts who have conducted limited research or have come in direct contact with complaints from victims, we can say that the number of battered women nationwide reaches into the millions.

While wife beating has only recently surfaced as a major social problem, it is highly doubtful that its incidence is increasing. Admittedly, some men who feel threatened by the concept of women's liberation may beat their wives to keep them in their place and to reassert their "manhood." But the truth is that men have beaten their wives with impunity for centuries.

HISTORICAL ATTITUDES TOWARD WOMEN

The historical roots of wife beating are ancient and deep. Frederick Engels (1948:53-58) placed its beginnings with the emergence of the first monogamous pairing relationships, which replaced group marriage and the extended family of early promiscuous primitive societies. This new arrangement came about because women sought protection from what Susan Brownmiller (1975:16) called "open season on rape" and because men wanted to authenticate and guarantee their identity and rights as fathers. Prior to the pairing marriage, women, as mothers, were the only discernible parents and were held in high esteem. But with the new "father right," the strictest fidelity was demanded of women. Polygamy and infidelity remained men's privileges, however. The cost to women for the "protection" of one man from the sexual ravages of other men came high. Monogamy brought about the complete subjugation of one sex by the other.

With the advent of the pairing marriage, the man seized the reins in the home and began viewing the woman as his property. The sole purpose of woman was seen as that of satisfying her husband's lust, bearing his children, and tending to his household. Women were relegated to certain parts of the home, isolated, guarded, and their public activities restricted. If a woman showed any signs of having a will or a mind of her own, she was beaten in the same way that a strong-willed horse might be whipped and finally subdued.

The church sanctioned the subjection of women to their husbands "in everything" (Ephesians 6:22-24). Abused wives were advised by priests that a husband's displeasure was best dispelled by the woman's increased devotion and meek submissiveness. Physical cruelty, even murder, of the wife or a serf, were allowed in medieval times (Davis, 1971:255) if it was inflicted for "disciplinary purposes." Women were burned at the stake for many reasons, including scolding and nagging, talking back, refusing to have intercourse, *miscarrying* (even though the miscarriage was caused by a kick or blow from the husband), and permitting sodomy (even though the husband who committed it was forgiven). These inhumane practices and attitudes toward women were incorporated into the dominant culture by law, allowing men to avoid responsibility for their own behavior.

In the 1880s, the British Parliament, through a series of legal reforms (Davis, 1971:311), began to deal with the sorry plight of the married woman. The law was changed to allow a wife who had been habitually beaten by her husband to the point of "endangering her life" to separate from him, though not to divorce him. Another law prohibited a husband from selling his wife or daughter into prostitution—but only if she were under 16 years of age. Special legislation was enacted to prevent a husband from keeping his wife under lock and key.

In our own country, a husband was permitted by law (Calvert, 1975:89) to beat his wife as long as he didn't use a switch any bigger around than his thumb. It was not until the end of the 19th century that such laws were repealed. An old town ordinance, still on the books in Pennsylvania in the 1970s (Fleming, 1975), prohibited a husband from beating his wife after 10 o'clock at night or on Sundays.

THE MARRIAGE CONTRACT

Despite recent gains of the women's movement in correcting some of the inequalities between the sexes, the legal and social authority of the husband in marriage still persists. Time-honored traditions and laws are not easily or quickly changed. According to early English common law, which is the basis for American jurisprudence, "The very being or legal existence of the woman is suspended during the marriage, or at least is incorporated and consolidated into that of the husband, under whose wing, protection, and cover she performs everything" (Blackstone, 1765). In other words, the husband and wife were regarded as one person in law, and the rights and property of the marriage were vested in one person—the husband. With few modifications, this is still true today.

The married woman's loss of identity begins with the loss of her name. She takes her husband's domicile; she becomes his legal dependent. Traditional marriage vows still exhort her to "love, honor, and *obey* " her husband. He is designated by both church and state as the head of household. This authority of the husband over his wife is reinforced by the courts, the Internal Revenue Service, the Census Bureau, economic dependence, and the socialization of the sexes. The marriage contract and the restrictions it imposes have been justified by the state's overriding interest in keeping the traditional family structure intact, for marriage is the mechanism by which the patriarchy is maintained.

The law says the husband is responsible for the support of the family, and the wife is responsible for the household and the children. With the notable exception of five states (Arizona, California, Idaho, New York, and Washington) where women recently won rights to joint management of community property, the husband has sole financial authority in marriage. The wife who does not have an outside income is thus dependent upon her husband's generosity and good will for her economic and physical well-being. If a husband decides to give her no money or clothing and provides her with only a roof over her head and groceries on the table, she has no legal recourse. In 1953, a Nebraska judge ruled (DeCrow, 1974:164-165) that the living standards of a family are not the concern of the court. That the home is maintained and the parties are living as husband and wife is all that is required by law, he said. A 1962 court decision in Connecticut (Weitzman, 1974:1187) was more specific about the obligation of the wife to perform her household and domestic duties *without compensation*. "A husband is entitled to benefit of his wife's industry and economy," the court ruled.

The economic disadvantage of the wife makes her vulnerable to the whim of a supposedly benevolent despot. In return for the promise of the protection and security of her husband, she is required to reshape her personality to conform to his expectations. Should she fail to accommodate herself and accede to his standards, he may abuse her economically, emotionally, and physically. When this happens and she seeks help, she is likely to find support systems of society are geared to keeping the marriage intact, no matter the danger to her well-being or that of the children.

THE FAILURE OF THE LEGAL SYSTEM

Today, wife beating is a crime just as any other crime that constitutes bodily harm: assault and/or battery, aggravated assault, intent to assault or to commit murder. But the law becomes ambiguous in its application when the parties involved are husband and wife. The sanctity of the family home and the adage that a man's home is his castle, which pervade the whole fabric of society, are reflected in the legal system. Police admit that a large percentage of the calls they receive are DD's (domestic disturbances), but they do not differentiate between family "squabbles" and incidents of violence. They seldom make arrests in either case.

A study conducted by the Kansas City (Missouri) Police Department in 1971-1972 revealed that 46,137 DD calls were received during one year.

Of the city's homicides, 40% were found to be cases of spouse killing spouse. In more than 85% of these homicides, police had been summoned at least once before the murder occurred, and in almost 50% of the cases, the police had been called to the scene five or more times within the two-year period prior to the homicide. Escalation of marital violence was also noted in figures for aggravated assault (domestic disturbance accounting for one third of these crimes) and the equally high percentage of repeated calls for help prior to the incident.

FBI statistics (Murphy et al.:n.d.) show that one out of every five officers killed in the line of duty in 1974 died trying to break up a family fight, and that the majority of injuries sustained by patrol officers are due to domestic disturbances. The danger to police may explain their reluctance to respond to DD calls and why many departments have instituted family crisis intervention training—training that places a high priority on teaching officers how to protect themselves in volatile home situations. But it does not explain why the police ironically persist in viewing these cases as mere family "spats." If these situations are perilous to trained police officers, they are certainly even more dangerous to the defenseless woman and her children.

The police are probably the worst possible choice for a woman to call to her rescue, according to Deputy Chief James D. Bannon who has been with the Detroit Police Department since 1949. Policemen, like most males, are imbued with perceptions of masculine-feminine roles which translate into dominance-submission terms. They perceive the husband as the boss and the wife as his subordinate. These attitudes develop naturally into a laissez-faire policy. "In Detroit, as in many other cities, the treatment of female victims of assault of the domestic variety could charitably be termed cavalier. Not so charitable, but perhaps more accurate, would be an allegation of misfeasance," Bannon declared in a speech before the American Bar Association in Montreal in 1975.

Police officers are usually directed by their superiors to avoid making arrests in domestic disputes except in cases of severe injury. In a training bulletin on "Techniques of Dispute Intervention," the nonarrest policy of the City of Oakland (California) Police Services (1975:2-3) is stated explicitly: "The police role in a dispute situation is more often that of a mediator and peacemaker than enforcer of the law." The officer is told that an arrest may only aggravate the dispute or create a serious danger for the arresting officers because a husband is likely to exert desperate resistance to prevent loss of face in front of his family. The manual goes on to say that when no "serious" crime has been committed but one of the parties demands arrest, the officer should attempt to explain the ramifications (loss of wages, bail procedures, court appearances, and other hardships) and "encourage the parties to reason with each other."

Implicit in these guidelines is the refusal of police to take wife beating seriously, even though it has been shown in their own experience and that of researchers that these beatings, when unchecked, are repeated and become more and more severe as time goes on. It is hard to imagine any other situation in which police would be officially advised to encourage a victim to "reason" with an attacker. Furthermore, encouraging victims to refrain from exercising their rights is in effect denying them their rights. Wife/victims are entitled to be apprised of the law and its procedures without prejudice. It is not the function of the police to give legal advice or to base decisions on what might happen. Nor is it the function of police to help the violent offender "save face" at the expense of the victim. The safety and protection of the victim should take priority over all other considerations.

While it is true that police in most jurisdictions cannot make an arrest unless they actually witness a misdemeanor, the victim still has the option of making a citizen's arrest. Usually she is not aware of that right, and the officer should be required to so inform her and to take the offender into custody if she chooses to make an arrest. Instead, police are prone to point out to the woman that if her husband is taken to the station he will be out in a few hours on bail or on his own recognizance and will probably return to give her an even more severe beating for turning him in. Additionally, she is reminded of her dependence upon her husband's paycheck, which he could lose if he were found guilty of the charges and jailed. Some women, fearing for their lives and faced with the realization that the system offers them no physical or economic protections, renege and drop the charges. By so doing they give law enforcers the excuse, "They won't follow through," for placing a low priority on cases of marital violence.

Two class action suits have recently been filed by wife/victims: one in federal court against the Oakland Police Department and the other in the state court against the New York City police and the Family Court clerks and probation officers because of their failure to provide protection to battered wives. The 102-page New York complaint charges that the police unlawfully refuse to make arrests and employees of the Family Court unlawfully refuse to allow victims to see judges to ask for orders of protection. In one of the complaints, a neighbor called the police, and when they arrived the beating was still going on. Even though the two officers had to pry the husband's hands from around the wife's neck, and several neighbors present cried, "Arrest him; he will kill her!" the police refused to do so. They merely shrugged, said, "There is nothing we can do. We can't do anything in marriage fights," and left.

If the husband is arrested or the wife files a complaint with the district attorney, the victim faces still another test. District attorneys, who are understaffed and overburdened with caseloads, tend to count stitches and rely on the availability of witnesses in deciding which cases they will prosecute. Rarely are there witnesses to violence in the home other than the children, who are routinely protected from making court appearances. Justice and protection of the victim are sacrificed for the "We'll only go with the cases we know we can win" philosophy. According to Sgt. Barry Whalley, who conducts family crisis intervention training for the Oakland Police Department, only one out of a hundred complaints filed ever reaches the courtroom. Bannon said that of 4,900 formal complaints filed in Detroit one year only 300 were tried in court.

When the police and district attorney do follow through and prosecute a wife-beating case, there is no assurance that the judge will take the case seriously. Judges also have a tendency to dismiss marital violence as family quarrels. If they find the husband guilty, more than likely they will let him off with a suspended sentence, probation, or a small fine. A classic case in New York City (Hart, 1975) was that of "Loretta," who brought charges in criminal court against her former common-law husband on five occasions for five different incidents within a year and a half. Each time she pressed charges, followed through, and testified in court, and each time the judge released "Thomas" on his worthless promise the he wouldn't do it again. The fact that Loretta had been hospitalized on at least two occasions and had lost an eye and part of an ear because of the savage beatings she had suffered obviously had no effect on the judges who heard her complaints.

The civil remedy—issuance of temporary restraining orders or orders of protection—is equally farcical. As many attorneys point out, they aren't worth the paper they are written on. When a man is of a mind to beat his wife, he'll do it. Violations of court orders are considered contempt of court offenses and are subject to the same restrictions as other misdemeanor arrests. The victim is generally referred back to her attorney to obtain another court order, which must again be served on the husband, to appear at another show cause hearing. The procedure, which requires costly and time-consuming paper work and court appearances, offers the woman no practical protection and, again, no guarantee that the offender will be incarcerated and the beatings stopped. For this reason, many attorneys who handle divorce and domestic relations cases refuse to obtain these orders of "protection" for their clients. Others continue to go through the motions on the outside chance that such an order will have a restraining effect on the husband.

A proposal for a three-year study to test the effectiveness of legal remedies for wife abuse has been submitted to the Ford Foundation by Nadine Traub, associate professor of Rutgers Law School, and Ann Marie Boylan, attorney-at-law. They contend that comparatively little attention has been given to the question of whether available legal remedies would be effective in reducing marital violence if, indeed, they were actually used and enforced to a greater extent. In addition to the usual legal avenues a wife may pursue (criminal charges, divorce, orders of protection, suing for damages, or using child abuse laws), the attorneys suggest it may be appropriate in some instances to ask the court to use the remedies of prosecution for obstruction of justice or pretrial detention. These remedies, which would protect the victim/plaintiff from threats or harmful assaults to "persuade" her to drop the charges or perjure her testimony, are seldom invoked. The legal system routinely has placed its emphasis upon the protection of the defendant's civil rights, among them the "rule of disclosure" requiring the complainant to disclose her current address to the defense. The plaintiff's right to physical protection and the prevention of intimidation of witnesses are rarely considered in marital violence cases.

This demonstration project would be most helpful in determining the facts about wife abuse laws and their effectiveness. While the grant application applies only to a test of New Jersey law, and laws differ somewhat from state to state, still the data from such a study could have an impact nationally by suggesting legislative reforms necessary to make state laws workable.

THE INADEQUACIES OF SOCIAL SERVICES

Many women are trapped in violent homes because they have no place to go and no means of supporting themselves and their children if they were to leave. Attempts to seek help from other sources can be as discouraging as calling the police to intervene. In the first place, most beatings take place at night or on weekends, when social agencies are closed. A woman, fleeing in the middle of the night and fearing for her life, often finds herself wandering the streets aimlessly not knowing where to turn or what to do.

The most pressing need is for emergency shelter. Although there are about 70 refuges for battered women and their children in England and a network of shelters across Scotland and Holland, few exist in the United States. Task forces across the country are grappling with this desperately urgent problem. Unfortunately, efforts to establish shelters are coming at a time when money is scarce, government budgets are being pared to the bone, and private foundations are cutting back on the number and size of grants. Also, past funding patterns show that federal monies are available for research but not for services, and less than one fifth of one percent of the billions of dollars granted annually by private foundations goes to women's projects (Tully, 1975:26).

In many localities, surveys of existing emergency housing reveal that a disproportionate number of beds are available to men rather than to women and that stays are generally for a maximum of three nights. Admissions in many instances are limited to alcoholics, former mental patients, or ex-prisioners. Few places are prepared to take in women with children, and those that do sometimes have rules that exclude sons over four years old. A traditional shelter may meet a victim's immediate need for refuge. But, because of the limitation on the number of nights she can stay, it protects her from immediate danger at best and allows for a "cooling off" period at least. It does not allow a battered woman enough time to reevaluate her situation, consider her options, and perhaps seek a more permanent solution to her predicament. More than likely she has no money and only the clothes on her back. She may have no work experience or job skills. She needs more time and the opportunity to acquire vocational counseling, training, and placement. The experience of the shelters set up specifically for battered women and their children shows that when they are allowed to stay for at least three weeks to a month, they are more likely to become independent. To give them time to get on their feet and make their own way, they need public assistance.

Runaway wives who apply for funds through the Aid for Dependent Children program (AFDC) are often turned away because the husband's income makes the family ineligible for welfare. The social services system doesn't bend for the wife who is trying to make a break from an unbearable situation and has no money of her own. Technically, she is neither homeless nor destitute. She has a husband who is obligated to support her and a home to which she can return. A woman cannot qualify for financial assistance unless she has filed for divorce and is established in a separate domicile of her own. But to establish that domicile, she needs money. Consequently, many victims are forced to return to their violent husbands.

Should a woman be lucky enough to have the money to rent a place, she may still need food, clothing, and other necessities. Welfare is not obtained instantaneously. In crowded urban areas where there is high unemployment, applicants sometimes have to wait as long as ten days to two weeks for the first interview to determine eligibility and, if they qualify, another two weeks or more for their first check.

Government services are no more prepared to meet emergencies than is the legal system. Rules and regulations are rigid and do not permit social workers the flexibility needed to respond adequately to crisis situations. Contingency funds to meet unusual emergencies are virtually nonexistent. Thus, victims are frequently referred to privately funded agencies which may then refer them to others. Victims who tenaciously follow every lead often report that they wind up full circle—back to the agency where they originally sought help, and, more likely than not, back to the home where they are in jeopardy of further physical abuse.

When it comes to mental health services, battered women are far more likely to be recipients than their irrationally violent husbands. Women are told to be more compliant and to be cautious about their own behavior, especially when their husbands are in a bad mood. They are given tranquilizers along with the "grin-and-bear-it" advice. Unable to change her situation, the wife often falls into depression and despair. The majority of women who sought refuge at Chiswick Women's Aid in England (Gayford, 1975) had spent time in mental institutions for depression or suicide attempts. In fact, some women have committed themselves as one means of getting away from their abusive husbands.

Few batterers, even those who may be genuinely remorseful when they see the damage they have wrought, seek treatment on their own. According to the League of Women Voters (1975), California law allows involuntary custody for up to 72 hours "if a person is a danger to himself, to others, or gravely disabled." After the 72-hour detention period for evaluation and treatment, if the person is still considered dangerous and will not accept voluntary treatment, a certification for intensive treatment for another 14 days can be obtained. When diagnosed as "imminently dangerous," a person can be held for a period not exceeding 90 days. If a woman's husband is dangerously violent, and she wants him hospitalized, she must go to court and show reasonable cause. The man, naturally, has the right to hire an attorney and request a jury trial contesting the decision to hospitalize.

Considering how battered women are treated when criminal charges are at issue, there is little reason to believe the victim would fare any better in taking this approach. Getting mental health professionals and judges to agree that the man is "dangerous," let alone "imminently dangerous," when wife beating is the only "symptom," is a bit far-fetched. It is far easier for a husband to get his wife committed when she is so depressed and tranquilized that she no longer has the will to resist. Besides, everyone she has turned to for help has told her that she is really to blame for her husband's violence.

THE "BLAME" BIAS

Mental health professionals and researchers generally view wife beating in terms of personal relationship and individual background. Concerned chiefly with the psychological interaction between the offender and the victim, they tend to adhere to theories of victimology, in which the victim is perceived as having provoked or instigated the offense. This translates into the old saw, "a wife has masochistic needs that are gratified by her husband's assaultive behavior." The husband is thus vindicated for his act of violence by the shifting of responsibility from the assailant to his victim.

Mother, who is traditionally blamed for all family ills—particularly the antisocial behavior of the males in her family—is blamed once again. Her punishment is the beating she "brought on herself."

One battered wife stated emphatically (Martin, 1976:3): "No one has to 'provoke' a wife-beater. He will strike out when he's ready and for whatever reason he has at the moment. I may be his excuse, but I have never been the reason." Indeed, reports from victims as to what triggered their beatings (she broke the egg yolk when she was cooking his breakfast, she raised her voice, she wore her hair in a ponytail, she prepared a casserole dish instead of fresh meat for dinner) indicate that the incidents are trivial in the extreme. Other women said their husbands came home late at night, and without any warning, started beating them as they lay fast asleep in bed. They had no idea what prompted their husbands' violence.

In *Practical Psychology for Physicians*, Ray Fowler (1975), the executive director of the American Association of Marriage and Family Counselors, describes the wife abuser as "generally an obsessional person who has learned how to trigger himself emotionally." A man may perceive a reasonable comment by his wife as a nagging remark or a whining complaint, mull it over and exaggerate it until, in his own mind, he provides himself with a justification for his behavior.

"There is no warrant for jumping to the conclusion that since suffering exists, there is therefore a tendency to incur it or enjoy it," according to Karen Horney (1973:261). Elizabeth Truninger (1971:260) agrees that the pattern and frequency of wife beating merely demonstrates that some women *tolerate* violence, not that they invite it. Reasons for a woman continuing to tolerate the beatings are myriad: she is afraid to leave, she feels ashamed or guilty and doesn't want anyone else to know; to admit the failure of her marriage is to admit her own personal failure as a woman; she is dependent upon her assailant. She has no place to go and no way to support the children on her own; she is unaware that she has any option but to stay. Underlying these reasons are the ways in which women are socialized to be emotionally and economically dependent upon men and the ways in which all of our institutions are geared to keep the family together, no matter what the consequences.

Batterers, for the most part, do not seek counseling or therapy. They usually feel their actions are justified, and they have no need of help. For this reason, and because they are seldom apprehended or detained by either the criminal justice or the mental health systems, little is known about batterers. What we do know we have learned primarily from the victims. At one time the court in Framingham, Massachusetts, referred husband/offenders to the psychiatric clinic for evaluation and treatment. The psychiatrists (Snell et al., 1964) found the husbands uncooperative and unwilling to admit there were any problems in their marriages that warranted outside intervention.

On the other hand, the wives, who wished to put a stop to the beatings, welcomed the opportunity for marital counseling. The doctors therefore interviewed the wives and wound up writing a paper called "The Wife-Beater's Wife" (Snell et al., 1964), the gist of which is the everpresent sexist line that "a husband's behavior may serve to fill a wife's needs even though she protests it." The doctors concluded, "We have come to feel that the offender cannot be adequately understood, and treatment and correctional measures appropriate to him devised, until one knows whom he has offended, how and why. One cannot understand the offender and his offense without having some understanding of the people with whom he has to deal."

That may be true to a certain extent, but, unfortunately, that is where these good doctors stopped. They took the easy way out because the wives were willing subjects. Psychiatrists, like all others in our society, are socialized to believe in sex-typed roles in marriage. In this study they saw role reversal as a causal factor in marital violence. They depicted the wives as efficient, masculine, frigid, and masochistic. The husbands they viewed as shy, passive, indecisive, and sexually inadequate. The beatings were the means by which husbands reasserted their masculinity and took revenge upon their castrating wives. "The devised treatment and correctional measures appropriate to the *offender*" were never determined, of course. Getting the victim to change *her* behavior became the modus operandi. The psychiatrists cited a measure of success in one instance where the husband continued to drink, "but in a more controlled manner, and with less violence in the home."

They also noted, "In none of the cases we studied did the husband express any intent to kill his wife, although some of the beatings were severe." As therapists, they seemed to be satisfied that their work had *lessened* the violence, admitting that it did not stop completely. The implication is that the men meant no real harm and that they should be encouraged to develop less explicit, physically injurious expressions of their male power over their wives.

The problem with psychiatry as a discipline is, Naomi Weisstein (1970: 210) says, that findings which are based upon "insight, sensitivity and intuition" rather than upon empirical evidence can confirm for all time the biases that one started out with. She also finds fault with the personality theory (1970:209) which "has looked for inner traits when it should have been looking at social context." If a psychiatrist accepts the traditionally defined sex roles as gospel, believes (as Freud did) that women are innately masochistic, and is convinced that somehow a battered wife precipitates the crimes committed against her, the woman doesn't have a chance. If the wife accepts her "feminine" role, she is set up for a slave-master marital relationship which in and of itself invites abuse. But the tradition-bound psychiatrist would see her "inner need" for abuse, not the social imperatives that made her vulnerable.

Those who operate refuges for battered women report that wife/victims who take advantage of their services are generally submissive and have a very low self-esteem. Most of them need assertiveness training because they have spent their lives being passive (feminine) and have made every effort to please their husbands in order to avoid beatings. The point is that these wives are in a no-win situation. If they are passive, they are doormats that invite abuse. If they are aggressive, they invite the beatings to put them in their place.

Nathan Caplan and Stephen D. Nelson (1974:101-102) complain that a "person-blame" bias arises from too much concentration on the victim and not enough on the offender. Person-centered research and clinical therapy may have validity, they say, but the danger is that the situation can be vastly oversimplified and the labeling of groups (in this case, women, who are already socially, politically, and economically vulnerable) reinforced. The alternative is a "situation-centered" examination of the problem, which takes into account the social variables involved. When studying wife beating, the institutional history of marriage, the lack of effective sanctions by relevant social agencies, and the general status of women must be taken into account.

More often, studies to determine factors that contribute to the practice of wife abuse concentrate on alcohol use, unemployment, jealousy, stress, "innate" male aggression, and victim provocation. While they may have a certain amount of value, in the long run their chief function is to provide the husband with an excuse for beating his wife. He can say, "I was drunk and didn't know what I was doing"; "She was pregnant, and I panicked because I couldn't face the added financial responsibility"; "I was distraught because I lost my job."

All the trails that are followed in an effort to determine the etiology of wife beating lead to some kind of excuse for or vindication of the assailant/husband. Researchers, therapists, and law enforcers often miss two very salient points: (1) There can be no justification for even a "little" violence. No matter what she may have said or done, no woman deserves to be beaten; (2) The underlying factor that breeds and perpetuates hostility between the sexes is the male-supremacist, patriarchal system which depends upon the sexist structure of the family unit and other social institutions.

As already discussed, violence, if allowed to continue, escalates in intensity. What begins as a slap can lead to a broken jaw the second time around and to murder the third. This chronology of events actually happened to one San Francisco woman (Martin, 1976:20). There is no way to "control" the severity of the beatings even if that were an appropriate goal, which it is not.

Wife beating is, without question, an example of power abuse. Therapists who support the oppressive status quo—the man-over-woman power relationship in marriage—only validate the man's right to exert power over his wife. Expecting the husband to be a benevolent despot is no guarantee that physical force will not be used. The prevalence of wife beating belies such expectations.

WHAT ABOUT THE CHILDREN?

Any solution to the problem of marital violence has to begin by making the public keenly aware of its prevalence and of how it affects the children in the home. An increasing number of people are becoming alarmed about the violence in our society. They berate the police for not protecting them on the streets. They protest the inordinate amount of violence in television programming, which they feel must relate to the increased incidence of muggings and rapes. They express their outrage against child abuse, but fail to see the correlation between child abuse and wife beating or any connection between wife beating and violence in the streets.

The seeds of violence begin in the home where much of the socialization of children takes place. Children who witness their mother's beatings or hear her cries in the middle of the night react with shock, fear, and guilt. They cringe in the corner not knowing what to do. They are afraid to interfere and feel guilty when they don't. Some children, who have been taught that the police are there to protect people from harm, will run to a neighbor to call the police. How the police officer handles the situation will have a strong effect on the children.

In Morton Bard's study (1971:161) of family violence in New York City's 30th Precinct, children were present in 41% of the cases in which police were called to intervene. "If this is typical, one can only speculate on the modeling effects of parental aggression on such children—not to speak of the effects of a variety of police behaviors on the perception of children in such situations," he says. If the police officers (usually male) identify with the husband and treat the incident lightly, they will be reinforcing the role models of violent imperious male and powerless female victim. But if police efficiently calm down the parents, and, whether or not an arrest is made, effectively communicate the attitude that violent behavior is not to be excused or tolerated, the children will receive healthier signals.

Richard Gelles's research (1972:173) shows that people who as children observed violence between their parents or who were themselves victims are more likely to become batterers and victims than people who never saw their parents fight or were not subject to corporal punishment as children. From his investigations, Gelles (1972:171) concluded, "Not only does the family expose individuals to violence and techniques of violence, the family teaches approval for the use of violence."

Violence in the home takes many forms. The wife very often acts as the buffer between father and child. She takes the husband's abuse, and he leaves the children alone. In many instances, however, the husband beats the wife *and* children. Sometimes the battered wife, in her desperation, will strike out against the children. Violence then follows the "pecking order" pattern: the husband beats the wife, the wife beats the child, and the child beats the dog.

In a study of 100 battered wives in England, Gayford (1975) found that 37% of the women admitted taking their frustrations out on their children, and 54% claimed their husbands committed acts of violence against the children. The breaking point for many of these women came when the children became victims of abuse, too. At that point these women resolved, or tried, to leave.

But leaving then may be too late if, as Gelles indicates, "merely" witnessing violence in the home as a child has a deleterious effect on adult marital behavior. Instead of reacting with abhorrence to the violence they saw, as one might hope or expect, the children tend to see violence in another way—as a way of life and a means of problem solving. If children are imbued with this concept, is it any wonder that violence extends beyond the home? The reluctance of the criminal justice system to enforce the law, the failure of social services to provide emergency support systems for victims and their families, the blaming of the victim and related social factors that tend to vindicate the perpetrator—all of these serve to condone the father's violence. It is not surprising then that many sons believe that violent behavior is an assertion of one's masculinity, not only excusable but expected of them.

Robert Whitehurst (1971:41) reminds us that "men are not programmed to be other than aggressive" and that "much of the aggressive hostility vented on wives must be seen as a product of our sexually schizoid culture." He concludes, "Our culture teaches men to be tough and ready to fight if necessary. To expect men to also become tender lovers and responsive husbands seems to be asking more than logic can allow."

Change will not come about by itself. To break through the cycle of violence that has our society in its grip is an enormous task, involving nothing less than a cultural revolution of attitudes and values. If we are to reduce aggression and violence in our society, we must begin with the children. They must be trained to relate to one another as individuals, as human beings rather than as stereotypes.

Seymour and Norma Feshbach (1973:95) believe that parents and school administrators need to find alternatives to physical punishment for discipline and behavior control. They also see a need to develop procedures that will enhance empathy in children as an inhibitory mechanism by which to check the use of violence. When the individual perceives another as similar to oneself, it is more difficult to injure that person. Through role-playing techniques, the child could learn to perceive situations from someone else's perspective and to experience the other person's feelings. Emphasis should be placed on the broad dimensions of similarity that unite us in our humanness rather than on the narrow ones that divide us into antagonism-inducing categories.

James W. Prescott (1975) alludes to pleasure and violence as having a reciprocal relationship in that the presence of one inhibits the other. He sees deprivation of touching, body contact, and movement as a basic cause for a number of emotional disturbances, including violence. Prescott backs his theory by citing studies on child abuse showing that parent abusers were invariably deprived of physical affection during childhood and studies of other cultures demonstrating that societies giving infants the greatest amount of physical affection had low crime and violence rates. Murray Straus (1977) points out, however, that the warmth and affection ideology of child rearing is already espoused in America. He claims additional research is needed to determine the social and psychological conditions that prevent some parents from exhibiting such behavior toward their children and then to translate the results into programs that will assist these parents.

Prescott also sees the double standard—the rigid values of monogamy, chastity, and virginity for women—as helping to produce physical violence. "The denial of female sexuality must give way to an acceptance and respect for it," Prescott (1975:18) says, "and men must share with women the responsibility for giving affection and care to infants and children." He recognizes, too, that to replace materialistic values with human values would mean drastic change in the socioeconomic system and men's concepts of work and home.

Recognition of the problems inherent in sex role stereotyping is not enough to change attitudes and behavior. Men, though they may accept the need for change intellectually, naturally resist giving up their power and privileges. Parents who are locked into inflexible masculine and feminine roles teach their children these same roles from birth. Teachers, too, are apt to treat boy and girl children differently. Researchers Lisa A. Servin and K. Daniel O'Leary (1975) have found that nursery schoolteachers are much more likely to react to a boy's behavior, bad or good, than to a girl's.

By thus rewarding boys for aggression and girls for passivity, however unconsciously, teachers mold behavior that will cause both sexes pain later.

Psychologist Marcia Guttentag and a research team (Tavris, 1975) designed a six-week curriculum to be offered in three large, ethnically diverse school districts in Boston. The course, aimed at counteracting stereotypical conditioning and raising the children's consciousness, was given to three age groups: kindergarten (age 5), fifth grade (10), and ninth grade (14). The methodology included reading stories, viewing films, acting out scenes from plays, and working on special projects. The children learned that it is possible for both sexes to share desirable personality traits—that is, men can be sensitive and warm, and women can be assertive and competent.

From tests administered before giving the course, the researchers found that most five-year-olds are already ripe old sexists. Children, no matter what their social class or economic background, had by then been thoroughly indoctrinated to "masculine" and "feminine"sex roles. Whether their mothers worked outside the home made no difference in their belief that boys are strong and can do all sorts of interesting things, and girls are weak and silly and are best kept at home.

Efforts to broaden the children's view of sex roles did not work as well as the researchers had hoped. The girls were consistently more ready to accept the new ideas, and some turned into feminist fledglings, aware of new vistas open to women and eager to experience new roles. Most of the fifth and ninth grade boys, however, persistently held to traditional concepts, and some became even more outspoken about a "woman's place."

The degree to which the students were positively influenced by learning about changing role concepts depended, in large part, upon the teacher's enthusiasm and the extensive use of class materials. But another influencing factor is the child's observation of adult behavior outside of the classroom. Children pick up far more from the ways in which adults act than from what they say. Boys can't help but observe that men have the power and that they, too, can have things their own way if they take the power their maleness commands in our society. Their observations, unfortunately, still reflect the reality.

CHANGING POLICE ATTITUDES

First, we need to deal with the immediacy and the danger involved in marital fights. We must find ways to stop the violence when it occurs and to prevent it from reoccurring. Still the most obvious thing to do, in spite of what has been said, is to call the police for protection. Neighbors, who hear a fight going on and have reason to believe it has become violent and therefore dangerous, should call the police immediately. Neighbors, friends, and relatives must be made to realize that once violence erupts, what transpires between husband and wife can no longer be shielded by concerns for privacy. When a husband abuses his wife physically, he automatically forfeits that right. Prompt action is required to protect the wife, and possibly the children, from severe injury. A quick phone call may even prevent a murder.

When the police receive domestic disturbance calls in which violence or the threat of violence is reported they must give them top priority. Those who receive and dispatch calls should be specially trained in distinguishing wife-beating calls from nonviolent family hassles. They should be made particularly aware of the danger involved so that they get sufficient information from the caller to forewarn the responding officers. Police departments also need to develop some method of separating wife-beating incidents from the usual categories of domestic disturbance or violent crime. When arrests are made for the specific crime (assault, battery, murder), the marital relationship between victim and offender should be noted and tabbed under the heading of spouse abuse. Quasilegal relationships should, of course, be included in this category. Such a system of recording and tabulating incidents would enable us to derive the statistics that are now nearly impossible to obtain. Cross-referenced filing of incidents by name and address is also necessary so that the dispatcher can run a check for any previous reports involving the same parties and determine the probable danger.

On arrival, police should treat these cases routinely, as they would any other investigation of violent crimes. Once a determination has been made that a crime has been committed, officers should be careful to gather evidence, determine the means of force used, and be aware of all possible corroborating witnesses, including the children. Fact finding is the job of the investigating officer. Under no circumstances should the police assume that the case won't go anywhere or that the victim will drop the charges. Therefore, a detailed report of the facts should be filed in every instance, whether or not an on-the-scene arrest is made.

The wife who claims to have been struck or physically abused by her husband should be treated as a victim, even though her injuries are not visible to the officer. Police should be sensitive to the trauma the woman has just experienced and the emotional as well as physical stress she may still be suffering. She may not be in a state where she can make necessary decisions about the case. If strong circumstantial and physical evidence exists in a felony case, the officer can proceed on his own and make an arrest for probable cause without the wife's cooperation. In a misdemeanor case, the officer is obliged to state why police cannot make an arrest, and advise the woman of her right to make a citizen's arrest. Should she choose not to exercise that right at the moment, the officer should nonetheless proceed with the investigation, which may serve to validate or disprove a complaint filed later with the district attorney. If the wife needs medical attention, the officer should see that she gets it. Police should have the information needed to refer the victim to appropriate agencies where she can find financial aid, emergency shelter, legal assistance, and counseling.

The husband should be viewed as a possible criminal suspect. As part of the fact-finding process, the officer needs to determine whether the incident was an accident, a matter of self-defense, or a criminal offense. If the officer determines during questioning that a crime has indeed been committed, then the husband must be apprised of his constitutional rights before he is interrogated. Regardless of personal feelings about a domestic situation, the officer should take the matter seriously at all times.

When possible, man-woman police teams should be sent out on marital violence calls. Experience shows that women officers have a high success rate in defusing volatile situations. With both sexes responding to these calls, and with each officer serving as a check on the other, there would be less chance for sex-biased reporting of incidents.

How police officers handle themselves in marital violence situations is crucial to their own safety, to the safety of others involved, to the perceptions of the assailant as to the seriousness of the act he has committed, to the trust and commitment of the victim to pursue the case, to the perceptions of the children about violence as accepted behavior, and to the confidence of witnesses in the criminal justice system.

A policy of arrest promotes the well-being of the victim. Many battered wives who have tolerated their husbands' violence in the past have felt alone in coping with the problem. The officer who takes the situation seriously and initiates legal action may give the wife the courage to proceed with her case and change her life situation. Documenting these cases, regardless of expected outcome, builds a record of the husband's actions and intent, which may prove useful for future prosecution. Additionally, the policy of arrest may place pressure on the prosecutor and the courts— pressure that may force them to join in the struggle to find adequate legal remedies and to institute programs that will prevent repeated offenses.

To strengthen the effectiveness of the temporary restraining order as an inhibitory measure to prevent further violence, arrangements were made recently in San Francisco, at the behest of an ad hoc committee of women, to computerize such orders. In this way, the officer can call in to communications, check whether there has been a previous restraining order, and take appropriate action. With this system the officer can no longer beg off from responsibility by referring the woman back to her attorney.

DIVERSIONARY MEASURES

Many people prefer some alternative to arrest and possible jail sentences for the violent husband. One reason given is that he is the "breadwinner," but few would think of using this excuse as a saving grace for an assailant whose victim was other than his wife. In an effort to bypass criminal procedures, and perhaps hold the marriage intact, various diversionary programs have been developed.

In Hayward, California, the police department has established Project Outreach. Mental health specialists, hired by the police, go out on marital violence calls with the responding officers on weekends, when most family fights occur. When the police feel relatively sure that they have successfully quelled the violence, they are free to leave, and the therapists stay on to counsel the couple. Additionally, up to ten counseling sessions are made available free of charge to couples who wish to receive such help. After working with the project for three years, Sue Gershenson, who is a psychiatric social worker, said at a California Senate Subcommittee hearing (1975:112) that she is "convinced that the combination of trained mental health professionals and police who are sensitive and trained in crisis intervention can not only help prevent marital violence, but can also provide assistance in the resolution of family disputes." An evaluation of the project revealed that the number of repeat DD calls to police has decreased.

Project Outreach can be helpful, indeed, if the psychiatric social workers who go out on police calls can persuade the husbands to take advantage of the counseling they offer. Danger lies, however, in viewing marital violence solely as a mental health problem and in measuring the success of the project by the reduction of calls to police. If a batterer rejects counseling, as so many of them do, the wife may decide that calling the police is useless.

Some counties have started Night Prosecutor Programs to mediate disputes in ongoing personal relationships. Hearings are held in various communities in Clackamas County, Oregon, as frequently as volume demands. Volunteer mediators are screened and trained by professionals. The emphasis is on resolution of problems rather than judging right and wrong. The Night Prosecutor Program in Columbus, Ohio, is coordinated by prosecutors and conducted by law students (Martin, 1976:112). If the situation is particularly volatile, the prosecutor or hearing officer may warn of possible legal consequences if the conflict continues. Officials who started this "Citizens Dispute Settlement" concept were motivated to find a way of handling "minor" cases such as "simple assaults" and family disputes in a supervised setting outside of the traditional judicial system, to alleviate caseload pressure on the court, thereby permitting a higher degree of attention to "serious" crimes. Such informal hearings also save money, they claim, by avoiding costly court proceedings. During the first year of this program, only 2% of 3,626 direct complaints resulted in criminal charges.

Here again, wife beating is seen as a minor offense, and the husband is let off with a warning. To make the woman believe that such hearings do something for her is a cruel hoax. What about her future safety? Warnings and threats are useless unless the district attorney is prepared to follow through if the husband calls the system's bluff.

A unique judicial process that seems far more helpful has been developed in Pima County, Arizona. Under the Pre-Trial Release Program, every criminal defendant eligible for release is interviewed by a trained investigator. If, during the initial interview at the county jail, the investigator finds that the alleged offender resides with the victim, a call is made to the Victim Witness Advocate (VWA) Program. A counselor there contacts the complainant to verify the information and asks what conditions of release she would like to recommend. The counselor then relays the wishes of the complainant to the Pre-Trial Release investigator, who so advises the judge.

"Battered women have been very practical about the conditions of release they would like," states David A. Lowenberg (1976), program coordinator of the VWA Program. Consequently, judges have been receptive to their wishes and have usually complied with the suggested conditions of release. Usually the defendant is released on his own recognizance to a relative's or friend's residence with the proviso that he not contact the victim by telephone or in person during the course of the judicial proceedings. A substantial number of wife/victims ask that the defendant be given treatment for severe alcohol or emotional problems.

"From the time a criminal complaint has been issued until the final case disposition, the VWA staff keeps the battered woman apprised of the status of her case and informs her of the date, time, and place of the trial," Lowenberg says. In addition, a member of the VWA staff will escort her to court and arrange day care for her children, if she needs these support services.

The alternative to treatment of wife beating as a crime is to treat it as a mental health problem. As previously discussed, getting a batterer to seek help is extremely difficult. Because he believes not only that he has the right to beat his wife but that other husbands are doing it, too, he considers his behavior to be "normal." Therefore, he believes he has no problem and no need for outside help. The only way to get him into therapy or counseling would be for a judge to order it as a condition of release. Lt. George Rosko of the San Francisco Police Department (Martin, 1976:118) suggests that a first-time offender be remanded to a counseling center in the same way that traffic violators are sent to traffic school. The batterer would be warned explicitly that if he "ever lays a hand on his wife again" he will be sent to jail. If judges would take such a hard-nosed position and make it stick, Rosko believes there would be a marked reduction in the incidents of wife abuse.

An assistant district attorney in Spokane proposes a quicker method of obtaining results: peer pressure. If men would stop making jokes about wife beating, if they would declare wife abuse off limits and bring pressure to bear upon offenders and let them know in no uncertain terms that such behavior is not acceptable, if men would work with batterers in much the same way as women are working with victims, we might well be on our way to solving the problem.

REFUGES FOR BATTERED WOMEN

Under present conditions, however, the need for emergency shelter for battered women and their children is paramount. Women have been trapped in violent homes out of fear and economic dependency or, as one victim put it (Martin, 1976:3), "because the social structure of my world says I cannot do anything about a man who wants to beat me."

Since feminist groups have made the plight of the battered woman a national issue and because the media have been so responsive in giving the subject public exposure, help is now on the way. Consortia, coalitions, or task forces are being formed across the country to provide emergency services and shelter for battered wives and their families. These groups usually start with women banding together to help women. Initiative may come from feminist groups, such as the National Organization for Women, the local women's center or switchboard, or the rape crisis hotline. In other instances, more established groups like the Commission on the Status of Women or the Y.W.C.A. may take it upon themselves to pull together a representative group of women, among whom are attorneys, social workers, mental health specialists, or members of Junior League and Soroptimists. Experts in fund raising and proposal writing are essential to such women's support coalitions.

Gradually these groups expand to form a second more community-oriented coalition which includes both men and women from the social service agencies that relate in any way to the various problems battered wives face. Among these agencies are the police, district attorney, court, legal aid, mental health association, family service agencies, welfare, government social service and mental health departments, emergency hospital physicians, child protective services, AFL-CIO community services, and alcohol and drug abuse programs. University schools of social work, sociology, psychology, medicine, nursing, and law may provide students to conduct research or field work that can be helpful in designing a workable program to provide for the varied needs of battered women.

Invariably the groups see the value in working together to coordinate available services and identify those that are lacking. Most notable is the lack of adequate emergency housing, which usually becomes a top priority of both the women's support coalition and the secondary community resource coalition.

In forming a shelter for battered women, it is essential that the second coalition see its function as supportive of the first. Experience shows the importance of women supporting women as *women* rather than as professionals "helping" clients find solutions to their problems. According to Sharon Vaughn (Martin, 1976:203), the professional "treatment" model automatically creates a barrier that serves to further isolate and dehumanize the woman who is already the victim not only of her violent husband or lover, but of society itself. Vaughn was instrumental in the founding of Women's House in St. Paul in 1974 and the Harriet Tubman Emergency Shelter for Women in Minneapolis in 1977. She contends that peer counseling is the crucial factor. Having the opportunity to talk with other women who have shared her own experience and seeing their strength growing as they cope with emotional and economic problems, the battered woman takes on a new sense of self. She no longer feels isolated and begins to see her own strengths. Even if she decides to return home, the bond between herself and the other women remains.

As soon as a refuge opens its doors, it is filled to capacity almost immediately and has a long waiting list. That this has been the experience of existing shelters throughout the world belies the popular assumption that the wife remains with her battering husband because she has a compelling need for such abusive treatment. The *need* is for an escape hatch— for a place to go. When help is really available, battered women take advantage of it in such numbers that shelters need to tap other resources, like private homes or traditional short-term accommodations, until a vacancy arises in the refuge.

Insofar as possible, under such crowded conditions, the shelter should maintain a homelike atmosphere, particularly for the children's sake. They have already been uprooted from their homes and their friends, and they, too, suffer from the traumatic effects of the violence they have seen or felt. Children often form the majority of the residents in the refuge. Services must be provided for them while the mother is trying to pull herself together and make plans for their future. Funding agencies often lop off from their budgets funds necessary for child care services under the premise that mothers should take responsibility for their own children. They fail to see that the children may have emotional problems requiring special professional attention and that the mother, in a state of recovery herself, needs peace and time in which to work through her personal problems. She may require medical treatment, therapy, assertiveness training, job rehabilitation and placement, legal counseling, or other services provided by the shelter and its support and resource coalitions. The wife/victim needs help in caring for her children while she is reevaluating her situation and pursuing new options—perhaps creating a whole new life for herself and her family.

The biggest problem shelter task forces face is funding. Somehow when women's projects come along the vast well of funding sources suddenly runs dry. Government pleads that there isn't enough money to cover the budgetary needs of already existing programs. Officials continue to pour large sums of money into research on violence rather than reorder priorities to provide vital services for victims. Private foundations, usually traditional and conservative in outlook, are more apt to put funds into programs that are less threatening to the ongoing family relationship. Because of the tremendous need for shelters—there should be, at the very least, one in each county—it is really incumbent upon communities to find local sources to assume responsibility and produce the necessary funding. This can probably be done best by not relying upon only a single source for funding. The combination of some government funds, private donations, small grants from local foundations, and community fund-raising events—while not all that sure or secure—keeps La Casa de las Madres going in San Francisco. Those shelters lucky enough to tie into government or foundation programs must face the fact that these grants are only for a specified period; they are not ongoing. The shelter must find other sources for future needs. One means of raising funds is to set up a business (telephone answering service, mail order, catering service) in the shelter itself. The women could receive training and experience so that they can later qualify for jobs and get out on their own.

REMEDIAL LEGISLATION

Because of conditions in the criminal justice system that allow for discretion and inequities, and because of the need to reorder government spending policies, remedial legislation is being introduced at both the state and federal levels. Legislation introduced in Congress would establish a national clearinghouse for information, research, training workers, funding shelters, and a national hot line. The bill is modeled after legislation that created the national centers for the prevention and treatment of rape and child abuse. Pennsylvania, which previously had no legal provisions for evicting an abusive husband from the home or for issuing protection orders, enacted such a law to provide relief for battered women. What is unique about the statute is that it covers anyone residing in the household; it therefore extends protection to women in "common law" marriages who are not usually covered under existing law in other states. The new law also eliminates the traditional proviso that the woman must file for divorce before she can obtain a restraining order.

Revisions to New York law are being offered by State Senator Carol Bellamy so that a woman who flees her home in fear for her life cannot be divorced later by her husband on grounds of "desertion." This quirk in the law had previously placed the wife/victim "at fault," and therefore at a disadvantage, in custody and financial settlement considerations in divorce proceedings. Legislation to fund, at least partially, four to six emergency shelters for battered women has passed in California. Bills introduced in Florida, Maryland, and California would require all social agencies (police, doctors, social workers, and others who come in direct contact with marital violence cases) to report them to a central state registry. In this way, data could be gathered which might prove helpful in suggesting other solutions. These bills have been rejected by state legislatures because this information gathering would be too costly. Yet these same legislators require statistics that are otherwise unobtainable to prove the need for other "battered wives" legislation, such as funding for shelters.

Women's legislative advocates should work with attorneys who specialize in family law, directors of emergency shelters for battered women, and women's organizations to assess the inadequacies in the law and to initiate changes.

CONCLUSION

Recent developments to alleviate the plight of the battered wife by beefing up the law and law enforcement or by establishing shelters for family victims are, admittedly, only stop-gap, band-aid measures. Such intervention only serves to stop immediate violence in a particular home and to prevent imminent injury or loss of life. There is no guarantee that it won't happen again with this couple, nor that violence will not erupt in other families. Intervention is not synonymous with prevention.

Hopefully, however, these emergency measures will serve as a catalyst for dramatic and widespread change in social attitudes. When we refuse to accept marital violence as a given in some homes, when we publicly deny the husband's misconceived notion that he has a right to beat his wife, when we recognize that children are being trained to violence—then we have already begun that process of change.

For too long we have placed value upon the institution of marriage in and of itself. For the most part, we have neglected or impeded the *quality* of the marital relationship. Marriage counseling comes after the fact—after the damage is done. So long as women are relegated to subservient positions in society and in the home, they can only be victims.

Sex roles, in and out of marriage, need to be re-examined and redefined. The concept that the man is head of household and sole breadwinner for the family must be eliminated. Laws that reinforce man-over-woman power relationships in marriage must be repealed. Family life classes should be instituted in early childhood—at preschool nurseries and in kindergarten—rather than in high school, when it is too late to counteract the effects of sex-role stereotyping. Teachers and parents alike need to be trained to overcome their own sexism so as not to infect the children.

Prevention of marital violence means a whole restructuring of our society so that equality between the sexes is guaranteed in marriage and the family, in the schools, in the work force, and in government. Only when marriage is seen as an egalitarian relationship or partnership will we be able to eliminate the "battered wife syndrome."

References

Bard, M. (1971). "The study and modification of intra-familial violence." Pp. 149-164 in The Control of Aggression and Violence: Cognitive and Psychological. New York: Academic Press.

Blackstone, W. (1765). Commentaries.

Brownmiller, S. (1975). Against Our Will. New York: Simon and Schuster.

California Senate Subcommittee on Nutrition and Human Needs (1975). Hearings on Marital Violence and Family Violence transcript, July 21.

Calvert, R. (1975). "Criminal and civil liability in husband-wife assaults." Pp. 88-91 in S.K. Steinmetz and M. Straus (eds.), Violence in the Family. New York: Dodd, Mead.

Caplan, N., and Nelson, S.D. (1974). "Who's to blame?" Psychology Today, (November):99-104.

City of Oakland Police Services (1975). "Techniques of dispute intervention." Training Bulletin III-J, (June 19).

Davis, E.G. (1971). The First Sex. New York: Putnam.

DeCrow, K. (1974). Sexist Justice. New York: Random House.

Durbin, K. (1974). "Wife-beating," Ladies Home Journal, (June).

Eisenberg, S., and Micklow, P. (1974). "The assaulted wife: 'catch 22' revisited." Unpublished manuscript. A version of this study will be published in Women's Rights Law Reporter.

Engels, F. (1948). The Origin of Family, Private Property and the State. Moscow: Progress.

Feshbach, S., and Feshbach, N. (1973). "The young aggressors." Psychology Today, (April):90-96.

Fleming, J. (1975). Wife abuse. Unpublished manuscript.

Gayford, J.J. (1975). "Wife battering: A preliminary survey of 100 cases." British Medical Journal, (January 25):194-197.

Gelles, R. (1972). The Violent Home. Beverly Hills: Sage.

Hart, A.W. (1975). "Thomas promised that he would." The New York Times, (June 10).

Horney, K. (1973). The Neurotic Personality of Our Time. New York: Norton.

Kansas City Police Department (1971-1972). Northeast Patrol Division Task Force. "Conflict management: Analysis/resolution." Unpublished manuscript.

League of Women Voters (1975). Challenge of the 70's.

Lowenberg, D.A. (1976). "Pima county services for battered women." Response, (December):3-4.

Martin, D. (1976). Battered Wives. San Francisco: Glide.

Murphy, R.B., McKay, E., Schwartz, J.A., and Liebman, D.A. (n.d.). "Training patrolmen as crisis intervention instructors." Unpublished manuscript.

Practical Psychology for Physicians (1975). Summer:75.

Prescott, J.W. (1975). "Body pleasure and the origins of violence." Bulletin of the Atomic Scientists, (November):10-20.

Servin, L.A., and O'Leary, K.D. (1975). "How nursery schools teach girls to shut up." Psychology Today, (December):57-58, 102-103.

Snell, J.E., Rosenwald, R.J., and Robey, A. (1964). "The wifebeater's wife." Archives of General Psychiatry, Volume II, (August):107-112.

Straus, M. (1977). "A social structural perspective on the prevention and treatment of wife-beating." In Maria Roy (ed.), Battered Women. New York: Van Nostrand-Reinhold.

Tavris, C. (1975). "It's tough to nip sexism in the bud." Psychology Today, (December):58, 102.

Truninger, E. (1971). "Marital violence: The legal solutions." Hastings Law Journal, 23(1) (November):260.

Tully, M.J. (1975). "Funding the feminists." Foundation News, (March/April):24-33.

Weisstein, N. (1970). " 'Kinder, kuche, kirche' as scientific law: Psychology constructs the female." Pp. 205-220 in R. Morgan (ed.), Sisterhood is Powerful. New York: Random House.

Weitzman, L. (1974). "Legal regulations of marriage: Tradition and change." California Law Review, 62(4) (July-September):1169-1288.

Whitehurst, R. (1971). "Violently jealous husbands." Sexual Behavior, (July).

15

The Prostitute as Victim

Jennifer James

In discussing the laws covering prostitution and their enforcement, James introduces the reader to an argument worthy of serious consideration: that rather than being victims of prostitution itself, prostitutes may be the victims of the laws against prostitution, the predominantly white middle class men these laws tend to protect, and the ways in which these laws are enforced. In addition, the author suggests that prostitution, while considered deviant and treated as an immoral and illegal activity of women, is in fact an aspect or extension of, not a contradiction of, the traditional female sex role in our society.

An important part of this chapter is the discussion of the economics of prostitution. James notes that because of economic discrimination directed against women in the legal but sex-segregated job market, prostitution is financially attractive and offers a life of more excitement and variety than would otherwise be available—especially to women without special skills. This chapter also provides a review of earlier explanations of prostitution, including physical and psychological "theories." In her review of the literature on the etiology of female crime in general, James concludes, as does Dorie Klein in Chapter 2, that little evidence can be mustered in support of any of these traditional attempts at causal explanation.

The last three sections of the chapter on child/parent relationships, sexual history, and incest and rape will continue to be discussed in the following chapter on juvenile prostitutes. James reports that adult prostitutes lacked parental guidance when they were young, were sexually active at a young age, and had been victimized by incest or rape to a greater extent than non-prostitutes. Statistics from her own research indicate that over half of the prostitutes in her study had been raped and over one-third had been multiple rape victims.

In concluding, she distinguishes between legalization and decriminalization of prostitution, and suggests that decriminalization is the least abusive method currently available to lessen the victimization of prostitutes as prostitutes. She argues, however, that decriminalization will do far less to lessen their victimization as women.

Reprinted from "The Prostitute As Victim" by Jennifer James, pp. 175-201, in *The Victimization of Women*, J.R. Chapman and M. Gates (eds.), © 1978 Sage Publications, Beverly Hills, by permission of the publisher.

Prostitution is often referred to as a "victimless crime" or a "crime without a complainant." These terms are used to characterize crimes, such as vagrancy, gambling, pornography, and prostitution, in which typically none of the involved citizens files a complaint with the police. Because the prostitute and her customer are involved in a mutually agreed upon relationship, neither party feels any need for the services or interference of the authorities—in contrast to the relationship between a burglar and his home-owner victim, in which the latter is quite clearly an involuntary participant in the interaction. Those who refer to the prostitute as a victim do so in a nonlegal sense. She is seen as a victim because of her life-style, her "immorality," or "degradation," or the presumption that she is exploited by pimps or others.

Many of those who view prostitutes as the victims of prostitution base their judgments on assumptions about the individual psychology—or pathology—of prostitutes. As Stein (1974:21-22) said about her attitude at the beginning of her study of call girls,

> I kept looking for signs that the women were really miserable or neurotic or self-destructive. I wanted them to be that way. I think I wanted call girls to be "sick" because I believed that anybody—at least any woman—who sold sexual access ought to be sick.

The plethora of myths about prostitutes, prostitution, and the effects of prostitution on its practitioners is an inevitable result of prostitution's illegality. Prostitutes are labeled as criminals, forced to lead undercover lives that are far removed from and inaccessible to "respectable" members of society. Aside from the customers (men who usually are far more interested in their own immediate needs and desires than in investigating the life-style of the prostitute, who may have a considerable psychological investment in maintaining their fantasies about prostitutes, and who, in any case, are unlikely to broadcast widely their experiences since they are committing an illegal act by patronizing a prostitute) the only other members of "respectable" society who ordinarily have contact with prostitutes are police officers and other members of the criminal justice system. In other words, police and jail records have been until recently our only source of "hard data" on prostitutes and prostitution. This is certainly a limited source of information, and one that raises an interesting possibility. Rather than being the victims of prostitution itself, prostitutes may be the victims of the laws against prostitution and the ways in which they are enforced.

DISCRIMINATORY LAW ENFORCEMENT

Violations of the prostitution statutes account for approximately 30% of most women's jail populations. Convicted prostitutes serve long jail sentences compared to other misdemeanants such as shoplifters or those involved in larceny or assault. The judicial attitude represented by these sentencing patterns has no justification when considered in reference to the traditional legal concerns of danger to person or property loss. Nor does the large number of women arrested for prostitution (33,306 in 1975, according to the Uniform Crime Reports of 1976) indicate the commitment of the criminal justice system to an effective, realistic campaign to eliminate prostitution. Each act of prostitution, after all, requires at least two participants: a seller *and* a buyer. Despite this incontrovertible fact, the arrest rate for customers is only two for every eight prostitutes arrested (Uniform Crime Reports, 1976). It has been estimated by Kinsey and others (1953) that about 20% of the male population has some contact with prostitutes. There are obviously many more customers than prostitutes, and yet the prostitutes seem to bear virtually the entire weight of legal reprisals. Since the prostitution laws in almost every state are neutral on their face, holding the prostitute and the customer equally culpable, the figures prove that prostitutes are the victims of discriminatory law enforcement.

Class Discrimination

The traditional justification for discriminatory enforcement of prostitution laws was stated by Davis (1937:752):

> The professional prostitute being a social outcast may be periodically punished without disturbing the usual course of society; no one misses her while she is serving out her term—no one, at least, about whom society has any concern. The man [customer], however, is something more than a partner in an immoral act; he discharges important social and business relations. . . . He cannot be imprisoned without deranging society.

This argument assumes a class difference between prostitutes and their customers: customers are middle- or upper-class "pillars of society"; prostitutes are lower-class "lumpenproletariat." While we may doubt that law enforcement should discriminate on the basis of class, the characterization of customers as middle class implied by Davis is accurate: most customers are middle class, married, white, professionals, or businessmen who live in the suburbs. The class of prostitutes, however, is not as easily categorized. For example, in one study (James, 1976a)[1] including 136 streetwalkers, 64% of the subjects reported their childhood family's income as middle or upper class. It is social mobility, as effected by societal application of the "deviant" label, that makes the common assumption of "prostitute = lower class" near absolute in fact. As Davis further stated, "The harlot's return is not primarily a reward for abstinence, labor, or rent. It is primarily a reward for loss of social standing." Benjamin and Masters (1964:93) also noted that "The economic rewards of prostitution are normally far greater than those of most other female occupations" in large part because the prostitute is paid not only for providing a service but also for incurring a loss of social status. The statistics on prostitutes' class standing as measured by income, education, and so on, are not at issue here. We are merely pointing out that, by "working the streets" as a prostitute, a woman becomes defined by the larger society as "lower class" and thus gains all of the liabilities pertaining to that social status. No parallel social process exists to label customers as deviant, and their higher-class status is therefore not affected by their illegal participation in prostitution.

The accepted status of customers, as opposed to that accorded to prostitutes, tends to protect these men from the possibility of involvement in the criminal justice system. Judging by the arrest statistics, the majority of customers seem to be either invisible to the police or else above the law. The latter is, of course, more likely, especially since "Agencies of social control do not operate with impunity; they must protect themselves from public reprisal and antipathy" (Kirk, 1972:24). Any attempt to routinely arrest, process, and label a large proportion of a politically powerful class (middle-class white males, in this case) can lead only to "organizational strain and trouble" (Chambliss, 1969:21). Harassment and labeling of social outcasts, on the other hand, has always been considered a reasonable way to gain public approval and support. It has been reported that 70% of the women who are now inmates in American prisons were initially arrested for prostitution, indicating the possible importance of prostitution law enforcement as a labeling device and of the jail experience as an introduction to other crime:

> The adolescent girl who is labeled a sex offender for promiscuity . . . may initially experience a conflict about her identity. Intimate association with sophisticated deviants [in jail], however, may provide an incentive to learn the hustler role . . . and thus resolve the status anxiety by gaining prestige through association with deviants, and later, experimentation in the deviant role. [Davis, 1971:305]

Finally, in considering the possible class differential between prostitutes and their customers it must be remembered that women in this society traditionally have no class standing of their own: they are considered to belong to the class of their closest male associate (father, brother, husband, or lover). The illegal, "deviant" status of prostitution means that the circle of those with whom a prostitute can form close associations is arbitrarily limited to a very small number of men, virtually all of whom are, or are considered to be, lower class. (This point will be amplified later in this chapter when we discuss the relationship between prostitutes and pimps.)

NATURE OF LAWS

A second justification for discriminatory enforcement of prostitution laws is implicit in the nature of the laws themselves. The control of overt prostitution is achieved in the United States through two main types of laws, those against loitering with the intent to commit an act of prostitution and offering or agreeing to an act of prostitution. The most common enforcement procedures involve the use of police officers as decoys. The officer behaves as he assumes a customer would behave and, when approached by a suspected prostitute, elicits evidence of intent. The prostitute is arrested if she mentions money and sexual service in her verbal exchange with the officer. These arrest techniques frequently involve the officer in the possibility of entrapment and questionable sexual exchanges. Some jurisdictions use civilian agents who complete acts of sexual intercourse before the arrest is made. These agents view themselves as protecting society by committing immoral acts for moral reasons. The use of female agents to solicit and arrest customers is rare because it requires a violation of appropriate behavior for women and an "unfair" use of female sexuality to entrap men. In most states, customers are rarely, if ever, arrested. A woman who has once been convicted of offering/agreeing, regardless of the circumstances, is subject to future arrests under loitering statutes as a "known prostitute." (A "known prostitute" is a woman who has been convicted of an act of prostitution within the past year.) If she is seen in the area "known to be inhabited by prostitutes" she may also be arrested for loitering. Loitering laws are frequently used by enforcement agencies to control individuals labeled as deviants.

It obviously is easier to arrest prostitutes—at least, streetwalkers[2]—than to arrest their customers. The location of the streetwalker's place of business in itself makes her an obvious target. Men may walk the streets freely whenever they wish; a woman downtown late at night with a male escort is ipso facto suspect. George R. Cole (1972:97) reports that a police expert, in delineating for police officers the "subjects who should be subjected to field interrogations," included "unescorted women or young girls in public places, particularly at night in such places as cafes, bars, bus and train depots, or street corners." Unescorted men or young boys in public places were not included in this list of suspect persons. Moreover, it is considered acceptable behavior for men to initiate conversations—including conversations with overt or covert sexual content—with female passers-by. This last point leads us to a discussion of *why* prostitutes have been made the victims of discriminatory law enforcement, aside from the argument of what is most convenient for the police.

CUSTOMERS

In this society, there are some behaviors which are considered acceptable for men but not for women, e.g., standing on a street corner alone at night or soliciting sexual conversations with strangers. Prostitutes are women who are simultaneously rewarded and punished for choosing to earn their living through patterns of behavior that are unacceptable for members of their sex. In other words, prostitutes are the victims of sex-role stereotyping. The sexual needs of customers are loosely defined as normal, except for those of a small percentage of "freaks" or perverts. In fact, the customers of prostitutes and their activities as such have enjoyed a long tradition of "normality." Even during periods when intensive official attempts to end the business of prostitution were underway—see descriptions by Anderson (1974) of Chicago, 1910-1915, and by Holmes (1972) of nationwide efforts at about the same time—customers' needs were accepted as "inevitable." At most, the men were chided for risking venereal disease and implored to practice self-control. Today, men who purchase the services of prostitutes are still considered normal (nondeviant), even though their actions may be seen as unpalatable, or even immoral, according to the personal standards of the observer. Customers of prostitutes are, of course, acting outside the law, but where the law and the accepted male sex role come into conflict, the norms of sexual role playing overshadow the power of the law to label deviance. Men are expected to have a wide variety of sexual needs and to actively seek fulfillment of those needs. As part of that search, men are allowed to illegally purchase the sexual services of women with relative impunity, as arrest statistics demonstrate.

A review of the acceptability of men's reasons for visiting prostitutes can be couched only as an impression of common attitudes. Having quantity in sexual partners has long been a praised accomplishment for men in many social groups. Although some restraint may be considered important after marriage, the attitude clearly is that a man who has been with many women has positive status. The epithet of the "Don Juan" or "stud" does not carry the connotation that "whore" or "promiscuous" does for women. The male "need" for sexual variety, a common subject in the commercial media and in sexual-joking behavior, and the desire for sex without emotional involvement are both frequently expressed as common, acceptable male sexual behavior, while they are both strongly rejected for women. Men with these desires and "needs," as well as traveling salesmen, convention attenders, participants in stag parties, and so forth, are all considered "natural" customers of prostitutes. The provision of sexual services to males by women is, in contrast, clearly labeled deviant. Males break few social rules in patronizing a prostitute; females break almost all the rules in becoming prostitutes. Streetwalkers, in particular, place themselves at the wrong end of the whore-madonna spectrum: they accept money for sex, they are promiscuous, they are not in love with their customers, they are not subtle, and they engage in "abnormal" or deviant sex acts—acts which "respectable" women are not expected to accept (e.g., anal intercourse). As mentioned earlier, even the streetwalker's place of business is a violation of her sex role.

Most importantly, however, the independent, promiscuous, overt sexuality of the prostitute challenges the traditional assumption that female sexuality is entirely dependent upon, and awakened only by, male sexuality. As Davis (1937) stated, "Women are either part of the family system, or they are prostitutes, members of a caste set apart." Unregulated sexuality is accepted from males; from females, however, whose sexual stability is the sine qua non of our family concept, ultrafamilial sex threatens the basic structures of society. So threatening is the idea of female sexual independence, that we have laws defining juvenile women who engage in sexual intercourse without official permission as deviants "in danger of falling into habits of vice." Because women and their sexuality are tied so closely to the family structure—that is, to a long-term relationship based on a complexity of economic, emotional, and sexual expectations dictated by law and custom—sexual interactions between male and female social equals are commonly more or less channeled and controlled by these social expectations. Prostitutes are not considered to be the social equals of their customers, however. As we have seen, customers are primarily middle or upper class, and prostitutes are considered to be lower class. Customers do not usually see prostitutes as being potential members of that section of womanhood to whom they may have to relate according to the prescribed roles of the family system, and they are therefore able to interact with prostitutes in a much freer way. Gagnon and Simon (1973:230) stated that,

> Since many of the organizing constraints on sexual activity are related to maintenance of the family and its future, the contact with the prostitute is significant, because it allows sexual expression without such controls on behavior.

It is true, of course, that the female sex role followed by nondeviant, nonprostitute women also consists in large part of barter transactions.

> Non-deviant male and female expectations concerning how women use [their] sexuality, and the exploitation of sexuality to achieve gain otherwise unavailable all add up to a routine exchange of sexual favors for pay. . . . The distinction between prostitution

and the mundane characteristics of the female sex role simply are not as distinct as one might hope [Rosenblum, 1975:182]

The point we are making here is that the less overtly pragmatic sexual transactions a man enters into with a nonprostitute are likely to involve or lead to a variety of consequences which may be legally, "morally," or emotionally binding. Moreover, the variety of sexual services a man can obtain from a nondeviant woman is likely to be smaller than that possible with a prostitute; and once a man enters into a long-term relationship with a woman, he has in a sense recognized her as his social equal and thus must "pay" more (e.g., a house, a car, clothes, and so on) for the same sexual service.

When the effects of sex-role stereotyping are taken into account, we can see that the perceived difference in class between the prostitute and her customers has a larger function than simply protecting the latter from social and legal labeling. One aspect of this function, for example, is that "many a client [customer] is sexually neutral or impotent with his wife and erotic or potent with a woman he can safely degrade—usually a prostitute" (Esselstyn, 1968:130). This supposed inferiority of the prostitute may be a matter of her presumed lower-class status alone, or it may include recognition of her "deviant" label: some men desire the excitement of sexual relations in an illegal, or "I'm OK, you're deviant," situation (James, 1976b).

More importantly, however, the perceived interclass nature of prostitution is an expression of the middle-class man's need for liberation from the sex-role stereotyping of his class. The accepted range of male sexual behavior in our society is considerably wider than the accepted behavior conventions of the middle class—and especially of middle-class women. Women defined as lower class, then, and particularly those who have been "set apart" by the label "deviant," must serve as substitutes for the middle-class women so firmly restricted by their class-related sex-role proscriptions. Prostitution allows men "to regress to an 'Id' state of complete freedom from all restraints of civilization and acculturation" (Winick and Kinsie, 1971:97), to move briefly in to the deviant subculture, secure in their class-guaranteed ability to return to 'normality.' As noted by Gagnon and Simon (1973:231),

The frequency of contacts with prostitutes by males at conventions and in other situations that are separated from the home suggests the loosening of social controls that are [sic] necessary for such contacts to take place.

The more highly restricted female sex role contains almost none of the sexual motivations and behaviors allowed to the male; nor does it allow a woman to serve as a professional accompanyist for those men who would rent her participation in sexual activities. Rather than stating, then, that a prostitute is a deviant human being and a prostitute's customer is a normal human being, it is actually more exact—and more telling—to say that a prostitute is a deviant *woman* and her customer is a normal *man*.

The puritan aspect of middle-class society means that the full acting out of the male sex role by middle-class males requires the existence of prostitution. As a result, the male need for purchased female sexual service is, and long has been, accepted as "inevitable" and therefore not to be punished. To have laws against prostitution almost seems to imply that some aspects of the male sex role itself are intolerable—or at least dangerously at odds with the conventions of middle-class society. Women are daily jailed, stigmatized, and exiled from "decent" society for their ability to recognize and deal with this conflict between male sexual needs and male social ideals.

ECONOMIC DISCRIMINATION

Far from being limited to the traditionally "private" sector of sexual behaviors, sex-role stereotyping has a pervasive influence in many public aspects of our society, including the economic system. Money-making options are still quite limited for women, especially for un- or low-skilled women. Recognition of this basic sex inequality in our economic structure helps us understand prostitution as an occupational choice for some women, rather than as a symptom of the immorality or deviance of individuals. There is evidence that some women, in choosing the occupation of prostitution, are reacting to their victimization by this sex-based economic inequality. Pomeroy (1965:175), for example, studied 175 prostitutes, up to 93% of whom were motivated by economic factors; he noted that "the gross income from prostitution is usually larger than could be expected from any other type of unskilled labor." Benjamin and Masters (1964:93) were also aware of this sex-based economic differential and its relationship to prostitution: "The economic rewards of prostitution are normally far greater than those of most other female occupations." According to Esselstyn (1968:129), "women are attracted to prostitution in contemporary America because the income is high and because it affords an opportunity to earn more, buy more, and live better than would be possible by any other plausible alternative." Davis (1937:750) summed up the economic pull of prostitution: "Purely from the angle of economic return, the hard question is not why so many women become prostitutes, but why so few of them do."

Some researchers claim to find an abnormal, perhaps even neurotic, materialism among prostitutes. Jackman et al. (1967:138), for example, state that:

> The rationalization by prostitutes violating social taboos against commercial sex behavior takes the form of exaggerating other values, particularly those of financial success, and for some the unselfish assumption of the financial burden of people dependent upon them.

However, as Greenwald (1970:200) more accurately points out,

> Economic factors helped to mold the entire society, the family structure, and therefore the very personalities of these girls [call girls] . . . the girls were caught up in the worship of material success.

In what way is the economic motivation of these women different from that of men who strive to attain a position on the executive level so that they can afford "the good life" and support the people dependent upon them? The majority of Americans, it would seem, share the desire for financial success. Prostitutes are women who, usually with good cause, see prostitution as their only means for moving from a three- to six-thousand-a-year income to the gracious living possible with $50,000 a year. It is important to note that this view of prostitutes contradicts the traditional stereotype of prostitutes as wretched creatures forced into prostitution by extreme economic deprivation. In one recent study of 136 streetwalkers (James, 1976a), 8.4% of the subjects claimed to have started prostitution because of economic necessity, while 56.5% were motivated by a desire for money and material goods—a desire which, due to sex-based economic discrimination, they saw no way to fulfill other than by prostitution. A typical comment by a streetwalker in that study referred to "the excitement of buying whatever you wanted without asking anybody . . . of having big sums of money that you never had before." Once accustomed to a higher income, as another subject of that study noted, "It would be pretty hard to go back to less money."

A person's choice of occupation is not limited solely by external realities. One's self-image plays an important part in one's perception of possible alternatives. If a man believes himself to have a "poor head for math," he will probably not be able to visualize himself attaining great success as a physicist. Women as a whole suffer from an especially narrow self-image in terms of occupational choices because of sex-role stereotyping. Traditionally, women's roles have been those of wife and mother, both of which are exclusively biological and service roles. The emphasis on service carries over into the definition of "new" traditional women's roles, such as teaching children, serving food or drink, and secretarial work. The importance of physical appearance in many of these occupations reinforces women's self-image as physical/biological objects, limited to the confines of their sex-role stereotype at work as well as at home. As Rosenblum (1975:169) argues, "Prostitution utilizes the same attributes characteristic of the female sex role, and uses those attributes towards the same ends. . . . " In other words, prostitution is a very natural extension of the female sex role into the occupational arena.

Some researchers (e.g., Esselstyn, 1968) believe that certain occupations lead women easily into prostitution. These occupations are those that adhere most closely to the traditional female service role, often emphasizing physical appearance as well as service. Clinard (1959:228) comments that "Quasi-prostituting experiences, such as those of a waitress who, after hours, accepts favors from customers in return for sexual intercourse, may lead to prostitution." It is not unusual for a woman who is required by her employer to flirt with customers and "be sexy" to find that the men with whom she must interact in business transactions relate to her as a sexual object or potential sex partner. Once she has been cast in this role of sex object, she may decide to make the best of a negative situation by accepting the "favors"—or the money—men are eager to give her for playing out the implications of the role. Again, these low-status service occupations are among the few occupational alternatives available to un- or low-skilled women.

INDEPENDENCE AND EXCITEMENT

Another possibility excluded by the traditional female sex role is financial independence. In a sense, then, a financially independent woman is a "deviant" woman. These roles are beginning to shift and broaden now, but there are still virtually no occupations available to un- or low-skilled women which allow the independence or provide the adventure of prostitution. Rosenblum (1975:177) states that the "specific precipitating factors" which cause women to choose prostitution as a profession "can be identified simply as independence and money." Data from the recent study (James, 1976a) mentioned earlier, support the assertion that independence is highly valued by many of the women who choose prostitution. When asked "Why did you leave home?" the largest category of responses by the subjects in that study was "desire for independence," and the second largest category was "dispute with family," which may also imply a desire for independence from the strictures of family life. Another question in that study, "What are the advantages of being a prostitute?", also revealed the value that independence has for these women. Although the economic motivation overwhelmed all other categories in the first responses, in the second responses, independence had first place. The search for an independent life-style can lead a young woman into a situation in which she sees prostitution as her only alternative: "It [her entrance into prostitution] was actually caused because I ran away [when I was] too young to get a job. So I either had the alternative to go back home or to prostitute. So there was no way I was going to go back home, and so I turned out [became a prostitute]." Davis (1971), Benjamin and Masters (1964), and Esselstyn (1968) also specifically mention independence as a motivating factor in the choice of prostitution.

For many women, the "fast life" of prostitution represents more than simply economic independence unobtainable within the conventions of the "straight" world's female sex role. The life-style of the prostitution subculture has itself proved attractive to a large number of women over the years. "Fondness for dancing and restaurant life" and the "tendency to vagabondage" comprise over one fourth of the "immediate causes of prostitution" listed by Kemp (1936:190). In tabulating "the factors in becoming prostitutes" of three groups of prostitutes, Pomeroy (1965:184) found 3% to 19% influenced by their perception of prostitution as "an easy life," 12 to 24 percent by the "fun and excitement" they found in the "fast life," and 14 to 38 percent by the fact that prostitution enabled them to meet "interesting people." Gray, in a study examining "why particular women enter prostitution" (1973:401), reported that "many of the respondents . . . felt intrigued by the description [by prostitutes] of prostitution which appeared exciting and glamorous . . . the initial attraction for the girls in this study was social as well as material" (pp. 410-411). Benjamin and Masters (1964:107) state that the life-style inherent in identification with the prostitution subculture continues to be a strong attraction after women have committed themselves to the profession: "There is an abundance of evidence that on the conscious level it is the *excitement* of the prostitute's life, more than any other single factor, which works to frustrate rehabilitation efforts." These excerpts from interviews with streetwalkers (from James, 1976a) illustrate some of the attractions of prostitution: "The glamour side . . . being able to be in with the in crowd . . . you really feel kind of good because you meet people who say, I wish I was like you—have diamond rings, a pocketful of money, and go out and drink"; "To see if I can get away with it before I get caught: a game, like"; "You don't have certain hours you have to work. You can go to work when you want, leave when you want . . . you don't have a boss hanging over you, you're independent"; "It's really kind of fun . . . it's a challenge."

The preceding discussion provides a substantial explanation of why some women choose prostitution rather than the economic dependence of the traditional wife's occupational role—as defined by the female sex-role —even when both options are available to them. Neither marriage nor extralegal monogamy provides or allows for the economic independence, the excitement, the adventure, or the social life available through prostitution. The basic fact of sexual objectification (exchanging sexual services for financial support) may be the same in either case, but, for many women, prostitution has benefits that outweigh the privileges—and limitations—of "respectable" women's roles. Winick and Kinsie (1971:75) refer to a rehabilitation program for prostitutes in Japan in the 1950s that included such traditional women's activities as arts and crafts and homemaking. The program failed, they report, because the prostitutes were simply not interested. As Greenwald discovered (1970:202), most prostitutes feel "overt hatred of routine, confining jobs." The traditional female occupations, including that of housewife, can be seen as among the most "routine, confining jobs" in this society, and thus present limited temptation to women who value the relative freedom of the "fast life." To sum up this section of our discussion: prostitution is one way for women to reject their victimization by our sex-biased economic system by choosing an independent and exciting, albeit "deviant," occupational lifestyle.

PIMPS

Thus far we have examined prostitutes as the victims of discriminatory law enforcement, sex-role stereotyping, and economic discrimination. Now we will take a look at prostitutes as victims of those who are traditionally assumed to be their primary oppressors: pimps. A common myth in this society pictures prostitutes as defeated women cowering under the coercion of brutal pimps. Kemp (1936:214), for example, stated that "in many cases friendship with a pimp may be considered the immediate cause of a woman's becoming a harlot. It is the man who leads her on." However, "friendship" and "leading on" are not necessarily coercive, and Kemp earlier (p. 190) stated that the influence of a pimp was the "immediate cause of prostitution" for only 8.3% of prostitutes. Gray (1973:412) found that the influence of pimps, when it was a factor, "was generally minimal." Data from the James (1976a) study showed a somewhat larger role for pimps in recruiting women for prostitution. It should be noted, however, that the influence of "girlfriends" was more than equal to the influence of pimps, that more than twice as many women reported choosing prostitution solely on their own initiative, and that our field experience leads us to agree with Gray that the pressure applied by pimps in recruiting women is generally minimal. One woman described her entrance into prostitution this way: "The only reason I got started was because of my old man's suggestion, because otherwise I don't think—maybe I would have, later. I liked the money; it was easy money."

Women in this society are socialized to feel they need a man to take care of them, to "take care of business," to "complete" them, to love them, to make a home with them; this is part of the traditional female sex role. Prostitutes are no exception to this rule. "Well, everybody wants a man," said one streetwalker. "You can get lonesome," explained another; "even though they laugh and say, if you're with that many men how can you get lonesome. But believe it or not, it's just like getting up at 8 o'clock in the morning, going to work, and coming home at 5 o'clock in the evening; it's just something you do to survive and that's it. There's no feelings involved." For many of these women, a relationship with a pimp means "just knowing that you have somebody there all the time, not just for protection, just someone you can go to." Because of their involvement in a deviant life-style, however, prostitutes must share their lives with men who understand the dynamics and values of their deviant subculture—men who will accept their violations of the traditional female sex role. Any man who lives with a prostitute will be called a pimp, although usually the only factors that distinguish a prostitute-pimp relationship from that of a "normal" marriage relationship, aside from the illegality of both roles, are the woman's status as sole "breadwinner" and often, the man's overt maintenance of two or more similar relationships simultaneously. It has become obvious that physical male abuse of females in marital relationships is common. As is true throughout society, women's socialized need for men is reinforced by the fact that a woman's status is determined by that of her man. A prostitute who can achieve a relationship with a "high class" pimp raises her standing in the subculture of prostitution. This rise in status pays important dividends in her interactions with other members of the subculture: "If you have a pimp, other guys on the street, they kind of leave you alone." Thus, confounding the scenario of the coercive pimp, one can often find prostitutes actively seeking to attach themselves to those pimps whose patronage they feel will be most beneficial.

Of course, not all prostitute-pimp relationships are desirable models of human social interaction. Some pimps are physically abusive, just as some husbands are. Perhaps prostitutes who experience abuse from their pimps are in a better position than nonworking wives with abusive husbands, in that prostitutes are financially more independent. On the other hand, prostitutes—whether they are married to their pimps or not—are likely to be taken less seriously by authorities, such as police, to whom they turn for help. This lack of respect and concern on the part of law enforcement personnel towards prostitutes also prevents prostitutes from seeking legal help when they are abused or assaulted by customers, which is not an uncommon occurrence. Faced with the attitude that she was "asking for it," or at least "had it coming to her," a prostitute who reports abuse from a customer or her pimp to the police is liable to feel more victimized by the discrimination of the legal system than by the violence of individual men (James, 1973).

REVIEW OF THEORIES

There is yet another way of looking at prostitutes as victims. Rather than seeing them as simply victims of prostitution itself and of societal reactions to prostitution, one can ask whether prostitutes are women with histories of victim experience that influenced them in their choice of occupation and life-style. We have seen that prostitution is an aspect of, not a contradiction to, the female sex role as it exists in this society; and yet the choice to prostitute is obviously heavily loaded with negative valuations, according to the judgment of the majority culture. What, then, determines which individual women will act out the prostitution components of the female sex role? What factors enable certain women to accept the deviant status conferred upon them by their choice of prostitution? Scores of researchers, theorists, and moralists have published their opinions on what is "wrong" with prostitutes, individually and as a class. At the end of the last century, for example, Lombroso (1898) cited physiological abnormalities and deficiencies as the cause of all female crime, including prostitution. Another researcher (Kemp, 1936), as late as 1936, stated that "from 30 to 50 percent of all prostitutes must be classed as feeble-minded." More recently, these discredited theories have been replaced by psychological evaluations of prostitutes, which are more "modern" sounding, if not necessarily more valid. "Latent homosexuality" has been seen as a main spring of prostitute motivation by some (e.g., Greenwald, 1970; Maerov, 1965; Hollender, 1961). Since homosexuality, like prostitution, is popularly considered deviance, the temptation to put all the "bad eggs" in one theoretical basket is perhaps understandable. There are no hard data, however, linking homosexuality, whether latent or overt, with female prostitution. Some researchers believe many prostitutes have an oedipal fixation. Winick and Kinsie (1971:83), for example, see prostitution as atonement for guilt produced by incestuous fantasies. This theory is impossible to disprove, since we cannot accurately measure the incidence of incestuous fantasies. On the other hand, it is impossible to prove their theory, or to prove that it applies more to prostitution than to other occupations. "Money is heavily loaded with all kinds of psychological conflicts. In our civilization, among many other things . . . it symbolizes the will to power and the ensuing unconscious guilt of having taken the father's place," Choisy states (1961: 1). Perhaps every women, prostitute and business executive alike, who desires economic independence is acting out oedipal fantasies. It seems unlikely, however, that many women are motivated solely or primarily by such a tenuous subconscious factor in making their occupational choice. Again, the literature provides virtually no hard data to justify including this theory among the significant prostitute motivating factors.

The myth that women become prostitutes because they are "oversexed" has been countered by the discovery that most prostitutes see their sexual activities with customers as purely business and usually get no sexual pleasure from them. Unfortunately, an opposite myth also exists: that of "the invariably frigid prostitute" (Maerov, 1965:692). Responding to this myth, Pomeroy (1965:183) reports that the 175 prostitutes he studied "were more sexually responsive in their personal lives than were women who were not prostitutes." As noted earlier, emphasis on physical appearance is an important aspect of the female sex role. "Movies, television, popular literature and, particularly, advertising make it seem that the cardinal sin a woman can commit is to be unattractive" (Greenwald, 1970: 201). Some researchers believe, with Greenwald, that prostitutes are motivated by the need to prove their attractiveness through sexual contact with many men. Taking the theory a step further, Winick and Kinsie (1971:35) state that

> many prostitutes apprehended by the police tend to be overweight and short. They often have poor teeth, minor blemishes, untidy hair, and are otherwise careless about their personal appearance. Docility and indifference are common. This leads one to conclude that such women may feel inadequate to compete in more traditional activities and thus more readily accept a vocation that involves the sale of something they may not value highly.

Winick and Kinsie do not seem to consider the fact that a large percentage of the prostitutes apprehended by the police are "hypes"—drug addicts working as prostitutes to support their habit—who form a special, lower class in the hierarchy of the "fast life." In any case, since it is demonstrably true that the majority of "unattractive" women do not become prostitutes, and since it is a matter of personal opinion what percentage of prostitutes is "unattractive," the importance of the Winick and Kinsie statement quoted above lies in its assumption that women's "traditional activities" are those which emphasize physical appearance. This assumption is very pervasive throughout society and is a major influence for women in the development of self-image—and self-image is always a factor in the individual's choice of occupation. Perhaps we could find women who became prostitutes because their "attractiveness" rating was not high enough for them to gain employment as receptionists or cocktail waitresses. On the other hand, prostitutes generally make more money than waitresses or receptionists, regardless of physical appearance, and the economic motivation may be statistically far more important than the psychological one presented by Greenwald and Winick and Kinsie. The last of these common psychological theories about prostitutes pictures them using their profession to act out their hostility toward men. Looking at this objectively, it would seem equally valid, except for the illegality of prostitution, to suggest that some women become elementary schoolteachers in order to act out their hostility toward children. Perhaps this motivation is real for some women, both teachers and prostitutes, but documentation is scarce.

Moving on from theories based on psychological evaluation, we will now consider some theories based on hard data about prostitute's lives—data obtained from prostitutes themselves. The James (1976) study and a few other recent studies indicate that the factors which enable some women to accept the deviant status inherent in prostitution can be tentatively identified as exposure to the prostitution life-style, certain patterns in child/parent relationships, and perhaps patterns of negative sexual experiences that lead to the development of a self-concept including a high degree of sexual self-objectification. The last two of these three factors can be seen as evidence that prostitutes are women with histories of victimization.

CHILD/PARENT RELATIONSHIPS

Parental abuse or neglect is widely considered a typical childhood experience of women who become prostitutes. Kemp (1936), Choisy (1961), Maerov (1965), Jackman et al. (1967), Esselstyn (1968), Greenwald (1970), Davis (1971), and Gray (1973) all mention unsatisfactory relationships with parents as a fact of life for these women. Whether the condition is simple neglect-by-absence or outright physical or psychological abuse, the result is generally considered to be alienation of the child from the parents and a consequent inability—greater or lesser, depending upon the circumstances—of the child to adequately socialize the conventional mores of "respectable" society. Data from the James (1976) study seem to reaffirm the prevalence of parental abuse/neglect experience among prostitutes. The mean age at which the women in that study left home permanently was 16.25 years. As previously mentioned, "dispute with family" was one of the major reasons given by these women for leaving home, and physical and emotional abuse also was a significant factor in separating many of them from their families. Of the 136 prostitutes in the James study, 65.4% had lived apart from their families for some period prior to moving out permanently, and 70.4% reported the absence from the family of one or more parents—most often the father—during the subject's childhood. Neglect, rather than abuse, was the pattern for the majority of James' subjects, although abuse was reported by a significant number. Some typical comments about relations with parents were: "We had a lack of communication problem, me and my parents, for a long time. I didn't even know how to approach them. I was scared to talk to them, because every time I did something wrong, they'd yell at me." "My mom didn't let us go out with boys. We were at home and always working. If anyone called up, we got cursed out and then a beating." "I felt isolated, and that's why I ran away. I just felt that my mother didn't care." "My step-father, it's been negative since he's been around . . . He hits me till I'm all stiff." One apparent area of neglect on the part of parents of women in this study was sex education. Compared to the 31 to 34 percent found by other researchers (e.g., Wittels, 1951; Sorensen, 1973) among normal female populations, only 15.4% of these prostitutes had learned about sex from their parents.

SEXUAL HISTORY

This lack of parental guidance may help to explain why many prostitutes apparently are more sexually active at an earlier age than the majority of women in the United States. A full 91.9% of the prostitutes in the James study, for example, were not virgins by the age of 18 (including 23% who had experienced intercourse by the age of 13 or younger), compared to the 74.9% of the black subjects and 19.9% of the white subjects studied by Kantner and Zelnick (1972). Although information on sexual experiences prior to first intercourse was not elicited through the questionnaires used in the James study, extensive interviews of the subjects in that study revealed a pattern similar to the one found by Davis (1971:301) in her study of 30 prostitutes: "The 'technical virginity' pattern typical of the middle-class female was not in evidence here. First sexual contacts typically involved sexual intercourse. . . . " More than one third of the subjects in the James study reported that they had no further sexual relationship with their first intercourse partner, while other studies have found 10 to 15 percent of their samples in this category (e.g., Eastman, 1972). That the superficial, nonemotionally charged nature of the first sexual intercourse of many of these women initiated a series of such encounters is supported by the fact that the mean number of private (not-for-profit) sexual partners of young adult subjects in the James study was 23. Making this figure even more significant is the fact that the mean number of persons with whom these subjects felt they had developed a "significant relationship" was only five.

Societal reactions to juvenile female sexual activity may be an influence on some women's entrance into prostitution, especially for those young women who are more sexually active and less discrete than the majority of their peers, as seems to be the case with many prostitutes. "At what number of lovers is a girl supposed to lose the status of a decent person?" asks Choisy (1961:1). Carns (1973:680) explains: "a woman's decision to enter coitus . . . implies that she is creating for herself a sexual status which will have a relatively pervasive distribution . . . she will be evaluated downwardly. Such is the nature of the male bond." Girls learn early society's moral valuation of their sexuality. For example, in discussing her childhood sex education, one streetwalker stated, "I think the basic theme of the whole thing was that it was a dirty thing but that it was a duty for a woman to perform, and if you fooled around, you were a prostitute." Female promiscuity, real or imputed, virtually guarantees loss of status in the majority culture: "I got pregnant and kicked out of the house and school." "I was accused of being promiscuous while I was still a virgin. They did that because I used to run around with a lot of guys." The labeling implied by such loss of status may be an important step in the process by which a woman comes to identity with, and thus begins to see as a possible alternative, a deviant life-style such as prostitution. For its youthful victims, the labeling impact of such status loss must strongly affect the development of an adult self-image. These women may attempt to rebuild their self-image by moving into a subculture where the wider society's negative labeling of them will not impede their efforts toward a higher status, although that status itself will be perceived as negative by the wider society.

However negative the long-term effects of juvenile promiscuity on a woman's social status, the short-term effects of contra-normative juvenile sexual activity may often appear quite positive to the young woman involved. Young women suffering from parental abuse or neglect, a common pattern for prostitutes, may be especially susceptible to the advantages of what Greenwald (1970:167) calls "early rewarded sex—that is, . . . engaging in some form of sexual activity with an adult for which they were rewarded. [These women] discovered at an early age that they could get some measure of affection, of interest, by giving sexual gratification." This type of positive sexual reinforcement, particularly when coupled with the cultural stereotype of women as primarily sexual beings, may cause some women to perceive their sexuality as their primary means for gaining status: "Sex as a status tool is exploited to gain male attention" (Davis, 1971:304). Since all women in our culture must somehow come to terms with the fact that their personal value is often considered as inseparable from their sexual value, it is not uncommon for female adolescents to use "sex as a status tool" through makeup, flirting, dating, petting, and so forth. Prostitutes, however, more often skip over the usual preintercourse socio-sexual activities in favor of an active and more-or-less promiscuous intercourse pattern. Victimization results when "there is a 'drift into deviance,' with promiscuity initially used as a status tool, but later becoming defined by the individual as having consequences for the foreclosure of alternative career routes" (Davis, 1971:300).

INCEST AND RAPE

There is some evidence (e.g. James, 1976c) that prostitutes are women who have also been the victims of less subtle negative sexual experiences. Specifically, the James study showed that prostitutes are disproportionately victimized by incest and rape compared to normal female populations. The only study populations with father-incest rates comparable to James' are those selected from the specialized samples of police reports or the case loads of child-protection agencies (e.g., DeFrancis, 1969). The effect of incest on the child involved is virtually unknown. Some researchers, e.g., Jaffe et al. (1975:691), prefer not to comment: "little is known of the physical and emotional effects of incest." Ferracuti (1972:179) states that "it is hardly proved that participation in incest . . . results in psychological disturbances." He notes, however, that "Frequently [victims of incest] become sexually promiscuous after the end of the incestuous conduct." DeFrancis (1969) found guilt, shame, and loss of self-esteem to be the usual reactions of child victims of sex offenses. These feelings often led to disruptive, rebellious behavior, and some older (i.e., adolescent) victims later became prostitutes. Sexual abuse "continued over a long period of time," as is usual with incest, was found by Gagnon (1965:192) to be "extremely disorganizing in its impact" on the victim. Weiner (1964:137) echoes Ferracuti in stating that "girls who begin incest in adolescence frequently become promiscuous following termination of the incest." In an earlier James study (1971) that included 20 adolescent prostitutes, a full 65% of these young subjects had been the victims of coerced sexual intercourse, with 84.7% of these experiences occurring while the subject-victim was aged 15 or younger. Over half (57.4%) of the prostitute population in James' later study had also been raped, and 36.2% of the women in this sample were multiple rape victims.

It is not possible, of course, to conclude that, because certain study populations of "deviant" women were disproportionately victims of rape and incest, these sex-related abuses were therefore the cause of deviance. On the other hand, the overfrequent victimization of these women, particularly in youth and childhood, is a fact—just as their status as "deviants" is a fact—and should not be lightly dismissed. We realize that incidences of sexual victimization such as incest do not occur in a social "vacuum" and are virtually always surrounded by a complexity of causal, mitigating, or aggravating factors. In fact, a large proportion of the available research on incest—like the majority of studies of other more common types of sexual experiences—focuses primarily on the family background of the victim-subject. Study of the *causes* of sexual behaviors and experiences should not be our only concern, however. What we want to emphasize here is the importance of evaluating the *effects* of certain sexual patterns and experiences on the life of the individual. A simultaneous evaluation of cause and effect would be the ideal, but such an evaluation is beyond the scope of this chapter. We second DeFrancis (1969:225) in his assertion that

> it would be valuable to conduct a longitudinal study to determine more accurately what the long-term effects are on a child victim of sexual abuse. There are many conjectures which should be tested. Does exposure to sexual abuse lead to prostitution, as so often asserted? Does it lead to delinquency; to promiscuous behavior; to confusion of sexual identity; or to marital problems? We know that serious family dislocations, impairment of interfamily relationships and emotional disturbance are some of the immediate consequences of sexual abuse, but how permanent or far reaching is this impact?

Another conjecture can be made on the effect of sexual abuse: early, traumatic sexual self-objectification may be one factor influencing some women toward entrance into prostitution or other "deviant" life-styles. Sexual self-objectification is experienced by all women in this society to some degree, due to the simultaneous cultural adoration and vilification of the female body and its sexuality (the familiar madonna-whore spectrum). It seems possible, however, that to be used sexually at an early age in a way that produces guilt, shame, and loss of self-esteem on the part of the victim would be likely to lessen one's resistance to viewing one's self as a salable commodity. The relationship between early sexual history— especially incidences of sexual victimization—and adult deviance needs, and deserves, further study.

CONCLUSION

There is no obvious victim in a typical act of prostitution. Willing seller meets willing buyer, and both parties receive some gratification from the encounter: money, on the one hand, and sexual and/or psychological satisfaction on the other. It is when we examine the entrance of women into prostitution and when we review the enforcement of anti-prostitution laws that we find elements of victimization coming into focus. Because prostitution is an expression of deviance from the traditional female sex role and therefore entails ostracism from the status and privileges of "respectability," entrance into the profession is typically preceded and facilitated by an inadequate parent/child relationship and the development of a negative or sexually objectified self-image. These personal factors are then compounded by sex-role stereotyping and sex-based economic discrimination. Only widespread changes in socio-sexual attitudes will effect changes in these patterns of victimization and their relationship to prostitution. In regard to victimization of prostitutes by discriminatory law enforcement, however, change is more readily available.

Most other countries have stopped trying to end prostitution and instead made various less-abusive legal arrangements for its regulation. In West Germany, for example, prostitution is considered a social necessity, and the government supports the building of pimp-free prostitution hostels where prostitutes can live and work in comfortable rooms with access to shopping centers, recreational facilities, and mandatory health inspection. The Netherlands use zoning laws to prevent street solicitation from offending the general public. A total of 100 member nations of the United Nations have eliminated the crime of prostitution and have abandoned experiments at regulation (United Nations, 1951). The criminal laws in those countries seek instead to control public solicitation and to discourage the pimps and procurers who live off the earnings of prostitutes.

Decriminalization would seem the least abusive method of dealing with prostitution in the United States. Decriminalization differs from legalization in that, instead of creating more legal involvement, it removes prostitution from the criminal code entirely. An ideal approach would be to put all sexual behavior in private between consenting adults outside the purview of the law, but this ideal must be balanced by the reality of public expediency. Failing the ideal, then, options for controls would depend upon the communities' concern about the overtness of sexual activities, the possible disease problems, business and zoning regulations, and age of consent. Taxation, health, and age requirements can be approached in a number of ways. The least abusive to the individual woman would be to require a small-business license and a health card. Prostitutes would obtain a license much as a masseuse does; her place of business would have to conform with zoning requirements; she would be required to report her income, be of age, and keep her health card current. Violations would mean revocation of the license and would be handled by a nonpolice agency. Regulations such as the above would, of course, still limit personal freedom in a purely private area. The nonlicensed prostitute could still be prosecuted, although she would be served a civil citation rather than a criminal one. Decriminalization, with some restrictions, is regarded as a provisional solution to victimization of prostitutes by the criminal justice system only while efforts are made to change the more fundamental causes of prostitution itself. As long as we retain our traditional sex-role expectations, however, we will have prostitution. As long as women are socialized into the traditional female role and see their alternatives limited by that role, prostitution will remain an attractive occupational option for many women. It is within the power of our legislatures to lessen the victimization of prostitutes as prostitutes, but to eliminate the victimization of prostitutes as women will be a longer, far more difficult struggle.

Notes

[1] Ongoing research (1974-1977) includes a sample of 240 female offenders, 136 of whom have been identified as prostitutes. This research is funded by the National Institute on Drug Abuse, No. DA0091801, "Female Criminal Involvement and Narcotics Addiction."

[2] Attempts are occasionally made to arrest women who work in houses or massage/sauna parlors, but arrest figures on these women are less than 5% of the total. Their prostitution is at least partially hidden by the offering of other, more legitimate services. Subtle prostitutes found on all social levels, e.g., call girls or conventioneers, are rarely arrested because they cause no direct affront to the public. Their sexuality is not explicit in their behavior.

References

Anderson, A. (1974). "Prostitution and social justice." Social Service Review (June):203.

Benjamin, H., and Masters, R. (1964). Prostitution and Morality. New York: Julien Press.

Carns, D. (1973). "Talking about sex: Notes on first coitus and the double sexual standard." Journal of Marriage and Family, 35:677-688.

Chambliss, W. (1969). Crime and the Legal Process. New York: McGraw-Hill.

Choisy, M. (1961). Psychoanalysis of the Prostitute. New York: Philosophical Library.

Clinard, M. (1959). Sociology of Deviant Behavior. New York: Rinehart.

Cole, G.R. (1972). Criminal Justice: Law and Politics. New York: Duxbury Press.

Davis, K. (1937). "The sociology of prostitution." American Sociological Review, 2:744-755.

Davis, N. (1971). "The prostitute: Developing a deviant identity," pp. 297-322 in J. Henslin (ed.), Studies in the Sociology of Sex. New York: Appleton-Century-Crofts.

DeFrancis, V. (1969). "Protecting the child victims of sex crimes committed by adults." P. 215 in final report, American Humane Association, Children's Division. Denver, Colorado.

Eastman, W. (1972). "First intercourse: Some statistics on who, where, when, and why." Sexual Behavior, 2:22-27.

Esselstyn, T.C. (1968). Prostitution in the U.S. Annals of the American Academy of Political and Social Sciences, (March):123-125.

Ferracuti, F. (1972). "Incest between father and daughter." Pp. 169-183 in H. Resnik and E. Wolfgang (eds.), Sexual Behaviors: Social, Clinical, and Legal Aspects. Boston: Little, Brown.

Gagnon, J. (1965). "Female child victims of sex offenses." Social Problems, 13:176-192.

Gagnon, J., and Simon, W. (1973). Sexual Conduct. Chicago: Aldine.

Gray, D. (1973). "Turning-out: A study of teen-age prostitution." Urban Life and Culture, (January):401-425.

Greenwald, H. (1970). The Elegant Prostitute. New York: Ballantine.

Hollender, M.H. (1961). "Prostitution, the body and human relatedness." International Journal of Psychoanalysis, 42:404-413.

Holmes, K. (1972). "Reflections by gaslight: Prostitution in another age." Issues in Criminology, (Winter):83.

Jackman, N., O'Toole, R. and Geis, G. (1967). "The self-image of the prostitute." Pp. 133-146 in J. Gagnon and W. Simon (eds.), Sexual Deviance. New York: Harper & Row.

Jaffe, A., Dynneson, L. and Ten Bensel, R. (1975). "Sexual abuse of children." American Journal of Disabled Children, 129:689-692.

James, J. (1971). "A formal analysis of prostitution." Final report to the Division of Research, State of Washington Department of Social and Health Services, Olympia, Washington.

_____ (1973). "The prostitute-pimp relationship." Medical Aspects of Human Sexuality. (November):147-160.

_____ (1976a). "Motivations for entrance into prostitution." In L. Crites (ed.), The Female Offender: A Comprehensive Anthology. University of Alabama Press (in press).

_____ (1976b). "Normal men and deviant women." Unpublished manuscript.

_____ (1976c). "Early sexual experience and prostitution." The American Journal of Psychiatry (in press).

Kantner, J., and Zelnik, M. (1972). "Sexual experience of young unmarried women in the United States." Family Planning Perspectives, 4:9-18.

Kemp, T. (1936). Prostitution: An investigation of its causes, especially with regard to hereditary factors. Copenhagen: Levin & Munskgaard.

Kinsey, A., Pomeroy, W. Martin, C., and Gebhard, P. (1953). Sexual Behavior in the Human Female. Philadelphia: Saunders.

Kirk, S. (1972). "Clients as outsiders: Theoretical approaches to deviance." Social Work, (March):24.

Lombroso, C. (1898). The Female Offender. New York: D. Appleton.

Maerov, A. (1965). "Prostitution: A survey and review of 20 cases." Psychiatric Quarterly, 39:675-701.

Pomeroy, W. (1965). "Some aspects of prostitution." Journal of Sex Research, (November):177-187.

Rosenblum, K. (1975). "Female deviance and the female sex role: A preliminary investigation." British Journal of Sociology, 25(June):69-85.

Sorensen, R. (1973). Adolescent Sexuality in Contemporary America. New York: World.

Stein, M.L. (1974). Lovers, Friends, Slaves. New York: Putnam's.

Uniform Crime Reports (1976). Crime in the United States. Washington, D.C.: United States Government Printing Office.

United Nations (1951). International Convention for the Suppression of the White Slave Traffic. United Nations Publishing.

Weiner, I. (1964). "On incest: A survey." Excerpta Criminologica, 4:137-155.

Winick, C., and Kinsie, P. (1971). The Lively Commerce. New York: New American Library.

Wittels, F. (1951). Sex Habits of American Women. New York: Eton.

16

Concurrent and Consecutive Abuse: The Juvenile Prostitute

Dorothy H. Bracey

This chapter explores the sorely neglected area of juvenile prostitution. Bracey, an anthropologist, provides a descriptive analysis of several young prostitutes. As an inquiry at the individual level, her study offers one explanation for why individual girls become prostitutes, depicting some of the immediate familial antecedents that lead to their "deviant" lifestyles. More needs to be known about family influences at the individual level. At the structural level, more also needs to be known about how juvenile prostitution relates to certain sexual patterns, values, and ideologies in our culture.

Both James in the previous chapter and Bracey would agree that the relationship of early sexual victimization and later deviance need to be studied more fully in understanding prostitution. As Martin noted in Chapter 14, it is also important to look at the larger structural conditions that contribute to a woman's, or girl's, decision to become a prostitute, including the general status of women in society, sex-based economic discrimination, the patriarchal characteristics of the family, the juvenile justice system and other social service systems more devoted to keeping the family intact rather than to helping women.

Further, in keeping with the overal theme of this book, readers should ask themselves how the organization of class and race as well as sex biases in our society might likewise trigger all kinds of prostitution. How, for example, does poverty and racism affect individual relationships between parents and their young and teenage daughters? Finally, what are the special circumstances related to the organization of adolescence in contemporary western society that may lead to a better understanding of the special case of teenage prostitution?

The young prostitute is not in trouble because she is on the street—she is on the street because she is in trouble. A growing body of evidence confirms the view that the juvenile hustler is not simply a runaway who has been deceived by a pimp or his "bottom woman" but is instead the product of a specific history, a history that most likely involves sexual abuse, incest, and some form of abandonment.

Although one of the earliest studies of juvenile prostitution (Grey,

1973) did not report a history of sexual abuse, a later study of adult prostitutes (James and Meyerding, 1976) did indicate that prostitutes as children experienced more sexual advances by elders, were more victimized by incest, and demonstrated a higher incidence of rape than women who were not prostitutes. A later study of teenage prostitutes (Bracey, 1979) also discovered over 50 percent of the girls reported seductive or forcible sexual advances by older men, often members of the family or household, before the girl reached puberty.

Later studies confirm these early tentative findings. A 1979 report indicates that subjects of child pornography as well as young prostitutes may have a history of sexual molestation in the home (Dulles, 1979:C11). The most authoritative data is probably that gathered by Silberman (1981) who reports that 61 percent of the over 200 teenage prostitutes questioned had been sexually molested by a father, father-figure, or male member of the household.

The exact relationship between early sexual molestation and juvenile prostitution will not be clear until there is a better understanding of the incidence of early sexual molestation in the general female population. The sexual abuse of children by relatives and friends is one of the last remaining taboos; that is, it is taboo to talk about it. It is therefore very difficult to gauge its frequency. One authority (Robinson, 1979) estimates that approximately 25 percent of adult females have been sexually molested as children. If this figure is even close to the truth, it indicates that the relationship between such molestation and juvenile prostitution is a complex one; although there is a greater incidence of such molestation among young prostitutes than in the female population generally, molestation is neither a necessary or sufficient condition to produce prostitution. Clearly, other factors must be present also.

Silberman offers one explanation:

> As the interviews wore on, it became apparent that an incestuous father or father-figure, when accompanied by a child's perception that no one will listen to her confused fears—or worse, will accuse her of lying—lays the foundation for prostitution. A lifestyle of *learned helplessness* ensues.

Bracey's study also revealed conditions that might lead to "learned helplessness." Over half the girls in this study reported parents who were heavily involved with drugs or alcohol, thus providing a model of dealing with problems by running away from them. In addition, parents under the influence of such substances are in no position much of the time to provide the understanding and support that might make it possible for a sexually molested child to come to terms with her situation.

James and Meyerding suggest a possible relationship among sexual molestation, lack of parental understanding and support, and a career of prostitution. They feel that "abusive sexual experiences may have a significant impact on the victims' developing self-identity and this may relate to the development of adult patterns of female sexual or occupational deviance such as prostitution." They conjecture that abusive sexual experiences in childhood may lead a victim to regard herself as a sexual object and they observe "that to be used sexually at an early age in a way that produces guilt, shame, and loss of self-esteem on the part of the victim would be likely to lessen one's resistence to viewing one's self as a saleable commodity."

This impression of low self-worth may be transmitted in other ways also. Families may let their children know that they are persons to be valued and prized or, alternatively, that they are unwanted, a source of trouble, and of little account. The judgments of adults influence the ways in which juveniles perceive and evaluate themselves. If their sense of self-worth is low, children will be ready to sell themselves cheaply; by turning to prostitution, they also turn that metaphorical sale into a literal one. The case of Jean provides an example of this process.

Jean did well in school but received no praise. Her parents did not consider education important for a girl and they encouraged her to think about an early marriage and to visualize her role in it as passive and subserviant: "A woman is a maid, a cook, and a prostitute to her husband," was Jean's mother's description of the female role. Jean married in her senior year in high school, but found her husband sexually inadequate. In one way, however, he did perform the role of instructor as her mother had taught her to expect—he taught her to use drugs. Jean left her husband and went to live with a woman friend who became her lover. Her parents were very upset upon learning of her lesbian relationship, and in a stormy scene, forbade her presence in the house. After a while Jean abandoned her lover and went to live with a man who shared her drug habit. He did not order or even overtly encourage her to become a prostitute; he simply expected her to pay for their drugs and living expenses. Although she had finished high school and appeared quite bright, she never considered any occupation other than prostitution. She has carried out her mother's prescription of the female role, albeit perhaps a bit more literally than was intended.

This case also helps to explain the relationship between the juvenile prostitute and her pimp. Both the Silberman and the Bracey studies emphasize that kidnapping, forcible administration of drugs or other methods of coercion are rare; instead, pimps supply a facsimile of the attention, approval, and understanding that the girls have not received at home; not having known real affection, the girls do not realize that they are accepting a cheap imitation.

Most of the pimps associated with juveniles are not the "classic" pimps or *Black Players* described by Christina and Edward Milner (1972). The majority of these men, with their distinctive clothes, customized cars, and large stables of attractive, adoring women, would not be bothered with the "small change" of juvenile prostitution. They consider juveniles to be hard to train, unstable, and dangerous, since a pimp caught with a juvenile is easier to convict and liable to far stiffer penalties than one who consorts with adults. The men in the lives of young prostitutes are the "macaroni" or "coffee-and-cake" pimps, the lower stratum of their trade who use prostitution only to supplement incomes produced by odd jobs, small-scale illegal enterprises, or welfare. They usually have only one girl and may view themselves as no different from the man whose wife supports him by waiting on tables while he goes to law school. The young prostitute has little trouble accepting this definition of their relationship, and she may readily fantasize for any listener about the boutique they will open with the money he is so carefully holding and investing for her.

Although threats of violence are far more common than violence itself in these relationships, violence is by no means totally absent. If a girl has not obeyed orders and needs to be taught a lesson, if she has not brought in enough money, if she has not shown the proper respect, a pimp may indeed resort to force. Although the girl may be frightened, indignant, or enraged during and immediately after such a beating, soon after she inevitably admits the justice of her man's anger and acknowledges his right to correct her. Her greatest fear is not his violence, but his apathy. As long as he cares enough about her to "teach her a lesson," he will not leave her. Her low opinion of herself convinces her that she is an unworthy recipient of care or effort. Her man's attacks are a dramatic form of the attention that she craves, while at the same time they reinforce her perception of herself as flawed and defective. Similarly, when her pimp shouts "whore" and "bitch" at her, she accepts those words both as insults and as accurate descriptions. Her self-esteem is so low that she cannot imagine being independent; there is a paradox in the fact that she needs someone to support her, to complete her, but the only support she can accept is that which supports her self-image of being unworthy. Thus the threats, abuse, and insults of the pimp are not only acceptable, they are eagerly sought, since the only alternative the girl can imagine is indifference and abandonment.

If abuse from her pimp is tolerated and sometimes welcomed as a form of attention, abuse from a john is accepted as one of the risks of the business. All prostitutes are vulnerable to the danger of a customer who gets satisfaction from inflicting pain, although women who work out of massage parlors, brothels, or jointly occupied apartments may have the protection of hired bouncers or, at least, of each other. The woman who works the streets and cannot have her tricks pre-screened is in the greatest peril. The young prostitute is in some ways the most vulnerable of all.

Since she often appears frail and inexperienced, she provides a particularly attractive target to the sadist. The girl who does not satisfy her customer or who refuses to engage in a particular type of sexual activity also runs the risk of physical abuse. Young prostitutes seem particularly prone to incite abuse when they attempt to deceive customers or use force against them; at least in some instances, this is done to provoke excitement, but the customer's rage may well get out of hand.

The younger and slighter she is, the prostitute is also a tempting target for muggers. Not only are juveniles often physically at a disadvantage compared to the men who prey upon them, they are also victims of the fact that some men do not think that it is a crime to attack or abuse a prostitute. Prostitutes are in the streets in high-crime areas late at night and by themselves. They often carry large sums of money. The chances of their complaining to the authorities are miniscule and the chances of such a complaint being taken seriously are even less. Any prostitute will hestitate to initiate contact with the police, even if it is for the purpose of protecting herself; a juvenile who may also be a sought-after runaway will be even more reluctant than an adult.

If she is apprehended by the police the young prostitute is confronted by a juvenile justice system that is not only ill-equipped to help her, but is even unwilling to acknowledge the nature of her problem. In some cases there is a benignly motivated effort to avoid stigmatizing a youngster with the label of prostitute; she will be described as a runaway or as a juvenile who has been associating with undesirables. If the authorities do focus their attention on the sexual nature of her acts, she may be defined as promiscuous. Regardless of the designation, if the family is seemingly intact, the juvenile court will have a strong tendency to return her to them and to consider its work done.

If, on the other hand, the system chooses to be outraged by the girl who has not only broken the rules enjoining female adolescent chastity but has done so publicly, defiantly, and for profit, she will probably be placed in an institution. (It is worthwhile noting that her adult counterpart will receive no more than a light fine for identical behavior.) In any case, once the juvenile is in the institution, emphasis will be placed on her delinquent behavior, not on the causes of it.

This should not be seen as an indictment of the juvenile justice system, but rather of the atmosphere of shame and ignorance which has made it impossible to do adequate research on the nature and consequences of early sexual experiences. As long as we pretend that incest and the seduction of children are rare events, as long as juvenile prostitution is viewed as an act of delinquency rather than as a manifestation of social and cultural forces that lead to troubled teenage young girls, it will not be possible to examine and deal with child prostitution realistically.

References

Bracey, Dorothy H. Baby-Pros: Preliminary Profiles of Juvenile Prostitutes. New York: John Jay Press, 1979.

Dulles, Georgia. "Child prostitution causes are sought." The New York Times, September 4, 1979.

Grey, Diana. "Turning out. A story of teen-aged prostitution." Urban Life and Culture, Vol. 1(4), 1973.

James, Jennifer and Jane Meyerding. "Motivations of women for entrance into prostitution," unpublished.

Milner, Christina and Richard Milner. Black Players. New York: Bantam, 1973.

Robinson, Shirley, quoted in "How children become prostitutes." Chicago Tribune, February, 1981.

Silberman, Mimi, quoted in "How children become prostitutes." Chicago Tribune, February, 1981.

17

Incest: Whose Reality, Whose Theory?

Sandra Butler

The recent history of the study of sexual violence within the context of the family is the subject of this chapter. Butler distinguishes between two types of analysis of incest that are prevalent in the literature: one, common among many practitioners and researchers alike, studies sexual violence as part of the family unit and its individual psychology; the other, the feminist analysis, studies sexual violence in terms of power structures in the family. The latter perspective does not deny the role of psychology in studying individuals and their development, but maintains that the general structure of the family unit be studied as it has developed specifically in our society.

This chapter continues to add weight to the now-familiar argument that the victimization of women is due in large part to the traditional roles that men and women are supposed to play in society; that the victimization of women is not simply a manifestation of an aberration of these sex roles. Thus it is the author's contention that "sexual assault is not an unnatural acting out of a particular configuration of family interaction or personality types, but is simply further along on the continuum of societally condoned male behaviors."

How does the family provide a setting for sexual violence according to this chapter? Butler argues that psychological theories seem to always end up justifying the abuser (the father) and serve to perpetuate the helplessness of the mother and the powerlessness of women in general. As you read the description of the child, mother, and father as presented in this chapter, think about how these two different theoretical approaches apply to the analysis of incest and how you would approach a study of the subject in your locality.

This piece attempts to look at the theory and the reality of incestuous assault; they are not the same. I am going to juxtapose the experience against the words of the theorists so that we can, as feminists, begin to understand the woman-blaming, misogyny and excuses at the foundation of the writing about incest.

The legal definitions and consequences of incest vary widely from state to state. The laws are inconsistent and rarely used to prosecute. In Califor-

Reprinted from *Aegis,* volume 29, P.O. Box 21033, Washington, D.C. 20009.

nia, the penalty for incest is sixteen months to two or three years in state prison. In other states, the penalties range from a small fine to twenty and thirty years imprisonment.

Because of inconsistencies in the law, I have formulated the following definition to encompass a range of abuses: Incestuous assault is any manual, oral or genital sexual contact or other explicitly sexual behavior that an adult family member imposes on a child by exploiting the child's vulnerability and powerlessness. The vulnerability of the child stems from specific lack of information about the unacceptability of the behavior because of her early state of psychological and psychosexual development. Her powerlessness stems from the inability to say "no" to an adult member of her family.

Incestuous assault is a reality in the lives of children of all races and classes. The only constant is that aggressors are overwhelmingly male and the victims are nearly always female.

Incestuous assault is like rape in that it is still viewed as a "sex" crime, most of the offenders are male and victims experience similar feelings of humiliation, fear, powerlessness and self-blame. But it is the differences that augment the suffering caused by this form of assault. One difference is that in an incestuous assault, there is always a close if not primary relationship between the offender and the victim. Second, the incestuous assault is not one-time "only" but continues for a long period during which it increases in sexual specificity. Third, the child is less likely to report the violation since her family is at stake and is more likely to be disbelieved if she does.

These differences point out the importance of understanding the family as the system in which incestuous assault occurs. At the same time, it is important to remember that families do not sexually abuse children, men do.

There is an urgent need for a feminist analysis of families and particularly families in which sexual violence occurs. We need to look closely at power in the family, who has it and why. Power can be translated through choice and we need to look at how those choices are exercised. Do women and children have the power to say "yes" when they do not have equal power to say "no"?

The issue of men's power in the family is rarely integrated in a non-feminist analysis of incest. Men have, at least in their homes if nowhere else, the power and the options that power affords them. Men who have little or no prestige or status in the larger world still have the ability to control the events and the people in their "castles." When prevailing social theory on incest begins to approach this aspect of male power, it turns away.

Non-feminist theorists do not move to look at male power in the family, but instead study sexual violence within the context of the family as a psychological unit. This analysis began during the 1960's when incest was first defined as a "transaction which protects and maintains the family from disintegration. It is a symptom of family dysfunction and utilized as a tension-reducing device."[1] According to Dr. Graves, "It's easier for the man to admit the problem if it's presented in terms of family dynamics. He's the one on the defensive and seeing it as a family problem will help him open up."[2] Incest is no longer seen as something which happens to a victim, but rather a sophisticated interplay between two victims within the context of the family.

Typically, the description of the family in which incestuous assault occurs is as follows: father rarely has a criminal record, has a good and steady work history, tends to be domineering and tyrannical and unable to deal well with adult women. He views his wife as rejecting and threatening. His wife is described as needy, insecure both in her own sense of self-worth and her "femininity," less interested in sex than her husband, immature and in need of approval. Is that family unfamiliar to any of us?

The theory that incestuous assaults occur when families become dysfunctional serves to excuse the offender. To assign to each family member a role in causing the incestuous assault is to imply that whatever happens to women and children in our homes can be traced back to something that is our fault. The promise held out to us by family systems theorists is that once we figure out as mothers and as children what we have done wrong, our victimization will stop. Men will simply stop hunting our flesh for reassurance of their power over us and their need for reminders of their sexual strength.

I suggest that incestuous assault is not an unnatural acting out of a particular configuration of family interaction or personality types but is simply further along on the continuum of societally condoned male behaviors. We must recognize incestuous assault as culturally and politically sanctioned violence against women and children.

Although it is necessary to look at individual psychopathology and psychosexual development as well as at ways in which the family system provides a context for sexual violence, we must also see incestuous assault as part of an established social structure built with stones engraved:

. . . children are the property of their parents and families
. . . blood is thicker than water
. . . men are kings in their castles
. . . a sexually successful man is a "ladykiller"
. . . the "little" woman stands loyally and firmly behind her man.

This conclusion is strenuously avoided throughout the literature on incest. In its place are psychological interpretations which bear little resemblance to reality and which serve to justify the abuser's actions and further maintain women's powerlessness.

THE CHILD

One of the earliest canons in the writing on incestuous assault is the assertion that children are not to be believed. To this day, this is the premise from which most non-feminist professionals begin. The most frequent model for training in mental health agencies is that of disbelief and assumed manipulation. Staff have been repeatedly trained with a variation on the following: "Don't believe them. Always try to think about why they are telling you what they are saying. What's in it for them and what do they expect to get from you as a result?"

The need to disbelieve has its origins in Freud's need to deny what he was hearing about his male associates from their daughters who were clients of his. Freud preferred to turn things around and focus his attention on the child's fantasies rather than on the adult's predatory behavior. Many clinicians still are taught that children want genitally specific contact with the adults in their immediate environment, fantasize it, and when angry may even make it up to punish the male figure.

In reality, from reports I've gathered, children go to great lengths to lie in order to assure us that incestuous assaults do *not* happen. I have never known a child who said she was assaulted who "made it up," but I do know of many who do not tell anyone until early adolescence or when they have a feeling of enough power to survive outside the protection of the family. By the time they tell us, either directly or more often by "acting out" behaviors such as running away, drug addiction, alcoholism, or suicide attempts, we find it easier to scrutinize the symptomatic behaviors rather than to believe the underlying reality that caused enough pain and rage to precipitate such extreme behavior.

Besides accusing children of making up stories, many who have written about incestuous assault begin with the view that it is the child who is the source of the blame, responsibility and seduction of the adult. In some instances, she is the "active seducer rather than the one innocently seduced."[3] Some children are "passive participants who seldom complain or resist"[4] and yet others "avoid guilt feelings by denying their enjoyment in the sexual experience."[5] These children not only instigated the incest, according to these writers, but even if they didn't, it was seen as proof that they were seductive by "their acquiescence and albeit masked pleasure."[6]

These assumptions are based on the observation that incestuous assault rarely begins with threats of physical harm or corporal abuse. Overlooked is the more subtle coercion of bribes, gifts or misrepresentation of moral standards. The child has no reason to feel threatened by an adult in her family and will assume that what the adult is telling her to do is alright. That is, after all, the training we give our children. They respond to an adult whose love is important to them by denying their own reality and perceptions. Women remembering such experiences thirty years later, still remember it felt "funny." One woman told me, "What your Daddy tells you to do can't be wrong. So you start to think that it's you that's wrong for feeling funny about it."

The fondling and touching, often gentle and non-threatening, gradually progress to specific genital contact and intercourse during a period of years. As the sexual activity escalates, the child makes an adaptive response in order to survive in her family environment. Her response is to endure her own victimization in silence, to keep the family intact.

Some youngsters feel further torn because they may be enjoying the only form of love and attention that is offered in their family and the special position it offers them. The child is caught in the knot of being hugely powerful—the one who holds the key to the secret—and yet completely powerless to do anything to stop it from continuing. In a few instances where women felt some closeness and enjoyment during the incestuous assault, remembering back, they consistently said it was "their fault" for letting it happen, their responsibility and badness. It becomes a double betrayal. One at the hands of their assailant and the other at the response of their bodies.

Most youngsters fail to report the abuse to others due to the fear that they will be blamed, or that no one will believe them. They are sure they will be punished, rejected, and even abandoned for bringing shame upon the family. It is, after all, the only family they have and assailants often warn repeatedly of the "trouble" that will result from their telling. The trouble is often vague and amorphous with intimations of dissolution of the family, jail for the man, and beatings by the mother. In other instances, the threats are more specific. Many women remembered being threatened with brutal violence against them, their mothers, their friends, anyone they might choose to confide in in the hope of ending the relationship. There is an endless parade of horrifying possibilities marched before the child, who most often responds with silence and repression.

How, then, can one researcher claim that, in his sample of 54 girls who were involved in incestuous relationships between the ages of 9-14, 46 of them had made "acceptable adaptations."[7] No definition of acceptable is noted.

This conclusion is repeated by other studies which state that incest prior to puberty causes no "long term damage to the child."[8] The terms "acceptable" and "damage" are most often defined (if at all) in terms of the adult woman's sexual response in a monogamous heterosexual model. If an adult woman who was sexually victimized as a child is "frigid," "promiscuous," or lesbian—all seen as sexual maladaptations—the incestuous assault is seen to have had a deleterious effect on her natural development as a woman. When these young girls grow into women who marry and, as wives, remain silent, such behavior is seen as an appropriate model for women's mental health and no "damage" is believed to have resulted.

The effects of incestuous assault are multiple and not measureable by these crude and disrespectful indicators. They are lasting, though they need not be permanent. They are, however, a consistent source of pain because there are very few interventions that are successful, caring, believing and healing. Most of our responses still compound the trauma and pain of the child and the rest of the family as well.

We are learning that women who were assaulted as children find it extremely difficult to enter a relationship based on trust and intimacy. There is often a fearful expectation of repeated rejection, fears of vulnerability and openness, and an inability to acknowledge their own power.

One woman I spoke with was married to a man she valued and with whom she was struggling to create a relationship based on friendship, trust, and caring. She told me, "Sometimes when he wants to do certain things sexually I just can't. They are the same things my father forced me to do when I was small. I know it's not the same and I know he loves me, but when I say 'no,' part of me feels like that little girl finally grown strong who is able to say the 'no' I couldn't say all those years ago. The other part of me feels guilty that I am saying 'no' to the wrong person and I really love my husband and am making him suffer for my own history."

This woman and many others I spoke with have little self-esteem, self-worth, and perspective on how arduous and lonely their struggle is and how sadly unnecessary it is to hold themselves responsible.

Besides the many professionals who respond with disbelief or blame, there are also those who tell us that the trauma may come not from the experience itself but from an uptight and puritanical society that cannot allow uninterrupted a tender and loving rite of passage without causing trouble and interfering.

Dr. Wardell Pomeroy writes in *Forum* magazine that he has known many cases of father-daughter incest which illustrate that this kind of relationship can be positive as well as negative. He reports that "incest between adults and younger children can also prove to be a satisfying and enriching experience."[9] James Ramey, Professor of Psychiatry, writes in the "SIECUS" newsletter that incest is a matter of "personal morality"[10] and that the laws concerning it are "overly harsh."[11]

The male interpretation appears to suggest that incest doesn't happen at all and we make it up. Or, if it does happen, however rarely and to lower class people, then it was because we were seductive and wanted it and we are to blame. And finally, that even if it does happen frequently and we were not seductive and encouraging, it is something that is a pleasurable experience and an enriching part of our growth into womanhood.

THE MOTHER

Most researchers view both the mother and the child as similarly responsible. The mother's assumed culpability is based on the following questions, "How can the incest continue without her knowledge? Why doesn't she do something about it?" These questions the experts proceed to answer as follows:

Mother is defined as the "cornerstone in the pathological family system."[12] Father is aided and abetted in his liaison by the "conscious or unconscious seduction by his daughter and by his wife's collusion."[13] She is "frigid, hostile and unloving."[14] Even when she does not sexually deny her husband, she is unable to respond and frustrates him."[15]

Another scholar suggests that incest begins when the "father and daughter felt abandoned because of the birth of a baby or the wife's developing some outside interests."[16] Additionally, mothers promote incest by "frustrating their husbands sexually or symbolically deserting them and encouraging their daughters to assume mothering functions."[17]

These interpretations are grounded in the premise that mothers are responsible for maintaining the family unit in a state of balance and equilibrium. This logic suggests that if she withdraws from that role by choice or necessity, then all that happens within the family unit is her fault. If she decides to get a job to augment the family income; if she is giving birth to another, often unplanned child; if she returns to school or develops outside interests; if she masks the pain of her life with too much alcohol; if she is invalided emotionally or physically; her daughters, usually the eldest, will often assume her function in the family. That includes cooking, cleaning and caring for the younger children and providing the attention the "head of the family" requires.

If incestuous assault should occur as an outgrowth of any of these alterations of "appropriate" family roles, the mother is held responsible. Why the father does not assume the wife's maternal role when she withdraws or is incapacitated seems to be ignored by these theorists. Instead, the man feels his "first right is to receive the services which his wife formerly provided, sometimes including sexual services."[18]

In contrast to these approaches, feminist scholar Dr. Judith Herman encapsulates the mothers' painful message to their daughters: "Your father first, you second. It is dangerous to fight back, for if I lose him, I lose everything. For my own survival I must leave you to your own devices. I cannot defend you and if necessary I will sacrifice you to your father."[19]

In a forthcoming book, Dr. Herman compassionately describes many mothers in incest families as "disabled." Untreated depression, alcoholism, psychosis, and repeated involuntary childbearing are cited by Dr. Herman. Fear, loss, isolation, and anger at being abandoned and powerless are the underpinning of most of these women's lives and those dimensions are rarely, if at all, mentioned in the literature.

After the secret has been disclosed, children feel more betrayed by their mother's inability to protect them than from their father's assault. Although feelings of disappointment and even contempt for fathers are reported, it is still easier to be angry at one who does not have power rather than at the legal and actual perpetrator.

It is important for us to understand that by viewing incestuous dynamics in this way, that is, holding a woman responsible for her husband's assault on her child, we are doubly punishing a woman for her pain, her powerlessness, and her passivity and, furthermore, intimating that none of this would have happened had she fulfilled her responsibilities.

Let us suppose that the mother is withdrawn, disabled, and cannot provide good role modeling for her daughter. Can we not conclude that her behavior is symptomatic of the oppression of women in this culture? If women are so robbed of power and strength that a mother feels she is unable to prevent her husband's assault on her daughter, then we need to look at women's oppression as a direct cause of incestuous assault. In some cases, a woman who was an incest victim herself may feel as powerless to stop her husband's assault on her daughter as she was to stop her father's assault on herself years before.

THE FATHER

I have reviewed how the children and the mothers are portrayed. Now let us look at the aggressors. They were described during the 1940's and 1950's as uniquely pathological, culturally different and rare, when they were mentioned at all. They were the men caught in the criminal justice process, whose lives were studied by the agencies that provided services to them and their families. These were therefore men in poor and fragmented families in the ghettoes of our cities. Or they were tyrannical men heading isolated rural families. The pictures of these men and the extrapolations drawn from their lives remain in much of the literature today. "These men were seen against a backdrop of deprivation and a need to appear as a strong patriarch while uncertain of their masculine identity."[20]

Nowadays, the incestuous male is described in more sympathetic psychological language. One factor often taken into account is the "sexual maladjustment and estrangement between the husband and the wife" coupled with the male's "poor impulse control."[21] Since these males were of normal intelligence and acceptable occupational and social adjustment, incarcerated men who were studied were described as "fully exploiting their position as the authoritarian head of the home, also acting in many ways like a caricature of an adolescent."[22]

Incestuous males are often described as being overwhelmed by a maelstrom of unmet needs: emotional, psychological, physical, and sexual. They are experiencing stress from one or a combination of job-related, mid-life related, economically related or sexually related pressures. These stresses are considered to be exacerbated by their wives' collusion and their children's compliance and inability to protect themselves. The man is a "psychological child in the physical guise of an adult."[23] Men who receive very little love and nurturing from their mothers " . . . become symbiotic personalities and want someone to satisfy their needs as adults"[24] and are presumably motivated because they had "mothers who were overly seductive or overly attentive."[25]

In a startling new piece of analysis, emphasis is placed on going beyond the need to "blame" and urging renewed application of "compassion,"[26] undoubtedly to be applied directly to the male offender. We are now to understand that these men are emotionally troubled and incest is not something that happens *to* a victim but rather something that happens between *two* victims, circling back to the suggestion that these men have been victimized by poor parenting (read "mothering").

The researcher whose analysis this is points out that incarcerating the abuser may "leave the family destitute."[27] Additionally there are suggestions in the recent literature that incest should be decriminalized: "Incarceration causes both economic and psychological hardship to the family."[28]

Lucy Berliner, a victim advocate experienced in sexual abuse cases, observed, "When was the last time we heard anyone voice those concerns about a bank robber or a car thief? Why are we concerned about the economic hardships when it involves incestuous assault?" Why, indeed?

Once again, our work, our images as women, our reality is being defined by males and male-defined clinicians, scholars and theorists. There *is* a "conspiracy of silence" and as feminists, we must break our part of the silence by speaking the truth of our lives and experiences so that the theory, the funding, the clinicians, and the criminal justice personnel will be made to respond to us with clarity, respect, and immediacy.

Fear, isolation, and secrecy are the underpinnings of powerlessness. We need to speak, to break the silences between our lives, to listen and to provide compassionate alternatives for the women and children brave and strong enough to speak out. Listening, believing, caring are the first steps for us to take to hear the sounds and shapes of each other's lives, each other's pain. Then we can begin to develop *our* theory, *our* analysis, *our* interventions in a way that reflects our lives and validates our experiences as women.

Notes

1 Cormier, B.M., Kennedy, M., Sangowicz, J., "Psychodynamics of Father-Daughter Incest," *Canadian Psychiatric Association Journal,* 7 (1962), 203.

2 Dr. Graves, Richard, cited in *Sexuality Today* newsletter, August 27, 1979.

3 Bender, L., and Blau, A., "The Reaction of Children to Sexual Relations with Adults," *American Journal of Orthopsychiatry,* 7 (1937), 500-18.

4 Sarles, R.M. "Incest: Symposium on Behavioral Pediatrics," *Pediatric Clinics of North America,* 22 (1975), 108.

5 Weiner, J.B., "Father-Daughter Incest," *Psychiatric Quarterly,* 36: 1132-38.

6 Bender, L. et al., *ibid.*

7 Rasmussen, A. "The Importance of Sexual Attacks on Children Less than 14 Years of Age for the Development of Mental Disease and Character Anomalies," *Acta Psychiatric Neurology,* 9 (1934), 351-434.

8 Sarles, R.M., *ibid.*

9 Pomeroy, Wardell, B., "A New Look at Incest," *Forum,* November 1976.

10 Ramey, James W., "Dealing With The Last Taboo," *SIECUS Report,* Vol VII, No. 5, (May, 1979).

11 *Ibid.*

12 Lustig, N., Dreser, J., Spellman, S. and Murray, T., "Incest: A Family Group Survival Pattern," *Archives of General Psychiatry,* 14 (1966), 31-40.

13 Henderson, D.J., "Incest: A Synthesis of Data," *Canadian Psychiatric Association Journal,* 17 (1972), 299.

14 Cormier, B.M. et al., *ibid.*

15 *Ibid.*

16 Henderson, D.J., *ibid.*

17 *Ibid.*

18 Herman, J., and Hirschman, L., "Father-Daughter Incest," *Signs: Journal of Women in Culture and Society* (Summer 1977).

19 *Ibid.*

20 Lustig, N. et al., *ibid.*

21 Summitt, R., and Kryso, J., "Sexual Abuse of Children; A Clinical Spectrum," *American Journal of Orthopsychiatry* (1978), 1237-1251.

22 Cormier, B.M., *ibid.*

23 Groth, N., Burgess, A., Holmstrom, L. and Sgroi, S., *Sexual Assault of Children and Adolescents.* (Lexington, Mass.: Lexington Books, D.C. Heath and Co.)

24 *Ibid.*

25 Lustig, N. et al., *ibid.*

26 Rosenfeld, A., "Incest: The Victim-Perpetrator Model," Submitted for Publication. (Dr. Rosenfeld is Assistant Professor of Psychiatry and Director of Child Psychiatry Training at the Dept. of Psychiatry at Stanford University. Reprints are available from him directly.)

27 *Ibid.*

28 Cooper, Ingrid, "Decriminalization of Incest—New Legal/Clinical Approaches," *McGill Clinic in Forensic Psychiatry* (June 1977).

18

Pornography and Repression: A Reconsideration

Irene Diamond

In this chapter the topic is pornography. A discussion of pornography in a general considera-tion of victimization of women is relevant because, as Diamond says, the real subject of pornography is not sex, but power and violence.

There are two points of view on pornography. The traditional perspective maintains that pornography is harmless and may even be beneficial—serving as a "safety outlet" for males by permitting the viewing of violent sex and thereby eliminating the desire to act that way. The alternative view, that of recent feminists, maintains that pornography is a serious social problem. They argue that since pornography depicts women as victims, it reinforces and fosters attitudes of domination of women. Further, Diamond claims, this leads to actual physical brutalization and victimization of women.

Following her basic position on pornography, Diamond reviews for the reader findings from a national commission on violence, attitude surveys, retrospective studies (convicted sex offenders who reported on their experiences with pornography prior to their committing crimes), laboratory studies, and social indicator studies. Diamond summarizes all types of available research and rejects the Commission on Pornography and Obscenity findings that pornography is harmless. In addition she raises an important question about the motivation of the state in permitting pornography in order to distract men from their powerless economic condition.

"Porn Is Here to Stay," sociologist Amitai Etzioni could assert with com-plete confidence in 1977,[1] by assuming that any attempt to abolish pornog-raphy would be tantamount to trying to eliminate sexual impulses. Pornography may in fact have the staying power suggested by Etzioni, not because of the "naturalness" of sexuality but rather because of the resilien-cy of the political and economic institutions which structure and shape sexual expression. If we regard pornography primarily as a medium for expressing norms about male power and domination which functions as

Reprinted from *Signs* 5:4 (1980) by Irene Diamond. By permission of The University of Chicago Press.

a social control mechanism for keeping women in a subordinate status, then we have to question the prevailing liberal attitudes toward the issue of pornography and repression, which Etzioni and other social scientists hold. My purpose here is to examine the assumptions and data upon which the liberal model rests.

Historically, efforts to control the distribution of pornography have emanated from societal forces bent on suppressing all sexual matters—from birth control to sex education to scientific studies—while opposing efforts have come from those promoting openness in sexual matters. Moreover, since John Wilkes's *An Essay on Woman* in the eighteenth century, pornography has been used as a vehicle for criticizing the prevailing social order. As a consequence of this history, contemporary wisdom in the social science and "progressive" intellectual communities chastizes all plans to control pornography as attempts to repress sexuality and maintain the established order by those who have unenlightened and unhealthy sexual attitudes. Predictably, Etzioni dismisses a 1976 poll indicating that a substantial majority of Americans approves of crackdowns on pornography by declaring that most of these persons "have difficulty accepting their own sexuality and feel that unless the authorities keep the lid on, their urges may erupt. A democratic society requires holding at bay these sexual anxieties and their repressive political expressions."[2] Leaving aside the genuine motivations of such persons, which we cannot presume to know, Etzioni's statement contains the conventional assumption that the content of pornography is sex and that the genre is essentially a medium for sexual expression. For example, in his history of pornography, H. Montgomery Hyde writes: "It is generally agreed that the essential characteristic of pornography is its sexuality. In order to come within the category of pornography, material must have the power to excite sexual passions."[3] Since free and unfettered sexual expression is valorized as a force leading to human liberation, liberals have associated pornography with the progressive and the good. For instance, Al Goldstein, editor of *Screw*, one of the many tabloids of the 1960s designed to expose the hypocrisies of society by shocking its sensibilities, has described pornography as "one of the most sane manifestations of the human condition."[4] And Paul Goodman, though obviously not a "porn pusher," shared Goldstein's presumptions regarding the "progressive" model and could call on the Supreme Court in 1961 to "set aside the definition of pornography as obscenity—just as it set aside the doctrine of separate but equal facilities—and to clarify and further the best tendency of the sexual revolution."[5] Interestingly, many commentators consider pornography a uniquely modern phenomenon which emerged during the seventeenth century in response to the strains of modernization.[6] Steven Marcus has argued that the social process accompanying industrialization and urbanization led to the splitting off of sexuality from the rest of life. It was in response to this increasingly repressive situation that pornography, which Marcus describes as "nothing more than a representation of the fantasies of infantile sexual life,"[7] emerged and flourished. Although the "newness" of pornography is by no means accepted by pornography historians or sexual historians, it is nonetheless an article of faith in the conventional wisdom that the so-called excesses of pornography—its tendency toward what has been euphemistically termed the "unaesthetic"—are solely attributable to the repression of sexuality in the society at large.

THE EMERGING CRITIQUE

In recent years, the conventional liberal interpretation of pornography has come under attack. The generally held presumption that pornography is about sexuality has been called into question. Reflecting on his brief career in a "porno-fac," Burton Wohl concluded: "The letting of blood, violence, is porno's bottom line and not even the insatiable marquis could get beyond it. Power depends on violence, bloodshed. And power is what pornography celebrates, illuminates—above all sublimates. The other stuff, the tumid-humid-licking-sticking-writhing-and fall is peripheral, a catalogue of ornaments like the botanical and architectural doodling in Renaissance painting."[8] This primacy of power and violence in pornography was first underscored in *Sexual Politics* (1970), where Kate Millett dramatically demonstrated the centrality of male domination and female subjugation in literary descriptions of sexual activity. Others before her may have noted the sadistic aspects of pornography, but no one had linked sexuality and cruelty to the maintenance of patriarchy. Moreover Millett argued that the growing permissiveness in sexual expression during the twentieth century had given greater latitude to the expression of male hostility.[9] Whereas Millett dealt with avant-garde pornographic literary artists of the twentieth century, Robin Morgan in "Goodbye to All That" (1970) exposed the woman hatred of Left-hippie underground papers such as *Rat:* "It's the liberal co-optative masks on the face of sexist hate and fear worn by real nice guys we all know and like, right? We have met the enemy, and he's our friend. And dangerous. . . . A genuine left doesn't consider anyone's suffering irrelevant or titillating."[10] Morgan was also one of those arrested in 1970 for invading Grove Press, a so-called pioneer publisher of erotic literature, on the grounds that "Grove's sadomasochistic literature and pornographic films dehumanize and degrade women."[11] Expanding on these critiques of pornographic avant-garde literature and underground newspapers, Andrea Dworkin wrote in 1974: "*Suck* is a typical counter-culture sex paper. Any analysis of it reveals that the sexism is all-pervasive, expressed primarily as sadomasochism, absolutely the same as, and not counter to, the parent cultural values."[12] Dworkin also stressed the effects of pornography on the self-images of women and men, but she never explicitly connected the violence of fiction to what she termed "herstory, the underbelly of history." It was Susan Brownmiller, in her examination of the history of rape (1975) who made the connection when she defined pornography as "the undiluted essence of anti-female propaganda" and equated its philosophy to that of rape. She charged that the open display of pornography promoted a climate in which acts of sexual hostility were not only tolerated but ideologically encouraged. Calling attention to the systematized, commercially successful propaganda machines dominating the Forty-Second Streets of the nation's cities,[13] Brownmiller became the first feminist since the social purity advocates of the 1870s to call for government censorship of pornography.

With the appearance of *Snuff* in 1975, a porn film which purported to show an actual sexual assault, murder, and dismemberment of a woman, feminist activities began to focus on the portrayal of sexual violence. The relationship between increased violence in pornography and the media and the increasing rate of rape was emphasized; in Robin Morgan's words: "Pornography is the theory, and rape the practice."[14] Moreover, feminists began to argue that the increasing degree of violence was a male response to feminism itself. Diana Russell, who helped to organize the first International Tribunal on Crimes against Women in 1976 and subsequently helped to form a San Francisco group called "Women against Violence in Pornography and Media," claimed that "the great proliferation of pornography since 1970—particularly violent pornography and child pornography—is part of the male backlash against the women's liberation movement. Enough women have been rejecting the traditional role of being under men's thumbs to cause a crisis in the collective male ego. Pornography is a fantasy solution that inspires non-fantasy acts of punishment for uppity females."[15] And in a similar vein Ellen Willis wrote: "The aggressive proliferation of pornography is . . . a particularly obnoxious form of sexual backlash. The ubiquitous public display of dehumanized images of the female body is a sexist, misogynist society's answer to women's demand to be respected as people rather than exploited as objects. All such images express hatred and contempt, and it is no accident that they have become more and more overtly sadomasochistic. . . . Their function is to harass and intimidate, and their ultimate implications are fascistic."[16]

This newly emerging analysis of pornography differs in several respects from conventional interpretations. For feminists, the "what" of pornography is not sex but power and violence, and the "who" of concern are no longer male consumers and artists but women. In the conventional model, women are invisible. No concern is expressed for women being degraded or abused in pornographic films, photographs, or shows; nor the women who might become the real-life victims of nonfantasy acts; nor women in general whose oppression is reinforced by distorted views of their nature. The invisibility of women in this conventional model is attributable to several factors: (1) the tendency of patriarchal society to define reality in terms of men's activities, (2) the tendency in liberal society to discuss pornography in relationship to abstract rights and principles disconnected from pornography's grim reality in actual communities; and (3) the belief shared by traditional moralists and liberationists alike that human sexuality has a fixed "naturally" given shape. Feminists maintain that women as a class are victimized in an ideological sense by pornography and that this leads to the actual physical victimization of individual women. Although feminists reject the "traditional moralist" notion that pornography is primarily about sex, and therefore evil, they tend to agree with the moralist argument that the effects of pornography are harmful. And yet, the two positions differ fundamentally in their definition of the wrongness of pornography: for the moralist pornography is a pleasure which substitutes for "higher" pleasures, thus destroying the "virtue" of the viewer; it is wrong because of what it does *not* lead to. According to Charles B. Keating, Jr., head of one of the most active national antipornography organizations: "The traditional Judeo-Christian ethic does not condemn pleasure as an evil in itself; it does condemn the pursuit of pleasure for its own sake, *as an end* rather *than a means,* deliberately excluding the higher purposes and values to which pleasure is attached. [The sex drive] serves the individual and the common good of the human race, only when it is creative, productive, when it ministers to love and life. When, however, it serves only itself, it becomes a perversion. . . . Every word by which the organs of sex are designated bears out this statement: genital, generative, reproductive, procreative."[17] The possibility that pornography may have consequences for victims other than the viewer is not the moralist's primary concern since patriarchal religions view the abused wife, rape victim, or brutalized actress as fallen women who are in large part responsible for their fate. The feminist, on the other hand, who is predominantly concerned with female victims, insists that pornography contributes to actual violence against women. Feminist analysis interprets pornography not merely as the reflection of men's sexual fantasies but primarily as one of the mechanisms that has sustained the systemic domination of women by men throughout history. Pornography, then, is not unique to a particular historical period; nevertheless, because it serves political purposes, its quantity and violent nature will proliferate in response to efforts to disturb power relationships between men and women. Moreover, feminists consider the so-called excesses of pornography a manifestation of a backlash rather than the conventional argument concerning the "repression of sexuality." These are the propositions suggested by a feminist interpretation of pornography. Does the available evidence support these propositions? If not, why not?

PORNOGRAPHY AND VIOLENT BEHAVIOR

In 1969 the President's Commission on the Causes and Prevention of Violence concluded that media violence can induce persons to act aggressively. However, a year later the Commission on Obscenity and Pornography concluded that exposure to pornography does not seriously promote antisocial behavior. Since 1970, this latter report has been continuously acclaimed within the liberal social science community for having definitely documented the benignity of pornography.[18] At worst pornography is harmless; at best it provides for "more agreeable and 'increased openness' in marital communications."[19] Thus, whereas the report on violence confirmed the accepted liberal credo that environment is an important determinant of human behavior, the report on obscenity and pornography rejected this notion. A social learning model was deemed appropriate in explaining the impact of violence in the media but was not deemed applicable to the impact of pornography. The disparate models and conclusions of two major government research reports produced by leading social scientists can only be understood in light of the prevailing liberal ideology of the late 1960s: violence by ordinary citizens in the midst of civil disorders and a purported crime wave was viewed unfavorably, while sex in the midst of the so-called sexual revolution was viewed most favorably. The respective commissions framed their research questions and designs accordingly.

As we might expect, the Pornography Commission assumed that its subject of concern was "explicit sexual materials." In fact the commission chose not to use "pornography" in its report because it felt that the term connoted disapproval of the materials in question.[20] By employing a neutral term the commission could also use its investigations to document the need for sex education. However, this seemingly genuine concern became confused with its primary goal of proving that anything associated with the expression of sexuality was good. These "biases" influenced the final report in several ways: the choice of research designs employed by the various investigators, the interpretation of the individual data sets, and the integration of the individual studies into the actual report. Because of the commission's agenda only a small percentage of the materials in both the report and its accompanying ten technical volumes actually deals with the impact of pornography on human behavior.

ATTITUDE SURVEYS

The commission's investigators undertook a wide variety of surveys designed to discover different populations' *attitudes* toward pornography and its effects. Opinion data, however interesting in terms of descriptive information, do not address the question of the empirical consequences of visual materials. By comparison, the violence commission did not conduct polls to determine which persons believed that the effects of violence in the media were harmful. The thrust of the pornography commission's attitude studies did suggest that educated persons, young persons, and men tended to believe that pornography was harmless and that it provided information about sex. That this information became the first data section of the effects-panel report suggests the conventional premise: "If enough of the right people believe it to be so, then it is so." Data indicating that sex offenders more often than nonoffenders also expressed agreement with pornography's socially desirable or neutral effects were not included.[21] The final report did not explore some of the fascinating material which surveys did uncover with regard to the politics of porn usage.[22]

RETROSPECTIVE STUDIES

Due to the ethical problems involved in human experimentation, retrospective studies are often used in social research, although it is very difficult if not impossible to establish causal relationships through the use of such designs. Here again it is worth noting that the Violence Commission did not undertake a single study that attempted to identify violent offenders and then to trace their use of violent materials. The Pornography Commission, however, conducted several retrospective studies of sex offenders, some with appropriate control groups and some without, and arrived at the conclusion that "empirical research . . . has found no reliable evidence to date that exposure to explicit sexual materials plays a significant role in the causation of delinquent or criminal sexual behavior among youth or adults."[23] This conclusion relied on the findings that sex offenders and "sex deviants" reported less exposure to erotica during adolescence than other adults, and that during adulthood sex offenders did not have significantly different exposure to erotica or report greater likelihood of engaging in "sociosexual" behavior following exposure.[24]

However, the technical reports reveal different usages of the term "sex offender" which are sometimes liberal and sometimes restrictive. In two of the four studies where controlled comparisons were made between offenders and other groups, rapists constituted a minority of the offenders, and exhibitionists, pedophiles, persons convicted of "taking indecent liberties," and homosexuals formed the majority.[25] Only in these studies do the data indicate fairly conclusively that "sex offenders" had less exposure to pornography during adolescence. In the Walker study, where "sex offenders" referred only to rapists, we find that with a total group of sixty incarcerated rapists use of pornographic materials during adolescence was not examined other than to determine at what age subjects first saw various kinds of pornography. The investigators indicate no statistically significant differences in age of first exposure but then note that "visual inspection of the means [of exposure] revealed a tendency . . . for the comparison groups to be exposed to pornography at an earlier age." Rapists indicated less frequent usage during adulthood, but of course these incarcerated subjects also reported that "pornography was not easy to obtain."[26] Rapists did report *collecting* pornography for a significantly longer time than other men's groups, but no data are presented as to whether collecting is more common among the one group or the other. And yet, on the basis of such data the investigators conclude that "sex offenders, if anything, tend to have less experience with pornography than other groups."[27]

Goldstein et al., the other study which isolated sex offender rapists, attempted a more sophisticated analysis of pornography usage. Twenty rapists plus a variety of different control groups were questioned about their use of pornographic materials during the past year, the rapists being asked to report on the year prior to their incarceration. On the basis of data derived in this manner the investigators concluded that rapists had less exposure to all stimuli and media.[28] During adolescence there were few significant differences. However, in the investigators' own published book, and not the official report, they discovered what they term "dramatic" differences during preadolescence (six to ten years): 30 percent of the rapists, as opposed to 2 percent of the control groups, reported exposure to hard-core pornographic photos. Also cited here is the finding that "only rapists stand out in reporting a significantly earlier age of peak experience," and "the rapists only report more frequent exposure than controls for the most vivid experience."[29]

In both the Goldstein and Walker studies, data on the question of behavioral impact tend to be questioned and interpreted away. The Walker study indicates that rapists "reported more frequently than the control group that pornography had led them to commit a sexual crime," but this response, it is argued, represents a "convenient, ready-made explanation" for their current situation (although the control group comprised incarcerated non-sex offenders). Moreover, although Walker notes that the ratings on the projective inkblot test "were only minimally reliable and demonstrated essentially no validity," he nevertheless concludes: "Expert clinical judges did not rate the fantasy productions of the sex offenders in response to projective stimuli as indicating significantly more pathological sexual thought, sexual arousal, or aggressive sexual inclinations."[30] Somewhat similarly, the Goldstein study notes that "only the rapists stand out from all other groups in containing a higher percentage who wished to imitate the portrayed activity." Yet, because only 57 percent of the rapists as opposed to 85 percent of the controls actually attempted to imitate some feature of their peak erotic stimulus, the rapists are then characterized as having "low-beam performance" in contrast to their high interest statements.[31] The crucial question of the circumstances under which "performance" occurs is not explored. Thus when only rapists are categorized as sex offenders the actual data do not suggest that rapists have typically been deprived of pornography, nor is there firm evidence that rapists do not imitate portrayed behavior.

That some of the deficiencies in the report are attributable to the restrictive categorization of rapists is also apparent in Propper's survey of young male (aged sixteen to twenty-one) reformatory inmates. The data that show these inmates reporting considerable experience with sexual materials are footnoted in the report with the comment: "*Only* 3% of the sample had been incarcerated for assault, and *only* 2% for sex offenses"[32] (emphasis added). Not included in the report itself are data indicating that 62 percent of these "juveniles" scored high on a "peer sex behavior index," which included such items as "gang-bangs" and "intentionally getting a girl drunk." Since scores on this index positively related to exposure to "erotic materials," Propper himself concluded that "contrary to the opinion that high exposure may inhibit sexual practices, the data suggest a greater amount of activity among those who are more highly exposed."[33]

EXPERIMENTAL LABORATORY STUDIES

Unlike the various commissions which have studied the impact of violence, the Pornography Commission did not undertake a single controlled laboratory study involving children. The commission noted this gap in its call for "Needed Additional Research" but explained that fears about the consequences of such studies had precluded them. Garry Wills has commented on the irony of this attitude: "The group first deferred to a social instinct that childhood exposure to 'pornography' would have a powerful effect, before going on to argue that exposure has no such effect—all on the basis of tests invalidated by that first deference to the view that it has such an effect!"[34] The fourteen laboratory studies which were conducted used either male college students or married couples as subjects, and only three of these studies were designed in a way that permitted exploration of the possible relationship between pornography and aggressive behaviors. Most examined the impact of viewing pornography on attitudes, reported feelings of sexual arousal, or reports of sexual behavior outside the laboratory,[35] and were not designed to consider the matter of aggressive sexual behavior. Moreover, in many of the experiments the materials which subjects were shown might be classified more properly as sex-education materials rather than the amalgam of sex, violence, and woman hatred which typifies pornography.

Of the three experiments that did deal with aggression, two were conducted by Donald L. Mosher and lacked the most elemental features of standard laboratory research—a control group. His designs were clearly derived from the popularly held theory that if persons are provided with a "safety outlet" for expressing their "normal" feeling of hostility and aggression toward women they will be less inclined to act on those feelings. On the basis of his finding that males who exhibited highly "sex-calloused" attitudes showed a decline in such attitudes after viewing pornography, the commission concluded that "fears" about learning such attitudes from the medium were "unwarranted." The fact that these subjects might have shown the same decline after watching "Mr. Rogers' Neighborhood" was simply ignored.[36]

Only one study was modeled on the extensively used experiments which enabled violence researchers to conclude that aggressive behaviors are learned from media presentations of aggression. Tannenbaum found that subjects delivered stronger shocks to a confederate after viewing an "erotic" film sequence than did subjects who viewed neutral or aggressive films. And even more significantly, when aggressiveness and eroticism were joined in the same presentation, subjects delivered the most intense shocks.[37] The commission's brief reference to this study was counterbalanced with the findings from Mosher's other study,[38] which lacked the most basic ingredient of experimental design and yet purported to show that subjects were less inclined to aggress verbally against a female after viewing pornography. No less questionable was the commission's extensive reliance on the now famous satiation study conducted by Howard, which has often been offered in the popular media as proof of the catharsis theory of aggression. Howard found that college students exhibited a decreased interest in pornographic materials after being fed large amounts in a short period of time.[39] Presumably, after getting a proper "dosage" interest is satisfied. The commission never questioned the validity of this experiment even though its own surveys indicated that pornography consumers are habitual consumers in the real world.

SOCIAL INDICATORY STATISTICS

The final type of evidence upon which the commission relied was longitudinal data on the availability of pornography and reported sex offenses in both the United States and Denmark. The commission argued that the number of rapes known to the police in the United States was a "crude" measure, in comparison with the more "refined" measure of arrests for rape.[40] Although rape and pornography had both increased during the decade, the commission concluded that if availability were related to the incidence of rape "one would have expected an increase of much greater magnitude than the available figures indicate." It must be said that the commission also noted that the data did not disprove a causal connection. Since the publication of the commission's report, however, it is the Danish data which have been proclaimed positive proof for the catharsis of "safety-outlet" theories. The Danes had gradually removed all legal restrictions on pornography during the 1960s, and the data appeared to indicate that sex crimes had taken a dramatic turn downward. Further research has shown, however, that certain crimes such as homosexual prostitution were no longer being included in the statistics, thus artificially deflating the overall sex-crime figure. More importantly, it is now evident that the incidence of rape did not decline but in all likelihood increased.[41] The effects report of the commission demonstrated a decline in rape in Denmark by combining the statistics for "rape" and "attempted rape." These data were "adapted" from statistics in the technical report by Ben-Veniste;[42] his raw data indicated a decline in "attempted rape," but he himself did not discuss the issue of a decline in rape.[43] Kutschinsky, in his study, reported slightly different figures for "rape" and concluded that the overall decline in sex-crimes had not occurred in the area of rape.[44] In 1976 both J. H. Court of Australia and Victory Bachy of Belgium published papers which reported new rape statistics released by the Copenhagen police that were considerably higher than those cited by Kutschinsky. According to Court, "the trend since 1969 indicates that there has been a rise to a new level higher than anything experienced in the previous decade."[45] The Danish experiment, then, has not proven that the proliferation of pornography leads to a decline in sexual assaults against women.

In retrospect, the conclusions of the Commission on Pornography and Obscenity that pornography is harmless are not warranted on the basis of the actual data that were available to it. One might well wonder why the Goldstein report to the commission contained partially analyzed data or why rape statistics were gathered so hastily, but the fact remains that the commission's dubious conclusions cannot be attributed to its lacking the advantages of more recent data. Instead of pointing out the defects of the report, social scientists such as Etzioni who adhere to the conventional model of pornography and repression argued that the commission's data provided incontrovertible support for their belief in the harmless impact of pornography. The power of the prevailing liberal model has effectively limited the quality of research in the area, but more valuable studies are now emerging. Edward Donnerstein and John Hallan, for example, in a variation of a typical laboratory study where subjects are angered by a confederate, report that subsequent exposure to erotica increases aggression against females more so than against males.[46] And work by Seymour Feshback and his students indicates that males exposed to sadomasochistic stories are more likely to be sexually aroused by rape stories, more likely to believe that victims enjoy rape, and more likely to say that they would behave like fictional rapists when assured of nonpunishment.[47] Other data which may also support the proposition that pornography contributes to actual violence against women include reports from some cities that areas with large numbers of pornography outlets tend to have disproportionately high rape rates, statements from police officers that rapists are often found with pornographic materials, and reports that wife batterers are often devotees of pornographic literature.[48]

At this point there are no systematic quantitative data to support the proposition that pornography will proliferate in response to efforts to increase women's power. However, I would argue that the relationship between pornography and violence against women is inexplicable without the assumptions of this second proposition. Recognition of an institutionalized sexual hierarchy where men are in the dominant position provides the only adequate explanation for the repeated selection of women as victims in both pornography and the real world. Liberal social science has tended not to document these patterns because its models do not acknowledge the existence of patriarchy. This crucial theoretical gap also leaves liberals unable to explain why the legitimization of the pornography trade in the 1970s has not resulted in the predicted loss of interest and sales. (Estimates for this trade in Los Angeles were $15 million in 1969 and $85 million in 1976. Shops increased from eighteen to 143.)[49] If, however, we do accept the idea that pornography is a political and economic mechanism for sustaining patriarchal power relationships between men and women, we must also consider the possibility that when women take on new economic roles and destabilize existing relationships there will be an increase in the use of violence and repression against women. To recognize these dynamics is to understand why pornography appears to grow both in its quantity and its violence in certain historical periods. F. E. Kenyon, a British psychiatrist, has argued: "The considerable output of pornography in Victorian times may have resulted not only from the repressive, puritanical and hypocritical society, but also as a reaction to emerging female emancipation. Similarly today the further threat of 'Women's Liberation' could be partly responsible for another outpouring of pornography."[50] Of course, not all classes of women were drawn out of the home in the nineteenth century, and the challenges to the sexual status quo were neither as widespread or fundamental as those occurring today. Thus sexual backlash may not have been a predominant feature of the Victorian period. Moreover, technological advances in the capacity to produce pornographic materials are a contributing factor to growth and can determine differences between various historical periods. And yet, since technology is not an autonomous force, printing advances have taken particular forms because of prevailing power relationships.

One final factor is relevant in considering the proliferation of pornography in the contemporary period. Capitalism has advanced to a consumer stage where its economic goals are readily served by the commoditization and exploitation of sexuality, although the structural dynamics specific to capitalism did not necessitate this particular mechanism for achieving the goals of increased consumption. Sexuality has been appropriated as the particular mechanism because of preexisting patriarchal relationships. But pornography may serve the interests of capitalism in yet another way, a notion which is dramatized in Pamela Hansford Johnson's comments on German fascism: "When the Nazis took on the government of Poland, they flooded the Polish bookstalls with pornography. This is a fact. Why did they do so? They did so on the theory that to make the individual conscious only of the need for personal sensation would make the social combination of forces more difficult. . . . The Nazi scheme was the deliberate use of pornography to the ends of social castration. The theory was, and it is worth considering that—permit all things for self-gratification, and you are likely to encourage withdrawal from any sort of corporate responsibility."[51] Although Johnson is calling attention to the consequences of self-indulgence, her analysis does suggest that the reaffirmation of male power and control promoted by pornography and the behaviors thereby encouraged serve to deflect attention from the complete absence of control which most men have over their economic roles within capitalist society.

Ultimately, however, any understanding of the nature of pornography will have to include new conceptualizations of human sexuality. For there are those who acknowledge that violence is endemic to pornography, and that men often act on these fantasies, but who still view these connections as a "natural" expression of human sexuality. Robert Stoller, a psychoanalyst, writes: "An essential dynamic in pornography is hostility. Perhaps the most important difference between more perverse and less perverse ('normal') pornography, as between perversion and 'normality,' is the degree of hostility (hatred and revenge fantasies) bound or released in the sexual activity. One can raise the possibly controversial question whether in humans (especially males) powerful sexual excitement can ever exist without brutality also being present."[52] Although Stoller recognizes the complexity of the prevailing pattern of male "sexual" behavior in patriarchal society, he does not acknowledge the possibility that this "natural" dynamic may in fact be structured by patriarchy. Admittedly, this is an extremely difficult proposition to test because patriarchy has been so universally dominant. In fact, in the laboratory it is difficult to distinguish sexual and violent arousal, a seeming confirmation of the "nature" argument. However, as far as I am aware, no experimental studies have considered how these arousal mechanisms are themselves conditioned by sexist attitudes. I would propose a laboratory study akin to the Tannenbaum experiment mentioned earlier,[53] with the crucial addition of a measure for subjects' adherence to patriarchal values to test whether there is any variability in the apparent physiological interconnection between violent and sexual arousal, and if so, whether attitudinal predispositions can account for the way the two covary. Admittedly such a study, no matter how imaginative and sensitive its design, would still be a very crude approximation of complex biohistorical processes, thus careful historical study in combination with field studies of noncapitalist-patriarchal systems might provide a more appropriate test. These suggestions are predicated on the belief that sexuality, as well as relations between the sexes, is a product of social existence and as such is subject to human will. From this perspective, arguments contending that pornography is only about violence and oppression, and has nothing in common with erotica, are no less limited than arguments which recognize only pornography's sexual nature. In fact, the simplified equation of pornography and violence may well gain a degree of political legitimacy, for it reinforces the traditional view that pornography is evil without necessarily challenging anyone's fundamental beliefs about sexuality. By comparison, the argument that pornography is intimately related to sexual life as presently constructed and cannot be understood apart from that reality promotes the notion that even the raw material of sex is shaped by society and its relations of domination. This more inclusive perspective points to the futility of efforts to discover the "true" or "natural" form of sexuality, highlights the partial truths contained within traditional moralist and liberationist beliefs, and further elucidates the feminist claim that the sexual revolution is not our revolution.

Notes

1 Amitai Etzioni, "Porn Is Here to Stay," *New York Times* (May 17, 1977), p. 35.

2 *Ibid.*

3 H. Montgomery Hyde, *A History of Pornography* (New York: Farrar, Straus & Giroux, 1965), p. 1.

4 Cited by Robert Yoakum in "An Obscene, Lewd, Lascivious, Indecent, Filthy, and Vile Tabloid Entitled *Screw,*" *Columbia Journalism Review* (March/April 1977), p. 46.

5 Paul Goodman, *Utopian Essays and Practical Proposals* (New York: Random House, 1962), p. 57.

6 David Foxon, "Libertine Literature in England, 1660-1745," *Book Collector* 1-3 (Spring, Summer, Winter, 1963): 306.

7 Steven Marcus, *The Other Victorians* (New York: Basic Books, 1964), p. 286.

8 Burton Wohl, "The Reluctant Pornographer," *Harper's Magazine* (December 1976), p. 91.

9 Kate Millett, *Sexual Politics* (New York: Doubleday & Co., 1969), pp. 42-45.

10 Robin Morgan, "Goodbye to All That," in *The American Sisterhood,* ed. Wendy Martin (New York: Harper & Row, 1972), p. 361.

11 Nancy Moran, "Nine Women Arrested in Five-Hour Sit-In at Grove Press," *New York Times* (April 14, 1970), p. 55.

12 Andrea Dworkin, *Woman Hating* (New York: E. P. Dutton, 1974), p. 78.

13 Susan Brownmiller, *Against Our Will* (New York: Simon & Schuster, 1975), p. 394.

14 Robin Morgan, *Going Too Far* (New York: Random House, 1977), p. 169.

15 Diana Russell, "On Pornography," *Chrysalis* 4 (1977): 12.

16 Ellen Willis, "Sexual Counterrevolution 1," *Rolling Stone* (March 24, 1977), p. 29.

17 Statement of Charles H. Keating, Jr., in the *Report of Commission on Obscenity and Pornography* (Washington, D.C.: Government Printing Office, September, 1970), p. 516, emphasis added.

18 For instance, Etzioni's claims which appeared in several leading newspapers around the country in 1977 were based on the findings of the commission report.

19 *Report of the Commission,* p. 194.

20 *Ibid.,* p. 3.

21 R. F. Cook and R. H. Fosen, "Pornography and the Sex Offender: Patterns of Exposure and Immediate Arousal Effects of Pornographic Stimuli," in *Technical Reports of the Commission on Obscenity and Pornography* (Washington, D.C.: Government Printing Office, 1970), 7:168.

22 For instance, Alan Berger and his colleagues in their survey of high school students concluded that "it is the boys who introduce the girls to these movies, and this suggests that dating may be one of the major mechanisms by which boys manage the introduction" (A. S. Berger, J. H. Gagnon, and W. Simon, "Pornography: High School and College Years," in *Technical Reports of the Commission,* 9:168).

23 *Report of the Commission,* p. 139.

24 *Ibid.,* p. 242.

25 In Cook and Fosen, the group of sixty-three sex offenders included sixteen rapists and ten attempted rapists, while in W. T. Johnson, L. Kupperstein, and J. Peters, "Sex Offenders' Experience with Erotica," in *Technical Reports of the Commission,* 7:164, the forty-seven sex offenders included eighteen rapists.

26 C. E. Walker, "Erotic Stimuli and the Aggressive Sexual Offender," in *Technical Reports of the Commission,* 7:111.

27 *Ibid.,* p. 130.

28 M. J. Goldstein et al., "Exposure to Pornography and Sexual Behavior in Deviant and Normal Groups," in *Technical Reports of the Commission,* vol. 7. The authors indicated that the data in the report were not completely analyzed, which presumably explains why the preadolescence material only appears in their 1973 book.

29 Michael J. Goldstein and Harold Stanford Kant with John J. Hartman, *Pornography and Sexual Deviance* (Berkeley: University of California Press, 1973), p. 73.

30 Walker, p. 128.

31 Goldstein and Kant, p. 75.

32 *Report of the Commission,* p. 221.

33 M. M. Propper, "Exposure to Sexually Oriented Materials among Young Male Prison Offenders," *Technical Reports of the Commission,* 9:363.

34 Garry Wills, "Measuring the Impact of Erotica," *Psychology Today* (August 1977), p. 33.

35 It is worth noting that in one study of married couples 11 percent of the women reported that they sought therapy after viewing hard-core porn films with their husbands. Cited in J. Mann, J. Sidman, and S. Starr, "Effects of Erotic Films on Sexual Behaviors of Married Couples," *Technical Reports of the Commission,* 8:217.

36 *Report of the Commission,* p. 201.

37 P. H. Tannenbaum, "Emotional Arousal as a Mediator of Communication Effects," *Technical Reports of the Commission,* 8:340.

38 *Report of the Commission,* p. 208.

39 J. L. Howard, C. B. Reifler, and M. B. Liptzin, "Effects of Exposure to Pornography," *Technical Reports of the Commission,* 8:97-133.

40 *Report of the Commission,* p. 229.

41 J. H. Court notes these changes in "Pornography and Sex Crimes: A Re-Evaluation in the Light of Recent Trends around the World," *International Journal of Criminology and Penology* 5 (1976): 129-57.

42 *Report of the Commission,* p. 231.

43 R. Ben-Veniste, "Pornography and Sex Crime—the Danish Experience," *Technical Reports of the Commission,* 7:253.

44 B. Kutschinsky, "Sex Crimes and Pornography in Copenhagen: A Survey of Attitudes," *Technical Reports of the Commission,* 7:3.

45 Court, p. 143; Victor Bachy, "Danish 'Permissiveness' Revisited," *Journal of Communication* 26, no. 1 (1976): 40-43.

46 Edward Donnerstein and John Hallan, "The Facilitating Effects of Erotica on Aggression against Women," *Journal of Personality and Social Psychology* (in press).

47 Seymour Feshbach, "Sex, Aggression, and Violence toward Women" (paper delivered at the American Psychological Association Annual Meeting, Toronto, September 1978). See also Neal Malamuth, Scott Haber, and Seymour Feshback, "Testing Hypotheses Regarding Rape: Exposure to Sexual Violence, Sex Differences, and the Normality of Rapists," *Journal of Research in Personality* (in press).

48 Data on areas from Cleveland (Police Department memo, Captain Carl I. Delau, August 1977), and Los Angeles (City Planning Department, "Study of the Effects of the Concentration of Adult Entertainment Establishments in the City of Los Angeles," June 1977 [mimeographed]); Mildred Daley Pagelow reported on wife batterers as devotees in *Women against Violence in Pornography and Media Newspage* 1, no. 7 (December 1977): 2; and in response to my question during a public talk on wife abuse (Detroit, November 1976), Commander James Bannon of the Detroit Police Department (also a holder of a Ph.D. in sociology with a specialization in sex roles) responded that "often we find that the man is trying to enact a scene in some pornographic pictures." Liberals have tended not to believe the opinions of police officers; this may explain why the commission ignored their reports about rape and pornography which were available to the commission.

49 J. H. Court, "Rape and Pornography in Los Angeles" (paper presented at the annual conference of Australian Psychological Society, Flinders University, South Australia, August 1977), p. 7.

50 F. E. Kenyon, "Pornography, Law, and Mental Health," *British Journal of Psychiatry* 126 (March 1975): 226.

51 Pamela Hansford Johnson, *On Iniquity* (New York: Charles Scribner's Sons, 1967), p. 26.

52 Robert Stoller, *Perversion: The Erotic Form of Hatred* (New York: Pantheon Books, 1975), p. 88.

53 See above (n. 37).

19

Sexual Harassment: The Experience

Catharine A. MacKinnon

Study after study has found that women at work experience sexual harassment. MacKinnon explains why sexual harassment has only recently been "discovered" and why it is a serious problem of victimization of women: it is coercion; it is unwanted sex under threat; it is sex that is economically enforced; it denies women the exercise of control over their lives. The victimization descriptions and the course that sexual harassment takes are graphically presented. Legal action open to women who are victimized by sexual harassment rather than sexual discrimination is very recent. The author identifies three events that the law takes into account in defining sexual harassment—the advance, the response, and the employment consequence.

MacKinnon cites the particular sensitivity that black women have shown to this form of sexual victimization and suggests their vulnerability may be even greater than that of white women. She points out that black women are economically in an even more precarious situation than white women and that being black has always meant being a target of sexual abuse historically in the U.S. Further, in a racist as well as sexist society, black women continue to be stereotyped as more sexually accessible than white women. In conclusion to this chapter, the author discusses the difference between free choice and coercion, pointing out that in the middle, between these two extremes, is "caring" which often occurs in typically women's jobs such as secretarial work and waitressing. Employment superiors may turn job-related attitudes and personal attention by women into "coerced" caring.

Most women wish to choose whether, when, where, and with whom to have sexual relationships, as one important part of exercising control over their lives. Sexual harassment denies this choice in the process of denying the opportunity to study or work without being subjected to sexual exactions. Objection to sexual harassment at work is not a neopuritan moral protest against signs of attraction, displays of affection, compliments, flirtation, or touching on the job. Instead, women

> are rattled and often angry about sex that is one-sided, unwelcome or comes with strings attached. When it's something a woman wants to turn off but can't (a co-worker or supervisor who refuses to stop) or when it's coming from someone with the economic power to hire or fire, help or hinder, reward or punish (an employer or client who mustn't be offended)—that's when [women] say it's a problem.

Women who protest sexual harassment at work are resisting economically enforced sexual exploitation.

This chapter analyzes sexual harassment as women report experiencing it. The analysis is necessarily preliminary and exploratory. These events have seldom been noticed, much less studied; they have almost never been studied *as* sexual harassment. Although the available material is limited, it covers a considerably broader range of incidents than courts will (predictably) consider to be sex discrimination. Each incident or facet of the problem mentioned here will not have equal *legal* weight or go to the same legal issue; not every instance or aspect of undesired sexual attention on the job is necessarily part of the legal cause of action. Some dimensions of the problem seem to contra-indicate legal action or to require determinations that courts are ill suited to make. The broader contextual approach is taken to avoid prematurely making women's experience of sexual harassment into a case of sex discrimination, no more and no less. For it is, at times, both more and less.

I envision a two-way process of interaction between the relevant legal concepts and women's experience. The strictures of the concept of sex discrimination will ultimately constrain those aspects of women's oppression that will be legally recognized as discriminatory. At the same time, women's experiences, expressed in their own way, can push to expand that concept. Such an approach not only enriches the law. It begins to shape it so that what *really* happens to women, not some male vision of what happens to women, is at the core of the legal prohibition. Women's lived-through experience, in as whole and truthful a fashion as can be approximated at this point, should begin to provide the starting point and context out of which is constructed the narrower forms of abuse that will be made illegal on their behalf. Now that a few women have the tools to address the legal system on its own terms, the law can begin to address women's experience on women's own terms.

Although the precise extent and contours of sexual harassment await further and more exacting investigation, preliminary research indicates that the problem is extremely widespread. Certainly it is more common than almost anyone thought. In the pioneering survey by Working Women United Institute, out of a sample of 55 food service workers and 100 women who attended a meeting on sexual harassment, from five to seven of every ten women reported experiencing sexual harassment in some form at some time in their work lives. Ninety-two percent of the total sample thought it a serious problem. In a study of all women employed at the United Nations, 49 percent said that sexual pressure currently existed on their jobs. During the first eight months of 1976, the Division of Human Rights of the State of New York received approximately 45 complaints from women alleging sexual harassment on the job. Of 9,000 women who responded voluntarily to a questionnaire in *Redbook Magazine*, "How do you handle sex on the job?" nine out of ten reported experiences of sexual harassment. Of course, those who experience the problem may be most likely to respond. Nevertheless, before this survey, it would have been difficult to convince a person of ordinary skepticism that 8,100 American women existed who would report experiencing sexual harassment at work.

Using the *Redbook* questionnaire, a naval officer found 81 percent of a sample of women on a navy base and in a nearby town reported employment-related sexual harassment in some form. These frequency figures must, of course, be cautiously regarded. But even extrapolating conservatively, given that nine out of ten American women work outside the home some time in their lives and that in April 1974, 45 percent of American women sixteen and over, or 35 million women, were employed in the labor force, it is clear that a lot of women are potentially affected. As the problem begins to appear structural rather than individual, *Redbook*'s conclusion that "the problem is not epidemic; it is pandemic—an everyday, everywhere occurrence" does not seem incredible.

One need not show that sexual harassment is commonplace in order to argue that it is severe for those afflicted, or even that it is sex discrimination. However, if one shows that sexual harassment in employment systematically occurs between the persons and under the conditions that an analysis of it as discrimination suggests—that is, as a function of sex as gender—one undercuts the view that it occurs because of some unique chemistry between particular (or aberrant) individuals. That sexual harassment does occur to a large and diverse population of women supports an analysis that it occurs *because* of their group characteristic, that is, sex. Such a showing supports an analysis of the abuse as structural, and as such, worth legal attention as sex discrimination, not just as unfairness between two individuals, which might better be approached through private law.

If the problem is so common, one might ask why it has not been commonly analyzed or protested. Lack of public information, social awareness, and formal data probably reflects less its exceptionality than its specific pathology. Sexual subjects are generally sensitive and considered private; women feel embarrassed, demeaned, and intimidated by these incidents. They feel afraid, despairing, utterly alone, and complicit. This is not the sort of experience one discusses readily. Even more to the point, sexual advances are often accompanied by threats of retaliation if exposed. Revealing these pressures enough to protest them thus risks the very employment consequences which sanctioned the advances in the first place.

It is not surprising either that women would not complain of an experience for which there has been no name. Until 1976, lacking a term to express it, sexual harassment was literally unspeakable, which made a generalized, shared, and social definition of it inaccessible. The unnamed should not be mistaken for the nonexistent. Silence often speaks of pain and degradation so thorough that the situation cannot be conceived as other than it is:

> When the conception of change is beyond the limits of the possible, there are no words to articulate discontent, so it is sometimes held not to exist. This mistaken belief arises because we can only grasp silence in the moment in which it is breaking. The sound of silence breaking makes us understand what we could not hear before. But the fact we could not hear does not prove that no pain existed.

As Adrienne Rich has said of this kind of silence, "Do not mistake it for any kind of absence." Until very recently issues analogous to sexual harrassment, such as abortion, rape, and wife beating existed at the level of an open secret in public consciousness, supporting the (equally untrue) inference that these events were infrequent as well as shameful, and branding the victim with the stigma of deviance. In light of these factors, more worth explaining is the emergence of women's ability to break the silence.

Victimization by the practice of sexual harassment, so far as is currently known, occurs across the lines of age, marital status, physical appearance, race, class, occupation, pay range, and any other factor that distinguishes women from each other. Frequency and type of incident may vary with specific vulnerabilities of the woman, or qualities of the job, employer, situation, or workplace, to an extent so far undetermined. To this point, the common denominator is that the perpetrators tend to be men, the victims women. Most of the perpetrators are employment superiors, although some are co-workers or clients. Of the 155 women in the Working Women United Institute sample, 40 percent were harassed by a male superior, 22 percent by a co-worker, 29 percent by a client, customer, or person who had no direct working relationship with them; 1 percent (N = 1) were harassed by a subordinate and 8 percent by "other."

As to age and marital status, *Redbook* finds the most common story is of a woman in her twenties fending off a boss in his sixties, someone she would never choose as a sexual partner. The majority of women who responded to the survey, in which 92 percent reported incidents of sexual harassment, were in their twenties or thirties, and married. Adultery seems no deterrent. However, many women were single or formerly married and ranged in age from their teens to their sixties. In the Working Women United Institute speak-out, one woman mentioned an incident that occurred when she was working as a child model at age ten; another reported an experience at age 55. The women in that sample ranged in age from 19 to 61. On further investigation, sexual harassment as a system may be found to affect women differentially by age, although it damages women regardless of age. That is, many older women may be excluded from jobs because they are considered unattractive sex objects, in order that younger women can be hired to be so treated. But many women preface their reports of sexual harassment with evaluations of their appearance such as, "I am fat and forty, but . . . "

Sexual harassment takes both verbal and physical forms. In the Working Women United Institute sample, approximately a third of those who reported sexual harassment reported physical forms, nearly two-thirds verbal forms. Verbal sexual harassment can include anything from passing but persistent comments on a woman's body or body parts to the experience of an eighteen-year-old file clerk whose boss regularly called her in to his office "to tell me the intimate details of his marriage and to ask what I thought about different sexual positions." Pornography is sometimes used. Physical forms range from repeated collisions that leave the impression of "accident" to outright rape. One woman reported unmistakable sexual molestation which fell between these extremes: "My boss . . . runs his hand up my leg or blouse. He hugs me to him and then tells me that he is 'just naturally affectionate.' "

There is some suggestion in the data that working class women encounter physical as well as verbal forms of sexual harassment more often than middle class and/or professional women, who more often encounter only the verbal forms. However, women's class status in the strict sense is often ambiguous. Is a secretary for a fancy law firm in a different class from a secretary from a struggling, small business? Is a nurse married to a doctor "working class" or "middle class" on her job? Is a lesbian factory worker from an advantaged background with a rich ex-husband who refuses to help support the children because of her sexual preference "upper class"? In any case, most women who responded to the *Redbook* survey, like most employed women, were working at white collar jobs earning between $5,000 and $10,000 a year. Many more were blue collar, professional, or managerial workers earning less than $5,000 or more than $25,000 a year. They report harassment by men independent of the class of those men.

The Working Women United Institute sample, in which approximately 70 percent reported incidents of sexual harassment, presented a strikingly typical profile of women's employment history. Almost all of the women had done office work of some kind in their work life. A quarter had done sales, a quarter had been teachers, a third file clerks, 42 percent had been either secretaries or receptionists, and 29 percent had done factory work. Currently, fifty-five were food service workers with the remainder scattered among a variety of occupations. The average income was $101-$125 per week. This is very close to, or a little below, the usual weekly earnings of most working women.

Race is an important variable in sexual harassment in several different senses. Black women's reports of sexual harassment by white male superiors reflect a sense of impunity that resounds of slavery and colonization. Maxine Munford, recently separated and with two children to support, claimed that on the first day at her new job she was asked by her employer "if she would make love to a white man, and if she would slap his face if he made a pass at her." She repeatedly refused such advances and was soon fired, the employer alleging she had inadequate knowledge and training for the job and lacked qualifications. His last statement before she left was: "If you would have intercourse with me seven days a week I might give you your job back." Apparently, sexual harassment can be both a sexist way to express racism and a racist way to express sexism. However, black women also report sexual harassment by black men and white women complain of sexual harassment by black male superiors and co-workers.

. . .

One might consider whether white women more readily perceive themselves as *sexually* degraded, or anticipate a supportive response when they complain, when they are sexually harassed by a black man than by a white man. Alternatively, some white women confide that they have consciously resisted reporting severe sexual harassment by black men to authorities because they feel the response would be supportive for racist reasons. Although racism is deeply involved in sexual harassment, the element common to these incidents is that the perpetrators are male, the victims female. Few women are in a position to harass men sexually, since they do not control men's employment destinies at work, and female sexual initiative is culturally repressed in this society.

As these experiences suggest, the specific injury of sexual harassment arises from the nexus between a sexual demand and the workplace. Anatomized, the situations can be seen to include a sexual incident or advance, some form of compliance or rejection, and some employment consequence. Sometimes these elements are telescoped, sometimes greatly attenuated, sometimes absent. All are variable: the type of incident or advance, the form of response, and the kind and degree of damage attributable to it.

The critical issues in assessing sexual harassment as a legal cause of action—the issues that need to be explored in light of women's experiences —center upon the definition of and the relationship among three events: the advance, the response, and the employment consequence. Critical questions arise in conceptualizing all three. Where is the line between a sexual advance and a friendly gesture? How actively must the issue be forced? If a woman complies, should the legal consequences be different than if she refuses? Given the attendant risks, how explicitly must a woman reject? Might quitting be treated the same as firing under certain circumstances? To get legal relief, must a job benefit be shown to be merited independent of a sexual bargain, or is the situation an injury in itself? When a perpetrator insists that a series of touchings were not meant to be sexual, but the victim experienced them as unambiguously sexual, assuming both are equally credible, whose interpretation controls when the victim's employment status is damaged? These issues will be explored here in the context of women's experiences. In addressing these questions, it is important to divide matters of persuasion from issues of fact, and both of these from issues which go to the core of the legal concept of the discrimination. The first distinguishes the good from the less good case; the second sets a standard of proof; the third draws a line between a legal claim and no claim at all.

Women's experiences of sexual harassment can be divided into two forms which merge at the edges and in the world. The first I term the *quid pro quo*, in which sexual compliance is exchanged, or proposed to be exchanged, for an employment opportunity. The second arises when sexual harassment is a persistent *condition of work*. This distinction highlights different facets of the problem as women live through it and suggests slightly different legal requirements. In both types, the sexual demand is often but an extension of a gender-defined work role. The victim is employed, hence treated, "as a woman." In the quid pro quo, the woman must comply sexually or forfeit an employment opportunity. The quid pro quo arises most powerfully within the context of horizontal segregation, in which women are employed in feminized jobs, such as office work, as a part of jobs vertically stratified by sex, with men holding the power to hire and fire women. In a job which is defined according to gender, noncompliance with all of the job's requirements, which may at the boss's whim come to include sexual tolerance or activity, operatively "disqualifies" a woman for the job. In sexual harassment as a condition of work, the exchange of sex for employment opportunities is less direct. The major question is whether the *advances themselves* constitute an injury in employment.

IMPACT OF SEXUAL HARASSMENT

Women's feelings about their experiences of sexual harassment are a significant part of its social impact. Like women who are raped, sexually harassed women feel humiliated, degraded, ashamed, embarrassed, and cheap, as well as angry. When asked whether the experience had any emotional or physical effect, 78 percent of the Working Women United Institute sample answered affirmatively. Here are some of their comments:

> As I remember all the sexual abuse and negative work experiences I am left feeling sick and helpless and upset instead of angry. . . . Reinforced feelings of no control— sense of doom . . . I have difficulty dropping the emotion barrier I work behind when I come home from work. My husband turns into just another man. . . . Kept me in a constant state of emotional agitation and frustration; I drank a lot. . . . Soured the essential delight in the work. . . . Stomachache, migraines, cried every night, no appetite. [Ellipses separate different person's responses.]

In the Working Women United Institute study, 78 percent of the women reported feeling "angry," 48 percent "upset," 23 percent "frightened," 7 percent "indifferent," and an additional 27 percent mentioned feeling "alienated," "alone," "helpless," or other. They tend to feel the incident is their fault, that they must have done something, individually, to elicit or encourage the behavior, that it is "my problem." Since they believe that no one else is subjected to it, they feel individually complicit as well as demeaned. Almost a quarter of the women in one survey reported feeling "guilty."

Judging from these responses, it does not seem as though women want to be sexually harassed at work. Nor do they, as a rule, find it flattering. As one explanation for women's apparent acquiescence, Sheila Rowbotham hypothesizes that (what amounts to) sexually harassed women are "subtly flattered that their sex is recognized. This makes them feel that they are not quite on the cash nexus, that they matter to their employer in the same way that they matter to men in their personal lives." While the parallel to home life lends plausibility to this analysis, only 10 percent of the women in the Working Women United Institute sample and 15 percent of the *Redbook* sample reported feeling "flattered" by being on the sex nexus. [In both surveys, women could indicate as many feelings as they felt applied to them.] Women do connect the harasser with other men in their lives, but with quite different results: "It made me think that the only reason other men don't do the same thing is that they don't have the power to." The view that women really want unwanted sex is similar to the equally self-serving view that women want to be raped. As Lynn Wehrli analyzes this:

Since women seem to "go along" with sexual harassment, [the assumption is that] they must like it, and it is not really harassment at all. This constitutes little more than a simplistic denial of all we know about the ways in which socialization and economic dependence foster submissiveness and override free choice.... Those women who are able to speak out about sexual harassment use terms such as "humiliating," "intimidating," "frightening," "financially damaging," "embarrassing," "nerve-wracking," "awful," and "frustrating" to describe it. These words are hardly those used to describe a situation which one "likes."

That women "go along" is partly a male perception and partly correct, a male-enforced reality. Women report being too intimidated to reject the advances unambivalently, regardless of how repulsed they feel. Women's most common response is to attempt to ignore the whole incident, letting the man's ego off the hook skillfully by *appearing* flattered in the hope he will be satisfied and stop. These responses may be interpreted as encouragement or even as provocation. One study found that 76 percent of ignored advances intensified. Some women feel constrained to decline gently, but become frustrated when their subtle hints of lack of reciprocity are ignored. Even clear resistance is often interpreted as encouragement, which is frightening. As a matter of fact, any response or lack of response may be interpreted as encouragement. Ultimately women realize that they have their job only so long as they are pleasing to their male superior, so they try to be polite.

Despite the feelings of guilt, self-loathing, and fear of others' responses, many women who have been sexually harassed do complain about it to someone—usually a woman friend, family member, or co-worker. About a quarter of them complain to the perpetrator himself. Those who complain, as well as those who do not, express fears that their complaints will be ignored, will not be believed, that they instead will be blamed, that they will be considered "unprofessional," or "asking for it," or told that this problem is too petty or trivial for a grown woman to worry about, and that they are blowing it all out of proportion. Carmita Wood's immediate supervisor, to whom she had reported incidents with her other superior at length, when asked to recall if she mentioned them, stated: "I don't remember specifically, but it was my impression, it was mentioned among a lot of things that I considered trivia."

Women also feel intimidated by possible repercussions of complaint, such as being considered a "troublemaker," or other men in their lives finding out about the incidents, men who typically believe they must have been asking for it. One article reports a man "recalling a woman purchasing clerk who had just received a 'really good raise' and then showed up at work 'all black and blue.' Her husband had 'slapped her around' because he thought the raise was a result of 'putting out.'" Women students (and women junior faculty) fear the repercussions of complaint more than the academic and professional consequences of the harassment itself.

Women's worst fears about the impact of complaint are amply justified. "Most male superiors treat it as a joke, at best it's not serious. . . . Even more frightening, the woman who speaks out against her tormentors runs the risk of suddenly being seen as a crazy, a weirdo, or even worse, a loose woman." Company officials often laugh it off or consider the women now available to themselves as well. One factory worker reports: "I went to the personnel manager with a complaint that two men were propositioning me. He promised to take immediate action. When I got up to leave, he grabbed my breast and said, 'Be nice to me and I'll take care of you.' "

Unions' response to women's complaints of sexual harassment by management has been mixed. Some union officials refuse to process grievances based upon claims of sexual harassment. In one such case, the complainant sued the union for breach of its duty of fair representation. Ms. Gates, the company's first and only woman employee, was hired as a janitor on the day shift, then reassigned to the night shift.

> While on the graveyard shift she was assigned to clean men's restrooms, to which she did not object except for the treatment which she allegedly received while doing her work. She complained that men were using the urinals while she was cleaning; that on occasions she was propositioned and chased around the restrooms, and that the company refused to place locks on the doors to prevent this from happening.

Her doctor stated that the resulting emotional breakdown made her physically unable to work the night shift. The company then fired her on the grounds that she was unable to perform the work for medical reasons. Through its woman president, the union maintained that the firing was for good cause and urged Ms. Gates to accept the company's offer of reinstatement under the same working conditions. When she refused, the union declined to process her claim, a decision the court held was for the union to make.

Firm union support was given to four women in another shop who complained to the union of sexual harassment by a male foreman. The National Labor Relations Board reportedly "decided that the foreman would have to apologize to each woman and from then on our relationship would be strictly business." The women found this inadequate. The union continued to pursue the issue, intervening directly in their relations with the perpetrator and working to change the pervasive attitude that "any woman who works in an auto plant is out for a quick make." It should be noted that this assumption is not limited to auto plants. Men in almost every working context attribute sexual desire to women workers based upon their mere presence as workers in that particular environment. This assumption is professed equally about women who are seen as anomalies on the job (any woman who would seek a male-defined work situation must be there because of men) as for those who are in women's jobs (any woman who would choose a feminine job must be looking for a man). Since no working context is excluded, one cannot conclude that women select particular jobs for sexual reasons. As with rape, the situation seems more to be that men wish to believe that women desire to be sexually attacked and to that end construct virtually any situation as an invitation. Constructed according to these images, women who do convey any sexuality whatever are assumed to be unselective: "If you express any sexuality at all, they just assume you're available to them—you know, just any-body."

As a further result of such attitudes, complaining to the perpetrator usually has little good effect. The refusal is ignored or interpreted as the no that means yes. If the no is taken as no, the woman often becomes the target of disappointed expectations. She is accused of prudery, unnatural-ness, victorianism: "What's the matter, aren't you liberated? I thought nothing bothered you." And lesbianism. The presumption seems to be that women are supposed to want sex with men, so that a women who declines sexual contact with this particular man must reject all sex, or at least all men. Noncooperative women (including women who carry resistance to the point of official complaint) are accused of trying to take away one of the few compensations for an otherwise meaningless, drab, and mech-anized workplace existence, one of life's little joys. This essentially justifies oppression on the basis of what it does for the oppressor. When the man is black and the woman white, the emotional blackmail, the "you're not the woman I took you for," often becomes particularly unfortunate. The American heritage of racism that portrayed the white woman as "too good" for the black man is now used to manipulate her white guilt, putting her in the position of seeming to participate in that system's castration of the black man if she declines to have sex with him, and in racist repression if she complains officially.

Women's confidence in their job performance is often totally shattered by these events. They are left wondering if the praise they received prior to the sexual incident was conditioned by the man's perception of the sexual potential in the relationship—or is it only that the later accusations of incompetence are conditioned by his perception of the lack of this possibility? Attempting to decline gracefully and preserve a facade of normalcy also has its costs: "We've all been so polite about it for so long to the point we are nauseated with ourselves."

Jokes are another form that the social control over women takes. Women who consider noncompliance dread the degradation of male hu-mor. At Carmita Wood's hearing, when she was describing disabling pains in her neck and arm which vanished upon leaving the job, the referee said,

"So you're saying, in effect, that [the professor] was a pain in the neck?" On being told the perpetrator's age, the referee remarked, "Young enough to be interested anyway." As the brief for Ms. Wood put it, "Nowhere is the existence of a persistent sexual harassment . . . questioned, it is merely treated lightly. Trivialization of sexual harassment has been a major means through which its invisibility has been enforced. Humor, which may reflect unconscious hostility, has been a major form of that trivialization. As Eleanor Zuckerman has noted, "Although it has become less acceptable openly to express prejudices against women, nevertheless, these feelings remain under the surface, often taking the form of humor, which makes the issues seem trivial and unimportant."

Faced with the spectre of unemployment, discrimination in the job market, and a good possibility of repeated incidents elsewhere, women usually try to endure. But the costs of endurance can be very high, including physical as well as psychological damage:

> The anxiety and strain, the tension and nervous exhaustion that accompany this kind of harassment take a terrific toll on women workers. Nervous tics of all kinds, aches and pains (which can be minor and irritating or can be devastatingly painful) often accompany the onset of sexual harassment. These pains and illnesses are the result of insoluble conflict, the inevitable backlash of the human body in response to intolerable stress which thousands of women must endure in order to survive.

Without further investigation, the extent of the disruption of women's work lives and the pervasive impact upon their employment opportunities can only be imagined. One woman, after describing her own experiences with sexual harassment, concluded:

> Many women face daily humiliation simply because they have female bodies. The one other female union member at my plant can avoid contact with everyone but a few men in her department because she stays at her work bench all day and eats in a small rest room at one end of her department.

For many women, work, a necessity for survival, requires self-quarantine to avoid constant assault on sexual integrity. Many women try to transfer away from the individual man, even at financial sacrifice. But once a woman has been sexually harassed, her options are very limited:

> If she objects, the chances are she will be harassed or get fired outright. If she submits, the chances are he'll get tired of her anyway. If she ignores it, she gets drawn into a cat-and-mouse game from which there is no exit except leaving the job.

Women do find ways of fighting back short of, and beyond, leaving their jobs. As has been noted, nonrejection coupled with noncompliance is a subtle but expensive form. One shuffles when one sees no alternative.

Women have also begun to oppose sexual harassment in more direct, visible, and powerful ways. The striking fact that black women have brought a disproportionate number of the sexual harassment lawsuits to date points to some conditions that make resistance seem not only necessary but possible. Protest to the point of court action before a legal claim is known to be available requires a quality of inner resolve that is reckless and serene, a sense of "this I won't take" that is both desperate and principled. It also reflects an absolute lack of any other choice at a point at which others with equally few choices do nothing.

Black women's least advantaged position in the economy is consistent with their advanced position on the point of resistance. Of all women, they are most vulnerable to sexual harassment, both because of the image of black women as the most sexually accessible and because they are the most economically at risk. These conditions promote black women's resistance to sexual harassment and their identification of it for what it is. On the one hand, because they have the least to fall back on economically, black women have the most to lose by protest, which targets them as dissidents, hence undesirable workers. At the same time, since they are so totally insecure in the marketplace, they have the least stake in the system of sexual harassment as it is because they stand to lose everything by it. Since they cannot afford any economic risks, once they are subjected to even a threat of loss of means, they cannot afford *not* to risk everything to prevent it. In fact, they often must risk everything even to have a chance of getting by. Thus, since black women stand to lose the most from sexual harassment, by comparison they may see themselves as having the least to lose by a struggle against it. Compared with having one's children starving on welfare, for example, any battle for a wage of one's own with a chance of winning greater than zero looks attractive. In this respect, some black women have been able to grasp the essence of the situation, and with it the necessity of opposition, earlier and more firmly than other more advantaged women.

Other factors may contribute to black women's leadership on this issue. To the extent they are sensitive to the operation of racism on an individual level, they may be less mystified that the sexual attention they receive is "personal." Their heritage of systematic sexual harassment under slavery may make them less tolerant of this monetized form of the same thing. The stigmatization of all black women as prostitutes may sensitize them to the real commonality between sexual harassment and prostitution. Feeling closer to the brand of the harlot, black women may more decisively identify and reject the spectre of its reality, however packaged.

The instances of sexual harassment described present straightforward coercion: unwanted sex under the gun of a job or educational benefit. Courts can understand abuses in this form. It is important to remember that affirmatively desired instances of sexual relationships also exist which begin in the context of an employment or educational relationship. Although it is not always simple, courts regularly distinguish bona fide relationships from later attempts to read coercion back into them. Between the two, between the clear coercion and the clear mutuality, exists a murky area where power and caring converge. Here arise some of the most profound issues of sexual harassment, and those which courts are the least suited to resolve.

In education, the preceptive and initiating function of the teacher and the respect and openness of the student merge with the masculine role of sexual mastery and the feminine role of eager purity, especially where the life of the mind means everything. The same parallel between the relationship that one is supposed to be having and the conditions of sexual dominance and submission can be seen in the roles of secretary and boss. Rosabeth Kanter notes that the secretary comes to "feel for" the boss, "to care deeply about what happens to him and to do his feeling for him," giving the relationship a tone of emotional intensity. Elsewhere, she sees that a large part of the secretary's job is to empathize with the boss's personal needs; she also observes that, since the secretary is part of the boss's private retinue, what happens to him determines what happens to her. Kanter does not consider that there may be a connection between the secretary's objective conditions and her feelings—sexual feelings included —about her boss.

Although the woman may, in fact, be and feel coerced in the sexual involvement in some instances of sexual harassment, she may not be entirely without regard for, or free from caring about, the perpetrator. Further investigation of what might be called "coerced caring," or, in the most complex cases, an "if this is sex, I must be in love" syndrome, is vital. It is becoming increasingly recognized that feelings of caring are not the only or even a direct cause of sexual desires in either sex. In light of this, it cannot be assumed that if the woman cares about the man, the sex is not coerced. The difficulties of conceptualization and proof, however, are enormous. But since employed women are supposed to develop, and must demonstrate, regard for the man as a part of the job, and since women are taught to identify with men's feelings, men's evaluations of them, and with their sexual attractiveness to men, as a major component of their *own* identities and sense of worth, it is often unclear and shifting whether the coercion or the caring is the weightier factor, or which "causes" which.

This is not the point at which the legal cause of action for sexual harassment unravels, but the point at which the less good legal case can be scrutinized for its social truths. The more general relationship in women between objective lack of choices and real feelings of love for men can be explored in this context. Plainly, the wooden dichotomy between "real love," which is supposed to be a matter of free choice, and coercion, which implies some form of the gun at the head, is revealed as inadequate to explain the social construction of women's sexuality and the conditions of its expression, including the economic ones. The initial attempts to establish sexual harassment as a cause of action should focus upon the clear cases, which exist in profusion. But the implications the less clear cases have for the tension between women's economic precariousness and dependency—which exists in the family as well as on the job—and the possibilities for freely chosen intimacy between unequals remain.

There is a unity in these apparently, and on the legal level actually, different cases. Taken as one, the sexual harassment of working women presents a closed system of social predation in which powerlessness builds powerlessness. Feelings are a material reality of it. Working women are defined, and survive by defining themselves, as sexually accessible and economically exploitable. Because they are economically vulnerable, they are sexually exposed; because they must be sexually accessible, they are always economically at risk. In this perspective, sexual harassment is less "epidemic" than endemic.

Women Workers in the Criminal Justice System

Introduction

Part 3 explores issues surrounding women working in the criminal justice system. The chapters in this section discuss the jobs, many of which are at the professional level, performed within the courts, law enforcement, and corrections. The focus in this section is on the functioning of women in these jobs, the occupational setting in which women work, the level of acceptance of women, the issues surrounding hiring substantial numbers of women and the promotion of women to high level positions in the criminal justice system. The section also deals with some of the legal recourses which are available to women who have experienced unjust treatment. One consequence of women entering into the system in increased numbers is that they become able in their professional capacities to influence and change social policy that affects women offenders and women victims of crime, as well as women workers themselves.

THE IMPACT OF WOMEN WORKERS
ON OFFENDERS AND VICTIMS

It is clear that there have been serious practical costs to our democratic principles as a nation from the past exclusion of women from the practice of law and related scholarship. Put in its boldest form: when few women were either in criminology or law, women victims and women offenders frequently did not receive equal treatment under the law. Inequities ranged from sexually discriminatory sentencing practices toward both female juveniles and female adult felons to the imposition of more severe criteria for women than men in order to be released on parole. One example of sentencing inequity is the once notorious Muncy Act in Pennsylvania which required judges to sentence women to an indefinite term at the penitentiary at Muncy while men were sentenced for a fixed amount of time and ended up serving a shorter sentence.[1] However, criminal laws and agency regulations which treat women differently than men are being changed, although the process has been slow and piecemeal. The sentencing provision in the Pennsylvania statute has been struck down by that state's supreme court as a violation of the Equal Protection Clause of the Fourteenth Amendment to the United States Constitution.[2] The following year a similiar law in Connecticut was struck down by a federal judge.[3]

Women undergraduates appear to be attracted to the fields of law and

criminology in growing numbers perhaps, in part, as a result of the women's movement and a new understanding of the need for more women
in these fields. In recent years women students have increased markedly
in numbers and, if the increase continues, their impact could be significant.[4] Students soon become tomorrow's professionals pursuing careers in
academic institutions, the law, prosecutors' offices, and other local, state,
and federal criminal justice agencies. The presence of large numbers of
women can have a real impact on stubborn discriminatory practices within
the legal system.

Bringing about policy changes has often meant battling in the courts.
A significant factor in the initiation and subsequent success of litigation
has been the growing availability of women lawyers. Those who are sympathetic to discrimination issues take on these cases with a special commitment and determination. It should be apparent, of course, that not all
women are sympathetic to such issues nor are all women feminists. Recall
Feinman's discussion in Chapter 7 in which women who on the surface
were reformers bent on improving women's prisons during the last century
were actually perpetuating sexual stereotypes about women.

Frequently the issue is not the law but its implementation. One such
case which serves as an example was brought by seventy-one women,
lasted over 2 1/2 years and was conducted by four different legal corporations arguing the case. The goal: to obtain the same police protection for
married women that already existed for single women and men. The suit
sought to reverse a long-standing practice in the New York City Police
Department of not arresting a husband who assaults his wife. Today, the
police policy is to arrest a husband who commits felonious assault or other
felonies against a wife.[5] Again, though the law may have changed, implementation is still in question as it depends on interpretation of departmental policy and individual officer discretion.

Any victory for equal protection under the law is a product of a long
chain of events which frequently starts with feminist political efforts to
gain economic, social, and political equality for women. In turn, the wom-
en's movement and the awareness it generates fuels interest in women's
criminality and their victimization, which attracts more women students
and so produces professionals who are able to challenge inequitable social
policies. One impact of the presence of female criminologists has been that
they and their students become a force for change. With the emergence of
more sophisticated professionals, we also find a better understanding of
social process and a recognition that legal changes do not always result in
implementation. Constant monitoring, the creation of procedural guidelines and their evaluation are essential components in meaningful social
change. Women working in professional and paraprofessional capacities in
the criminal justice system have in the past worked for fair treatment of

women offenders. Such treatment, not always accorded males, is essential for our criminal justice system—the essence of which should be to provide equal and fair treatment for all offenders, female and male alike. Women working in the system are becoming a catalyst for change in this direction.

THE IMPACT OF WOMEN WORKERS ON PRACTITIONERS

Women have experienced a great deal of difficulty in the United States in gaining entrance to occupations which traditionally have employed primarily men. The criminal justice system with its many different and varied positions—police officer, correctional officer, parole officer, judge, prosecutor, defense attorney—has always had many strong barriers to equal employment. Even after discrimination in employment in the public sector was a violation of federal and many state laws, the attitude changes necessary for abiding by the law with good faith and thereby treating women fairly have changed little.[6] Moreover, each instance of employment discrimination requires remediation on a case by case complaint filing—a slow and often personally painful course of action.

Of all the components of the criminal justice system, the judicial branch appears to have made the greatest strides in recent years, yet few women are to be found in the prestige positions such as judgeships. However, more women are going to law school today than ever before. In 1967, 4 percent of all law degrees were awarded to women; in 1978, the figure had risen to 26 percent.[7] After graduation some women are employed subsequently in offices of public prosecutors and public defenders. But few women have received appointments to clerk under prominent judges; this is one of the routes frequently followed by men aspiring to judgeships. Other avenues taken by men include serving as a U.S. district attorney, conducting a private practice which involves trial work, and being a state legislator.[8] The increased hiring of women at lower levels in the field of law such as assistant district attorney may be explained as a result of the fact that clearly defined job criteria exist (having a law degree and having passed the bar examination are concrete credentials). Or perhaps it is the fact that the myths about the need for physical prowess in the role of lawyer, judge, and prosecutor cannot be established. However, other myths concerning the unsuitability of women for legal work have been created. For example, notions that the male is more suitable for the bench because he projects greater authority and because he possesses higher status by virtue of being a male continue to influence judicial selection (see Chapter 20).

In policing and corrections, of course, myths abound. There is a perpetuation of the view that only men can do the job, that strength, physical size, and bravery are essential job criteria and are exclusively male attributes. Chapters 23 and 24 address these issues for police work and Chapter 25 examines these claims as they relate to the corrections field. It is worth noting that in police work 80 to 85 percent of all tasks are of a social service nature and that, although it has been well known for some time, it has not lessened the myths about the physical nature of the work. These stereotypes about jobs and about the characteristics of women and men have strongly affected the willingness of administrators to hire more than token numbers of women as officers.[9] Once hired, women are subjected to harassment on the job and frequently face reduced opportunities to demonstrate their value to the organization, whether a police agency, a corrections department, or a prosecutor's office.

"Comparable Value"

Almost two decades ago the Civil Rights Act of 1964 was passed by Congress. The Act prohibits discrimination in employment on the basis of sex as well as race. The year prior to its passage Congress adopted the Equal Pay Act of 1963 which states that equal pay for equal work is the law of the land. The Civil Rights Act is more broadly based, however, and is not limited to claims of equal pay for equal work. But until 1981 the broader meaning had not been successfully tested in the courts. In 1981 when the Supreme Court heard a case involving Oregon jail matrons, it ruled that they are entitled to seek relief in court using the Civil Rights Act. The women claimed that they have been discriminated against in their pay scale because of their sex since the male deputy sheriffs who guard prisoners earn $200 more a month than the women. The women argued that they do similiar work but not equal or the same work as that of the men. This is an important case because the Supreme Court ruled that the women were entitled to claim discrimination even though the case does not meet the more narrowly defined Equal Pay Act standard of equal pay for equal work. Instead, the Court said, the case falls under the broader scope of the Civil Rights Act of 1964. The ruling takes women's groups and labor groups a step closer to one of their goals which is to use the Civil Rights Act to bring lawsuits under the theory of "comparable worth." The standard of comparable worth holds that jobs of comparable difficulty or value to an organization should receive comparable pay. Many say that the comparable worth principle is the only way to upgrade compensation in fields traditionally occupied by women. The Oregon case represents the first indication that the courts may in the future rule that "comparable worth" lawsuits may be brought using the Civil Rights Act and it is a potentially important ruling for women challenging low pay scales. However, at this time, the Court has said that the Oregon ruling refers only to this particular case and cannot be used as a precedent in other labor cases that might deal with "comparable worth."

WOMEN AND CRIMINAL JUSTICE PROFESSIONALISM—THE FUTURE

Continual overseeing by the courts and local human rights commissions, as well as monitoring by women activists and concerned citizens, will be essential in the coming decades if women in sufficient numbers are to be given a chance to "prove themselves" in these agencies. This is necessary not only to show that they can do the job and that they intend to stay around but to assure implementation of laws designed to promote equality of opportunity. Several of the chapters in this section make the point that there are distinct groups that must be convinced of women's rights and capabilities; these are superiors in agencies, co-workers, clients, and the public.

Others would say that it is not enough to convince specific groups of women's basic rights and capabilities; that it is also necessary to examine the way work in our society is structured in relation to women's roles and status. There are several theories of women's status in the labor force.[10] Among these theories two, status attainment and marxist feminism, seem particularly useful in understanding women's disadvantaged situation in the working world of the criminal justice system.

Status attainment theory places the cause of women's lack of employment success on women's own values, attitudes, training and experiences which are shaped from birth by traditional sex role assignments. In other words, the educational experiences of women, their employment, aspirations, and their related attitudes are all said to be the result of society's attitudes and expectations of women as childbearers and rearers. Thus, this theory argues, women start at a disadvantage when they enter the job market because neither their occupational training nor earlier education and experience have prepared them for prestigious, high level jobs. Their work careers, then, have been viewed by society, and hence by many women, as secondary to marriage and motherhood. Accordingly, women's expectations of themselves are modest. Moreover, they do not anticipate that the job market will react favorably to them. Women, in other words, have been "socialized" to be less bold and assertive in entering occupations, in looking for opportunities to be valuable to the organization, and in looking for promotions. This position is close to the victim-blaming approach outlined by Karmen in the Introduction to Part 2.

The second theory, marxist feminism, argues that women's worth has been devalued over the years in the marketplace mainly because she receives no salary working at home. Her unwaged labor is considered essential by capitalism because: (1) it produces and nurtures children (future workers); (2) it provides basic support to the male worker; and (3) it ensures an intact family unit which is a consumer of products from cleaning supplies to furniture and grass seed. According to this theory, women's housework is encouraged and reinforced by males and the patriarchal system. Thus, when the woman goes out into the labor market, it is assumed she will make a less useful contribution to the organization than the man because she has always worked for no wages in the past. Further, it is hoped (by her fellow male workers) that she will not be too successful. Good jobs are always scarce and men, understandably, find the existing competition stiff enough without the addition of a new pool of workers. Women are sources of cheap labor available during times of economic expansion and are readily fired during periods of economic contraction. This makes the labor market always a "buyer's market."

In times of economic hardship (recession, inflation) the hiring and promotion of women in jobs not traditionally designated to women becomes even more problematic as personnel policies become more conservative. Women are to the professional and paraprofessional systems (e.g., policing) much like what the minority and immigrant workers are to the mining and agricultural industries. That is, they represent a willing, indeed eager, pool of workers to be employed and discarded at the convenience of the organization. Chapter 22 discusses hurdles police departments create for women trying to obtain jobs as police officers. The first chapter in this section, Chapter 20, discusses the judicial selection process and also explains how barriers are erected to keep women out of that field. Chapter 21 turns to an analysis of women professionals working as lawyers, a disproportionate number of whom practice criminal law. There are many impediments faced by women lawyers and Chapter 21 describes the part the profession itself takes in perpetuating the predominance of males.

Other ways that occupations attempt to prevent women from entering (or staying in once hired) are detailed in Chapters 23 and 24. Both are about police work. In one case the issue is the physical capability of women (Chapter 23) and in the second (Chapter 24) the issue is cowardice and charges created to call into question women's suitability (here black women) for the work. Following the chapters on courts and law enforcement, this section turns to the field of corrections. The reader will find that a similiar situation is encountered by women corrections officers, especially when they attempt to work in all-male prisons. The problems she faces are explicitly set forth in Chapter 25.

One final area not dealt with in any depth in this volume and deserving of serious study is the dual role that women workers must play at home as well as at work. This problem is considered for women lawyers in

Chapter 21. In addition, the unrecognized work and support of the wives of male workers in the criminal justice system is virtually ignored by contemporary researchers. One significant exception is the study of policemen's wives by Arthur and Elaine Niederhoffer.[11] They describe in detail the critical interconnection between work and home life, and the significant roles policemen's wives perform for their husbands.

The overall purpose of Part 3, Women Workers in the Criminal Justice System, is to provide the reader with a view of the scope of criminal justice roles as they are handled today by women who encounter from the system and society neither full acceptance nor full rejection as women working in criminal justice.

Notes

[1] (Act of July 25, 1913), P.L. 1311, Pa. Stat. Ann. tit. 61, §566(1964).

[2] Commonwealth v. Daniels, reported at 37 U.S.L.W. 2063(1968).

[3] United States ex rel. Robinson v. York, 281 F.Supp. 8(D.Conn.1968).

[4] At John Jay College of Criminal Justice, The City University of New York, the only college devoted entirely to criminal justice majors, there were in 1973 nineteen percent women in the undergraduate body while in 1980 forty-three percent were women. It would seem that women had begun to see careers in criminal justice as a real possibility while formerly this was not the case. "Student Data Statistics," John Jay College of Criminal Justice, 1980.

[5] *The New York Times*, June 27, 1978, p. A16.

[6] Equal Pay Act and Equal Employment Opportunity provisions of the Civil Rights Act of 1964, which is found at 78 Stat. 253, 42 U.S.C. 2000e et seq.(1964).

[7] *Digest of Educational Statistics*. HEW: National Center for Education Statistics. Washington D.C.1979 and *Degrees Awarded to Women: An Update*. 1979. HEW: National Center for Education Statistics. Washington D.C.

[8] Feinman, Clarice, *Women in Criminal Justice*. New York: Praeger,1980, p. 102.

[9] *The New York Times*, January 27, 1981. A report on the swearing in of a new police class indicates the 184 recruits out of a class of 885 are women. A twenty percent female hiring ratio is exceptionally high; few other departments in the country have approached it. See Price and Gavin, Chapter 22 and Townsey, Chapter 23, herein.

[10] Sokoloff, Natalie J. *Between Money and Love: The Dialectics of Women's Home and Market Work*. New York: Praeger, 1980.

[11] Arthur and Elaine Niederhoffer. *The Police Family: From Station House to Ranch House*. Lexington, Mass.: D.C. Heath, 1978.

20

A Sexist Selection Process Keeps Qualified Women off the Bench

Susan Ness

Ness, focusing on the federal judiciary, describes the institutional nature of discrimination in the appointment of judges, one of the highest status positions in our society. Ness describes how the judicial selection process works against the chances of women being appointed. Consider the barriers she cites: restrictive criteria (the "15 year rule"), double standards (women but not men are required to have judicial experience before a federal appointment), and male domination (e.g., in the form of the "old boy network") amongst those doing the selecting. Thus it is not the sexism of any one individual making appointments but rather a system deeply rooted in favor of men (institutionalized sexism) that prevents women from attaining federal judgeships in any significant numbers. Consider which of the three facets used in the selection process contribute the most toward women being bypassed for federal judicial appointment.

The recent appointment of Sandra Day O'Connor as the first woman to the Supreme Court, notwithstanding, Ness's theme of a sexist selection process in the judiciary remains quite valid. While a breakthrough after one hundred and ninety-two years of male justices, the philosophy of Justice O'Connor on sexual equality and the role the courts play in it is not yet clear. Second, it is also unclear what degree of influence Justice O'Connor will have as the only woman on the Supreme Court. Third, we would suggest, as women enter male-dominated occupations, it is important to question their commitment to women's issues.

One of the last white male bastions, the federal judiciary, boasting only 1.1 percent women and 4 percent blacks, is on the brink of the largest expansion in its history. The omnibus judgeship bill now awaiting action by House-Senate conferees would create 145 to 150 new judgeships, thus increasing the size of the federal judiciary by more than 25 percent. Women and minorities will fill a significant number of these new positions only if the president and members of the Senate change the present selection process to provide equal access for these traditionally ignored groups.

Reprinted with permission from Susan Ness, "A Sexist Selection Process Keeps Qualified Women Off the Bench," *The Washington Post,* March 26, 1978.

379

The Marston affair, which recently focused public attention on the selection process for federal judges and U.S. attorneys, did not, however, reveal the devastating impact that process has had on the appointment of women.

Even when compared with other traditionally male-dominated occupations, the federal judiciary—the upholder of equal rights in the United States—is at the bottom of the heap. The percentage of women construction workers (6.4 percent), welders and flame cutters (6.3 percent), and even female locomotive engineers (2.1 percent), exceeds the 1.1 percent of federal judges who are women.

The paucity of women federal judges is shocking:

• No woman has ever served on the Supreme Court.

• Only 51 women have ever served on the federal bench in its almost 200-year history.

• Only two women have ever been appointed to the U.S. Court of Appeals.

• Only one out of the 97 authorized Courts of Appeals judgeships is now held by a woman.

• Only 45 of the 525 authorized federal judgeships are now held by women.

Against this background, candidate Jimmy Carter assured women's groups at the 1976 Democratic national convention that he would appoint more women to the federal bench. How has he performed? During his first 14 months in office, President Carter made 38 nominations for federal judgeships; only two were women. Of his 10 appointments to the U.S. Court of Appeals, not one was a woman. Yet Labor Department statistics show that more than 41,000, or 9 percent, of the attorneys practicing in the United States today are women. Today, five years later, there are more than 70,000 female attorneys practicing in the United States.

Why is it important to have more women on the bench? Basic fairness demands it. It is a disgrace for a nation which prides itself on equality to have only males deciding the critical legal issues of our day. An all-male Supreme Court decided in *Geduldig v. Aiello* that excluding pregnancy-related conditions from coverage under disability insurance, while including coverage of prostate-related conditions, is not discriminatory. An all-female Supreme Court would never have reached that decision.

Do we lack women attorneys qualified to be judges? Governor Jerry Brown of California dispelled that myth by appointing 42 women to state judgeships. One of those women, Rose Elizabeth Bird, was selected to be chief justice of the California Supreme Court.

Not a lack of qualified women, but the method of judicial selection, has preserved the federal bench as a male domain. That process, complex and decentralized, is encumbered with many of the same barriers which blocked women during Carter's search for cabinet and sub-cabinet appointees:

- Selection criteria tend to favor men.
- A double standard prevails in applying the selection criteria.
- Primarily men—the "old boy network"—make the selections.

Certain selection criteria have the effect of barring women from the judiciary. A Justice Department guideline disqualifies, except in unusual circumstances, qualified candidates who have practiced law for less than 15 years. Since women and minorities have only recently gained access to legal training in significant numbers, the "15-year rule" works to exclude women. Had the 15-year rule been applied in California, the present chief justice of that state's supreme court would not now occupy the bench.

A double standard in the application of selection criteria is another major obstacle in the path of would-be women jurists. For example, all seven of the women and minority members who have been nominated to federal judgeships by the Carter administration have had previous judicial experience. But only 35 percent of the white male district court nominees and 28 percent of the circuit court appointees had such experience.

The highest hurdle for women, however, is the overwhelming predominance of men in the judicial selection process. Although the Constitution gives the president the power to appoint federal judges with the advice and consent of the Senate, the political reality of the appointments process, as Attorney General Griffin Bell recently acknowledged, is that "the Senate nominates and the president confirms."

The senators, who until the appointment of Muriel Humphrey constituted an all-male club, make their selections based on a variety of factors. Many senators treat judicial appointments as political patronage—a way of rewarding campaign contributors, former elected officials and loyal staff.

Research by Susan Tolchin, director of the Washington Institute for Women in Politics, indicates that some senators have considered it politically necessary to recommend a black or a member of a particular ethnic or religious group for a judgeship, but until very recently no one has perceived a similar political need to satisfy women's groups.

At the behest of the president, a growing number of senators have set up selection panels to screen candidates for U.S. district court judgeships and to forward the names of the top five applicants either to the senator or to the White House for final selection. Passage of the omnibus judgeship bill will undoubtedly prompt more senators to create such panels. Attorney General Bell's recent praise for these panels, however, may be premature.

Selection panels may not look like patronage, but almost all the 15 panels established to date have merely institutionalized the old-boy network which senators previously relied upon to make judicial nominations. Even though women are a majority of the population, and the panels purport to reflect a state's diversity, 78.3 percent of these panels' members are male. Of the attorneys on the panel, 92.4 percent are men. No panel is chaired by a woman. No bar association recommended a woman attorney to fill a slot on any of the panels.

With so few women, and even fewer female attorneys, represented, it is no wonder that hardly any panels have recommended women for judicial appointments.

For example, Senator Jacob Javits' six-member judicial selection panel, set up 8 years ago, has no women. Senator Daniel Patrick Moynihan's recently established 10-member panel includes only one woman—a non-lawyer. Not surprisingly, the first five out of six vacancies on the district court in New York were filled by men. This despite the fact that New York has one of the highest concentrations of women attorneys in the country as well as a very active women's bar.

By executive order last year, President Carter created nominating commissions to screen candidates for U.S. appeals court judgeships. These panels, made up largely of early campaign supporters, include lawyers and non-lawyers alike. Although the Carter administration speaks of seeking for qualified women and minorities to appoint to the bench, it did not require its hand-picked panels to search out members of these groups for consideration. None of Carter's initial 10 panels is chaired by a woman. And while 73 percent of the male panelists are lawyers, only 36 percent of the women panel members are attorneys.

One way of significantly increasing the chances for qualified women and minorities to be appointed would be for the Carter administration, which is currently revising its executive order setting up the nominating panels, to include a requirement for searching out candidates from groups traditionally overlooked in the selection process.

Even after an individual has been selected by either a senator or the White House as a potential jurist, the male-dominated screening process continues. The name is sent to the 14-member American Bar Association Committee on the Federal Judiciary. Although not affiliated with the federal government, this group nonetheless has been given the power to evaluate the legal qualifications of all designees. The committee, which takes great pride in having reviewed more than 1,000 individuals over a 25-year period, lost its all-male status only recently when a woman was appointed by the president of the ABA.

In 1977, the Carter administration called upon the National Bar Association, a black group, to review the qualifications of judicial candidates. Apparently no one at the White House has thought to ask a women's bar group or a legal panel of representatives from women's rights organizations to conduct similar reviews.

Thus, we see a combination of restrictive criteria, apparent double standards and the male-dominated selection process perpetuating an essentially white male judiciary. The omnibus judgeship bill gives the administration and the Senate an unparalleled opportunity to redress this imbalance.

Women's groups, such as the National Women's Political Caucus, and other public interest groups are vigorously lobbying on these appointments. They are acutely aware that these lifetime appointees will be making law on civil rights and women's rights issues for years to come.

21

Women in a Male-Dominated Profession: The Women Lawyers

Michelle Patterson and Laurie Engelberg

In this chapter the authors explain how professions which offer economic and political power to their members have been a male domain generally closed to women. Professions, such as law and medicine, are unique since they have the power to set their own performance standards and they are able to control who enters and how the work is evaluated. These special characteristics of professions have worked against women.

In the legal profession the exclusion of women starts with law school admission, and continues thereafter. In law school women are scrutinized more severely than men; they must out-perform men scholastically. Upon graduation, women tend to have greater difficulty finding jobs in law firms. On the job, women are paid less than men. Moreover, as you read about the law profession, notice the important part that sex role stereotyping plays in keeping women out of the profession, in the first place, and in determining how they function as professionals once they have become lawyers, in the second place. It is especially interesting to note that a greater percentage of women than men specialize in criminal law, one of the lowest paying specialties in the legal profession. Men dominate the more prestigious and more lucrative specialties.

In addition, despite the high status of the profession and the many years of training, it is still the women in the profession who bear the primary burden of child rearing, not the men, and this despite the extremely high rate of employment (67-84 percent) of women lawyers. Patterson and Engelberg conclude that career women in the professions, generally confronted with conflicting home and work demands, have resorted to individual strategies of career management. This chapter not only describes and analyzes these and other problems women encounter as workers in law, but it also suggests ways to change the profession so as to enable women greater access and success in legal careers.

Extracted from "Women in Male-Dominated Professions" by Michelle Patterson and Laurie Engelberg in *Women Working: Theories and Facts in Perspective*, Ann Stromberg and Shirley Harkess (eds.), by permission of Mayfield Publishing Co. Copyright © 1978 by Ann H. Stromberg and Shirley Harkess. Footnotes have been edited and renumbered.

Although the past several decades have witnessed a striking increase in female labor force participation, the professions have not opened to women in substantial numbers. The professions are at the top of the American occupational hierarchy in terms of the power and prestige they confer on their practitioners. The major professions of medicine, law, and higher education have been in existence for centuries. Begun as medieval guilds reserved to men, they have remained bastions of male dominance.

This chapter explores the place of women in the traditionally male world of one of these three professions. The most significant fact about women in these three professions is that there are so few of them. Beyond this, women in these professions are likely to hold less desirable positions than men and to be paid less for equivalent work. In short, the position of women in the professions has traditionally been, and continues to be, a marginal one. . . .

THE PROFESSIONS

Almost everyone knows what occupations are considered professions in the United States, and most people have a rough idea of the characteristics that describe the professions. These characteristics have as much to do with formalized privilege and power as with the type of training or work involved in the professions. The "professionalization" of an occupation allows practitioners to lay claim to an exclusive market for their particular service.

Sociological definitions describe an "ideal type" or model rather than any actual profession; a particular profession will only approximate the attributes of the ideal type. The traditionally accepted characteristics that are used to distinguish professions are: (1) a basis of systematic theory and wide knowledge of a specialized technique obtained by a long period of intensive training; (2) authority based on this knowledge and recognized by both the clientele of the professional group and the larger community; (3) autonomy (based on the claim of unique expertise) in the exercise of the skills, in the training of new entrants, and in the evaluation and control of practice of the profession; (4) a code of ethics and professional culture developed by formal professional associations, inculcated by professional schools, and regulating the relations of professionals with clients and with colleagues; and (5) an intense commitment to the profession based on the required long investment in professional training and on a strong sense of identification with the work.[1]

Although specialized knowledge and skill are frequently used to define the professions, the possession of special expertise also becomes an ideology when used by a group to advance its claim to be a profession.[2] Knowledge itself does not give power; however, exclusive knowledge does give power, particularly when government grants a particular group the exclusive right to use or to evaluate a body of knowledge or skill. A profession has to organize and act as an interest group first to pressure the government to convey this right to it and later to promote itself and protect itself from groups with competing aims that may threaten its exclusive authority.

In brief, then, a profession can be defined as an organized occupation that makes a claim to special, esoteric competence and to concern for the quality and benefits to society of its work. By virtue of this claim, it is given the exclusive right to perform a particular type of work, to control the training for and access to it, and to control the way the work is performed and how it is evaluated.[3] Professions thus have monopolies over particular markets for particular services.

Professions maintain their monopolies and their control partly by devising and promoting models of the professional practitioner. These models, which the professions seek to maintain at all costs, depict the practitioner as having the requisite knowledge, skill, and commitment to serve the community properly. The practitioner almost always has one other attribute (supported in recent years by media characterizations): he is male. In fact, men have continued to dominate the professions, in large part, as a result of this model of the practitioner. The public expects professionals to be men, and women professionals tend to be viewed as oddities. The near-monopoly of men over the professional monopolies contributes greatly to the dominant position of men in American society.

With these models of practitioners, the professions in the United States have traditionally been sex-typed. According to Robert K. Merton, "Occupations can be described as 'sex typed' when a very large majority of those in them are one sex and when there is an associated normative expectation that this is as it should be."[4] For example, at present about 97 percent of doctors and 93 percent of lawyers are male. The subordinate professions, such as nursing and librarianship, have traditionally been female-dominated. As Cynthia Epstein observes:

> The more nearly a profession is made up entirely of members of one sex, the less likely it is that it will change its sex composition in the future and the more affected will be the performance of those few members who are not of that sex. Sex-typing tends to be a self-perpetuating process operating according to the dynamics of the self-fulfilling prophecy.[5]

That such sex-typing is not the result of the inherent nature of the work performed is demonstrated by the fact, noted below, that in other countries women comprise the majority in professions that are considered "male" in the United States.

When an occupation becomes sex-typed, the sex of the members of the minority becomes occupationally salient. Those whose sex does not fit the model of the practitioner of their profession will be viewed as "deviant" and treated accordingly by patients or clients. R. Barker compares the uncertainty in social interactions experienced by these atypical practitioners with that of the physically disabled:

[Such people] can never be sure what the attitude of a new acquaintance will be, whether it will be rejective or accepting, until the contact has been made. This is exactly the position of the adolescent, the light-skinned Negro, the second-generation immigrant, the socially mobile person, and the woman who has entered a predominantly masculine occupation.[6]

A woman in a male profession, then, is forced to be self-conscious, burdened by the feeling that she is "on." She must calculate the impression she is making and counteract possible wrong assumptions about and misperceptions of her by others.[7] Behavior that would be viewed favorably in a male may be interpreted as demonstrating a woman's lack of suitability for her profession:

Men, according to many attorneys, expect a woman to be emotional, so they read irrationality into her every word and gesture. "If a man gives the riot act to his secretary when she's made a mistake, he runs a tight ship," comments one female attorney. "Let a woman do the same thing and she's neurotic." Her female colleague agrees: "When a male attorney gets into a heated discussion over a point of law, he's a dynamic ball of fire. Should a woman attorney get equally excited, she's overwrought, easily agitated, and taking the matter personally."[8]

Displays of behavior that are thought to be "typically female" conflict with the woman's role as a professional. On the other hand, for many women exceptional professional competence may conflict with their role as "woman." Matina Horner found that women were much more likely than men to be disconcerted, troubled, or confused by the prospect of success in a typically male profession.[9] She found that women tend to see success as being accompanied by a loss of femininity, social rejection, and personal or societal destruction, and she concluded they may have an unconscious motive to avoid success. Later researchers have more clearly identified this phenomenon as a "fear of sex-atypical behavior" coupled with a motive to avoid the costs involved in violating sex-role norms. In any case, women see themselves as having to manage the effects of role deviation if they choose male-dominated professions.

The result is that women find it harder to get into and remain in the professions than men do. Problems of access to, entry of, and persistence in professional training are forerunners of difficulties faced by women in the professions. Once they have joined the professional ranks women must be far more conscious of competing demands on them than men, and problems of career management, including maintenance and advancement, come to the fore. . . .

LAW

The situation of women in law is remarkably similar to that of women in medicine where 7 percent of American women are doctors. Only about 3 percent of the more than 300,000 practicing attorneys in the United States are female.[10] Again, international comparisons are instructive. For example, more than 30 percent of the lawyers in the Soviet Union are women.[11] On the other hand, in this country more than 98 percent of the secretaries, stenographers, and typists working in the legal field are women.[12] Women and men in law, like those in medicine, are sex-segregated in an occupational hierarchy: the lawyers and judges are almost invariably men, while the clerks, paralegal workers, and secretaries who work for them are usually women.

The low participation of women in law too had its genesis in open discrimination on the basis of sex. As late as 1869, when the Illinois State Bar refused to admit a woman, the United States Supreme Court upheld this action, with one justice declaring that "the natural and proper timidity and delicacy which belongs to the female sex evidently unfit it for many of the occupations of civil life."[13] Ironically, that same year the first American woman was admitted to the bar association in the state of Iowa. A year later, in 1870, the first woman graduated from an American law school. However, Harvard Law School, venerating tradition, waited more than 130 years from its founding, before it began to admit women in 1950. As late as the fall of 1969, neither Notre Dame University nor Washington and Lee University had ever admitted a female student to its law school.[14]

In recent years less open forms of sex discrimination, many of them apparently operating before a student even applies for law school, have kept women from becoming lawyers. In the academic year 1969-70, women constituted only 1.7 percent of all law school applicants. By 1972-73 this proportion had risen to a still low 7.4 percent.[15] Beatrice Dinerman found that law schools admitted they scrutinized women's applications with greater care in evaluating ability, motivation, and the effects of marital status.[16] Another survey, conducted about the same time as Bysiewicz's, found that one-half of all lawyers, both male and female, felt that women encountered resistance at the point of admission to law school.[17]

Perhaps one reason that women seem to be deterred from applying to law school in the first instance is a widely held conception of law as a masculine field—a conception supported by the fact that only 3 percent of American lawyers are women. Many lawyers, both male and female, believe that there is something inherently masculine about the practice of law. The argument, related by Dinerman, runs like this:

> The law is born of conflict, and its practice, almost by definition, must be aggressive and warlike in nature. To be successful an attorney must have a fighting disposition. He should have mental alertness, unusual self-confidence, a logical mind and a non-retiring personality. These qualifications, many contend, are not the type of traits normally associated with the feminine personality. Female attributes, such as softness, gentleness and pacifism, just aren't characteristics that make for effective lawyers.[18]

Whatever the reasons for women's traditionally low participation in law schools, once the schools, under the impetus of the women's movement, began actively to encourage women to apply, their participation increased substantially. The proportion of women law students more than quadrupled in ten years: women constituted 23 percent of all law students in 1975, compared to 5 percent in 1965. The increase in women among first-year law students was even more dramatic, with three law schools having 1975 entering classes that were more than half women.[19]

James White's major study found that, once in law school, women were at least equal to men scholastically.[20] A survey of Columbia Law School students found that women received proportionately more academic honors than men, surpassed men in class rank, and surpassed men in law review participation. Indeed, law schools generally report that women outperform men scholastically.[21] In contrast to medicine, the dropout rates for male and female law students are virtually identical, as are the reasons for their attrition.[22]

After completing law school, women confront another barrier to the practice of law: finding a job. In a 1969 study, law schools reported difficulty convincing law firms to interview their finest female graduates, and female attorneys agreed that the most serious roadblock to a legal career was the difficulty of finding a first job.[23] In a matched sample of male and female Harvard Law School graduates, Dorothy Glancy found that women had more job interviews than men but men received a significantly greater number of job offers.[24] The position of women in law was well summarized by Professor Frederica Lombard of Wayne State University Law School, chairperson of the Committee on Women in Legal Education of the Association of American Law Schools:

> The real problem facing women lawyers is getting a job. The discrimination is somewhat less blatantly stated now than it was seven years ago when I got out of law school, but that is the only change. And if law firms do hire women, they still shunt them into estates and trusts. They tell us we're good at working with widows and orphans.[25]

A United States government publication advises women planning to make a career in the law:

Women's opportunities seem best in those law specialties where their contributions to the field have already been recognized. Some of these are real estate and domestic relations work, women's and juvenile legal problems, probate work (about a third of all women judges are probate judges), and patent law for those who have the required training in science.[26]

Women lawyers do tend to cluster in the specialties where their "opportunities seem best." Like women physicians, they seem to manage their careers in two major ways: by choice of specialty and by choice of type of practice (discussed below). Table 1 shows the specialties indicated by White's sample when respondents were asked to describe their legal work at the time of the survey. The most striking finding concerns the relative proportions of men and women in general practice. Nearly half the men characterized themselves as general practitioners, while less than a third of the women did so. A similar avoidance of general practice and a greater tendency to specialize was noted among women in medicine. There may be fewer women generalists in both law and medicine because general practitioners are in the front line of their profession in terms of initial consultation by the patient or client and initial decisions about the legal or medical problems. It is the general practitioner who refers the person to a specialist. The bias against a woman lawyer or physician may be undercut somewhat if she receives clients or patients after initial introductions or referrals from a male lawyer or physician, who fits more closely the model of the professional practitioner.[27] White suggests that:

The woman makes a conscious choice to avoid general practice because she believes that a special skill will reduce or overcome sex discrimination. Or, the relative absence of women in general practice may mean only that some employers hire women for specialized positions in probate, tax and other fields.[28]

Table 2, which presents data on the type of work actually performed by lawyers, gives a better idea of the specialties attorneys actually practice. According to White's study, men dominate litigation and corporate work. Women predominate, to a significant degree, in trusts and estates and domestic relations—and these are the traditional female domains in the profession.[29] White found a surprisingly high proportion of women engaged in litigation, given the common belief that women are rarely trial lawyers, but his data reveal nothing about the type or size of the litigation they handle. Women may try only cases of relatively little importance, and, therefore, of low visibility. On the whole, women lawyers are engaged either in low-prestige specialties, such as domestic relations, in which there are large proportions of female clients, or in specialties such

Table 1   Specialties of Attorneys by Sex

	Women	Men
Specialty in law	(N = 654)	(N = 1115)
General practice	31.4%	49.0%
Litigation	7.0	7.2
Corporate	5.2	3.8
Tax	4.8	3.5
Trusts and estates	4.1	1.1
Criminal	4.1	2.1
Labor	1.8	2.2
Real estate	1.5	1.7
Domestic relations	0.3	0.0
Other (including nonlaw)	39.8	29.4

Source: James J. White, "Women in the Law," *Michigan Law Review* 65 (1967): 1064, exhibit 7. Reprinted by permission of the publisher and the author.

Table 2   Type of Work Performed by Attorneys by Sex

	Women	Men
Type of work	(N = 575)	(N = 952)
Trusts and estates	60.0%	52.7%
Real estate	51.0	52.8
Domestic relations	49.8	38.6
Litigation	45.6	58.5
Corporate	42.0	53.8
Tax	31.0	27.9
Criminal	27.7	28.0
Labor	7.3	11.8

Source: James J. White, "Women in the Law," *Michigan Law Review* 65 (1967): 1063, exhibit 6. Reprinted by permission of the publisher and the author.

as trusts and estates where firms can put them in "back rooms," making sure they do not have contact with big clients who, the firms claim, would find it unacceptable to deal with women.

The second area in which women lawyers, like their medical counterparts, engage in career management is in their choices of type of practice. There is a smaller proportion of women than men in the private sector—71 percent of all women lawyers compared to 82 percent of all men lawyers.[30] Among those in private practice, women are much more likely to practice alone than are men: 41 percent of women attorneys are sole practitioners, compared to 35 percent of the men. Conversely, only 20 percent of the women are in law firms, while 35 percent of the men are. Among those in firms, fewer women are partners (joint owners of the firm rather than employees): only 65 percent of the women are partners, while 79 percent of the men are. Women are least represented in middle-sized firms. White found that one-fifth of the men (21.7 percent) were in firms of five to thirty people, but only one-tenth (10 percent) of the women were.[31] It seems that women must either "go it alone" (or virtually so) in a very small practice or join the extremely large firms that can more easily tolerate "deviant" practitioners and where they may remain anonymous.

Finding private practice less inviting than their male colleagues do, a slightly higher proportion of the women turn to government positions: 14 percent of female attorneys are employed by the government at one level or another, compared to 10.5 percent of males.[32] But, while men tend to use government employment as a stepping-stone into private practice, a large proportion of women make it a career.[33]

Finally, a much higher proportion of female attorneys (13.2 percent) than males (4.7 percent) are inactive or retired, despite the fact that there are no significant age differences.[34] For the most part, the inactivity of women attorneys is attributable to child rearing. A 1970 study of Harvard Law School graduates found that at the time of the survey 98 percent of the men but only 84 percent of the women were employed.[35] Of the women who were not employed, 90 percent had left the profession because they had very young children. White found that 85.5 percent of the males who responded to his survey were employed full-time and none said that they were not working.[36] Among women attorneys, 65.3 percent were working full-time, another 12.1 percent were working part-time, and 12.9 percent were not working at the time of the study. The record for women without children, however, was remarkably similar to that of the men; 83.5 percent of the single women and 74.5 percent of the married women without children were employed full-time and an additional 5.5 percent and 4 percent, respectively, were employed part-time. It was married women with children who had to bear the primary burden of child rearing and who found that career and family were incompatible. Only 44.5 percent of the married women with children were employed full-time, although another 22.2 percent were employed part-time. More than one-quarter of the married women with children (25.7 percent) were not working at the time of the study.

That women attorneys are discriminated against in salaries as well as hiring is almost universally recognized by practicing lawyers of both sexes (88 percent of the women and 80 percent of the men believe this).[37] Women attorneys are clearly paid less than men. The average annual salary differential between females and males the first year out of law school is $1,500. Within ten years this discrepancy grows to between $9,000 and $18,000 a year.[38] Dinerman and White found differences even when they controlled for variations in the amount of time worked, experience, class rank, participation on the law review while in law school (an honor), and type of work performed.[39] The differences in income that remain, after accounting for these factors, are simply a function of sex discrimination. . . .

CONCLUSION

Because their monopolies are repositories of significant economic and political power, the professions have been slow to yield to women. As we have seen, women in professions do not share the same situations as their male colleagues. Women face a host of problems—from initial, and sometimes continuing, overt discrimination to lower pay, less prestigious positions, and circumscribed specialties. They represent a very small minority, and their role in the professions can be characterized as marginal. Confronted with these barriers and with conflicting sex-role demands throughout their careers, professional women have resorted to individual strategies of career management.

Women have to be far more conscious about managing their careers than men. All professionals manage their careers to some extent, but for men career management is generally part of a larger process of career development. A man's career is managed not to maintain his position as a professional, but to develop and improve his opportunities. For a woman, career management may overshadow career development. She is forced to manage her career simply to maintain it, not only to improve it. The perceptions of fellow professionals and the public at large as to appropriate "female" behavior and specialties must be taken into account and managed by women, often by choosing types of practice that will be more readily accepted.

Events that may be of no consequence to male career development become problems to be managed by women professionals. For example, marriage and family are part of or at least consistent with a male professional's career development. For a woman, they constitute potential conflicts with career development and problems to be managed. The predominant structure of the contemporary American family and its accompanying sex-role differentiation create a double standard of expectations whereby the family and home are assumed to be the primary responsibility of the woman, even if she also holds a professional position. As long as women are primarily responsible for running the household and rearing the children, they will have to work at managing their careers in order simply to maintain them, much less make it to the top. Changes in the direction of an equal sharing of familial responsibilities will allow greater opportunities for the participation of women in the professions and reduce somewhat the need for career management. But such individual solutions are not enough.

In the late 1960s increasing numbers of professional women began to see their "private troubles" as public issues. They began to document their marginality in the professions, demonstrating that the paucity of women was a result both of real social constraints and of conscious and nonconscious discrimination. The need for constant career management on the part of women came to be seen as stemming directly from the fact that the structures of the professions were designed over the course of time to accommodate the work needs of the male professional routinely. Narrow, inflexible, and resistant to change, these structures are major impediments to the full participation of women. Higher education well illustrates this:

> Leaves of absence for research, reduced teaching loads upon the assumption of large administrative responsibilities, joint appointments for persons with expertise in two fields, and part-time appointments for senior faculty—these are just some of the adjustments men have built into the system to allow for the demands upon their time and energies. Increasingly, requirements and expectations are being made flexible to accommodate militant minority groups, yet no provisions are made in academia for the added burdens of married career women. The academic man is not expected to make a choice between his family and his work; indeed, he is not expected to "raise" a family or be a "helpmate" to his spouse in the same sense that a woman is. But it is this choice—between family and career—that men routinely thrust upon married women by requiring them to comport themselves as though they were men—men who have molded the work structure to suit their gender.[39]

Suggestions for changing the professions to produce greater flexibility include the additions of routine leaves of absence for "nonprofessional" reasons, and split and part-time positions.

Joining together in professional organizations and activist groups, women professionals began to focus public attention on these inequities and to exert pressure to bring about change. Their efforts to open up the professions to women, coupled with the attention they drew to the low-paying, low-prestige, dead-end nature of most women's jobs, led more young women to break away from the ghetto of traditional women's occupations. A national survey of freshmen entering college in the fall of 1975 found that one woman in six (16.9 percent) is planning a career in business, engineering, law, or medicine. This figure represents a 2-percent increase over 1974 and nearly triple the proportion in 1966, when only 5.9 percent of women college entrants planned such careers. A substantial influx of women into the professions will of itself end the marginality of women's roles and will go a long way toward making women's career management a normal part of their career development.

Notes

[1] See e.g., William J. Goode, "The Theoretical Limits of Professionalization," in *The Semi-Professions and Their Organization*, ed. Amital Etzioni (New York: Free Press, 1969), pp. 266-313; Ernest Greenwood, "Attributes of a Profession," *Social Work*, July 1957, pp. 44-45; Edward Gross, *Work and Society* (New York: Thomas Y. Crowell Company, 1958), p. 77; Robert Perrucci and Joel E. Gerstl, *Profession without Community: Engineers in American Society* (New York: Random House, 1969) pp. 10-14.

[2] Eliot Freidson, "Professions and the Occupational Principle," in *The Professions and Their Prospects*, ed. Eliot Friedson (Beverly Hills: Sage Publications, 1973), p. 30.

[3] Cf. *Ibid.*, pp. 19-38.

[4] Correspondence quoted in Cynthia Fuchs Epstein, *Woman's Place: Options and Limits in Professional Careers* (Berkeley and Los Angeles: University of California Press, 1971), p. 152. Also see Cynthia B. Lloyd, ed., *Sex, Discrimination, and the Division of Labor* (New York: Columbia University Press, 1975).

[5] *Ibid.*, p. 165.

[6] R. Barker, "The Social Psychology of Physical Disability," *Journal of Social Issues* 4 (1948):33.

[7] Erving Goffman, *Stigma: Notes on the Management of Spoiled Identity* (Englewood Cliffs, N.J.: Prentice-Hall, 1961), p. 14.

[8] Beatrice Dinerman, "Sex Discrimination in the Legal Profession," *American Bar Association Journal* 55 (1969): 953.

[9] Matina F. Horner, "Fail: Bright Women," *Psychology Today*, November 1969, pp. 36-38; idem, "Femininity and Sucessful Achievement: A Basic Inconsistency," in *Roles Women Play: Readings toward Women's Liberation*, ed. Michele H. Garskof (Belmont, Calif.: Brooks/Cole Publishing Company, 1971), pp. 97-122.

[10] Gail McK. Beckman, "A Comparison of Woman in the Legal Profession in Scotland and America," *New York State Bar Journal* 42 (1970): 20-24; Arlene M. Simolike, "Ladies Create a New Trend in Legal Practice," *New York State Bar Journal* 45 (1973):15-18; Soule and Standley, "Perceptions of Sex Discrimination."

[11] Beckman, "Comparison of Women"; Doris L. Sassower, "Woman and the Law: The Second Hundred Years," *American Bar Association Journal* 57 (1971): 329-32; Simoloke, "Ladies Create a New Trend."

[12] *1969 Handbook on Women Workers.*

[13] Bradwell v. State, 83 U.S. 130, 141 (1972) (Bradley, J., concurring).

[14] Beckman, "Comparison of Women"; Dorothy J. Glancy, "Women in Law: The De-

pendable Ones," *Harvard Law School Bulletin* 21 (1970): 23-33; Anne Thornton and Linda Davis, "Women at Harvard Law School," *Harvard Law School Bulletin* 21 (1970): 34-35.

[15] Shirley Raissi Bysiewicz, "1972 AALS Questionnaire on Women in Legal Education," *Journal of Legal Education* 25 (1973): 503-13.

[16] Dinerman, "Sex Discrimination."

[17] Soule, B. and Standley K., "Perceptions of Sex Discrimination in the Law," *American Bar Association Journal,* 52 (1973), 1145.

[18] Dinerman, "Sex Discrimination," p.953.

[19] James P. White, "Legal Education: A Time of Change." *American Bar Association Journal* 62 (1976): 335-338; Martha Grossblat and Bette H. Sikes, eds., *Women Lawyers: Supplementary Data to the 1971 Lawyer Statistical Report* (Chicago: American Bar Foundation, 1973).

[20] James J. White, "Women in the Law," *Michigan Law Review* 65 (1967): 1051-122.

[21] Dinerman, "Sex Discrimination."

[22] Bysiewicz, "1972 AALS Questionnaire"; Dinerman, "Sex Discrimination."

[23] Dinerman, "Sex Discrimination."

[24] Glacy, "Women in Law."

[25] *New York Times,* October 22, 1971, p. 25.

[26] Verna E, Griffin, *Employment Opportunities for Women in Legal Work* (Washington, DC: Government Printing Office, 1958), p.12.

[27] Patterson, "Sex and Specialization," p.320.

[28] White, "Women in the Law," p.1064.

[29] Epstein, *Woman's Place;* Glancy, "Women in Law"; White, "Women in the Law."

[30] Grossblat and Sikes, *Women Lawyers,* p.8.

[31] White, "Women in the Law," p. 1058.

[32] Grossblat and Sikes, *Women Lawyers,* p.8.

[33] White, "Women in the Law," p.1059.

[34] Grossblat and Sikes, *Woman Lawyers,* pp.4, 8.

[35] Glacy, "Women in Law."

[36] White, "Women in the Law," p.1065.

[37] Soule and Standley, "Perceptions of Sex Discrimination," p. 1145.

[38] Beckman, "Comparison of Women"; White, "Women in the Law," pp.1055-56.

[39] Dinerman, "Sex Discrimination"; White, "Women in the Law."

22

A Century of Women in Policing

Barbara Raffel Price and Susan Gavin

Price and Gavin open this chapter, the first of three on the police, by providing a much needed historical context for a study of women police officers. They follow this with a discussion of the situation today. The message is clear: after more than a century of women serving as police officers, they still have not been accepted by the male members of the occupation. The successes have been few and the progress of sexual integration, where identifiable, has been painfully slow.

This chapter offers several related explanations of why the problem of sex discrimination in law enforcement has been so resistant to solution. Two separate sets of reasons are put forth. First, the authors describe principles of social change and how sex role stereotyping and related attitudes operate to continue discrimination. Second, they discuss the police organization itself and how it reflects, through specific practices such as job assignments, the way the larger social structure treats women and how societal attitudes and the social system help to perpetuate male police attitudes about the male nature of police work. In effect, the police departments are both shaped by the social system and they contribute to the social structure by reinforcing it. What suggestions might you have to remedy this situation?

THE BEGINNINGS

Women appeared on the criminal justice scene as a response to social forces in the late 1800s and early 1900s. Rapid industrialization was accompanied by a host of problems: the breakdown of the family, endemic poverty, an increase in youth- and female-related crime, child labor, and social disorganization.[1] The late 1800s also marked the appearance of the first significant organized women's movement.[2] Known as suffragettes, they lobbied for the right to vote and questioned the notion that "a woman's place is in the home." Some women began to look outside the home for self-fulfillment and an opportunity to help alleviate some of the mushrooming social problems. The fact that increasingly more criminal offenders were women and children further created a need for women professionals. Even in today's more liberated age, there are special problems associated with women in custody supervised only by male staff.[3] The processing of juveniles, in particular, came to be dominated by the values of therapeutic justice that created jobs for professional social workers who were mostly women.[4] In the course of these events, women became involved in police work as a part of wider social developments.

The first women in police-related work were assigned tasks which were essentially custodial in nature. Between 1877 and 1888, there were 16 cities which had appointed police matrons to attend to women and children in custody awaiting trial.[5] In 1893, the Chicago police force appointed Mrs. Marie Owen to the detective bureau in order to assist in cases involving women and children. This did not represent a rethinking of the role of women in police work, but appears to have been a way to create a job for a policeman's widow.[6]

The first documented appointment of a woman with police powers occurred in 1905 during the Lewis and Clark Exposition in Portland, Oregon.[7] There were apparently large numbers of young women soliciting the attention of lumbermen, miners, laborers, and vacationers "on sprees." The city fathers of Portland hired Lola Baldwin to help cope with this problem. Her efforts were so successful that a permanent Department of Public Safety for the Protection of Young Girls and Women was created.[8] Other cities began to hire women police officers, but the scope of their work was generally limited to cases involving children and women. The role of the woman police officer during this period was altogether compatible with progressive movements both for women's rights and humane treatment of young offenders.

It was not until 1910 that the first regularly rated policewoman was appointed. Mrs. Alice Stebbins Wells, a graduate theological student and ardent social worker from Los Angeles, believed that protective and preventative work with women and children would be most effective if services were delivered by sworn policewomen.[9] She circulated a petition to this effect and then addressed it to the city council and police commissioner. Mrs. Wells's work resulted in her appointment to the Los Angeles Police Department as a fully empowered policewoman with the rank of detective.[10] The appointment of Mrs. Wells attracted wide attention, especially from other energetic women searching for solutions to America's social problems. Overwhelmed by lecture requests, Mrs. Wells made a series of tours in the United States and Canada between 1912 and 1914.[11] By 1915, at least 16 cities had recognized the need for women police officers and added them to their departments.[12] One woman even became chief of police in Milford, Ohio.[13]

It is quite likely that Mrs. Wells influenced the increased use of female police officers during this period.[14] Most of the women hired during the period came from social work backgrounds. Their duties generally included supervision of public places of recreation, responsibility for female suspects, and missing persons. Due to the background of these women and the nature of their assignments, it is hardly surprising that female police officers came to be viewed as specialized social workers.[15]

Organized feminism had become a deeply rooted force in American life by 1915. With women's associations springing up in most cities, the idea of organizing a policewoman's society occurred to Alice Wells. In May, 1915, The International Association of Policewomen was created with Mrs. Wells as its first president. The Association dedicated itself to providing police departments and the general public with information on women police, searching for better standards and improving the role of policewomen.[16]

With the entrance of the United States into World War I, women were hired to fill vacant police positions and to perform quasipolice functions related to their earlier duties, such as keeping prostitutes away from military camps, returning runaway girls, and supervising amusement areas near the camps.[17] While America's men were fighting overseas to make the world "safe for democracy," women also became increasingly caught up in the war effort and appeared in even larger numbers in the work force. By the end of World War I, policewomen were employed in over 220 American cities.[18]

The 1920s was a period of prosperity and economic expansion. The women's movement was strong, the economy good, and the idea of women police seemed to have taken hold. The success of women officers around military camps and the efforts of The International Association of Policewomen no doubt aided the movement in quickly spreading across the country. In 1922, The International Association of Chiefs of Police passed a resolution stating that policewomen were indispensable to the modern police department.[19] At the same time, the general public became comfortable with the notion of crime prevention as a legitimate function of police departments and with the presence of female police officers. Yet, female officers were usually relegated to the women's bureau, were promotable only within that unit, and received less pay than male officers.[20]

The 1930s were, of course, an altogether different time. Unemployment soared; poverty and related social ills were rampant. The central focus of President Roosevelt's economic policy, the New Deal, was to reduce poverty by creating jobs for men.[21] The underlying assumptions of the New

Deal were that employed wage earners would support their wives and children; widows would receive Aid For Dependent Children. Single women, though, didn't appear to have the interest of the federal government. Perhaps Roosevelt's "brain trust" thought their fathers would take care of them. In any event, police jobs for women nearly disappeared, and The International Association of Policewomen disbanded due to lack of funds.[22]

World War II fueled the economy and turned wage earners into soldiers. America was ripe (again) for policewomen. In the 1940s, however, women were pretty much limited to the role of auxiliary police.[23] With the end of the war and the return of millions of young men, families became the order of the day.[24] The nation experienced a baby boom, and once again a woman's place seemed to be in the home. The Eisenhower years were characterized by political normalcy and economic prosperity. The primary work of women continued to be the raising of children and maintenance of homes newly built in innumerable new suburbs. Whether women were actually content with their domestic lot is an open question, but there is no evidence of militancy to secure paying jobs. The concern of Americans for equal rights and fair employment, such as there was, extended at first only to racial discrimination.

In the 1960s, the concern for social justice accelerated.[25] The Kennedy Administration was built on an implicit promise of Camelot,[26] and the Johnson Administration, which followed, was committed to a war on poverty. The postwar babies were grown and out of the home and their mothers were looking for new ways to find fulfillment. Younger women (perhaps because of improved contraceptives, especially the pill) were able to make choices which were not available to their mothers, and a great many chose not to get married, or not to have children, or to postpone children until their careers were launched. Among those who had young children, many became working mothers for these reasons or simply in order to meet family expenses. The women's movement captured the hearts and imaginations of many American women. Several influential writers (Germaine Greer,[27] Betty Friedan,[28] Kate Millet,[29] and others), supported by media attention on the role of women, created a new women's movement unprecedented since the Suffragettes.

At the turn of the century, equality meant the right to vote; in the 1960s, it meant the right to work. Once again, general social developments influenced the administration of police services. In an age of "affirmative action," police departments were required to show that the absence of women was not a consequence of systematic prejudice against women; and female employees demanded they be allowed to do the same work as males, and so have the same opportunities for promotion and salary.[30] This then is the situation today. Women are more interested than ever before

in working in areas traditionally dominated by men, and the law is supportive of that right. Whether the police profession will actually become
sexually integrated, or whether the events of the past decade will prove
to be merely a part of a cycle which brings women into the work force and
then pushes them back into the home, is still unanswered. However, the
unprecedented involvement of the law in the civil rights of women and
minorities suggests that women are unlikely to leave the working world
to any substantial extent in the future.

THE PRESENT SITUATION

Today, women police are to be found in all aspects of police work and in
all types and sizes of departments—municipal, state, and federal. Tables
1, 2, and 3 illustrate the numbers of women employed in 1978 in the ten
largest police departments. For comparison we have also given, where
available, 1974 figures on women employed by these same departments in
an effort to describe recent gains.

In 1974, the general work force was 39 percent female; by 1978, this
figure had risen to 48 percent.[31] Data on women in policing show that
increases in large departments were not nearly of the same magnitude
(Table 3). Only in Detroit was there a big increase (13.1 percent) in the
number of sworn female officers. Also, note that an intensive effort was
made in 1972 in Washington, D.C., both to increase the number of women
employed and to systematically evaluate their performance.

As women became aware of the inferior status they held as members
of women's bureaus in police departments, they pressed for promotions
commensurate with their years of experience and performance. In response, police administrators utilized a Catch 22: women could only be
promoted within their own bureaus because they had not had the full
"police experience" of being on the street, i.e., patrol duty. Of course,
women had been systematically denied opportunities in the past for general patrol assignments. Energetic women fought to turn this situation
around by gaining the right to work in the same capacity as male officers
in order to earn the same pay and the same promotion opportunities.
Therefore, in examining the data in the charts, the percentage of women
in patrol assignments is one critical indicator of the integration of women
in policing (Table 3). Both the percentages of women on patrol and the
gains in these percentages over the four-year period make it clear that
women have a long way to go before they are commonplace in police
departments.

The problem of achieving sexual equality in policing has been exacerbated by the fact that many urban police departments have recently been

forced to reduce in size due to municipal budgetary problems. (Tables 1 and 2 show that only Houston has not undergone a retrenchment of personnel.) The significance of this situation is found in the fact that now male officers will be competing for even more limited promotion opportunities than ever before and they will be less sympathetic to personnel reform measures demanded by women's groups, minorities, and civil rights commissions. The impact of decreasing opportunities in policing will have an overall conservatizing effect on hiring procedures and reform.

However, it may be that the constriction of police departments is a temporary situation which future growth in the national economy will eliminate. Whatever the case, it is clear that this is a very recent phenomenon and cannot explain the low numbers of women in police work. Women have been pushing for reform since the early 1970s with the law backing their efforts. The issues run much deeper. We will look now at other factors which have worked against the sexual integration of policing.

WHY WOMEN AREN'T FULLY ACCEPTED IN THE POLICE OCCUPATION

It is apparent from history, employment figures, and talks with police that women have had a great deal of difficulty in moving into police work in large numbers. Few departments have made a total commitment to hire women and, after hiring, to utilize them in all police functions. This is so in spite of Title VII of the Civil Rights Act of 1964 and the Equal Opportunity Act of 1972, which specifically prohibits discrimination against public employees on the basis of sex. The picture is not all bleak. Table 4 shows increased use of women in patrol work from 1974 to 1978. Even in New York City where the absolute numbers of women police decreased (largely due to firing recently hired officers as part of the city's fiscal crisis), those on the force were more widely used for general patrol function. Table 4 gives encouraging data for the future because as women participate in basic police work, promotional opportunities may open up. As women move up into management, they will have a voice in pressing for stronger affirmative action policies.

Why has sexual integration not yet been successful in the police occupation? All available information indicates that, for the most part, women can perform successfully; numerous evaluations document women's effectiveness in all phases of work, including patrol.[32] Moreover, individual male police, at all ranks, will acknowledge (off the record) the ability of females to be good police officers. The resistance can be explained on the basis of two phenomena: (1) the social change process and the critical role that attitudes play in it; and (2) the impact of police attitudes shaped by the organizational structure, and in turn, reinforcing its social structure.

In order to understand the critical role that police attitudes play in preventing women from participating in police work, it is necessary to review how social change takes place. Social change theory identifies three separate levels within society in which change can be initiated: the social structure (the stable characteristics of the society, e.g., government, educational system, the family); the technology of society (the accumulated skills, methods, tools, machinery); and the culture of the society (its values, attitudes, ideologies). Change can begin in any one of these areas, but until it has been assimilated at all three levels of the society, social change is not part of the fabric of society. For example, courts (which are part of the social structure) can mandate a policy of nondiscriminatory hiring, but until people accept the idea, until it permeates the values of those who will implement it, and until a technology or method is developed to operationalize the court ruling, the new hiring policy is unlikely to be successful. Hence, that specific aspect of social change has not come about. Social change theory recognizes that it is much easier to initiate change in the social structure or in the technical components than it is at the cultural level. In effect, attitudes die hard.

It is a relatively straightforward matter to introduce into society a specific technological change since most technological innovations do not challenge accepted and cherished values. It is more difficult to initiate a structural change (integration of women into policing is such a case) which requires altering people's attitudes. People cling longest to their own beliefs. If you believe things are one way, or that something is "right," it is hard to see the matter in a new light. Very few police react emotionally to the introduction of new technology into policing (for example, mobile radios), but almost every police officer, as well as many others, carries "a whole baggage of myths, images, and symbols to the issue of female equality."[33]

In order to understand the attitudes of police toward their work and to grasp the depth of police feelings about their work, especially the conviction that it is men's work requiring, above all, physical strength and bravery, we must recognize that two powerful determinants have converged to shape attitudes. The first factor pertains to the historical beginnings of policing when its technology was so rudimentary that physical strength was necessary and was the major qualification for becoming a police officer. Few techniques were available to the police other than muscle; the police role was defined as maintaining order by intimidation. The attributes for selection to police departments were size, physical power, and an inclination for "mixing it up" with anyone who defied police authority. This belief in the importance of strength and power to do police work has lingered and is, in part, a measure of the limited evolution of the occupation. But also, it is illustrative of how slowly attitudes die, especially when reinforced by the organization.

The second factor deals with why the organization has reinforced these attitudes over the years. Recent research indicates that the opportunity structure of an organization helps to determine the behavior of employees.[34] The opportunity structure results from the hierarchy of the organization which defines the range and amount of vertical mobility available to job incumbents. In policing, that hierarchy has always been rigid (no lateral entry) with a very narrow pyramid at the top. Of those promoted, many have been involved in the more dangerous, most prized, but limited opportunity of arresting street criminals. Crimefighting and the "good" arrest are the surest ways to be promoted in most departments. The problem is that the great majority of police work (80 to 85 percent) involves not law enforcement activities but rather service-related tasks. There are neither enough felons on the streets for all police to be promoted nor are there enough top positions available. In fact, as a result, those personnel who are promoted may be ill-equipped for a supervisory position and the responsibility of a higher level position.[35]

And so the lack of attention to meaningful criteria, the rewarding of an officer's arrest record, the limited number of middle management and administrative positions, and the historically established qualifications for police work—all serve to perpetuate attitudes about policing being man's work. Moreover, for the first 75 years, those women who were in police departments did not present serious challenges to these attitudes or to the organization. While they were called policewomen, they functioned only where their suitability for youth work and guarding female prisoners was recognized and accepted by their male co-workers. Because they were not assigned regular patrol duty, they had no opportunity to prove themselves in those activities which the organization tended to reward, nor were they even eligible for promotion within the organization's total hierarchy.

In 1968, when women were first assigned to patrol duty in Indianapolis, the potential for major change in their status existed for the first time.[36] The implications can be best understood in terms of the challenge that a new pool of human resources presented to males. Consider, again, the concept of the opportunity structure of the department and the potential upheaval to the organization which resulted when women challenged the departmental personnel policy of isolating them from many aspects of police work, especially patrol. Relative opportunity tends to create self-fulfilling prophecies; those with the most opportunity appear to be the most worthy and tend to advance the fastest. Those with the fewest opportunities appear least valuable and tend to advance the least.[37] If males work in all phases of policing and if women are defined as suitable

Table 1   *Women Police Officers in the Ten Major Police Departments in 1974*

Police Department	Total Size of Dept.	Total Women in Dept.	Percent of Women in Dept.	Patrol	
				No. Women on Patrol	Percent Women (of Total Personnel)
New York City	35,653	759	2.10	414	1.20
Chicago	14,935	*	–	*	–
Los Angeles	10,137	148	1.50	0	0
Philadelphia	9,247	69	0.75	0	0
Detroit	6,106	30	0.49	0	0
Washington D.C.	5,558	268	4.80	161	2.90
Baltimore	4,150	9	0.21	1	0.02
Boston	2,877	14	0.49	11	0.38
St. Louis	2,822	9	0.32	2	0.07
Houston	2,792	*	–	*	–

*Unavailable.

Table 2   *Women Police Officers in the Ten Major Police Departments in 1978*

Police Department	Total Size of Dept.	Total Women in Dept.	Percent of Women in Dept.	Patrol	
				No. Women on Patrol	Percent Women (of Total Personnel)
New York City	24,891	495	2.0	329	1.30
Chicago	13,258	439	3.3	282	2.10
Los Angeles	7,071	169	2.4	33	0.50
Philadelphia	8,397	160	1.9	76	0.91
Detroit	5,818	792	13.6	514	8.80
Washington D.C.	4,890	308†	6.3	219†	4.50
Baltimore	3,300	68	2.1	*	–
Boston	2,167	53	2.4	*	–
St. Louis	2,018	40	2.0	15	0.74
Houston	2,915	266	9.1	100	3.40

*Unavailable.
†Approximate.

Table 3   *Percent Increase of Women Police Officers from 1974-1978*

Police Department	Percent Increase of Women on Patrol	Percent Increase of All Women Officers
New York City	0.1	– 0.1
Chicago	–	–
Los Angeles	0.5	0.9
Philadelphia	0.91	1.15
Detroit	8.8	13.1
Washington D.C.	1.6	1.5
Baltimore	–	1.89
Boston	–	1.91
St. Louis	0.67	1.68
Houston	–	–

Note: 1974 data are drawn from *Uniform Crime Reports,* Federal Bureau of Investigation (Washington D.C.: U.S. Government Printing Office), 1974, and *Deployment of Female Police Officers in the United States,* International Association of Chiefs of Police and the Police Foundation (Washington D.C.: Police Foundation), 1974. 1974 was used as the comparison year because national figures were not compiled on women on patrol until IACP conducted its survey on female officers that year. 1978 data was generated by telephone interviews.

Table 4   *Use on Patrol of Available Women Police Officers for 1974 and 1978*

Police Department	1974		1978	
	%	Women/Patrolling	%	Women/Patrolling
New York City	54.5	759/414	66.0	495/329
Chicago	*	–	64.0	439/282
Los Angeles	0	148/0	19.5	169/33
Philadelphia	0	69/0	47.5	160/76
Detroit	0	30/0	64.8	792/514
Washington D.C.	60.0	161/268	71.1	368/219†
Baltimore	11.0	1/9	*	68/*
Boston	78.0	11/14	*	53/*
St. Louis	22.0	2/9	37.5	40/15
Houston	*	–	37.6	266/100

*Unavailable.
†Approximate.

for limited assignments only, the men will be more valued by the organization. They will also have more chances to make arrests or do those things which the organization rewards, thereby having the greatest opportunity for promotion. As women became integrated into departments in the early 1970s, the competition for upper level positions widened because the women's skills and characteristics now had to be considered. (In many departments their superior education, a result of earlier sex discrimination at entrance, stood the women in good stead for management jobs.)[38] In addition to the understandable interest of the male police to reduce competition, there is another element operating.

The traditional police attitudes about the inherently masculine nature of police work make the prospect of having a female superior particularly offensive to some male officers. The specter of women sergeants is probably as significant a factor in male police officers' unwillingness to support women on patrol as is the additional competition for promotion that women can represent. Data from Washington, D.C., New York City, and other communities[39] which have favorably evaluated women on patrol have not changed the conviction of most male police that women are not competent and lack the stamina and the aggressiveness for the job. Contributing to these beliefs is the difficulty some men have in taking orders from a woman sergeant. The idea itself violates their self-image and the organizationally and socially conditioned belief that they are engaged in men's work. Many see the possibility of women as equal co-workers and even bosses as not just unpleasant but unwise. People who think this way do not take to facts which contradict their attitudes.

If police feel so strongly about the issue of women becoming fully integrated into law enforcement, the community also appears to agree. The public takes its cues from the experts (the police officers) who say that women will not be adequate for the job and, in fact, may jeopardize citizen safety. In the past, the community has taken many of its attitudes about police work both from the police and the media which fosters the "John Wayne" syndrome of policing.[40] Little pressure, then, comes from the immediate community for police to conform to equal hiring opportunities as defined by the law. What pressure is felt stems from (1) new federal policies such as recommended standards for employing women found in the National Advisory Commission on Criminal Justice Standards and Goals; (2) a growing body of legal decisions on equal hiring and promotional opportunities; and (3) a widening feminists' orientation in the larger society. But in terms of immediate pressure from the local community to conform to legal requirements, the threat of losing federal monies is probably the only factor that prompts strong local pressure on the police.

For years, small numbers of policewomen have been used as undercover operatives in vice work, and in more recent years they have been assigned similar functions in narcotics units. This is truly dangerous work. Frequently they have no partner, no method of communication for assistance, and no weapon. Police departments have never viewed this work as too dangerous for women to engage in. Routine patrol, however, which has high visibility, the accompanying authority of the uniform, the availability of a weapon, and direct communication to the department, has until very recently been called hazardous work for which women are not suited.

Those departments that have added women to their patrol units and have administratively supported their arrival find it important to develop resocialization strategies for their male officers so that they may begin to accept the presence of women on the force and deal with them as officers. Such steps are important not only for the success of new women, but for the safety of men and the general effectiveness of the department.

Various evaluations and internal assessments have attributed women with:

— Causing few citizen complaints;
— Improving the department's image;
— Improving the department's service capability, since many women possess previous training in such areas as social work, nursing, and probation;
— Increasing the crime suppression capability through the use of alternative deployment strategies;
— Impelling the department to reevaluate many of its policies, especially selection and training practices.

Organizations promote their own myths; they are reinforced by incumbents who believe themselves to be served by the myths. These myths, in turn, affect behavior. Do we want our police to reflect a police technology of the nineteenth century? Or do we want them to reflect the changes of the twentieth century which recognize that law enforcement is a professionalizing occupation demanding sensitive, well-trained people? It has become increasingly important to bring to policing the full range of human resources available in our community, as citizens demand higher quality police—citizen interactions from their law enforcement agencies. Some women will be found unsuitable for this demanding work. Sometimes men are also found to be unsuitable for police work. One police administrator has noted that this is not a compelling reason for discontinuing the use of men in policing.[41]

Notes

1 Levine, Murray and Levine, Adeline, *A Social History of Helping Services,* New York: Appleton-Century-Crofts, 1970, p. 24.

2 For a general discussion of the early womens' movement see Flexner, Eleanor, *Century of Struggle: The Women's Rights Movement in the United States,* Cambridge: Harvard University Press, 1975.

3 The case of Joanne Little is illustrative of the problems which can arise. She was guarded by a male jailor in a small jail in North Carolina and claimed that he attempted to rape her whereupon she killed him in self-defense.

4 For a discussion of the therapeutic model see Platt, Anthony M., *The Child Savers,* Chicago: University of Chicago Press, 1969.

5 Owings, Chloe, *Women Police,* Montclair, NJ: Patterson Smith, 1969, pp. 98-99.

6 *Ibid.,* p. 99.

7 Horne, Peter, *Women in Law Enforcement,* Springfield, IL: Charles C. Thomas, 1975, p. 18.

8 *Ibid.,* p. 18.

9 Owings, *op. cit.,* p. 101.

10 *Ibid.,* p. 102.

11 *Ibid.,* p. 103-104.

12 Horne, *op. cit.,* p. 19.

13 *Ibid.,* p. 19.

14 Simpson, Antony, "The Changing Role of Women in Policing," *Law Enforcement News,* Vol. 2, No. 3, March 1976, p. 84.

15 *Ibid.,* pp. 21-22.

16 Wells, Alice, "Reminiscences of a Policewoman," *The Police Reporter,* September 1929, p. 23.

17 Owings, *op. cit.,* pp. 107-115.

18 Horne, *op. cit.,* p. 19.

19 *Ibid.,* p. 19.

20 *Ibid.,* p. 20.

21 For a discussion of the New Deal see Schlesinger, Arthur, *The Age of Roosevelt,* Boston: Houghton Mifflin, 1975.

22 Simpson, *op. cit.,* p. 85.

23 Horne, *op. cit.,* p. 20.

24 For a general discussion of the postwar years see Allen, Frederick Lewis, *The Big Change: America Transforms Itself, 1900-1950,* New York: Harper & Row, 1952.

25 For an interesting and critical discussion see Cloward, Richard and Piven, Frances, *Regulating the Poor,* New York: Vintage Books, 1971.

26 Schlesinger, Arthur, *A Thousand Days: John F. Kennedy in the White House,* Boston: Houghton Mifflin, 1965.

27 Greer, Germaine, *The Female Eunuch,* New York: McGraw-Hill, 1971.

28 Friedan, Betty, *The Feminine Mystique,* New York: Dell, 1975.

29 Millet, Kate, *Sexual Politics,* Garden City, NY: Doubleday, 1970.

30 For a discussion of women's rights according to the Civil Rights Act of 1964, see *Women and The Law,* The American Civil Liberty Foundation of Pennsylvania, Philadelphia.

31 Source: U.S. Department of Labor Statistics, 1978.

32 See, for example, Bloch, Peter B. and Anderson, Deborah, *Policewomen on Patrol: Final Report,* Washington, D.C.: Washington, D.C. Police Foundation, 1974, and Sichel, Joyce L., Friedman, Lucy N., Quint, Janet C., Smith, Michael E., *Women on Patrol: A Pilot Study of Police Performance in New York City,* New York: Vera Institute, 1977.

33 Bouza, Anthony V., *Police Administration,* New York: Pergamon Press, 1978, p. 89.

34 Kanter, Rosabeth Moss, *Men and Women of the Corporation,* New York: Basic Books, 1977.

35 *Police,* p. 423.

36 Donovan, Edwin J., "Women on Patrol," mimeographed report, New York City Police Department, undated.

37 *Op. cit.*

38 For a discussion of the higher educational level of women police, see Price, B.R., "Female Police Executives," *Journal of Police Science and Administration,* Vol. 2, No. 2, 1974, pp. 219-226.

39 See, for example, the findings of women on patrol in New York City who were studied for seven months in 1977. It was found that, by and large, patrol performance of the women was more like that of the men than it was different. See *Women on Patrol: A Pilot Study of Police Performance in New York City,* Rockville, MD: National Criminal Justice Reference Service, 1977. Also see "Women Mounties Match the Men," *Liaison,* Vol. 2, 1975, p. 7, which reported, "While excelling in some areas, the women have also maintained the high standards expected from all recruits, even in such 'male' pursuits as physical and firearms training."

40 Price, Robert and Price, Barbara R., "Should the Police Officer Know What's Happening?" in *The Police in Society,* eds. E.C. Viano and J.H. Reiman, Lexington, MA: Lexington Books, 1975.

41 Bouza, Anthony V., *Police Administration,* New York: Pergamon Press, 1978, p. 90.

23

Female Patrol Officers: A Review of the Physical Capability Issue

Roi D. Townsey

This chapter deals with the issue of the physical capability of women police. It meets head on and clearly refutes the commonly expressed myth that policing is essentially male work because only men have the physical strength needed to perform on patrol. Using data collected from police departments across the nation, Townsey demonstrates that women have been found to be as physically able as men to perform on patrol. She also details how many police physical agility exams are not job-related. Moreover, she argues, since women can be trained to be as agile as men for the job, physical agility should not be used as a selection criteria prior to training. Yet 9 out of 10 agencies require agility tests be passed first. In these ways physical entrance tests for policing discriminate against women, thereby eliminating disproportionate numbers of women applicants.

This chapter summarizes findings from eight different types of police departments across the country which evaluated women on patrol. It also gives data on 221 city police departments and 36 state departments demonstrating the prevalence of agility tests before training. This chapter, like the chapter by Patterson and Engelberg on the law, identifies solutions to discriminatory practices.

The seventies witnessed significant circumstances in American policing. Among such was extensive debate as to whether or not women are suited for the police patrol function. Given the exhaustive scrutiny of this issue, one might reasonably expect the eighties to include no further debate on the physical capability of female police officers. However, recognizing the growing and widespread use of stringent physical agility tests for initial selection of police recruits, and related justifications, the question of the physical capability of women as patrol officers remains primary.

In this chapter I will: (1) overview the status of women in policing; (2)

The research from which this paper is drawn was supported by the Office of Justice and Research Statistics, U.S. Department of Justice. The national survey data is presented in *A Progress Report on Women in Policing,* by Cynthia G. Sulton and Roi D. Townsey (Washington, D.C.: Police Foundation, 1981).

outline the conclusion that women are as capable as men as patrol officers; (3) display the disparate impact of stringent physical tests upon female police applicants; and (4) identify and recommend a nondiscriminatory type of physical agility test and alternative training methods for police agencies in support of equal employment opportunity for women in policing.

THE STATUS OF WOMEN IN MUNICIPAL POLICING

Since the mid-sixties there has been considerable progress in the hiring and deployment of women in law enforcement agencies.[1] No longer are women subject to differential hiring criteria and inferior compensation; nor are they relegated solely to women's or juvenile bureaus. Following the 1963 Equal Pay Act, the 1972 Revenue Sharing Act, the 1972 amendment to Title VII of the 1964 Civil Rights Act, the 1978 Pregnancy Discrimination Act, subsequent Equal Employment Opportunity Commission guidelines, and successful litigation, it appears women are hired, compensated, trained, and generally deployed throughout municipal police agencies without reference to their gender.

Although it is fact that women are no longer subject to differential hiring criteria and inferior compensation, it is less factual that they are not measurably performing traditional duties. Very few would argue that women have been fully accepted as patrol officers. Largely, duties of female officers and male attitudes remain as they were prior to the 1972 amendment to Title VII. It is not uncommon to find female officers overwhelmingly assigned to desk duties and juvenile matters. Neither is it uncommon to hear of " . . . muttered insults and open jibes and sometimes even a hostile refusal to recognize a woman's presence" (Giordano, 1981: 15). Moreover, cases of open resistance of male officers to ride with women still occur and many commanding officers reportedly honor the related requests. It is relevant to note that the status and job responsibilities of female officers remain virtually traditional even in major and enlightened agencies. There are, for example, fewer female officers in New York City than there were during the mid-seventies. Presently, there are 699 female officers (including the 142 at the Police Academy); there were 725 prior to massive layoffs as a result of the 1975 fiscal crisis. Reports note that the duties of female officers in New York City remain significantly traditional, although the agency's Policewoman's Bureau was disbanded in 1968. Giordano (1981:15) writes that " . . . the chances of running into a female cop in New York City are almost as poor as the chances of finding a subway without graffiti." Having conducted a two-month study of female officers in New York City, Giordano indicates that approximately 50 percent (n = 338) of the agency's female officers are assigned to patrol. However, she indicates that " . . . there are usually not even two women cops per precinct per shift on the streets." Circumstances such as these exist across the entire country, and they lend support to the observation that although women have been variedly assigned to patrol duties since 1968, they have not been fully integrated.

SCIENTIFIC TESTING

The patrol capability of female officers was scientifically appraised during the seventies most notably in eight different police settings. Five of these performance evaluations concern the patrol capability of female officers in municipal policing (Washington, D.C.—Bloch and Anderson, 1974; New York City—Sichel et al., 1977; Denver Colorado—Bartlett and Rosenblum, 1977; Newton, Massachusetts—Kizziah and Morris, 1977; and Philadelphia, Pennsylvania—Bartell Associates, 1978); two concern the capability of women as state troopers (California Highway Patrol, 1976; Pennsylvania State Police, 1974); and one concerns the patrol capability of female officers in county policing (St. Louis County, Missouri—Sherman, 1975).

Purpose. Primarily, the purpose of these evaluations was to determine whether or not women are physically able to perform the police patrol function. Each evaluation entailed comparing two (one male and one female) patrol groups using measures such as supervisory ratings, patrol observation of policing style, citizens' opinions, arrest rates, sick time, complaints, and commendations. More specifically:

(1) *the Washington, D.C.* evaluation addressed the advantages and disadvantages of hiring women on an equal basis with men and the effects of employing a substantial number of women on patrol;

(2) *the New York City* evaluation was directed in great part for developing guidelines to assist the department in increasing the effectiveness of female patrol officers;

(3) *the Denver* evaluation aimed at pinpointing areas of policing in which female officers performed differently than male officers and related effects;

(4) *the Newton, Massachusetts* evaluation sought: a) to determine if female officers were treated equally with men and if their performance was on par with the performance of men; and b) to determine if women had been integrated into the police department;

(5) *the Philadelphia, Pennsylvania* evaluation addressed the capability of female officers in high crime rate patrol areas;

(6) *the California State Highway Patrol* evaluation addressed the general

feasibility of hiring female troopers; whereas (7) *the Pennsylvania State Police* evaluation aimed at pinpointing the performance capability of female troopers vis a vis male troopers; and

(8) *the St. Louis County, Missouri* evaluation sought to extend previous study findings of the effectiveness of female officers within the city setting to the suburban setting.

Results. Compositely, these performance evaluations indicate that women perform the patrol function in the municipal, county, and state police settings as ably as men, and that it is feasible to hire and deploy women as officers the same as men. Noted differences generally concern the following.

(1) *Arrest Rates.* Women required arrest assistance more often than men. Also, women made less arrests. However, in Washington, D.C., female officers sustained a higher conviction rate making it likely that they made fewer unnecessary arrests or higher quality ones (Bloch and Anderson, 1974:25).

(2) *Policing Style.* Female officers performed less aggressively and involved themselves in "preventive" activity less often than male officers.

(3) *Shooting Ability.* Men had significantly better shooting rates.

(4) *Sick Time.* Women assumed more sick leave due to injuries.

(5) *Discipline.* Women (in Philadelphia, for example) had significantly more sustained disciplinary infractions.

(6) *Agility.* Men were found to be stronger and more agile than women. However, attempts in Philadelphia to relate strength to patrol performance were unsuccessful (Bartell Associates, 1978:xv).

PHYSICAL AGILITY TESTING

The increased utilization of women in policing is directly attributable to the legislation noted at the outset and subsequent litigation; particularly litigation concerning the issue of physical agility testing.[2]

In 1973, 54 percent of the departments responding to a personnel survey used a physical agility test for male police applicants, while only 31 percent used this selection criterion for female police applicants (Eisenberg, et al., 1973:19). However, since 1973 the function of female officers has greatly diversified. Even more importantly, between 1973-1979 the rate of female representation among all law enforcement personnel increased from 1.7 percent (FBI, 1974:166) to 3.38 percent (Sulton and Townsey, 1981), and so has the use of physical agility tests by police agencies.

The most recent survey findings relating to the use of physical agility tests were collected in 1979 by the Police Foundation of Washington, D.C., as part of a federally funded assessment of the status of women in policing

(Sulton and Townsey, 1981). The Police Foundation surveyed 47 state police agencies and 387 municipal police agencies serving populations of 50,000 and above to determine the extent to which women are used as sworn police officers, as well as the extent to which various selection criteria (such as physical agility tests) affect the hiring and retention of female officers.[3] Specifically, Foundation findings show that 78 percent of the municipal and 91 percent of the state police agencies surveyed use a physical agility test for the hiring of both men and women. More specifically, findings outline that *western* and *north central* municipal agencies and those serving smaller populations of 50,000-49,999 require physical agility tests in greater proportions. Relatedly, the mean numbers of female police officers in these regions and population areas are relatively low and/or significantly comparable to early 1970 numbers (Sulton and Townsey, 1981). Only three of the state police agencies surveyed do not require physical agility testing. Relatedly, female representation is significantly low on the vast majority of state police forces (see Tables 1 and 2). Recognizing this, it is likely more than an unfounded notion that physical agility tests are but a means of opponents to women on patrol to counter the related influx.

Under Title VII, all applicants for a position requiring physical strength and agility must be given an opportunity to demonstrate their ability to perform the work in question. *Bowe v. Colgate-Palmolive Co.*, 416 F.2d 711 (7th Cir. 1969). Further, although gender is a bona fide occupational qualification (BFOQ) in certain cases, the Equal Employment Opportunity Commission (EEOC) Guidelines on Sex Discrimination bar the refusal to hire a female applicant because of characteristics attributed to women as a class. As well, although jobs may be classified as "heavy" and "light," it is unlawful to label a job as "male" or "female." Thus, if lifting and carrying heavy objects and persons are a part of job performance, female applicants must be afforded an opportunity to demonstrate their ability. Moreover, the Fifth Circuit Court of Appeals has, for example, dictated that jobs which require a great deal of strength must be made available to applicants on an individual basis. *Weeks v. Southern Bell Telephone & Telegraph Co.*, 408 F.2d 228 (5th Cir. 1969).

Since the early seventies female police applicants have been required to pass the same physical agility test administered to male applicants. Generally, the physical agility test administered by a police agency emphasizes upper body strength and eliminates a highly disproportionate number of female applicants. Numerous municipal and state police agencies employ physical agility tests which assess rapid reflexes, high degrees of speed coordination, dexterity, endurance, and strength. However, it is unlawful for these physical fitness standards (purportedly measured in physical agility tests) to be applied in a discriminatory manner to bar opportunities

Table 1   Municipal Departments Using Physical Agility Tests before Training, by Population and Region

	50,000-99,999		100,000-249,999		250,000-499,999		500,000+		Total	
	#	%	#	%	#	%	#	%	#	%
Yes	109	87.90	56	96.55	24	96.00	12	85.71	201	90.95
No	15	12.10	2	3.45	1	4.00	2	14.29	20	9.05
Total	124	100.00	58	100.00	25	100.00	14	100.00	221	100.00

	Northeast		North Central		South		West		Total	
	#	%	#	%	#	%	#	%	#	%
Yes	36	85.71	59	92.19	49	90.74	57	93.44	201	90.95
No	6	14.29	5	7.81	5	9.26	4	6.56	20	9.05
Total	42	100.00	64	100.00	54	100.00	61	100.00	221	100.00

Source: Sulton and Townsey, Police Foundation, Washington, D.C. 1981

Table 2   Use of Physical Agility Tests in State Departments, by Region

	Northeast		North Central		South		West		Total	
	#	%	#	%	#	%	#	%	#	%
Yes	8	100.00	4	57.14	6	54.55	10	100.00	28	77.78
No	0	.00	3	42.86	5	45.45	0	.00	8	22.22
Total	8	100.00	7	100.00	11	100.00	10	100.00	36	100.00

Source: Sulton and Townsey, Police Foundation, Washington, D.C. 1981.

to women. Further, following the U.S. Supreme Court's ruling in *Griggs v. Duke Power Co.*, 401 U.S. 423 (1971), police agencies, like other employers, must demonstrate the job-relatedness of criteria which have disparate impact on one sex or the other. Thus, although police agencies have latitude, under constitutional requirements, in establishing employment standards, an employment practice that places a disproportionate burden on women may be a basis for requiring that the practice be shown to have a valid purpose. *Washington v. Davis*, 426 U.S. 229 (1976). Consequently, although police agility tests involving swimming, running, carrying, jumping, and the like measure attributes that are bona fide occupational qualifications for police jobs, agencies using them must guard against disproportionate impact on protected groups (such as women), and must make certain that the tests meet standards of job-relatedness and validation. In point of this, courts have invalidated police department physical agility tests which included such exercises as pushups, situps, broad jumps, and obstacle courses because of disparate impact (*Harless v. Duck*, 619 F.2d 611 (6th Cir. 1980). Specifically, in *Officers for Justice v. Civil Service Commission* (395 F. Supp. 378 (N.D. Cal. 1979), the court recognized that the physical agility test used by the San Francisco Police Department had "substantial disparate impact upon women." It noted that a selection device (such as a physical agility test) that has an adverse impact on women may be allowed only if it is job-related, thereby measuring skills necessary to perform patrol work. The San Francisco physical agility test then before the court had been passed by only 2 of 166 female applicants, whereas 63 percent of the male applicants had passed. Moreover, the test measured only physical skills used in emergency situations. It did not address aspects of patrol work that emphasized skills such as "teamwork, intelligence, judgment, patience, and verbal skills as more important aids to patrol officers in emergency situations." In light of inconclusive evidence as to the extent to which the skills measured by the physical agility test were related to patrol performance, the court found that the validity of the test had not been established. However, courts have also upheld the use of physical agility tests in spite of disparate impact on underrepresented groups. For example, in *Hail v. White*, 334 F. Supp. 930, *aff'd in part, rev'd in part*, 459 F.2d 725 (1st Cir. 1972), the court upheld a strength and agility test on the ground that the test was substantially job-related, although it disqualified a significant number of female applicants.

Note One: Disparate Impact

The Houston (Texas) Police Department. The fact that physical agility tests eliminate a disproportionate number of female police applicants is common knowledge. The use of a physical agility test by the Houston Police Department, like the use of such by numerous others, is illustrative of this observation.

The Houston Police Department has a very impressive and higher than average complement of female officers—n=181; 6.2 percent.[4] However, this agency employs a rigorous physical agility test (labelled "Work Sample Test") which clearly disqualifies a highly disproportionate number of female applicants.

In March 1977, Lifson, Wilson, Ferguson and Winick (LWFW, management consultants) conducted a validity study of Houston's police officer selection, training and promotion criteria and procedures. The Work Sample Test, which is administered to both male and female applicants, is a result of a selection recommendation of the LWFW validity study.

The Work Sample Test which must be passed before an applicant is investigated and approved for appointment, entails: running; jumping hurdles; a pull-up on a 7'6" wall, remaining at the top of the wall for a specified period; a 6' wall climb; and dragging a 65-pound dummy. All "events" are to be completed within 60 seconds. Should an applicant fail any one of the "events" the entire examination must be repeated. Two subsequent attempts are allowed an applicant after an initial failure. As noted, a disproportionate number of female applicants fail the Work Sample Test initially. A disproportionate number also fail upon each re-take.

Department data show that although the rate of application of women increased from 16.0 percent in 1976 to 20.0 percent in 1978, the rate of actual representation of women on the force remains below the labor representation rate (39.89) of women in the Houston Standard Metropolitan Statistical Area (SMSA). Moreover, (remaining mindful of the female labor force representation rate) the most recent department data show that of a total of 205 women of one applicant group in 1978, only 13.1 percent (n=27) were approved for investigation. Indications suggest that failure of the Work Sample Test is directly related to this and subsequent low approved percentages. This is reasoned as it is also reported that the very vast majority of female applicants meet the department's eligibility requirements and pass the preliminary interview (the only process points preceding the Work Sample Test). Thus, it is reasonable to deduce that the small percentages of women approved for investigation (the process point following successful completion of the Work Sample Test) is directly attributable to disproportionate failure of the Work Sample Test. Nonetheless, as noted, Houston has an impressive complement of female officers. This agency recruits on a massive basis covering 12 states. In this effort, directed primarily at black men, the agency acquires applications from a large number of qualified women. Sound speculation notes that given this agency's massive recruitment strategy and the application response of women, their impressive complement of capable female officers could be even more impressive were it not for the disproportionate impact of the Work Sample Test. Interestingly, the Work Sample Test has yet to be validated, and there are reports that there are no seven-feet walls within the city limits.

Note Two: Nondiscriminatory Physical Agility Testing

The Miami (Florida) Police Department. The Miami Police Department administers a physical agility test to determine whether applicants are capable of completing training at the Police Academy. Thus, it pointedly assesses agility potential. Formerly, there were separate physical agility tests for men and women. However, the current physical agility test is the same for both applicant groups. Department records show that both sexes pass the test in proportionate numbers. Previously, the physical agility test was scored on a "pass/fail" basis and was found to have an adverse impact upon women. It was modified in 1974 to a point system. This modification has seemingly corrected the previous disparity between the numbers of men and women who pass the physical agility test. The test includes a five feet wall climb which women master proportionately.

If an applicant fails the physical agility test, he or she is placed on a six-weeks hold, allowing for successful completion of the physical agility test within this time period. Of those who initially fail the examination, 95 percent (proportionate numbers of men and women) successfully complete it upon retake. Problematic physical feats for women are pushups and broad jumps. However, applicants' agility potential, rather than present fitness, is assessed; thus, women pass the test proportionately.

Between 1967 and 1979, the number and percent of female officers increased steadily. In 1967, 1969, 1974, 1976, and 1979, respectively, female police officers composed 2.9 percent (n=14), 1.0 percent (n=10), 4.2 percent (n=34), 6.2 percent (n=49), and 7.2 percent (n=49). While the total strength of the department increased 96 percent from 1970 to 1976, the complement of female officers increased 390 percent and has remained constant to date. The 1974-76 percentage increase of female officers is attributable in large part to the marked increase of minority female officers who joined the Miami police force during this time period and the department's amendments in selection and training procedures emphasizing an applicant's potential to complete academy training (Sulton and Townsey, 1981: Appendix D). These amendments are the results of a consent decree between the City of Miami and the U.S. Department of Justice which addresses race and sex discrimination in hiring. The 1977 consent decree directs that 56 percent of new hires be members of three "affected classes" —blacks, latins, and women. In 1979, the Miami Police Department undertook a major recruitment drive aimed at recruiting members of the three "affected" classes. Although the department has had considerable difficulty attracting black male applicants, it has not had any difficulty attracting female applicants. For example, between 1975 and 1978, 783 persons applied for the position of police officer of whom 15.0 percent (n = 125) were women.

Note Three: Alternative Training

The New Jersey State Police. Although opponents to women on patrol continue to argue that women cannot succeed in rigorous physical training, events of 1980, like numerous ones of the seventies, indicate that this is not the case. In February 1980, the New Jersey State Police (at the direction of the U.S. Deparment of Justice) began an all-female state trooper class, which consisted of 104 women chosen from more than 1,600 female applicants. Although 70 percent of the 104 women dropped out before the completion of the training class, much about rigorous training and women was learned. In conjunction with New Jersey's Seton Hall University, New Jersey State Police officials determined that women, with some *minor* modifications in the physical training program, can be made as physically fit as men.

At the outset of the training class, instructors addressed the anticipated problem of a high injury rate among female recruits (foot injuries had plagued women in preceding classes). As expected, foot injuries began with the start of the running-in-formation exercise. Women noted that the required ankle-high sneakers were uncomfortable and they did not feel confident in them. The state police considered the complaint and authorized low shoes, which was followed by a drop in the number of foot injuries to almost zero. From that point on, instructors modified the physical training course (*without lowering standards*) where necessary and discovered that women reached the levels of function required of state troopers.

The New Jersey State Police report that although women are generally smaller and weaker than men, they can meet standards if specially designed exercises are used. (Graduates of the all-female class ranged from 5'1 1/2" tall and 105 pounds to 5'9" and 158 pounds.) Because the upper body strength of women is less than that of men, the New Jersey State Police placed more emphasis on lower body strength through the use of karate and judo. Women who experienced difficulty were urged to engage in extra weight training, using progressively heavier weights. They did so and met required standards relating to physical strength.

Firearms training is very often difficult for female recruits. At New Jersey it was discovered that women's "weak" hands were weaker than those of most men.[5] However, this weakness was overcome by recruits engaging in special exercises to strengthen their grip.

At the outset, female recruits were found to be significantly more reluctant to use their fists in training events than male recruits. However, the New Jersey State Police report that this reluctance was overcome by women who were determined to meet the required standard.

The New Jersey State Police experience clearly notes that women can withstand rigorous training providing progressive development is afforded.

CONCLUSIONS AND RECOMMENDATIONS

That police officers should meet certain physical standards to be capable of performing the patrol function cannot be countered. However, this obvious fact does not relieve police agencies of their duty under Title VII and EEOC instructives to not only develop non-discriminatory means of measuring physical fitness, but to also use strictly job-related fitness mechanisms that provide equal employment opportunity to all applicant groups. Clearly, whether intended or not, physical agility tests as used by a growing number of municipal agencies have disparate impact on female applicants. A great number of physical agility tests have the effect of measuring physical fitness through the use of irrelevant standards voiding the test of required criterion-related validity. This major flaw rests on the fact that generally the physical agility test administered by a police department appraises abilities (e.g., standing broad jumps, vertical jumps, situps, pushups, swimming, etc.) that police officers, as part of their job activities, are not required to perform. Moreover, generally physical agility tests produce scores that do not positively correlate with later training and job performance scores (Fischer, 1980:31-32). However, the use of physical agility tests do support the traditional biases against women in policing generally, and women on patrol in particular; and they do so to effective degrees.

Substantively, stringent physical agility tests are recognized by some law enforcement observers as providing (as did past discriminatory eligibility and selection requirements and training practices) a personnel strategy to limit the entry (and consequently the growth and impact) of women into general policing—namely, the patrol function. Thus, although research of the seventies convincingly shows that women are generally as capable as men in the patrol function, the eighties find police agencies strongly supporting the use of typically stringent physical agility tests as a selection criterion although such tests disqualify a disproportionate number of capable female applicants.

In response to this predicament, women must remain mindful of supportive legislation and litigation and must continue to challenge in all arenas discriminatory personnel practices. This remains a must in spite of the certain uphill climb, given the fate of an equal protection claim that allowed the U.S. Supreme Court to uphold a medical plan (that excluded pregnancy and pregnancy-related disorders, although it covered voluntary medical procedures like vasectomies, see *Geduldig v. Aiello,* 417 U.S. 484 (1974) and *General Electric v. Gilbert,* 429 U.S. 125 (1976), because " . . . it made no distinction between pregnant men and pregnant women" (Lewin, 1980:4).

A major argument against the use of a physical agility test prior to training (as is the case in Houston) is based on the observation that women can be trained to be as agile as physically fit men generally are upon application, and thus perform adequately in the patrol function. The noted New Jersey experience and case studies of the Metropolitan Police Department (Washington, D.C.), the Miami Police Department, the Denver Police Department, the Houston Police Department, and the Detroit Police Department show this to be so (Sulton and Townsey, 1981: Chapter III). Contrary to acknowledging this observation, however, the Police Foundation survey findings show that 91 percent of municipal and state police agencies require that the agility test be passed before training (Sulton and Townsey, 1981). Relatedly, findings show only 10 to 12 major police agencies to have female complements at or above the national sample average of 3.38 percent.

Police agencies committed to equal employment opportunity for women should employ physical agility tests which primarily measure agility potential and they should structure training programs which are developmental in nature, allowing recruits to progressively attain the required level of physical competence.

Notes

[1] For a detailed overview of the evolution of women in policing, see *"Evolution" in Women Police Officers: A Personnel Study* by Sulton and Townsey, 1981.

[2] For detailed analyses of other litigated issues of particular importance to women in policing (i.e., height and weight requirements; veterans' preference; sexual harassment; and pregnancy and related maternity benefits), see "Litigation" in Sulton and Townsey, 1981.

[3] Response Rates: 73.9 percent—municipal agencies; 71.4 percent—state agencies.

[4] 1978 department data.

[5] The weak hand is the left hand in a right-handed person, and vice versa; recruits were required to properly fire weapons with both hands.

References

Bartlett, Harold and Arthur Rosenblum (1977). Policewoman Effectiveness. Denver: Civil Service Commission and the Denver Police Department.

Bloch, Peter and Deborah Anderson (1974). Policewomen on Patrol: Final Report. Washington, D.C.: Police Foundation.

Bowe v. Colgate-Palmolive Co., 416 F. 2d 711 (7th Cir. 1969), revising in part 272 F. Supp. 332 (S.D. Ind. 1967).

Eisenberg, Terry, Deborah Ann Kent, and Charles R. Wall (1973). Police Personnel Practices in State and Local Governments. Washington, D.C.: International Association of Chiefs of Police and Police Foundation.

Federal Bureau of Investigation (1974). Uniform Crime Reports. Washington, D.C.: Government Printing Office.

Fischer, Charles H. (1980). "City's exercise in job sex bias: get physical fitness test in shape." The National Law Journal (November):31-32.

Geduldig v. Aiello, 417 U.S. 484 (1974).

General Electric Co. v. Gilbert, 429 U.S. 125 (1976).

Giordano, Mary Ann (1981). "Women cops—the blue line fades." Daily News (January):17.

Griggs v. Duke Power Co., 401 U.S. 424 (1971).

Hail v. White, 334 F. Supp. 930, affirmed in part, revised in part 459 F.2d 725 (1st Cir., 1972).

Kizziah, Carol and Mark Morris (1977). Evaluation of Women in Policing Program: Newton, Massachusetts. Oakland: Approach Associates.

Lewin, Tamar (1980). "Courts more hospitable to minorities than to women in bias suits, study says." The National Law Journal (October):4.

Pennsylvania State Police Female Trooper Study (1974). Harrisburg: Pennsylvania State Police.

Sherman, Lewis J. (1975). "Evaluation of policewomen on patrol in a suburban police department." Journal of Police Science Administration 3 (December):434-438.

Sichel, Joyce, Lucy N. Friedman, Janet C. Quint, and Michael E. Smith (1977). Women on Patrol: A Pilot Study of Police Performance in New York City. New York: Vera Institute of Justice.

Sulton, Cynthia and Roi D. Townsey (1981). Women Police Officers: A Personnel Study. Washington, D.C.: Police Foundation.

The Study of Police Women Competency in the Performance of Sector Police Work in the City of Philadelphia (1978). State College, Pennsylvania: Bartell Associates, Inc.

Washington v. Davis, 426 U.S. 229 (1976).

Weeks v. Southern Bell Telephone and Telegraph Co., 408 F.2d 228 (5th Cir. 1969), revising 277 F. Supp. 117 (1967).

White v. Nassau County Police Department, 15 FEP 261 (1977).

Women Traffic Officer Project: Final Report (1976). Sacramento: Department of California Highway Patrol.

24

Why Two Women Cops Were Convicted of Cowardice

Claudia Dreifus

Since the 1967 riots, the Detroit Police Department has had a history of violence, racism, and sexism. In 1974 when a black mayor took office only 18 percent of all officers in the department were black in a city whose citizens were 50 percent black. Today 40 percent of the department is black. However, institutionalized racism continues. For example, 70 percent of the officers brought up on charges are black, even though citizens' allegations of police brutality are primarily against white officers. In terms of the sexism in the department, after a strong affirmative action order in 1973 the department hired one woman for every man until a backlog of 1500 applicants had been exhausted, but in 1980 only 12 percent of the department was female, 63 percent of whom are black. As one of many incidents, in 1977 a woman officer reporting for duty found her squad car strewn with dead rats. In addition, the police union had shown little interest in protecting its black and female members. *

It is against this background that Dreifus describes the case of two women officers accused of cowardice after an incident with a black male citizen in which their supervisor intervened, moved in on and was attacked by the man. While both of the women were eventually acquitted of the cowardice charges, within weeks of their rehiring they were again dismissed, this time on the basis of city budgetary problems. Recall that in the Price and Gavin chapter (Chapter 22), Detroit in 1978 had the highest percentage of women officers of all cities studied. When Detroit had financial problems in 1979, 271 women were fired, eliminating in one stroke almost half of the gains of an affirmative action program instituted under the black mayor that had put them out front nationally.

The chapter provides a graphic study of the impact of sexism and racism on workers in the field of law enforcement. What are some of the institutionalized mechanisms by which racism and sexism can be shown to have occurred? What were some of the individual attitudes that clearly expressed hostility to blacks and women? Can you make an argument for how these sexist and racist attitudes and institutionalized structures supported each other to produce the particular incident described in this chapter?

Reprinted with permission from Claudia Dreifus, "Why Two Women Cops Were Convicted of Cowardice," *Ms Magazine*, April 1981.

* The above information was obtained from Georgia Christagau, "Police Study: Women Cops on Trial in Detroit." *The Village Voice*, Vol. 25(31) 1980.

One other point you should consider is: Discussions about hostility of police officers against women and minority races are not uncommon. It is much more common than such discussions of racism and sexism among lawyers, another white, male-dominated occupation. Can you suggest any reasons why observers are less critical of the higher status legal profession's hostility toward and discrimination against women than that of the police department?

It was nearly midnight on August 26, 1979. Officers Glenda Rudolf and Katherine Perkins of Detroit's police department were cruising through a working-class black neighborhood when they saw something odd. "Look, Perk," Rudolf exclaimed. "I think I see a naked man over there." And sure enough, Calvin Rowell, 30, nude from head to toe, with a huge Doberman pinscher at his side, was standing in the middle of Second Avenue and Hazlewood Street, burning dollar bills and shouting about the evils of white people.

The two women, who are themselves black, looked at the scene and burst out laughing.

Katherine Perkins sent an immediate radio message to headquarters explaining that there was a naked man in the street, that the situation was under control. They followed the standard procedure for requesting back-up. Still laughing, the women left their scout car and approached Rowell. "Hey, brother, what are you doing in the middle of the street with no clothes on?" Glenda Rudolf inquired as she began extinguishing flames on the burning money.

"Don't do that, sister," Rowell intoned. "That's white man's money. That's what keeps us apart."

Rudolf chuckled and kept on. Suddenly, from behind her, car 13-71 and Sergeant Paul Janness screeched onto the scene. Janness, who is white, immediately jumped out of his car and began moving in on Rowell. The black man charged the sergeant screaming something about a "blue-eyed devil." *Whap! Blap!* in an instant, Rowell had decked the sergeant and was pounding him against the pavement. What happened next is not clear. Glenda Rudolf claims that she and Perkins piled on top of the two brawling men; that she hit Rowell with a flashlight, forcing him to release Janness. Then Katherine Perkins moved toward Rowell and attempted to handcuff him. According to the women, Janness barked something to the effect of "Don't cuff him, I'm going to beat his — ass." Sergeant Janness denies he ever said such a thing. In any event, a few seconds later, scout car 13-94 arrived with officers Vikki Hubbard and Lawrence Estelle; they would later say that they saw the women do nothing to aid the sergeant.

Rudolf and Perkins claim that Hubbard and Estelle arrived too late to witness any help.

From beginning to end, it all took no more than two minutes. For Katherine Perkins and Glenda Rudolf, those two minutes were the beginning of a yearlong ordeal that would result in their becoming the first Americans, civilian or military, to be convicted of cowardice since the Korean War.

Some background: Detroit is a city where antagonisms between the police and the black community have always been sharp; the devastating 1967 riot was partly a reaction to what blacks saw as unrestrained abuses by what was then an all-white police force. When Coleman Young, a black, ran for mayor in 1974, he pledged to integrate the police department. As soon as he was elected, Young instituted a massive affirmative action hiring program that brought hundreds of blacks into policing; the old guard of angry white career officers retaliated with everything from lawsuits to violence. Incidents of white cops drawing guns on black cops occurred; an assassination plot by white officers against a black sergeant was uncovered; racial harassment in the precinct houses was common. Then, in 1975, a federal court ordered that affirmative action hiring be extended to women: for every white male hired or promoted, a female would have to be hired or promoted. From that time on, Detroit aggressively recruited women into law enforcement. By the spring of 1980, 12 percent of the department was female, one of the highest percentages in the country; 63 percent of those women officers were black.

Katherine Perkins had been trying to become an officer since 1971. "I thought I could do something different," she explained one morning in Detroit while sitting in her attorney's office. "I felt the need to communicate—do you understand? The white officers just didn't know how to communicate with us." She also hoped that the job would work changes in her own life. Now 35, she had married young, had her four kids young, and had, within the confines of a traditional marriage, a fairly restricted existence. "I was so sheltered in my marriage," she explains, "that during the 1967 riot, my husband came home and said, 'My God, they just burned down Twelfth Street,' and I didn't know what he was talking about. The riot changed me. I wanted to be involved afterward."

"Involvement" meant enrolling in Wayne County Community College, a part-time job at a home for juvenile offenders, and starting to apply for the patrol officer position. "I remember once applying," she recalled, "This must have been in 1971 or 1972—before the Supreme Court ruled that you can't discriminate against women because we are shorter or because we weigh less than men. Well, this white officer took my application and tore it up right in my face. I only had a high school diploma at the time and I'm five-foot-two-inches tall. He said, 'You might be able to get two years of college, Katherine, but you'll never grow. Come back when you grow!' " Short but determined, she kept coming back.Finally in 1977, after the court-ordered affirmative action program was put into full effect, she was hired.

"The police academy was the hardest thing I'd ever tried," she explains. "The sergeants and the lieutenants just yelled and yelled and yelled. They had no compassion or understanding of why some of us were there. I didn't want to be treated differently from any other rookie, but the women were treated worse."

After the academy, Perkins was assigned to the Woodward Precinct—the 13th, and there, she says, she ran straight into male hostility. "They had this attitude, 'You want to be here? Well, you can do it without my help.' The men seemed to be so psyched out on this six-foot/two-hundred-dred-twenty-pound image of what a cop should be. It was ridiculous. Any *fool* can shoot a gun. What you really need is intelligence and sensitivity—and that's what women bring to the job."

So from the first, Katherine Perkins never fitted into that tight little male world of the police precinct. But at the time it happened, the Rowell incident seemed routine to her. She would never have given Calvin Rowell another thought, had not, within an hour of the incident, rumors started floating that she and Rudolf were to be "jammed" for some kind of malfeasance. "When officers started coming up to me that night and telling me I was going to be charged, I couldn't figure out why," she recalled. "The next day at roll call, there was this sergeant and he was running off at the mouth about how 'if a women wants to become a patrol officer, she had better know how to handle herself on the street.' After roll call, Lieutenant Ronald Karchefski, who was our superior, called me and Rudolf into his office and said he was going to bring us up on charges. I said, 'What charges?' He said, 'Cowardice.' I said, 'That's a lie!' then he ordered us to make written statements on the incident—which we did. We said that we weren't cowards. Later, we were charged with making a false statement for saying that. I got ten-days' pay penalty for it."

From that moment on, Katherine Perkins decided that she was going to fight. "I knew from that minute that they were going to find me guilty and that there was going to be no fairness to this," she explained. "I mean, why weren't they charging the sergeant with anything? I figured that if I did wrong, he did wrong. Why weren't they charging him with threatening a civilian? Why weren't they thinking about how the incident was under control until *he* got there? I'll tell you why. Because in Detroit, it's the sergeants and the lieutenants who make the charges and it's the patrol officers who get charged. Besides, there was something else to this . . . a message to the blacks and the women: 'If you get out of line, the same thing will happen to you that's happened to Katherine Perkins.' "

The specifics of what happened to Katherine Perkins and Glenda Rudolf are that just before Christmas in 1979, they were officially charged with three offenses: cowardice; making a false statement in saying that they'd helped Janness; making a false statement when they'd accused the sergeant of threatening Rowell. A few months later, two departmental trial boards met. The first trial board found the women guilty of the first two offenses; the third charge was dropped. What the trial board was saying was that they found Janness truthful when he said that the women were cowards, but not truthful when he said he'd never threatened the naked man. The second trial board reviewed the evidence, heard new witnesses, and then reaffirmed the opinion of the first.

By mid-March, Perkins and Rudolf were officially fired, their guns and badges removed. At that point, the women—who were never personally close anyway—chose different courses of action. Katherine Perkins moved to appeal her case to the next highest body—the board of police commissioners; Glenda Rudolf, who had a different lawyer and was being represented by her union (the Detroit Police Officers Association), appealed to an outside impartial arbitrator. It was Rudolf's view that the board of commissioners with its record of upholding 89 percent of all trial-board decisions would never go against the brass on a case this big.

In June, the board of commissioners reluctantly acquitted Katherine Perkins on the cowardice charge, on the grounds that the legal definition of cowardice required that a person "acted or failed to act out of fear." There never had been any question of fear on the part of either woman; they were laughing at Calvin Rowell, not running from him. So while the board found her technically innocent of cowardice, it did convict her of making a false statement by claiming "to have taken certain action to terminate the assault on Sergeant Janness and subdue the officer's assailant, when in fact she took no such action." On a warm June afternoon, Katherine Perkins returned to her beat. Glenda Rudolf, still unemployed, bitterly waited for an arbitrator to rule on her innocence.

Glenda Rudolf and I are sitting in a downtown Detroit Howard Johnson's on a pleasant June morning: Rudolf is telling me about the long road that brought her from teaching to nursing to law enforcement. "I was always a bit of a tomboy as a kid," she says with a warm laugh. "My folks were pretty well-off, they're educators—Ph.D.s—but I was a pretty wild kid. I ran with a motorcycle gang. Talk about macho, I was *tough*. In my whole life, I never dreamed anyone would dare call me a coward." A tall, lanky woman—athletic—Rudolf gives off a mixed sense of strength and vulnerability.

As we talk, a beefy-looking man, middle-aged, Central Casting's perfect vision of the "Undercover Columbo," enters, sits down at the table next to us; he wears very obvious electronic equipment. "I used to see stuff like that around the precinct," Rudolf says matter-of-factly, "it's used for surveillance." With the realization that we're being tailed and taped, we get up, leave the restaurant—only to discover that wherever we stroll we seem to "pick up" hefty-looking guys with police department prep-sets, walkie-talkies. "I'm not surprised by this," Rudolf says. "A few weeks ago, I found this guy hanging out on my telephone pole, saying he was making repairs. Ain't nothing wrong with my phone, except that I'm getting a lot of crank calls in the middle of the night. My phone now clicks all the time. I guess somebody somewhere is really unused to seeing a woman say no to the brass. They can't figure it, so they just try to keep an eye on me."

When Deputy Chief of Police James Bannon was asked why someone might want to be following a reporter and Glenda Rudolf, he denied that any of his people were involved. "The chief has directed Perkins and Rudolf, in their own best interests, to let this go away," he said. "They have to function. However, this department, its members, would never be permitted to make that kind of surveillance."

Later, we drive around in her car, away from the electronic eavesdropping. "I was working as a nurse in 1977 and hating it," she recalled. "My sister was already a patrol officer. She said, 'Why don't you sign up? It's good money, good benefits, and you can change some attitudes—you can do some good.' So I joined and I liked the work. But it was rough. Down at the precinct, there was a lot of sexual and racial harassment. Guys would come in and say, 'I wonder if Rudolf thinks she's a *bad* bitch!' Or they'd tell me, 'In order to get ahead on this job, you have to jump on the jolly pole.' There was big pressure to act like a man if you were a patrol officer. Some of the women, they'd try to act tougher than the men. My attitude was always to do what I had to do and not to be ashamed of being a woman."

The incident. Glenda Rudolf gives off an ironic laugh when she speaks of it. "It was more funny than anything else. Actually, there was no problem until the sergeant arrived. Then, everything happened real fast and suddenly the sergeant was getting hit. Till the day I die, I *know* I got in on the fight and that I hit Rowell with my flashlight. You know, for a while I was afraid that they were going to charge me with brutality on that. At the trial board, the sergeant testified that Rowell had just let go of him spontaneously. Rowell let go because *I* forced him to."

Like Katherine Perkins, Rudolf thought of the incident as routine. But after she had taken Calvin Rowell to Detroit General Hospital, Rudolf began hearing rumors that she was to be charged. "It started with one of the male officers talking to me at the hospital," she recalls. "He said, 'Girl, look at your clothes—they're not even dirty.' I said, 'I don't wear dirty clothes to work.' He said, 'Well, at the precinct, they're thinking of jamming you and Perkins.' When he said that, I thought that they were going to enter our names in the book down at the precinct where they write you up if you've done something wrong. 'The Gig Book.' Cowardice? It never entered my mind. To me, cowardice is somebody running to their scout car and driving off. And I've heard stories like that. I've heard stories of male officers doing just that."

At the 13th Precinct that night, Glenda Rudolf did her usual paperwork. At one point, Paul Janness, who in addition to being her supervisor was Rudolf's good friend, brought her his injury report to witness. "Now do you think if I had been a coward or had even thought of the incident as something unusual, I would have signed the report?" Glenda Rudolf asks, "I'm no fool. Well, I just signed that report—I didn't even read it. Later that morning, I even called Paul at home to see how he was feeling. He said he wasn't even going to go to the doctor about it—maybe he'd go to the medical center. I told him to call me if there was anything I could do."

The very next day, after roll call, Glenda Rudolf was stunned to hear that she might actually be charged. "I just couldn't imagine why Paul, who wasn't even going to a doctor for this, would make it into a big thing. Well, I don't think he initiated the charges anyway. I think what happened was that rumors got around the precinct that he'd been beaten up, while we supposedly just stood by. The story fell right into a lot of guys' fears. The men were always saying that you could never count on women to back you up in a pinch. Well, one thing led to another and before anyone could stop it—pow!—you had these incredible charges. This whole thing is really about embarrassment. You have a lot of cops on our shift who are very prejudiced. This thing was blown out of proportion because a black guy hit a white supervisor and we didn't kill him. If we had killed him, it would have been a horse of a different color."

Paul Janness will not speak to reporters, but Gerald Storch of the Detroit News spoke to several of Janness's friends—anonymously—who said he didn't want to make the cowardice accusation. One colleague told Storch, "He didn't want to file the charges. I was surprised to hear that he did." Another said, "He just wishes now the whole thing had never happened." However, Lieutenant Karchefski told Storch that the charges developed because "the sergeant said he wanted to write them up for misconduct—that was the same night. I spoke to him the following day to see if he still felt strongly about it and he did."

So there it was. Rudolf, who in her two-and-a-half years on the force had been shot at, been knifed, captured a rapist, suddenly became known as the coward cop. Interestingly, the night after the Rowell incident, Perkins and Rudolf fought and captured a man with a gun who tried to kidnap them. For much of the winter of 1979, Rudolf remained at her job at the 13th—working, oddly enough, within a few feet of Paul Janness, who remained her supervisor. "It was incredibly weird," she says. "He couldn't look me in the face. All the time I was out on patrol, I kept wondering what was happening. After all, if I really was a coward, the supervisors shouldn't have allowed me to go out on patrol—I'd be a danger to the citizenry and to the other officers."

Then, in March, 1980, after the trial board met, she was fired.

Unemployment was difficult. Ineligible for unemployment insurance, single, isolated, she had few sources of support—emotional or financial. To pay her bills, she lived off checks from friends and relatives; to keep sane, she did volunteer work for Catholic Big Sisters and spent her time searching for witnesses who could clear her. "I found Calvin Rowell at one point," she declares. "And he was unbelievably frightened. He said that he thought they'd given him too many drugs at the hospitals and he was afraid that if he testified for me, they'd commit him again." Good things sometimes happened—a chance to tell her story on the "Phil Donahue Show" and to the *New York Times*—but mostly she had to deal with crank calls, a broken engagement, and lots of "friends" who disappeared.

When Katherine Perkins was acquitted of the cowardice charge by the board of commissioners, it should have cheered Glenda Rudolf since it virtually assured her vindication; instead, it depressed her. Rudolf's own ruling from the arbitrator was weeks, probably months, away. "The board of commissioners ruled for Perkins only because they knew an arbitrator would eventually clear me," she said. "They hardly ever go against a trial board. They just didn't want to be embarrassed by having a contrary ruling from an outside body. So now Perkins is back at work and I'm still unemployed."

The day after our interview, Glenda Rudolf went to church . "I asked the priest," she told me later, "to bless me in my heart because I'm a strong person and I want to be stronger yet so that I can fight this charge. I'm someone who's in the middle of something that's a lot bigger than me or Katherine Perkins. Everything that's happened to me has to do with some men not liking women doing equal work to them. That's the truth about this story, that's the truth."

The truth about the Perkins-Rudolf case is like *Rashomon*. Talk to three Detroiters and you'll get three different theories. Robert Cohn, lawyer for Katherine Perkins, puts it into a political context. "This case has everything to do with racism and sexism," he explains. "We've got a police department that's thirty percent black—twelve percent female. The blacks and the women who come in are idealistic. But soon, they find themselves getting hauled up on crazy charges by the white brass. This case hasn't happened in a vacuum. Seventy percent of those officers brought to trial board for disciplinary reasons are black—and the charges are made up by the white sergeants and lieutenants. As a tactic to defeat affirmative action, it works. It's getting harder and harder to recruit blacks into police work in this town. People tell their friends: 'Don't join. You'll get into worse trouble than you would if you stayed on the street.' The whole thing is getting really embarrassing to Mayor Young."

Bernard Feldman, Glenda Rudolf's lawyer, thinks of the charges as a series of accidents: "The lieutenant who originally wrote them up called what happened 'cowardice.' No one pulled this out of the system along the line. No one looks. That's the way things go in a bureaucracy. They charged the women on very weak facts."

Deputy Chief of Police James Bannon, a man with a Ph.D. in sex roles, disagrees: "The charge was cowardice because the rule was clear. The rule very simply stated that shirking of duty in time of danger was cowardice. To the people drafting the charges, it seemed an appropriate charge. It's obvious in retrospect that they were not very sensitive to the social issues involved."

Social issues? "Well, no one says that courage is not a female trait. Women are brave in childbirth," Bannon adds. "But physical courage is an expectation we have of men, not women. We have an obligation to resocialize women, and, as we see here, it has to happen at earlier stages."

In mid-July, Glenda Rudolf came to the point where further unemployment seemed unbearable. When her union called her with a proposed deal, she reluctantly accepted it: the department would take her back before the arbitrator ruled if she would accept the Perkins verdict—innocent of cowardice, guilty of making a false statement. "I knew that the arbitrator would totally clear me," she explained, "but I just couldn't afford to wait any more . . . the money. They assigned me to a new precinct and there, everyone was very curious about me. Oh, a couple of chauvinist men stood around and said, 'Here come the cluck, cluck.' Mostly, people wanted to know what happened during the incident, and I told them: 'Nothing . . . really nothing.'"

Five weeks after Glenda Rudolf returned to work, she, Katherine Perkins, and 690 other Detroit police officers were laid off their jobs because of a municipal financial crunch; 271 of those furloughed were female. In one shot, almost half the gains of the affirmative action program were eliminated.

"If anyone wants to know what this case is really about, it's about these layoffs," Glenda Rudolf says bitterly. "Our case provided the rationalization for them. The men sit around the precincts now and they say: 'The women, it's a good thing they're gone. Women weren't good cops, anyway. Look at what happened with Perkins and Rudolf.'"

25

Doing Time with the Boys: An Analysis of Women Correctional Officers in All-Male Facilities

Cheryl Bowser Petersen

Studies on women corrections officers are very scarce. In recent years women have, at their insistence so as to be eligible for promotion and other organizational rewards, begun to work in all-male prisons and jails. Studies exploring this new work setting for women are also scarce and seldom appear as rigorous social science research. Petersen's work is a rare exception.

In this chapter the author reports on her own experiences as a corrections officer in an all-male prison. As a participant observer, Petersen examines the impact on both male officers and male inmates to the presence of female officers. She employs classic research methods: first, she describes the several techniques used in collecting her data (the methodology); then her findings are presented; and finally, conclusions are offered.

Her most important finding is that male officers were more hostile and gave the women guards more trouble than male inmates. In this regard, recall the earlier discussion of sexual harassment of women on the job (Chapter 19). Petersen's finding should not now surprise the reader familiar with the policing occupation and the introduction of women into that formerly exclusive male area. As you read this chapter, consider the reasons for male guard hostility, drawing on what you know of sexism and occupational dynamics. Refer back to earlier articles in this section for support for your arguments. Also, consider the sexist reasons inmates might want women officers around.

INTRODUCTION[1]

For the first time in the history of the Wisconsin Division of Corrections, women are being hired as correctional officers (guards) in all-male prisons. Because these institutions have previously been staffed almost entirely with men, the employment of female officers is an issue surrounded by many unanswered questions.[2] It is not, however, the purpose of this study to address all of these questions. Instead, this chapter will be limited to an exploration of three areas which affect the potential employability of women guards in male prisons:

1.   The reactions of male prisoners (or "residents") to female officers;
2.   The reactions of male officers to female officers; and
3.   Whether women can and/or should function in all guard positions throughout an institution.

These issues will be examined through a review of the relevant literature, a ten-month participant observation study of women guards in a male prison and an analysis of both inmate questionnaires and face-to-face interviews with male and female officers at three test institutions.

How the less aggressive, more nuturant and "nicer" female will fare in what has traditionally been defined as a conflict-ridden, all-male environment is an interesting question indeed. Unfortunately, there is little research which addresses the specific issue of women guards in male prisons. There is, however, a greater amount of research on women in policing. Similar to corrections, the police world has traditionally been thought of as a high-conflict, male-dominated profession which places much emphasis on toughness and physical aggression. Additionally, because both police officers and correctional officers may end up in situations requiring them to pat search a clothed subject of the opposite sex, the privacy issue is relevant for women in both fields.

There are, of course, some distinctions between women guards and women police officers. For example, the issue of privacy is somewhat more significant for female guards in male prisons than it is for women police officers because guards may be more likely to be required to perform strip searches. In addition, guards are sometimes required to supervise shower procedures. Furthermore, because residents of a prison have probably been isolated from the opposite sex for a much greater time than a subject who is likely to be apprehended by a police officer, it could be suggested that women guards can more easily become the target of sexual advances by the population which they "serve." However, an interview with one attractive female police officer revealed that she, at least, ultimately arrested a male subject for repeatedly pinching her while on duty.[3] Conversely, none of the women guards interviewed had ever been physically harassed by a male inmate.

Because of the similarities between women in corrections and women in policing, the literature review will attempt to explore the situations of women in both fields. In addition, other relevant documents, such as the employee evaluations of women guards, incident reports, etc., will be examined. It is hoped that this will provide a useful theoretical framework against which to analyze the results of this current research.

WOMEN IN LAW ENFORCEMENT
REVIEW OF THE LITERATURE

A significant issue in the employment of women in law enforcement related fields is the reaction of male colleagues and supervisors to the women. Because this has been a male-dominated area for so many years, one would except the presence of women officers to generate a certain amount of hostility and uncertainty as would any other significant change in the professional status quo. That this is true is suggested by the initial employee evaluations of the first two women correctional officers hired at Kettle Moraine Correctional Institution in Wisconsin. The evaluations state, "resented by most of her peers and they have stated so," and "most capable and can work cooperatively with others, but is rejected by some staff and residents . . . finds it hard to secure respect. . . ."[4]

Literature on women in law enforcement also suggests that women are rejected by their male counterparts. A survey of sheriff's deputies found that male deputies expressed negative attitudes about the performance of women officers in hazardous situations.[5] This finding is consistent with the findings of Silverman and Vega,[6] Arofat and McCahrey (1975) and Block and Anderson.[7]

Some women hold values which preclude assignment to particular job areas. Mary Hamelton wrote, "Policewomen have taken up policemanship, not with the idea of replacing men in this work, but for the purpose of aiding and assisting them, in a quiet, unassuming way, to prevent crime."[8] What Hamelton implies, of course, is that only a subservient, background role is proper for women in law enforcement. Confirming the notion that women are often precluded from job areas because of their own feelings of inadequacy and propriety is the finding by Vega and Silverman,[9] which indicated that a full 20 percent of the female officers interviewed felt that women should not be considered for patrol assignments.

Despite which positions women in corrections and law enforcement fill, they are considerably underrepresented in both corrections and law enforcement. Data from 1978 show that only 3 percent of Wisconsin law enforcement officers and correctional officers are women. Yet, the Statistical Abstract of the United States shows that, in the same year, women comprised a full 42 percent of the labor force.

In addition to being underrepresented in corrections and law enforcement, it is also true that women, once hired in these fields, are not treated in a manner comparable to male personnel. Knoohuizen and Gulman found that the Chicago Police Department treated women differently from the application process through on-the-job training and experience.[11] Fleming suggests that one reason for this differential treatment is the average male officer's tendency to be protective toward women.[12] Fleming cites the Indianapolis Police Department as an example of this type of protectiveness. Indianapolis was the first city in the United States to put a women in a regular patrol car. One patrol unit was comprised solely of two women. They patrolled a section which overlapped a number of other areas. As a result, Fleming states that male dispatchers only gave the women assignments when no other unit was available. Furthermore, she states that when the women were called, the assignments were limited to stereotypically feminine assignments (e.g., family arguments, first aid, juvenile-related tasks, etc.). The Block and Anderson study confirms this notice of male protectiveness and suggests that if it is not counteracted, women will not have a full opportunity to demonstrate their ability in law enforcement.

One recent study of national police selection standards[13] suggests that a number of police departments require higher education for women than men. This study also found that women often have different height and weight requirements, take entrance exams which differ in emphasis from those given to male applicants, and are trained separately from the men. Hence, when women are assigned to traditionally male jobs (e.g., patrol work) they perform poorly because they have not been properly selected, nor have they received appropriate training.

There are many examples of sex discrimination in job assignment. The Iowa State Reformatory in Anamosa, Iowa had two female correctional officers employed as of May 4, 1978. At that time, they were allowed to work only in the inner visiting room, the control center, and the tower. Because of these job limitations, one of the female correctional officers filed a union grievance against the institution. Referring to the pending hearing, Calvin Auger,[14] Superintendent of the Iowa State Men's Reformatory, stated:

> If she loses at that level, we have reason to believe that she will file a discrimination suit with either the state or federal civil rights commission. If we lose, we then will demand that they (the women) work in any and all areas as do all other correctional officers and perform all duties that they do.

Regarding Auger's last statement (i.e., "If we lose, we will then demand that they . . . perform all duties. . . . "), one may speculate about why the long overdue promise that all persons in the same classification must function similarly seems to be an implicit threat.

At a criminal justice training seminar, several women spoke of the professional difficulties which they had encountered. Barbara Bellande of the Silverbow County Sheriff's Department spoke of the unwillingness of male colleagues to take her on a "gun call" (e.g., an assignment where there is the potential for gun use) because she was a woman.[15] Arlina Howell, a former probation officer, pointed out that women were not considered capable of handling male probationers and were usually assigned an all-female caseload.[16] All women at the seminar indicated that, after "proving" themselves, most of the problems disappeared for them as individuals. However, the same prejudices about women in general often remained to plague other women coming into the field.

LEGAL ISSUES

Three pieces of federal legislation have been the basis for most challenges to discriminatory employment practices:

1. Section 1981 of the Civil Rights Act;
2. The Fourteenth Amendment to the United States Constitution;
3. Title VII of the Civil Rights Act of 1964.

Title VII of the Civil Rights Act of 1964, as amended, states that "It shall be an unlawful employment practice for an employer to fail or refuse to hire or to discharge any individual, or otherwise to discriminate against any individual with respect to his compensation, terms, conditions, or privileges of employment because of such individual's race, color, religion, sex or national origin." The 1972 amendment to Title VII makes such employment illegal whether practiced by public or private employers.

Recent decisions of the U.S. Supreme Court lend support to the argument that sexually discriminatory employment practices are also illegal under the "equal protection" clause of the Fourteenth Amendment. Furthermore, the intent of the agency in promulgating a particular employment practice is not the controlling factor. The Court stated in *Griggs* that "good intent or absence of discriminatory intent does not redeem discriminatory employment procedures or testing mechanisms that are unrelated to job capability.[17]

Minimum weight and height requirements have been shown to have a disparate impact on Hispanic Americans, Orientals, and women.[18] Additionally, the courts have taken a hard look at physical strength tests. In one case the court made a distinction between brute force and leverage strength and noted that " . . . the ability to use 'brute force' is not a necessary skill to perform job functions."[19]

The question of whether or not sex is a bona fide occupational qualification in a correctional setting is a question which remains largely unanswered in any unequivocal legal sense. A prisoner incarcerated at the Wisconsin State Prison requested that injunctive relief be granted prisoners at that prison against the use of women guards.[20] Apparently no final decision was made, for two years later another inmate at the Wisconsin Kettle Moraine Correctional Institution filed a second complaint (through the Inmate Complaint System) against the use of women officers.[21] He followed his complaint with a letter (dated March 2, 1978) to this author. The California Court of Appeals upheld the denial of the State Personnel Board to certify an ordained female chaplain for employment in a male correctional facility.[22] The personnel board found that the male only certification requirement for this position constituted a "bona fide occupational qualification reasonably necessary to the normal operation of the prison."

The right to privacy is a significant concern in the employment of women guards in male prisons. Although no general legal rule of thumb has yet been established by the courts, it is logical to assume that the definition of sex as an occupational qualification is dependent, at least in part, upon the privacy accomodations in the various institutions. Barbary Yaffe, attorney for the Wisconsin Department of Administration, wrote:

> I am of the opinion that the conditions in Wisconsin's maximum security facilities are sufficiently different from those existing in Alabama so that there is no reason to discontinue the employment of female correctional officers.[23]

SEXUAL EXPLOITATION OF WOMEN IN LAW ENFORCEMENT

Women who choose to work in a male-dominated environment, such as that of law enforcement, are often thought to be somewhat atypical and somehow lacking in feminity. In light of this notion, it is interesting to note the fact that in the spring of 1977 the Boise, Idaho Chief of Police dismissed seven female members of his police force because he feared that they *might* be homosexual.[24] No pre-termination hearing was held in any of the cases.

Women who enter male-dominated fields such as law enforcement are the subjects of a great deal of speculation about their sex lives. The wife of an inmate incarcerated in the Wisconsin State Prison-Waupun wrote:

> . . . I strongly disapprove of this (i.e., women officers) in some ways, such as allowing them to work within the prison. One of the positions within the prison is the visiting room. I have observed her (a women officer) eyeing up the inmates as though she were man-hungry. Also, on her first day, she wanted to help "shake down" (i.e., pat search) the men when visiting was over.[25]

It is interesting to note, however, that carefully scrutinizing (or "eyeing up") inmates for contraband, inappropriate behavior, etc., is one of the duties of all visiting area officers—whether that officer is male or female. Post-visit "shake down" is also part of the routine duties specific to the visiting area. One may question whether the tenor of the above letter would have been the same had the officer involved been male rather than female.

Consistent with the above, the Police Foundation[26] found that the majority of the policemen's wives who were studied were very much against the sexual integration of the police force. The researchers noted that jealousy was one of the major reasons for the antipathy of the police wives toward female officers. Similarly, the Silverman and Vega study[27] found that a full 45 percent of the male officers surveyed felt that female officers would use their sex as a device for enhancing their position with the police department. The same study also found that 36 percent of the male officers surveyed felt female officers would be sexually exploited.

Finally, an incident report written by Officer Gary Henderson at Wisconsin Correctional Institute (Fox Lake), indicates that the speculation about the sexual lives of the female officers does not always remain a mere undercurrent among male officers. Officer Henderson wrote:

> . . . (a male resident) made other remarks to (a female officer) about her sleeping with him that (a male officer) laughed about . . . I do not agree with (the female officer) being in the housing units, but I do not feel that she should have to put up with another officer . . . making indecent and insulting remarks about her. . . . [28]

The Block and Anderson study compared the field patrol work of male officers with that of female officers.[29] The study found that, in general, men and women performed patrol work in a similar manner. Furthermore, the study also revealed that the arrests made by both male and female officers are equally likely to produce convictions. One distinction did emerge. Although arrests made by both sexes were equally effective, women made fewer arrests than their male counterparts. Since police discretion involves the power to overlook minor offenses when an arrest would prove counter-productive, it is not clear whether the women produced too few arrests or the men produced too many arrests.

Sherman found that policemen and policewomen with equal time and experience in field patrol work perform similarly.[30] In 1972 the Police Foundation compared the performance of 86 policewomen on Washington's metropolitan force with an equal number of male officers.[31] Only two relevant differences emerged:

1. The men showed greater willingness to take formal action.
2. Women officers acted less physically aggressive.

Much of the literature on women in law enforcement is consistent with the Police Foundation's finding that female officers tend to act less aggressively than their male counterparts. Whether this reduced aggression is positive or negative is unclear. Fleming reveals that many female officers feel that brawn is not as essential to the job as male officers believe it to be.[32] She further notes that women officers feel that male officers often create more difficulty by "acting tough." One Los Angeles policewomen stated,

A lot of these guys feel that they have to assert their virility. More often than not, they end up turning a situation which could have been diffused into a full-scale brawl.[33]

Conversely, Silverman and Vega found that both college and non-college groups of male officers tended to downgrade the effectiveness of female officers in handling situations with a potential for violence.[34] However, it is clear that the police subculture has traditionally *required* a more assertive, "macho" method of dealing with potentially violent situations (Reis, 1971). This requirement may mean that the diffusion method used by female officers is not acceptable—even though the outcome may be the same or better than a more aggressive technique. Consistent with this is the finding by Silverman and Vega that women officers generally had to perform at a superior level in order to be considered adequate as officers.

While there is no concensus about the best way to handle potentially violent situations, there is evidence to indicate that women are somewhat more effective than men in *diffusing* potential violence. One study found that male/female police teams used force only 62 percent as often as male/male teams.[35] Female nurses in all-male mental institutions seem to have a similar advantage over their male counterparts. Dr. Milton Greenblatt, Commissioner of the Massachusetts Department of Mental Health, stated, " . . . female nurses on male wards, even on very disturbed wards, seem to have a good effect on the anger, belligerence and violent tendencies. . . . "[36]

Further illustration of this undefined female "quality" comes from a St. Louis housing project.[37] Four women became security guards at the Pruitt-Igoe housing project, a housing project reputed to be one of the most dangerous in the country. The women guards performed the same functions as the men and *as successfully as the men*. The only difference was that the women evoked a different (i.e., more favorable) response from the residents of the housing project. In explaining this different response, Sherman noted:

. . . the male guards frequently exacerbate conflict rather than resolve it . . . men by their attitudes and behavior tend to elicit more anger and violence . . . the women tend to diffuse violent situations by their intervention style. Since the four women guards at Pruitt-Igo are big . . . and quite formidable in appearance, some other, more subtle psychological factors are involved in eliciting hostility.[38]

Tanley posits an alternative explanation for this phenomenon. He suggests that many criminals are given to value systems which make it heroic to "take on" another man—especially if he is a police officer.[39] This same value system, however, makes it cowardly to attack a woman, even though she is a police officer. Tanley further notes that loss of status (among one's peers) can be a persuasive means of controlling individuals in such situations. In commenting on Tanley's hypothesis, Police Chief Wayne Heikkila proposed that this chivalrous behavior on the part of the male criminals will disappear when law-breakers realize that an arrest by a female officer is just as valid as one by a male officer.[40]

While the research noted above suggests that women are more effective than men in diffusing potential violence, one study found that both male and female officers obtained similar results in handling angry or violent citizens.[41] While this one inconsistent finding should not be ignored—especially in an area of study as new as women in law enforcement—the bulk of the literature does, indeed, point to the superior effectiveness of women in diffusing potential violence. However, whether diffusion is the best technique to employ in conflict situations is an unanswered question among law enforcement practitioners (Reis, 1971).

Anomia (a sense of self-to-other alienation) has traditionally been a problem among police officers. One interesting study found that female officers are not as significantly affected by anomia as male officers.[42] Furthermore, this study also found that women police officers do not suffer as severely as their male counterparts from job dissatisfaction. These findings are of consequence because anomia (or alienation), high authoritarianism, and feelings of job dissatisfaction can be related to job effectiveness and psychological "fitness" for police duties.

To conclude this review of the literature has uncovered several distinctions between male and female law enforcement personnel. They are:

1. Female officers tend to take formal action less often than their male counterparts.
2. Women officers act less aggressively than male officers.
3. Women officers seem to diffuse potential violence more effectively than male officers.
4. Women officers suffer less than men from feelings of alienation, job dissatisfaction, and high authoritarianism.

It is necessary to interpret these differences with caution. The amount of time and experience in a profession and the level of acceptance by the work group can influence work-related behavior. In a study of jail personnel, Rankin and Easterday found no significant attitudinal differences between sworn officers and civilian staff.[43] The authors argue that this similarity in attitude is due, in large part, to the fact that both civilians and sworn officers develop an awareness of the problems and pressures of the job and that this awareness influences staff attitudes more than their particular employment classification or background. Thus, on one hand, it may be suggested that women officers haven't been in the profession long enough to "develop an awareness of the problems and pressures on their job." On the other hand, this isolation from the sub-culture may allow women officers to develop their own awareness of job pressures and problems without the (possibly biasing) effects of tutelage by older officers. Further, as women in our society, they may bring other values and modes of behaving to this situation that could benefit police and corrections work.

METHODOLOGY

As noted earlier, it is the intent of this study to explore three issues relevant to the employment of female correctional officers in all-male institutions. Those issues are:

1. The reactions of residents to female correctional officers.
2. The reactions of male officers and supervisors to female officers.
3. The ability of female officers to function effectively in various positions within the institution.

The following four institutions were chosen as sites in which these three areas could be studied:

1. Wisconsin State Prison—Waupun (maximum security)
2. Wisconsin Correctional Institute—Fox Lake (medium security)
3. Kettle Moraine Correctional Institute (medium security)
4. Wisconsin Correctional Institute—Oakhill (minimum security)

Interviews and questionnaire distribution occurred at only the first three institutions. Oakhill was the site at which the participant observation phase of this research occurred. As noted earlier, the security level and privacy accomodations (two variables that seem to be related to each other) may affect the performance of women guards. Therefore, in order to both increase the external validity of this present research and address security level as it affects women guards, test institutions with various security classifications (all of which employ women officers) were chosen.

In order to effect a successful analysis of the above issues, the following data collection techniques were employed:

1. Face-to-face interviews with both male and female officers at three test institutions.
2. Distribution of attitudinal questionnaires to a sample of inmates at three test institutions.
3. Participant observation at a fourth test institution.

A questionnaire, designed to assess attitudes toward women officers, was distributed to a random sample of 40 residents at each of three test institutions (KMCI, WSP, and WCI—Fox Lake). This questionnaire was pre-tested by a small group of inmates and guards at WCI-Oakhill. A Likert scale was used to facilitate analysis. To prevent against response bias, the data collection instrument was structured so that half of the items reflected a positive attitude toward women while the other half reflected a negative attitude.

In an attempt to create the least amount of inconvenience and to insure that security requirements were not violated, the institutions were invited to have input on any research area in which the manner of implementation was felt to be problematic. As a result, questionnaire distribution was slightly different at each test institution.[44]

A small sample of correctional officers at each of the three test institutions was chosen to participate in an unstructured, face-to-face interview. It was the intent of these interviews to assess staff attitudes toward female correctional officers. All of the female officers at each institution were interviewed. Additionally, six male officers from each institution were selected to participate in an interview.[45] Because of the lack of previous research in this area, it was felt that an unstructured interview schedule would encourage respondents to discuss any aspect of the topic they felt was relevant, thus facilitating a more sensitive analysis of the issues than would otherwise have been possible.

While an attempt was made to select officers as randomly as possible, time constraints and institutional security prohibited interviewing third-shift officers (11:00 p.m. to 7:00 a.m.) in the same proportion as officers from the other two shifts. Because the participant observation phase of the study revealed attitudinal differences among shifts, the lack of a good, stratified sample may have biased the interview results somewhat.[46] Alternatively, one can suggest that the lack of a proportionate number of third-shift officers would have little impact because of their isolation from both inmates and other officers. It is, however, unclear exactly to what extent and in what direction the bias (if any) did occur.

Finally, it seemed that the best way to gain a broad overview of the role and status of women correctional officers in male facilities was through participant observation of women officers in a male prison. Therefore, on August 16, 1977 the author accepted a position as a correctional officer at an all-male, minimum security prison in Wisconsin where she remained employed for approximately ten months. The researcher was one of the first two women hired for any officer position at Oakhill; however, during the course of the ten-month participant observation study, six more women guards were hired.

RESEARCH FINDINGS

1. *Response Rate.* Of the 120 inmates randomly selected to participate in this study, 79 percent (95) completed and returned questionnaires. The majority of those persons were single and between the ages of 20 and 30. Most had no post-high school education and had been incarcerated for 6 to 24 months at the time of the study. A comparison of specific demographic information about the inmate respondents with data detailing such characteristics for the total adult population in Wisconsin's correctional institutions reveals a similarity between characteristics of the sample population and the total population. One difference, however, is that the age of the total population is somewhat younger than that of the sample population (e.g., more persons in the total population are in the "below 20" classification, and fewer are in the "40 and above" classification). Because analysis of the questionnaire data revealed an association between the prisoner/respondent age and attitude toward female correctional officers, this age difference between the sample population and the total population may somewhat affect the external validity of the study.[47]

Finally, the responses of the maximum and medium security samples reflect some attitudinal differences.[48] This is of consequence because the medium security sample included a somewhat larger number of cases. As a result, the responses of the total sample population may more heavily reflect the (different) attitudes of medium security inmates.

2. *Reaction of Male Prisoners Toward Female Officers.* Analysis of inmate questionnaires indicates a moderately positive attitude toward women correctional officers. (Table 1 presents the data resulting from the questionnaires). There were, however, a large number of neutral responses. This may indicate that many inmates simply don't care about the sex of their "captors." As one respondent wrote, "A screw is a screw whether it's a male or a female."

As one might predict, there was a correlation between attitude and respondent's age[49] and education.[50] The data show a relationship between attitude and length of incarceration.[51] Because the wives of prisoners are said to resent the use of female correctional officers, one might expect to find an association between attitude and marital status. This, however, was not the case.[52]

Many residents indicated that the presence of women officers improves the atmosphere of the institution. A majority of respondents agreed that "the presence of women officers in male institutions improves the atmosphere of the institution" (58 percent) and that, "the presence of women officers has a tendency to reduce tension and hostility" (49 percent). Seventy-two percent agreed that "most residents are more careful about good grooming and behavior when there are female officers present." One respondent wrote, "I think it is real beautiful that Waupun have the female officers working here: It's an honor." Another man wrote, "It makes me feel more like a human being." Along similar lines, another respondent indicated that, "They (women officers) seem to bring a feeling of not being incarcerated . . . a little pizzazz into prison life." Many respondents alluded specifically to the aesthetic aspect of environmental change brought about by women officers and commented that it was nice to see a "pretty face," hear a "soft voice," and not have to "look at bearded faces all of the time." One respondent wrote, "I feel that it adds a little pleasantness to the atmosphere . . . anyone likes to see a woman smile."

Responses from the questionnaire indicated that, in general, the threat of physical assault by a resident was not a real concern for female guards. Only 14 percent of the respondents indicated that most residents would be more likely to threaten a female officer than a male officer. If such an assault were to occur, 65 percent of the respondents indicated that they would be more likely to protect a female officer than a male. While most respondents did indicate that it would be unlikely for a female to be the target of an inmate attack, several inmates did question the efficacy with which a female could break up a fight between two inmates or exercise the necessary physical force to preserve institutional order. One respondent, however, wrote, " . . . a female may be able to work things out where a male may cause a bigger hassle."

None of the research techniques employed uncovered even one incident where a female officer was the object of physical abuse by a resident. Further, this researcher, as an officer, never felt herself to be a more vulnerable "target" than her male counterparts. While none of the female officers in this study expressed concern over the possibility of physical assault, all of the male officers interviewed (and most of the male officers with which this author interacted during the participant observation phase of this study) indicated great concern about the ability of female officers to protect themselves, other officers, and inmates.

It is obvious that sex is an issue of some concern to persons segregated within a single-sexed, total institution. Opportunity for interaction with

Table 1 Responses to the Inmate Questionnaire

Questionnaire Item	Agree	Neutral	Disagree	Total Number of Respondents for Each Item
1. The presence of women correctional officers improves the atmosphere of the institution.	55 (58%)	20 (21%)	20 (21%)	95 (100%)
2. The majority of residents feel that female officers are more easily conned than male officers.	23 (24%)	26 (27%)	46 (48%)	95 (99%)*
3. Most residents feel that female officers do their job as well as male officers.	59 (62%)	17 (18%)	19 (20%)	95 (100%)
4. Most residents will try harder to obey the rules when supervised by female officers than by males.	35 (37%)	30 (32%)	30 (32%)	95 (101%)*
5. The presence of women officers make the lack of sex more frustrating.	38 (40%)	19 (20%)	38 (40%)	95 (100%)
6. Most residents would be more likely to threaten women than men officers.	14 (15%)	15 (16%)	66 (69%)	95 (100%)
7. Most residents would be more likely to protect a women officer who is being physically threatened.	62 (65%)	17 (18%)	16 (17%)	95 (100%)
8. Most women officers will have a great deal of difficulty with residents making improper advances at them.	34 (36%)	22 (23%)	39 (41%)	95 (100%)

Statement				
9. Women officers have a harder time gaining resident respect than male officers.	26 (27%)	18 (19%)	51 (54%)	95 (100%)
10. Most male officers don't like to work with female officers in all-male correctional institutions.	53 (56%)	26 (27%)	16 (17%)	95 (100%)
11. Most women officers will be as effective in tense situations as male officers.	36 (38%)	22 (23%)	37 (39%)	95 (100%)
12. Most residents resent having women in all-male institutions.	26 (27%)	22 (23%)	47 (49%)	95 (99%)*
13. The presence of women officers will reduce homosexuality.	21 (22%)	21 (22%)	53 (55%)	95 (99%)*
14. The presence of women officers has a tendency to reduce tension and hostility within an institution.	47 (48%)	18 (19%)	30 (32%)	95 (100%)
15. Most residents are more careful about good behavior when there are female officers present.	68 (72%)	13 (14%)	14 (15%)	95 (101%)*
16. There should be more female officers in all-male institutions.	60 (63%)	18 (19%)	17 (18%)	95 (100%)
17. It's all right for a woman officer to supervise a housing unit alone.	39 (41%)	17 (18%)	39 (41%)	95 (100%)
18. Residents are not as free to say what they want when there are women officers in all-male institutions.	49 (52%)	14 (15%)	32 (34%)	95 (101%)*
19. Residents tend to compete jealously for the attention of female officers.	31 (33%)	25 (26%)	39 (41%)	95 (100%)

*Percentages do not total 100% due to rounding.

the opposite sex is severely limited and controlled in prisons. Buffum,[63] suggests that these very restrictions, and a concommitant lack of social cues suggestive of sexual activity, inhibits sexual responsiveness. This may suggest that the employment of women correctional officers in male institutions would be a particular hardship for prisoners in that it would make the lack of sex more frustrating. A significant minority (36 percent) also felt that female officers would have a great deal of difficulty with residents making improper advances at them. One respondent wrote:

> They (women) come here looking and smelling good; what's a man that's done a lot of time supposed to think . . . I feel a woman officer makes the men more uptight. Every man out to out-do one another. . . .

In addition, 33 percent of the respondents felt that residents compete jealously for the attention of female officers.

It is clear that there is some inmate consensus about the fact that the employment of women officers makes the lack of sex more frustrating to prisoners. However, there was not the *overwhelming* agreement that had been anticipated. Despite this, most of the male officers represented in this study (both through interviews and the participant observation phase) indicated that the sexual attractiveness of women officers was a serious problem. One male officer stated:

> If a woman is nice to a resident in line with doing their job, the residents blow it out of proportion and fall in love with them (the woman). They (the residents) don't understand that the woman is just doing her job.

Another male officer stated, "The potential for rape is greater for women. This (homosexual rape) is a possibility for male guards also, but it is less of a possibility. . . . Also, a woman may take a liking to one of the residents. . . . "

In summary, it is clear that the women officers are not disliked by the male inmates. In fact, quite to the contrary, the women seem to be received quite positively by the inmates. One of the primary reasons the women are so greatly liked is that they fulfill a role as sex objects to the inmates. Another reason they are liked (one which is not necessarily inconsistent with the first) by the inmates is because of their different style of intervention. This assertion is verified by the participant observation stage of this research which revealed that male officers who adopted this less aggressive style of intervention are also well liked.

3. *Reaction of the Male Officers Toward the Women Officers.* Both participant observation and interviews indicated that the male officers initially responded to the female guards with hostility. Additionally, 56 percent of the inmate respondents indicated that male officers resented females. The fact that

even inmates were aware of the hostility of male officers toward female officers is significant because officers are counseled in their training, by the officer subculture and by their supervisors, to present a unified front to inmates. Furthermore, while interview results suggest that this hostility decreased with time, participant observation suggests that, rather than disappearing, the hostility simply became less visible.

This study revealed much speculative interest in the sexual activities of the female officers and thus is consistent with the literature on women in law enforcement. During the participant observation phase of the study, this researcher heard a variety of allegations about the sexual behavior of on-duty female officers. These rumors involved almost two-thirds of *all* female officers employed in Wisconsin's male facilities.[54] Sexual interaction was alleged to have occurred between female officers and both male officers and male inmates; such interaction was asserted to have occurred in a variety of "nooks and crannies" within the institutions (from cornfield to institution library). Rumors traveled from institution to institution via a very effective communication network and came complete with names and other specifics.

Most of the officers who were interviewed, both male and female, verified the existence of sexual rumors about the women. This verification was not solicited in any way by the interviewer. One male interviewee said, of a female colleague, "She gave half of the male population the 'clap' (i.e., venereal disease)." That such a sensitive topic was discussed with an unknown researcher by over half of those interviewed suggests this issue generates intense feelings.

Most of the allegations of sexual misconduct made against the women were spread informally through the officer subculture. Very few of the rumors involved a formal complaint to (or investigation by) prison officials. This lack of investigation is perhaps more debilitating to the integrity of female officers because they are never found "innocent" or "guilty." Instead, they are forever under suspicion of sexual deviance. Thus, sexual harassment is perpetuated. It was clear from both formal interviews and informal interaction with the female officers that these rumors not only caused much discomfort but, in addition, have created employment-related problems. At least one officer quit her job, while another woman asserts that, although ostensibly terminated for an inability to communicate well, she was fired for sex-related reasons. A third woman, on leave during the time of the interview, was uncertain about whether she would return to her job because of the rumors about her unborn child's heritage. Another woman, under an investigation for (allegedly) having intercourse in the institution kitchen with a male colleague, was removed temporarily from her shift, while the male officer remained untouched. Finally, another woman was, at the time of writing, deciding whether to file civil charges of slander against two male colleagues who had made unfounded sexual allegations about her. It could, of course, be argued that the women have simply imagined these rumors in response to their marginal acceptance by the officer subculture. However, the existence of these rumors can be verified by the fact that male interviewees also admitted these allegations. Furthermore, the problem had become so acute at Oakhill that, during an officer in-service training session, prison administrators admonished all staff from further involvement in such behavior.

It is difficult to explain why this phenomenon exists. One possible explanation is that once a woman steps outside of her accepted stereotype (for example, by taking a "man's job"), she is no longer considered a "normal" woman. Consequently, she is defined as a deviant. That these allegations of deviance result in sexual harassment is an ironically "fitting" punishment for a woman who chooses to go beyond her traditional sexual role.

An additional alternative interpretation of this phenomenon can be found in an examination of the correctional officer sub-culture. The existence of this subrosa culture was discovered during the participant observation phase of the study and was verified in the literature by David Duffee[55] and others. While the Oakhill officer group was somewhat lacking in cohesion, there were specific mores which informally governed many aspects of job-related behavior (e.g., interaction with prison administrators). Some of the primary tenets of this subgroup seemed to be:

1.   Don't be too friendly with the inmates. Don't get involved; it's just a job.
2.   Don't allow yourself to be "conned." Never take the side of an inmate.
3.   Don't "make waves."
4.   Stand up for your brother officer whether he's right or wrong. Don't "snitch" . . . solidarity among officers is important.
5.   Don't trust the people "up front" (e.g., prison administrators).

Even though Oakhill officers were not unified in many respects, the above rules received at least lip service from the majority of officers. "Punishment" of some form was meted out to those who deviated from subcultural norms. For example, non-participants in a union strike did not conform to the rule stressing officer solidarity. As a result, those officers were ostracized from the work group. Because there is an effective intra-institution communication network, non-strikers were unable to escape negative sanctions by transferring to another facility.

Women do not fit easily into this sub-culture. They already threaten the professional status quo (or "made waves") simply by their presence. Both participant observation and interview results revealed that women were severely resented by male officers even before they began their first day on the job. Furthermore, as indicated by responses to the open-ended questions on the inmate questionnaire, interviews and participant observation, female officers use a more personal method of interaction with inmates than the male officers. This is consistent with the literature on sex-related differences which suggests that women have a higher need to affiliate and is contrary to the norm which stresses the importance of impersonal interaction with inmates. Finally, interviews and participant observation indicate that women officers were often thought to be more easily "conned" than their male counterparts: this is also in violation of subcultural norms. These deviations from group mores kept women on the periphery of the work group. Because of this, females had even less loyalty to group norms. This, in turn, alienated them further from their co-workers. Sexual rumors may be punishment for this perceived separation from the sub-culture and its governing mores.

4. *Job Performance of Women Officers.* Both male and female officers seemed confused about how women should function in cases where privacy was a concern. While women officers could not "strip search" a male resident except in "emergency situations," the term "emergency situation" was never clearly defined. Confusion seemed to exist about whether or not females could "pat search" the men. One female guard said, "One day they tell me I must 'shake down' the men, and the next day they say I can't." Similar situations include medical appointments in the community (i.e., if a woman guard "escorts" a male prisoner, should he disrobe in her presence or should she wait elsewhere and increase the potential for escape, contraband smuggling, etc.), surveillence of bathrooms and shower areas, etc.).

Continued uncertainty in these areas seem to have generated negative consequences. The women are hesitant about doing "pat searches," etc. because they don't know from day-to-day what their role is. The male guards, on the other hand, feel that the women are avoiding a major (unpleasant) part of their job-related responsibilities. One male guard said, "the worst part of this job is 'shaking down' those grungy mother f__."

While neither the Division of Correction, nor the courts, have yet made any definitive decision about privacy concerns, it is clear that both the structural accommodations and the security level of the particular institution will influence any such decision. Additionally, it seems important to note that medical practitioners have been immune from censure for examining opposite-sexed persons in various stages of undress. While this situation is not analogous in many respects to that of a woman guard in a male institution, it seems worthwhile to remember the existence of such professional immunity. It is possible that a similar type of immunity—although certainly *much* more limited—be granted to female guards.

CONCLUSION

The employment of female correctional officers in male correctional facilities is very new. There is almost no research which addresses this specific issue. Because of the lack of previous research, several techniques were used to explore this topic: (1) participant observation; (2) unstructured, face-to-face interviews; (3) inmate questionnaires; and (4) review of other relevant research.

In general, the reaction of the residents to the women guards seemed positive. However, the employment of women guards had some unfavorable consequences for male residents. Many men felt at least some frustration because they could "look at but not touch" the women guards. Privacy was also a problem. Despite a desire to interact with persons of the opposite sex, most men did not like to perform intimate bodily functions in view of female officers.

There is some confusion about the role of female officers in situations where privacy is a concern. The fact that there is confusion about this rather critical dilemma indicates that the Wisconsin Division of Corrections has either neglected to provide a clear policy statement or has failed to effectively communicate this policy to relevant staff of the individual institutions. This lack of a definitive stance by the division seems to exacerbate not only the existing hostility between male and female officers, but also the potential for a civil suit. While the almost nonexistent case law on this issue clearly provides little guidance, the division can ill-afford to allow policy to remain its current amorphous form.

All of the research techniques employed uncovered some hostility of male officers toward women officers. Most of the officers who were interviewed indicated that this hostility decreased after the women had been employed for a while. This is consistent with the literature. Additionally, participant observation suggested that, ostensibly at least, time did lessen this initial hostility. However, observation also suggested that the hostility rather than abating simply became less visible. As suggested in the text of this report, such dormant hostility seems to be manifested in a covert fashion (e.g., sexual rumors, "setting the women up," etc.).

Questionnaire responses indicated that the majority of respondents felt women officers do their jobs as well as male officers. However, interviews and questionnaires did reveal some concern about the ability of women to maintain institutional order and to protect themselves and others. That is clearly a concern in defining a guard's ability to function effectively. However, whether this concern is valid or simply a function of a stereotypic bias is unclear. The literature points to the superior effectiveness of women in diffusing potential violence. Questionnaire responses, however, rather evenly divided on this issue (statement No. 11). If this perceived superiority does exist (and at least one study suggests that it does not), it is not clear what causes it. Whether it is a function of chivalrous behavior on the part of men (and, hence, perhaps a short-lived phenomena), a different style of intervention used by women or some other subtle factor is not known.

There are, of course, a multitude of other factors to consider in employing female guards in male institutions. This study has attempted to address some of them. Some have deliberately been neglected. For example, it has been proposed that the use of female staff affects rehabilitation in a positive sense and facilitates reintegration of the offender into society. While an interesting assertion, this issue is clearly beyond the scope of the current study.

Notes

1 Revised version of this paper was presented at the American Society of Criminology meeting, November 1980. The author would like to thank Andrew Basinas and Larry Alberts, administrators at WCI-Oakhill, where participant observation phase of this study was conducted. Although employing a social science researcher as a prison guard could have been threatening to many prison administrators, both men gave me their full support. A very special thanks goes to David Pope of the Wisconsin Division of Corrections; Tom Eversen and William Rankin from the Wisconsin Council on Criminal Justice; Professor Michael Hakeem of the University of Wiconsin; and Dr. Robert Petersen of Abt Computer Graphics, Inc.

2 Until recently, women did not even fill traditionally female positions (e.g., clerical, nurses, etc.) in all-male institutions.

3 Interview with Officer Utterback of the LaCrosse Police Department, LaCrosse, Wisconsin, June 1979.

4 Employee evaluations (dated November 1975) for the first two women correctional officers hired at Wisconsin Correctional Institution, Fox Lake.

5 Hindman, R., "A Survey Related to the Use of Female Law Enforcement Officers," *The Police Chief*, 1975.

6 Silverman and Vega, *Women Peace Officers as Viewed by Their Male Counterparts in Three Different Police Departments*, Department of Crime and Justice, University of South Florida.

7 Bloch, P. and D. Anderson, *Policewomen on Patrol: A Final Report*, Washington, D.C.: Police Foundation, 1974.

8 Hamilton, M., *Police in America*, New York: Arno Press, 1971.

9 Silverman and Vega, *supra* n. 6.

10 Knoohuizen, B. and R. Gutman, *Women in Police Work in Chicago*, A Report of the Chicago Law Enforcement Study Group, Evanston, Illinois, 1974.

11 Fleming, A., *New on the Beat: Women Power in the Police Force*, New York: McCann and Geaghegan, Inc., 1975.

12 Bloch and Anderson, *supra* n. 7.

13 Eisenburg and Wall, *Police Personnel Practices in State and Local Government*, Washington, D.C.: Police Foundation, December 1973.

14 Auger, Calvin, Warden of Iowa State Men's Reformatory, in a letter to Darrell Kolb, Security Chief of Wisconsin Division of Corrections, May 7, 1975.

15 *Women and the Criminal Justice System: Training Seminar Report and Recommendations*, University of Montana, May 1975.

16 Milton, C., *Women in Policing*, Washington, D.C.: Police Foundation, 1972.

17 Griggs v. Duke Power Company, 401 U.S. 224, 431 (1971).

18 Smith v. City of East Cleveland, 363 F. Supp. 1131 (N.D. Ohio, 1973).

19 *Ibid.*

20 Petition submitted by a prisoner incarcerated at the Wisconsin State Prison, Waupun, Dodge County Circuit Court, State of Wisconsin.

21 A formal complaint dated February 9, 1978 filed through the inmate complaint system at Kettle-Moraine Correctional Institution.

22 Long v. California State Personnel Board, 116 Cal. Rptr. 562 (1974).

23 Yaffe, B., Attorney, Wisconsin Department of Administration, memo re Dorthard v. Rawlinson to Robert Fox II, Director of Affirmative Action Office, September 6, 1977.

24 "When Women Cops Get the Ax in Boise," in *Mother Jones*, August 1977.

25 A letter to Manuel Carbollo, Secretary, Department of Health and Social Services, January 18, 1975.

26 Milton, *supra* n. 16.

27 Silverman and Vega, *supra* n. 6.

28 Henderson, Sgt. Gary, Officer, WCI-Fox Lake, in an Incident Report dated September 9, 1976.

29 Bloch and Anderson, *supra* n. 7.

30 Sherman, Lewis, in a personal interview on February 13, 1974 regarding an in-progress evaluatory project on women patrol officers.

31 Milton, *supra* n. 16.

32 Fleming, *supra* n. 11.

33 *Ibid.*

34 Silverman and Vega, *supra* n. 6.

35 Bloch, Anderson, and Gervais, *Policewomen on Patrol*, Washington, D.C.: Police Foundation, 1973.

36 *Ibid.*

37 Sherman, L., "A Psychological View of Women in Policing," *Journal of Police Science and Administration*, December 1973.

38 *Ibid.*

39 Taney, "Women in Law Enforcement: An Expanded Role," *Police Magazine*, November/December 1969.

40 Personal interview with Police Chief Wayne Heikkela, Menominee Police Department, September 1978, Menominee, Wisconsin.

41 Bloch and Anderson, *supra* n. 7.

42 Ayas, R., "The Mental Miasmas—A Police Personnel Problem," *Police III*, July/August 1959; Chivast, J., "Value Conflicts in Law Enforcement," *Journal of Crime and Delinquency*, 1965.

43 Rankin, W. and J. Easterday, *Survey of Attitudes and Perceptions of Custodial Staff in Jails: Civilian Versus Sworn Officers*, Madison, Wisconsin, Wisconsin Council on Criminal Justice. Presented to the National Conference on Criminal Justice Evaluation, Washington, D.C., February 23, 1977.

44 At one institution the researcher personally distributed and monitored the question-

naire and verbally explained the background of the study and instructions for questionnaire completion. At the third institution the questionnaires were distributed by the inmate "runner" to the selected respondents during a time when all inmates were locked in their cells. All of these questionnaires had an attached cover letter explaining the purpose of the study and instructions for questionnaire completion.

[45] Although the researcher was employed as a correctional officer at the time of data collection, it was decided that her status remain confidential in order to insure unbiased research results. Despite all attempts at concealment, there were occasions when the researcher's dual role became known. However, the information was not divulged to any person directly participating in the study. Therefore, it was felt that research results were not biased in any appreciable way.

[46] Differences between the shifts include the following: Because first shift hours (7:00 am to 3:00 am) are the most sought-after, only the men with the greatest seniority are "rewarded" with this shift. As a result, officers on this shift are more experienced. The requirements of their job have become routinized and on-the-job decisionmaking is less tension producing than it is for rookies.

[47] In order to speculate on the magnitude and direction of this bias, it seems important to note that the age of the sample was lowered by not including Wisconsin Correctional Institution-Green Bay. This is an adult institution which houses the majority of young adult offenders sentenced under the Youthful Offender Act. Thus the more youthful age of those responding to the questionnaires was not the result of a self-selection process (i.e., a process whereby persons with certain attitudes/characteristics select themselves out of a sample by non-response) which would have introduced a more damaging attitudinal bias than would the pragmatic exclusion of a prison with younger offenders.

[48] Chi square analysis was significant at the .001 level with four degrees of freedom.

[49] Chi square analysis was significant at the .001 level with six degrees of freedom.

[50] Chi square analysis was significant at the .001 level with four degrees of freedom.

[51] Chi square analysis was significant at the .001 level with four degrees of freedom.

[52] Chi square analysis was significant at the .10 level with four degrees of freedom.

[53] Buffum, P., *Homosexuality in Prison,* U.S. Department of Justice, Law Enforcement Assistance Administration, February 1972.

[54] There were almost no rumors involving allegations of male sexual misconduct; those rumors that did circulate involved males as only a peripheral figure (i.e., as a partner to a female officer) and were stated in a laudatory rather than disparaging manner.

[55] Duffee, David, "The Officer Subculture," 1972.

References

Ayas, R. "The mental miasmas—A police personnel problem," Police III, July/August, 1959; Chivast, J. "Value conflicts in law enforcement," in Journal of Crime and Delinquency, 1965.

Bloch, P. and Anderson, D. Policewomen on Patrol: A Final Report, Washington, D.C.: Police Foundation, 1974.

Bloch, Anderson, and Gervais, Policewomen on Patrol, Washington, D.C.: Police Foundation, 1973.

Buffum, P. Homosexuality in Prison, U.S. Department of Justice, Law Enforcement Assistance Administration, February 1972.

Duffee, David. "The officer subculture," 1972.

Eisenburg, Kent and Wall. Police Personnel Practices in State and Local Government, Washington, D.C.: Police Foundation, December 1973.

Fleming, A. New on the Beat: Women Power in the Police Force. New York: McCann and Geaghegan, Inc., 1975

Griggs v. Duke Power Company, 401 U.S. 224, 431 (1971).

Hamilton, M. Police in America. New York: Arno Press, 1971.

Hindman, R. "A survey related to the use of female law enforcement officers," in The Police Chief, 1975.

Knoohuizen, B. and Gutman, R. Women in Police Work in Chicago. A Report of the Chicago Law Enforcement Study Group, Evanston, Illinois, 1974.

Long v. California State Personnel Board, 116 Cal Rptr. 562, (1974).

Milton, C. Women in Policing. Washington, D.C.: Police Foundation, 1972.

Rankin, W. and Easterday, J. "Survey of attitudes and perceptions of custodial staff in jails: civilian versus sworn officers." Madison, Wisconsin: Wisconsin Council on Criminal Justice. Presented to the National Conference on Criminal Justice Evaluation, Washington, D.C., February 23, 1977.

Sherman, L. "A Psychological View of Women in Policing," in Journal of Police Science and Administration, December 1973.

Silverman and Vega. Women Peace Officers as Viewed by Their Male Counterparts in Three Different Police Departments. Department of Crime and Justice, University of South Florida.

Smith v. City of East Cleveland, 363 F. Supp. 1131 (N.D. Ohio, 1973).

Smith v. City of East Cleveland, 363 F. Supp. 1131, 1141 (N.D. Ohio, 1973).

Taney. "Women in law enforcement: an expanded role," in Police Magazine, November/December 1969.

University of Montana. Women and the Criminal Justice System: Training Seminar Report and Recommendations. University of Montana, 1975.

PART 4

The Future

Introduction

This final section on future directions of women and the criminal justice system should be understood as a modest beginning, not a conclusion.

The chapter by Rafter and Natalizia was chosen for several reasons. First, the authors capture many issues that have been considered important throughout this book on women, institutionalized sexism, and the criminal justice system. In fact, they make reference to several of the articles included in this book and recognize the importance of looking at women in the criminal justice system as offenders, as victims, and as employees. Second, they not only pose questions and present a theoretical analysis, but they make noteworthy recommendations on how women might resist the effects of sexism operative in the criminal justice system today. It is hoped that the readers will explore in detail the varied recommendations that Rafter and Natalizia make throughout the chapter.

This chapter illustrates the nature of a radical critique of the criminal justice system in relation to women. Historically, while traditional criminology and sociology studied social deviance, it was the radical or marxist criminologists who began to look at the underlying power relationships between those groups who defined deviance, the groups who became defined as deviant, as well as the societal response to deviance. Thus, the major scholarly critique of the inequities that operate within the criminal justice system originated with the radical criminological community. Rafter and Natalizia follow in this tradition.

Rafter and Natalizia argue that sexism is not mere prejudice but a function of capitalism. Therefore, with the elimination of capitalism, women's oppression, including that within the criminal justice system, should end. We would argue, on the other hand, that capitalism did not invent sexism, nor will the oppression of women simply disappear under other political and economic systems. Yet, sexist relations take on their own particular form within the context of contemporary capitalism and are an important element in understanding and changing the treatment of women throughout our own criminal justice system.

The postscript to this book was written with three goals in mind: to demonstrate to the reader (1) that long-term forecasts are difficult at this point to make; (2) that the issues as developed in the preceding chapters require thought, research, and action directed toward changing the sexist nature of society and its impact on the criminal justice system; and (3) that no simple solutions exist for the problems that are raised throughout the readings. It is also in this spirit that the editors in the postscript have tried to point out their own differences, as well as similarities, in their understanding of the problems women face as offenders, victims, and criminal justice workers. It is the responsibility of all those concerned about these problems and issues to look at the variety of theoretical and empirical approaches and evaluate all the available material in understanding the causes, consequences, and future directions of women and their relationship to the criminal justice system.

26

Marxist Feminism: Implications for Criminal Justice

Nicole Hahn Rafter and Elena M. Natalizia

CAPITALISM, SEXISM, AND THE DILEMMAS OF RESISTANCE

Capitalism and sexism are intimately related, and it is this relationship that accounts for the inferior status traditionally given to women by the American criminal justice system. Sexism is not merely the prejudice of individuals; it is embedded in the very economic, legal, and social framework of life in the United States. The criminal justice system, as one part of that institutional framework, reflects the same sexist underpinning that is evidenced throughout capitalist society.

Capitalism relies upon the traditional structure of monogamy and the nuclear family to fulfill its economic potential. The division of labor essential to the capitalist system is one that cuts off those who produce from control over the means of production. And it dictates that men shall be the chief producers of goods, while women shall function primarily as nurturers of the next generation of producers. In a capitalist society,

> Men and women are brought up for a different position in the labor force: the man for the world of work, the woman for her family. This difference in the sexual division of labor in society means that the relationship of men as a group to production is different from that of women. . . . Female production in the family means that the commodity producer, the husband, and the future producers, the children, survive to produce commodities which are exchanged. The separation of male/female roles is thus materially as well as ideologically part of the way in which capitalism is maintained.[1]

As long as women continue to accept an auxiliary role within the economic system, capitalism can flourish, especially when supported by other institutions—schools, churches, legal systems—which reinforce women's adherence to traditional sex role models.

The rejection of traditional female roles and increased militancy among

Reprinted by permission of the authors.

working-class women challenge capitalist structures which assume that women are supporters rather than initiators of economic policy. For women to refuse to be relegated either to traditional, nonpaying roles within the family or to unskilled, poorly paid positions in the workplace is a threat to an economic system whose primary goal is maximization of profits.

It becomes clear that, as women struggle for equal access to economic and social power, the enemy is not so much the men who presently exercise that power as it is the capitalist system which assigns males and females to roles that yield the greatest economic profit. The bourgeois, commerce-based mentality which prompts men to exploit women for the sake of economic gain must be overcome if women are to achieve true equality. Recognition of this is essential if we are to restructure the criminal justice system to provide equal rights for women. As Engels has expressed it, "The legal inequality of the two partners [male and female] . . . is not the cause but the effect of the economic oppression of women."[2]

The basic implication of Marxism for feminism, then, is that equality and freedom for women will not be fully realized until the capitalist system is superceded and we develop a classless society—an economic and political system in which men and women share equally in production and its rewards. The ultimate implication of Marxist feminism is, in other words, revolution.

Some Marxist criminologists would stop there. They would deny the possibility of valid Marxist involvement in criminal justice, rejecting efforts to improve upon the current justice system as mere reformism. To attempt to improve a capitalist system of social control, they would argue, is to subscribe to a misguided meliorism which will function, in the long run, merely to bolster capitalism.[3]

On the other hand, it can be argued—and this is the position we endorse here—that to wait until the revolution, to turn one's back on the criminal justice system, especially on the treatment of women by that system, is naive. To respond in such a way is to acquiesce to a status quo which oppresses women and to ignore the pressing problems of women, particularly working-class women, in the here and now. Furthermore, the refusal to deal with current problems is a nondialectical response: It pictures capitalism as a monolithic, undifferentiated monster instead of recognizing that the capitalist system in fact encompasses contradictions—some of which can be used to undercut that system.

Rather than magisterially ignoring the contradictions of capitalism and the needs of women involved in criminal justice (as victims, offenders, practitioners), we must identify, analyze, and use these contradictions to further the cause of economic and social equality. Those who ground their feminism in Marxism must be willing to risk accusations of "mere reformism" as they work to promote both the feminist and Marxist causes. Our argument, in short, is that there is a difference between reformism and resistance.

FEMALES AND THE LAW

Legal policy and structures evolve in response to the particular system of morals prevalent in a given society. This means that, in a capitalist system, law reflects a bourgeois moral code which restricts women to specific roles within the economic scheme. Women are properly chattel of the dominant men in their lives (husbands, fathers, lovers, pimps), and women's work is defined as unworthy of significant remuneration. Violations of the moral code defining women's proper role are labeled deviant and punished by stringent sanctions. Law becomes an instrument of social control over women and a means of preserving the economic status quo.

Historically, the entire justice system in America has been dominated by men. Our legal framework "has been codified by male legislators, enforced by male police officers, and interpreted by male judges. Rehabilitation programs have been administered by males. The prison system has been managed by men, primarily for men."[4] Even more significant to the class analysis presented here, these legal functionaries as representatives of the dominant bourgeois ideology serve as conduits through which bourgeois morality becomes codified in our legal structures. Thus, "in order to understand sexism within the criminal justice system, one must analyze the class nature of that system and how it is rooted in the class structure of advanced monopoly capitalism."[5]

The legal apparatus within capitalist society serves to oppress women in two basic ways. The first is paternalism, the restriction of women through enactment of "chivalrous" statutes ostensibly aimed at their protection. For example, differential sentencing statutes, which allow women to be incarcerated for longer periods than men for similar offenses, have traditionally been justified on the grounds of their rehabilitative potential. Notwithstanding the presumably benevolent motivation behind such legislation, however, it is discriminatory, serving to reinforce the stereotype of women as weak and in need of extra protection by virtue of their "natural differences."

Likewise, chivalrous motives are the ostensible grounds for a particularly discriminatory instrument for the oppression of female juveniles—status offense statutes. These statutes specify that juveniles can be prosecuted for behaviors or conditions that would not be illegal if committed or manifested by an adult, such as running away, incorrigibility, and being in danger of falling into vice. Although theoretically applying to juveniles of both sexes and all economic levels, these laws reflect efforts to uphold bourgeois standards of femininity—standards glorifying submissiveness, docility, and sexual purity. That these statutes function with sexual bias is borne out by studies revealing that the prosecution rate for status offenses is much higher among girls than among boys, and that female status offenders are punished more severely than are boys who commit more serious property or violent offenses.[6] And, as in the case of their adult counterparts, low-income and minority girls bear most of the burden of such sanctions.[7] At an early age, therefore, these girls learn that deviance from economically based sex role patterns will result in legal sanctions, despite the chivalrous intent of our justice system.

The second way in which the legal system oppresses women is through its almost total failure to respond to issues of concern to women. Wife abuse, sexual harassment, incest, rape, production of unsafe methods of birth control, forced sterilization for eugenic purposes—these are critically important problems to women, whose needs the legal system has either failed to consider or has glossed over with token, ad hoc efforts. Such problems, moreover, have the greatest significance for poor and working-class women, indicating that class is at least as critical as sex in the struggle to obtain legal equality for women.

Despite the frequent use of law as a tool of patriarchal capitalism, however, the legal system has the potential for advancing the equality of women. This could be achieved by means of several specific steps, including the following:

1. Adoption of the Equal Rights Amendment. An important means of eliminating discrimination against women of all ages and in all situations, the ERA would make equality of the sexes a fact of law rather than a matter to be determined on an ad hoc basis by judges and legislators. The ERA would require revision of the entire justice system, eliminating sexist wording in statutes, differential sentencing provisions, poorer treatment programs in correctional institutions for women, and so on. In addition, it would provide a strong legal foundation for court action against discriminatory practices within the criminal justice system.

2. Affirmative action toward women and minorities in law-related professions. Active recruitment of women and minorities by the legal profession would help alter the white male-dominated system which presently codifies, administers, and interprets our laws. Such efforts, however, must also ensure that these persons be reasonably representative of the poor and working classes.

3. Removal of status offense jurisdiction from the juvenile courts. Status offenses are matters of morality rather than of law; as such, they should be removed from our legal system and dealt with by nonjudicial means.

This step would rid the system of inherently discretionary laws which are used to discriminate against female juveniles of low-income backgrounds.

THE CRIMINOLOGY OF WOMEN

Like law, traditional criminology embodies capitalist values. Until recently most theorists ignored women entirely, thereby relegating them to their "proper" place of insignificance. The work of those few criminologists who have dealt with women has usually been dominated by stereotypes of the "bad" woman. The main effect of these stereotypes has been to enforce conformity to class-based stereotypes of the good woman, one who (in contrast to the witch, temptress, or prostitute) does not challenge patriarchy. Recently, however, theorists such as Dorie Klein, June Kress, and Carol Smart have challenged the class and sexual biases of traditional criminology, indicating ways in which criminological work on women can be reoriented to serve feminist and Marxist goals.[8]

These critics call for a new criminology of women which will take as its starting point a critical attitude toward sexual stereotypes and their class implications. They also call for a move away from what Smart refers to as "orthodox, control-oriented criminology, which has been involved in serving the needs of administrators and policy-makers,"[9] and the substitution of a new value-oriented theoretical framework based on the needs of women and the underclasses.[10]

What might the research agenda of this new criminology look like? The recommendations that follow indicate some directions that the criminology of women might profitably take in the near future:

1. An important threshold requirement is simply for more data on crime by women and female criminals. As the District of Columbia Commission on the Status of Women pointed out, "The paucity of data on the female offender is only slightly less disturbing than the lack of concern. Neither the criminal justice system nor the public even knows who the female offender is, much less what her needs and problems are."[11] The current failure of key sources to give information by sex often makes impossible the separate or comparative study of females. One obvious means of overcoming the data gap would be to require that government publications on crime present all relevant statistics with breakdowns by sex.

If the vacuum in crucial information is to be filled, another key need is for more "women only" studies—research that focuses on women without necessarily including comparative data on men. With this recommendation, however, go two important qualifications. First, a moratorium should be declared on certain types of "women only" criminological research, such as studies of types of female offenders (e.g., "the prostitute") that do not build into their research designs a focus on social class factors and, as appropriate, the double standard of sexual morality. Second, after "women only" studies have produced a body of information as extensive as that which exists on men, it would be best to abandon most mono-sex research designs. As Michael Hindelang has pointed out,

> Sociologists . . . should incorporate the sex variable into existing and emerging theories. Certainly the tendency of sociological theorists of the 1950's and 1960's to restrict their theories to males *by design* . . . represented a decision to focus on residual variance (after sex had been controlled—i.e., ignored) and thereby represented a missed opportunity to include in theoretical explanations a powerful predictor of involvement in illegal activity.[12]

Generation of data on crime by women and their inclusion in criminological studies will, then, help block the old "assumption that women are inessential and invisible"[13]; the effect will be a general strengthening of the quality of criminological findings.

2. Another major need is for extensive research on the social contexts of crime by women and the punishment of female offenders. Some of the research questions here can be fairly global. For example, what is the relationship between rates of property crime by women and women's restricted access to jobs, especially in periods of economic depression? What relationship obtains at various times and places between criminal justice institutions and others that socially control women (the welfare system, mental health system, and so on)? Others among the research questions should be highly particular, aimed at detailed analyses of the relationship between women's socioeconomic position and the crimes committed by them in specific social contexts, both past and present. What effect, for example, did the banning of midwifery (and concomitant transfer of control over birthing to male physicians) have on the rates of conviction of women for abortion and murder (i.e., death of the mother as a result of abortion) in selected cities in the nineteenth century? How did divorce laws affect conviction rates of women for adultery and bigamy in specific areas in the early twentieth century? Such specialized studies, taking into account the diversity and fluidity of women's history, will help pinpoint the effects of variables such as class, race, and age. They will help reveal the diversities and contradictions of capitalism, showing the varying effects of capitalist social control systems as different groups of women encounter the criminal justice system.

3. Also needed is research on the attitudes of criminal justice personnel toward women who enter the system through a variety of routes (as victims, offenders, and workers within the system). One especially useful subarea of study here would be elucidation of the class relationships be-

tween women who help run the criminal justice system and the female offenders they control.[14]

FEMALES AS VICTIMS

Although women in capitalist society are victimized by the same offenses as are men, some types of victimization are inherently or virtually the domain of women. These include rape, incest, wife abuse, sexual harassment on the job, and prostitution, all of which are rooted in the traditional patriarchal concept of women as sexual chattel.

Rape is an act that symbolizes the political and economic oppression of women in capitalist society. Traditionally, rape has been regarded as a property crime, an offense whose victim is the man whose property (i.e., wife or daughter) has been defiled.[15] This interpretation is reinforced by the fact that, in most jurisdictions, it is legally impossible for a man to rape his wife, for she is his possession and he may demand sexual gratification from her at will.[16] Patriarchal capitalism thus reduces the body and spirit of women to their property value and then takes from them the control over that property.

Furthermore, the handling of rape cases within the criminal justice system, including very low conviction rates for alleged rapists, reinforces notions of woman as temptress and seducer who, in effect, makes herself vulnerable to sexual attack.[17] Rather than viewing rape as an act of violence in which sex is used as an instrument of oppression, the justice system often regards it as the "natural," though perhaps improper, response of males to seductive women.

Closely related to the sexual victimization of adult women is the sexual abuse suffered by young girls at the hands of fathers and other older males in the family. Although incest is a widespread and pervasive problem, it has only recently come to the attention of the criminal justice system. Like rape, incest reflects the patriarchal nature of the family; the father dominates and all other family members, especially women, must submit to his will. In addition to possible physical injury, the incest victim suffers untold emotional damage, particularly if she attempts to prosecute the offender within our complex and often insensitive criminal system.[18]

Wife battering is another common and frightening example of the chattel system under which women have traditionally lived. Recognizing that "a marriage license is for many people a hitting license," Murray Straus sees sexist cultural patterns and institutions as contributors to men's assaultive behavior and women's inability to defend themselves or escape[19] Research confirms this, indicating that wife abuse is most likely to occur in familial patterns most closely following the patriarchal model (the male dominating a nurturing, submissive woman).[20]

The response of the justice system to this problem is dismally inadequate. Although technically husbands can be prosecuted under statutes outlawing assault, battery, or intent to murder,

> the law becomes ambiguous [in its application] when the parties involved are husband and wife. The sanctity of the family home and the adage that a man's home is his castle, which pervade the whole fabric of society, are reflected in the legal system. Police admit that a large percentage of the calls they receive are DD's (domestic disturbances), but they do not differentiate between family "squabbles" and incidents of violence. They seldom make arrests in either case.[21]

Our patriarchal society, by keeping women dependent on their husbands and failing to provide adequate legal protection to abused wives, continues to perpetuate this insidious form of victimization of women.

For many women, sexual harassment on the job has become a form of extortion in which forced sex is the price of a job. Penalties for noncompliance with this type of victimization, which ranges from unwanted staring to forcible rape, include failure to be hired, demotions, and outright firing.[22] A woman who fails to conform to her established role as sex object can be made to feel the full effect of the male economic power structure; and the results for such a woman are often a drop in status and loss of a job.[23]

> Male sexual harassment, which until recently has been a completely acceptable idea . . . , [is] a practice that has kept working women both individually and collectively locked into a position of economic inferiority. Men accordingly have successfully insured their domination of modern work, hence society, because the patriarchy cannot lose control of its material base. The sexual harassment of working women is an issue of enormous significance.[24]

From the perspective of Marxist criminology, the traditional "crime" of prostitution is instead another victimization of women, a matter of sexual slavery rather than sexual immorality. The prostitute may be seen, in fact, as the archetype of woman's traditional role of sex partner to man; however, because she performs this role outside the nuclear family model—and does it for profit—she is punished by bourgeois moral codes upholding a double standard of morality for men and women. Her relationship to a pimp is a pattern of victimization and exploitation, reflecting patriarchal standards and the economic powerlessness of women. But the most serious victimization may be that which the prostitute faces at the hands of the criminal justice system in its discriminatory, class-based enforcement of prostitution laws. K. Davis provided the classic justification for such discrimination:

The professional prostitute being a social outcast may be periodically punished with-out disturbing the usual course of society; no one misses her while she is serving out her term—no one, at least, about whom society has any concern. The man [customer], however, is something more than a partner in an immoral act; he discharges important social and business relations. . . . He cannot be imprisoned without deranging socie-ty.[25]

The social status of white, middle-class, married customers is a protective shield which often guards them against prosecution, keeping them "either invisible to the police or else above the law."[26] The prostitute, on the other hand, is considered "lower class" by virtue of her profession and is regard-ed as an expendable commodity.

What would an alternative, egalitarian system look like in its handling of women as victims? Most important, it would undertake a massive commitment to the female victim, including the following:

1. Mandatory education in public schools on rape, incest, and employ-ment rights. In addition, training of females in self-defense should be offered by the schools.

2. Employment of female staff in all parts of the criminal justice system dealing with female victims.

3. Training of all law enforcement personnel in the problems unique to female victims.

4. Establishment of rape crisis centers and shelters, and of other support systems to encourage bonding among female victims.

5. Encouragement of women who wish to prosecute men who have victimized them, and the provision of legal assistance for these women.

In addition, necessary legal reforms would include the following:

1. Removal of the husband exemption in rape statutes.

2. Making restraining orders against abusive husbands a more effective legal tool for battered women.

3. Recognition of self-defense as a legitimate legal defense for women who retaliate against men who repeatedly batter them.

4. Legalization of prostitution or, at the very least, sanctions directed equally at all parties involved.

5. Adoption of laws criminalizing sexual harassment on the job. Sexual harassment should be established as adequate grounds for leaving a job without forfeiting unemployment compensation.

Such an alternative system would also attempt to demythologize the nuclear family. Freeing women from imprisoning beliefs in the overriding importance of loyalty to the home and hearth would better enable them to leave an abusive husband or family and seek the help they need. The "save the marriage at all costs" philosophy of many law enforcement personnel and judges in dealing with cases of physical and sexual abuse would be abandoned in recognition of the primary need for women to maintain their physical and psychological well-being. Furthermore, all homemakers would be entitled to financial remuneration for their efforts on behalf of their families and would receive equal treatment in all matters pertaining to credit, pensions, contracts, and so on. Thus women who choose the role of wife and mother would still be able to maintain economic independence.

FEMALES AS OFFENDERS

When we look at the female offender, we must keep in mind the subjective nature of crime and deviance as defined by law based on capitalism. Our legal system focuses its attention on individual pathology, particularly of the poor, rather than on exploitative systems in its definitions of crime and deviance.[27] For example, the woman who turns to prostitution as an economic alternative that is superior to working as a waitress or in a factory is labeled criminal: Not only has she violated standards of female purity, but, moreover, in so doing she has demonstrated that she is "sick" and in need of "rehabilitation." Yet at the same time, the corporate executive who knowingly pollutes the environment or manufactures unsafe products is considered to be engaging in normal competitive business practices, often outside the purview of stringent legal sanction. Radical criminology would shift the focus from individual deviance to systemic oppression and exploitation. War-making for profit, inequities between rich and poor, racial and sexual discrimination, denial of basic human rights—these are the true acts of criminality which are largely ignored by the legal system.

Examination of the types of offenses women commit reveals them to be rooted in the subordinate, economically dependent position of women and in the bourgeois morality which our laws embody. Women

are . . . first, petty offenders in the area of "consumerism," which reflects their position as houseworkers in "straight" society. They shoplift, use illicit drugs purchased from men . . . and pass bad checks. Second, they may act as accomplices to men in offenses such as robbery. Third, . . . prostitution affords . . . women the opportunity to earn their living through their sexuality. . . . As surrogate wives and lovers, prostitutes serve the same functions of sexual work and nurturance that other women do. Fourth, women "on the streets" are harassed for vagrancy and drunkenness much as men in their situation are, chivalry notwithstanding. Fifth, juvenile females are apprehended for status offenses, such as running away. And finally, women commit "crimes of passion," primarily against husbands and lovers, and strike out sometimes at children as well, which may reflect emotional frustration created by sexist roles.[28]

The female offender is usually not violent; for the most part, she engages in petty property offenses or crimes that violate traditional concepts of the proper female role.

It has long been held that women offenders fare better than men in the criminal justice system, because of the "chivalry factor" mentioned earlier, which inclines law enforcement and judicial officials to show more leniency to females than to males.[29] Evidence indicates, however, that this chivalrousness benefits some women more than others—in particular, the few white middle- or upper-class women coming in any contact with the criminal justice system. Furthermore, it appears to be extended to female suspects only when they behave in a stereotypic fashion—that is, crying, pleading for release for the sake of their children, claiming that men have led them astray. Female suspects who are hostile and aggressive, on the other hand, are frequently arrested.[30] It seems, then, that "the police might be involved in punishing women who violate their sex-role expectations rather than those who violate the law."[31] Statistics on males and females held in pretrial detention indicate the women are not granted any special leniency at this stage of the criminal justice process. Although fewer women than men are detained awaiting trial, women are jailed for committing much less serious offenses.[32]

The selective application of chivalrousness to affluent white women can be seen in examining the population of our jails and prisons. Historically, chivalry has been a racist and class-based concept; the gallantry of the ideal knight was not extended to the minority or poor woman.[33] Furthermore, "the term chivalry implies basic forms of human interaction befitting a model of political paternalism. If the gentle treatment women are said to enjoy is based on this political inferiority, we should be aware of the high price paid for the so-called benefits of chivalry."[34] Chivalrousness should be seen as a tool for the preservation of patriarchy rather than as a benign effort to treat women with special kindness.

Sexism pervades the juvenile justice system in many of the same ways seen in the adult system. As mentioned previously, status offense statutes are used to punish "immoral," though noncriminal, female juveniles; often, the sanctions are more severe than those given more serious juvenile male offenders. One blatant form of sexism within the juvenile justice system is evident in the frequency with which girls in custody are questioned about their sexual behavior and subjected to vaginal examinations, regardless of the nature of the offense.[35] In 1977, for example, it was reported that all girls brought before family court in New York City were being tested for venereal disease, even if the charge was not sexual in nature.[36] Such practices reflect bourgeois notions of female sexuality.

Likewise, adult women have found themselves victims of a discriminatory, selectively enforced system. Provisions for differential sentencing of males and females for the same offense are a standard part of many states' laws—not all of them operating to women's advantage. As recently as 1973, for example, Iowa statutes provided that a woman could be incarcerated for five years for a misdemeanor while a man could be held for a maximum of one year.[37] Women have been subjected to indeterminate sentences more frequently than men, giving judges and correctional officials the opportunity to hold them longer for identical offenses.[38]

One might expect that such overly sexist practices would be unhesitatingly invalidated by court action. There have been some victories, but equal protection challenges to differential sentencing statutes have generally failed.[39] Rather, our legal system has acted to legitimize sex-based discrimination and denial of equal protection. As Carolyn Temin points out, "The lesson is . . . unavoidable. Freedom from sex-based discrimination will not come through judicial expansion of existing constitutional guarantees. The history of the fight against sex-based discrimination in criminal sentencing statutes presents a strong example of the necessity for the Equal Rights Amendment."[40]

As we emphasized earlier, passage of the ERA would be the cornerstone of an egalitarian system of justice in which women would be afforded full and equal protection of the law. Every form of sexism—both overt and implicit—must be eliminated from our laws. Women of all social classes must be assured of equal treatment at every stage of the criminal justice process, and all vestiges of patriarchal chivalrousness must be rejected as efforts to keep woman in her proper social and economic place in the capitalist hierarchy. Vigorous court action must be taken against discriminatory laws and practices in the justice system, and women who attempt to fight such discrimination must receive full support. Massive educational efforts are also needed so that all women, particularly those of the lower economic strata, are made fully aware of their legal rights and the forms of redress available when those rights are violated.

INCARCERATED WOMEN

For well over a century, the goal of rehabilitation has been the basis for the correctional system's work with female offenders. This goal means, in effect, that offenders are afflicted with the "sickness" of criminality; their cure inevitably takes the form of their being trained to conform to middle-class standards of behavior. In both theory and practice, this is class biased, sexist, and paternalistic. A fundamental implication of Marxist feminism for policy in the incarceration of women is that the old goal of rehabilitation must be replaced by one of empowerment. Whereas rehabilitation implies efforts to change the prisoner, empowerment seeks to offer her opportunities to overcome class-based and sexual oppression. Whereas the goal of rehabilitation assumes the superiority of the rehabilitator, policy guided by the goal of empowerment assumes the integrity of the offender's own value system and seeks to enable her to increase control over her life.

The typical female offender, even before she reaches jail, is already among the persons most victimized by capitalism. She comes from a racial or ethnic minority group, is poor and in poor health, is likely to have a history of physical abuse, and is the sole supporter of one or more children. She is likely to be dependent on alcohol or drugs and has few educational or vocational resources. "Most of these women are caught in a web of dependency which they do not know how to break."[41] While it is surely these women who most need empowerment to overcome class and sexual oppression, our current correctional system operates as if designed to victimize them further.

One way in which jails and prisons oppress female inmates is by encouraging passivity. Health care is poor and seldom addresses the needs of women. Diets are high in starches, resulting in loss of physical energy among inmates and in weight gains.[42] Psychotropic drugs are often administered freely, to ensure inmate passivity.[43] These institutions offer little in the way of recreation—indeed, in many jails there are no opportunities for women to exercise.[44] The inmates' lack of access to people who might help (lawyers, nurses, or even—as in the Joan Little case—a matron who might help ward off attackers) also contributes to passivity.

Second, jails and prisons oppress female inmates by encouraging conformity to sex role stereotypes. The sexual biases of our penal institutions are perhaps most vividly demonstrated by the numerous studies showing that, in nearly all respects, women's institutions are inferior to those for men.[45] That is, correctional systems start with the assumption that discrimination may occur on the basis of sex. So it is not surprising that women's institutions stress sex role socialization. Women in prison are perpetually infantilized by routines and paternalistic attitudes ("Time to get up, girls") which make them feel weak, helpless, dependent.[46] Programs, when offered, train female prisoners in cleaning, cooking, cosmetology, sewing, typing—in short, train them to serve men or middle-class women and work to resocialize them in "proper" gender roles.[47] Female prisoners are closely watched and sternly punished even for unaggressive homosexual activity.[48] Traditionally, women's prisons have administered to inmates large doses of "moral" training designed to transform fallen women into ladies.

A third way in which jails and prisons oppress women is by severing their ties with the outside world. That it is difficult for incarcerated women to maintain old community ties and establish new ones is, in part, a function of the relative isolation of women's institutions. Many states, in efforts to keep women out of local jails, remove them to other facilities where they have less access to lawyers, visitors, even telephones than do their male counterparts back in the local jails.[49] Women's prisons are often located in rural areas—where, it was believed at the time these institutions were built, inmates could be isolated from evil influences. And there are so few federal prisons for women that federal prisoners are likely to be held at great distances from their homes. Geographic isolation aside, it is also true that there are few opportunities for women to receive furloughs, work release, or release to special programs such as those for substance abusers. For example, Ruth Glick and Virginia Neto found work release opportunities for women to be "extremely rare, involving only two percent of the total prison inmates and one percent of jail inmates."[50]

The current correctional system, then, often operates to entrench female inmates in dependency. How can it reorient itself toward the goal of empowerment?

Central to long-range planning must be the transfer of prisoners from these oppressive institutions to community-based facilities. More immediately, women must be given equal access not only to recreation and job training within the walls but also to furlough programs, work release, and special programs outside. Because women are so often solely responsible for their children, special opportunities should be made for contact visits between mothers and children.[51]

All forms of treatment that reinforce (no matter how unintentionally) conformity to sex roles, from job training to such casual remarks as calling women "girls," should be eliminated. Feminist therapists should be added to staffs, and to ensure that they serve inmates rather than institutional needs, these therapists should not be assigned administrative duties. Administrative grievance procedures should be established in all institutions so that inmates can take action on their own behalf[52]; toward the same end, inmate organizations should be actively encouraged.

Through such means, incarcerated women can be empowered to start breaking the bonds of institutional, sexual, and class oppression.

WOMEN AS CRIMINAL JUSTICE SYSTEM PERSONNEL

From the perspective of Marxist feminism flow two central implications for employment of women in criminal justice. First, equal access to jobs of all types and at all levels must be provided for women generally; and second, access to such jobs must be provided for working-class women in particular.

Hiring and Sex

Of all areas of public service employment, criminal justice probably discriminates most on the basis of sex.

> Despite Federal legislation and numerous court decisions outlawing sex discrimination, women remain underrepresented in every [criminal justice] employment category except clerical and secretarial. They are systematically excluded from many jobs based on irrational and outdated sex role stereotyping, uniformly receive lower pay for the same work as their male counterparts, and are generally denied opportunities for training and career advancement.[53]

But in arguing for equal employment opportunity for women in criminal justice, it is important not to rely on contentions that women are somehow specially qualified for such positions by their sex (not to argue, for example, that the presence of women officers will "cool out" violent situations).[54] This sex-stereotyping argument is self-defeating; its ultimate effect, historically, has been to lock women employees into sex role-specific jobs—of which there are few in criminal justice. Women penetrated the criminal justice system by using this argument,[55] but they simultaneously closed off their access to jobs where "womanliness" might be affronted.

The following recommendations indicate some steps that must be taken if the goal of equal employment in the criminal justice system is to be realized:

1. Affirmative action must be pursued aggressively: Funds should be withheld from and legal action taken against agencies that cannot show, on a yearly basis, significant improvement in the employment of women at all levels.

2. Agencies that are being sexually integrated should provide training to make male personnel sensitive to problems related to sexual discrimination and sexual harassment.

3. Academic programs in criminal justice—and in 1978 there were over 2,300 such programs nationwide—are a major training ground for personnel in the field. Yet despite the enormous potential of these programs for reducing sex biases and encouraging women to enter criminal justice, criminal justice education frequently functions instead to perpetrate traditional prejudices. We recommend that program accreditation and government funds (including student loans and faculty grant support) be withheld from academic programs whose course content shows the presence of sex biases. We also recommend that criminal justice programs take the initiative in boycotting sexist texts, such as those by Donald Gibbons and by Edwin Sutherland and Donald Cressey.[56] Such steps would do

much to ensure that academic programs do not merely breed the prejudices that now bar women from jobs in criminal justice.

4. All future studies of employment by criminal justice agencies must be designed to include data on sex differentials. The *Report of the LEAA Task Force on Women* pointed to the "overwhelming" obstacle to employment of women created by the absence of "systematic collection and analysis of statistics on women employed in criminal justice professions."[57] Yet three years later, an LEAA study entitled (significantly enough) the *National Manpower Survey of the Criminal Justice System* demonstrated nothing so vividly as lack of interest in and commitment to increased employment of women.[58] Like most current publications on hiring in criminal justice, the *Manpower Survey* paid far more attention to racial than sexual imbalances.

Hiring and Social Class

Historically, when the criminal justice system has opened the doors of employment to women, those few permitted to pass through have been either middle-class women or working-class women who identify strongly with middle-class values. The achievement of such women in penetrating new job markets should not be slighted, but it is nonetheless true that the main impact of this achievement has been to strengthen the power of the criminal justice system to impose middle-class values, often sexual in nature, on lower-class offenders.[59]

It is very important, therefore, as women move into criminal justice-related work, that positions be opened mainly to working-class women—those who most need the jobs in any case, and whose presence will minimize the class divisions which have, historically, separated professional from offender. Although it would be naive to hope that even the hiring of sizable numbers of working-class women would bring about real change in the class-supportive functions of the criminal justice system as a whole, such an emphasis would provide a guard against some of the more extreme forms of class-based sex role prejudices which have been imposed, in the past, in the name of justice.

CONCLUSION

The perspective of radical criminology implies dramatic changes for women within criminal justice. With its adoption, women victims, offenders, and professionals would at last receive equal treatment within what has long been an oppressive and discriminatory system. Criminality would be redefined, legal codes revamped, sexist and class-based practices ended, and patriarchal notions of women's proper role within capitalism discard-

ed. Such changes offer a way to resist the current depradations of capitalism, and they would also be steps toward more revolutionary forms of
sexual and economic equality.

Notes

1 Sheila Rowbotham, *Woman's Consciousness, Man's World* (Baltimore, Md.: Penguin Books, 1973), p. 61.

2 Frederick Engels, *The Origin of the Family, Private Property and the State* (New York: International Publishers, 1972), pp. 136-37.

3 This Marxist position is critically analyzed by Steven Spitzer in "Left-Wing Criminology—An Infantile Disorder?" in *Radical Criminology: The Coming Crises*, James A. Inciardi, ed.
(Beverly Hills, Calif.: Sage, 1980), pp. 169-90.

4 Ray R. Price, "The Forgotten Female Offender," *Crime & Delinquency*, April 1977, p. 102.

5 June Kress, "Bourgeois Morality and the Administration of Justice," *Crime and Social
Justice*, Winter 1979, p. 45.

6 Meda Chesney-Lind, "Judicial Enforcement of the Female Sex Role: The Family Court
and the Female Delinquent," *Issues in Criminology*, Fall 1973, pp. 51-69; Law Enforcement
Assistance Administration, *Children in Custody, 1975* (Washington, D.C.: Govt. Printing Office,
1979), p. 8.

7 Meda Chesney-Lind, "Juvenile Delinquency: The Sexualization of Female Crime," *Psychology Today*, July 1974, p. 45.

8 Dorie Klein, "The Etiology of Female Crime: A Review of the Literature," *Issues in
Criminology*, Fall 1973, pp. 3-30; Kress, "Bourgeois Morality and Administration of Justice";
Klein and Kress, "Any Woman's Blues"; Carol Smart, *Women, Crime and Criminology: A Feminist
Critique* (London, England: Routledge & Kegan Paul, 1976).

9 Smart, *Women, Crime and Criminology*, p. 3.

10 Spitzer, "Left-Wing Criminology," p. 181, observes in connection with the issue of
value-oriented criminology that "for Marx and those who seek to follow his method it is
impossible to achieve a watertight separation between 'facts' and 'values.' While most positivists operate within a philosophical universe in which values may be parsed from facts and
held in abeyance while 'scientific' investigation proceeds, for Marx all knowledge which we
generate about the world must bear some relationship to our needs and purposes." If our
"needs and purposes" are revolutionary, it is necessary to shape our research agendas with
them in mind.

11 District of Columbia Commission on the Status of Women, 1972, as quoted in General
Accounting Office, *Female Offenders: Who Are They and What Are the Problems Confronting Them?*
(Washington, D.C.: Govt. Printing Office, 1979), p. 3.

12 Michael J. Hindelang, "Sex Differences in Criminal Activity," *Social Problems*, December
1979, p. 154.

13 Smart, *Women, Crime and Criminology*, p. 1.

14 For a good beginning along this line, see Estelle B. Freedman, "Their Sisters' Keepers:
An Historical Perspective on Female Correctional Institutions in the United States: 1870-
1900," *Feminist Studies*, vol. 2, no. 1 (1974), pp. 77-95.

15 Klein and Kress, "Any Woman's Blues," p. 37.

16 Nancy L. Yasutake, "The Marital Rape Exemption: Its History, Application and Present
Status" (Master's Thesis, Boston, Northeastern University, College of Criminal Justice, June
1980).

17 Lee H. Bowker, *Women, Crime, and the Criminal Justice System* (Lexington, Mass.: Lexington Books, 1978), pp. 115-22.

18 Kee MacFarlane, "Sexual Abuse of Children," in *The Victimization of Women,* Jane R. Chapman and Margaret Gates, eds. (Beverly Hills, Calif.: Sage, 1978), pp. 81-109.

19 Murray Straus, "Sexual Inequality, Cultural Norms and Wife-Beating," as quoted in Dorie Klein, "Can This Marriage Be Saved? Battery and Sheltering," *Crime and Social Justice,* Winter 1979, p.22.

20 *Ibid.,* pp. 24-25.

21 Del Martin, "Battered Women: Society's Problem," in *Victimization of Women,* Chapman and Gates, eds., p. 115.

22 Lin Farley, *Sexual Shakedown* (New York: Warner Books, 1978).

23 Laura J. Evans, "Sexual Harassment: Women's Hidden Occupational Hazard," in *Victimization of Women,* Chapman and Gates, eds., pp. 206-07.

24 Farley, *Sexual Shakedown,* p. 15.

25 K. Davis, "The Sociology of Prostitution," *American Sociological Review,* vol. 2 (1937), p. 752, as quoted in Jennifer James, "The Prostitute as Victim," in *Victimization of Women,* Chapman and Gates, eds., p. 177.

26 James, "Prostitute as Victim," pp. 177-78.

27 Klein and Kress, "Any Woman's Blues," pp. 34-37.

28 *Ibid.,* p. 41.

29 *Ibid.;* Elizabeth F. Moulds, "Chivalry and Paternalism: Disparities of Treatment in the Criminal Justice System," in *Women, Crime & Justice,* Susan K. Datesman and Frank R. Scarpitti, eds. (New York: Oxford University Press, 1980), pp.277-99.

30 Lois B. DeFleur, "Biasing Influences on Drug Arrest Records: Implications for Deviance Research," as cited in Meda Chesney-Lind, "Chivalry Reexamined: Women and the Criminal Justice System," in Bowker, *Women, Crime and the Criminal Justice System,* p. 203.

31 Chesney-Lind, "Chivalry Reexamined," p. 203.

32 *Ibid.,* pp. 207-08.

33 Klein and Kress, "Any Woman's Blues," p. 44.

34 Moulds, "Chivalry and Paternalism," p. 278.

35 Meda Chesney-Lind, "Judicial Paternalism and the Female Status Offender," *Crime & Delinquency,* April 1977, p. 125.

36 Gail Armstrong, "Females under the Law—'Protected' but Unequal," *Crime & Delinquency,* April 1977, p. 116.

37 Chesney-Lind, "Chivalry Reexamined," p. 211.

38 GAO, *Female Offenders,* p. 25.

39 Chesney-Lind, "Chivalry Reexamined," pp. 211-12; Carolyn E. Temin, "Discriminatory Sentencing of Women Offenders: The Argument for ERA in a Nutshell," in *Women, Crime & Justice,* Datesman and Scarpitti, eds., pp. 255-76.

40 Temin, "Discriminatory Sentencing of Women Offenders," p. 257.

41 GAO, *Female Offenders,* p. 4.

42 Judith Resnik and Nancy Shaw, "Prisoners of Their Sex: Health Problems of Incarcerated Women," in *Prisoners' Rights Sourcebook: Theory, Litigation, and Practice,* vol. 2, Ira Robbins, ed. (New York: Clark Boardman, 1980).

43 Ruth M. Glick and Virginia V. Neto, *National Study of Women's Correctional Programs* (Washington, D.C.: Law Enforcement Assistance Administration, 1977), pp. 67-69.

44 GAO, *Female Offenders,* p. 32.

45 *Ibid.;* Glick and Neto, *National Study of Women's Correctional Programs;* Judith Resnick, Statement before the Subcommittee on Courts, Civil Liberties, and the Administration of Justice of the Committee on the Judiciary, U.S. House of Representatives, Oct. 11, 1979.

46 Kathryn W. Burkhart, *Women in Prison* (Garden City, N.Y.: Doubleday, 1973).

47 Glick and Neto, *National Study of Women's Correctional Programs,* p. xxiv, quote with amuse-

ment from a serious recommendation that women prisoners be trained in the dairy industry; the recommendation was based on the ground that women have a natural affinity for udders and understanding of mammary infections.

48 Burkhart, *Women in Prison*, p. 377; Kress, "Bourgeois Morality and the Administration of Justice," p. 47.

49 GAO, *Female Offenders*.

50 Glick and Neto, *Female Offenders*, p. xvi.

51 *Ibid.;* Kathleen Haley, "Mothers behind Bars: A Look at the Parental Rights of Incarcerated Women," in *Women, Crime & Justice*, Datesman and Scarpitti, eds., pp. 339-53.

52 Resnik, Statement before the Subcommittee on Courts, Civil Liberties, and the Administration of Justice.

53 Law Enforcement Assistance Administration, *Report of the LEAA Task Force on Women* (Washington, D.C.: LEAA, 1975), p. 14.

54 Some examples of this position are mentioned by James B. Jacobs, in "The Sexual Integration of the Prison's Guard Force: A Few Comments on *Dothard v. Rawlinson,*" *University of Toledo Law Review*, Winter 1979, pp. 389-418; at times Jacobs himself appears to endorse this position.

55 See, for example, Chloe Owings, *Women Police: A Study of the Development and Status of the Women Police Movement* (New York: Frederick H. Hitchcock, 1925).

56 Donald G. Gibbons, *Society, Crime and Criminal Careers*, 3d ed. (Englewood Cliffs, N.J.: Prentice-Hall, 1977); Edwin Sutherland and Donald Cressey, *Criminology*, 10th ed. (Philadelphia: J. B. Lippincott, 1978). These and other texts received low ratings in an unpublished evaluation of ten criminology textbooks for sex bias by Elise Sklar, "The Treatment of Women in Current Criminology Literature" (Boston: Northeastern University, College of Criminal Justice, July 1979).

57 LEAA, *Report of the LEAA Task Force on Women*, p. 14.

58 LEAA, *Summary Report, The National Manpower Survey of the Criminal Justice System*, vol. 1 (Washington, D.C.: LEAA, 1978).

59 See, for example, "Indiana Woman's Prison," in *Indiana's State Institutions*, Peter Sletterdahl, ed. (Indianapolis, 1928), pp. 54, 72.

Postscript: The Future of Women and the Criminal Law

Natalie J. Sokoloff and Barbara Raffel Price

On November 5, 1873 Susan B. Anthony and thirteen other women voted in an election in Rochester, New York. Anthony was convicted for casting her vote on the federal charge of "having voted without the lawful right to vote."[1] Although she could have received a maximum sentence of three years in prison, Anthony was only fined $100. She refused to pay the money, hoping to be incarcerated so that the way would be open for a direct review of her case by the Supreme Court.[2] The judge did not oblige her and her conviction held although she never paid the fine. Through the demands of the contemporary women's movement, Susan B. Anthony is honored officially by her country with a one dollar coin engraved with her likeness. Her "deviance" in 1873 has made her a national hero with the passage of time.

When Anthony died in 1906 would she have predicted that political equality would still not be a reality for women in 1980? Could she have predicted a women's movement would still be necessary one hundred years later? One can speculate that she might have forecasted, as did others, that 100 years from her time women would have gained full equality with men in political, economic, and social sectors of society.

Susan B. Anthony's story illustrates the enormous difficulties in making long-term forecasts. Still the question of what the future holds for women and the criminal law is important to consider.

We would like to be able to provide an optimistic forecast. We would like to be able to say that equal treatment for all women before the law will be a reality by 2000. In fact, we wish we could predict that in the near future there would be: improved laws and better enforcement of crimes against women (rape, incest, wife battering, discrimination in employment), stronger laws to protect women from the more recently accepted types of female victimization (sexual harassment, pornography, unnecessary mutilating operations like hysterectomies and mastectomies) and those not yet widely recognized by officials (production of unsafe methods of birth control, involuntary childbirth for all women and coerced sterility of poor and racial/ethnic women), and more humane and substantive rehabilitation programs with equal opportunities in non-sexist education, training, and placement for women offenders.

We would like to forecast these developments, but both history and the onslaught against recent feminist reforms in the 1980s makes it inadvisable. Most importantly, as has been argued throughout this book, the kinds of changes possible for women within the criminal justice system, in large part, depends on what happens outside the criminal justice system itself. The nature of the legal and criminal justice systems reflects the distribution of political and economic power within the larger society, which is highly influenced by race, class, and sex.

Despite the fact that the legal system reflects these many biases of society, overt sexism has been signficantly reduced over the last decade. Many of these changes can be attributed to the political strength of the women's movement. In spite of these important changes, many nonsexist laws are either ignored or enforced only sporadically. Fundamental social change is a long-term, contradictory process. We must understand both the strengths and limitations of formal legal changes that occur within a society organized for the benefit of those in power—men over women, rich over poor, white over people of color.

Recall that although the women's movement began in the 1830s with the abolitionist movement to end slavery, it took women almost 100 years to achieve the right to vote. And in 1920, with the passage of the 19th Amendment giving women the vote, most people mistakenly believed that women's complete equality had been obtained. The women's movement as a consequence faded from the political scene.[3] History showed that women's complacency was in error, yet the need for renewed activism was not identified until the mid 1960s. It took until as recently as 1971 for women to be declared to be the "persons" of the 14th Amendment and to be entitled to the equal protection of the law.[4] In spite of many changes that have been generated in the law itself, women are still not equal to men in their daily lives. Three examples, one on spouse abuse, one on tax laws, and one on income inequality, illustrate the law's limitations.

Toward the end of 1970 almost half of the states had passed laws making spouse abuse a crime, a direct result of the political action of the women's movement. However, experience has shown that most of these laws do not provide sufficient protection for women and most fail to incorporate any support services for abused women. Thus, although the laws are "on the books," wife abuse continues because the causes of the abuse that the law seeks to deter and remedy are so deeply ingrained in our culture. Moreover, the law itself is not totally impartial with regard to wife abuse. As one author describes the situation: "Battered women exist because women as a class lack political, economic and social power which limit their options, because of the culture of [male] violence, and because the legal system has condoned the husband's right to physically 'punish' his wife (Eisenberg, 1977). In some states, the first beating is legal; in others, based on the ancient 'rule of thumb' or the right of a husband to strike his wife with a stick not thicker than his thumb, the severity of the beating is the criterion (Gringold, 1976)."[5]

Second, while changes in the tax laws have been demanded so that certain childcare deductions are permitted for employed women, men cannot deduct childcare as bona fide expenses enabling them to work. Such rulings reflect entrenched and deep-rooted beliefs about the correct or appropriate role for women. The predominantly male lawmakers continue to cast women in the childcare role while discouraging men from sharing equitably in homemaking and childcare tasks. Thus, the structure of women's lives is still commonly such that they cannot pursue many of the better paying, more challenging, higher status jobs; that they must seek out only those jobs that fit with their domestic responsibilities. This socially created and legally supported sexual division of labor is surrounded with a supporting set of attitudes and values and is intimately connected to the material benefits—better jobs and better pay—men experience in the job market today. Neither men's privileged economic position and social status nor traditional attitudes and values surrounding the sexual division of labor yield to rapid change. As a result, while we would like to be able to predict a speedy end to this situation, most women entering the employment arena will need to continue to hold down two separate jobs—one in the world of paid employment, the other in the world of unpaid employment in the home.

Third, there are many employment laws written to guarantee that women not be discriminated against in recruitment, employment, promotion, and income. But most women are trained for and recruited into those jobs primarily available for them—sex-segregated jobs—as nurses rather than doctors, as secretaries rather than office managers.[6] This means that women are employed in jobs with lower pay, lower status, and little political power. In fact, women are paid fifty-nine cents for every dollar that a man is paid at year-round, full-time employment. She must work ten days for every six days worked by a man to earn the same income.[7]

If we consider that the differential in pay between men and women has held rather steady for the past forty years, from the time when the law officially discriminated against women to today when federal and state laws specifically prohibit discrimination in employment, it becomes clear that as legal equality for women has increased, actual equality (e.g., occupational and economic) in everyday life has not necessarily followed. In short, we must be very cautious about predicting that laws, by themselves, will soon solve the problems women face in our society.

Law in our society is not static. Substantive laws change, in part, as struggles between groups and social classes emerge, forcing the criminal justice system and its legal apparatus to respond. Laws concerning women's rights have changed in just this way, as has been noted throughout this book. In spite of the limitations of the law, it is important to acknowledge the positive effects that changes in the laws have had for women. The Civil Rights Act of 1964, the Equal Employment Opportunity Commission, the right of women to be treated as persons and not as the property of their husbands, the right of women to choose to have an abortion or not, the right of women offenders to the same sentencing procedures as men— all make a very real difference in the lives of women each and every day. And yet, these laws are not without challenge.

Gains in the law and recent reforms won by women during the 1960s and 1970s have come under attack as the tide of political conservatism has gained momentum with increasing economic crises since the mid 1970s. Specifically, the Reagan administration has weakened regulations in the federal law on discrimination in higher education, employment, in school athletic policy, and in sexual harassment guidelines.[8] These hard-won regulations guaranteeing a modicum of equality for women and minorities have been criticized by high officials such as the vice-president of the United States as "burdensome, unnecessary or counterproductive Federal regulations."[9] Readers, having now covered the material in this book, can judge the accuracy of that statement for themselves. In addition, conservatives have tried to impose new regulations against women, such as attempts to recriminalize abortion. All these actions demonstrate to us how fragile the laws, by themselves, can be. Despite these many problems, we are still optimistic; but any optimism held for women's equality under and before the law is based on the existence of a renewed women's movement to protect and extend gains made in the previous period.

Predicting the future is not only precarious; it is also controversial. Indeed, the two editors of this book are inclined to approach the future in different ways. One of us sees major conflict in this society being between women (as a group) and men (as a group). Moreover, to the degree the women's movement is successful in achieving legal equality for women (and thus, economic, political, and social equality), a reduction in some of the conditions that promote crime, both by women and by those who victimize women, can be anticipated. And finally, to the extent that policy-making agencies are better representative of the sexual ratio in society, they should be able to better advocate the needs of women. As this happens, we will find more equitable treatment of women who have been accused or convicted of crime. More women policy makers is a need that extends to the state and federal lawmakers where presently women are not found in substantial or sufficient numbers to adequately represent women as laws are made.[10] For this to occur more women must be employed at every level in the criminal justice system. This position holds that equal employment will happen but the confidence in this forecast is less strong given the fact that we have already entered the 1980s.

The other of us sees that in addition to the changes recommended to better women's position in the preceding paragraph, that far broader changes in the organization of our society must also occur. Since the legal and criminal justice systems reflect and perpetuate the class, race, and sex biases of the larger society, this position is based on the argument that a basic transformation in economic, political, racial, and sexual systems of power and domination are all necessary conditions for women's legal equality to be meaningful. Thus, according to this line of thought, the women's movement must expose the links between sexism, capitalism, and racism. In order to transform women's position in society, the women's movement must build coalitions with minorities, trade unions, and a wide range of political organizations which are fighting for fundamental social change.

It is important for the reader to understand that the positions of both editors are equally valid, hence the art of predicting the future for women and the criminal justice system is made much more difficult a task.

In spite of our differences, we wanted this book to go beyond the descriptive questions about women, crime, and the criminal justice system. We wanted to raise issues about the underlying social relations, especially those around organized sexism, and the context in which laws operate (1) to define certain women as criminals, (2) to respond to certain groups of women as victims of crime, and (3) finally, to encourage (or discourage) women to join men as workers in the criminal justice system. Only in this way will the rights of all people—women, men, and children—be guaranteed.

Notes

1 Section 19 of the Civil Rights Act of 1870, 16 Stat. 144.

2 Babcock, Barbara Allen, A.E. Freedman, E.N. Norton, S.C. Ross. *Sex Discrimination and the Law: Causes and Remedies.* Boston: Little, Brown & Co., 1975, p. 10.

3 Koedt, Anne, Ellen Levine, Anita Rapone (eds.). *Radical Feminism.* New York: Quadrangle/The New York Times Book Co., 1973, p. 14.

4 Reed v. Reed 404 US 71, 92 S. Ct. 251, 30 L.Ed. 2d 225 (1971).

5 Richardson, Laurel Walum. *The Dynamics of Sex and Gender: A Sociological Perspective.* Boston: Houghton Mifflin Co., 1981, p. 121.

6 Traditionalists argue that if only women had the right kind of motivation and training, they too could become doctors, lawyers, bank presidents, etc. However, if all women who wanted these jobs were "properly" motivated and trained for them, and indeed qualified, there would not be enough high status, prestigious jobs for the candidates. The problem is

not the women but the way work is organized in our society. For further elaboration on this very important issue, see Natalie J. Sokoloff, *Between Money and Love: The Dialectics of Women's Home and Market Work.* New York: Praeger, 1980.

7 U.S. Department of Labor, Bureau of Labor Statistics. *Perspectives on Working Women: A Databook.* Bulletin 2080. Washington, D.C.: U.S. Government Printing Office, 1980.

8 Attempts to legally restrict women are seen in challenges by Congress in the early 1980s against the following legislation: Title VII (jobs), Title IX (education), the Equal Employment Opportunities Commission, Pregnancy Discrimination Act, Women's Educational Equity Act, Domestic Violence Prevention Act, protection against sexual harassment of employed women, and women's reproductive rights. In addition, food stamps were dangerously cut, racially integrated education was seriously questioned, enforcement of fair housing laws was defeated as was the Children's Health Assurance Program, and the Civil Rights Voting Act was challenged in Congress. Unfortunately, the list continues.

9 Raines, Howell. "U.S. Begins Deregulation Review on Rights and Ecology Guidelines," *New York Times,* August 13, 1981, P. A15.

10 The percentage of women state legislators ranges from 1 percent in Mississippi to 29 percent in New Hampshire, with the national average 12 percent at the state level. In the U.S. Congress 4 percent of all members are women. *National Directory of Women Elected Officials 1981.* Washington, D.C.: National Women's Political Caucus, 1981, pp. 8-10

DATE DUE